Fourth Joint Conference on Lexical and Computational Semantics

(*SEM 2015)

Denver, Colorado, USA
4 – 5 June 2015

ISBN: 978-1-5108-0444-9

Printed from e-media with permission by:

Curran Associates, Inc.
57 Morehouse Lane
Red Hook, NY 12571

Some format issues inherent in the e-media version may also appear in this print version.

Printed by Curran Associates, Inc. (2015)

Association for Computational Linguistics
209 N. Eighth Street
Stroudsburg, Pennsylvania 18360

Phone: 1-570-476-8006
Fax: 1-570-476-0860

acl@aclweb.org

Additional copies of this publication are available from:

Curran Associates, Inc.
57 Morehouse Lane
Red Hook, NY 12571 USA
Phone: 845-758-0400
Fax: 845-758-2634
Email: curran@proceedings.com
Web: www.proceedings.com

*SEM 2015: Joint Conference on Lexical and Computational Semantics

The **Joint Conference on Lexical and Computational Semantics (*SEM)** provides a forum of exchange for the growing number of NLP researchers working on different aspects of semantic processing. After the previous editions of *SEM in Montreal (2012), Atlanta (2013), and Dublin (2014), the 2015 edition will take place in Denver on June 4 and 5 and is colocated with SemEval and NAACL. As in 2014 at COLING, also on this occasion *SEM and SemEval chose to coordinate their programs by featuring a joint invited talk. In this way, *SEM aims to bring together the ACL SIGLEX and ACL SIGSEM communities.

The acceptance rate of *SEM 2015 was quite competitive: out of 98 submissions, we accepted 36 papers for an overall acceptance of 37%. The acceptance rate of long paper that were accepted for oral presentation (18 out of 62) is 29%. The papers cover a wide range of topics including distributional semantics; lexical semantics and lexical acquisition; formal and linguistic semantics; discourse semantics; lexical resources, linked data and ontologies; semantics for applications; and extra-propositional semantics: sentiment and figurative meaning.

The *SEM 2015 program consists of oral presentations for selected long papers and a poster session for long and short papers.

Day One, June 4th:

- Joint *SEM SemEval keynote talk by **Marco Baroni**;
- Oral presentation sessions on distributional semantics, lexical semantics, and extra-propositional semantics;
- Poster session.

Day Two, June 5th:

- Keynote talk by **Preslav Natkov**;
- Oral presentation sessions on semantics for applications, lexical resources and ontologies, formal semantics, and discourse semantics;
- *SEM Best Paper Award.

We cannot finish without saying that *SEM 2015 would not have been possible without the considerable efforts of our area chairs, their reviewers, and the computational semantics community in general.

We hope you will enjoy *SEM 2015,

Martha Palmer, University of Colorado Boulder, General Chair
Gemma Boleda, University of Trento, Program Co-Chair
Paolo Rosso, Universitat Politècnica de València, Program Co-Chair

*SEM 2015 Chairs and Reviewers

General Chair

Martha Palmer, University of Colorado Boulder

Program Co-Chairs

Gemma Boleda, University of Trento
Paolo Rosso, Universitat Politècnica de València

Publication Co-Chairs

Marc Franco-Salvador, Universitat Politècnica de València
Enrique Flores, Universitat Politècnica de València

Area Chairs

Distributional semantics:
Edward Grefenstette, Google DeepMind

Lexical semantics, lexical acquisition, WSD:
Hwee Tou Ng, National University of Singapore

Lexical resources, linked data, ontologies:
Paul Buitelaar, National University of Ireland, Galway

Formal and linguistic semantics:
Aurelie Herbelot, University of Cambridge

Discourse semantics:
Graeme Hirst, University of Toronto

Semantics for applications (textual entailment, IE, QA, summarization, social media):
Alessandro Moschitti, Qatar Computing Research Institute

Extra-propositional semantics (sentiment, metaphor, irony, figurative meanings, etc.):
Tony Veale, University College Dublin

Program Committee

Apoorv Agarwal, Eneko Agirre, Guadalupe Aguado-de-Cea, Nicholas Asher, Timothy Baldwin, Francesco Barbieri, John Barnden, Roberto Basili, Núria Bel, Islam Beltagy, Emily M. Bender, Igor Boguslavsky, Johan Bos, Antal van den Bosch, Paul Buitelaar, Marine Carpuat, Fabio Celli, Grzegorz Chrupała, Yee Seng Chan, Christian Chiarcos, Robin Cooper, Bonaventura Coppola, Anna Corazza, Danilo Croce, Walter Daelemans, Daniel Dahlmeier, Thierry Declerck, Rodolfo Delmonte, Georgiana Dinu, Judith Eckle-Kohler, Katrin Erk, James Fan, Manaal Faruqui, Vanessa Wei Feng, Claire Gardent, Andrew Gargett, Aniruddha Ghosh, Stephan Gouws, Jorge Gracia, Edward Grefenstette, Gregory Grefenstette, Weiwei Guo, Sebastian Hellmann, Iris

Hendrickx, Aurélie Herbelot, Delia Irazú Hernández Farías, Graeme Hirst, Dirk Hovy, Richard Johansson, Shafiq Joty, Dimitri Kartsaklis, Douwe Kiela, Adam Kilgarriff, Valia Kordoni, Anna Korhonen, Jayant Krishnamurthy, Germán Kruszewski, Angeliki Lazaridou, Yoong Keok Lee, Alessandro Lenci, Guofu Li, Patricia Lichtenstein, Annie Louis, Wei Lu, Marie-Catherine de Marneffe, Lluís Màrquez, David Martinez, Sebastian Martschat, Yashar Mehdad, Diana McCarthy, John Philip McCrae, Louise McNally, Dmitrijs Milajevs, Shachar Mirkin, Saif Mohammad, Andrea Moro, Alessandro Moschitti, Philippe Muller, Preslav Nakov, Roberto Navigli, Malvina Nissim, Hwee Tou Ng, Vincent Ng, Nghia The Pham, Siddharth Patwardhan, Sameer Pradhan, Laurette Pretorius, Tamara Polajnar, John Prager, Stephen Pulman, Antonio Reyes, Sebastian Riedel, German Rigau, Tim Rocktäschel, Horacio Rodriguez, Michael Roth, Mehrnoosh Sadrzadeh, Gilles Sérasset, Eyal Shnarch, Jennifer Spenader, Christian Stab, Armando Stellato, Mark Stevenson, Carlo Strapparava, Stan Szpakowicz, Stefan Thater, Ivan Titov, Sara Tonelli, Kateryna Tymoshenko, Christina Unger, Olga Uryupina, Alessandro Valitutti, Tony Veale, Eva Maria Vecchi, Laure Vieu, Andreas Vlachos, Carl Vogel, Gabriela Vulcu, Joachim Wagner, Janyce Wiebe, Annie Zaenen, Roberto Zamparelli, Fabio Massimo Zanzotto, Heike Zinsmeister.

Table of Contents

Neural Networks for Integrating Compositional and Non-compositional Sentiment in Sentiment Composition
Xiaodan Zhu, Hongyu Guo and Parinaz Sobhani 1

Compositional Distributional Semantics with Long Short Term Memory
Phong Le and Willem Zuidema 10

A Hybrid Distributional and Knowledge-based Model of Lexical Semantics
Nikolaos Aletras and Mark Stevenson 20

Distributional semantics for ontology verification
Julien Corman, Laure Vieu and Nathalie Aussenac-Gilles 30

Combining Seemingly Incompatible Corpora for Implicit Semantic Role Labeling
Parvin Sadat Feizabadi and Sebastian Padó 40

Identification of Caused Motion Construction
Jena D. Hwang and Martha Palmer 51

A Methodology for Word Sense Disambiguation at 90% based on large-scale CrowdSourcing
Oier Lopez de Lacalle and Eneko Agirre 61

Learning Structures of Negations from Flat Annotations
Vinodkumar Prabhakaran and Branimir Boguraev 71

A New Dataset and Evaluation for Belief/Factuality
Vinodkumar Prabhakaran, Tomas By, Julia Hirschberg, Owen Rambow, Samira Shaikh, Tomek Strzalkowski, Jennifer Tracey, Michael Arrigo, Rupayan Basu, Micah Clark, Adam Dalton, Mona Diab, Louise Guthrie, Anna Prokofieva, Stephanie Strassel, Gregory Werner, Yorick Wilks and Janyce Wiebe 82

Non-Orthogonal Explicit Semantic Analysis
Nitish Aggarwal, Kartik Asooja, Georgeta Bordea and Paul Buitelaar 92

Combining Mention Context and Hyperlinks from Wikipedia for Named Entity Disambiguation
Ander Barrena, Aitor Soroa and Eneko Agirre 101

Collective Document Classification with Implicit Inter-document Semantic Relationships
Clint Burford, Steven Bird and Timothy Baldwin 106

SGRank: Combining Statistical and Graphical Methods to Improve the State of the Art in Unsupervised Keyphrase Extraction
Soheil Danesh, Tamara Sumner and James H. Martin 117

Towards Semantic Language Classification: Inducing and Clustering Semantic Association Networks from Europarl
Steffen Eger, Niko Schenk and Alexander Mehler 127

Ideological Perspective Detection Using Semantic Features
Heba Elfardy, Mona Diab and Chris Callison-Burch 137

Mapping Different Rhetorical Relation Annotations: A Proposal
Farah Benamara and Maite Taboada 147

Dissecting the Practical Lexical Function Model for Compositional Distributional Semantics
Abhijeet Gupta, Jason Utt and Sebastian Padó 153

Event Extraction as Frame-Semantic Parsing
Alex Judea and Michael Strube 159

Competence in lexical semantics
Andras Kornai, Judit Ács, Márton Makrai, Dávid Márk Nemeskey, Katalin Pajkossy and Gábor Recski 165

Extending a Single-Document Summarizer to Multi-Document: a Hierarchical Approach
Luis Marujo, Ricardo Ribeiro, David Martins de Matos, João Neto, Anatole Gershman and Jaime Carbonell 176

Reading Between the Lines: Overcoming Data Sparsity for Accurate Classification of Lexical Relationships
Silvia Necsulescu, Sara Mendes, David Jurgens, Núria Bel and Roberto Navigli 182

Multi-Level Alignments As An Extensible Representation Basis for Textual Entailment Algorithms
Tae-Gil Noh, Sebastian Padó, Vered Shwartz, Ido Dagan, Vivi Nastase, Kathrin Eichler, Lili Kotlerman and Meni Adler 193

Leveraging Preposition Ambiguity to Assess Compositional Distributional Models of Semantics
Samuel Ritter, Cotie Long, Denis Paperno, Marco Baroni, Matthew Botvinick and Adele Goldberg 199

Learning to predict script events from domain-specific text
Rachel Rudinger, Vera Demberg, Ashutosh Modi, Benjamin Van Durme and Manfred Pinkal 205

Combining Open Source Annotators for Entity Linking through Weighted Voting
Pablo Ruiz and Thierry Poibeau 211

Automatic Generation of a Lexical Resource to support Semantic Role Labeling in Portuguese
Magali Sanches Duran and Sandra Aluísio 216

Can Selectional Preferences Help Automatic Semantic Role Labeling?
Shumin Wu and Martha Palmer 222

Implicit Entity Recognition in Clinical Documents
Sujan Perera, Pablo Mendes, Amit Sheth, Krishnaprasad Thirunarayan, Adarsh Alex, Christopher Heid and Greg Mott . . . 228

A Distant Supervision Approach to Semantic Role Labeling
Peter Exner, Marcus Klang and Pierre Nugues . . . 239

Discovering Hypernymy Relations using Text Layout
Jean-Philippe Fauconnier and Mouna Kamel . . . 249

The complexity of finding the maximum spanning DAG and other restrictions for DAG parsing of natural language
Natalie Schluter . . . 259

Incremental Semantic Construction Using Normal Form CCG Derivation
Yoshihide Kato and Shigeki Matsubara . . . 269

Dependency-Based Semantic Role Labeling using Convolutional Neural Networks
William Foland and James Martin . . . 279

A State-of-the-Art Mention-Pair Model for Coreference Resolution
Olga Uryupina and Alessandro Moschitti . . . 289

Resolving Discourse-Deictic Pronouns: A Two-Stage Approach to Do It
Sujay Kumar Jauhar, Raul Guerra, Edgar Gonzàlez Pellicer and Marta Recasens . . . 299

Graph-based Coherence Modeling For Assessing Readability
Mohsen Mesgar and Michael Strube . . . 309

Conference Program

Thursday, June 4

08:50–10:30 **Block 1 - Distributional semantics**
Session Chair: Martha Palmer

08:50–09:00 ***Welcome***

09:00–10:00 Joint *SEM / SemEval keynote talk by **Marco Baroni**
Playing ficles and running with the corbons: What (multimodal) distributional semantic models learn during their childhood

10:00–10:30 *Neural Networks for Integrating Compositional and Non-compositional Sentiment in Sentiment Composition*
Xiaodan Zhu, Hongyu Guo and Parinaz Sobhani

10:30–11:00 ***Coffee break***

11:00–12:30 **Block 2 - Distributional semantics**
Session Chair: Ed Grefenstette

11:00–11:30 *Compositional Distributional Semantics with Long Short Term Memory*
Phong Le and Willem Zuidema

11:30–12:00 *A Hybrid Distributional and Knowledge-based Model of Lexical Semantics*
Nikolaos Aletras and Mark Stevenson

12:00–12:30 *Distributional semantics for ontology verification*
Julien Corman, Laure Vieu and Nathalie Aussenac-Gilles

12:30–14:00 ***Lunch break***

Thursday, June 4 (continued)

14:00–15:30 **Block 3 - Lexical semantics**
Session Chair: Gemma Boleda

14:00–14:30 *Combining Seemingly Incompatible Corpora for Implicit Semantic Role Labeling*
Parvin Sadat Feizabadi and Sebastian Padó

14:30–15:00 *Identification of Caused Motion Construction*
Jena D. Hwang and Martha Palmer

15:00–15:30 *A Methodology for Word Sense Disambiguation at 90% based on large-scale CrowdSourcing*
Oier Lopez de Lacalle and Eneko Agirre

15:30–16:00 ***Coffee break***

16:00–17:00 **Block 4 - Extra-propositional semantics**
Session Chair: Tony Veale

16:00–16:30 *Learning Structures of Negations from Flat Annotations*
Vinodkumar Prabhakaran and Branimir Boguraev

16:30–17:00 *A New Dataset and Evaluation for Belief/Factuality*
Vinodkumar Prabhakaran, Tomas By, Julia Hirschberg, Owen Rambow, Samira Shaikh, Tomek Strzalkowski, Jennifer Tracey, Michael Arrigo, Rupayan Basu, Micah Clark, Adam Dalton, Mona Diab, Louise Guthrie, Anna Prokofieva, Stephanie Strassel, Gregory Werner, Yorick Wilks and Janyce Wiebe

17:00–19:00 **Poster session with lightning talks intro**

Non-Orthogonal Explicit Semantic Analysis
Nitish Aggarwal, Kartik Asooja, Georgeta Bordea and Paul Buitelaar

Combining Mention Context and Hyperlinks from Wikipedia for Named Entity Disambiguation
Ander Barrena, Aitor Soroa and Eneko Agirre

Collective Document Classification with Implicit Inter-document Semantic Relationships
Clint Burford, Steven Bird and Timothy Baldwin

Thursday, June 4 (continued)

SGRank: Combining Statistical and Graphical Methods to Improve the State of the Art in Unsupervised Keyphrase Extraction
Soheil Danesh, Tamara Sumner and James H. Martin

Towards Semantic Language Classification: Inducing and Clustering Semantic Association Networks from Europarl
Steffen Eger, Niko Schenk and Alexander Mehler

Ideological Perspective Detection Using Semantic Features
Heba Elfardy, Mona Diab and Chris Callison-Burch

Mapping Different Rhetorical Relation Annotations: A Proposal
Farah Benamara and Maite Taboada

Dissecting the Practical Lexical Function Model for Compositional Distributional Semantics
Abhijeet Gupta, Jason Utt and Sebastian Padó

Event Extraction as Frame-Semantic Parsing
Alex Judea and Michael Strube

Competence in lexical semantics
Andras Kornai, Judit Ács, Márton Makrai, Dávid Márk Nemeskey, Katalin Pajkossy and Gábor Recski

Extending a Single-Document Summarizer to Multi-Document: a Hierarchical Approach
Luis Marujo, Ricardo Ribeiro, David Martins de Matos, João Neto, Anatole Gershman and Jaime Carbonell

Reading Between the Lines: Overcoming Data Sparsity for Accurate Classification of Lexical Relationships
Silvia Necsulescu, Sara Mendes, David Jurgens, Núria Bel and Roberto Navigli

Multi-Level Alignments As An Extensible Representation Basis for Textual Entailment Algorithms
Tae-Gil Noh, Sebastian Padó, Vered Shwartz, Ido Dagan, Vivi Nastase, Kathrin Eichler, Lili Kotlerman and Meni Adler

Leveraging Preposition Ambiguity to Assess Compositional Distributional Models of Semantics
Samuel Ritter, Cotie Long, Denis Paperno, Marco Baroni, Matthew Botvinick and Adele Goldberg

Thursday, June 4 (continued)

Learning to predict script events from domain-specific text
Rachel Rudinger, Vera Demberg, Ashutosh Modi, Benjamin Van Durme and Manfred Pinkal

Combining Open Source Annotators for Entity Linking through Weighted Voting
Pablo Ruiz and Thierry Poibeau

Automatic Generation of a Lexical Resource to support Semantic Role Labeling in Portuguese
Magali Sanches Duran and Sandra Aluísio

Can Selectional Preferences Help Automatic Semantic Role Labeling?
Shumin Wu and Martha Palmer

Friday, June 5

09:00–10:30 **Block 1 - Semantics for applications**
Session Chair: Paolo Rosso

09:00–10:00 *60 Years Ago People Dreamed of Talking with a Machine. Are We Any Closer?*
Keynote by Preslav Nakov

10:00–10:30 *Implicit Entity Recognition in Clinical Documents*
Sujan Perera, Pablo Mendes, Amit Sheth, Krishnaprasad Thirunarayan, Adarsh Alex, Christopher Heid and Greg Mott

10:30–11:00 ***Coffee break***

11:00–12:00 **Block 2 - Semantics for applications; Lexical resources and ontologies**
Session Chair: Alessandro Moschitti

11:00–11:30 *A Distant Supervision Approach to Semantic Role Labeling*
Peter Exner, Marcus Klang and Pierre Nugues

11:30–12:00 *Discovering Hypernymy Relations using Text Layout*
Jean-Philippe Fauconnier and Mouna Kamel

12:00–13:30 ***Lunch break***

Friday, June 5 (continued)

13:30–15:00 **Block 3 - Formal semantics**
Session Chair: TBD

13:30–14:00 *The complexity of finding the maximum spanning DAG and other restrictions for DAG parsing of natural language*
Natalie Schluter

14:00–14:30 *Incremental Semantic Construction Using Normal Form CCG Derivation*
Yoshihide Kato and Shigeki Matsubara

14:30–15:00 *Dependency-Based Semantic Role Labeling using Convolutional Neural Networks*
William Foland and James Martin

15:00–15:30 ***Coffee break***

15:30–17:00 **Block 4 - Discourse semantics**
Session Chair: TBD

15:30–16:00 *A State-of-the-Art Mention-Pair Model for Coreference Resolution*
Olga Uryupina and Alessandro Moschitti

16:00–16:30 *Resolving Discourse-Deictic Pronouns: A Two-Stage Approach to Do It*
Sujay Kumar Jauhar, Raul Guerra, Edgar Gonzàlez Pellicer and Marta Recasens

16:30–17:00 *Graph-based Coherence Modeling For Assessing Readability*
Mohsen Mesgar and Michael Strube

17:00 **Best Paper Award and closing**

Invited Talks

Playing ficles and running with the corbons:
What (multimodal) distributional semantic models learn during their childhood
Marco Baroni, University of Trento

Joint work with: Angeliki Lazaridou, Marco Marelli (University of Trento),
Raquel Fernandez (University of Amsterdam), Grzegorz Chrupała (Tilburg University)

Distributional semantic methods have some a priori appeal as models of human meaning acquisition, because they induce word representations from contextual distributions naturally occurring in corpus data without need for supervision. However, learning the meaning of a (concrete) word also involves establishing a link between the word and its typical visual referents, which is beyond the scope of classic, text-based distributional semantics. Since recently several proposals have been put forward about how to induce multimodal word representations from linguistic and visual contexts, it is natural to ask if this line of work, besides its practical implications, can help us to develop more realistic, grounded models of human word learning within the distributional semantics framework.

In my talk, I will report about two studies in which we used multimodal distributional semantics (MDS) to simulate human word learning. In one study, we first measured the ability of subjects to link a nonce word to relevant linguistic and visual associates when prompted only by exposure to minimal corpus evidence about it. We then simulated the same task with an MDS model, finding its behavior remarkably similar to that of subjects. In the second study, we constructed a corpus in which child-directed speech is aligned with real-life pictures of the objects mentioned by care-givers. We then trained our MDS model on these data, and inspected the generalizations it learned about the words in the corpus and the objects they might denote.

The results highlight interesting issues not only for distributional semantics (can we build meaningful word representations from very limited contexts? are such representations reasonably human-like?), but also for the study of human language acquisition (are we "done" with learning a word once we associate it to a referent? do we incrementally refine our word representations? is an explicit cross-situational mechanism really necessary?).

60 Years Ago People Dreamed of Talking with a Machine. Are We Any Closer?

Preslav Nakov, Qatar Computing Research Institute (QCRI)

Joint work with Marti Hearst (UC Berkeley)

The 60-year-old dream of computational linguistics is to make computers capable of communicating with humans in natural language. This has proven hard, and thus research has focused on sub-problems. Even so, the field was stuck with manual rules until the early 90s, when computers became powerful enough to enable the rise of statistical approaches. Eventually, this shifted the main research attention to machine learning from text corpora, thus triggering a revolution in the field.

Today, the Web is the biggest available corpus, providing access to quadrillions of words; and, in corpus-based natural language processing, size does matter. Unfortunately, while there has been substantial research on the Web as a corpus, it has typically been restricted to using page hit counts as an estimate for n-gram word frequencies; this has led some researchers to conclude that the Web should be only used as a baseline.

In this talk, I will reveal some of the hidden potential of the Web that lies beyond the n-gram, with focus on the syntax and semantics of English noun compounds. I will further show how these ideas apply to a number of NLP problems, including syntactic parsing and machine translation, among others. Finally, I will share some thoughts about the future of lexical semantics and machine translation, in view of the ongoing deep learning revolution.

Neural Networks for Integrating Compositional and Non-compositional Sentiment in Sentiment Composition

Xiaodan Zhu & Hongyu Guo
National Research Council Canada
1200 Montreal Road, M50
Ottawa, ON K1A 0R6, Canada
{xiaodan.zhu,hongyu.guo}@nrc-cnrc.gc.ca

Parinaz Sobhani
EECS, University of Ottawa
800 King Edward Avenue
Ottawa, ON K1N 6N5, Canada
psobh090@uottawa.ca

Abstract

This paper proposes neural networks for integrating compositional and non-compositional sentiment in the process of *sentiment composition*, a type of semantic composition that optimizes a sentiment objective. We enable individual composition operations in a recursive process to possess the capability of choosing and merging information from these two types of sources. We propose our models in neural network frameworks with structures, in which the merging parameters can be learned in a principled way to optimize a well-defined objective. We conduct experiments on the Stanford Sentiment Treebank and show that the proposed models achieve better results over the model that lacks this ability.

1 Introduction

Automatically determining the sentiment of a phrase, a sentence, or even a longer piece of text is still a challenging problem. Data sparseness encountered in such tasks often requires to factorize the problem to consider smaller pieces of component words or phrases, for which much research has been performed on bag-of-words or bag-of-phrases models (Pang and Lee, 2008; Liu and Zhang, 2012). More recent work has started to model *sentiment composition* (Moilanen and Pulman, 2007; Choi and Cardie, 2008; Socher et al., 2012; Socher et al., 2013), a type of semantic composition that optimizes a sentiment objective. In general, the composition process is critical in the formation of the sentiment of a span of text, which has not been well modeled yet and there is still scope for future work.

Compositionality, or non-compositionality, of the senses of text spans is important for language understanding. Sentiment, as one of the major semantic differential categories (Osgood et al., 1957), faces the problem as well. For example, the phrase *must see* or *must try* in a movie or restaurant review often indicates a positive sentiment, which, however, may be hard to learn from the component words. More extreme examples, e.g., slangs like *bad ass*, are not rare in social media text. This particular example can actually convey a very positive sentiment even though its component words are very negative. In brief, a sentiment composition framework that can consider both compositional and non-compositional sentiment is theoretically interesting.

From a more pragmatical viewpoint, if one is able to reliably learn the sentiment of a text span (e.g., an ngram) holistically, it would be desirable that a composition model has the ability to decide the sources of knowledge it trusts more: the composition from the component words, the non-compositional source, or a *soft* combination of them. In such a situation, whether the text span is actually composable may be blur or may not be a concern.

In general, the composition of sentiment is a rather complicated process. As a glimpse of evidence, the effect of negation words on changing sentiment of their scopes appears to be a complicated function (Zhu et al., 2014). The recently proposed neural networks (Socher et al., 2013; Socher et al., 2011) are promising, for their capability of modeling complicated functions (Mitchell, 1997) in

*Proceedings of the Fourth Joint Conference on Lexical and Computational Semantics (*SEM 2015)*, pages 1–9,
Denver, Colorado, June 4–5, 2015.

general, handling data sparseness by learning low-dimensional embeddings at each layer of composition, and providing a framework to optimize the composition process in principled way.

This paper proposes neural networks for integrating compositional and non-compositional sentiment in the process of sentiment composition. To achieve this, we enable individual composition operations in a recursive process to possess the capability of choosing and merging information from these two types of sources. We propose our models in neural network frameworks with structures (Socher et al., 2013), in which the merging parameters can be learned in a principled way to optimize a well-defined objective. We conduct experiments on the Stanford Sentiment Treebank and show that the proposed models achieve better results over the model that does not consider this property.

2 Related work

Composition of sentiment Early work on modeling sentiment does not examine semantic composition closely (Pang and Lee, 2008; Liu and Zhang, 2012), as mentioned above. Recent work has considered sentiment-oriented semantic composition (Moilanen and Pulman, 2007; Choi and Cardie, 2008; Socher et al., 2012; Socher et al., 2013), or simply called sentiment composition in this paper. For example, Moilanen and Pulman (2007) used a collection of hand-written compositional rules to assign sentiment values to different granularities of text spans. Choi and Cardie (2008) proposed a learning-based framework. The more recent work of (Socher et al., 2013) proposed models based on neural networks that do not rely on any heuristic rules. Such models work in a bottom-up fashion over a tree to infer the sentiment label of a phrase or sentence as a composition of the sentiment expressed by its constituting parts. The approach leverages a principled method, the forward and backward propagation, to optimize the system performance. In this paper, we follow the neural network approach to integrate compositional and non-compositional sentiment in sentiment composition.

Prior knowledge of sentiment Integrating non-compositional sentiment into the composition process can be viewed as introducing some prior sentiment knowledge, as in general the sentiment of a word or a phrase perceived independent of its context is often referred to as *prior* sentiment. Word-level prior sentiment is typically annotated in manual sentiment lexicons (Wilson et al., 2005; Hu and Liu, 2004; Mohammad and Turney, 2010), or learned in an unsupervised or semisupervised way (Hatzivassiloglou and McKeown, 1997; Esuli and Sebastiani, 2006; Turney and Littman, 2003; Mohammad et al., 2009). More recently, sentiment indicators, such as emoticons and hashtags, are utilized (Go et al., 2009; Davidov et al., 2010; Kouloumpis et al., 2011; Mohammad, 2012; Mohammad et al., 2013a). With enough data, such freely available (but noisy) annotation can be used to learn the sentiment of ngrams. In our study, we will investigate in the proposed composition models the effect of automatically learned sentimental ngrams.

3 Prior-enriched semantic networks

In this paper, we propose several neural networks that enable each composition operation to possess the ability of choosing and merging sentiment from lower-level composition and that from non-compositional sources. We call the networks Prior-Enriched Semantic Networks (PESN). We present several specific implementations based on RNTN (Socher et al., 2013); the latter has showed to be a state-of-the-art sentiment composition framework. However, the realization of a PESN node is not necessarily only tied with RNTN.

Figure 1 shows a piece of PESN. Each of the three big nodes, i.e., N_1, N_2, and N_3, corresponds to a node in a constituency parse tree; e.g., N_3 may correspond to the phrase *not a must try*, where N_1 and N_2 are *not* and *a must try*, respectively. We extend each of the nodes to possess the ability to consider sentiment from lower-level composition and non-compositional sources. In node N_3, knowledge from the lower-level composition is represented in the hidden vector i_3, which is merged with non-compositional knowledge represented in e_3, and the merged information is saved in m_3. The black box in the center performs the actual merging, which integrates the two knowledge sources in order to minimize an overall objective function that we will discuss in detail later. The recursive neural networks and the forward-backward propagation over structures (Socher et al., 2013; Goller and Kchler, 1996) provide a principled way to optimize the whole network.

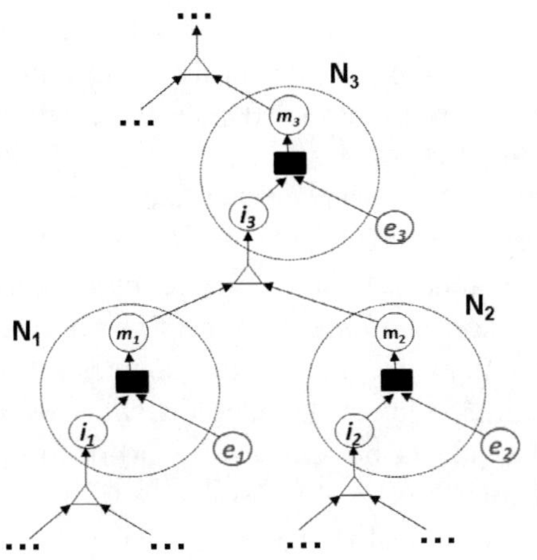

Figure 1: A prior-enriched semantic network (PESN) for sentiment composition. The three nodes, N_1, N_2, and N_3, correspond to three nodes in a constituency parse tree, and each of them consider sentiment from lower-level composition (i_1, i_2, i_3) and from non-compositional sentiment (e_1, e_2, e_3).

3.1 Regular bilinear merging

The most straightforward way of implementing a PESN node is probably through a regular bilinear merging. Take node N_3 in Figure 1 as an example; the node vector m_3 will be simply merged from i_3 and e_3 as follows:

$$m_3 = tanh(W_m \begin{bmatrix} i_3 \\ e_3 \end{bmatrix} + b_m) \quad (1)$$

Again, vector i_3 contains the knowledge from the lower-level composition; e_3 is a vector representing non-compositional sentiment information, which can be either from human annotation or automatically learned resources. Note that in the network, all hidden vectors m and i (including word embedding vectors) have the same dimensionality d, but the non-compositional nodes, i.e., the nodes e , do not necessarily have to have the same number of elements, and we let l be their dimensionality. The merging matrix W_m is *d-by-(d+l)*.

As in this paper we discuss PESN in the framework of RNTN, computation outside the nodes N_1, N_2, N_3 follows that for the standard three-way tensors in RNTN. That is, the hidden vector i_3 is computed with the following formula:

$$i_3 = tanh(\begin{bmatrix} m_1 \\ m_2 \end{bmatrix}^T V_r^{[1:d]} \begin{bmatrix} m_1 \\ m_2 \end{bmatrix} + W_r \begin{bmatrix} m_1 \\ m_2 \end{bmatrix}) \quad (2)$$

where, $W_r \in \mathbb{R}^{d \times (d+d)}$ and $V_r \in \mathbb{R}^{(d+d) \times (d+d) \times d}$ are the matrix and tensor of the composition function used in RNTN, respectively, each of which is shared over the whole tree in computing vectors i_1, i_2, and i_3.

3.2 Explicitly gated merging

Compared to the regular bilinear merging model, we here further explicitly control the input of the compositional and non-compositional semantics. Explicitly gating neural network has been studied in the literature. For example, the long short-term memory (LSTM) utilizes *input gates*, together with *output gates* and *forget gates*, to guide memory blocks to remember/forget history (Hochreiter and Schmidhuber, 1997).

For our purpose here, we explore an *input gate* to explicitly control the two different input sources. As shown in Figure 2, an additional gating layer g_3 is used to control i_3, e_3 explicitly.

$$g_3 = \sigma(\begin{bmatrix} W_{g_e} e_3 \\ \\ W_{g_i} i_3 \end{bmatrix} + b_g) \quad (3)$$

$$m_3 = tanh(W_m(g_3 \otimes \begin{bmatrix} i_3 \\ e_3 \end{bmatrix}) + b_m) \quad (4)$$

The sign $\otimes$ is a Hadamard product; σ is a logistic sigmoid function instead of a $tanh$ activation, which makes the gating signal g_3 to be in the range of [0, 1] and serve as a soft switch (not a hard binary

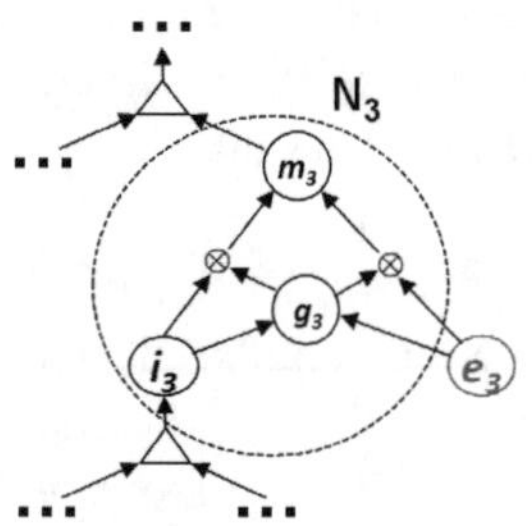

Figure 2: An input-gated network that explicitly controls the compositional and non-compositional sentiment input.

0/1 switch) to explicitly gate i_3 and e_3. Note that elsewhere in the network, we still use $tanh$ as our activation function. In addition, $W_{g_e} \in \mathbb{R}^{d \times l}$ and $W_{g_i} \in \mathbb{R}^{l \times d}$ are the weight matrices used to calculate the gate vector.

3.3 Confined-tensor-based merging

The third approach we use for merging compositional and non-compositional knowledge employs tensors, which are able to explore multiplicative combination among variables. Tensors have already been successfully used in a wide range of NLP tasks in capturing high-order interactions among variables. The forward computation of m_3 follows:

$$m_3 = tanh(\begin{bmatrix} i_3 \\ e_3 \end{bmatrix}^T V_m^{[1:d]} \begin{bmatrix} i_3 \\ e_3 \end{bmatrix} + W_m \begin{bmatrix} i_3 \\ e_3 \end{bmatrix}) \quad (5)$$

where $V_m^{[1:d]} \in R^{(d+l) \times (d+l) \times d}$ is the tensor m that defines multiple bilinear forms, and the matrix W_m is as defined in the previous models.

As we focus on the interaction between i_3 and e_3, we force each slice of tensor, e.g. $V_m^{[k]}$, to have zero-valued blocks. More specifically, the top-right *d-by-l* block of the piece matrix $V_m^{[k]}$ ($k \in \{1...d\}$) and the bottom-left *l-by-d* block are non-zero parameters, used to capture multiplicative, element-pair interactions between i_3 and e_3, while the rest block are set to be zero, to ignore interactions between those variables within i_3 and those within e_3. This does not only make the model focus on the interaction between vector i and e, it also helps significantly reduce the number of parameters to estimate, which, otherwise, could potentially lead to overfitting. We call this model confined-tensor-based merging.

3.4 Learning and inference

Objective The overall objective function in learning PESN, following (Socher et al., 2013), minimizes the cross-entropy error between the predicted distribution $y^{sen_i} \in \mathbb{R}^{c \times 1}$ at a node i and the target distribution $t^i \in \mathbb{R}^{c \times 1}$ at that node, where c is the number of sentiment categories. PESN learns the parameters that are used to merge the compositional and non-compositional sentiment so that the merging operations integrate the two sources in minimizing prediction loss. The neural network over structures provides a principled framework to optimize these parameters.

More specifically, the error over an entire sentence is calculated as a regularized sum:

$$E(\theta) = \sum_i \sum_j t_j^i \log {y^{sen_i}}_j + \lambda \left\|\theta\right\|^2 \quad (6)$$

where, λ is the regularization parameter, $j \in c$ denotes the j-th element of the multinomial target distribution, θ are model parameters that will be discussed below, and i iterates over all nodes i_x (e.g., i_1, i_2, and i_3) in Figure 1, where the model predicts sentiment labels.

Backpropagation over the structures To minimize $E(\theta)$, the gradient of the objective function with respect to each of the parameters in θ is calculated efficiently via backpropagation through structure (Socher et al., 2013; Goller and Kchler, 1996), after computing the prediction errors in forward propagation with formulas described above.

Regular bilinear merging The PESN implemented with simple bilinear merging has the following model parameters: $\theta = (V_r, W_r, W_m, W_{label}, L)$. As discussed above, V_r and W_r are the tensor and matrix in RNTN; W_m is the weight matrix for merging the compositional and non-compositional sentiment vectors. L denotes the vector representations of the word dictionary, and W_{label} is sentiment classification matrix used to predict sentiment label at a node. Backpropagation on the regular bilinear merging node follows a standard derivative computation in a regular feed-forward network, which we skip here.

Explicitly gated merging In this model, in addition to W_m, we further learn two weight matrices W_{g_i} and W_{g_e}, as introduced in Formula 3 and 4 above. Consider Figure 2 and let δ^{m_3} denote the error messages passed down to node m_3. The error messages are passed back to i_3 directly through the Hadamard product and also through the gate node g_3. The former, denoted as $\delta^{i_3,dir}$, is calculated with:

$$\delta^{i_3,dir} = (\delta^{m_3} \otimes g_3)[1:d] \quad (7)$$

where, g_3 is calculated with Formula 3 above in the forward process; $[1:d]$ means taking the first d elements of the vector yielded by the Hadamard product; the rest $[d+1:d+l]$ elements of the Hadamard production are discarded, as we do not update e_3, which is given as our prior knowledge.

The error messages passed down to gate vector g_3 is computed with

$$\delta^{g_3} = \delta^{m_3} \otimes \begin{bmatrix} i_3 \\ e_3 \end{bmatrix} \otimes s'(g_3) \quad (8)$$

where, $s'(.)$ is the element-wise derivative of logistic function, which can be calculated only using $s(.)$, as $s(.)(1-s(.))$. The derivative of W_{g_i} can be calculated with:

$$\frac{\partial E^{g_3}}{W_{g_e}} = (\delta^{g_3}[1:d])e_3^T \quad (9)$$

Similarly, partial derivatives over W_{g_i} can be calculated. These values will be summed to the total derivative of W_{g_i} and W_{g_e}, respectively. With these notations, the error messages passed down to i_3 through the gate can then be computed with:

$$\delta^{i_3,gate} = W_{g_i}^T(\delta^{g_3}[d+1:d+l]) \quad (10)$$

and the total error messages to node i_3 is then:

$$\delta^{i_3,total} = (\delta^{i_3,dir} + \delta^{i_3,gate} + \delta^{i_3,local}) \otimes f'(i_3) \quad (11)$$

where $\delta^{i_3,local}$ is the local error message from the sentiment prediction errors performed at the node i_3 itself to obtain the total error message for i_3, which is in turn passed down through regular RNTN tensor to the lower levels. $f'(.)$ is the element-wise derivative of $tanh$ function.

Confined-tensor-based merging In confined-tensor-based merging, the error messages passed to the two children i_3 and e_3 is computed with:

$$\delta^{i_3,e_3} = (W_m^T \delta^{m_3}) \otimes f'(\begin{bmatrix} i_3 \\ e_3 \end{bmatrix}) + \delta^{tns} \quad (12)$$

where,

$$\delta^{tns} = \sum_{k=1}^{d} \delta_k^{m_3} (V_m^{[k]} + (V_m^{[k]})^T) \begin{bmatrix} i_3 \\ e_3 \end{bmatrix} \otimes f'(\begin{bmatrix} i_3 \\ e_3 \end{bmatrix}) \quad (13)$$

where the error messages to i_3 are the first d numbers of elements of δ^{i_3,e_3}. The rest elements of δ^{i_3,e_3} are discarded; as mentioned above, we do not update e_3 as it is given as the prior knowledge. We skip the derivative for the W_{m_3}. While the derivative of each slice $k (k = 1, \ldots, d)$ of the tensor V is calculated with:

$$\frac{\partial E^{m_3}}{V_m^{[k]}} = \delta_k^{m_3,down} \begin{bmatrix} i_3 \\ e_3 \end{bmatrix} \begin{bmatrix} i_3 \\ e_3 \end{bmatrix}^T \quad (14)$$

Again, the full derivative for V_m and W_m is the sum of their derivatives over the trees. After the error message passing from m_3 to i_3 is obtained, it can be summed up with the local error message from the sentiment prediction errors at the node i_3 itself to obtain the total error message for i_3, which is in turn used to calculate the error messages passed down as well as the derivative in the lower-level tree.

4 Experiments

4.1 Data

We use the Stanford Sentiment Treebank (Socher et al., 2013) in our experiments. The data contain about 11,800 sentences from the movie reviews that were originally collected by Pang and Lee (2005).

The sentences were parsed with the Stanford parser (Klein and Manning, 2003). Phrases at all the tree nodes were manually annotated with sentiment values. We use the same split of the training and test data as in (Socher et al., 2013) to predict the sentiment categories of the roots (sentences) and the phrases, and use the same evaluation metric, *classification accuracy*, to measure the performances.

4.2 Obtaining non-compositional sentiment

In our experiments, we explore in sentiment composition the effect of two different types of non-compositional sentiment: (1) sentiment of ngrams automatically learned from an external, much larger corpus, and (2) sentiment of ngrams assigned by human annotators.

Following the method proposed in (Mohammad et al., 2013b), we learn sentimental ngrams from Tweets. The unsupervised approach utilizes *hashtags*, which can be regarded as conveying freely available (but noisy) human annotation of sentiment. More specifically, certain words in tweets are specially marked with the hash character (#) to indicate the topic, sentiment polarity, or emotions such as joy, sadness, angry, and surprised. With enough data, such artificial annotation can be used to learn the sentiment of ngrams by their likelihood of co-occurring with such hashtagged words.

More specifically, a collection of 78 seed hashtags closely related to *positive* and *negative* such as *#good, #excellent, #bad,* and *#terrible* were used (32 positive and 36 negative). These terms were chosen from entries for *positive* and *negative* in the Roget's Thesaurus. A set of 775,000 tweets that contain at least a positive hashtag or a negative hashtag were used as the learning corpus. A tweet was considered positive if it had one of the 32 positive seed hashtags, and negative if it had one of the 36 negative seed hashtags. The association score for an ngram w was calculated from these pseudo-labeled tweets as follows:

$$score(w) = PMI(w, positive) - PMI(w, negative) \quad (15)$$

where PMI stands for pointwise mutual information, and the two terms in the formula calculate the PMI between the target ngram and the pseudo-labeled positive tweets as well as that between the ngram and the negative tweets, respectively. Accordingly, a positive *score(.)* indicates association with positive sentiment, whereas a negative score indicates association with negative sentiment.

We use in our experiments the bigrams and trigrams learned from the dataset with the occurrences higher than 5. We assign these ngrams into one of the 5 bins according to their sentiment scores obtained with Formula 15: $(-\infty, -2]$, $(-2, -1]$, $(-1, 1)$, $[1, 2)$, and $[2, +\infty)$. Each ngram is now given a one-hot vector, indicating the polarity and strength of its sentiment. For example, a bigram with a score of -1.5 will be assigned a 5-dimensional vector $[0, 1, 0, 0, 0]$, indicating a weak negative. Note that PESN can also take into other forms of sentiment embeddings, such as those learned in (Tang et al., 2014).

In addition, the Stanford Sentiment Treebank contains manually annotated sentiment for each individual phrase in a parse tree, so we use such annotation but not other manual lexicons, by assuming such annotation fits the corpus itself the best. Specifically, we use bigram and trigram annotation in the treebank. Note that even longer ngrams are much sparser and probably less useful in general, one may learn sentiment for multi-word expressions of a larger length, which we will leave as future work.

4.3 Results

Overall prediction performance Table 1 shows the accuracies of different models on Stanford Sentiment Treebank. We evaluate the models on 5-category sentiment prediction at both the sentence (root) level and at all nodes (including roots).[1] The results reported in Table 1 are all based on the version 3.3.0 of the Stanford CoreNLP[2] and our implementation of PESN on it. The CoreNLP includes a java implementation of RNTN.[3] To make the results reported in the table comparable, we trained the

[1]The package only gives approximate accuracies for 2-category sentiment, which are not included here in the table.

[2]http://nlp.stanford.edu/sentiment/code.html

[3]The matlab code used in (Socher et al., 2013) is not published.

Models	sentence-level (roots)	all phrases (all nodes)
(1) RNTN	42.44	79.95
(2) Regular-bilinear (auto)	42.37	79.97
(3) Regular-bilinear (manu)	42.98	80.14
(4) Explicitly-gated (auto)	42.58	80.06
(5) Explicitly-gated (manu)	43.21	80.21
(6) Confined-tensor (auto)	42.99	80.49
(7) Confined-tensor (manu)	**43.75**†	**80.66**†

Table 1: Model performances (accuracies) on predicting 5-category sentiment at the sentence (root) level and phrase-level on Stanford Sentiment Treebank. The numbers in the bold font are the best performances achieved on the two tasks. Both results are statistically significantly better ($p < 0.05$) than the corresponding RNTN results.

RNTN models with the default parameter[4] and run the training from 5 different random initializations, and report the best results we observed.

The rows in the table marked with *auto* are models using the automatically learned ngrams, and those marked with *manu* using manually annotated sentiment for bigrams and trigrams. Note that the non-compositional sentiment of a node is only used to predict the sentiment of phrases above it in the tree. For example, in Figure 1 discussed earlier, the effect of e_1 and e_2 will be used to predict the sentiment of i_3 and other node i above, but not that of i_1 and i_2 themselves, avoiding the concern of using the annotation of a tree node to predict the sentiment of itself.

The models in general benefit from incorporating the non-compositional knowledge. The numbers in the bold font are the best performance achieved on the two tasks. While using the simple regular bilinear merging shows some gains, the more complicated models achieve further improvement.

Above we have seen the general performance of the models. Below, we take a closer look at the prediction errors at different depths of the sentiment treebank. The *depth* here is defined as the longest distance between a tree node and its descendant leafs. In Figure 3, the x-axis corresponds to different depths and y-axis is the accuracy. The figure was drawn with the RNTN and the model (7) in Table 1, so as to study the compositional property in the ideal situation where the lexical has a full coverage of bigrams and trigrams.

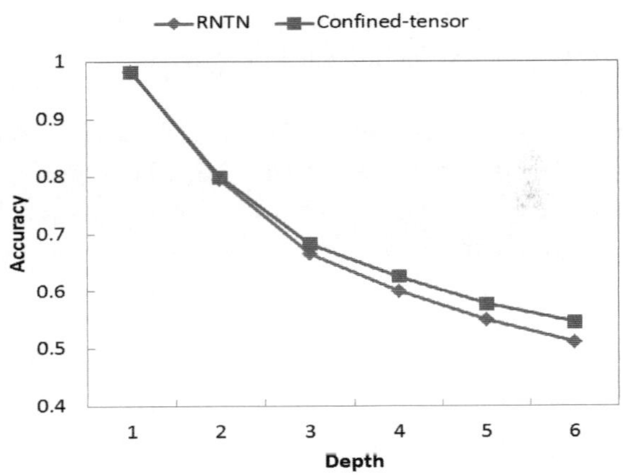

Figure 3: Errors made at different depths in the sentiment tree bank.

The figure shows that using the confined tensor to combine holistic sentiment information outperforms the original RNTN model that does not consider this, starting from depth 3, showing the benefit of using holistic bigram sentiment. The improvement increases at depth 4 (indicating the benefit of using trigram sentiment), and then was propagated to the higher levels of the tree. As discussed above, we only use non-compositional sentiment of a node to predict the sentiment of the phrases above it in the tree but not the node itself. And the system still needs to balance which source it trusts more, by optimizing the overall objective.

Although the empirical improvement may depend on the percentage of non-compositional instances in a data set or the sentiment that need to be learned holistically, we present here the first effort, according to our knowledge, on studying the concern of in-

[4]java -mx8g edu.stanford.nlp.sentiment.SentimentTraining -numHid 25 -trainPath train.txt -devPath dev.txt -train -model model.ser.gz

tegrating compositional and non-compositional sentiment in the semantic composition process.

5 Conclusions and future work

This paper proposes models for integrating compositional and non-compositional sentiment in the process of sentiment composition. To achieve this, we enable each composition operation to be able to choose and merge information from these two types of sources. We propose to implement such models within neural network frameworks with structures (Socher et al., 2013), in which the merging parameters can be optimized in a principled way, to minimize a well-defined objective. We conduct experiments on the Stanford Sentiment Treebank and show that the proposed models achieve better results over the model that does not consider this property.

Although the empirical improvement may depend on the percentage of non-compositional instances in a data set or the sentiment that need to be learned holistically, we present here the first effort, according to our knowledge, on studying the basic concern of integrating compositional and non-compositional sentiment in composition. While we focus on sentiment in this paper, investigating compositional and non-compositional semantics for general semantic composition with neural networks is interesting to us as an immediate future problem, as such models provide a principled way to optimize the overall objective over the sentence structures when we consider both compositional and non-compositional semantics.

References

Yejin Choi and Claire Cardie. 2008. Learning with compositional semantics as structural inference for subsentential sentiment analysis. In *Proceedings of the Conference on Empirical Methods in Natural Language Processing*, EMNLP '08, pages 793–801, Honolulu, Hawaii.

Dmitry Davidov, Oren Tsur, and Ari Rappoport. 2010. Enhanced sentiment learning using Twitter hashtags and smileys. In *Proceedings of the 23rd International Conference on Computational Linguistics: Posters*, COLING '10, pages 241–249, Beijing, China.

Andrea Esuli and Fabrizio Sebastiani. 2006. SENTIWORDNET: A publicly available lexical resource for opinion mining. In *In Proceedings of the 5th Conference on Language Resources and Evaluation*, LREC '06, pages 417–422.

Alec Go, Richa Bhayani, and Lei Huang. 2009. Twitter sentiment classification using distant supervision. Technical report, Stanford University.

Christoph Goller and Andreas Kchler. 1996. Learning task-dependent distributed representations by backpropagation through structure. In *In Proc. of the ICNN-96*, pages 347–352, Bochum, Germany. IEEE.

Vasileios Hatzivassiloglou and Kathleen R. McKeown. 1997. Predicting the semantic orientation of adjectives. In *Proceedings of the 8th Conference of European Chapter of the Association for Computational Linguistics*, EACL '97, pages 174–181, Madrid, Spain.

S. Hochreiter and J. Schmidhuber. 1997. Long short-term memory. *Neural Computation*, 9(8):1735–1780.

Minqing Hu and Bing Liu. 2004. Mining and summarizing customer reviews. In *Proceedings of the 10th ACM SIGKDD International Conference on Knowledge Discovery and Data Mining*, KDD '04, pages 168–177, New York, NY, USA. ACM.

Dan Klein and Christopher D. Manning. 2003. Accurate unlexicalized parsing. In *Proceedings of the 41st Annual Meeting on Association for Computational Linguistics - Volume 1*, ACL '03, pages 423–430, Sapporo, Japan. Association for Computational Linguistics.

Efthymios Kouloumpis, Theresa Wilson, and Johanna Moore. 2011. Twitter sentiment analysis: The Good the Bad and the OMG! In *Proceedings of the 5th International AAAI Conference on Weblogs and Social Media*.

Bing Liu and Lei Zhang. 2012. A survey of opinion mining and sentiment analysis. In Charu C. Aggarwal and ChengXiang Zhai, editors, *Mining Text Data*, pages 415–463. Springer US.

Tom M Mitchell. 1997. Machine learning. 1997. *Burr Ridge, IL: McGraw Hill*, 45.

Saif M. Mohammad and Peter D. Turney. 2010. Emotions evoked by common words and phrases: Using Mechanical Turk to create an emotion lexicon. In *Proceedings of the NAACL-HLT Workshop on Computational Approaches to Analysis and Generation of Emotion in Text*, LA, California.

Saif Mohammad, Cody Dunne, and Bonnie Dorr. 2009. Generating high-coverage semantic orientation lexicons from overtly marked words and a thesaurus. In *Proceedings of the Conference on Empirical Methods in Natural Language Processing: Volume 2*, EMNLP '09, pages 599–608, Singapore.

S. Mohammad, S. Kiritchenko, and X. Zhu. 2013a. NRC-Canada: Building the state-of-the-art in sentiment analysis of tweets. In *Proceedings of the International Workshop on Semantic Evaluation*, SemEval '13, Atlanta, Georgia, USA, June.

Saif M. Mohammad, Bonnie J. Dorr, Graeme Hirst, and Peter D. Turney. 2013b. Computing lexical contrast. *Computational Linguistics*, 39(3):555–590.

Saif Mohammad. 2012. #emotional tweets. In *Proceedings of the First Joint Conference on Lexical and Computational Semantics*, *SEM '12, pages 246–255, Montréal, Canada. Association for Computational Linguistics.

Karo Moilanen and Stephen Pulman. 2007. Sentiment composition. In *Proceedings of RANLP 2007*, Borovets, Bulgaria.

Charles E Osgood, George J Suci, and Percy Tannenbaum. 1957. *The measurement of meaning*. University of Illinois Press.

Bo Pang and Lillian Lee. 2005. Seeing stars: Exploiting class relationships for sentiment categorization with respect to rating scales. In *Proceedings of the Annual Meeting of the Association for Computational Linguistics*, ACL '05, pages 115–124.

Bo Pang and Lillian Lee. 2008. Opinion mining and sentiment analysis. *Foundations and Trends in Information Retrieval*, 2(1–2):1–135.

Richard Socher, Jeffrey Pennington, Eric Huang, Andrew Y. Ng, and Christopher D. Manning. 2011. Semi-supervised recursive autoencoders for predicting sentiment distributions. In *Conference on Empirical Methods in Natural Language Processing*.

Richard Socher, Brody Huval, Christopher D. Manning, and Andrew Y. Ng. 2012. Semantic compositionality through recursive matrix-vector spaces. In *Proceedings of the Conference on Empirical Methods in Natural Language Processing*, EMNLP '12, Jeju, Korea. Association for Computational Linguistics.

Richard Socher, Alex Perelygin, Jean Y. Wu, Jason Chuang, Christopher D. Manning, Andrew Y. Ng, and Christopher Potts. 2013. Recursive deep models for semantic compositionality over a sentiment treebank. In *Proceedings of the Conference on Empirical Methods in Natural Language Processing*, EMNLP '13, Seattle, USA. Association for Computational Linguistics.

Duyu Tang, Furu Wei, Nan Yang, Ming Zhou, Ting Liu, and Bing Qin. 2014. Learning sentiment-specific word embedding for twitter sentiment classification. In *Proceedings of ACL*, Baltimore, Maryland, USA, June.

Peter Turney and Michael L Littman. 2003. Measuring praise and criticism: Inference of semantic orientation from association. *ACM Transactions on Information Systems*, 21(4).

Theresa Wilson, Janyce Wiebe, and Paul Hoffmann. 2005. Recognizing contextual polarity in phrase-level sentiment analysis. In *Proceedings of the Conference on Human Language Technology and Empirical Methods in Natural Language Processing*, HLT '05, pages 347–354, Stroudsburg, PA, USA. Association for Computational Linguistics.

Xiaodan Zhu, Hongyu Guo, Saif Mohammad, and Svetlana Kiritchenko. 2014. An empirical study on the effect of negation words on sentiment. In *Proceedings of ACL*, Baltimore, Maryland, USA, June.

Compositional Distributional Semantics with Long Short Term Memory

Phong Le and **Willem Zuidema**
Institute for Logic, Language and Computation
University of Amsterdam, the Netherlands
{p.le,zuidema}@uva.nl

Abstract

We are proposing an extension of the recursive neural network that makes use of a variant of the long short-term memory architecture. The extension allows information low in parse trees to be stored in a memory register (the 'memory cell') and used much later higher up in the parse tree. This provides a solution to the vanishing gradient problem and allows the network to capture long range dependencies. Experimental results show that our composition outperformed the traditional neural-network composition on the Stanford Sentiment Treebank.

1 Introduction

Moving from lexical to compositional semantics in vector-based semantics requires answers to two difficult questions: (i) what is the nature of the composition functions (given that the lambda calculus for variable binding is no longer applicable), and (ii) how do we learn the parameters of those functions (if they have any) from data? A number of classes of functions have been proposed in answer to the first question, including simple linear functions like vector addition (Mitchell and Lapata, 2009), non-linear functions like those defined by multi-layer neural networks (Socher et al., 2010), and vector matrix multiplication and tensor linear mapping (Baroni et al., 2013). The matrix and tensor-based functions have the advantage of allowing a relatively straightforward comparison with formal semantics, but the fact that multi-layer neural networks with non-linear activation functions like sigmoid can approximate any continuous function (Cybenko, 1989) already make them an attractive choice.

In trying to answer the second question, the advantages of approaches based on neural network architectures, such as the recursive neural network (RNN) model (Socher et al., 2013b) and the convolutional neural network model (Kalchbrenner et al., 2014), are even clearer. Models in this paradigm can take advantage of general learning procedures based on back-propagation, and with the rise of 'deep learning', of a variety of efficient algorithms and tricks to further improve training.

Since the first success of the RNN model (Socher et al., 2011b) in constituent parsing, two classes of extensions have been proposed. One class is to enhance its compositionality by using tensor product (Socher et al., 2013b) or concatenating RNNs horizontally to make a deeper net (Irsoy and Cardie, 2014). The other is to extend its topology in order to fulfill a wider range of tasks, like Le and Zuidema (2014a) for dependency parsing and Paulus et al. (2014) for context-dependence sentiment analysis.

Our proposal in this paper is an extension of the RNN model to improve compositionality. Our motivation is that, like training recurrent neural networks, training RNNs on deep trees can suffer from the vanishing gradient problem (Hochreiter et al., 2001), i.e., that errors propagated back to the leaf nodes shrink exponentially. In addition, information sent from a leaf node to the root can be obscured if the path between them is long, thus leading to the problem how to capture long range dependencies. We therefore borrow the long short-term memory (LSTM) architecture (Hochreiter and Schmidhu-

*Proceedings of the Fourth Joint Conference on Lexical and Computational Semantics (*SEM 2015)*, pages 10–19,
Denver, Colorado, June 4–5, 2015.

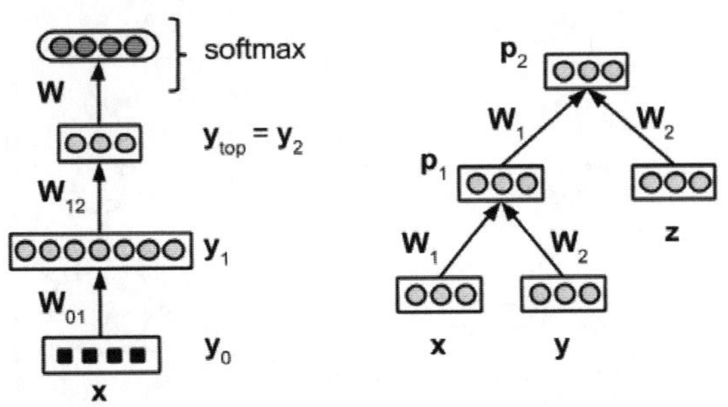

Figure 1: Multi-layer neural network (left) and Recursive neural network (right). Bias vectors are removed for the simplicity.

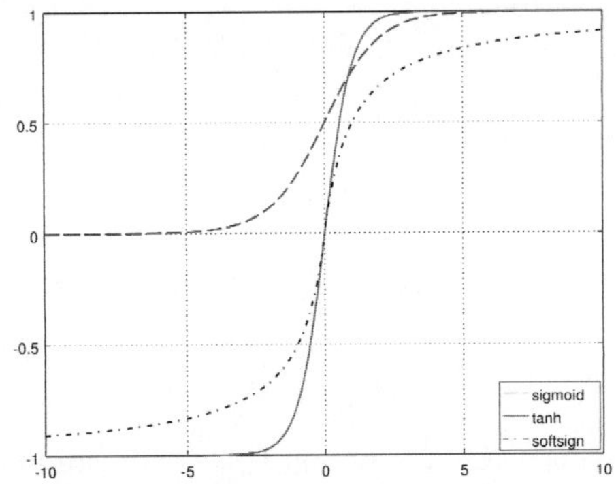

Figure 2: Activation functions: $\text{sigmoid}(x) = \frac{1}{1+e^{-x}}$, $\tanh(x) = \frac{e^{2x}-1}{e^{2x}+1}$, $\text{softsign}(x) = \frac{x}{1+|x|}$.

ber, 1997) from recurrent neural network research to tackle those two problems. The main idea is to allow information low in a parse tree to be stored in a memory cell and used much later higher up in the parse tree, by recursively *adding* up all memory into memory cells in a bottom-up manner. In this way, errors propagated back through structure do not vanish. And information from leaf nodes is still (loosely) preserved and can be used directly at any higher nodes in the hierarchy. We then apply this composition to sentiment analysis. Experimental results show that the new composition works better than the traditional neural-network-based composition.

The outline of the rest of the paper is as follows. We first, in Section 2, give a brief background on neural networks, including the multi-layer neural network, recursive neural network, recurrent neural network, and LSTM. We then propose the LSTM for recursive neural networks in Section 3, and its application to sentiment analysis in Section 4. Section 5 shows our experiments.

2 Background

2.1 Multi-layer Neural Network

In a multi-layer neural network (MLN), neurons are organized in layers (see Figure 1-left). A neuron in layer i receives signal from neurons in layer $i-1$ and transmits its output to neurons in layer $i+1$. [1] The computation is given by

$$\mathbf{y}_i = g\big(\mathbf{W}_{i-1,i}\mathbf{y}_{i-1} + \mathbf{b}_i\big)$$

where real vector $\mathbf{y}_i$ contains the activations of the neurons in layer i; $\mathbf{W}_{i-1,i} \in \mathbb{R}^{|\mathbf{y}_i|\times|\mathbf{y}_{i-1}|}$ is the matrix of weights of connections from layer $i-1$ to layer i; $\mathbf{b}_i \in \mathbb{R}^{|\mathbf{y}_i|}$ is the vector of biases of the neurons in layer i; g is an activation function, e.g. *sigmoid*, *tanh*, or *softsign* (see Figure 2).

For classification tasks, we put a *softmax* layer on the top of the network, and compute the probability of assigning a class c to an input $\mathbf{x}$ by

$$Pr(c|\mathbf{x}) = \text{softmax}(c) = \frac{e^{u(c,\mathbf{y}_{\text{top}})}}{\sum_{c'\in C} e^{u(c',\mathbf{y}_{\text{top}})}} \quad (1)$$

where $\big[u(c_1, \mathbf{y}_{top}), ..., u(c_{|C|}, \mathbf{y}_{top})\big]^T = \mathbf{W}\mathbf{y}_{top} + \mathbf{b}$; C is the set of all possible classes; $\mathbf{W} \in \mathbb{R}^{|C|\times|\mathbf{y}_{top}|}$, $\mathbf{b} \in \mathbb{R}^{|C|}$ are a weight matrix and a bias vector.

Training an MLN is to minimize an objective function $J(\theta)$ where θ is the parameter set (for classification, $J(\theta)$ is often a negative log likelihood). Thanks to the back-propagation algorithm (Rumelhart et al., 1988), the gradient $\partial J/\partial\theta$ is efficiently computed; the gradient descent method thus is used to minimize J.

2.2 Recursive Neural Network

A recursive neural network (RNN) (Goller and Küchler, 1996) is an MLN where, given a tree structure, we recursively apply the same weight matrices at each inner node in a bottom-up manner. In order to see how an RNN works, consider the following example. Assume that there is a constituent

[1] This is a simplified definition. In practice, any layer $j < i$ can connect to layer i.

with parse tree $(p_2\ (p_1\ x\ y)\ z)$ (Figure 1-right), and that $\mathbf{x}, \mathbf{y}, \mathbf{z} \in \mathbb{R}^d$ are the vectorial representations of the three words x, y and z, respectively. We use a neural network which consists of a weight matrix $\mathbf{W}_1 \in \mathbb{R}^{d \times d}$ for left children and a weight matrix $\mathbf{W}_2 \in \mathbb{R}^{d \times d}$ for right children to compute the vector for a parent node in a bottom up manner. Thus, we compute p_1

$$\mathbf{p}_1 = g(\mathbf{W}_1\mathbf{x} + \mathbf{W}_2\mathbf{y} + \mathbf{b}) \quad (2)$$

where $\mathbf{b}$ is a bias vector and g is an activation function. Having computed p_1, we can then move one level up in the hierarchy and compute p_2:

$$\mathbf{p}_2 = g(\mathbf{W}_1\mathbf{p}_1 + \mathbf{W}_2\mathbf{z} + \mathbf{b}) \quad (3)$$

This process is continued until we reach the root node.

Like training an MLN, training an RNN uses the gradient descent method to minimize an objective function $J(\theta)$. The gradient $\partial J/\partial\theta$ is efficiently computed thanks to the back-propagation through structure algorithm (Goller and Küchler, 1996).

The RNN model and its extensions have been employed successfully to solve a wide range of problems: from parsing (constituent parsing (Socher et al., 2013a), dependency parsing (Le and Zuidema, 2014a)) to classification (e.g. sentiment analysis (Socher et al., 2013b; Irsoy and Cardie, 2014), paraphrase detection (Socher et al., 2011a), semantic role labelling (Le and Zuidema, 2014b)).

2.3 Recurrent Networks and Long Short-Term Memory

A neural network is *recurrent* if it has at least one directed ring in its structure. In the natural language processing field, the simple recurrent neural network (SRN) proposed by Elman (1990) (see Figure 3-left) and its extensions are used to tackle sequence-related problems, such as machine translation (Sutskever et al., 2014) and language modelling (Mikolov et al., 2010).

In an SRN, an input $\mathbf{x}_t$ is fed to the network at each time t. The hidden layer $\mathbf{h}$, which has activation $\mathbf{h}_{t-1}$ right before $\mathbf{x}_t$ comes in, plays a role as a memory store capturing the whole history $(\mathbf{x}_0, ..., \mathbf{x}_{t-1})$. When $\mathbf{x}_t$ comes in, the hidden layer updates its activation by

$$\mathbf{h}_t = g(\mathbf{W}_x\mathbf{x}_t + \mathbf{W}_h\mathbf{h}_{t-1} + \mathbf{b})$$

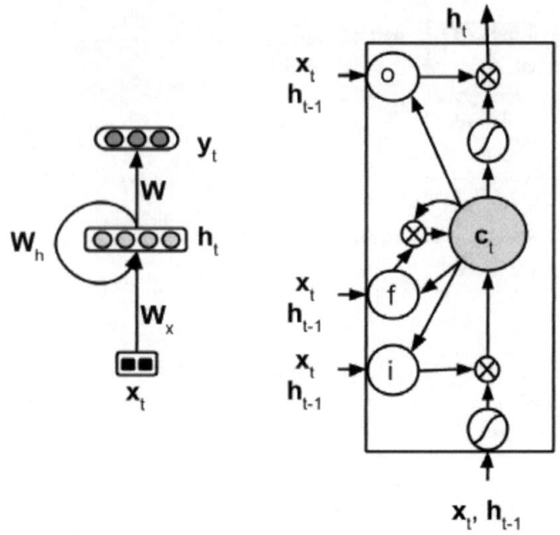

Figure 3: Simple recurrent neural network (left) and long short-term memory (right). Bias vectors are removed for the simplicity.

where $\mathbf{W}_x \in \mathbb{R}^{|\mathbf{h}| \times |\mathbf{x}_t|}$, $\mathbf{W}_h \in \mathbb{R}^{|\mathbf{h}| \times |\mathbf{h}|}$, $\mathbf{b} \in \mathbb{R}^{|\mathbf{h}|}$ are weight matrices and a bias vector; g is an activation.

This network model thus, in theory, can be used to estimate probabilities conditioning on long histories. And computing gradients is efficient thanks to the back-propagation through time algorithm (Werbos, 1990). In practice, however, training recurrent neural networks with the gradient descent method is challenging because gradients $\partial J_t/\partial \mathbf{h}_j$ ($j \leq t$, J_t is the objective function at time t) vanish quickly after a few back-propagation steps (Hochreiter et al., 2001). In addition, it is difficult to capture long range dependencies, i.e. the output at time t depends on some inputs that happened very long time ago. One solution for this, proposed by Hochreiter and Schmidhuber (1997) and enhanced by Gers (2001), is *long short-term memory* (LSTM).

Long Short-Term Memory The main idea of the LSTM architecture is to maintain a memory of *all* inputs the hidden layer received over time, by *adding up* all (gated) inputs to the hidden layer through time to a memory cell. In this way, errors propagated back through time do not vanish and even inputs received a very long time ago are still (approximately) preserved and can play a role in computing the output of the network (see the illustration in Graves (2012, Chapter 4)).

An LSTM cell (see Figure 3-right) consists of a memory cell c, an input gate i, a forget gate f, an output gate o. Computations occur in this cell are given below

$$
\begin{aligned}
\mathbf{i}_t &= \sigma\big(\mathbf{W}_{xi}\mathbf{x}_t + \mathbf{W}_{hi}\mathbf{h}_{t-1} + \mathbf{W}_{ci}\mathbf{c}_{t-1} + \mathbf{b}_i\big) \\
\mathbf{f}_t &= \sigma\big(\mathbf{W}_{xf}\mathbf{x}_t + \mathbf{W}_{hf}\mathbf{h}_{t-1} + \mathbf{W}_{cf}\mathbf{c}_{t-1} + \mathbf{b}_f\big) \\
\mathbf{c}_t &= \mathbf{f}_t \odot \mathbf{c}_{t-1} + \\
&\quad \mathbf{i}_t \odot \tanh\big(\mathbf{W}_{xc}\mathbf{x}_t + \mathbf{W}_{hc}\mathbf{h}_{t-1} + \mathbf{b}_c\big) \\
\mathbf{o}_t &= \sigma\big(\mathbf{W}_{xo}\mathbf{x}_t + \mathbf{W}_{ho}\mathbf{h}_{t-1} + \mathbf{W}_{co}\mathbf{c}_t + \mathbf{b}_o\big) \\
\mathbf{h}_t &= \mathbf{o}_t \odot \tanh(\mathbf{c}_t)
\end{aligned}
$$

where σ is the sigmoid function; $\mathbf{i}_t$, $\mathbf{f}_t$, $\mathbf{o}_t$ are the outputs (i.e. activations) of the corresponding gates; $\mathbf{c}_t$ is the state of the memory cell; $\odot$ denotes the element-wise multiplication operator; $\mathbf{W}$'s and $\mathbf{b}$'s are weight matrices and bias vectors.

Because the sigmoid function has the output range $(0, 1)$ (see Figure 2), activations of those gates can be seen as normalized weights. Therefore, intuitively, the network can learn to use the input gate to decide when to memorize information, and similarly learn to use the output gate to decide when to access that memory. The forget gate, finally, is to reset the memory.

3 Long Short-Term Memory in RNNs

In this section, we propose an extension of the LSTM for the RNN model (see Figure 4). A key feature of the RNN is to hierarchically combine information from two children to compute the parent vector; the idea in this section is to extend the LSTM such that not only the output from each of the children is used, but also the contents of their memory cells. This way, the network has the option to store information when processing constituents low in the parse tree, and make it available later on when it is processing constituents high in the parse tree.

For the simplicity [2], we assume that the parent node p has two children a and b. The LSTM at p thus has two input gates i_1, i_2 and two forget gates f_1, f_2 for the two children. Computations occuring in this LSTM are:

[2]Extending our LSTM for n-ary trees is trivial.

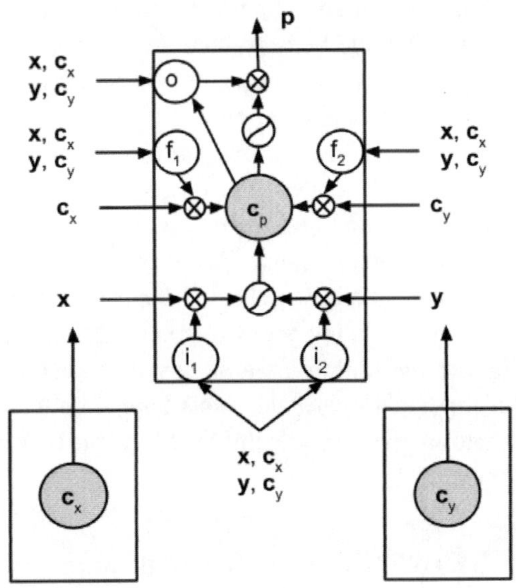

Figure 4: Long short-term memory for recursive neural network.

$$
\begin{aligned}
\mathbf{i}_1 &= \sigma\big(\mathbf{W}_{i1}\mathbf{x} + \mathbf{W}_{i2}\mathbf{y} + \mathbf{W}_{ci1}\mathbf{c}_x + \mathbf{W}_{ci2}\mathbf{c}_y + \mathbf{b}_i\big) \\
\mathbf{i}_2 &= \sigma\big(\mathbf{W}_{i1}\mathbf{y} + \mathbf{W}_{i2}\mathbf{x} + \mathbf{W}_{ci1}\mathbf{c}_y + \mathbf{W}_{ci2}\mathbf{c}_x + \mathbf{b}_i\big) \\
\mathbf{f}_1 &= \sigma\big(\mathbf{W}_{f1}\mathbf{x} + \mathbf{W}_{f2}\mathbf{y} + \mathbf{W}_{cf1}\mathbf{c}_x + \mathbf{W}_{cf2}\mathbf{c}_y + \mathbf{b}_f\big) \\
\mathbf{f}_2 &= \sigma\big(\mathbf{W}_{f1}\mathbf{y} + \mathbf{W}_{f2}\mathbf{x} + \mathbf{W}_{cf1}\mathbf{c}_y + \mathbf{W}_{cf2}\mathbf{c}_x + \mathbf{b}_f\big) \\
\mathbf{c}_p &= \mathbf{f}_1 \odot \mathbf{c}_x + \mathbf{f}_2 \odot \mathbf{c}_y + \\
&\quad g\big(\mathbf{W}_{c1}\mathbf{x} \odot \mathbf{i}_1 + \mathbf{W}_{c2}\mathbf{y} \odot \mathbf{i}_2 + \mathbf{b}_c\big) \\
\mathbf{o} &= \sigma\big(\mathbf{W}_{o1}\mathbf{x} + \mathbf{W}_{o2}\mathbf{y} + \mathbf{W}_{co}\mathbf{c} + \mathbf{b}_o\big) \\
\mathbf{p} &= \mathbf{o} \odot g(\mathbf{c}_p)
\end{aligned}
$$

where $\mathbf{u}$ and $\mathbf{c}_u$ are the output and the state of the memory cell at node u; $\mathbf{i}_1$, $\mathbf{i}_2$, $\mathbf{f}_1$, $\mathbf{f}_2$, $\mathbf{o}$ are the activations of the corresponding gates; $\mathbf{W}$'s and $\mathbf{b}$'s are weight matrices and bias vectors; and g is an activation function.

Intuitively, the input gate i_j lets the LSTM at the parent node decide how important the output at the j-th child is. If it is important, the input gate i_j will have an activation close to 1. Moreover, the LSTM controls, using the forget gate f_j, the degree to which information from the memory of the j-th child should be added to its memory.

Using one input gate and one forget gate for each child makes the LSTM flexible in storing memory and computing composition. For instance, in a complex sentence containing a main clause and a dependent clause it could be beneficial if only information about the main clause is passed on to higher levels. This can be achieved by having low values for the input gate and the forget gate for the child node that covers the dependent clause, and high values for the gates corresponding to the child node covering (a part of) the main clause. More interestingly, this LSTM can even allow a child to contribute to composition by activating the corresponding input gate, but ignore the child's memory by deactivating the corresponding forget gate. This happens when the information given by the child is temporarily important only.

4 LSTM-RNN model for Sentiment Analysis [3]

In this section, we introduce a model using the proposed LSTM for sentiment analysis. Our model, named LSTM-RNN, is an extension of the traditional RNN model (see Section 2.2) where traditional composition function g's in Equations 2- 3 are replaced by our proposed LSTM (see Figure 5). On top of the node covering a phrase/word, if its sentiment class (e.g. positive, negative, or neutral) is available, we put a softmax layer (see Equation 1) to compute the probability of assigning a class to it.

The vector representations of words (i.e. word embeddings) can be initialized randomly, or pretrained. The memory of any leaf node w, i.e. $\mathbf{c}_w$, is 0.

Similarly to Irsoy and Cardie (2014), we 'untie' leaf nodes and inner nodes: we use one weight matrix set for leaf nodes and another set for inner nodes. Hence, let d_w and d respectively be the dimensions of word embeddings (leaf nodes) and vector representations of phrases (inner nodes), all weight matrices from a leaf node to an inner node have size $d \times d_w$, and all weight matrices from an inner node to another inner node have size $d \times d$.

[3]The LSTM architecture was already applied to the sentiment analysis task, for instance in the model proposed at `http://deeplearning.net/tutorial/lstm.html`. Independently from and concurrently with our work, Tai et al. (2015) and Zhu et al. (2015) have developed very similar models applying LTSM to RNNs.

Training Training this model is to minimize the following objective function, which is the cross-entropy over training sentence set $\mathcal{D}$ plus an L2-norm regularization term

$$J(\theta) = -\frac{1}{|\mathcal{D}|}\sum_{s\in\mathcal{D}}\sum_{p\in s}\log Pr(c_p|\mathbf{p}) + \frac{\lambda}{2}||\theta||^2$$

where θ is the parameter set, c_p is the sentiment class of phrase p, $\mathbf{p}$ is the vector representation at the node covering p, $Pr(c_p|\mathbf{p})$ is computed by the softmax function, and λ is the regularization parameter. Like training an RNN, we use the mini-batch gradient descent method to minimize J, where the gradient $\partial J/\partial\theta$ is computed efficiently thanks to the back-propagation through structure (Goller and Küchler, 1996). We use the AdaGrad method (Duchi et al., 2011) to automatically update the learning rate for each parameter.

4.1 Complexity

We analyse the complexities of the RNN and LSTM-RNN models in the forward phase, i.e. computing vector representations for inner nodes and classification probabilities. The complexities in the backward phase, i.e. computing gradients $\partial J/\partial\theta$, can be analysed similarly.

The complexities of the two models are dominated by the matrix-vector multiplications that are carried out. Since the number of sentiment classes is very small (5 or 2 in our experiments) compared to d and d_w, we only consider those matrix-vector multiplications which are for computing vector representations at the inner nodes.

For a sentence consisting of N words, assuming that its parse tree is binarized without any unary branch (as in the data set we use in our experiments), there are $N-1$ inner nodes, N links from leaf nodes to inner nodes, and $N-2$ links from inner nodes to other inner nodes. The complexity of RNN in the forward phase is thus approximately

$$N \times d \times d_w + (N-2) \times d \times d$$

The complexity of LSTM-RNN is approximately

$$N \times 6 \times d \times d_w + (N-2) \times 10 \times d \times d + (N-1) \times d \times d$$

If $d_w \approx d$, the complexity of LSTM-RNN is about 8.5 times higher than the complexity of RNN.

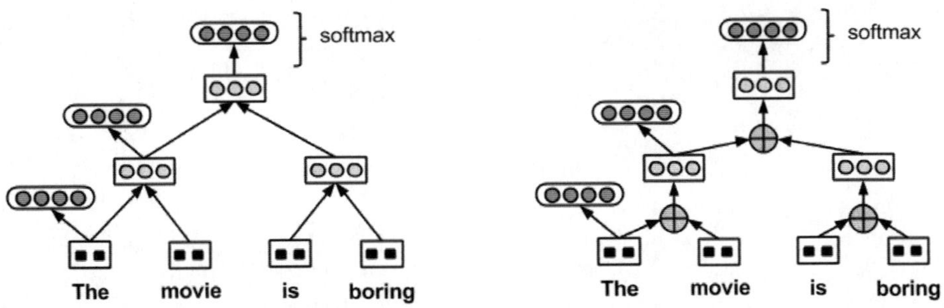

Figure 5: The RNN model (left) and LSTM-RNN model (right) for sentiment analysis.

In our experiments, this difference is not a problem because training and evaluating the LSTM-RNN model is very fast: it took us, on a single core of a modern computer, about 10 minutes to train the model ($d = 50, d_w = 100$) on 8544 sentences, and about 2 seconds to evaluate it on 2210 sentences.

5 Experiments

5.1 Dataset

We used the Stanford Sentiment Treebank[4] (Socher et al., 2013b) which consists of 5-way fine-grained sentiment labels (very negative, negative, neutral, positive, very positive) for 215,154 phrases of 11,855 sentences. The standard splitting is also given: 8544 sentences for training, 1101 for development, and 2210 for testing. The average sentence length is 19.1.

In addition, the treebank also supports binary sentiment (positive, negative) classification by removing neutral labels, leading to: 6920 sentences for training, 872 for development, and 1821 for testing.

The evaluation metric is the accuracy, given by $\frac{100 \times \#correct}{\#total}$.

5.2 LSTM-RNN vs. RNN

Setting We initialized the word vectors by the 100-D GloVe[5] word embeddings (Pennington et al., 2014), which were trained on a 6B-word corpus. The initial values for a weight matrix were uniformly sampled from the symmetric interval $[-\frac{1}{\sqrt{n}}, \frac{1}{\sqrt{n}}]$ where n is the number of total input units.

[4]http://nlp.stanford.edu/sentiment/treebank.html

[5]http://nlp.stanford.edu/projects/GloVe/

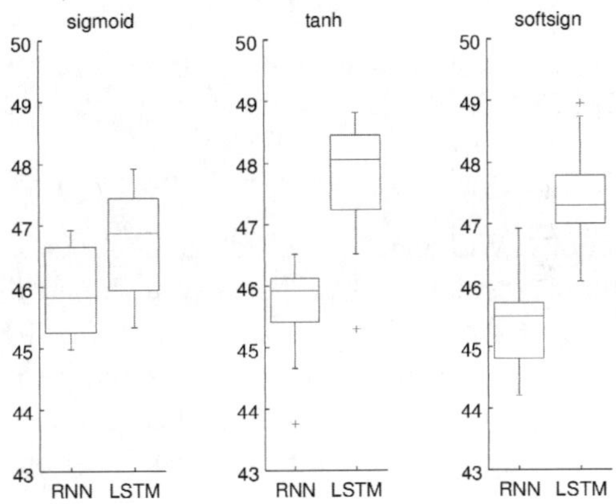

Figure 6: Boxplots of accuracies of 10 runs of RNN and LSTM-RNN on the test set in the fine-grained classification task. (LSTM stands for LSTM-RNN.)

For each model (RNN and LSTM-RNN), we tested three activation functions: softmax, tanh, and softsign, leading to six sub-models. Tuning those sub-models on the development set, we chose the dimensions of vector representations at inner nodes $d = 50$, learning rate 0.05, regularization parameter $\lambda = 10^{-3}$, and mini-batch-size 5.

On each task, we run each sub-model 10 times. Each time, we trained the sub-model in 20 epochs and selected the network achieving the highest accuracy on the development set.

Results Figure 6 and 7 show the statistics of the accuracies of the final networks on the test set in the fine-grained classification task and binary classification task, respectively.

It can be seen that LSTM-RNN outperformed RNN when using the tanh or softsign activation

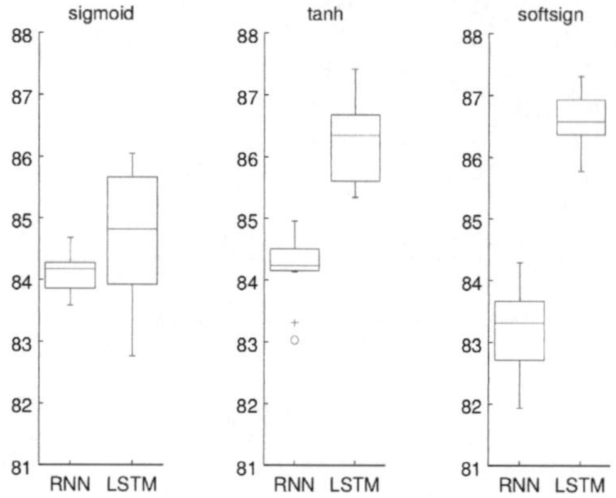

Figure 7: Boxplot of accuracies of 10 runs of RNN and LSTM-RNN on the test set in the binary classification task. (LSTM stands for LSTM-RNN.)

functions. With the sigmoid activation function, the difference is not so clear, but it seems that LSTM-RNN performed slightly better. Tanh-LSTM-RNN and softsign-LSTM-RNN have the highest median accuracies (48.1 and 86.4) in the fine-grained classification task and in the binary classification task, respectively.

With the RNN model, it is surprising to see that the sigmoid function performed well, comparably with the other two functions in the fine-grained task, and even better than the softsign function in the binary task, given that it was not often chosen in recent work. The softsign function, which was shown to work better than tanh for deep networks (Glorot and Bengio, 2010), however, did not yield improvements in this experiment.

With the LSTM-RNN model, the tanh function, in general, worked best whereas the sigmoid function was the worst. This result agrees with the common choice for this activation function for the LSTM architecture in recurrent network research (Gers, 2001; Sutskever et al., 2014).

5.3 Compared against other Models

We compare LSTM-RNN (using tanh) in the previous experiment against existing models: Naive Bayes with bag of bigram features (BiNB), Recursive neural tensor network (RNTN) (Socher et al., 2013b), Convolutional neural network (CNN) (Kim, 2014), Dynamic convolutional neural network

Model	Fine-grained	Binary
BiNB	41.9	83.1
RNTN	45.7	85.4
CNN	48.0	<u>88.1</u>
DCNN	48.5	86.8
PV	48.7	87.8
DRNN	<u>49.8</u>	86.6
with GloVe-100D		
LSTM-RNN	48.0	86.2
with GloVe-300D		
LSTM-RNN	**49.9**	**88.0**

Table 1: Accuracies of the (tanh) LSTM-RNN compared with other models.

(DCNN) (Kalchbrenner et al., 2014), paragraph vectors (PV) (Le and Mikolov, 2014), and Deep RNN (DRNN) (Irsoy and Cardie, 2014).

Among them, BiNB is the only one that is not a neural net model. RNTN and DRNN are two extensions of RNN. Whereas RNTN, which keeps the structure of the RNN, uses both matrix-vector multiplication and tensor product for the composition purpose, DRNN makes the net deeper by concatenating more than one RNNs horizontally. CNN, DCNN and PV do not rely on syntactic trees. CNN uses a convolutional layer and a max-pooling layer to handle sequences with different lengths. DCNN is hierarchical in the sense that it stacks more than one convolutional layers with k-max pooling layers in between. In PV, a sentence (or document) is represented as an input vector to predict which words appear in it.

Table 1 (above the dashed line) shows the accuracies of those models. The accuracies of LSTM-RNN was taken from the network achieving the highest performance out of 10 runs on the development set. The accuracies of the other models are copied from the corresponding papers. LSTM-RNN clearly performed worse than DCNN, PV, DRNN in both tasks, and worse than CNN in the binary task.

5.4 Toward State-of-the-art with Better Word Embeddings

We focus on DRNN, which is the most similar to LSTM-RNN among those four models CNN, DCNN, PV and DRNN. In fact, from the results reported in Irsoy and Cardie (2014, Table 1a), LSTM-

RNN performed on par[6] with their 1-layer-DRNN ($d = 340$) using dropout, which is to randomly remove some neurons during training. Dropout is a powerful technique to train neural networks, not only because it plays a role as a strong regularization method to prohibit neurons co-adapting, but it is also considered a technique to efficiently make an ensemble of a large number of shared weight neural networks (Srivastava et al., 2014). Thanks to dropout, Irsoy and Cardie (2014) boosted the accuracy of a 3-layer-DRNN with $d = 200$ from 46.06 to 49.5 in the fine-grained task.

In the second experiment, we tried to boost the accuracy of the LSTM-RNN model. Inspired by Irsoy and Cardie (2014), we tried using dropout and better word embeddings. Dropout, however, did not work with LSTM. The reason might be that dropout corrupted its memory, thus making training more difficult. Better word embeddings did pay off, however. We used 300-D GloVe word embeddings trained on a 840B-word corpus. Testing on the development set, we chose the same values for the hyper-parameters as in the first experiment, except setting learning rate 0.01. We also run the model 10 times and selected the networks getting the highest accuracies on the development set. Table 1 (below the dashed line) shows the results. Using the 300-D GloVe word embeddings was very helpful: LSTM-RNN performed on par with DRNN in the fine-grained task, and with CNN in the binary task. Therefore, taking into account both tasks, LSTM-RNN with the 300-D GloVe word embeddings outperformed all other models.

6 Discussion and Conclusion

We proposed a new composition method for the recursive neural network (RNN) model by extending the long short-term memory (LSTM) architecture which is widely used in recurrent neural network research.

[6]Irsoy and Cardie (2014) used the 300-D word2vec word embeddings trained on a 100B-word corpus whereas we used the 100-D GloVe word embeddings trained on a 6B-word corpus. From the fact that they achieved the accuracy 46.1 with an RNN ($d = 50$) in the fine-grained task and 85.3 in the binary task, and our implementation of RNN ($d = 50$) performed worse (see Table 6 and 7), we conclude that the 100-D GloVe word embeddings are not more suitable than the 300-D word2vec word embeddings.

The question is why LSTM-RNN performed better than the traditional RNN. Here, based on the fact that the LSTM for RNNs should work very similarly to LSTM for recurrent neural networks, we borrow the argument given in Bengio et al. (2013, Section 3.2) to answer the question. Bengio explains that the LSTM behaves like low-pass filter "hence they can be used to focus certain units on different frequency regions of the data". This suggests that the LSTM plays a role as a lossy compressor which is to keep global information by focusing on low frequency regions and remove noise by ignoring high frequency regions. So composition in this case could be seen as compression, like the recursive auto-encoder (RAE) (Socher et al., 2011a). Because pre-training an RNN as an RAE can boost the overall performance (Socher et al., 2011a; Socher et al., 2011c), seeing LSTM as a compressor might explain why the LSTM-RNN worked better than RNN without pre-training.

Comparing LSTM-RNN against DRNN (Irsoy and Cardie, 2014) gives us a hint about how to improve our model. From the experimental results, LSTM-RNN without the 300-D GloVe word embeddings performed worse than DRNN, while DRNN gained a significant improvement thanks to dropout. Finding a method like dropout that does not corrupt the LSTM memory might boost the overall performance significantly and will be a topic for our future work.

Acknowledgments

We thank three anonymous reviewers for helpful comments.

References

Marco Baroni, Raffaella Bernardi, and Roberto Zamparelli. 2013. Frege in space: A program for compositional distributional semantics. In A. Zaenen, B. Webber, and M. Palmer, editors, *Linguistic Issues in Language Technologies*. CSLI Publications, Stanford, CA.

Yoshua Bengio, Nicolas Boulanger-Lewandowski, and Razvan Pascanu. 2013. Advances in optimizing recurrent networks. In *Acoustics, Speech and Signal Processing (ICASSP), 2013 IEEE International Conference on*, pages 8624–8628. IEEE.

George Cybenko. 1989. Approximation by superpositions of a sigmoidal function. *Mathematics of control, signals and systems*, 2(4):303–314.

John Duchi, Elad Hazan, and Yoram Singer. 2011. Adaptive subgradient methods for online learning and stochastic optimization. *The Journal of Machine Learning Research*, pages 2121–2159.

Jeffrey L. Elman. 1990. Finding structure in time. *Cognitive science*, 14(2):179–211.

Felix Gers. 2001. Long short-term memory in recurrent neural networks. *Unpublished PhD dissertation, École Polytechnique Fédérale de Lausanne, Lausanne, Switzerland.*

Xavier Glorot and Yoshua Bengio. 2010. Understanding the difficulty of training deep feedforward neural networks. In *International conference on artificial intelligence and statistics*, pages 249–256.

Christoph Goller and Andreas Küchler. 1996. Learning task-dependent distributed representations by backpropagation through structure. In *International Conference on Neural Networks*, pages 347–352. IEEE.

Alex Graves. 2012. *Supervised sequence labelling with recurrent neural networks*, volume 385. Springer.

Sepp Hochreiter and Jürgen Schmidhuber. 1997. Long short-term memory. *Neural computation*, 9(8):1735–1780.

S. Hochreiter, Y. Bengio, P. Frasconi, and J. Schmidhuber. 2001. Gradient flow in recurrent nets: the difficulty of learning long-term dependencies. In Kremer and Kolen, editors, *A Field Guide to Dynamical Recurrent Neural Networks*. IEEE Press.

Ozan Irsoy and Claire Cardie. 2014. Deep recursive neural networks for compositionality in language. In *Advances in Neural Information Processing Systems*, pages 2096–2104.

Nal Kalchbrenner, Edward Grefenstette, and Phil Blunsom. 2014. A convolutional neural network for modelling sentences. In *Proceedings of the 52nd Annual Meeting of the Association for Computational Linguistics (Volume 1: Long Papers)*, pages 655–665, Baltimore, Maryland, June. Association for Computational Linguistics.

Yoon Kim. 2014. Convolutional neural networks for sentence classification. In *Proceedings of the 2014 Conference on Empirical Methods in Natural Language Processing (EMNLP)*, pages 1746–1751, Doha, Qatar, October. Association for Computational Linguistics.

Quoc Le and Tomas Mikolov. 2014. Distributed representations of sentences and documents. In *Proceedings of the 31st International Conference on Machine Learning (ICML-14)*, pages 1188–1196.

Phong Le and Willem Zuidema. 2014a. The inside-outside recursive neural network model for dependency parsing. In *Proceedings of the 2014 Conference on Empirical Methods in Natural Language Processing*. Association for Computational Linguistics.

Phong Le and Willem Zuidema. 2014b. Inside-outside semantics: A framework for neural models of semantic composition. In *NIPS 2014 Workshop on Deep Learning and Representation Learning*.

Tomas Mikolov, Martin Karafiát, Lukas Burget, Jan Cernockỳ, and Sanjeev Khudanpur. 2010. Recurrent neural network based language model. In *INTERSPEECH*, pages 1045–1048.

Jeff Mitchell and Mirella Lapata. 2009. Language models based on semantic composition. In *Proceedings of the 2009 Conference on Empirical Methods in Natural Language Processing*, pages 430–439.

Romain Paulus, Richard Socher, and Christopher D Manning. 2014. Global belief recursive neural networks. In *Advances in Neural Information Processing Systems*, pages 2888–2896.

Jeffrey Pennington, Richard Socher, and Christopher D Manning. 2014. Glove: Global vectors for word representation. *Proceedings of the Empiricial Methods in Natural Language Processing (EMNLP 2014)*, 12.

David E Rumelhart, Geoffrey E Hinton, and Ronald J Williams. 1988. Learning representations by backpropagating errors. *Cognitive modeling*, 5.

Richard Socher, Christopher D. Manning, and Andrew Y. Ng. 2010. Learning continuous phrase representations and syntactic parsing with recursive neural networks. In *Proceedings of the NIPS-2010 Deep Learning and Unsupervised Feature Learning Workshop*.

Richard Socher, Eric H. Huang, Jeffrey Pennington, Andrew Y. Ng, and Christopher D. Manning. 2011a. Dynamic pooling and unfolding recursive autoencoders for paraphrase detection. *Advances in Neural Information Processing Systems*, 24:801–809.

Richard Socher, Cliff C. Lin, Andrew Y. Ng, and Christopher D. Manning. 2011b. Parsing natural scenes and natural language with recursive neural networks. In *Proceedings of the 26th International Conference on Machine Learning*, volume 2.

Richard Socher, Jeffrey Pennington, Eric H Huang, Andrew Y Ng, and Christopher D Manning. 2011c. Semi-supervised recursive autoencoders for predicting sentiment distributions. In *Proceedings of the Conference on Empirical Methods in Natural Language Processing*, pages 151–161.

Richard Socher, John Bauer, Christopher D Manning, and Andrew Y Ng. 2013a. Parsing with compositional vector grammars. In *Proceedings of the 51st Annual Meeting of the Association for Computational Linguistics*, pages 455–465.

Richard Socher, Alex Perelygin, Jean Y Wu, Jason Chuang, Christopher D Manning, Andrew Y Ng, and

Christopher Potts. 2013b. Recursive deep models for semantic compositionality over a sentiment treebank. In *Proceedings EMNLP*.

Nitish Srivastava, Geoffrey Hinton, Alex Krizhevsky, Ilya Sutskever, and Ruslan Salakhutdinov. 2014. Dropout: A simple way to prevent neural networks from overfitting. *The Journal of Machine Learning Research*, 15(1):1929–1958.

Ilya Sutskever, Oriol Vinyals, and Quoc VV Le. 2014. Sequence to sequence learning with neural networks. In *Advances in Neural Information Processing Systems*, pages 3104–3112.

Kai Sheng Tai, Richard Socher, and Christopher D Manning. 2015. Improved semantic representations from tree-structured long short-term memory networks. *arXiv preprint arXiv:1503.00075*.

Paul J Werbos. 1990. Backpropagation through time: what it does and how to do it. *Proceedings of the IEEE*, 78(10):1550–1560.

Xiaodan Zhu, Parinaz Sobhani, and Hongyu Guo. 2015. Long short-term memory over tree structures. *arXiv preprint arXiv:1503.04881*.

A Hybrid Distributional and Knowledge-based Model of Lexical Semantics

Nikolaos Aletras
Department of Computer Science,
University College London,
Gower Street,
London WC1E 6BT
United Kingdom
nikos.aletras@gmail.com

Mark Stevenson
Department of Computer Science,
University of Sheffield,
Regent Court, 211 Portobello,
Sheffield S1 4DP
United Kingdom
mark.stevenson@sheffield.ac.uk

Abstract

A range of approaches to the representation of lexical semantics have been explored within Computational Linguistics. Two of the most popular are distributional and knowledge-based models. This paper proposes hybrid models of lexical semantics that combine the advantages of these two approaches. Our models provide robust representations of synonymous words derived from WordNet. We also make use of WordNet's hierarcy to refine the synset vectors. The models are evaluated on two widely explored tasks involving lexical semantics: lexical similarity and Word Sense Disambiguation. The hybrid models are found to perform better than standard distributional models and have the additional benefit of modelling polysemy.

1 Introduction

The representation of lexical semantics is a core problem in Computational Linguistics and a variety of approaches have been developed. Two of the most widely explored have been knowledge-based and distributional semantics.

Knowledge-based approaches make use of some external information source which defines the set of possible meanings for each lexical item. The most widely used information source is WordNet (Fellbaum, 1998), although other resources, such as Machine Readable Dictionaries, thesaurii and ontologies have also been used (see Navigli (2009)).

One advantage of these resources is that they represent the various possible meanings of lexical items which makes it straightforward to identify ones that are ambiguous. For example, these resources would include multiple meanings for the word *ball* including the 'event' and 'sports equipment' senses. However, the fact that there are multiple meanings associated with ambiguous lexical items can also be problematic since it may not be straightforward to identify which one is being used for an instance of an ambiguous word in text. This issue has lead to significant exploration of the problem of Word Sense Disambiguation (Ide and Véronis, 1998; Navigli, 2009).

More recently distributional semantics has become a popular approach to representing lexical semantics (Turney and Pantel, 2010; Erk, 2012). These approaches are based on the premise that the semantics of lexical items can be modelled by their context (Firth, 1957; Harris, 1985). Distributional semantic models have the advantages of being robust and straightforward to create from unannotated corpora. However, problems can arise when they are used to represent the semantics of polysemous words. Distributional semantic models are generally constructed by examining the context of lexical items in unannotated corpora. But for ambiguous words, like *ball*, it is not clear if a particular instance of the word in a corpus refers to the 'event', 'sports equipment' or another sense which can lead to the distributional semantic model becoming a mixture of different meanings without representing any of the meanings individually.

This paper proposes models that merge elements of distributional and knowledge-based approaches to lexical semantics and combines advantages of both techniques. A standard distributional semantic model

*Proceedings of the Fourth Joint Conference on Lexical and Computational Semantics (*SEM 2015)*, pages 20–29,
Denver, Colorado, June 4–5, 2015.

is created from an unannotated corpus and then refined using WordNet. The resulting models can be viewed as enhanced distributional models that have been refined using the information from WordNet to reduce the problems caused by ambiguous terms when models are created. Alternatively, it can be used as a version of the WordNet hierarchy in which distributional semantic models are attached to synsets. Thereby creating a version of WordNet for which the appropriate synsets can be identified more easily for ambiguous lexical items that occur in text.

We evaluate our models on two standard tasks: lexical similarity and word sense disambiguation. Results show that the proposed hybrid models perform consistently better than traditional distributional semantic models.

The reminder of the paper is organised as follows. Section 2 describes our hybrid models which combine information from WordNet and a standard distributional semantic model. These models are augmented using Latent Semantic Analysis and Canonical Correlation Analysis. Sections 3 and 4 describe evaluation of the models on the word similarity and word sense disambiguation tasks. Related work is presented in Section 5 and conclusions in Section 6.

2 Semantic Models

First, we consider a standard distributional semantic space to represent words as vectors (Section 2.1). Then, we make use of the WordNet's clusters of synonyms and hierarchy in combination with the standard distributional space to build hybrid models (Section 2.2) which are augmented using Latent Semantic Analysis (Section 2.3) and Canonical Correlation Analysis (Section 2.4).

2.1 Distributional Model

We consider a semantic space D, as a word by context feature matrix, $L \times C$. Vector representations consist of context features C in a reference corpus. We made use of pre-computed publicly available vectors[1] optimised for word similarity tasks (Baroni et al., 2014). Word co-occurrence counts are extracted using a symmetric window of two words over a corpus of 2.8 billion tokens obtained by concatenating ukWaC, the English Wikipedia and the British National Corpus. Vectors are weighted using positive Pointwise Mutual Information and the set of context features consists of the top 300K most frequent words in the corpus.

2.2 Hybrid Models

2.2.1 Synset Distributional Model

We assume that making use of information about the structure of WordNet can reduce noise introduced in vectors of D due to polysemy. We make use of all noun and verb synsets (excluding numbers and compounds) that contain at least one of the words in L to create a vector-based synset representation, H. Where H is a synset by context feature matrix, i.e. $S \times C$. Each synset vector is generated by computing the centroid of its lemma vectors in S (i.e. the sum of the lemma's vectors normalised by the number of the lemmas in the synset). For example, the vector of the synset *car.n.01* is computed as the centroid of its lemma vectors, i.e. *car, auto, automobile, machine* and *motorcar* (see Figure 1).

2.2.2 Synset Rank Model

The Synset Distributional Model provides a vector representation for each synset in WordNet which is created using information about which lemmas share synset membership. An advantage of this approach is that vectors from multiple lemmas are combined to form the synset representation. However, a disadvantage is that many of these lemmas are polysemous and their vectors represent multiple senses, not just the one that is relevant to the synset. For example, in WordNet the lemma *machine* has several possible meanings, only one of which is a member of the synset *car.n.01*.

WordNet also contains information about the relations between synsets, in the form of the synset hierarchy, which can be exploited to re-weight the importance of context features for particular synsets. We employ a graph-based algorithm that makes use of the WordNet is-a hierarchy. The intuition behind this approach is that context features that are relevant to a given synset are likely to be shared by its neighbours in the hierarchy while those that are not relevant (i.e. have been introduced via an irrelevant sense of a synset member) will not be. The graph-based algorithm increases the weight of context features

[1] http://clic.cimec.unitn.it/composes/semantic-vectors.html

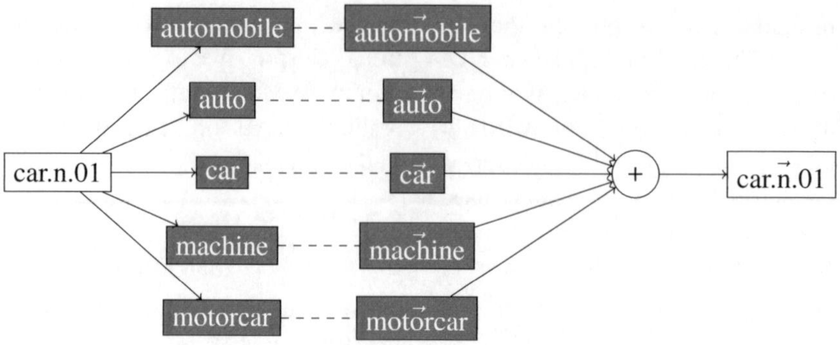

Figure 1: In the Synset Distributional Model the vector representing a synset (white box) is computed as the centroid of its lemma vectors (grey boxes)

that synsets share with neighbours and reduces those that are not shared.

PageRank (Page et al., 1999) is a graph-based algorithm for identifying important nodes in a graph that has been applied to a range of NLP tasks including word sense disambiguation (Agirre and Soroa, 2009) and keyword extraction (Mihalcea and Tarau, 2004).

Let $G = (V, E)$ be a graph with a set of vertices, V, denoting synsets and a set of edges, E, denoting links between synsets in the WordNet hierarchy. The PageRank score (Pr) over G for a synset (V_i) can be computed by the following equation:

$$Pr(V_i) = d \cdot \sum_{V_j \in I(V_i)} \frac{1}{O(V_j)} Pr(V_j) + (1-d)\mathbf{v} \quad (1)$$

where $I(V_i)$ denotes the in-degree of the vertex V_i and $O(V_j)$ is the out-degree of vertex V_j. d is the damping factor which is set to the default value of $d = 0.85$ (Page et al., 1999). In standard PageRank all elements of the vector $\mathbf{v}$ are the same, $\frac{1}{N}$ where N is the number of nodes in the graph.

Personalised PageRank (PPR) (Haveliwala et al., 2003) is a variant of the PageRank algorithm in which extra importance is assigned to certain vertices in the graph. This is achieved by adjusting the values of the vector $\mathbf{v}$ in equation 1 to prefer certain nodes. The values in $\mathbf{v}$ effectively initialises the graph and assigning high values to nodes in $\mathbf{v}$ makes them more likely to be assigned a high PPR score.

For each context feature c in C if $c \in LM$ where LM contains all the lemma names of synsets in S, we apply PPR to assign importance to synsets. The score of each synset S_c in the personalisation vector $\mathbf{v}$, is set to $\frac{1}{|S_c|}$ where $|S_c|$ is the number of synsets that context feature i belongs. The personalisation value of all the other sysnets is set to 0.

We apply PPR over WordNet for each context feature using UKB (Agirre et al., 2009) and obtain weights for each synset-context feature pair resulting to a new semantic space H_{p}, $S \times C$, where vector elements are weighted by PageRank values. Figure 2 shows how the synset scores are computed by applying PPR over WordNet given the context feature *car*. Note that we use the context features of the distributional model D.

2.3 Latent Semantic Analysis

Latent Semantic Analysis (LSA) (Deerwester et al., 1990; Landauer and Dumais, 1997) has been used to reduce the dimensionality of semantic spaces leading to improved performance. LSA applies Singular Value Decomposition (SVD) to a matrix X, $W \times C$, which represents a distributional semantic space. This is a form of factor analysis where X is decomposed into three other matrices:

$$X = U \Sigma V^T \quad (2)$$

where U is a $W \times W$ matrix of row vectors where its columns are eigenvectors of XX^T, Σ is a diagonal $W \times C$ matrix containing the singular values and V is a $C \times C$ matrix of context feature vectors where its columns are eigenvectors of $X^T X$. The multiplication of the three component matrices results in the original matrix, X. Any matrix can be decomposed perfectly if the number of singular values is no smaller than the smallest dimension of X. When

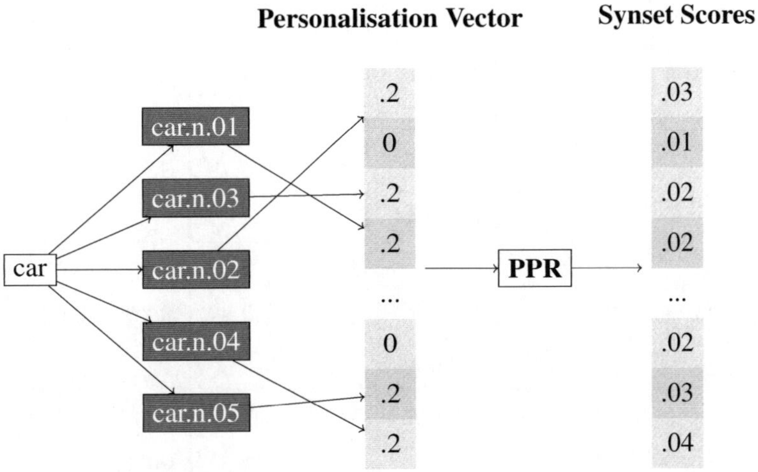

Figure 2: In the Synset Rank Model, each synset (grey boxes) is assigned with a score by computing PPR over WordNet. The personalisation vector (grey array) is initialised by assigning probabilities only to the synsets that include the context feature as a lemma name.

fewer singular values are used then the matrix product is an approximation of the original matrix. LSA reduces the dimensionality of the SVD by deleting coefficients in the diagonal matrix Σ starting with the smallest. The approximation of matrix X retaining the K largest singular values, $\tilde{X}$, is then given by:

$$\tilde{X} \approx U_K \Sigma_K V_K^T \quad (3)$$

where U_K is a $W \times K$ matrix of word vectors, Σ_K is a $K \times K$ diagonal matrix with singular values and V_K is a $K \times C$ matrix of context feature vectors.

We apply LSA on the Synset Distributional Model, H and the Synset Rank model, H_p to obtained the reduced semantic spaces $\tilde{H}$ and $\tilde{H}_\mathrm{p}$ respectively.

2.4 Joint Representation using CCA

Recent work has demonstrated that distributional models can benefit from combining alternative views of data (see Section 5). H and H_p provide two different views of the synsets and we incorporate evidence from both to learn a joint representation using Canonical Correlation Analysis (CCA) (Hardoon et al., 2004). Given two multidimensional variables $\mathbf{x}$ and $\mathbf{y}$, CCA finds two projection vectors by maximising the correlations of the variables onto these projections. The function to be maximised is:

$$\rho = \frac{E[xy]}{\sqrt{E[x^2]E[y^2]}} \quad (4)$$

The dimensionality of the projection vectors is lower or equal to the dimensionality of the original variables.

The computation of CCA directly over H and H_p is computationally infeasible because of their high dimensionality (300K). We apply CCA over the reduced spaces learned using LSA, $\tilde{H}$ and $\tilde{H}_\mathrm{p}$ to obtain two joint semantic spaces following a similar approach to Faruqui and Dyer (2014). These are the spaces H^*, resulting from the projection of the Synset Distributional Model $\tilde{H}$, and H_p^*, resulting from the projection of the Synset Rank Model $\tilde{H}_\mathrm{p}$.

3 Word Similarity

3.1 Computing Similarity

Since hybrid models represent words as synset vectors, similarity between two words can be computed following two ways. First, we compute similarity between two words as the **maximum** of their pairwise synset similarity. On the other hand, similarity can be computed as the **average** pairwise synset similarity using the synsets that the two words belong. Similarity is computed as the cosine of the angle between word or synset vectors.

3.2 Data

We make use of six standard data sets that have been widely used for evaluating lexical similarity and relat-

Max						
Model	**WS-353**	**WS-Sim**	**WS-Rel**	**RG**	**MC**	**MEN**
Distributional Model						
D	0.62	0.70	**0.59**	0.79	0.72	**0.72**
Hybrid Models - Full						
H	0.49	0.60	0.36	0.69	0.64	0.58
H_{p}	0.58	0.67	0.49	0.82	**0.86**	0.63
Hybrid Models - LSA						
$\tilde{H}$	0.55	0.69	0.42	0.71	0.71	0.54
$\tilde{H}_{\mathrm{p}}$	0.58	0.68	0.46	0.85	**0.86**	0.55
Hybrid Models - CCA						
H^*	**0.67**	**0.76**	0.57	0.81	0.79	**0.72**
H_{p}^*	0.52	0.62	0.41	**0.86**	0.80	0.56

Table 1: Spearman's correlation on various data sets. Maximum similarity between pairs of synsets.

edness. First, we make use of **WS-353** (Finkelstein et al., 2001) which contains 353 pairs of words annotated by humans. Furthermore, we make use of the similarity (**WS-Sim**) and relatedness (**WS-Rel**) pairs of words created by Agirre et al. (2009) from the original WS-353 data set.

We also made use of the **RG** (Rubenstein and Goodenough, 1965) and **MC** (Miller and Charles, 1991) data sets which contain 65 and 30 pairs of nouns respectively. Finally, we make use of the larger **MEN** data set (Bruni et al., 2012) which contains 3,000 pairs of words that has been used as image tags. Annotations are obtained using croudsourcing.

3.3 Model Parameters

The parameters we need to tune are the number of the top components in LSA spaces, $\tilde{H}$ and $\tilde{H}_{\mathrm{p}}$, and CCA spaces, H^* and H_{p}^*. For the LSA spaces, we tune the number of the top k components in RG. We set $k \in \{50, 100, ..., 1000\}$ and select the value that maximises performance which is $k = 700$ for $\tilde{H}$ and $k = 650$ for $\tilde{H}_{\mathrm{p}}$. For the joint spaces learned using CCA, we also tune the number of the top l correlated features in RG. We set $l \in \{10, 20, ..., 650\}$ and select the value that maximises performance which is $l = 250$ for H^* and $l = 40$ for H_{p}^*.

3.4 Evaluation Metric

Performance is measured as the correlation between the similarity scores returned by each proposed method and the human judgements. This is the standard approach to evaluate word and text similarity tasks, e.g. (Budanitsky and Hirst, 2001; Agirre et al., 2009; Agirre et al., 2012). Our experiments use Spearman's correlation coefficient.

3.5 Results

Table 1 shows the Spearman's correlation of similarity scores generated by each model and human judgements of similarity across various data sets by taking the maximum pairwise similarity score of two words' synsets. The first row of the table shows the results obtained by the word distributional model of Baroni et al. (2014). The full hybrid models H and H_{p} perform consistently worse than the original distributional model D across data sets. The main reason is that a large number of synsets contain only one lemma name which might be polysemous. For example, the only lemma name of the synsets 'ball.n.01' (*'round object that is hit or thrown or*

Average						
Model	**WS-353**	**WS-Sim**	**WS-Rel**	**RG**	**MC**	**MEN**
Distributional Model						
D	0.62	0.70	0.59	0.79	0.72	0.72
Hybrid Models - Full						
H	0.61	0.71	0.52	0.72	0.65	0.64
H_{p}	0.65	0.73	0.56	0.79	0.81	0.58
Hybrid Models - LSA						
$\tilde{H}$	0.59	0.70	0.48	0.68	0.68	0.63
$\tilde{H}_{\mathrm{p}}$	0.65	0.73	0.56	**0.81**	**0.86**	0.58
Hybrid Models - CCA						
H^*	**0.70**	**0.77**	**0.64**	0.78	0.84	**0.74**
H^*_{p}	0.61	0.69	0.52	0.72	0.76	0.62

Table 2: Spearman's correlation on various data sets. Average pairwise similarity between pairs of synsets.

kicked in games') and 'ball.n.04' (*'the people assembled at a lavish formal dance'*) is 'ball'. In this case, the synset vector in H and the lemma vector in D are identical and still polysemous. This problem does not hold in H_{p} and therefore the correlations are higher for that semantic space but still lower than those obtained for D. Applying LSA on H and H_{p} improves results but correlations are still lower than those obtained using D[2]. On the other hand, the joint space learned by applying CCA, H^*, produces consistently better similarity estimates than D while outperforms all the other models in the majority of the data sets. That confirms our main assumption than incorporating information obtained from a large corpus and a knowledge-base improves word vector representations.

Table 2 shows the Spearman's correlation of similarity scores generated by each model and human judgements of similarity across various data sets by taking the average pairwise similarity score of two words' synsets. Results show that using the average rather than the maximum system similarity improves results for almost all data sets. For example, the best hybrid model, H^*, achieves correlations that are between 2% and 12% than D for the majority of data sets, although performance is 1% lower for the RG data set. This improved performance suggest that human judgements of word similarity are based on the relation between all the senses of two given words rather than just the most similar ones.

[2]Note that Baroni et al. (2014) found that applying SVD to D did not improve performance over using the full space.

4 Word Sense Disambiguation

4.1 Data

We test the efficiency of our hybrid models on the English All Words tasks of Senseval-2 (Palmer et al., 2001) and Senseval-3 (Snyder and Palmer, 2004), two standard data sets for evaluating WSD. Our experiments focus on the disambiguation of nouns in these data sets.

4.2 Word Sense Tagging

A simple approach to all-words WSD was implemented in which each sense of an ambiguous word is compared against its context and the most similar chosen.

For example suppose that we want to disambiguate

Nouns	Senseval-2		Senseval-3	
	Precision	Recall	Precision	Recall
Hybrid Models - Full				
H	0.46	0.45	0.37	0.36
H_p	**0.65**	**0.63**	**0.50**	**0.48**
Hybrid Models - LSA				
$\tilde{H}$	0.45	0.44	0.39	0.37
$\tilde{H}_\mathrm{p}$	0.60	0.58	0.46	0.45
Hybrid Models - CCA				
H^*	0.44	0.43	0.36	0.34
H^*_p	0.61	0.60	0.48	0.46

Table 3: Results obtained by hybrid models on SenseEval-2 and SenseEval-3 data sets (nouns only).

the word *bank* in the following sentence:

"Banks provide payment services."

Assume that the word *bank* consists of two senses *'bank.n.01'* and *bank.n.02* defined as *'sloping land (especially the slope beside a body of water)'* and *"a financial institution that accepts deposits and channels the money into lending activities'* respectively.

First we consider the vectors of all the possible noun synsets containing the word *bank* as a synset name. Then for each context word (*provide*, *payment* and *service*) that exists in our semantics spaces we compute a centroid vector from its constituent senses. Finally, we compute a context vector for the entire context by summing up all the context word vectors. We select the synset of the target word that its vector has the highest cosine similarity to the context vector.

4.3 Model Parameters

The parameters we need to tune are the same as for the word similarity task and we use the best settings obtained for that task. We also experimented with varying the number of surrounding sentences used as context by testing values between ±1 and ±4. The best performance was obtained using a context created from the sentence containing the target word and ±1 sentences surrounding it.

4.4 Evaluation Metrics

Word sense disambiguation systems are evaluated by computing precision and recall. Precision measures the proportion of disambiguated words that have been correctly assigned with a sense. Recall measures the proportion of words disambiguated correctly out of all words available for disambiguation.

4.5 Results

Table 3 shows the results obtained by using our hybrid models on the two word sense disambiguation data sets. The full Synset Rank model H_p is consistently better method in terms of precision and recall in both data sets. On the other hand, it is somewhat surprising that dimensionality reduction and integration of semantic spaces do not help in improving performance. That is the $\tilde{H}_p$ and H^*_p models achieve lower precision and recall than the fuller H_p.

The Synset Distributional models H, $\tilde{H}$ and H^* consistently fail to perform well. The difference in precision and recall compared to the Synset Rank models is between 12% and 19%. This suggests that the knowledge-based weighting of the context features generates less noisy vectors for sense tagging.

The pattern of results observed for the WSD task is somewhat different to those obtained for word similarity, where applying LSA and CCA improved performance (see Section 3). The most likely explanation of this difference is that WSD requires the model to represent the possible senses of each ambiguous word. It is also important that these senses correspond to the ones used in the relevant lexicon (WordNet in this case). The Synset Rank model H_p does this by making use of information from WordNet. However, these synset representations are disrupted by LSA and CCA which compress the semantic space by extracting general features from them. This is not a problem for word similarity since there is no need to model the senses found in the lexicon.

5 Related Work

Dealing with polysemy in distributional semantics is a fundamental issue since the various senses of a word type are conflated in a single vector. Previous work tackled the problem through vector adaptation, clustering and language models (Erk, 2012). Vector adaptation methods modify a traditional (i.e. polysemous) target word vector by applying pointwise operations such as addition or multiplication to that and the surrounding words in a sentence (Mitchell and Lapata, 2008; Erk and Padó, 2008; Thater et al., 2011; Van de Cruys et al., 2011). Alternatively, clustering methods have been used to cluster together the different contexts a target word appears assuming that each cluster of contexts captures a different sense of the target word (Dinu and Lapata, 2010; Erk and Pado, 2010; Reisinger and Mooney, 2010). Language models have also been used to remove polysemy from word vectors by predicting words that could replace the target word given a context (Deschacht and Moens, 2009; Washtell, 2010; Moon and Erk, 2013). More recently, Polajnar and Clark (2014) applied context selection and normalisation to improve the quality of word vectors. Our hybrid models are related to the vector adaptation methods since we modify the synset vectors using its lemmas' vectors to remove noise.

Our work is also inspired by recent work on improving classic distributional vector representations of words by incorporating information from different modalities. For example, researchers have developed methods that make use of both visual and contextual information to improve word vectors (Bruni et al., 2011; Silberer et al., 2013; Lazaridou et al., 2014). Following a similar direction, Faruqui and Dyer (2014) found that learning joint spaces from multilingual vector spaces using CCA improves the performance of standard monolingual vector spaces on semantic similarity. Fyshe et al. (2014) showed that integrating textual vector space models with brain activation data when people are reading words achieves better correlation to behavioural data than models of one modality.

Our hybrid models are also closely related to a supervised method proposed by Faruqui et al. (2015). Their method refines distributional semantic models using relational information from various semantic lexicons, including WordNet, by making linked words in these lexicons to have similar vector representations. While our models are also based on using information from WordNet for refining vector representations, they are fundamentally different. They create synset vectors in an unsupervised fashion and more importantly can be used for sense tagging.

6 Conclusions

This paper proposed hybrid models of lexical semantics that combine distributional and knowledge-based approaches and offer advantages of both techniques. A standard distributional semantic model is created from an unannotated corpus and then refined by (1) using WordNet synsets to create synset vectors; and (2) applying a graph-based technique over WordNet to reweight synset vectors. The resulting hybrid models can be viewed as enhanced distributional models using the information from WordNet to reduce the problems caused by ambiguous terms when models are created. Results show that our models perform better than traditional distributional models on lexical similarity tasks. Unlike standard distributional approaches the techniques proposed here also model polysemy and can be used to carry out word sense disambiguation.

References

Eneko Agirre and Aitor Soroa. 2009. Personalizing PageRank for word sense disambiguation. In *Proceedings of the 12th Conference of the European Chapter of the Association for Computational Linguistics (EACL '09)*, pages 33–41, Athens, Greece.

Eneko Agirre, Enrique Alfonseca, Keith Hall, Jana Kravalova, Marius Pasca, and Aitor Soroa. 2009. A study on similarity and relatedness using distributional and wordnet-based approaches. In *Proceedings of Human Language Technologies: The 2009 Annual Conference of the North American Chapter of the Association for Computational Linguistics (NAACL-HLT '09)*, pages 19–27, Boulder, Colorado.

Eneko Agirre, Mona Diab, Daniel Cer, and Aitor Gonzalez-Agirre. 2012. Semeval-2012 task 6: A pilot on semantic textual similarity. In *Proceedings of the First Joint Conference on Lexical and Computational Semantics-Volume 1: Proceedings of the main conference and the shared task, and Volume 2: Proceedings of the Sixth International Workshop on Semantic Evaluation*, pages 385–393. Association for Computational Linguistics.

Marco Baroni, Georgiana Dinu, and Germán Kruszewski. 2014. Don't count, predict! a systematic comparison of context-counting vs. context-predicting semantic vectors. In *Proceedings of the 52nd Annual Meeting of the Association for Computational Linguistics (Volume 1: Long Papers)*, pages 238–247, Baltimore, Maryland.

Elia Bruni, Giang Binh Tran, and Marco Baroni. 2011. Distributional semantics from text and images. In *Proceedings of the Workshop on GEometrical Models of Natural Language Semantics (GEMS '11)*, pages 22–32, Edinburgh, UK, July.

Elia Bruni, Gemma Boleda, Marco Baroni, and Nam-Khanh Tran. 2012. Distributional semantics in technicolor. In *Proceedings of the 50th Annual Meeting of the Association for Computational Linguistics: Long Papers-Volume 1*, pages 136–145, Jeju Island, Korea.

Alexander Budanitsky and Graeme Hirst. 2001. Semantic distance in WordNet: An experimental, application-oriented evaluation of five measures. In *Proceedings of the workshop on "WordNet and other Lexical Resources" at the Second Annual Meeting of the North American Association for Computational Linguistics*, Pittsburgh, PA.

Scott Deerwester, Susan T. Dumais, George W. Furnas, Thomas K. Landauer, and Richard Harshman. 1990. Indexing by latent semantic analysis. *Journal of the American Society for Information Science*, 41(6):391–407.

Koen Deschacht and Marie-Francine Moens. 2009. Semi-supervised semantic role labeling using the Latent Words Language Model. In *Proceedings of the 2009 Conference on Empirical Methods in Natural Language Processing*, pages 21–29, Singapore.

Georgiana Dinu and Mirella Lapata. 2010. Measuring distributional similarity in context. In *Proceedings of the 2010 Conference on Empirical Methods in Natural Language Processing*, pages 1162–1172, Cambridge, MA.

Katrin Erk and Sebastian Padó. 2008. A structured vector space model for word meaning in context. In *Proceedings of the 2008 Conference on Empirical Methods in Natural Language Processing*, pages 897–906, Honolulu, Hawaii.

Katrin Erk and Sebastian Pado. 2010. Exemplar-based models for word meaning in context. In *Proceedings of the ACL 2010 Conference Short Papers*, pages 92–97, Uppsala, Sweden.

Katrin Erk. 2012. Vector space models of word meaning and phrase meaning: A survey. *Language and Linguistics Compass*, 6(10):635–653.

Manaal Faruqui and Chris Dyer. 2014. Improving vector space word representations using multilingual correlation. In *Proceedings of the 14th Conference of the European Chapter of the Association for Computational Linguistics*, pages 462–471, Gothenburg, Sweden.

Manaal Faruqui, Jesse Dodge, Sujay K Jauhar, Chris Dyer, Eduard Hovy, and Noah A Smith. 2015. Retrofitting word vectors to semantic lexicons. In *Proceedings of the 2015 Conference of NAACL*, Denver, Colorado.

C. Fellbaum, editor. 1998. *WordNet: An Electronic Lexical Database*. The MIT Press, Cambridge, MA, London.

Lev Finkelstein, Evgeniy Gabrilovich, Yossi Matias, Ehud Rivlin, Zach Solan, Gadi Wolfman, and Eytan Ruppin. 2001. Placing search in context: The concept revisited. In *Proceedings of the 10th international conference on World Wide Web*, pages 406–414, New York, USA. ACM Press.

J. Firth. 1957. A synopsis of linguistic theory 1930-1955. In *Studies in Linguistic Analysis*.

Alona Fyshe, Partha P. Talukdar, Brian Murphy, and Tom M. Mitchell. 2014. Interpretable semantic vectors from a joint model of brain- and text- based meaning. In *Proceedings of the 52nd Annual Meeting of the Association for Computational Linguistics (Volume 1: Long Papers)*, pages 489–499, Baltimore, Maryland.

David Hardoon, Sandor Szedmak, and John Shawe-Taylor. 2004. Canonical correlation analysis: An overview with application to learning methods. *Neural computation*, 16(12):2639–2664.

Z. Harris. 1985. Distributional structure. In J. Katz, editor, *The Philosophy of Linguistics*, pages 26–47. Oxford University Press, New York.

Taher Haveliwala, Sepandar Kamvar, and Glen Jeh. 2003. An analytical comparison of approaches to personalizing PageRank. Technical Report 2003-35, Stanford InfoLab.

N. Ide and J. Véronis. 1998. Introduction to the special issue on word sense disambiguation: The state of the art. *Computational Linguistics*, 24(1):1–40.

Thomas K Landauer and Susan T Dumais. 1997. A solution to plato's problem: The latent semantic analysis theory of acquisition, induction, and representation of knowledge. *Psychological review*, 104(2):211.

Angeliki Lazaridou, Elia Bruni, and Marco Baroni. 2014. Is this a wampimuk? cross-modal mapping between distributional semantics and the visual world. In *Proceedings of the 52nd Annual Meeting of the Association for Computational Linguistics (Volume 1: Long Papers)*, pages 1403–1414, Baltimore, Maryland.

Rada Mihalcea and Paul Tarau. 2004. TextRank: Bringing order into texts. In *Proceedings of International Conference on Empirical Methods in Natural Language Processing (EMNLP '04)*, pages 404–411, Barcelona, Spain.

George A Miller and Walter G Charles. 1991. Contextual correlates of semantic similarity. *Language and cognitive processes*, 6(1):1–28.

Jeff Mitchell and Mirella Lapata. 2008. Vector-based models of semantic composition. In *Proceedings of ACL-08: HLT*, pages 236–244, Columbus, Ohio.

Taesun Moon and Katrin Erk. 2013. An inference-based model of word meaning in context as a paraphrase distribution. *ACM Transactions on Intelligent Systems and Technology (TIST)*, 4(3):42.

Roberto Navigli. 2009. Word Sense Disambiguation: a survey. *ACM Computing Surveys*, 41(2):1–69.

Lawrence Page, Sergey Brin, Rajeev Motwani, and Terry Winograd. 1999. The PageRank citation ranking: Bringing order to the web. Technical Report 1999-66, Stanford InfoLab.

Martha Palmer, Christiane Fellbaum, Scott Cotton, Lauren Delfs, and Hoa Trang Dang. 2001. English tasks: All-words and verb lexical sample. In *The Proceedings of the Second International Workshop on Evaluating Word Sense Disambiguation Systems*, pages 21–24, Toulouse, France.

Tamara Polajnar and Stephen Clark. 2014. Improving distributional semantic vectors through context selection and normalisation. In *Proceedings of the 14th Conference of the European Chapter of the Association for Computational Linguistics*, pages 230–238, Gothenburg, Sweden. Association for Computational Linguistics.

Joseph Reisinger and Raymond J. Mooney. 2010. Multi-prototype vector-space models of word meaning. In *Human Language Technologies: The 2010 Annual Conference of the North American Chapter of the Association for Computational Linguistics*, pages 109–117, Los Angeles, California.

Herbert Rubenstein and John B Goodenough. 1965. Contextual correlates of synonymy. *Communications of the ACM*, 8(10):627–633.

Carina Silberer, Vittorio Ferrari, and Mirella Lapata. 2013. Models of semantic representation with visual attributes. In *Proceedings of the 51st Annual Meeting of the Association for Computational Linguistics (Volume 1: Long Papers)*, pages 572–582, Sofia, Bulgaria.

Benjamin Snyder and Martha Palmer. 2004. The english all-words task. In *Senseval-3: Third International Workshop on the Evaluation of Systems for the Semantic Analysis of Text*, pages 41–43, Barcelona, Spain.

Stefan Thater, Hagen Fürstenau, and Manfred Pinkal. 2011. Word meaning in context: A simple and effective vector model. In *Proceedings of 5th International Joint Conference on Natural Language Processing*, pages 1134–1143, Chiang Mai, Thailand.

Peter D. Turney and Patrick Pantel. 2010. From frequency to meaning: Vector space models of semantics. *Journal of Artificial Intelligence Research*, 37:141–188.

Tim Van de Cruys, Thierry Poibeau, and Anna Korhonen. 2011. Latent vector weighting for word meaning in context. In *Proceedings of the 2011 Conference on Empirical Methods in Natural Language Processing*, pages 1012–1022, Edinburgh, Scotland, UK.

Justin Washtell. 2010. Expectation vectors: A semiotics inspired approach to geometric lexical-semantic representation. In *Proceedings of the 2010 Workshop on GEometrical Models of Natural Language Semantics (GEMS)*, pages 45–50, Uppsala, Sweden.

Distributional semantics for ontology verification *

Julien Corman
IRIT, University of Toulouse
julien.corman@irit.fr

Nathalie Aussenac-Gilles
CNRS
IRIT, University of Toulouse
aussenac@irit.fr

Laure Vieu
CNRS
IRIT, University of Toulouse
vieu@irit.fr

Abstract

As they grow in size, OWL ontologies tend to comprise intuitively incompatible statements, even when they remain logically consistent. This is true in particular of lightweight ontologies, especially the ones which aggregate knowledge from different sources. The article investigates how distributional semantics can help detect and repair violation of common sense in consistent ontologies, based on the identification of consequences which are unlikely to hold if the rest of the ontology does. A score evaluating the plausibility for a consequence to hold with regard to distributional evidence is defined, as well as several methods in order to decide which statements should be preferably amended or discarded. A conclusive evaluation is also provided, which consists in extending an input ontology with randomly generated statements, before trying to discard them automatically.

1 Introduction

Ontology learning from texts deals with the automated extraction of knowledge from linguistic evidence. This article investigates a slightly different problem, which is how Natural Language Processing may provide hints for the identification of statements of an input ontology which are unlikely to hold if the rest of it does. As a minimal example, consider the following set Δ of statements, from DBpedia (Mendes et al., 2012), and assume that Δ is a subset of a larger set of statements K (for instance DBpedia itself, or some subset of it) :

Ex 1.
Δ = { (1) `keyPerson`(*Caixa Bank*, *CEO*),
(2) `keyPerson`(*BrookField Office Properties*, *Peter Munk*)
(3) `occupation`(*Peter Munk*, *CEO*) }

There is a clear violation of common sense in Δ : the individual *CEO* must be both a key person of *Caixa Bank*, and the occupation of another individual (*Peter Munk*), who is himself a key person of some company. Detecting such cases within (larger) sets of logical statements is of particular interest in OWL, which facilitates the aggregation of knowledge from multiple sources with overlapping signatures, yielding datasets in which several incompatible understandings of a same individual or predicate may coexist. This easily leads to undesired inferences, even when the dataset is logically consistent.[1] But as the example illustrates, the problem may also occur within a single knowledge base, especially if it has been built semi-automatically, and/or is issued from a collaborative effort.

Another problem of interest consists in deciding which statement(s) should be preferably discarded or amended in order to get rid of the nonsense. In example 1, without further information, it would be intuitively relevant to discard or modify either (1) or (2). Unfortunately though, Δ alone does not give any indication of which of the two should be preferably discarded. But the whole input ontology $K \supset$

* The research reported here was supported by a Marie Curie FP7 Career Integration Grant, Grant Agreement Number PCIG13-GA-2013-618550.

[1] and *coherent* in the Description Logics sense, i.e. whose signature contains unsatisfiable DL atomic concepts/OWL named classes

*Proceedings of the Fourth Joint Conference on Lexical and Computational Semantics (*SEM 2015)*, pages 30–39,
Denver, Colorado, June 4–5, 2015.

Δ may. To keep the example simple, let us assume that *Peter Munk*, *CEO* and occupation do not appear in $K \setminus \Delta$. Then a reasonable assumption is that the overall understanding of keyPerson within K should be the decisive factor. If it generally ranges over person functions (i.e. if in most instances of the relation according to K, the second argument is a person function), then it is to be understood as "has as a key person someone whose function is", and (2) should be preferably discarded. Alternatively, if keyPerson generally ranges over human beings, then (1) should be preferably discarded.

The article investigates the use of linguistic evidence to solve both of these problems : identifying violations of common sense, and selecting the statement(s) to be preferably amended or discarded. This may be viewed as a small paradigm shift, in that it questions an assumption commonly made in the knowledge extraction literature, namely that manually crafted knowledge strictly prevails over the one obtained from linguistic sources. By default, the case of a consistent[2] input ontology K will be studied, but section 6 discusses the application of the approach to an inconsistent K as well.

As a concrete contribution, section 5 evaluates the adaptation of relatively simple techniques issued from named entity classification/ontology population, and based on distributional semantics. To illustrate how this works, let us assume that the only other appearance of keyPerson within K is the following OWL statement :

(4) hasRange(keyPerson, Person)

i.e. in FOL :

(4) $\forall xy(\texttt{keyPerson}(x, y) \rightarrow \texttt{Person}(y))$

Then $K \models \psi_1 = \texttt{Person}(\textit{CEO})$, and $K \models \psi_2 = \texttt{Person}(\textit{Peter Munk})$. Assume also that there are other instances of Person according to K, and that most of them are actually human beings (like *Peter Munk*). Then ψ_1 is an undesirable consequence of K, whereas ψ_2 on the other hand reinforces it.

Distributional semantics characterizes a word (or possibly a multi word unit) by some algebraic representation of the linguistic contexts with which it is observed. These representations have already been used for ontology population, for instance by (Tanev and Magnini, 2008), the main intuition being that individuals denoted by linguistic terms with similar contexts tend to instantiate the same classes. The underlying linguistic phenomenon is known as *selectional preference*, i.e. the fact that some contexts tend to select or rule out certain categories of individuals : e.g. the context "*X* was born in" tends to select a human being, whereas "*X* was launched" tends to rule it out. Back to the example, one can expect the similarity between the distributional representation of the term "C.E.O" and other terms denoting instances of Person according to K to be relatively low, hindering the plausibility of ψ_1 with regard to K. In other words, ψ_1 should stand as an outlier among consequences of K, and therefore is probably undesirable. Conversely, the similarity between "Peter Munk" and terms denoting other instances of Person should be relatively high. For simplicity, suppose that (1), (2), (3) and (4) are the only 4 statements of K which are candidate for removal. Then in order to give up the belief in ψ_1 while preserving ψ_2, it is necessary to discard (1), and retain (2) and (4). It is also sufficient to discard (1), i.e. discarding (3) as well would result in an unnecessary information loss. So in this case, the evidence provided by distributional semantics should suggest the removal of (1), or at least its modification, which is also intuitively the correct solution.

Section 4 formalizes this approach, by defining a score which estimates the plausibility of some consequences a subbases Γ of K, given distributional evidence. Section 5 then provides an original evaluation of this strategy, based on the prior extension of a small OWL ontology with randomly generated statements. The approach is evaluated for both problems, i.e. the identification of undesired consequences and statements. Performances of several forms of distributional representations are also compared. Section 6 discusses immediate applications, in particular for (consistent and inconsistent) ontology debugging. Finally, section 7 considers possible extensions of this framework, as well as their limitations. Section 2 is a brief overview of related works in the fields of ontology learning and debugging, whereas section 3 introduces notational conventions, and lists some preliminary requirements to be met by the input K.

[2]and coherent (see footnote 1)

2 State of the art

Ontology learning from texts (Cimiano, 2006; Buitelaar et al., 2005) aims to automatically build or enriching a set of logical statements out of linguistic evidence, and is closely related to the field of information extraction. The work presented here borrows from a subtask called ontology population (which itself borrows from named entity classification), but only when the individuals and concepts of interest are already known (Cimiano and Völker, 2005; Tanev and Magnini, 2008; Giuliano and Gliozzo, 2008), which is not standard. A comparison may also be drawn with the use of linguistic evidence by (Suchanek et al., 2009) for information extraction in the presence of conflicting data.

But the objective of the present work is different, pertaining to ontology debugging, which covers a wide range of techniques, from syntactic verifications (Poveda-Villalón et al., 2012) to anti-patterns detection (Roussey and Zamazal, 2013), both based on common modeling mistakes, or the submission of models (Ferré and Rudolph, 2012; Benevides et al., 2010) or consequences (Pammer, 2010) of the input ontology to the user. As discussed in section 6, the framework depicted here presents an interesting complementarity with debugging techniques developed in the Description Logics community, prototypically based on diagnosis (Friedrich and Shchekotykhin, 2005; Kalyanpur et al., 2006; Qi et al., 2008; Ribeiro and Wassermann, 2009), because they require the prior identification of some undesired consequence of K (be it $\bot$). But distributional evidence may also provide a principled way of selecting most relevant diagnoses among a potentially large number of candidates, as well as an alternative to their exhaustive computation, which has been shown costly by (Schlobach, 2005).

3 Conventions and presuppositions

The prototypical input is a set of statements in OWL DL or OWL 2, although the approach may be generalized to other representation languages. OWL DL and OWL 2 are based on Description Logics (DL), which are themselves decidable fragments of first-order logic (FOL). The OWL notation is preferred to the DL one for readability, and FOL translations are given when not obvious.

An *ontology* is just understood here as a (finite) set of logical statements. A *class* will designate a named class in OWL, i.e. a FOL unary predicate, like `Person`, whereas a *named individual*, or just *individual*, designates a constant, like *Peter Munk*.

The input ontology K must provide English terms denoting some of its named individuals (e.g. the term "Peter Munk"). These terms are prototypically named entities, but may also occasionally be common nouns (or common noun phrases), as shown in example 1 with "C.E.O". There may be multiple terms for a same individual. The approach cannot handle polysemy though, in particular the fact that some individuals of K may have homonyms (within K or not), for instance that the term "JFK" can stand for a politician, airport or movie. Ideally, no distributional representation should be built for individuals of K with potential homonyms. Some of them may be identified with simple strategies, like checking the existence of a Wikipedia disambiguation page. On the opposite, labels for classes of K (prototypically common nouns or common noun phrases, which are arguably more ambiguous) are never used during the process.

4 Proposition

Given a subbase Γ of the input ontology K (possibly K itself), the ontology verification strategy presented in introduction relies on the evaluation of a set Ψ_Γ of consequences of Γ. This section first defines a score $\mathrm{sc}_\Gamma(\psi)$ for each $\psi \in \Psi_\Gamma$, which intuitively evaluates the plausibility of ψ wrt Γ, provided some distributional representation for each named individual appearing in Ψ_Γ. Then it discusses how this score can be used to select statements of the input ontology K which, according to distributional evidence, should be preferably discarded, or at least amended.

4.1 Plausibility of a consequence $\psi \in \Psi_\Gamma$

For the experiments described in section 5, Ψ_Γ is the set of consequences of Γ of the form $A(e)$ or $\neg A(e)$, with e a constant (like *CEO*) and A a unary predicate (like `Person`), and for which linguistic occurrences of a term denoting e could be retrieved. Possible extension of Ψ_Γ with other types of formulas is discussed in section 7.

Let ψ be a formula of Ψ_Γ, of the form $A(e)$, e.g. $\psi = \texttt{Person}(\textit{CEO})$ or $\psi = \texttt{Person}(\textit{Peter Munk})$. Then $\text{inst}_\Gamma(A)$ will designate all instances of A according to Γ for which linguistic occurrences could be retrieved, i.e. $\text{inst}_\Gamma(A) = \{e' \mid A(e') \in \Psi_\Gamma\}$, and $\text{inst}_\Gamma(A) \setminus \{e\}$ will be called the *support set* for $A(e)$. Similarly, $\text{inst}_\Gamma(\top)$ will designate all named individuals appearing in Ψ_Γ.

Let $\text{sim}(e_1, e_2)$ be a measure of similarity between the distributional representations of individuals e_1 and e_2 (prototypically the cosine similarity between some vector representations of the linguistic contexts of e_1 and e_2). Then for each $e' \in \text{inst}_\Gamma(A) \setminus \{e\}$, if $\text{sim}(e, e')$ is lower than what could be expected if e' was a random individual of $\text{inst}_\Gamma(\top) \setminus \{e\}$ (i.e. not necessarily an instance of A), the hypothesis that $A(e)$ is an outlier within Ψ_Γ will be reinforced.

For instance, in example 1, let $\psi = \texttt{Person}(\textit{CEO})$ and $\Gamma = K$. Then the support set $\text{inst}_\Gamma(A) \setminus \{e\}$ is composed of all other instances of Person according to Γ. For each individual e' of this support set, if $\text{sim}(\textit{CEO}, e')$ is lower than what can be expected for a random individual of K with linguistic occurrences (and different from *CEO*), then the confidence in $\texttt{Person}(\textit{CEO})$ should decline. Conversely, if $\text{sim}(e, e')$ is higher that expected, the hypothesis that ψ is in line with Ψ_Γ will be reinforced.

Here is a cost-efficient and relatively simple method to compute a plausibility score $\text{sc}_\Gamma(A(e))$. Let $S = \text{inst}_\Gamma(A) \setminus \{e\}$ designate the support set for Γ and e, and $|S|$ the cardinality of S, i.e. the number of other instances of A according to Γ. And let us assume a set W of $|S|$ randomly chosen elements of $\text{inst}_\Gamma(T) \setminus \{e\}$, i.e. of $|S|$ individuals which are different from e, but not necessarily instances of A. Finally, let the random variable $X^\Gamma_{e,|S|}$ model the expected value of $\sum_{e' \in W} \frac{\text{sim}(e,e')}{|S|}$, i.e. the mean of the similarities between e and each individual of W. In other words, if $|S|$ individuals were randomly chosen instead of those of the support set, $X^\Gamma_{e,|S|}$ models what the average similarity between e and these individuals can be expected to be. Then the plausibility $\text{sc}_\Gamma(A(e))$ of $A(e)$ can be defined by :

Definition 4.1. If $S = \text{inst}_\Gamma(A) \setminus \{e\}$, then $\text{sc}_\Gamma(A(e)) = p(X^\Gamma_{e,|S|} \leq \sum_{e' \in S} \frac{\text{sim}(e,e')}{|S|})$

$\text{sc}_\Gamma(A(e))$ estimates of how surprisingly high the similarity between e and the individuals of the support set S is, considering the overall similarity between e and the individuals of Γ.

For the evaluation described in section 5, the random variable $X^\Gamma_{e,|S|}$ was assumed to follow a beta distribution $\text{Beta}(\alpha, \beta)$, which intuitively allows taking the size $|S|$ of the support set into account. For instance, if $S = \{e'\}$, i.e. $|S| = 1$, then *ceteris paribus* a high similarity between e and e' will be less informative than an equally high average similarity between e and all elements of a large S. Stated another way, the lower $|S|$ is, the more uniform the distribution of $X^\Gamma_{e,|S|}$ should be. This can be obtained by setting $X^\Gamma_{e,|S|} \sim \text{Beta}(m|S| + 1, (1 - m)|S| + 1)$, where m is the average similarity between e and all other individuals of the signature of Γ, i.e. $m = \sum_{e' \in \Gamma \setminus \{e\}} \frac{\text{sim}(e,e')}{|\Gamma|-1}$.

A possible interrogation here is the choice of $\text{inst}_\Gamma(A) \setminus \{e\}$ as the support set for $A(e)$. For instances, if $\psi = \texttt{Person}(\textit{Peter Munk})$, a case could be made for using $\text{inst}_\Gamma(\neg A)$ as well, i.e. for exploiting the (dis)similarity between *Peter Munk* and individuals which, according to K, are instances of $\neg\texttt{Person}$.[3] This is quite unrealistic though from a linguistic point of view, which can be intuitively seen in this example by replacing *Peter Munk* with *CEO*. Assume for instance that *Thelonious Monk* and *Beijing* are (reliable) instances of Person and ¬Person respectively according to Γ. There is no reason to expect that $\text{sim}(\textit{CEO}, \textit{Beijing}) > \text{sim}(\textit{CEO}, \textit{Thelonious Monk})$. In other words, it is implausible to assume that elements of $\text{inst}_\Gamma(\neg A)$ should *a priori* share similar contexts.

Interestingly enough, and for the same reason, the support set for a consequence of Γ of the form $\neg A(e)$ is not $\text{inst}_\Gamma(\neg A)$, but $\text{inst}_\Gamma(A)$, which yields :

Definition 4.2. If $S = \text{inst}_\Gamma(A)$, then $\text{sc}_\Gamma(\neg A(e)) = p(X^\Gamma_{e,|S|} \geq \sum_{e' \in S} \frac{\text{sim}(e,e')}{|S|})$

[3] i.e. $\Gamma \models \neg\texttt{Person}(e')$ not only $\Gamma \not\models \texttt{Person}(e')$

4.2 Linguistic compliance of Γ

This does not directly address the second problem mentioned in introduction though. For practical ontology verification, it is also desirable to identify the cause of this nonsense, i.e. statements (*axioms* in the DL terminology) which are intuitively problematic. For instance, in example 1, computing $\text{sc}_\Gamma(\psi)$ for each $\psi \in \Psi_K$ may signal that the consequence ψ_1 is unlikely to hold wrt the larger ontology K. And discarding either (1) or (4) is sufficient to get rid of the belief in ψ. But given the additional assumptions made about K, discarding the former is preferable, in that discarding the latter would also result in the loss of ψ_2. In other words, some subbases of K (like $K \setminus (1)$ here) are more relevant than others (e.g. $K \setminus (4)$), which can be simply captured as follows. Let $\text{comp}(\Gamma)$ be an estimation of the compliance of a subbase Γ of K with the gathered linguistic evidence. A straightforward option consists in setting $\text{comp}(\Gamma)$ to be the mean of the scores of evaluated consequences for Γ, i.e. :

Definition 4.3. $\text{comp}(\Gamma) = \sum_{\psi \in \Psi_\Gamma} \frac{\text{sc}_\Gamma(\psi)}{|\Psi_\Gamma|}$

Then a strict partial order $\prec$ over 2^K can simply be defined by $\Gamma_1 \prec \Gamma_2$ iff either $\text{comp}(\Gamma_1) < \text{comp}(\Gamma_2)$, or ($\text{comp}(\Gamma_1) = \text{comp}(\Gamma_2)$ and $\Gamma_1 \subset \Gamma_2$),[4] and a subbase Γ of K can be viewed as optimal if it is maximal wrt $\prec$.[5]

In practice though, identifying optimal subbases is a non trivial task. To see this, note that the function to be maximized is not directly a function of the statements in Γ, but of Ψ_Γ, i.e. some of the consequences of Γ. So even if one could identify a subset Ψ' of Ψ_K which maximizes this function, there may not exist a subbase Γ of K such that $\Psi_\Gamma = \Psi'$. Another difficulty comes from the fact that for two subbases Γ_1 and Γ_2 of K, and a consequence $\psi \in \Psi_{\Gamma_1} \cap \Psi_{\Gamma_2}$, it doesn't hold in general that $\text{sc}_{\Gamma_1}(\psi) = \text{sc}_{\Gamma_2}(\psi)$, because the support set for ψ in Γ_1 may differ from its support set in Γ_2. In particular, it may be the case that $\Gamma_1 \subseteq \Gamma_2$ but $\text{sc}_{\Gamma_1}(\psi) > \text{sc}_{\Gamma_2}(\psi)$, which greatly reduces the possible uses of monotonicity (if $\Gamma_1 \subseteq \Gamma_2$, then $\text{Cn}(\Gamma_1) \subseteq \text{Cn}(\Gamma_2)$) to optimize the exploration of 2^K. More generally, if the optimal subbases of K are small (say twice smaller that K), it can be rightfully argued that dropping so many statements for the sake of linguistic evidence is not a viable debugging strategy.

Therefore a more plausible application scenario is one in which the search space has been previously circumscribed, either by setting a maximal (small) number of statements to discard, or by identifying a set of potentially erroneous statements, through *axiom pinpointing*, as explained in section 6. This is also why the evaluation presented in section 5 focuses on the simplest possible case, i.e. the removal from K of one statement only, whereas the integration of distributional evidence to more complex debugging strategies is discussed in section 6.

As an alternative to the function comp, and in order to avoid the fact that a same consequence may have different plausibility scores wrt two subbases of K, one may choose to discard unlikely consequences based on their respective scores in K, i.e. to use the score $\text{comp}_K(\Gamma)$,[6] defined by :

Definition 4.4. $\text{comp}_K(\Gamma) = \sum_{\psi \in \Psi_\Gamma} \frac{\text{sc}_K(\psi)}{|\Psi_\Gamma|}$

This solution is arguably less satisfying, but more amenable to optimizations. A trivial example is that of a subbase Γ_1 with $\max_{\psi \in \Psi_{\Gamma_1}} \text{sc}_K(\psi) < \text{comp}_K(\Gamma_2)$ for some already evaluated subbase Γ_2, in which case no subbase of Γ_1 can be optimal wrt $\prec$.

Additionally, instead of taking the mean of the scores of evaluated consequences of Γ, one may want to penalize the subbases of K with the most unlikely consequences, which gives a standard (total) lexicographic ordering $\preceq_{lex}$ on 2^K, defined as follows. Let $\boldsymbol{\omega}_\Gamma = \omega_\Gamma^1, .., \omega_\Gamma^{|\Psi_\Gamma|}$ be the vector of formulas of Ψ_Γ order by increasing score sc_Γ, and let $\text{sc}_\Gamma(\boldsymbol{\omega}_\Gamma) = \text{sc}_\Gamma(\omega_\Gamma^1), .., \text{sc}_\Gamma(\omega_\Gamma^{|\Psi_\Gamma|})$. Then $\preceq_{lex}$ is defined by $\Gamma_1 \preceq_{lex} \Gamma_2$ iff either $\text{sc}_{\Gamma_1}(\boldsymbol{\omega}_{\Gamma_1}) = \text{sc}_{\Gamma_2}(\boldsymbol{\omega}_{\Gamma_2})$, or (there is a $1 \leq i \leq |\Psi_{\Gamma_2}|$ such that $\text{sc}_{\Gamma_1}(\omega_{\Gamma_1}^j) = \text{sc}_{\Gamma_2}(\omega_{\Gamma_2}^j)$ for all $1 \leq j < i$, and either $\text{sc}_{\Gamma_1}(\omega_{\Gamma_1}^i) < \text{sc}_{\Gamma_2}(\omega_{\Gamma_2}^i)$ or $|\Psi_{\Gamma_1}| = i - 1$). Then

[4] The assumption is made that a minimum of syntactic information should be lost whenever possible, i.e. Γ_1 and Γ_2 are primarily viewed as bases, not as theories. In particular, if $\text{Cn}(\Gamma_1) = \text{Cn}(\Gamma_2)$, but $\Gamma_1 \not\subseteq \Gamma_2$ and $\Gamma_2 \not\subseteq \Gamma_1$, then Γ_1 and Γ_2 are not comparable wrt $\prec$. Redundancies in this view should also be preserved when possible, i.e. if $\text{Cn}(\Gamma_1) = \text{Cn}(\Gamma_2)$ and $\Gamma_1 \subset \Gamma_2$, then $\Gamma_1 \prec \Gamma_2$ still holds.

[5] There may be several several optimal subbases.

[6] or more generally $\text{comp}_{\Gamma'}(\Gamma)$, for some $\Gamma' \supseteq \Gamma$

as previously, a strict partial order $\prec$ over 2^K can be defined by $\Gamma_1 \prec \Gamma_2$ iff either $\Gamma_1 \prec_{lex} \Gamma_2$, or ($\Gamma_1 =_{lex} \Gamma_2$ and $\Gamma_1 \subset \Gamma_2$).

Again, $\text{sc}_K(\psi)$ may be used instead of $\text{sc}_\Gamma(\psi)$, yielding the lexical ordering $\preceq_{lex_K}$. This last possibility corresponds to a relatively intuitive operation, which consists in giving up in priority the most implausible consequences of K. All four possibilities are evaluated in what follows.

5 Evaluation

The dataset used for this evaluation is a fragment of the fisheries ontology from the NEON project.[7] It has been automatically built out of 10 randomly selected named individuals, applying a module extraction procedure, followed by a trimming algorithm. The fragment contains 1038 (logical) statements, and involves 71 named individuals (mostly geographical or administrative entities), the least expressive underlying DL being $\mathcal{SI}$.

The linguistic input is a small corpus of approximately 6300 web pages, retrieved with a search engine, using the labels of named individuals of F as queries. The HTML documents were cleaned with the BootCat library (Baroni and Bernardini, 2004).

The construction of the distributional representations of the named individuals of F was basic, the use of more elaborate methods (SVD,...) being left for future work. The approach presented in this article remains generic enough to be applied to most existing distributional frameworks, the only requirement being a real-valued similarity measure.

Two different forms of linguistic contexts were alternatively tested. The first option considers as a context any n-gram ($2 \leq n \leq 5$) without punctuation mark which immediately precedes or follows a term t denoting an individual of F. The other option is a more customized one, extracting sequences of lemmatized words (*lemmaPOS* in what follows) surrounding t, in a shifting window of 3 to 5 tokens + the size of t, ignoring certain categories of word. Part-of-speech tagging was performed thanks to the Stanford Parser (Toutanova et al., 2003), with a pre-trained model for English. If *Cont* designates the set of contexts observed with at least 2 individuals, then an individual was represented by the vector of its respective frequencies with each context $c \in Cont$. Different possibilities were compared to weight these frequencies. The pointwise mutual information (PMI) was used in a standard way for n-grams and lemmaPOS contexts (with possible negative resulting frequencies set to 0). Following (Giuliano and Gliozzo, 2008), the self-information *self*(c) was also used for n-grams, defined by *self*$(c) = -\log p(c)$, the probability $p(c)$ being estimated thanks to the Microsoft Web N-gram Services. A combined weighting by PMI and self-information was also tested for n-grams. These alternative settings are represented by capital letters in tables 1 and 2 : LP for lemmaPOS with PMI, and NP, NS and NPS for n-grams with PMI, self-information and both respectively.

The ontology F has been extended for the sake of the evaluation, with statements randomly generated out of its signature. The underlying assumption is that adding such statements to F is very likely to generate violations of common sense (although nothing prevents in theory the generation of plausible statements too). The goal for the evaluation was then to automatically retrieve proper consequences of each extension of F on the one hand, and the random statements themselves on the other hand.

To prevent any misunderstanding, it should be emphasized that this is not a realistic application case. The input ontology was selected for its quality, and degraded through random statement generation, allowing an arguably artificial, but also very objective evaluation procedure (the only bias may come from randomly generated statements which are actually plausible). By contrast, using a non modified input dataset, and evaluating whether or not the axioms/consequences spotted by the algorithm are actually erroneous is a complex and subjective task, with a possibly low inter-annotator agreement.

The generation procedure randomly selects a statement $\phi \in F$, and yields a statement ϕ' with the same syntactic structure as ϕ, but in which individuals and predicates have been replaced by random individuals and predicates appearing in F. For instance, if $\phi = \forall xy(A(x) \wedge r(x,y) \rightarrow \neg B(y))$, then $\phi' = \forall xy(C(x) \wedge s(x,y) \rightarrow \neg D(y))$, with C and D (resp. s) randomly chosen among classes (resp. binary predicates) of the signature of F.

100 randomly generated statements $\phi_1, \ldots, \phi_{100}$

[7] http://www.neon-project.org/nw/Ontologies

	rank	p-val
LP	4.15 / 216.1	<0.001
NP	9.73 / 216.1	<0.001
NS	7.33 / 216.1	<0.001
NPS	5.59 / 216.1	<0.001

Table 1: Average ranking among Ψ_{K_i} of the lowest-ranked formula of $\Psi_{K_i}^{rand}$, and p-value for the rankings of all formulas of all $\Psi_{K_i}^{rand}$

were added independently to F, yielding 100 input ontologies $K_1, \ldots, K_{100}$, such that each K_i was consistent, and that there was at least one consequence of the form $A(e)$ or $\neg A(e)$ entailed by K_i but not by F, with e sharing at least one linguistic context with some other individual of F. All 100 input ontologies are available online.[8]

The first part of the evaluation was performed as follows. For each K_i and each $\psi \in \Psi_{K_i}$, the plausibility $\mathrm{sc}_{K_i}(\psi)$ was computed as in definitions 4.1/4.2, and Ψ_{K_i} was ordered by increasing plausibility.[9] Within Ψ_{K_i} are consequences which were not initially entailed by F, but have been obtained after the extension of F with the random statement ϕ_i. So in a sense, these consequences are randomly generated too, and therefore one may expect many of them to convey absurd information (for instance `Architect`(*Belgium*)), or at least to be outliers (like `Person`(*CEO*) in ex 1) within Ψ_{K_i}. Let $\Psi_{K_i}^{rand}$ designate these additional consequences, i.e. $\Psi_{K_i}^{rand} = \Psi_{K_i} \setminus \Psi_F$. If $\psi \in \Psi_{K_i}^{rand}$, and if $\mathrm{sc}_{K_i}(\psi)$ is actually lower than for most other formulas of Ψ_{K_i}, this would indicate that the plausibility score, as formulated in definitions 4.1/4.2, is actually a good estimator.

In order to evaluate this, column "rank" in table 1 gives the average ranking (for all 100 ontologies) within Ψ_{K_i} of the formula $\psi_i \in \Psi_{K_i}^{rand}$ with lowest score. The lower this ranking, the more efficient the plausibility score is at detecting outlier consequences. Column "pVal" gives the probability (t-test) for the cumulated rankings of all formulas in all $\Psi_{K_i}^{rand}$ to be as low as the observed ones, if all consequences in all Ψ_{K_i} had been randomly ordered.

Results are convincing, with a significant p-value for all four settings. For most ontologies (75/100), there was only one formula in $\Psi_{K_i}^{rand}$. A closer look at the data revealed that, for the best setting (LP), in most of theses cases (57/75), the only formula in $\Psi_{K_i}^{rand}$ was also the one with lowest plausibility in Ψ_{K_i}, over 216.1 on average, i.e. the only randomly generated consequence was also the least plausible one according to linguistic evidence. This is very encouraging, especially considering the relatively small number of named individuals (71) in F, i.e. the fact that the support to evaluate the plausibility of a consequence $\psi \in \Psi_{K_i}$ was limited. On the other hand, performances were generally poor when the cardinality of $\Psi_{K_i}^{rand}$ was important ($> 0.25 * |\Psi_{K_i}|$), which may be explained by the fact that support sets for some classes of F were significantly modified after the extension of F with ϕ_i.

As for the settings, unsurprisingly, the two most beneficial (but unfortunately incompatible) factors were the use of lemmatized contexts on the one hand (LP), and the queries over the Web N-gram corpus on the other hand (NS and NPS)

The second part of the evaluation focused on the retrieval of the random statements $\phi_1, .., \phi_{100}$, for the LP setting only, because it gave the best results in the previous experiment. For each extended base K_i, all immediate subbases $\Gamma_{i,1}, .., \Gamma_{i,|F|+1}$ of K_i were generated, i.e. each $\Gamma_{i,j}$ was such that $K_i = \Gamma_{i,j} \cup \{\phi_j\}$ for some statement ϕ_j of K_i. The different $\Gamma_{i,j}$ were ordered by decreasing compliance score $\mathrm{comp}(\Gamma_{i,j})$ (resp. $\mathrm{comp}_{K_i}(\Gamma_{i,j})$), or by decreasing lexicographic ordering $\preceq_{lex}$ (resp. $\preceq_{lex_{K_i}}$).[10] Intuitively, this yields a ranking on K_i where the least reliable statements wrt linguistic evidence should appear first : if $\phi_j \in K_i$, and if the subbase of K_i obtained by discarding ϕ_j (i.e. $\Gamma_{i,j}$) has a higher linguistic compliance score than K_i, then discarding $\Gamma_{i,j}$ can be viewed as an improvement over K_i. And if $\Gamma_{i,j}$ is among the best ranked subbases of K_i, then ϕ_j is among the least reliable statements of K_i wrt distributional evidence. For instance, in example 1, one may expect the subbase $K \setminus (1)$ to have a maximal linguistic compliance score among immediate subbases of K (or to be

[8] http://www.irit.fr/~Julien.Corman/index_en.php

[9] The ranking was a strict ordering : if two consequences had the same score, one of them was randomly designated as strictly lower ranked.

[10] Again, the ranking was randomly turned into a strict ordering (see footnote 9).

	rank	p-val
$\text{comp}(\Gamma)$	7.86 / 80.03	< 0.001
$\text{comp}_{K_i}(\Gamma)$	8.05 / 80.03	< 0.001
$\preceq_{lex}$	6.51 / 80.03	< 0.001
$\preceq_{lex_{K_i}}$	2.47 / 80.03	< 0.001

Table 2: Average ranking of the randomly generated statement ϕ_i for each K_i, and p-value for the rankings of all ϕ_i

maximal wrt the lexicographic ordering), such that (1) is the best candidate for removal. So back to the test data, if $K_i = F \cup \{\phi_i\}$, i.e. if ϕ_i is, among the $|F+1|$ statements of K_i, the one which has been randomly generated, and if $\Gamma_{i,i} = K_i \setminus \phi_i$ is among the best ranked immediate subbases of K_i, this would indicate that the linguistic compliance score in definitions 4.3 (resp. 4.4), or the corresponding lexicographic ordering $\preceq_{lex}$ (resp. $\preceq_{lex_{K_i}}$) is actually a good estimator of faulty statements.

An additional precaution was taken in order to avoid artificially good results. For most statements $\phi_j \in K_i$, discarding ϕ_j did not have any impact on the set $\Psi_{\Gamma_{i,j}}$ of consequences to be evaluated, i.e. $\Psi_{\Gamma_{i,j}} = \Psi_{K_i}$, and therefore $\text{comp}(\Gamma_{i,j}) = \text{comp}(K_i)$. Let $\Delta_i \subseteq K_i$ be the set of statements whose removal did have an impact instead (on average, there were 79.3 statements in Δ_i). Then the compliance of a subbase $\Gamma_{i,j}$ of K_i was evaluated only if $\phi_j \in \Delta_i$, i.e. only if the removal of ϕ_j made a difference. K_i was also added to this set of evaluated subbases, yielding a ranking of $79.03 + 1 = 80.03$ bases on average.

Results are again positive. Column "rank" in table 2 gives the average ranking of $\Gamma_{i,i}$, i.e. the base obtained after the removal of the randomly generated statement ϕ_i. Both lexicographic orderings outperformed the compliance scores (i.e. the mean of plausibility scores), and the best configuration was the fourth presented in section 4.2, using $\text{sc}_{K_i}(\psi)$ as a plausibility score instead of $\text{sc}_{\Gamma_{i,j}}(\psi)$.

6 Applications

This section describes a few concrete use cases of the propositions made in section 4. A first basic but useful application is the identification of undesired consequences of a consistent input ontology K. As illustrated by example 1, violations of common sense often go unnoticed in publicly available OWL datasets, even though effective procedures can detect inconsistency[11] in most DLs. This is correlated with the overall sparse usage of negation in OWL, yielding ontologies which are consistent by default rather than by design. The identification of such cases can be very simply performed, by returning to the user the formulas of Ψ_K with lower plausibility scores, like `Person`(CEO) in example 1. Axiom pinpointing algorithms (Schlobach and Cornet, 2003; Kalyanpur et al., 2007; Horridge, 2011) may then be used to compute all *justifications* for each returned consequence ψ, i.e. all (set-inclusion) minimal subsets of K which have ψ as a consequence.

In a more automated fashion, the greedy trimming approach described in (Corman et al., 2015) returns n statements of K which are candidate for removal, n being given as a parameter, by incrementally selecting the immediate subbase of Γ with maximal linguistic compliance score, starting with $\Gamma = K$.

But inconsistent[12] ontology debugging may also benefit from distributional evidence. As discussed in section 2, state-of-the-art approaches to ontology debugging suffer from the number of candidate outputs, i.e. of (set-inclusion) maximal consistent subsets of K, as well as from the cost of their computation. If the set $\mathcal{J}$ of justifications for the inconsistency of K is known though, and if some (discriminant enough) preference relation $\preceq_a$ over $\bigcup \mathcal{J}$ can be obtained, then *prioritized base revision*, as it is defined in (Nebel, 1992), provides a principled and computationally attractive solution to these problems. Even if the whole process cannot be depicted here, $\preceq_a$ may actually be obtained through distributional evidence, by evaluating, for each statement $\phi \in \bigcup \mathcal{J}$, the plausibility of some consequences of candidate subbases in which ϕ does or does not appear. The support set in this case is reduced to consequences of the "safe" part of K, i.e. $K \setminus \bigcup \mathcal{J}$.

7 Extensions

A first straightforward extension of this framework consists in taking more complex classes into ac-

[11] or incoherence (see footnote1)

[12] or incoherent (see footnote 1), or for which a set of undesired consequences has already been identified

count. OWL (and most Description Logics) favor the recursive construction of arbitrarily complex classes out of the signature of Γ, and this mechanism could naturally be used to extend Ψ_Γ with more consequences of the form $C(e)$, where C is one of these complex classes. For instance, in example 1, if C_1 and C_2 are respectively defined by $\forall x(C_1(x) \Leftrightarrow \exists y(\texttt{occupation}(y,x))$ and $\forall x(C_2(x) \Leftrightarrow \exists y(\texttt{occupation}(x,y))$, then Ψ_K can be extended "for free" with $C_1(\textit{CEO})$ and $C_2(\textit{Peter Munk})$. Unfortunately, if Ψ_Γ^+ is the set of all consequences of Γ which can be built this way, there is in general no finite subset Ψ_Γ of Ψ_Γ^+ such that $\Psi_\Gamma \models \psi$ for all $\psi \in \Psi_\Gamma^+$. Therefore the complex classes to be used must be selected, which is not trivial. Intuitively, some complex classes are more relevant than other (e.g. the class of "physical objects owned by someone" may be linguistically relevant, but probably not "Moldavian or Muslim lawyers whose father lives in an apartment").

Another simple variation of the framework presented here consists in setting Ψ_Γ to be all consequences of Γ of the form $e_1 \neq e_2$, i.e. the fact that that e_1 and e_2 are not the same individual according to Γ. The unique name assumption is not made in OWL, which means that two distinct named individuals can be interpreted identically, and therefore these consequences do not hold by default. They may be explicitly stated in Γ (owl:differentIndividuals(e_1, e_2)), but are in most cases entailed by Γ, provided it contains some form of negation (e.g. instances of two disjoint classes cannot be the same individual). If Γ_1 and Γ_2 are two subbases of K such that $\Gamma_1 \models e_1 \neq e_2$, but $\Gamma_2 \not\models e_1 \neq e_2$, and if the similarity between e_1 and e_2 is lower than expected, then *ceteris paribus*, Γ_1 will be preferred to Γ_2.

Conclusion

This article is centered on the use of distributional representations of (labels of) named individuals of an input ontology K, in order to identify and repair violations of commonsense within K. For a set of statements $\Gamma \subseteq K$, and Ψ_Γ a specific set of consequences of Γ, a score $\mathrm{sc}_\Gamma(\psi)$ is attributed to each $\psi \in \Psi_\Gamma$, which evaluates the plausibility of ψ wrt Γ according to distributional evidence. Several methods based on this plausibility score are then proposed in order to compare two subbases Γ_1 and Γ_2 of K, leading to the identification of potentially erroneous statements. An evaluation is provided, which consists in extending a test ontology with randomly generated statements before trying to spot them automatically, with significant results. A more thorough evaluation is still required though, testing in particular the impact of a higher number of named individuals and/or classes. Scalability of the approach may also be limited by its heavy reliance on a reasoner. Finally, potential improvements may come from using more elaborated distributional representations, like the one described in (Mikolov et al., 2013).

References

Baroni, M. and S. Bernardini (2004). BootCaT: Bootstrapping Corpora and Terms from the Web. In *LREC proceedings*.

Benevides, A., G. Guizzardi, B. Braga, and J. Almeida (2010). Validating modal aspects of OntoUML conceptual models using automatically generated visual world structures. *Journal of Universal Computer Science 16*(20).

Buitelaar, P., P. Cimiano, and B. Magnini (2005). *Ontology Learning from Text: Methods, Evaluation And Applications*. IOS Press.

Cimiano, P. (2006). *Ontology learning and population from text: algorithms, evaluation and applications*. Springer.

Cimiano, P. and J. Völker (2005). Towards large-scale, open-domain and ontology-based named entity classification. In *RANLP proceedings*.

Corman, J., N. Aussenac-Gilles, and L. Vieu (2015). Trimming a consistent OWL knowledge base, relying on linguistic evidence. In *LangAndOnto proceedings*.

Ferré, S. and S. Rudolph (2012). Advocatus Diaboli–Exploratory Enrichment of Ontologies with Negative Constraints. *EKAW proceedings*.

Friedrich, G. and K. Shchekotykhin (2005). A general diagnosis method for ontologies. In *ISWC proceedings*.

Giuliano, C. and A. Gliozzo (2008). Instance-based ontology population exploiting named-entity substitution. In *COLING proceedings*.

Horridge, M. (2011). *Justification based explanation in ontologies*. Ph. D. thesis, the University of Manchester.

Kalyanpur, A., B. Parsia, M. Horridge, and E. Sirin (2007). Finding all justifications of OWL DL entailments. In *The Semantic Web*. Springer.

Kalyanpur, A., B. Parsia, E. Sirin, and B. Cuenca-Grau (2006). Repairing unsatisfiable concepts in OWL ontologies. In *ESWC proceedings*.

Mendes, P. N., M. Jakob, and C. Bizer (2012). DBpedia: A Multilingual Cross-domain Knowledge Base. In *LREC proceedings*.

Mikolov, T., K. Chen, G. Corrado, and J. Dean (2013). Efficient estimation of word representations in vector space. *ICLR proceedings*.

Nebel, B. (1992). Syntax-based approaches to belief revision. *Belief revision 29*, 52–88.

Pammer, V. (2010). *Automatic Support for Ontology Evaluation*. Ph. D. thesis, Graz University of Technology.

Poveda-Villalón, M., M. C. Suárez-Figueroa, and A. Gómez-Pérez (2012). Did you validate your ontology? OOPS! In *ESWC proceedings*.

Qi, G., P. Haase, Z. Huang, Q. Ji, J. Z. Pan, and J. Völker (2008). A kernel revision operator for terminologies - algorithms and evaluation. In *ISWC proceedings*.

Ribeiro, M. M. and R. Wassermann (2009). Base revision for ontology debugging. *Journal of Logic and Computation 19*(5).

Roussey, C. and O. Zamazal (2013). Antipattern Detection: How to Debug an Ontology without a Reasoner. In *WODOOM 2013 proceeding*.

Schlobach, S. (2005). Diagnosing terminologies. In *AAAI proceedings*.

Schlobach, S. and R. Cornet (2003). Non-standard reasoning services for the debugging of description logic terminologies. In *IJCAI proceedings*.

Suchanek, F. M., M. Sozio, and G. Weikum (2009). SOFIE: a self-organizing framework for information extraction. In *International World Wide Web conference proceedings*.

Tanev, H. and B. Magnini (2008). Weakly supervised approaches for ontology population. In *conference on Ontology Learning and Population proceedings*.

Toutanova, K., D. Klein, C. D. Manning, and Y. Singer (2003). Feature-rich part-of-speech tagging with a cyclic dependency network. In *NAACL proceedings*.

Combining Seemingly Incompatible Corpora for Implicit Semantic Role Labeling

Parvin Sadat Feizabadi and **Sebastian Padó**
Institut für Maschinelle Sprachverarbeitung
University of Stuttgart, Germany
{parvin.feizabadi,pado}@ims.uni-stuttgart.de

Abstract

Implicit semantic role labeling, the task of retrieving locally unrealized arguments from wider discourse context, is a knowledge-intensive task. At the same time, the annotated corpora that exist are all small and scattered across different annotation frameworks, genres, and classes of predicates. Previous work has treated these corpora as incompatible with one another, and has concentrated on optimizing the exploitation of single corpora. In this paper, we show that *corpus combination* is effective after all when the differences between corpora are bridged with domain adaptation methods. When we combine the SemEval-2010 Task 10 and Gerber and Chai noun corpora, we obtain substantially improved performance on both corpora, for all roles and parts of speech. We also present new insights into the properties of the implicit semantic role labeling task.

1 Introduction

Semantic role labeling (SRL) is the task of identifying semantic arguments of predicates in text. It is an important step in text analysis and has applications in information extraction (Christensen et al., 2010), question answering (Shen and Lapata, 2007; Moreda et al., 2011) and machine translation (Wu and Fung, 2009; Xiong et al., 2012) . A large body of work exists on algorithms for SRL (Gildea and Jurafsky, 2002; Srikumar and Roth, 2011). Their success is closely connected to the availability of two large, hand-constructed semantic role resources, FrameNet (Fillmore et al., 2003) and PropBank (Palmer et al., 2005). They used to concentrate on *overt* semantic roles, that is, semantic roles that are realized within the local syntactic structure of the predicate.

Recent years have seen a broadening of the focus in SRL to *implicit semantic roles*, that is all roles that remain locally unrealized but can be retrieved in the (typically prior) context (Ruppenhofer et al., 2010). In the following example annotated with PropBank roles (cf. Section 2), the target predicate *come* has two roles, a locally realized one (A1, the entity in motion), it, and an implicit role mentioned in the previous sentence (A4, the goal):

> Well, sir, it's [$_{A4}$ this lonely, silent house] and the queer thing in the kitchen . ... I thought [$_{A1}$ it] had **come** again.

Implicit SRL is useful to complete predicates' argument structures for inference (Mirkin et al., 2010) and paraphrasing (Roth and Frank, 2013), or to assess the coherence of discourse (Burchardt et al., 2005). It however requires (even) more training data than traditional SRL. One reason is that potential arguments come from the whole text rather than just the sentence. Another one is that most of the powerful syntactic features that are a staple in traditional SRL are unavailable across sentence boundaries. Unfortunately, existing corpora for implicit SRL are quite small: The task requires full-text annotation, which is time-consuming and pushes semantic role frameworks to their limits (Palmer and Sporleder, 2010). It is also hard to do consistently, and can only be crowdsourced in limited settings (Feizabadi and Padó, 2014). Thus, even though multiple systems for implicit SRL exist (among others, Tonelli and Delmonte (2011), Laparra and Rigau (2012), Silberer

*Proceedings of the Fourth Joint Conference on Lexical and Computational Semantics (*SEM 2015)*, pages 40–50,
Denver, Colorado, June 4–5, 2015.

and Frank (2012)), results are still relatively poor.

In this paper, we focus on the fact that the corpora that exist for implicit SRL differ not only in the semantic role frameworks used (FrameNet vs. PropBank), but also in genre (newswire vs. novels), and classes of annotated predicates (verbs vs. nouns). As a result, they are generally regarded as incompatible, and previous work has concentrated on getting most out of individual corpora, or spending annotation effort on focused extensions of these corpora. Instead, we will follow the intuition that the performance of implicit SRL can be improved significantly by *combining corpora*, using simple domain adaptation techniques to bridge the differences between them. We combine the two largest datasets for implicit SRL, the SemEval-2010 Task 10 dataset (Ruppenhofer et al., 2010) and the Gerber and Chai dataset (Gerber and Chai, 2012). This combination achieves improvements across all target and semantic roles despite the differences in genre, domain, and parts of speech. Our analyses indicates that the properties of the implicit SRL task – where syntactic features play a relatively minor role compared to semantic and discourse features – are responsible for this picture, and mean that models can actually profit from complementarity between combined corpora.

Plan of the paper. Section 2 summarizes the resource and model situation in SRL. Section 3 defines a simple system for implicit SRL that uses domain adaptation. Sections 4 and 5 report experiments and provide analysis. Section 6 concludes.

2 Traditional and Implicit SRL

This section first describes existing resources for traditional and implicit SRL (frameworks and corpora). Then it outlines the state of the art in modeling.

2.1 Frameworks for Semantic Roles

Almost all contemporary work on SRL is based on one of two frameworks: FrameNet and PropBank.

FrameNet is a dictionary and corpus annotated in the Frame Semantics paradigm (Fillmore et al., 2003). In Frame Semantics, the meaning of predicates (verbs, nouns, or adjectives) is conveyed by frames, conceptual structures which represent situations and define salient entities. Semantic roles describe these salient entities and are therefore located at the level of frames. E.g., the verb *approach* is analyzed as an instance of the frame ARRIVING, with the roles THEME, SOURCE, GOAL:

> [$_{\text{Theme}}$ He] was **approaching** [$_{\text{Source}}$ from behind and slightly to the right of Sharpe].

Frame Semantics also offers an analysis of unrealized roles, called Null Instantiations, that distinguishes three classes. Indefinite non-instantiations (INIs) are interpreted generically. Constructional non-instantiations (CNI) include, e.g., passives. Finally, definite non-instantiations (DNIs) have a specific interpretation and often refer to expressions in the context. DNIs correspond to the pre-theoretic concept of implicit roles. The FrameNet corpus, however, does not annotate the antecedents of DNIs, so it cannot be used directly as training data for implicit SRL.

PropBank The second major framework for semantic role annotation is PropBank (Palmer et al., 2005). It defines a set of general semantic roles named ARG0-ARG5 of which ARG0 and ARG1 are interpreted as proto-agent and proto-patient (Dowty, 1991), respectively. The higher-numbered roles receive more predicate-specific interpretations. These "core" roles are complemented by adjunct roles such as MNR (manner) or TMP (time). For example,

> Jim Unruh ... said [$_{A1}$ he] is **approaching** [$_{A2}$ next year] [$_{MNR}$ with caution].

PropBank has annotated the WSJ part of the Penn Treebank, i.e., newswire text, exhaustively with semantic roles. While it originally concentrated on verbs, the NomBank project (Meyers et al., 2004) extended the annotation scheme to nouns. PropBank does not have a specific taxonomy of null instantiations like FrameNet, but it can nevertheless be used equally for implicit role annotation.

2.2 Annotated Corpora for Implicit SRL

FrameNet and PropBank are both very large corpora, covering tens of thousands of instances. Corpora with implicit role annotation are generally much smaller; the main corpora are summarized in Table 1.

Ruppenhofer et al. Arguably the first corpus with a substantial set of annotations for implicit roles was

Corpus	Scheme	POS	Genre	# predicates	# instances	# implicit roles
Ruppenhofer et al. (2010)	FrameNet	V, N	Novels	801	1575	245
Gerber & Chai (2012)	PropBank	N	Newswire	10	1253	1172
Moor et al. (2013)	FrameNet	V	Newswire	5	1992	242
Feizabadi & Padó (2014)	FrameNet	V	Novels	10	384	363

Table 1: Size of available English corpora with implicit semantic role annotation

created for SemEval 2010 Task 10 (Ruppenhofer et al., 2010). This dataset covers a number of chapters from Arthur Conan Doyle short stories and provides full-text annotation of both explicit and implicit semantic roles. The texts were annotated manually with FrameNet roles. This dataset is a de-facto standard benchmark for implicit SRL.

Gerber and Chai. A study by Gerber and Chai (2012) investigated implicit arguments of NomBank nominalizations. They extended a part of the PropBank corpus with implicit roles for 10 nominal predicates, of which they annotated all instances.

Further Corpora with Implicit Role Annotation. Moor et al. (2013) created a corpus with all annotated instances for five verbs with the goal of focused improvement of implicit SRL. Feizabadi & Padó (2014) investigated the use of crowdsourcing to create annotations for implicit roles. Both corpora are more restricted in size and scope than the first two.

2.3 Models for Semantic Role Labeling

Traditional SRL. A broad range of models have been proposed for "traditional", i.e., local SRL (Palmer et al., 2010). The task can be seen as a sequence of two classification tasks, predicate disambiguation and role labeling. Earlier models modeled them in a pipeline architecture, but recent works demonstrates the benefits of joint inference (Srikumar and Roth, 2011; Das et al., 2014). SRL models have drawn on a wide variety of features from two main groups: syntactic features describing the structural relation between predicate and argument candidate, and semantic features describing role and candidate. A general observation is that SRL models are lexically specific to a substantial degree, i.e., do not generalize very well between predicates, so that the availability of annotations remains a bottleneck.

Implicit SRL was formulated by SemEval 2010 Task 10 in two versions. The "full task" includes identification of all (explicit or implicit) semantic roles of the target predicate. The "null instantiation task" is the subtask of the full task concerned only with the identification and labeling of antecedents for implicit roles. It assumes that predicates and overt roles are already available. We follow the lead of almost all models for implicit SRL on the null instantiation task. Structurally, it can be approached similarly to role identification in traditional SRL.

The first systems on large-coverage implicit SRL adopted traditional SRL modeling techniques (Chen et al., 2010; Tonelli and Delmonte, 2010). but struggled with the scarcity of training data for the complex task. Work since then has concentrated on tapping into novel knowledge and data sources. There are three main directions. The first one is knowledge about *semantic types*. This includes Ruppenhofer et al. (2011) who extract semantic types for null instantiations from FrameNet and Laparra and Rigau (2012) who learn distributions over semantic types for each role from explicit role annotations in FrameNet. Similarly, Roth and Frank (2013) retrieve overt instances of implicit roles from comparable corpora. The second direction is *discourse level knowledge*. Laparra and Rigau (2013) and Gorinski et al. (2013) treat implicit SRL as a task similar to anaphor resolution, which motivates the use of several features of discourse such as distance and salience. A third set of studies concentrated on simply obtaining *more annotated instances*. Silberer and Frank (2012) use an entity-based coreference resolution model to automatically extended the training set. Moor et al. (2013) and Feizabadi and Padó (2014) manually construct focused corpora (cf. Section 2.2).

3 Combining Corpora for Implicit SRL

3.1 Rationale and Challenges

Despite the progress made by on implicit SRL, as discussed in the previous section, *data sparsity* remains the main bottleneck. This has two main reasons.

First, the set of constitutents included in the search for each role is very large, potentially including the whole discourse. To address this problem, implicit SRL systems typically concentrate on a window of n sentences, typically the sentence with the predicate and its preceding discourse. Second, the powerful class of syntactic features becomes largely unavailable beyond sentence boundaries.

This situation calls for large, richly annotated corpora. Unfortunately, the annotation effort that has been expended on implicit role has been distributed over a number of different corpora, all of which are fairly small (cf. Section 2.2). The question that we are asking in this paper is: *Can data from existing corpora be combined rather than spending annotation effort on yet another corpus?*

We will consider the combination of the standard benchmark, the SemEval 2010 Task 10 dataset (Ruppenhofer et al., 2010) (henceforth SEMEVAL), with the corpus with the largest number of implicit roles, the Gerber and Chai (2012) corpus (henceforth GERBERCHAI). The main challenge in this endeavour is that these corpora have very different properties (cf. Table 1). Consequently, a number of challenges arise for data combination. Below we discuss them, our expectations, and our strategies to address them.

Challenge: Differences in Role Framework. SEMEVAL was annotated with FrameNet roles, while GERBERCHAI was annotated with PropBank roles. While semi-automatic conversion schemes now exist in both directions, we decided to adopt the PropBank paradigm, working on the basis of the semi-automatically converted SEMEVAL annotation provided by the task organizers. The reasons are twofold: (a), we believe that, in parallel to results on traditional SRL, PropBank roles should be generally easier to label than FrameNet roles; (b), this effect should be particularly pronounced when facing sparse data problems, as is the case here.

Challenge: Differences in Parts of Speech. SEMEVAL covers both verbal and nominal predicates, while GERBERCHAI contains only nominal predicates (cf. Table 1). Given the absence of syntactic features from implicit SRL, we believe that this is not a huge impediment. We will, however, evaluate on a per-POS basis to test this assumption.

Challenge: Differences in Genre/Domain. Also, SEMEVAL is based on novels dealing with everyday affairs, while GERBERCHAI consists of newswire text focusing on finance and politics. It is well known that the performance of NLP models degrades when applied across domains and genres. This holds for traditional SRL (Carreras and Màrquez, 2005) and is likely to extend to the implicit variant. For this reason, we believe that it is crucial to apply domain adaptation methods to ensure that reasonable generalizations can be learned. See Section 3.3 for details.

3.2 A Simple Implicit SRL System

We now describe the simple classification-based system for implicit SRL that we will use in our experiments. Like many systems from the literature, it focuses on the "null instantiation" step (cf. Section 2.2) – i.e., we assume that overtly realized roles are already available. The architecture of our system is inspired by the system by Laparra and Rigau (2012) which is among the best-performing systems on SEMEVAL.

Our system decomposes the task into two steps: (1), Determining a set of implicit roles that should be identified in context; (2) Determining the antecedents of these missing roles. For the first step, we extract the *predominant role set* (i.e., most frequently realized set) for each predicate by searching the predicate in a large corpus, OntoNotes (Hovy et al., 2006). We assume that all instances of the predicate realize these roles and select the subset that is not realized overtly for inclusion in the second step.

We phrase the second step as binary classification. The items to be classified are triples ⟨target predicate, implicit role, candidate realization⟩. The set of candidate realizations is defined as all constituents from the target predicate's sentence and the two prior sentences which do not fill an explicit role for the target. We employ a Naive Bayes classifier that can deal relatively well with sparse data.[1] We use 10 features, shown in Table 1 which attempt to capture relevant syntacto-semantic and the discourse features.

3.3 Domain Adaptation

The standard assumption in machine leaning is that data are independent and identically distributed, that is, drawn from the same underlying population. This

[1] We also experimented with other classifiers including SVMs, but did not achieve better results.

Name	Description
Expected roles	Set of roles required by the target predicates (based on PropBank and NomBank). This feature serves as a delexicalized target representation.
Semantic Type	Semantic type of the candidate realization's head word (WordNet supersenses) or, if pronoun, of the next content words in the coreference chain
Word Frequency	Lemma frequency of the candidate filler's head word
POS	Part of Speech of candidate realization's head word
Constituent type	The constituent type of the candidate filler, e.g. NP, PP, VP, etc.
Distance	Distance between candidate realization and target predicate (in sentences)
Salience	Whether the candidate realization's head word is included in a non-singleton coreference chain
Previous Role	Whether the candidate realization has overtly realized any semantic role in the dataset
Same Role	Whether the candidate realization has realized the implicit role as an overt role in the dataset
Role Percentage	The percentage with which the candidate realization has realized the implicit role

Table 2: Feature Set (above: syntacto-semantic features; below: discourse features)

assumption is violated if the test data differs substantially from the training data, and consequently the performance of models learned on the training data suffers on the test data. Since this situation arises frequently, the field of *domain adaptation* has developed (Jiang, 2008). In our application, SEMEVAL and GERBERCHAI can be understood as two domains.

We adopt Daumé's (2007) simple but effective *feature augmentation* method which makes use of some training data in both source and target domain. Each feature is stored in three variants: a general version, a source version and a target version. Each of the two domains (source and target) activates two versions, the general one and its specific one, which can also be given a Bayesian interpretation (Finkel and Manning, 2009). In this manner, the model balances global and domain-specific trends against each other. As an example, the "expected roles" feature (cf. Table 2), which is shaped by subcategorization, is a likely candidate for changess across domains, due to sense shifts. In contrast, we would not expect the part-of-speech features of realization candidates to undergo major changes across domains.

4 Experiment 1

We present three experiments. Experiment 1 extends the SEMEVAL training data with out-of-domain data from GERBERCHAI and evaluates on SEMEVAL. Experiment 2 swaps the setup, extending the GERBERCHAI dataset with SEMEVAL data and evaluating on GERBERCHAI. Experiment 3 aims at providing a better understanding of these observations.

4.1 Experimental Setup

Design. In this experiment, we evaluate our approach on the SEMEVAL dataset (SEMEVAL is the target domain and GERBERCHAI is the source domain). Since there is an established split of SEMEVAL into training and test parts, we simply use the test part for evaluation, and designate the SEMEVAL training part as well as GERBERCHAI for training.

We compare four experimental scenarios (cf. Table 3): (1) The standard "in-domain" setup that only uses SEMEVAL, as assumed by most studies on the dataset. (2) A pure "out-of-domain" setup where we use only GERBERCHAI as training data. Of course, there is reason to believe that this strategy will perform quite poorly. (3) A simple "concatenation" setup where we train on the union of GERBERCHAI and the SEMEVAL training corpus. (4) The feature augmentation setting where we train on the combined corpus, but apply Daumé's (2007) learning method.

Preprocessing. SEMEVAL comes pre-parsed with the Collins (Collins, 1997) parser. We parsed GERBERCHAI with the same parser, ignoring the Penn Treebank gold trees. Since all datasets are manually annotated with semantic roles, no overt SRL is necessary. Coreference information, which we require for some features, is available from manual annotation in the SEMEVAL test part, but not for the other datasets. We computed coreference chains with the Stanford CoreNLP tools (Manning et al., 2014).

Evaluation. We evaluate implicit role predictions with precision, recall, and F_1 score, following the official SemEval 2010 Task 10 guidelines. Note that

Training Set	Pr.	Rec.	F_1
(1) SEMEVAL train (in-domain)	0.10	0.20	0.13
(2) GERBERCHAI (out-of-domain)	0.12	0.08	0.10
(3) SEMEVAL train + GERBERCHAI, concat.	0.11	0.19	0.14
(4) SEMEVAL train + GERBERCHAI, feature augmentation	**0.13**	**0.30**	**0.18**
Laparra and Rigau (2013)	0.12	0.16	0.14

Table 3: Evaluation of implicit SRL (PropBank roles) on the SEMEVAL test set

% of GERBERCHAI	Pr.	Rec.	F_1
0	0.10	0.20	0.13
5	0.13	0.29	0.17
10	**0.14**	**0.31**	**0.19**
15	0.13	0.31	0.18
20	0.13	0.30	0.18
100	0.13	0.30	0.18

Table 4: Results on SEMEVAL test, training on SEMEVAL train plus varying amounts of data from GERBERCHAI

according to the guidelines, the true positives include all predictions that match the gold span indirectly through a (manually annotated) coreference chain.

Baseline. All previous studies on the SEMEVAL dataset used the FrameNet annotation, and without access to the actual predictions we cannot directly compare our predictions to theirs. We are grateful to Laparra and Rigau who agreed to share the predictions of their 2013 model with us, which is, at the time of writing, the system with the second-best reported scores. We converted the predictions into the PropBank format, using the FrameNet-to-PropBank mapping provided by the task organizers.

Upper bound. Implicit SRL systems typically trade off recall against precision by restricting the search space. Our system uses two heuristics: It restricts search to the current and two preceding sentences and to the predominant role set (cf. Section 3.2). The upper bound in recall on SEMEVAL test that can still be achieved in this setting is 60.1%.

4.2 Results

Table 3 shows the results of the four experimental conditions defined above and the comparison system, the converted Laparra and Rigau (2013). Our system, trained in-domain (1), achieves a performance comparable to Laparra and Rigau, albeit with a different precision-recall trade-off. Not surprisingly, pure out-of-domain training (2) does not perform well either. Simple data concatenation (3) leads to a minimal numeric improvement, but indicates that the datasets are indeed rather different.

We see a substantial improvement in performance when feature augmentation (4) is used. There is not only a major improvement in recall (+10 percentage points) but also a smaller improvement in precision (+3 points). We tested the difference to the in-domain model (1) for significance with bootstrap resampling (Efron and Tibshirani, 1993) and found it to be higly significant ($p<0.01$). In sum, we see an improvement of 5% F-Score, despite the differences between the corpora, when feature augmentation is used. Notably, we achieve a high recall, despite the upper bound imposed by the filtering heuristics.

Unfortunately, it is rather difficult to pinpoint individual instances whose improvements can be interpreted in a linguistically meaningful way. A comparative feature ablation study for models (1) and (4) showed that discourse features such as Previous Role (cf. Table 2) are among the most important features in (4), while they are almost useless in (1). This indicates that discourse-level features particularly profit from the inclusion of out-of-domain data.

Analysis by Amount of Out-of-Domain Data. Since GERBERCHAI is about ten times as large as the SEMEVAL training set, we wondered whether the out-of-domain GERBERCHAI data is "overwhelming" the SEMEVAL data. Keeping the SEMEVAL test set for evaluation, we combined SEMEVAL train with subsets of GERBERCHAI in increments of 5% of the total number of predicates. The results, shown in Table 4, show that almost the complete benefit of the GERBERCHAI data is already present when we add 5% of GERBERCHAI, and we achieve the optimal result by adding 10%. The results are marginally higher than when we add the complete GERBERCHAI (difference not significant). Our take away is that, in contrast to the proposal by Moor et al. (2013), we do not require many annotations for each predicate: the results are best when the in-domain and out-of-domain corpora have about the same size.

Training Set	Verbal predicates Pr.	Rec.	F_1	Nominal predicates Pr.	Rec.	F_1
(1) SEMEVAL train ("in-domain")	0.11	0.20	0.14	0.10	0.21	0.14
(2) GERBERCHAI train ("out-of-domain")	0.09	0.12	0.10	0.07	0.11	0.09
(3) SEMEVAL train + GERBERCHAI, concat.	0.11	0.18	0.13	0.11	0.21	0.14
(4) SEMEVAL train + GERBERCHAI, feature aug.	0.13	**0.30**	**0.18**	**0.14**	**0.32**	**0.20**
Laparra and Rigau (2013)	**0.15**	0.20	0.17	0.09	0.11	0.09

Table 5: Evaluation of implicit SRL (PropBank roles) on the SEMEVAL test set, by target part of speech

Training Set	A0 Pr.	Rec.	F_1	A1 Pr.	Rec.	F_1	A2 Pr.	Rec.	F_1
(1) SEMEVAL train ("in-domain")	0.19	0.29	0.23	0.09	0.26	0.13	0.06	0.10	0.07
(2) GERBERCHAI ("out-of-domain")	0.19	0.34	0.24	0.03	0.06	0.03	0.0	0.0	0.0
(3) SEMEVAL train + GERBERCHAI, concat.	0.23	0.34	0.27	0.08	0.22	0.11	0.0	0.0	0.0
(4) SEMEVAL train + GERBERCHAI, feature aug.	**0.24**	**0.42**	**0.31**	**0.11**	**0.37**	**0.17**	0.09	**0.24**	0.13
Laparra and Rigau (2013)	0.21	0.28	0.24	0.10	0.13	0.11	**0.13**	0.19	**0.15**

Table 6: Evaluation of implicit SRL (PropBank roles) on the SEMEVAL test set, by role

Analysis by Predicate POS. Since GERBERCHAI contains only noun targets, we could hypothesize that its inclusion improves results in SEMEVAL specifically for nominal predicates. To test this hypothesis, we evaluated verbal and nominal predicates separately. The results in Table 5 are actually comparable across parts-of-speech. Even though the benefit is somewhat smaller for verbs, there is still a substantial improvement (+4.1% F_1 for verbs; +5.9% F_1 for nouns). In contrast, studies on traditional SRL found only small (albeit consistent) improvements for extending training sets with instances of targets with different parts-of-speech (Li et al., 2009).

We believe that this is the case because implicit SRL, as discussed in Section 2.3, can rely less on syntactic features but must make predictions on the basis of semantic and discourse features, which are more comparable across target parts of speech. Consider these two examples – one verbal and one nominal predicate – of implicit A0 roles. Both occur in the same sentences as their predicates, but outside their syntactic domains:

SEMEVAL: The wagonette was **paid off** ... while [$_{A0}$ we] started walking.
GERBERCHAI: His ... house ... is up for **sale** to pay for [$_{A0}$ his] lawyers.

While the role realizations are quite different structurally (subject vs. posessive), they are similar on the semantics and discourse levels: both are pronouns referring to agent-like entities and are realized in the immediately following discourse.

Analysis by Role. Finally, we performed an evaluation by individual semantic roles, shown in Table 6, to assess to what extent differences in role distribution between SEMEVAL and GERBERCHAI influence the improvements. We concentrate on A0 through A2, since A3 and A4 are so infrequent in SEMEVAL that evaluation results are not reliable.

Not surprisingly, we see the overall best results for A0, followed by A1 and A2. The improvement for combining corpora correlates with the overall performance: +7% F_1 for A0, +4% for A1, +6% for A2. The overall pattern of a major boost to recall and a minor one to precision are also stable across roles. Thus, corpus combination seems to benefit all roles as well. A notable observation is the inability of the naive out-of-domain models (2) and (3) to correctly predict any A2 roles. The reason is that for the nominal targets in GERBERCHAI, A2 is an *incorporated role*, that is, realized by the predicate itself. This pattern hardly occurs in SEMEVAL. Interestingly, the domain adaptation model (4) manages to extract relevant information from GERBERCHAI. Nevertheless, the fact that (4) is still worse than Laparra & Rigau (2013), which is trained just in-domain, indicates that more informative features for A2 are also necessary.

Training Set	A0 Pr.	A0 Rec.	A0 F_1	A1 Pr.	A1 Rec.	A1 F_1
(1) GERBERCHAI ("in-domain")	0.15	0.10	0.12	0.18	0.23	0.16
(4) SEMEVAL + GERBERCHAI, feature augmentation	**0.19**	**0.13**	**0.15**	**0.26**	**0.35**	**0.30**

Table 7: Evaluation of implicit SRL (PropBank roles) on the SEMEVAL test set, by role

Training Set	Pr.	Rec.	F_1
(1) GERBERCHAI (in-domain)	0.16	0.10	0.12
(2) SEMEVAL (out-of-domain)	0.11	0.06	0.07
(3) SEMEVAL + GERBERCHAI, concat.	0.16	0.09	0.11
(4) SEMEVAL + GERBERCHAI, feature augmentation	**0.24**	**0.18**	**0.21**
Upper bound: Gerber & Chai (2012)	0.58	0.44	0.50

Table 8: Evaluation of implicit SRL (PropBank roles) on GERBERCHAI (3-fold CV)

5 Experiment 2

In Experiment 2, we use a combination of GERBERCHAI and the complete SEMEVAL for training and evaluate on GERBERCHAI. The main question is whether the addition of the (much smaller) SEMEVAL corpus to GERBERCHAI can improve performance.

We consider the same four conditions as in Experiment 1. To obtain reliable results, we split GERBERCHAI into three equal-sized parts and report averages over three cross-validation runs where we always use two thirds for training and one third for testing. Evaluation also is performed as before, with the exception that in the absence of manually annotated coreference chains, we only count direct matches as true positives. The upper bound for recall on this dataset (using the same 3-sentence window and predominant role set) is rather low, at 44%, which reflects the structural tendency of nominalizations to realize few roles locally.

Unfortunately, we do not have a directly comparable competitor, since Laparra and Rigau did not run their system on GERBERCHAI data. The results obtained by Gerber and Chai (2012) are not directly comparable, since their approach was hand-tailored towards nominal implicit SRL in the newswire domain. It incorporates a large number of detailed linguistic resources (Penn Treebank, Penn Discourse Bank, NomBank, FrameNet) and assumes gold standard information on all levels. We therefore see this system as an upper bound rather than as a competitor.

The results are shown in Table 8. The overall patterns are very similar to Experiment 1: out-of-domain training (2) works worse than in-domain training (1), and simple concatenation (3) does not improve over in-domain training. With feature augmentation, however, we see a significant improvement of 9% in precision, recall and F_1. The difference is highly significant at $p<0.01$. This confirms the effectiveness of corpus combination, despite the small size of the added SEMEVAL dataset compared to GERBERCHAI. It is also clear, however, that the results are much worse than the upper bound set by Gerber and Chai.

Table 7 subdivides the results by semantic roles for (1), as the in-domain baseline, and (4), as the best model. Again, we see improvements for both A0 and A1, both regarding precision and recall. Interestingly, the improvements as well as the performance for A1 exceed those for A0 – a difference to the SEMEVAL results, where we found the best results for A0.

6 Experiment 3

In Experiments 1 and 2, we have found an improvement for including out-of-domain data. However, it is unclear so far whether the improvements are simply due to the increased amount of training data, or to the training data becoming more *varied*. To distinguish between these two hypotheses, Experiment 3 keeps the total size of the training set constant and varies the proportions of the two source corpora, SEMEVAL and GERBERCHAI, in 10% increments, from 100% SEMEVAL to 100% GERBERCHAI. The size of the training set is limited by the smaller one of the training sets (SEMEVAL, cf. Table 1).

As before, we apply feature augmentation and train models, which we now evaluate on both the SEMEVAL and GERBERCHAI test sets. If the improvements we have seen before are solely due to the larger size of the training sets, we expect to see the highest performance for the 100% in-domain training

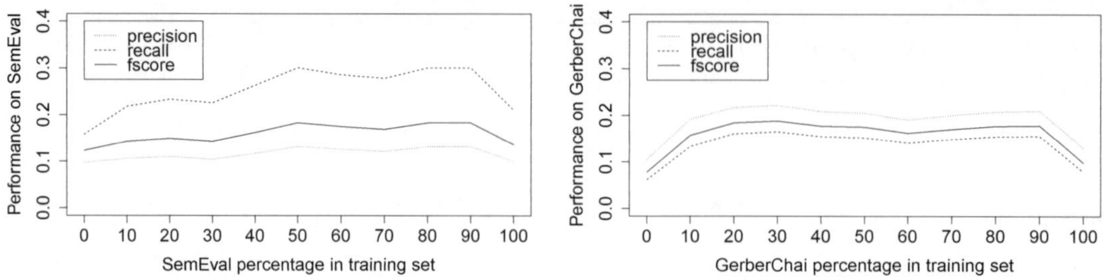

Figure 1: Evaluation of models trained on a constant-size training set with changing composition

set, and decreasing performance with more out-of-domain data. If however variety is important, we expect to see a maximum somewhere between the two extremes, at the point where there is enough out-of-domain training data to introduce variety but not enough to overwhelm the in-domain data.

Figure 1 shows the results. On both test sets, we do *not* see the best result for 100% in-domain data – there is a substantial improvement moving from 100% to 90% in-domain data (from 0.13 to 0.18 F-Score on SemEval and from 0.10 to 0.18 on GerberChai). On the SemEval test set, the result for 90% is the (tied) best result. We see minor variation until roughly the 50-50 split and then a mild degradation to the cases where the GerberChai training data dominates, consistent with Experiment 1. On the GerberChai test set, we see a more symmetrical picture, with relatively constant performance for almost all mixtures. We see degradation for the both "pure" (100%) training sets, but still better performance for in-domain than for out-of-domain (100% GerberChai: 0.10; 100% SemEval: 0.08).[2]

Overall, the results are compatible with the second, but not the first hypothesis: the models do seem to profit from the combination of different corpora even when this does not involve larger training sets.

7 Conclusion

This paper has reviewed the state-of-the-art in implicit semantic role labeling (SRL) where scarcity of training data is the major bottleneck. We have argued that rather than annotating new datasets, researchers should gauge the potential for *combining existing corpora*, even if they are very different at first glance.

We have presented experiments on two standard corpora, the SemEval 2010 Task 10 corpus (novels) and Gerber and Chai's nominalization corpus (newswire). They demonstrate that systems trained on either corpus can benefit substantially from combination with the other one. More specifically, we find that (a) domain adaptation techniques are helpful to bridge the differences between corpora; (b) improvements from corpus combination apply surprisingly uniformly to different roles and different parts of speech; (c) improvements can be obtained from relatively small amounts of "out-of-domain" data.

Further analyses have indicated that it is indeed the *complementarity* of the corpora, rather than the addition of training data, which is responsible for the improvement. This suggests that rather than annotating as many instances as possible, researchers should concentrate on annotating instances that are as *varied* as possible, similar to uncertainty sampling in active learning (Lewis and Gale, 1994). In future work, we will experiment with combining more than two corpora to test the scalability of the present approach.

An open question is to what extent the benefits that we see for implicit SRL generalize to other tasks. We believe that two factors combine to give us the present picture: the first one is the set of properties of implicit SRL as a task where semantic and discourse features play important roles. The second one is simply the low baseline performance; overall better models are presumably harder to improve.

Acknowledgments. We would like thank Roman Klinger for helpful suggestions.

[2]Note that these numbers do not match Experiment 2, since the training set in this experiment is much smaller.

References

Aljoscha Burchardt, Anette Frank, and Manfred Pinkal. 2005. Building text meaning representations from contextually related frames – a case study. In *Proceedings of the International Conference on Computational Semantics*, pages 66–77, Tilburg, Netherlands.

Xavier Carreras and Lluís Màrquez. 2005. Introduction to the CoNLL-2005 Shared Task: Semantic Role Labeling. In *Proceedings of the Conference on Computational Natural Language Learning 2005*, pages 152–164, Ann Arbor, MI.

Desai Chen, Nathan Schneider, Dipanjan Das, and Noah A. Smith. 2010. SEMAFOR: Frame argument resolution with log-linear models. In *Proceedings of the International Workshop on Semantic Evaluation*, pages 264–267, Uppsala, Sweden.

Janara Christensen, Mausam, Stephen Soderland, and Oren Etzioni. 2010. Semantic role labeling for open information extraction. In *Proceedings of the NAACL HLT 2010 First International Workshop on Formalisms and Methodology for Learning by Reading*, pages 52–60, Los Angeles, CA.

Michael Collins. 1997. Three generative, lexicalised models for statistical parsing. In *Proceedings of the 35th Annual Meeting of the Association for Computational Linguistics*, pages 16–23, Madrid, Spain.

Dipanjan Das, Desai Chen, André FT Martins, Nathan Schneider, and Noah A Smith. 2014. Frame-semantic parsing. *Computational Linguistics*, 40(1):9–56.

Hal Daumé III. 2007. Frustratingly easy domain adaptation. In *Proceedings of the Annual Meeting of the Association for Computational Linguistics*, pages 256–263, Prague, Czech Republic.

David Dowty. 1991. Thematic Proto-Roles and Argument Selection. *Language*, 67:547–619.

Bradley Efron and Robert J. Tibshirani. 1993. *An Introduction to the Bootstrap*. Chapman and Hall, New York.

Parvin Sadat Feizabadi and Sebastian Padó. 2014. Crowdsourcing annotation of non-local semantic roles. In *Proceedings of the Annual Meeting of the European Chapter of the Association for Computational Linguistics*, pages 226–230, Gothenburg, Sweden.

Charles J. Fillmore, Christopher R. Johnson, and Miriam R.L. Petruck. 2003. Background to FrameNet. *International Journal of Lexicography*, 16(3):235–250.

Jenny Rose Finkel and Christopher D Manning. 2009. Hierarchical Bayesian Domain Adaptation. In *Proceedings of Human Language Technologies: The 2009 Annual Conference of the North American Chapter of the Association for Computational Linguistics*, pages 602–610, Boulder, Colorado, USA.

Matthew Gerber and Joyce Y Chai. 2012. Semantic role labeling of implicit arguments for nominal predicates. *Computational Linguistics*, 38(4):755–798.

Daniel Gildea and Daniel Jurafsky. 2002. Automatic labeling of semantic roles. *Computational Linguistics*, 28(3):245–288.

Philip Gorinski, Josef Ruppenhofer, and Caroline Sporleder. 2013. Towards weakly supervised resolution of null instantiations. In *Proceedings of the International Conference on Computational Semantics*, pages 119–130, Potsdam, Germany.

Eduard H Hovy, Mitch Marcus, Martha Palmer, Lance Ramshaw, and Ralph Weischedel. 2006. OntoNotes: The 90% Solution. In *Proceedings of the Joint Human Language Technology Conference and Annual Meeting of the North American Chapter of the Association for Computational Linguistics*, pages 57–60, New York City, NY.

Jing Jiang. 2008. A literature survey on domain adaptation of statistical classifiers. Technical report, Department of Computer Science, University of Illinois at Urbana-Champaign.

Egoitz Laparra and German Rigau. 2012. Exploiting explicit annotations and semantic types for implicit argument resolution. In *Proceedings of the International Conference on Semantic Computing*, pages 75–78, Palermo, Italy.

Egoitz Laparra and German Rigau. 2013. Sources of evidence for implicit argument resolution. In *Proceedings of the International Conference on Computational Semantics*, pages 155–166, Potsdam, Germany.

David D. Lewis and William A. Gale. 1994. A sequential algorithm for training text classifiers. In *Proceedings of the 17th Annual International ACM SIGIR Conference on Research and Development in Information Retrieval*, pages 3–12, Dublin, Ireland.

Junhui Li, Guodong Zhou, Hai Zhao, Qiaoming Zhu, and Peide Qian. 2009. Improving nominal SRL in Chinese language with verbal SRL information and automatic predicate recognition. In *Proceedings of the Conference on Empirical Methods in Natural Language Processing*, pages 1280–1288, Singapore.

Christopher D. Manning, Mihai Surdeanu, John Bauer, Jenny Finkel, Steven J. Bethard, and David McClosky. 2014. The Stanford CoreNLP natural language processing toolkit. In *Proceedings of the Annual Meeting of the Association for Computational Linguistics: System Demonstrations*, pages 55–60, Baltimore, MD.

Adam Meyers, Ruth Reeves, Catherine Macleod, Rachel Szekely, Veronika Zielinska, Brian Young, and Ralph Grishman. 2004. The NomBank project: An interim report. In *Proceedings of the HLT-NAACL 2004 workshop on Frontiers in Corpus Annotation*, pages 24–31, Boston, MA, USA.

Shachar Mirkin, Ido Dagan, and Sebastian Padó. 2010. Assessing the Role of Discourse References in Entailment Inference. In *Proceedings of the 48th Annual Meeting of the Association for Computational Linguistics*, pages 1209–1219, Uppsala, Sweden.

Tatjana Moor, Michael Roth, and Anette Frank. 2013. Predicate-specific annotations for implicit role binding: Corpus annotation, data analysis and evaluation experiments. In *Proceedings of the International Conference on Computational Semantics*, pages 369–375, Potsdam, Germany.

Paloma Moreda, Hector Llorens, Estela Saquete, and Manuel Palomar. 2011. Combining semantic information in question answering systems. *Information Processing & Management*, 47(6):870–885.

Alexis Palmer and Caroline Sporleder. 2010. Evaluating FrameNet-style semantic parsing: the role of coverage gaps in FrameNet. In *Proceedings of the International Conference on Computational Linguistics*, pages 928–936, Beijing, China.

Martha Palmer, Daniel Gildea, and Paul Kingsbury. 2005. The proposition bank: An annotated corpus of semantic roles. *Computational Linguistics*, 31(1):71–106.

Martha Palmer, Dan Gildea, and Nianwen Xue. 2010. *Semantic Role Labeling*. Morgan & Claypool.

Michael Roth and Anette Frank. 2013. Automatically identifying implicit arguments to improve argument linking and coherence modeling. In *Proceedings of the Joint Conference on Lexical and Computational Semantics*, pages 306–316, Atlanta, GA.

Josef Ruppenhofer, Caroline Sporleder, Roser Morante, Collin Baker, and Martha Palmer. 2010. SemEval-2010 Task 10: Linking events and their participants in discourse. In *Proceedings of the International Workshop on Semantic Evaluation*, pages 45–50, Uppsala, Sweden.

Josef Ruppenhofer, Philip Gorinski, and Caroline Sporleder. 2011. In search of missing arguments: A linguistic approach. In *Proceedings of the Conference on Recent Advances in Natural Language Processing*, pages 331–338, Hissar, Bulgaria.

Dan Shen and Mirella Lapata. 2007. Using semantic roles to improve question answering. In *Proceedings of the Joint Conference on Empirical Methods in Natural Language Processing and Conference on Computational Natural Language Learning*, pages 12–21, Prague, Czech Republic.

Carina Silberer and Anette Frank. 2012. Casting implicit role linking as an anaphora resolution task. In *Proceedings of the Joint Conference on Lexical and Computational Semantics*, pages 1–10, Jeju Island, South Korea.

Vivek Srikumar and Dan Roth. 2011. A joint model for extended semantic role labeling. In *Proceedings of the Conference on Empirical Methods in Natural Language Processing*, pages 129–139, Edinburgh, United Kingdom.

Sara Tonelli and Rodolfo Delmonte. 2010. VENSES++: Adapting a deep semantic processing system to the identification of null instantiations. In *Proceedings of the International Workshop on Semantic Evaluation*, pages 296–299, Uppsala, Sweden.

Sara Tonelli and Rodolfo Delmonte. 2011. Desperately seeking implicit arguments in text. In *Proceedings of the ACL 2011 Workshop on Relational Models of Semantics*, pages 54–62, Portland, OR, USA.

Dekai Wu and Pascale Fung. 2009. Semantic roles for SMT: A hybrid two-pass model. In *Proceedings of the Annual Meeting of the North American Chapter of the Association for Computational Linguistics*, pages 13–16, Boulder, CO.

Deyi Xiong, Min Zhang, and Haizhou Li. 2012. Modeling the translation of predicate-argument structure for SMT. In *Proceedings of the Annual Meeting of the Association for Computational Linguistics*, pages 902–911, Jeju Island, South Korea.

Identification of Caused Motion Constructions

Jena D. Hwang
University of Colorado at Boulder
Boulder, CO 80309
hwangd@colorado.edu

Martha Palmer
University of Colorado at Boulder
Boulder, CO 80309
martha.palmer@colorado.edu

Abstract

This research describes the development of a supervised classifier of English Caused Motion Constructions (CMCs) (e.g. *The goalie kicked the ball into the field*). Consistent identification of CMCs is a necessary step to a correct interpretation of semantics for sentences where the verb does not conform to the expected semantics of the verb (e.g. *The crowd laughed the clown off the stage*). We expand on a previous study on the classification CMCs (Hwang et al., 2010) to show that CMCs can be successfully identified in the corpus data. In this paper, we present the classifier and the series of experiments carried out to improve its performance.

1 Introduction

While natural language processing performance has been improved through the recognition that there is a relationship between the semantics of the verb and the syntactic context in which the verb is realized (Guildea and Palmer, 2002), sentences where the verb does not conform to the expected syntax-semantic patterning behavior remain problematic.

1. The goalie kicked the ball into the field.
2. The crowd laughed the clown off the stage.

These sentences are semantically related – an entity causes a second entity to go along the path described by the prepositional phrase: in 1, the goalie causes the ball to go into the field, and in 2, the crowd causes the clown to go off the stage.

While only the verb in the first sentence is generally identified as a verb of motion that can appear in a caused motion context, both are examples of caused motion constructions (CMCs) (Goldberg, 1995). The verb *laugh* of sentence 2 is normally considered an intransitive manner of speaking verb (e.g. *The crowd laughed at the clown*), but in this sentence, the verb is coerced into the caused motion interpretation and the semantics of the verb gives the manner in which the movement happened (e.g. *the crowd caused the clown to move off the stage by means of laughing*). The semantics parallel one another: both sentences have a causal argument responsible for the event, an argument in motion, and a path that specifies the initial, middle, or final location, state or condition of the argument in motion (Hwang et al., 2013).

Thus, if the semantic interpretation is strictly based on the expected semantics of the verb and its arguments, it fails to include the relevant information from the CMC. Accurate semantic role labelling requires that NLP classifiers accurately identify these coerced usages in data.

In a previous study, we carried out preliminary work on the supervised identification of CMCs (Hwang et al., 2010). The pilot study was conducted in a highly controlled environment over a small portion of Wall Street Journal (WSJ) data. The annotation of CMCs were limited to 1.8K instances of WSJ data. In the pilot, we were able to establish a classifier predicting CMC with high accuracy (87.2% precision, 86.0% recall, and 0.866 f-score).

In a subsequent study, we developed a detailed set of criteria for identifying CMCs to insure the

*Proceedings of the Fourth Joint Conference on Lexical and Computational Semantics (*SEM 2015)*, pages 51–60,
Denver, Colorado, June 4–5, 2015.

production of consistent annotation with high inter-annotator agreement (Hwang et al., 2014). Through the semantic typing of the CMCs, the annotation guidelines defining CMCs were further refined from the guidelines used during the pilot study. Using the newly established criteria for annotation, we extended the annotation over the complete WSJ, and further included the Broadcast News and Webtext for the annotation of CMC. This study resulted in over 20K instances of CMC annotation.

In this paper, we carry out a supervised classification of the CMC. This study further expands on a pilot study with the larger set of high-quality annotated data for the further training and testing of CMC classifiers.

2 Caused Motion Constructions

CMCs are defined as having the coarse-grained syntactic structure of Subject Noun Phrase followed by a verb that takes both a Noun Phrase Object and a Prepositional Phrase: (NP-SBJ (V NP PP)); and the semantic meaning 'The agent, NP-SBJ, directly causes the patient, NP, to move along the path specified by the PP' (Goldberg, 1995). This construction is exemplified by the following sentences:

3. Frank sneezed the tissue off the table.
4. John stuffed the letter in the envelope.
5. Sally threw a ball to him.

However, not all syntactic structures of the form (NP-SBJ (V NP PP)):

6. Mary kicked the ball to my relief.
7. Jen took the highway into Pennsylvania.
8. We saw the bird in the shopping mall.

In 6, the PP does not specify a direction or a path. In 8, PP indicates the location in which the "seeing" event happened, not a path along which "we" caused "the bird" to move. Though the PP in 7 expresses a path, it is not a path over which Jen causes "the highway" to move.

3 Experimental Setup

3.1 Corpora

Our data comes from the latest version of OntoNotes, version 5.0, (Weischedel et al., 2012). Gold annotations for Penn Treebank, PropBank, and Verb Sense Annotation are available for all of OntoNotes corpora. As we did for the pilot study, we use the Wall Street Journal (WSJ) corpus. This corpus contains over 846K words selected from the non "strictly" financial (e.g., daily market reports) portion of the Wall Street Journal included in the Penn Treebank II (Marcus et al., 1994). We also pull from the smaller of the two WebText (WEB) data sets published in OntoNotes. This corpus contains 85K words selected from English weblogs. This portion of the data is not to be confused with the the larger 200K word web data, which is a separate corpus in OntoNotes. The third corpus used in our experiments is the 200K word Broadcast News (BN) data. OntoNotes' BN data contains news texts from broadcasting sources such as CNN, ABC, and PRI (Public Radio International).

3.2 Data Selection

In order to narrow the data down to a more manageable size for annotation, we exclude instances that can be deterministically categorized as NON-CMCs using the gold Penn Treebank annotation of the corpora. To do this we first select all sentences with the base syntactic form (NP-SBJ (V NP PP)) based on the Penn Treebank gold annotation.

Additionally, we use a set of heuristics (a smaller set than the pilot) to further select instances of potential CMCs. Instances which satisfy the following three conditions are extracted for annotation:(1) an NP exists in the verb phrase; (2) at least one PP exists in the verb phrase; and (3) the NP precedes the PP in the verb phrase.

For the remaining data, already annotated instances from the pilot study are separated out for double-checking. We also set aside instances that can be deterministically categorized as NON-CMC: instances with the function tags ADV, EXT, PRD, VOC, or TMP. These sentences are kept for a quick verification at the annotation stage that they indeed are cases of NON-CMCs and labeled as such.

3.3 Added Syntactic Complexity

In the pilot study, we had excluded passive instances (e.g. *Coffee was shipped from Colombia by Gracie.*), instances with traces in the object NP or PP including questions, relative clauses, and subordinate clauses (e.g. *What did Gracie ship from Colombia?* and *It was Gracie that shipped coffee from Colombia.*) and instances in which the verb is a conjunct to the main verb in the sentence (e.g. *chop* in *He peeled the potatoes and chopped them into a bowl*), opting to match sentences by their surface structure. For the current study, our data selection includes instances that retain an underlying syntactic form (NP-SBJ (V NP PP)). In effect, we extend the syntactic variability in the data.

Form	WSJ	BN	WEB
Questions/ Rel. clauses	2.3%	3.9%	2.6%
Passives	4.4%	4.6%	1.6%
Conjuncts	7.9%	10.2%	16.3%
Other clauses	46.3%	41.2%	37.3%
Other	41.4%	44.1%	44.7%

Table 1: Syntactic forms found in data. Other clauses include both subordinate and complement clauses.

Table 1 shows the breakdown of the syntactic forms in the current data. The pilot data was solely restricted to the "Other" category. More than half of all the syntactic forms represented in our current data add to the syntactic complexity beyond that of the pilot dataset, and lower our baseline classifier performance significantly.

3.4 Labels and Classfiers

The annotated data includes 4 major types of CMCs (Hwang et al., 2014). CMC types are listed below:

- **Displacement:** These CMCs express a (concrete or abstract) change of location of an entity (e.g. *The goalie kicked the ball into the field.* or *The market tilted the economy into recession.*). This is the most prototypical CMC type.
- **Change of Scale:** These CMCs express a change in value on a linear scale (e.g. *Torrential rains raised the water level to 500ft.*).
- **Change of Possesion:** These CMCs express a change of possession (e.g. *John gave a book to Mary*).
- **Change of State:** These CMCs express a change of attribute of an item (e.g. *I smashed the vase into pieces.*)

The experiments presented in this paper are geared towards the identification of: (1) all 4 types unified under a single label and (2) the "Displacement" type of CMCs (1 of the 4 types). We build two binary classifiers – one for each of the two labels. We will refer to the former classifier as "CMC classifier" and the latter as the "DISPLACE classifier". Table 2 shows the classification label distribution across the three corpora.

For all our experiments, 80% of the annotated data is randomly selected as the training/development data and the remaining 20% is set aside as the test/evaluation set. For our experiments, we use a Support Vector Machine (SVM) classifier with a linear kernel. In particular, we use LIBSVM (Chang and Lin, 2001) as our training and testing software. We use a 5-fold cross-validation process for the development stage.

3.5 Features

The features encode syntactic and semantic information that targets four elements in the sentence: (1) the verb, which expresses the event or the situation of the sentence, (2) the preposition, which instantiates the path information in a caused motion sentence, (3) the complement of the preposition, which covers the rest of the prepositional phrase, (4) the cause argument, which is recovered from the subject of the sentence or the prepositional by-phrase in a passive sentence, and (5) the undergoer argument, which is recovered from the direct object position of the sentence or from the subject position in a passive sentence. We will discuss the cause and undergoer argument recovery in further detail later.

3.5.1 Feature Sets

The **baseline** feature set is encoded by the **verb lemma** – the lemmatized and case-normalized verb. The verb lemma feature is the baseline feature for all our experiments. Following are the semantic and syntactic features sets used in our experiments. Anytime we use the terms "Full Set" or full feature set, we are referring to a set of features that includes all of the feature sets below for each of the four

	WSJ		WEB		BN	
CMC	2250	14.8%	533	29.2%	703	18.6%
NONCMC	12959	85.2%	1291	70.8%	3073	81.4%
DISPLACE	1261	8.3%	412	22.6%	511	13.5%
NONDISPLACE	13948	91.7%	1412	77.4%	3265	86.5%

Table 2: CMC and DISPLACE label distribution in training and test data

elements as noted above.

Features encoding **semantic** information are as following:

- **Nominal Entity** features which are automatically generated using BBNs IdentiFinder (Bikel et al., 1999). The IdentiFinder annotates relevant noun phrases with labels such as "Persons", "Time", "Location", or "Organization".
- **PropBank Frameset** features specify the verb's sense based on its subcategorization frame. This is extracted from the gold annotation provided by Ontonotes.
- **Ontonotes Verb Sense** features which specify the verb's sense. The semantics of these features are generally finer grained than what the PropBank framesets encode. These features are also provided as gold annotation in OntoNotes.
- **VerbNet Class** features that encode each of the VerbNet classes in which the verb is a member. A verb can be a member of one or more classes.
- **Preposition Type** features obtained from the automatic preposition labeller developed in a recent study by (Srikumar, 2013). The labeller introduces a set of 32 roles to disambiguate semantics of prepositions as used in sentences (e.g. *from* in *Her sudden death **from** pneumonia* ... (Cause) vs. *She copied the lines **from** the film.*(Source))

Features encoding **syntactic** information include:

- **Part of Speech Tag** of the lexical item in the syntactic parse.
- **Dependency Relation Tag** of the lexical item in a dependency parse.

Please note that while we depend on the phrasal trees for the data selection process, for feature extraction, we employ the CLEAR dependency parses (Choi, 2012). These parses have been automatically converted from the Penn Treebank phrasal trees. The decision to encode syntactic features from the dependency parses rather than from phrasal parses was based on the flexibility and the amount of additional information we gain through the dependency parse type. After a series of experimental runs with features from both parse types, it was determined that further syntactic features based on the phrase trees produced relatively similar performance to that of its counterpart labels on the dependency trees. However, the dependency labels are functionally finer grained than phrase structure labels for those syntactic elements that are most relevant to the CMCs.

3.5.2 Cause & Undergoer Argument Recovery

We make a pre-processing pass of the data to recover these arguments when possible. The recovered arguments are as following:

- **Passive Sentences:** For passive sentences, the complement of the *by*-prepositional phrase is recovered as the cause argument and the subject is recovered as the undergoer argument.
- **Conjunctions:** Given two verbal conjuncts sharing the subject, as in *"He cut the peppers and diced the tomatoes"*, the CLEAR dependency parse places the conjunction and the second conjunct as dependents of the first verb. This means that in dependency trees the two conjuncts' access to the cause argument is not symmetrical. The argument *He* is accessible to the verb *diced* via the verb *cut*, as the argument is a direct dependent of the verb *cut* and not the verb *diced*. To recover the arguments of the

	WSJ			WEB			BN		
	P	R	F	P	R	F	P	R	F
Baseline	61.23	37.56	0.4656	75.6	55.7	0.641	71.4	53.6	0.612
Baseline+P	**75.00**	74.67	0.7483†	78.0	**80.2**	**0.791**†	**84.8**	75.7	0.800†
Full Set	74.00	**77.78**	**0.7584**†	**79.0**	78.3	0.787†	84.1	**82.9**	**0.835**†
Annotator Agreement			0.667			0.764			0.606

Table 3: System performance on CMC label classification.
Statistically significant change from the Baseline feature set is marked with a †.

	WSJ			WEB			BN		
	P	R	F	P	R	F	P	R	F
Baseline	66.80	63.89	0.6531	72.7	58.5	0.649	71.3	55.9	0.626
Baseline+P	**76.33**	74.21	**0.7525**†	73.4	70.7	0.720	80.0	70.6	0.750†
Full Set	72.52	**75.40**	0.7393†	**76.5**	**79.3**	**0.778**†	**80.6**	**77.5**	**0.790**†

Table 4: System performance on DISPLACE label classification.
Statistically significant change from the Baseline feature set is marked with a †.

second verb conjunct we reach for the dependent on the first conjunct as necessary.

- **Subordinate clauses:** For verbs that are found in subordinate clauses whose head node is a verb (also called matrix verb) such as an infinitival clause (e.g. *He [plans]*-HEAD *to* ***cut*** *the peppers into pieces*), or a relative clause (e.g. *Joe [cut]*-HEAD *the tomatoes Mary* ***washed***.), we reach for the head node's arguments to fill in the missing cause and theme arguments. If there is an intervening relative pronoun (e.g. *Joe cut the tomatoes* ***that*** *Mary washed*), the relative pronoun is retrieved as the argument (either as cause or theme depending whether or not the subordinate clause is a passive), instead.

3.5.3 POS Tags & Dependency Relation Tags

After a series of experiments, it was determined that the part of speech and the dependency relation features might be too fine grained to provide useful information to the classifier. Thus, all of the features expressed by the part of speech and the dependency relation are featurized in the following manner.

- **Part of Speech Tags:** (1) Cardinal numbers (CD), pronouns (PRP), and gerundial (VBG) and participial (VBN) forms of verbs are featurized as found (one feature per tag). (2) Rest of the verb forms are mapped to the base tag VB. (3) Plural nouns are mapped to their singular counterparts. (4) Adjectives and adverbs are mapped to the base tag JJ and RB, respectively. (5) Rest are given the tag: OTHER.

- **Dependency Relation Labels:** (1) Relations specifying subjects, direct object, and agent (oblique of a passive sentence), and relations specifying the object of the preposition, complement clauses, and relative clauses are featurized as found (one feature per tag). (2) Complement clauses (e.g. *pcomp*, *acomp*) are grouped under a single *comp* label. (3) Modifiers (e.g. *partmod*, *advmod*) are grouped under the *mod* label. (4) Rest are given the tag: OTHER.

4 Classifier Experiments

Tables 3 and 4 show the precision and recall percentages and the f-score values for our experiments. Here we show results for three feature combinations: the **Baseline** set encoded from the verb's lemma, the **Baseline** plus the preposition feature set (**Baseline+P**), and the **Full Set** that includes all of the features listed in Section 3.5. The best performance values are bold-faced. The significance of a feature set's performance was evaluated via a chi-squared test (McNemar, $p < 0.05$). Statistically significant change from the **Baseline** feature set is marked with a †. Additionally, for the CMC classification we show the inter-annotator agreement

(Gold) f-score (Hwang et al., 2014). Our best performances in CMC classification as measured by the f-score are comparable or higher than the inter annotator agreement f-score.

4.1 Syntactic vs. Semantic Features

With the exception of the DISPLACE classifier on the WEB corpus, both the **Baseline+P** and the **Full Set** of features perform significantly better than the **Baseline** in both sets of experiments. It is interesting that the **Baseline+P** set performs just as well and sometimes better than the full set of feature consistently across the corpora, though the differences in the values are not statistically significant.

In order to gain a better understanding of the performance on the full set of features, the full feature set was divided into syntactic features and semantic features as described in Section 3.5. As a means of control, both the syntactic and semantic feature sets also include the features for the verb lemma and the preposition. Out of the different feature combinations examined, the distinction between semantic and syntactic features is the most salient. Table 5 shows the system performance values for the syntactic and semantic features. We also show the performance of the **Baseline+P** plus VerbNet class (**Baseline+PV**) feature set, as it gives better insight into the semantic feature performance.

The numbers indicate that the semantic features have a consistently higher performance than the syntactic features. The syntactic feature sets, perform significantly lower than the full feature sets and they barely pass the **Baseline** features in performance. In fact, the syntactic features are significantly lower than the **Baseline+P** features, despite the fact that, just like the semantic features, they include the verb lemma feature and the preposition feature. This suggests, that the syntactic features even in the presence of the lexical features are not strongly predictive of caused motion constructions. Moreover, these numbers seem to indicate that the performance on the full set of features likely comes from the semantic feature performance.

Amongst the semantic features, the **Baseline** feature, the **Baseline+P** feature, and the feature for VerbNet class membership of the verb (i.e. **Baseline+PV**) give the highest results. With the exception of the CMC classifier on the BN corpus, the numbers for the **Baseline+PV** set are not significantly different from either the semantic feature or the full feature set performance. Other semantic combinations were also tested, but they did not result in any particular change from the semantic feature set and the full feature set.

The semantic features perform as the most predictive features. This finding makes intuitive sense. Recall that during the data selection stage, we selected for instances that show syntactic compatibility with CMCs. Although syntactic variability still exists in the selected data (e.g. relative clauses and passive sentences), because of the data selection stage based on syntax, the task of identification comes primarily down to the semantic distinction between existing sentences. Additionally, some of the existing syntactic differences are neutralized by the cause and undergoer argument pre-processing stage described in Section 3.5.2. Thus, it stands to reason that most of the useful contributions come from the lexical items themselves and the semantics of the verb and its arguments.

Finally, the baseline system of the DISPLACE classification shows either a similar or improved performance over the CMC classifier. The overall performances across the different feature sets show similar values. Given that DISPLACE makes up a smaller percentage of the total data as shown in Section 3.4 (e.g. DISPLACE label for WSJ accounts for just under 9% of the total test and training data), the comparable performance is likely indicative that the DISPLACE label represents a more semantically coherent phenomenon than the CMC label.

4.2 Removing Frequent NON-CMC Verbs

In this experiment, we remove the top 25 highly frequent verbs[1] that do not appear in a CMC usage from both the training and testing data[2]. Their semantics are not compatible with the established definitions of CMCs. For example, verbs like *be*, *do*, or *have* cannot have caused motion usages, and verbs

[1]We effectively went down the list of the most frequent verbs in our WSJ data, and stopped at the first verb that could be judged as compatible and non-contrary to the established definitions of CMCs. 25 is the number of verbs in this list before the first CMC-compatible verb was reached.

[2]Top 25 verbs include: *accuse, base, be, build charge, create, do, fall, file, find, have, hold, keep, leave, offer, open, play, prevent, produce, quote, reach, rise, see, use*, and *view*.

CMC Classification									
	WSJ			WEB			BN		
	P	R	F	P	R	F	P	R	F
Syntactic	63.79	41.11	0.5000	76.6	55.7	0.645	72.4	54.3	0.620
Semantic	71.02	72.44	0.7173	77.3	64.2	0.701	80.5	76.4	0.784
Baseline+PV	71.78	76.89	0.7425	78.8	77.4	0.781	85.9	82.9	0.844

DISPLACE Classification									
	WSJ			WEB			BN		
	P	R	F	P	R	F	P	R	F
Syntactic	66.80	63.89	0.6531	73.8	58.5	0.653	72.3	58.8	0.649
Semantic	72.94	73.81	0.7337	76.3	70.7	0.734	74.3	79.4	0.768
Baseline+PV	74.81	76.59	0.7569	78.7	72.0	0.752	82.8	75.5	0.790

Table 5: System performance on semantic and syntactic features.

like *keep*, *leave*, or *prevent* are contrary to the semantics of CMCs. By removing large number of NON-CMC instances, we focus on how well the classifier performs on truly ambiguous cases. Furthermore, because these verbs have no instances of CMCs or DISPLACEs, only the negative label was reduced in size. Effectively, the removal of the verbs increases the proportion of the positive labels in the corpora. The numbers are shown in Table 6.

	CMC		DISPLACE	
Corpus	Before	After	Before	After
WSJ	14.8%	18.3%	8.86%	10.2%
WEB	29.2%	33.1%	24.2%	25.6%
BN	18.6%	21.6%	14.3%	15.7%

Table 6: Removed lemma count and effect on CMC label

Tables 7 and 8 show the precision and recall percentages and the f-score values when the instances of the most frequent NON-CMC verbs are removed from the training and testing data.

There is a general improvement in performance after the removal of the verbs from the data. The most marked improvement is in the WEB models (both CMC and DISPLACE) and the BN model's DISPLACE label classification. In particular the recall value shows improvement in these classifier models. As we have seen before, the **Baseline+PV** set and the full feature set show the best predictions. There is no noticeable improvement in the WSJ classifiers except for a slight (statistically insignificant) increase in the baseline values.

4.3 Random Downsampling of Negative Labels

As we have seen in Section 3.4, the CMC and the DISPLACE instances in WSJ are outnumbered by the negative, NON-CMC labels. The previous experiment on removing NON-CMC verbs effectively brought up the percentage of positive labels for the CMC and DISPLACE labels to 20% and 11%, respectively. However, label proportions of 20-80 or, worse, 11-89 are still highly unbalanced. Several studies have shown that in cases of training size imbalance, downsampling data can help with the performance of supervised classifiers (Weiss and Provost, 2001; Kubat and Matwin, 1997). Thus, for this experiment, we randomly downsample the negative labels in the WSJ training data to increase the percentage of positive labels[3]. For the sake of simplicity, we base the downsampling proportions on the CMC label: we cut the negative label so that the CMC label makes up 25% (Downsample1 "D1") and 30% (Downsample2 "D2")of the total data. The proportions of the DISPLACE labels are, therefore, 14.0% (D1)and 16.8% (D2), respectively.

Table 9 shows the performance of the WSJ models on the downsampled training set. The results indicate that the downsampling of the negative labels in the training data leads to increased performance. We have also tested the semantic feature set and the **Baseline+P** feature set as well. Their performances

[3]The downsampling was only applied to the training set, altering the distribution of labels only for the training data. The test set remains identical from its previous distribution in Section 4.2

	WSJ			WEB			BN		
	P	R	F	P	R	F	P	R	F
Baseline	63.32	40.67	0.4953	69.0	54.7	0.611	75.7	60.0	0.669
Baseline+P	71.71	71.56	0.7164	80.7	86.8	0.836	79.2	81.4	0.803
Baseline+PV	70.97	73.33	0.7213	81.6	87.7	0.845	79.6	83.6	0.815
Semantic	69.37	68.44	0.6890	74.6	80.2	0.773	77.1	84.3	0.805
Full Set	73.88	76.67	0.7525	76.2	87.7	0.816	79.5	82.9	0.811

Table 7: System performance on CMC label classification with frequent NON-CMC verbs removed.

	WSJ			WEB			BN		
	P	R	F	P	R	F	P	R	F
Baseline	63.25	58.73	0.6091	70.3	63.4	0.667	71.1	57.8	0.638
Baseline+P	72.77	67.86	0.7023	74.1	76.8	0.754	79.4	75.5	0.774
Baseline+PV	74.89	69.84	0.7228	76.1	81.7	0.788	79.8	81.4	0.806
Semantic	71.81	64.68	0.6806	73.8	75.6	0.747	74.5	77.5	0.760
Full Set	73.60	73.02	0.7331	76.7	84.1	0.802	81.4	81.4	0.814

Table 8: System performance on DISPLACE label classification with frequent NON-CMC verbs removed.

are approximately equal with no significant difference from the **Baseline+PV**, so we do not include those numbers.

We observe a large increase in the recall values, resulting in the overall improvement of the classifiers trained on downsampled data[4] . Interestingly, with the random downsampling of the training data, we see a boost in the full feature set's performance far more than the **Baseline+PV** set's performance. In fact, in all cases we observed that the full features now show a significantly higher performance than the other features (McNemar, $p < 0.05$). The observed results for the two downsampled classifiers are not statistically distinct from one another.

CMC Classification:				
	D1		D2	
	R	F	R	F
Baseline	55.33	0.5900	68.00	0.6207
Baseline+PV	86.00	0.7866	89.11	0.7886
Full Set	88.89	0.8180	91.33	0.8171
DISPLACE Classification:				
	D1		D2	
	R	F	R	F
Baseline	69.05	0.6705	75.40	0.6798
Baseline+PV	85.32	0.7776	88.10	0.7776
Full Set	88.10	0.8177	91.27	0.8084

Table 9: Classification performance with downsampled training data.

5 Final Considerations and Future Work

We have presented our work on the automatic classification of CMCs in corpus data using the annotated data produced in our earlier study (Hwang et al., 2014). Our studies have shown that we can achieve the identification of caused motion instances at a higher rate than the inter-annotator agreement scores, the best performance that can be realistically expected. We have also shown that semantic information is highly indicative of the caused motion phenomenon, confirming our general intuition that the caused motion construction is a semantic phenomenon. We have also carried out cross-genre experiments, which we were not able to include in this paper in the interest of length. In these experiments, we find that syntax provides scalable features that generalize well across different types of text, producing better results in cross-genre experiments. We have also shown that the downsampling of the negative label has a positive impact on the classification of the labels.

[4]We only show the recall values in Table 9 as the increase observed in the f-score was mainly due to the recall values.

This work has made use of various gold annotations for the purposes of feature extraction. The most obvious next step in this investigation will involve experimentation with automatically obtained features. Additionally, we hope to examine the impact of further features. As the experiments have shown, the lexical and semantic features (lemma, preposition, VerbNet classes) surface as strong predictors of CMCs. It follows from this, that we should expand the feature search to other semantic information. One particular set of features that might be interesting, would be based on FrameNet frames. Since FrameNet's frames represent different conceptual semantic domains, features from FrameNet may be instrumental at capturing and highlighting the semantics of CMCs that are spread across VerbNet classes of differing semantic types. Moreover, it would also be interesting to expand on the lexical features: lexical features can be extended to not just the verb of the sentence but also to the noun phrases. Further investigation into using resources like WordNet (Miller, 1995; Fellbaum et al., 1998) might be needed to remedy sparse data issues that lexical features based on words from the noun phrases might create.

Acknowlegements

We gratefully acknowledge the support of the National Science Foundation Grant NSF-IIS-1116782, A Bayesian Approach to Dynamic Lexical Resources for Flexible Language Processing. Any opinions, findings, and conclusions or recommendations expressed in this material are those of the authors and do not necessarily reflect the views of the National Science Foundation. We also gratefully acknowledge the support of DARPA/IPTO funding under the GALE program, DARPA/CMO Contract No. HR0011-06-C-0022, VN Supplement, and funding under the BOLT and Machine Reading programs. HR0011-11-C-0145 (BOLT) FA8750-09-C-0179 (M.R.).

References

Daniel M. Bikel, Richard Schwartz, and Ralph Weischedel. 1999. An algorithm that learns what's in a name. *Machine Learning: Special Issue on NL Learning*, 34.

Chih-Chung Chang and Chih-Jen Lin. 2001. LIBSVM: A library for support vector machines. *ACM Transactions on Intelligent Systems and Technology*, 2(3):27:1–27:27.

Jinho Choi. 2012. *Optimization of Natural Language Processing Components for Robustness and Scalability*. Ph.D. dissertation, University of Colorado at Boulder, Boulder, Colorado.

Cristiane Fellbaum, Joachim Grabowski, and Shari Landes. 1998. Performance and confidence in a semantic annotation task. In Christiane Fellbaum, editor, *WordNet: An Electronic Database*. The MIT Press.

Adele E. Goldberg. 1995. *Constructions: A Construction Grammar Approach to Argument Structure*. University Of Chicago Press.

Dan Guildea and Martha Palmer. 2002. The necessity of parsing for predicate argument recognition. In *40th Meeting of the Association for Computational Linguistics*, Philadelphia, PA, July.

Jena D. Hwang, Rodney D. Nielsen, and Martha Palmer. 2010. Towards a domain independent semantics: Enhancing semantic representation with construction grammar. In *Proceedings of the NAACL HLT Workshop on Extracting and Using Constructions in Computational Linguistics*, pages 1–8, Los Angeles, California, June. Association for Computational Linguistics.

Jena D. Hwang, Martha Palmer, and Annie Zaenen. 2013. Representing paths of motion in representing paths of motion in VerbNet. In Tracy Holloway King and Valeria de Paiva, editors, *From Quirky Case to Representing Space*. CSLI Online Publications.

Jena D. Hwang, Annie Zaenen, and Martha Palmer. 2014. Criteria for identifying and annotating caused motion constructions in corpus data. In *Proceedings of the Ninth International Conference on Language Resources and Evaluation (LREC'14)*, Reykjavik, Iceland.

Miroslav Kubat and Stan Matwin. 1997. Addressing the curse of imbalanced training sets: One-sided selection. *Proceedings of the Fourteenth International Conference on Machine Learning*.

Mitchell Marcus, Grace Kim, Mary Ann Marcinkiewicz, Robert Macintyre, Ann Bies, Mark Ferguson, Karen Katz, and Britta Schasberger. 1994. The penn treebank: Annotating predicate argument structure. In *ARPA Human Language Technology Workshop*, pages 114–119.

George A. Miller. 1995. Wordnet: a lexical database for english. *Communications of the ACM*, 38(11):39–41.

Vivek Srikumar. 2013. *Semantics of Role Labeling*. Ph.D. dissertation, University of Illinois at Urbana-Champaign, Urbana, IL.

Ralph Weischedel, Sameer Pradhan, Lance Ramshaw, Jeff Kaufman, Michelle Franchini, Mohammed El-Bachouti, Nianwen Xue, Martha Palmer, Jena D. Hwang, Claire Bonial, Jinho Choi, Aous Mansouri, Maha Foster, Abdel aati Hawwary, Mitchell Marcus, Ann Taylor, Eduard Hovy, Robert Belvin, and Ann Houston, 2012. *OntoNotes Release 4.99*, February.

Gary M. Weiss and Foster Provost. 2001. The effect of class distribution on classifier learning. Technical report, Rutgers University.

A Methodology for Word Sense Disambiguation at 90% based on large-scale CrowdSourcing

Oier Lopez de Lacalle
University of the Basque Country
oier.lopezdelacalle@ehu.eus

Eneko Agirre
University of the Basque Country
e.agirre@ehu.eus

Abstract

Word Sense Disambiguation has been stuck for many years. In this paper we explore the use of large-scale crowdsourcing to cluster senses that are often confused by non-expert annotators. We show that we can increase performance at will: our in-domain experiment involving 45 highly polysemous nouns, verbs and adjective (9.8 senses on average), yields an average accuracy of 92.6 using a supervised classifier for an average polysemy of 6.1. Our proposal has the advantage of being cost-effective and being able to produce different levels of granularity. Our analysis shows that the error reduction with respect to fine-grained senses is higher, and manual inspection show that the clusters are sensible when compared to those of OntoNotes and WordNet Supersenses.

1 Introduction

Word sense ambiguity is a major hurdle for accurate information extraction, summarization and machine translation. The utility of Word Sense Disambiguation (WSD) depends on the accuracy and on how useful the sense distinctions are. The first issue is quantitative, as it can be measured using a WSD system on certain dataset. The second examines whether the sense distinctions are appropriate, which varies from application to application. Although usefulness can be explored in a downstream application (Agirre et al., 2008), it is usually assessed subjectively, discussing the quality of the sense distinctions (Palmer et al., 2007). Both issues (performance and usefulness) are linked to the granularity of the sense inventory, and conflict with each other: finer granularity might produce more useful distinctions but the accuracy would be worse, and vice-versa.

WordNet (Fellbaum, 1998) is the most widely used resource to build word sense disambiguation tools and word sense annotated corpora, including recent large efforts (Passonneau et al., 2012), but its fine-grainedness has been mentioned to be a problem (Hovy et al., 2006; Palmer et al., 2007).

We think that a desiderata for a sense inventory would be that it provides useful sense distinctions and useful performance across a large range of applications. We would also add that it should be tightly integrated with WordNet, given its prevalence on NLP applications, and we thus focus on sense inventories which are mapped to WordNet.

In order to asses usefulness, we need specific measures. Downstream application is difficult, and unfeasible for new proposals, as a full-fledged sense inventories and associated annotations are necessary. We can instead estimate usefulness of proposed sense inventories using several proxy measures:

- High **polysemy**. Note that polysemy alone could be misleading, as a word with many senses might be skewed to a single sense: 99% of occurrences could belong to a single sense, while the rest are only seen once. Besides the absolute polysemy, we can use the accuracy of the **most frequent sense** (MFS, estimated in train data and applied to test data) as a simple

*Proceedings of the Fourth Joint Conference on Lexical and Computational Semantics (*SEM 2015)*, pages 61–70,
Denver, Colorado, June 4–5, 2015.

and effective indication of skewness. High polysemy and low MFS are desirable properties.

- High performance, as measured the accuracy of a supervised system trained on hand-annotated data. The higher the **accuracy**, the better.

- Flexible sense granularity, that is, the ability to produce different degrees of polysemy and accuracy, from fine-grained to coarse-grained. When comparing sense inventories with different granularities, absolute MFS and supervised performance are not enough. We propose to use **error reduction** of the supervised system with respect to the MFS as a measure of the balance between low MFS and high supervised performance. The larger the error reduction the better.

- Manual inspection of the sense distinctions, as a complement to quantitative measures.

We propose to use crowdsourced annotations (Passonneau and Carpenter, 2014) to cluster WordNet senses that are often confused by non-expert annotators. Our method can provide clusters at different levels of granularity. We show that we can construct clusters yielding around 90% accuracy for 45 words, with higher error reduction with respect to MFS than fine-grained senses. By construction, we merge senses which are often confused by annotators, yielding sensible sense clusters, as corroborated by manual inspection.

The paper is structured as follows. Section 2 mentions related work. We then present the annotations, followed by the clustering procedure. Section 5 report the main experiments. Section 6 compares our clustering to that of OntoNotes followed by a comparison to WordNet Supersenses. Section 8 draws the conclusions.

2 Related Work

Our work is close to (Passonneau and Carpenter, 2014) in that we use the same dataset and annotations presented in that work. They present a comparison of conventional expert-guided annotation model with a probabilistic annotation model that does not take agreement into account.

Previous efforts to cluster WordNet senses in order to produce coarse-grained inventories have shown that improved results can be obtained, but we think our approach fits the desiderata better. For instance, clustering together senses which have the same Semantic File (also called Supersenses) allowed the best supervised WSD system to date (Zhong and Ng, 2010) to increase accuracy from 58.3% to 82.6% in the Semeval 2007 all-words dataset (Navigli et al., 2007). Semantic Files are useful, but don't allow to provide flexible sense inventories.

The OntoNotes project (Hovy et al., 2006) devised a manual grouping method which explicitly sought 90% accuracy. Although the method was shown to be successful, the fixed sense groupings had to be produced manually, included complex mappings to WordNet (cf. Section 6), and was a limited exercise, with annotations for around 4900 words. Our work is similar in spirit to OntoNotes, but use a different methodology which allows for flexible granularity, as the annotation is done at the fine-grained level, and the clustering is done later fully automatically.

Automatic clustering algorithms are not new. (Tou Ng et al., 1999) propose to use annotator agreement to cluster senses, reporting higher inter-annotator agreement after clustering. We are in part inspired by their approach, as we extend it from two annotators to a sample with 25 annotators, and validate the approach with WSD systems.

The rest of approaches use other sources of information. Peters et al. (1998) make use of the WordNet hierarchy to group close senses. Mihalcea and Moldovan (1999) present similar approach that is based in the structure of WordNet. Tomuro (2001) presents are more principled algorithm based on *Minimum Description Length*. A work which is closely related to our work is (Agirre and Lopez de Lacalle, 2003), in which they examine a variety of information sources to cluster WordNet word senses, including a hierarchical clustering based on distributional information. Snow et al. (2007) present a supervised learning algorithm that learns merging senses and make use of wide range of WordNet-based and corpus-based features. (Navigli et al., 2007) mapped WordNet to the top level sense distinctions in the Oxford Dictionary of

English. All the above rely on automatic measures, while our method is based on human annotations.

3 MASC Crowdsourced annotations

The corpus used in the experiments is part of the Manually Annotated Sub-Corpus of the Open American National Corpus, which contains a subsidiary word sense sentence corpus consisting of approximately one thousand sentences per word annotated with WordNet 3.0 sense labels (Passonneau et al., 2012). In this work we make use of a publicly available subset of 45 words (17 nouns, 19 verbs and 9 adjective, see Table2) that have been annotated, 1000 sentences per target word, using crowdsourcing (Passonneau and Carpenter, 2014). The authors collected between 20 and 25 labels for every sentence. They showed that a probabilistic annotation model based on crowdsourced data was effective, with favorable quality when compared to a conventional expert-guided annotation model.

4 Clustering Procedure

Having access to multiple annotations of the same item allows to identify correlations among senses of a word. In particular, we can mine how many times the annotators confused 2 particular senses of a word. If two senses are confused very often, it will signal that the annotators find the differences between the two senses difficult to discriminate in context. We also want to note that, in some cases, the context might be underspecified, and several senses might hold at the same time. We left this second phenomena for a future study.

We built a confusion matrix for each target word counting how many times two distinct senses are annotated in the same instance. More formally, the confusion of two senses of a target word conf(s_1, s_2) is defined as follows:

$$\frac{1}{I}\sum_{i=1}^{I}\frac{1}{\binom{J_i}{2}}\sum_{m=1}^{J_i-1}\sum_{n=m+1}^{J_i}\mathbb{I}((y_{i,n}=s_1\wedge y_{i,m}=s_2)\vee (y_{i,n}=s_2\wedge y_{i,m}=s_1))$$

where I is number of instances of the word, J_i is the number of turkers that annotated instance i, and $y_{i,m}$ is the annotation of turker m in instance i. Finally, $\mathbb{I}(s)=1$ iff the condition expressed in s is true.

We cluster the senses based on the information in the confusion matrix, i.e. two senses (s_1, s_2) will tend to be in the same cluster if conf(s_1, s_2) is high. We used agglomerative hierarchical clustering for the sake of simplicity, as we obtain one hierarchy of senses in one go, and then used different cuts in the hierarchy to obtain clusters of different sense granularities.

In order to obtain the target coarse-grained inventory, the procedure was the following: (0) we start at the leaves of the hierarchy, that is, with the fine-grained senses; (1) we train and test a word sense disambiguation algorithm on development data using the current sense distinctions (see the next Section for details); (2) if the accuracy is higher than 90%, or if there are only two senses left, we stop and output the current sense distinctions; (3) we go up one level in the hierarchical cluster, joining together the two senses with highest confusion score, and go to step (1). Note that the algorithm does not guarantee obtaining 90% on the training data. Once the coarse-grained senses are obtained, we train the word sense disambiguation on the development data and test over held-out data, yielding the final accuracy scores.

In order to contrast results, we also produced hierarchies of senses based on random clustering, where the clusters yield the same sense granularity as those of the confusion-based clustering explained above. We produced 10 random clustering for each word, and averaged over the runs to obtain the final accuracy.

5 Experiments

The gold standard is based on the multiple annotations in the corpus, but a single sense was selected as the correct one, following (Passonneau and Carpenter, 2014), which use a probabilistic annotation model (Dawid and Skene, 1979). We split the 1000 examples for each word into development and test, sampling 85% (and 15% respectively) at random, preserving the overall sense distribution.

The Word Sense Disambiguation algorithm of choice is *It Make Sense* (IMS) (Zhong and Ng, 2010), which reports the best WSD results to date. IMS is a freely available Java implementation[1],

[1] http://www.comp.nus.edu.sg/~nlp/

which provides an extensible and flexible platform for researchers interested in using a WSD component. Following Lee and Ng (2002), IMS adopts support vector machines as the classifier and integrates the state of the features extractors including parts-of-speech of the surrounding words, bag of words features, and local collocations as features.

IMS provides ready-to-use models trained with examples collected from parallel texts , SEMCOR (Miller et al., 1993), and the DSO corpus (Ng and Lee, 1996). In our experiments we train IMS with the train examples of the crowdsourced MASC. We used IMS out-of-the-box, using the default parametrization and built-in feature extraction. We compare results obtained with IMS against the Most Frequent Sense (MFS), which was estimated using the training corpus. Both systems (IMS and MFS) could be trained on fine-grained senses, on coarse-grained senses induced from the confusion matrix using the 90% threshold described above ($\text{Coarse}_{\text{conf}}$) and coarse-grained senses induced from random clustering using the 90% threshold ($\text{Coarse}_{\text{random}}$). We also used sense clusters from OntoNotes and WordNet Supersenses (cf. Sections 6 and 7) .

5.1 Main results

The results of the six systems on development and test data are shown in Table 1, showing that we successfully attained an accuracy over 90% on average. The results for random clustering show that not any clustering yields meaningful results. Due to variation of the random sense-hierarchies, we calculated the upper and lower margins with 95% of confidence level (79.2-80.0 accuracy in test). The results show that random clustering performs significantly lower than the confusion based clustering. The results in development and test are very similar, confirming that the confusion information is stable in our in-domain scenario.

All in all, as Table 2 shows, 30 words out of the 45 attain an accuracy higher than 90% in test (14 out of 17 nouns, 11 out of 19 verbs and 5 out of 9 adjectives). The precision for the words which do not attain 90% is 87.4% on average, and 85.4% for adjective, being the lowest. The polysemy is reduced from 9.8 to 6.2.The appendix shows detailed information for each target word. In all but 3 words coarse-grained accuracy is above fine-grained. Note that MFS and IMS produce the same results in 11 words out of 45. We will revisit MFS in Section 6.

Figure 1 plots, on top, the results (on test) grouped on MFS and IMS for easier comparison. The figure also plots the error reduction of each coarse-grained inventory with respect to fine-grained. The higher

	Development		Test	
	MFS	**IMS**	**MFS**	**IMS**
Fine-grained	47.2	73.2	46.2	73.1
$\text{Coarse}_{\text{random}}$	60.4	79.9	60.2	79.6
$\text{Coarse}_{\text{conf}}$	84.2	92.9	84.1	92.6

Table 1: Development and test results using cross-validation (left side) and test results (right side) for IMS and MFS using three sense inventories.

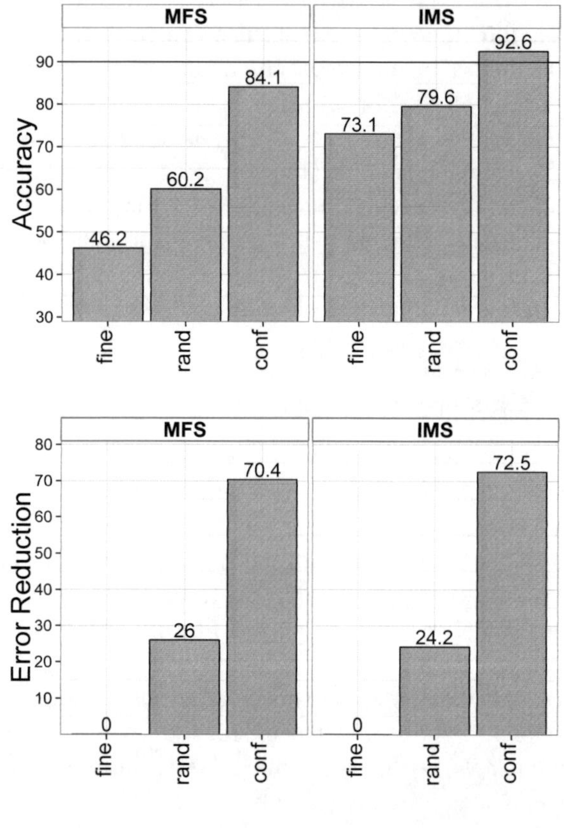

Figure 1: Accuracy on test of sense granularities and methods (top) and error reduction with respect to fine-grained (bottom), for the three sense inventories.

software.html

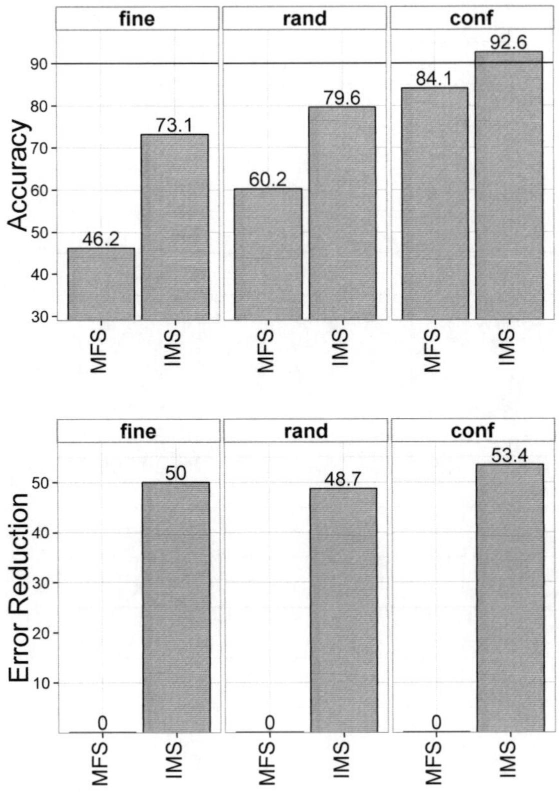

Figure 2: Accuracy of sense granularities and methods (top) and error reduction of IMS with respect to MFS (bottom), for the three sense inventories.

error reduction of our coarse-grained inventory with respect to the random clustering shows that the **clusters are meaningful**, and that the performance gain is not an artifact of reducing the sense inventory[2].

Figure 2 plots, on top, the results (on test) grouped on each sense inventory. The figure also plots the error reduction of IMS with respect to MFS in each coarse-grained inventory. The better error reduction of IMS with respect to MFS for our coarse-grained inventory shows that **our clusters are easier to learn**, in that reducing the sense inventory increases the delta with respect to the MFS baseline. Note that reducing the sense inventory is not enough to show this effect, as exemplified by the fact that the error reduction for the random clusters is lower than for the fine-grained senses.

[2]Note that, by construction, $\text{Coarse}_{\text{random}}$ and $\text{Coarse}_{\text{conf}}$ have the same granularity.

5.2 Flexible clustering

As we reached 90% of accuracy with relatively high polysemy, we also checked whether MFS could reach 90% of accuracy if we continued to cluster senses. The experiments in development confirmed that MFS gets above 90% at expenses of coarser grained senses than IMS does: On average, the fine-grained polysemy (9.8) would drop to 4.4, compared to the 6.2 when clustering to reach 90% using IMS. When we obtain MFS>90% 17 words have 2 senses and 40 words reach to 90% of accuracy, whilst when IMS>90% only 5 words are reduced to 2 senses and 42 words reach to 90%. This shows that it makes more sense to cluster senses using the performance of IMS as stopping criteria, as the polysemy is preserved better.

In case we continued clustering senses until we have 2 senses for each word, IMS would reach 98.2% and MFS 95.7%, with an error reduction of 58% over the MFS. Note that this error reduction compares favorably to that of our clustering when stopping at IMS>90%, showing that we could have kept clustering senses further without losing predictive power. These figures show that we could stop at arbitrary performance figures at the cost of obtaining highly skewed clusters (indicated by the high MFS value). We will revisit high MFS in Section 6.

6 Comparison to OntoNotes senses

In order to perform a qualitative study and check whether our sense clusters make sense, we decided to compare them to another coarse sense inventory which is mapped to WordNet. We chose Ontonotes 5.0 (Hovy et al., 2006), which also had the goal of attaining 90% sense accuracy. Alternatively, we could have used the Oxford Dictionary of English, which was mapped automatically to WordNet 2.1 (Navigli et al., 2007) but we preferred to factor out automatic mappings and version differences from the analysis.

Ontonotes contains lexical entries for 35 of our target words. The relation between the sense inventory of WordNet and OntoNotes is complex. Given that our work clusters WordNet senses, we focused on the 18 words where the OntoNotes senses where composed of one or several WordNet senses and where all WordNet senses were covered[3]. Table 2

[3]The rest of words include senses not mapped to Word-

Word	Fine-grained #S	Fine-grained IMS	Fine-grained Mfs	Conf #S	Conf IMS	Conf Mfs	Random IMS	Random Mfs	ON #S	ON IMS	ON Mfs	SS #S	SS IMS	SS Mfs
common-j	10	70.5	39.0	7	87.0	83.6	74.3	46.9	-	-	-	1	100	100
fair-j	11	88.8	67.3	11	88.8	67.3	88.8	67.3	-	-	-	2	95.9	93.9
full-j	9	78.5	45.1	8	92.4	66.7	80.2	54.2	-	-	-	2	98.6	98.6
high-j	8	86.3	71.9	7	94.5	86.3	87.1	74.6	-	-	-	2	97.9	92.5
late-j	8	84.9	52.1	7	87.0	70.5	87.5	58.5	-	-	-	2	98.6	98.6
long-j	10	78.0	49.3	6	98.7	98.7	79.8	53.6	-	-	-	2	90.0	86.7
normal-j	5	81.9	66.0	4	85.4	79.9	83.8	72.2	-	-	-	1	100	100
particular-j	7	85.0	51.0	6	94.6	66.7	89.5	60.0	-	-	-	1	99.3	99.3
poor-j	6	76.2	52.4	2	94.6	62.6	88.2	73.6	-	-	-	2	100	100
board-n	10	88.9	79.9	9	93.8	93.1	89.8	80.9	7	88.9	79.9	5	89.6	79.9
book-n	12	56.3	64.4	11	88.9	89.6	58.3	65.3	-	-	-	5	65.9	71.1
color-n	9	65.5	32.4	2	99.3	99.3	85.6	76.8	-	-	-	4	84.8	73.8
control-n	12	79.5	46.6	6	96.6	93.8	82.8	52.0	-	-	-	8	78.1	46.6
date-n	9	80.1	24.1	4	91.5	65.2	84.2	43.4	-	-	-	5	91.5	85.1
family-n	9	64.3	26.6	2	100	100	79.7	64.9	-	-	-	3	99.3	99.3
image-n	10	70.6	49.0	7	90.9	85.3	74.6	59.0	-	-	-	7	77.6	60.8
land-n	12	57.6	20.8	6	96.5	92.4	62.9	43.2	-	-	-	6	62.5	28.5
level-n	9	69.9	52.1	7	94.5	94.5	74.6	59.3	7	85.6	77.4	5	77.4	53.4
life-n	15	58.0	21.7	5	89.5	88.8	67.3	43.8	-	-	-	10	65.0	46.2
number-n	12	87.7	71.2	11	92.5	86.3	89.6	73.9	-	-	-	5	89.0	71.2
paper-n	8	76.4	41.0	2	100	100	87.7	72.4	-	-	-	5	83.3	74.3
sense-n	6	93.8	38.6	6	93.8	38.6	93.8	38.6	6	93.8	38.6	3	94.5	66.9
time-n	11	90.1	48.4	7	94.5	93.4	89.7	51.7	-	-	-	5	92.9	48.4
way-n	13	72.1	55.8	7	91.2	78.9	78.6	62.4	-	-	-	8	78.2	59.9
window-n	9	75.9	38.6	3	91.7	60.7	84.9	59.3	-	-	-	4	90.3	62.8
work-n	8	69.8	20.5	2	85.9	79.5	80.9	63.1	-	-	-	5	75.1	38.5
add-v	7	40.3	49.3	2	91.0	91.0	74.3	77.1	3	90.3	90.3	6	40.3	49.3
appear-v	8	64.4	47.3	5	87.7	63.0	69.2	59.6	5	87.7	63.0	5	87.7	63.0
ask-v	8	78.3	36.4	6	96.5	96.5	83.9	53.8	-	-	-	3	100	100
find-v	17	62.4	28.4	13	86.5	85.8	65.7	30.8	6	80.9	58.9	7	75.2	41.8
fold-v	6	93.2	83.7	6	93.2	83.7	93.2	83.7	5	93.2	83.7	4	94.6	83.7
help-v	9	61.2	36.0	6	99.3	97.1	69.3	48.7	3	100	97.8	4	73.4	59.7
kill-v	16	63.9	59.7	11	89.6	86.8	67.0	62.5	9	89.6	86.8	7	82.6	81.2
know-v	12	63.1	35.4	7	89.2	77.9	64.8	40.3	7	81.5	48.7	2	100	100
live-v	8	73.5	47.6	3	97.3	94.6	82.5	66.9	-	-	-	3	91.2	87.8
lose-v	12	64.4	50.7	3	93.8	93.8	76.6	69.1	6	70.5	58.2	7	75.3	64.4
meet-v	14	69.7	28.9	2	86.6	59.9	83.5	61.1	7	82.4	52.1	8	78.9	59.9
read-v	12	82.8	73.9	11	85.1	80.6	84.5	76.1	8	82.1	75.4	4	91.0	88.8
say-v	12	64.9	35.7	7	96.1	96.1	67.5	44.0	6	96.1	92.2	3	100	100
serve-v	16	73.1	40.7	11	88.3	83.4	76.4	46.1	7	80.0	49.7	6	81.4	65.5
show-v	13	75.7	27.5	9	94.2	93.7	79.1	41.6	-	-	-	5	81.5	32.8
suggest-v	5	74.3	63.5	3	97.3	97.3	81.0	73.3	3	91.2	81.8	1	99.3	99.3
tell-v	9	57.6	38.9	6	86.1	83.3	69.2	54.6	4	94.4	92.4	3	97.9	97.2
wait-v	5	70.2	36.6	3	96.2	92.4	82.2	66.1	3	96.2	92.4	4	76.3	64.9
win-v	5	72.81	60.5	2	100	99.3	87.9	82.3	-	-	-	4	76.9	70.1
AVG 45 words	9.8	73.1	46.2	6.2	92.6	84.1	79.6	60.2	-	-	-	4.7	84.2	73.3
AVG 18 words	10.2	69.9	48.8	6.0	91.5	83.2	76.8	59.6	5.7	88.0	73.2	4.3	86.2	74.3

Table 2: The 45 words, with PoS, polysemy, IMS and Mfs accuracy for fine-grained, our clustering (Conf.), random clustering, OntoNotes coarse-grained senses (ON, cf. Section 6) and Supersenses (SS, cf. Section 7). The bottom rows report averages for the 45 words and the 18 words in OntoNotes.

Net, or cases where one WordNet sense was mapped to several
OntoNotes senses

Conf	ON	WN	#	Gloss
1	1	1	421	Make an addition (to); join or combine or unite with others; increase the quality, quantity, size or scope of
1	1	2	115	State or say further
1	1	6	94	Constitute an addition
1	1	3	92	Bestow a quality on
2	2	4	47	Make an addition by combining numbers
2	2	5	44	Determine the sum of

Table 3: Senses for add-v in WN, OntoNotes (ON) and our clusters (Conf), including frequencies in train and glosses.

Conf	ON	WN	#	Gloss
1	2	1	449	a position on a scale of intensity or amount or quality
1	2	2	197	a relative position or degree of value in a graded group
1	6	3	143	a specific identifiable position in a continuum or series or especially in a process
5	5	7	18	an abstract place usually conceived as having depth
6	5	8	13	a structure consisting of a room or set of rooms at a single position along a vertical scale
2	1	4	11	height above ground
4	3	6	3	a flat surface at right angles to a plumb line
3	4	5	2	indicator that establishes the horizontal when a bubble is centered in a tube of liquid

Table 4: Senses for level-v in WN, OntoNotes (ON) and our clusters (Conf), including frequencies in train and glosses.

Conf	ON	WN	#	Gloss
1	1	1	285	give help or assistance; be of service
1	1	3	217	be of use
1	1	6	194	contribute to the furtherance of
1	1	2	80	improve the condition of
2	1	4	21	abstain from doing; always used with a negative
5	3	8	4	improve; change for the better
3	2	5	0	help to some food; help with food or drink
4	2	7	0	take or use

Table 5: Senses for help-n in WN, OntoNotes (ON) and our clusters (Conf), including frequencies in train and glosses.

lists those 18 words. We leave the analysis of the rest of words for further work, as they raise issues about overlapping sense boundaries, and our main goal is to check the quality of our method to group fine-grained senses.

Table 2 shows the statistics for those 18 words. Overall, the average polysemy of our clusters is higher and the performance of IMS on our clusters is also higher. We take this as an indication of the good quality of our clusters. On the other hand, the MFS on our clusters is considerably higher, which could mean that our algorithm has a tendency to lump together frequent senses, casting doubts on the quality of the clusters.

We selected three words for illustration, depending on the difference in number of clusters. Tables 3 to 5 show the senses of those four words[4]. In the case of add-v (Table 3), the clusters produced by our algorithm are the same as OntoNotes. For level-n (Table 4), although the number of clusters is the same, we group WordNet sense #3 together with senses #1 and #2, while OntoNotes keeps it separate. Note that sense #3 is very frequent, and as such it is lumped into a coarse grained sense which covers most of the occurrences. WordNet sense #8, on the contrary, is grouped by Ontonotes with #7, while we keep them separate. We think that in both cases, one could argue that our clusters make as much senses as those of OntoNotes, even if the distribution of our

[4]Note that coarse senses not in WordNet are not included.

cluster is more skewed than that of Ontonotes.

In the case of help-v (Table 5) our clusters produces more senses than those in Ontonotes. We think that sense #4, which is always used with a negative, can be sensibly considered a separate sense. Senses #5 and #7 are very similar, but being unattested in the train data, our algorithm is unable to cluster them.

In summary, the analysis of those (and other) examples shows that, in general, the sense clusters produced by our algorithm make sense. In a way, this was to be expected, as the clustering decisions depend on how often the volunteers confused the use of two senses. Our analysis also shows that our clustering does have an undesired tendency to cluster together frequent senses, while senses which occur rarely the train data are usually kept separate, adding artificially to the overall polysemy figure.

In the future we would like to study whether it is possible to make our algorithm more robust to this tendency to join frequent senses, perhaps discounting frequency from confusion measures.

7 Comparison to Supersenses

We also perform a qualitative study comparing our coarse grained senses to WN Supersenses. Supersenses are based on the lexicographer file names for WordNet, where all senses of the word that belong to the same lexicographer file (e.g. the artifact file) are joined together. They include 15 sense for verbs and 26 for nouns. Although WordNet also provide supersenses for adjective and adverbs, these are not semantically motivated and do not provide any higher abstraction (Johannsen et al., 2014).

Table 2 show the results for the target 45 words (adjectives included). The average polysemy of the supersenses is lower for all parts of speech with respect to our clustered senses and OntoNotes. Note that, word-wise, polysemy varies significantly: many words keep one or two senses, while others maintain high polysemy level (roughly similar to fine-grained senses). IMS and MFS performances are similar to OntoNotes.

Tables 6 to 8 show the differences in clustering for the same set of words (*add-v*, *level-n*, and *help-n*). In the case of add-v (Table 6), we produce two coarse grained sense against the 5 supersenses. The only coarse sense in Supersenses groups the arithmetic operation with *state or say further*, begin both *communication* senses, while our algorithm keeps groups them in separate sense clusters.

For level-n (Table 7) our algorithm produces more senses than the number of supersenses (6 *vs* 4). Supersenses of *state* and *attribute* are distributed between our clusters #1 and #2. Our clusters #3, #4 and #6 are lumped together as an *artifact*, although it would make sense to keep them separated. Finally, in the case of help-n (Table 8), we obtain the same amount of senses, but grouping differs considerably. For example, WordNet senses #3 and #4 are grouped under the *stative* supersense, although the definition and use of the two senses are completely different. On the other hand, our cluster #1 comprises the most frequent 4 senses.

Overall, the comparison of supersenses and our confusion-based coarse grained senses show complicated overlaps, contrary to OntoNotes, in which most of the clusters in one are subsumed in the other. Each of the sense groupings represent very different sense inventories. This shows the difficulty of having a *universal* sense representation that is useful for any application at hands. Actually, the choice of the inventory will depend on the angle of the meanings required by the application.

8 Conclusions and Future Work

This work explores the use of crowdsourced annotations to cluster senses that are often confused by non-expert annotators. Our method can provide clusters at different levels of granularity. We show that, for instance, we can construct clusters yielding around 90% accuracy for 45 words, with higher error reduction with respect to MFS than fine-grained senses. By construction, we merge senses which are often confused by annotators, yielding sensible sense clusters, as corroborated by manual inspection. The comparison to OntoNotes groupings fares well, with similar groupings, while the comparison to Supersenses shows that Supersenses follow a different grouping criterion, with overlapping clusters. The main weakness of our method seems to be the tendency to cluster together frequent senses.

This work is a small contribution towards the design of an ambitious annotation effort enabling

Conf	SS	WN	#	Gloss
1	change	1	421	make an addition (to); join or combine or unite with others; increase the quality, quantity, size or scope of
1	stative	6	94	constitute an addition
1	possession	3	92	bestow a quality on
1	communication	2	115	state or say further
2	communication	5	44	determine the sum of
2	cognition	4	47	make an addition by combining numbers

Table 6: Senses for add-v in WN, Supersenses (SS) and our clusters (Conf), including frequencies in train and glosses.

Conf	SS	WN	#	Gloss
1	state	2	197	a relative position or degree of value in a graded group
1	state	3	143	a specific identifiable position in a continuum or series or especially in a process
1	attribute	1	449	a position on a scale of intensity or amount or quality
2	attribute	4	11	height above ground
5	cognition	7	18	an abstract place usually conceived as having depth
6	artifact	8	13	a structure consisting of a room or set of rooms at a single position along a vert. scale
4	artifact	6	3	a flat surface at right angles to a plumb line
3	artifact	5	2	indicator that establishes the horizontal when a bubble is centered in a tube of liq.

Table 7: Senses for level-n in WN, Supersenses (SS) and our clusters (Conf), including frequencies in train and glosses.

Conf	SS	WN	#	Gloss
1	social	1	285	give help or assistance; be of service
1	social	6	194	contribute to the furtherance of
1	body	2	80	improve the condition of
1	stative	3	217	be of use
2	stative	4	21	abstain from doing; always used with a negative
5	change	8	4	improve; change for the better
3	consumption	5	0	help to some food; help with food or drink
4	consumption	7	0	take or use

Table 8: Senses for help-n in WN, Supersenses (SS) and our clusters (Conf), including freq. in train and glosses.

widespread use of high accuracy WSD. For the near future we would like to improve the error reduction with respect to the MFS trying to factor out sense frequency from clustering decisions. We would also like to check out-of-domain corpora, and to contrast the results of our confusion-based clusters with respect to other sense-clustering methods. Finally, we are aware that the final validity our technique needs to be shown in a downstream application.

Acknowledgments

This work was partially funded by MINECO (CHIST-ERA READERS project – PCIN-2013-002-C02-01, and SKaTeR project – TIN2012-38584-C06-02), and the European Commission (QTLEAP – FP7-ICT-2013.4.1-610516). The IXA group is funded by the Basque Government (A type Research Group).

References

Eneko Agirre and Oier Lopez de Lacalle. 2003. Clustering wordnet word senses. In *Proceedings of the Conference on Recent Advances on Natural Language Processing (RANLP'03)*, pages 11–18, Bulgary.

E. Agirre, T. Baldwin, and D. Martinez. 2008. Improving Parsing and PP attachment Performance with Sense Information. In *Proceedings of the 46th Annual Meeting of the Association for Computational Linguistics (ACL/HLT'08)*, pages 317–325, Columbus, USA.

A. P. Dawid and A. M. Skene. 1979. Maximum likelihood estimation of observer error-rates using the em algorithm. *Applied Statistics*, 28(1):20–28.

C. Fellbaum. 1998. *WordNet: An Electronic Lexical Database*. MIT Press.

Eduard Hovy, Mitchell Marcus, Martha Palmer, Lance Ramshaw, and Ralph Weischedel. 2006. Ontonotes: The 90% solution. In *Proceedings of HLT-NAACL 2006*, pages 57–60.

Anders Johannsen, Dirk Hovy, Héctor Martínez Alonso, Barbara Plank, and Anders Søgaard. 2014. More or less supervised supersense tagging of twitter. In *Proceedings of the Third Joint Conference on Lexical and Computational Semantics (*SEM 2014)*, pages 1–11, Dublin, Ireland, August. Association for Computational Linguistics and Dublin City University.

Yoong Keok Lee and Hwee Tou Ng. 2002. An empirical evaluation of knowledge sources and learning algorithms for word sense disambiguation. In *Proceedings of the 2002 Conference on Empirical Methods in Natural Language Processing*, pages 41–48. Association for Computational Linguistics, July.

Rada Mihalcea and Dan I. Moldovan. 1999. A method for word sense disambiguation of unrestricted text. In *Proceedings of the 37th Annual Meeting of the Association for Computational Linguistics*, pages 152–158, College Park, Maryland, USA, June. Association for Computational Linguistics.

G.A. Miller, C. Leacock, R. Tengi, and R.Bunker. 1993. A Semantic Concordance. In *Proceedings of the workshop on Human Language Technology (HLT'93)*.

R. Navigli, K. C. Litkowski, and O. Hargraves. 2007. SemEval-2007 Task 07: Coarse-Grained English All-Words Task. In *Proceedings of the 4th International Workshop on Semantic Evaluations (SemEval-2007) in conjunction with ACL*, pages 30–35, Prague, Czech Republic.

H. T. Ng and H. B. Lee. 1996. Integrating multiple knowledge sources to disambiguate word sense: an exemplar-based approach. In *Proceedings of the 34th annual meeting on Association for Computational Linguistics*, ACL '96, pages 40–47, Stroudsburg, PA, USA. Association for Computational Linguistics.

Martha Palmer, Hoa Trang Dang, and Christiane Fellbaum. 2007. Making fine-grained and coarse-grained sense distinctions, both manually and automatically. *Natural Language Engineering*, 13(2):137–163.

Rebecca J. Passonneau and Bob Carpenter. 2014. The benefits of a model of annotation. *Transactions of the Association for Computational Linguistics*, 2(1-9):311–326.

Rebecca J. Passonneau, Collin F. Baker, Christiane Fellbaum, and Nancy Ide. 2012. The MASC word sense corpus. In Nicoletta Calzolari (Conference Chair), Khalid Choukri, Thierry Declerck, Mehmet Uur Doan, Bente Maegaard, Joseph Mariani, Asuncion Moreno, Jan Odijk, and Stelios Piperidis, editors, *Proceedings of the Eight International Conference on Language Resources and Evaluation (LREC'12)*, Istanbul, Turkey, may. European Language Resources Association (ELRA).

W. Peters, I. Peters, , and P. Vossen. 1998. Automatic sense clustering in eurowordnet. In *Proceedings of the First International Conference on Language Resources and Evaluation*, pages 409–416, Granada, Spain.

Rion Snow, Sushant Prakash, Daniel Jurafsky, and Andrew Y. Ng. 2007. Learning to merge word senses. In *Proceedings of the 2007 Joint Conference on Empirical Methods in Natural Language Processing and Computational Natural Language Learning (EMNLP-CoNLL)*, pages 1005–1014, Prague, Czech Republic, June. Association for Computational Linguistics.

Noriko Tomuro. 2001. Tree-cut and a lexicon based on systematic polysemy. In *Proceedings of the Second Meeting of the North American Chapter of the Association for Computational Linguistics*, Pittsburgh, USA.

Hwee Tou Ng, Chung Yong Lim, and Shou King Foo. 1999. Siglex99: Standardizing lexical resources.

Z. Zhong and H. T. Ng. 2010. It makes sense: A wide-coverage word sense disambiguation system for free text. In *Proceedings of the ACL 2010 System Demonstrations*, pages 78–83, Uppsala, Sweden.

Learning Structures of Negations from Flat Annotations

Vinodkumar Prabhakaran
Department of Computer Science
Columbia University
New York, NY, USA
vinod@cs.columbia.edu

Branimir Boguraev
IBM Watson
Thomas J. Watson Research Center
Yorktown Heights, NY, USA
bran@us.ibm.com

Abstract

We propose a novel method to learn negation expressions in a specialized (medical) domain. In our corpus, negations are annotated as 'flat' text spans. This allows for some infelicities in the mark-up of the ground truth, making it less than perfectly aligned with the underlying syntactic structure. Nonetheless, the negations thus captured are correct in intent, and thus potentially valuable. We succeed in training a model for detecting the negated predicates corresponding to the annotated negations, by re-mapping the corpus to anchor its 'flat' annotation spans into the predicate argument structure. Our key idea—re-mapping the negation instance spans to more uniform syntactic nodes—makes it possible to re-frame the learning task as a simpler one, and to leverage an imperfect resource in a way which enables us to learn a high performance model. We achieve high accuracy for negation detection overall, 87%. Our re-mapping scheme can be constructively applied to existing flatly annotated resources for other tasks where syntactic context is vital.

1 Introduction

Accounting for extra-propositional aspects of meaning in text is a very active NLP research area in recent years, exploring different aspects of meaning such as *factivity* (Saurí and Pustejovsky, 2009), *uncertainty/hedging* (Farkas et al., 2010), *committed belief* (Prabhakaran et al., 2010), and *modalities* (Prabhakaran et al., 2012a). Among these, negation detection has generated special interest because of demonstrated needs for negation detection capability in practical applications such as information retrieval (Averbuch et al., 2004), information extraction (Meystre et al., 2008), sentiment analysis (Wiegand et al., 2010; Councill et al., 2010), and relation detection (Chowdhury and Lavelli, 2013).

Accurately detecting negations is especially important in systems processing medical/clinical text. Consider the segment *"Mild hyperinflation without focal pneumonia"*, taken from a patient's clinical record. It indicates the absence of *focal pneumonia* in the patient. Not capturing this extra-propositional aspect of negation concerning *focal pneumonia* will lead to wrong—and harmful—inferences in downstream processing, e.g. by a clinical decision support system. The need for sophisticated negation detection capabilities in clinical text is even more urgent given the broadening spectrum of applications in this domain: clinical question answering (Lee et al., 2006), clinical decision support (Demner-Fushman et al., 2009), medical information extraction (Uzuner et al., 2010), medical entity relation mining (Tymoshenko et al., 2012), patient history tracking (Raghavan et al., 2012), etc. Our motivation for detecting negations in medical texts also stems from practical concerns of an operational medical question answering (QA) system (Ferrucci et al., 2013).

Most recent approaches to negation detection adopt supervised machine learning techniques to learn the phraseology of negation-containing expressions. They often follow a two step process—detection of negation *cues* ("no", "without", ...), followed by detection of their associated *scopes*. Cue detection is a relatively simple task, since the set of cue words is not large. Determining the scope of

*Proceedings of the Fourth Joint Conference on Lexical and Computational Semantics (*SEM 2015)*, pages 71–81,
Denver, Colorado, June 4–5, 2015.

a negation cue, on the other hand, is more challenging. Negation constructs do not necessarily apply to entire sentences: in the earlier example, *Mild hyperinflation* is not negated. The scope detection task is to identify the part(s) of the sentence that come under the scope of a negation cue. Scope detection is crucial for interpreting negations, and to that end, the BioScope corpus (Vincze et al., 2008) was released, with annotations of both negation cues *and* their associated scopes.

The fact that these scopes are represented only as text-spans is a drawback of BioScope. Without being anchored to a syntactic analysis of the sentences in which they occur, BioScope's scope annotations suffer from a variety of inconsistencies of mark-up. They also may, and occasionally do, fail to align with the underlying syntactic structures (Vincze et al., 2011; Stenetorp et al., 2012). Such inconsistencies make it hard for a system to learn the actual syntactic patterns connecting negation cues and their scopes—which are, after all, the real object of negation interpretation.

The insight that we develop in this paper is that a scope span can be associated with one or more nodes in the syntactic analysis of a negated expression, and that these will be further connected—in a systematic way—to the negation cue node. Mapping loosely and/or inconsistently bounded spans to unique syntactic nodes (and configurations thereof) reduces the noise inherent in BioScope. The learning task for scope detection would now be the easier one of learning negation scoping patterns from syntactic representations.

To elaborate on this, we look at BioScope's issues in some detail (Section 3.1). Our intent here, however, is not to offer a review or criticism of the corpus, nor to suggest how to correct those issues. Given that we *do want* to use BioScope (we motivate our choice of BioScope separately in Section 2), we propose a new method for learning how to detect negated constructs which are rooted in syntactic structure elements, and therefore directly usable by downstream components, many of which typically assume awareness of syntax. Our method is to re-map BioScope's scope span annotations onto the syntactic space and then to use those annotations' corresponding node structure(s) to train a system to automatically detect negated syntactic nodes. As outlined earlier, due to the re-mapping, many syntactic inconsistencies would not be seen by the learner, which now is trained on cleaner data and consequently, faces a simpler learning problem.

We verify that our re-mapping process identifies the correct negated syntactic node with high accuracy (93%); this validates the approach we propose here. Our supervised learning system, trained using re-mapped scope nodes to detect them automatically, obtains an overall accuracy of 87%, using automatically tagged cues. In the light of state-of-the-art performance figures, ours is a novel, constructive and pragmatic approach which allows us to leverage effectively an important resource, despite its representational imperfections, and to utilize the essential 'nuggets' it captures and exposes—namely the expressions of negated predicates. This strategy can also be applied to other tasks where syntactic context is important but resources are annotated by text spans only (e.g. hedge detection (Farkas et al., 2010)).

The rest of the paper is grounded in discussion of related work, and of BioScope and its annotations (Section 2), highlighting some relevant details of the issues with these (Section 3). We then outline the syntactic framework we use in Section 4. Section 5 presents our re-mapping of BioScope, and Section 6 offers experiments and results. In Section 7, we compare our performance with previously published studies. Section 8 concludes the paper.

2 Background

Early approaches in negation detection were limited in the nature of negation they were concerned with. The prime example here, NegEx (Chapman et al., 2001), took a view of negation interpretation to be "determining whether a finding or disease ... is present or absent". From such a standpoint, the notion of scope is limited, since the scope is always the finding or disease that follows a negation cue. While this works well for simpler expressions of negations, it tends to fail for more complex negation constructs. More recent approaches attempt to tackle the variability in scopes encountered in broader data by using statistical learning methods grounded in publicly available corpora with cue and scope annotations.

The first such corpus was BioScope (Vincze et

al., 2008), which annotates negation cues and associated scopes in 3 genres—medical abstracts, scientific papers and clinical records. The BioNLP Event Extraction (EE) shared task corpus (Kim et al., 2009) also marks negation in the event annotations on sentences from molecular biology literature. Most recently, the *SEM 2012 shared task corpus (Morante and Blanco, 2012) marks negations, their foci, and scopes in sentences from Conan Doyle stories in an attempt to extend the research on negation to the general domain. Both the BioNLP-EE and *SEM corpora capture negations within—and therefore aligned with—syntactic analyses. Thus they deploy annotation schemes which assume downstream consumers of some granular negation representation, learnable from the annotated resource(s). However, the language in both of them differs greatly from the language encountered in clinical text, making them unsuitable for our QA system requirements. In contrast, BioScope matches our genre of clinical text. As an additional plus, it captures negation in a task-independent, linguistically motivated framework, which enables the building of systems applicable to a wider range of domains.

BioScope's negation-scope-as-span annotation framework, however, limits th corpus utility. Various approaches have used it to train negation scope span detection systems, and many have shown the importance of deep syntactic features in that task (e.g., (Ballesteros et al., 2012; Velldal et al., 2012; Zou et al., 2013)). They share a drawback: they are optimized for predicting the spans *as they are annotated* in BioScope—despite its various syntactic inconsistencies. For example, Ballesteros et al. (2012) use manual rules to detect the voice (passive or active) of a verb phrase; this is motivated by an annotation guideline for whether to include verb subjects in the span or not. In reality, what matters in the end is whether a detection system can capture the underlying phenomenon of negation that the annotations stand to represent, and not whether it can accurately replicate the representational choices the annotations follow. In light of this, our approach differs from the conventional ones, in that it mitigates the effects of inconsistencies in BioScope's original annotations by re-mapping it, as we explain in Section 5 below.

3 BioScope Corpus

The BioScope corpus (Vincze et al., 2008) is annotated for hedges and negations in sentences from biomedical domain; in this work, we use only the negation annotations. A negation (or hedge) annotation comprises a cue and a corresponding scope. The scope (hereafter BioScopeScopeSpan) is marked as a contiguous text-span including the associated cue annotation (BioScopeCue). BioScope contains sentences from three sub-genres—abstracts, full papers, and clinical records. We use all three sub-corpora. We divide each sub-corpus into 'Train' (70%), 'Dev' (15%) and 'Test' (15%) sets through random sampling. We use sentences in the Train and Dev sets to build and select best models and report the results obtained by our best models on Dev and Test sets.

3.1 Issues Challenging the Use of BioScope

BioScope is an important resource that has helped deeper understanding of various linguistic aspects of negation in a task independent manner. But, as we saw in the preceding sections, while demonstrating the importance of syntactic context for negation detection, recent efforts share the frustration arising from the fact that BioScopeScopeSpan annotations do not align with underlying syntactic structure. This problem is further exacerbated by inconsistencies in the corpus annotation. From a performance-driven point of view alone, negation detection systems trained over BioScope annotations are optimized to match the annotated spans in the corpus (as discussed in Section 2). However, for a negation detection system followed by downstream components implementing negation-driven inference, spans alone are not sufficient—especially spans which do not align with syntax. Negated expressions need to be captured within their syntactic context, and for this, we need the uniformity of syntax structures.

The misalignment issues of BioScopeScopeSpan annotations with respect to the underlying syntactic structures have already been extensively studied (Vincze et al., 2011; Stenetorp et al., 2012). Vincze et al. (2011) point out infelicities and mismatches, comparing BioScope annotations with the more syntactically oriented negated event annotations in the BioNLP-EE corpus (Kim et al., 2009). Inconsistencies are largely due to 'loose' annotation guidelines for BioScope, which are not rigorous enough in ensuring that annotation spans align with syntactic analyses. Given our position in this work—utilize BioScope, despite its shortcomings, in an alternative framework of analysis and training (see Section 2)—we explain some of the commonly occurring inconsistencies in this section. For this purpose, we use example annotations *e1-e5* from BioScope. (**Boldface** denotes BioScopeCue annotations and *italics* denotes corresponding BioScopeScopeSpan annotations as present in the BioScope corpus.)

One of the main source of inconsistencies within the syntactic space is with regard to the inclusion or exclusion of subjects of propositions. For example, in *e1*, the annotations identify the negation span to be the entire clause following the word *but*, including its subject and object. However, in *e2*, only the object of the predicate is marked as the negation scope (Figure 1). Vincze et al. (2011) state that "the treatment of subjects [in BioScope] remains problematic since in BioScope it is only the complements that are usually included within the scope of a keyword (that is, subjects are not with the exception of passive constructions and raising verbs)". Leaving aside the rationale for such a guideline, we note that such an inconsistency is harmful: proper interpretation of negated propositions does require a subject, and making annotations consistent by ignoring subjects, if present, does not help downstream components. Additionally, it makes the learning of contexts of negated propositions difficult.

e1: The cDNA hybridized to multiple transcripts in pre-B and B-cell lines, but *transcripts were* ***not*** *detected at significant levels in plasmacytoma, T-cell, and nonlymphoid cell lines.*

e2: Moreover, cAMP activators did ***not*** *activate NF-kappa B in Jurkat cells.*

Another problem with BioScopeScopeSpan annotations stems from the requirement that such annotations should have contiguous spans. For example, since sentence *e3* is a passive construction, the corresponding BioScopeScopeSpan annotation captures the subject (*mechanism*) as well. The contiguity requirement then forces the proposition *IFNs mediate this inhibition*—which modifies the subject but is itself not negated (Figure 2)—to be included within the BioScopeScopeSpan and therefore to be interpretable as negated. Clearly, there may be arbitrary intervening text in such, and similar, constructions, again making the learning task difficult.

e3: However, *the mechanism by which IFNs mediate this inhibition has* ***not*** *been defined.*

Sometimes, the BioScopeScopeSpan annotation boundaries do not align with syntactic constituents. For example, in *e4*, the BioScopeScopeSpan annotation excludes the determiner *the* from the scope while in *e5*, the determiner *the* is part of the scope. This might be due to the guideline that the scope should include the cue as well, causing to extend the scope annotation leftward until it covers the cue word (*absence*). Still, we are left with a span boundary which crosses, partially, a noun phrase boundary.

e4: Tal-1 transcription was shown to be monoallelic in Jurkat, a T-cell line that expresses tal-1 in the ***absence*** *of apparent genomic alteration of the locus.*

e5: The effects of selenium were specific for NF-kappa B, since *the activity of the transcription factor AP-1 was* ***not*** *suppressed.*

A system trained and optimized on how well it predicts the BioScopeScopeSpan boundaries suffers from also being forced to learn such syntactic inconsistencies along with the syntactic patterns that truly capture negation. In addition to learning the actual negation patterns, such a system is also forced to learn artifacts of annotation guidelines like: when to include or exclude subjects and when to include or exclude determiners. In order to circumvent this, we propose an approach in which we first re-map BioScope annotations onto nodes in the syntactic tree, and then train a system using features derived from the nodes, and node configurations, providing the context for the negation cue and scope nodes. We next describe the syntactic framework we use and then explain our approach in detail.

4 Syntactic Framework

Negation, as a language device, is naturally conceptualized as applying to fully instantiated predicate-argument clusters. We therefore use predicate argument graphs as structural abstractions of syntax trees. Additional advantages of these abstractions include their affinity for having extra-propositional

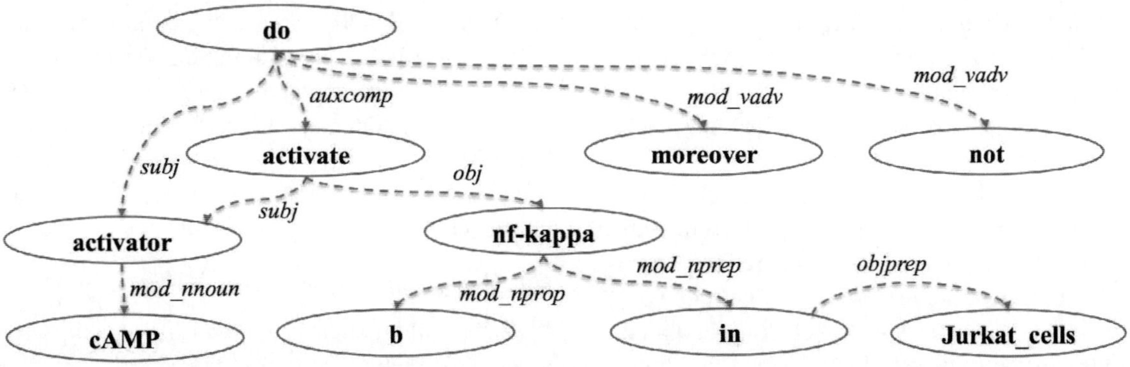

Figure 1: PAS for *e2*: "Moreover, cAMP activators did not activate NF-kappa B in Jurkat cells"

aspects of meaning 'layered' onto the representation (precedents in prior studies can be found in e.g. (Saurí and Pustejovsky, 2009; Diab et al., 2009)), and their pervasive use in a state-of-the-art QA system—for question analysis, candidate generation, and analysis of passage evidence (Ferrucci et al., 2010; Ferrucci, 2012)—which is at the heart of our medical adaptation (Ferrucci et al., 2013).

We use predicate-argument structure (PAS) (McCord et al., 2012) derived from dependency parses produced by the English Slot Grammar parser (McCord, 1990). In addition to normalizing across different tree structures expressing essentially the same meaning, PAS provides a simplified view over 'raw' syntactic trees, gathering all arguments to a predicate from local, and distant, parse tree nodes (see (McCord et al., 2012) for details). Figures 1 and 2 show the PASes for examples *e2* and *e3*. By localizing the logical arguments to a proposition, predicate-based representation provides direct access to *all* arguments of e.g. a verb frame: an important requirement for extracting context-denoting syntactic features.

PAS-based view into sentences offers unambiguously uniform treatment of some of the issues highlighted in the previous section. For example, going back to *e2*, and the rationale for including or excluding subjects in the scope of a negation, we observe that verb nodes in the PAS always have fully instantiated frames, with subject arguments bound to the

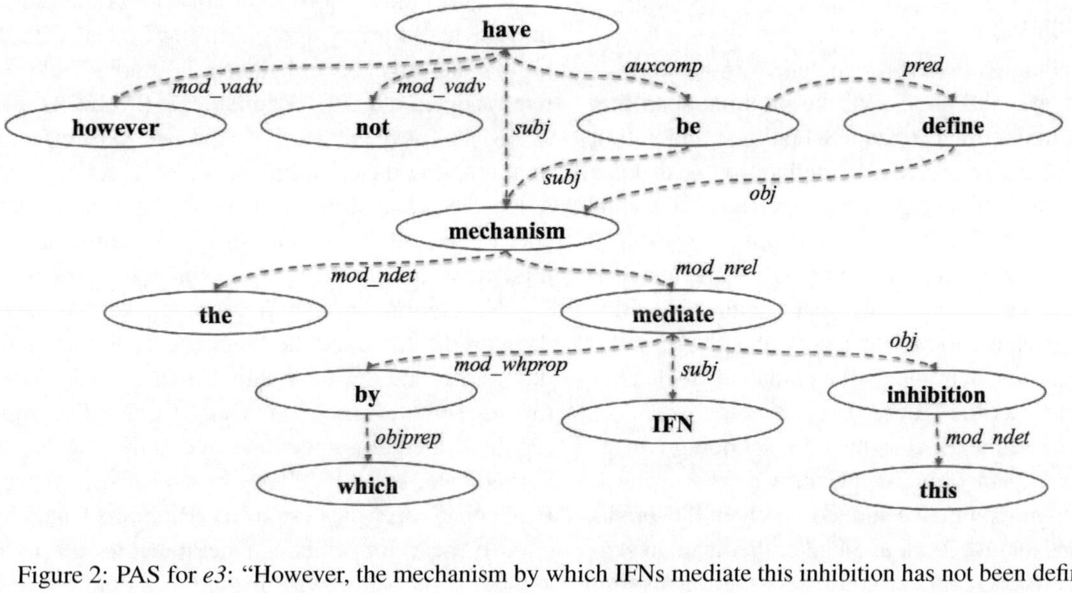

Figure 2: PAS for *e3*: "However, the mechanism by which IFNs mediate this inhibition has not been defined."

predicate nodes corresponding to the deep syntactic subject: observe how *activator* is 'subj' both to *do* and *activate*. Thus whether to include a subject into a verb scope (e.g. *not activate*) becomes largely irrelevant, and a PAS-based scope rendering can always include subjects. As another example, for the PAS for *e3*, the granular analysis of the arguments to the predicate for *define* can be leveraged to designate the predicate node for *mechanism* as the scope of the negation *not (defined)*, while excluding the *IFN mediate inhibition* subtree from the same scope.

5 Learning Negations from Re-mapped BioScope

Our goal is a system for automatic identification of negations and their scopes within the PAS of a sentence. Our resource for this is BioScope, with its text-based span annotations. We propose a novel approach, realized as a two-step process:

(1) **BioScope-to-PAS mapping**: map BioScope's text-span cue and scope annotations to PAS nodes (CuePredicate and NegatedPredicate) by identifying the predicate nodes in the PAS of the sentence that best capture the annotations.

(2) **NegatedPredicate learning**: train a statistical model to automatically identify the scope predicate using features from the PAS context of cue and scope predicates.

5.1 BioScopeScopeSpan-to-NegatedPredicate Mapping

Having obtained PASes for sentences in the corpus, we mark the PAS node with the minimal span that contains the entire BioScopeScopeSpan annotation as the NegatedPredicate. We define the 'span' of a PAS node to be the span of text covered by the subtree rooted at that node, which includes the spans of all of its descendants. Similarly, we mark the PAS node with the minimal span that contains the BioScopeCue annotation as the CuePredicate.

For example, in Figure 1, the predicate labeled *not* was marked as the CuePredicate and the predicate labeled *do* was marked as the corresponding NegatedPredicate. In order to perform a sanity check on our re-mapping, we judged whether the predicate nodes that we mark as NegatedPredicate in sentences from our Dev set are in fact the ones being negated. Of the 470 sentences containing negations, 13 (2.8%) failed to parse, breaking the mapping. In other words, our mapping strategy has coverage of about 97.2%. Of the sentences where a NegatedPredicate was obtained, our mapping achieved an accuracy of 92.8% in finding the correct negated predicate.

5.2 NegatedPredicate Learning

We now build a supervised learning system which, given a CuePredicate in a sentence, will identify its corresponding NegatedPredicate. For every predicate p in a sentence PAS with a CuePredicate, we create an instance <CuePredicate, p>. The instance <CuePredicate, p> is assigned *true* if p is the corresponding NegatedPredicate. For all other p in the PAS, <CuePredicate, p> is assigned *false*.

We extract three types of features for each instance <CuePredicate, p>: 1) *token features* (word lemma and POS tag) of CuePredicate and p, 2) *syntactic context features* (token features of parent predicates and all argument predicates) of CuePredicate and p, and 3) *predicate pair features* (is CuePredicate argument of p or vice versa?; distance between CuePredicate and p; relative position of CuePredicate and p).

We use the ClearTk (Ogren et al., 2008) framework to build our system and perform experiments. We use quadratic kernel SVMs in all our experiments. The ClearTK wrapper for SVM-Light (Joachims, 2006) internally shifts the prediction threshold using sigmoid fitting to deal with the highly skewed class imbalance (around 5% of positive cases) in our data. Prior studies (Prabhakaran et al., 2012b) have shown this approach to be effective in addressing the class imbalance problem.

During prediction, given an unseen sentence PAS and a CuePredicate (either GOLD or automatically predicted) in it, we need to find the corresponding NegatedPredicate. We iterate over all candidate predicates c in the sentence PAS and apply our trained model to assign a *true* or *false* value to <CuePredicate, c>. For any CuePredicate in a sentence there must be one and only one NegatedPredicate, since BioScope corpus marks a single BioScopeScopeSpan for every BioScopeCue. We choose the c for which <CuePredicate, c> is assigned a *true* value with the highest confidence as

	On Dev			On Test		
	Precision	Recall	F-measure	Precision	Recall	F-measure
Clinical	95.68	95.68	95.68	96.15	96.9	96.53
Abstracts	94.4	94.4	94.4	95.42	96.9	96.15
Papers	79.22	96.83	87.14	85.29	98.31	91.34
Overall	92.36	95.11	93.71	94.13	97.09	95.58

Table 1: Performance of our CuePredicate detection on Dev and Test sets

the NegatedPredicate. If <CuePredicate, c> is assigned a *false* value for all c, we choose the c with the least confident *false* assignment as the NegatedPredicate.

6 Experiments and Results

The most commonly used metric to evaluate negation scope span detection is Percentage of Correct Scopes (PCS). PCS measures the percentage of exact matches between predicted and actual scope spans. Since our task is different—negated predicate detection as opposed to negated span detection—we report the Percentage of Correct Scope Predicates (PCSP) obtained in our experiments. Models built from the composite training corpus comprising training corpora of all three genres (see Section 3) perform better than models built separately over each sub-corpus. We report results separately for each sub-corpus, as well as for the entire corpus, and compare them with a strong baseline.

6.1 Gold vs. Predicted CuePredicates

We report results for the NegatedPredicate detection task obtained using GOLD CuePredicates as well as predicted CuePredicates. In order to measure the performance on predicted CuePredicates, we built a CuePredicate detector using linear kernel SVM to detect whether a predicate is a negation cue or not. We use three types of features: 1) *token features* (lemma and POS) of the predicate, 2) *linear context* (token features of the token after the predicate in the sentence; features of tokens before the predicate turned out to be not useful), and 3) *syntactic context* (token features of parent and argument predicates). As shown in Table 1, our CuePredicate tagger obtained F-measures in the range of state-of-the-art results on negation cue detection using the BioScope (90-96% F-measure (Velldal et al., 2012)).

6.2 Baseline NegatedPredicate Predictor

Since this formulation of the task is new, we built a strong baseline system appropriate for it. In our baseline, we predict the NegatedPredicate to be the parent predicate of the CuePredicate, if the CuePredicate is a terminal node in the PAS (this will cover the most common cues such as *no* and *not*). If the CuePredicate is not a terminal node (which covers the cases of verbal negation cues such as *failed*), we choose the CuePredicate itself as the NegatedPredicate. Columns 1 and 3 of Table 2 show PCSP obtained by the baseline algorithm on our Dev and Test sets respectively using GOLD CuePredicates. Columns 5 and 7 show corresponding results using predicted CuePredicates.

6.3 Our NegatedPredicate Predictor

The results obtained by our NegatedPredicate detection system (Section 5.2) on Dev and Test sets using GOLD CuePredicates is shown in Columns 2 and 4 of Table 2. Our system outperforms the baseline by a large margin in all cases, with especially high performance in clinical records. We obtain an overall PCSP of 90.2% and 89.2% on Dev and Test sets respectively. The results we obtain in Test set are in the range of what we obtain using Dev set, which shows that our system does not overfit to our Dev set. On applying our system on predicted CuePredicates, the overall results (columns 6 and 8) decrease by around 3-5% from using GOLD CuePredicates. The overall PCSP value of 86.8% obtained on the Test set reflects the accuracy of our end-to-end system on a blind test. Note that this is a conservative estimate since we penalize our system for failed parses where the mapping step could not find a GOLD NegatedPredicate to compare against.

	Gold Cues (On Dev)		Gold Cues (On Test)		Predicted Cues (On Dev)		Predicted Cues (On Test)	
	Baseline	System	Baseline	System	Baseline	System	Baseline	System
	(1)	(2)	(3)	(4)	(5)	(6)	(7)	(8)
Clinical	83.45	97.12	88.37	100.00	82.01	93.53	87.60	96.90
Abstracts	81.34	89.18	79.07	84.50	76.49	83.96	77.52	82.56
Papers	73.02	79.37	81.36	86.44	66.67	71.43	77.97	83.05
Overall	80.85	90.21	82.06	89.23	76.81	85.11	80.49	86.77

Table 2: Percentage of Correct NegatedPredicate (PCSP) on Dev and Test sets

7 Comparison with Previous Approaches

Comparing our system with previously published approaches to negation scope detection is not straightforward, essentially because our and their tasks are different: negated predicate detection vs. negated scope span detection. The resulting difference in evaluation metrics makes PCS numbers reported elsewhere not directly comparable with our PCSP results presented in Table 2. To make such a comparison meaningful, we transform (reverse map) the NegatedPredicates we identify back into text spans and use those to derive PCS values better aligned with previously published ones. (Note that these PCS numbers are still not directly comparable, due to differences in experiment setup, e.g. cross validation vs. held out test set.

Transforming the NegatedPredicates back to BioScopeScopeSpan annotations is not trivial. As discussed in Section 5.1, we choose NegatedPredicate to be the predicate node that minimally covers BioScopeScopeSpan. Hence, the span of a NegatedPredicate may include text spans that were originally not part of the corresponding BioScopeScopeSpan annotation. Therefore, we built a statistically trained system to predict whether the span of a descendant node of a NegatedPredicate should, or should not, be included in reverse mapping that NegatedPredicate to the corresponding BioScopeScopeSpan.

We use the same set of features and learning configuration as we used for NegatedPredicate learning (Section 5.2). Our transformation obtained high accuracy (94.9%) for the clinical records. However, it was a harder task for abstracts (66.1%) and papers (73.1%) which contain more complex sentences.

We applied this transform on the predicate nodes identified by our end-to-end system (Section 6.3) in order to derive PCS values. In Table 3, we compare these PCS values against four previous studies above (due to lack of space, we do not discuss their techniques here), as well as with a baseline of our own where we use the covered text of the predicate node and all of its descendants as scopes used in the comparison. Our system (with transform) obtains higher PCS values than all other reported studies on the clinical records. The PCS values obtained for the abstracts and papers sub-corpora are lower, but still in comparable range to the other studies. It is important to note that the main source of error here is the NegatedPredicate-to-BioScopeScopeSpan trans-

	Morante09	Ballestros12	Velldal12	Ours (With Covered Text)		Ours (With Transform)		Zou13
				On Dev	On Test	On Dev	On Test	
	(1)	(2)	(3)	(4)	(5)	(6)	(7)	(8)
Clinical	70.75	89.06	89.41	88.49	89.92	91.37	**92.25**	85.31
Abstracts	66.07	68.92	**72.89**	35.45	35.27	61.94	58.53	76.90
Papers	41.00	61.43	**68.09**	33.33	23.73	53.97	47.46	61.19
Overall	-	-	-	50.85	49.55	69.57	66.82	-

Table 3: PCS measures from previous BioScope span detection approaches and our end-to-end system.
Col. 1-3: end-to-end systems (Morante and Daelemans, 2009), (Ballesteros et al., 2012), and (Velldal et al., 2012);
Col. 4-7: our end-to-end system with different ways of obtaining the spans in our Dev and Test sets;
Col. 8: (Zou et al., 2013) system using GOLD cues (often 5-10% higher than using predicted cues)

form step, with its inherent lower accuracies for these two corpora, as reported above. We emphasize that for practical applications this transformation is of little use: what matters more, certainly for a negation detection system feeding downstream components, are the PCSP values presented in Section 6.

8 Discussion and Conclusion

The results for our system, with reverse mapping, offer indirect evidence for our observation in Section 3.1: training a system to predict BioScopeScopeSpan boundaries would require it also to learn inconsistencies in BioScope annotations. This is a hard learning task, given the noise discussed in Section 3.1. Indeed, our results for learning the reverse-mapping transformation show that it is harder to learn the specific annotation criteria in BioScope than to learn the structural patterns expressing negations (which, as we saw in Section 6, obtained close to 90% accuracy). While we had to build a system to transform nodes back to spans for the purposes of comparative analysis, such a system has no role in our quest for practical negation detection and representation.

This substantiates our strategy of using BioScope, *as is*, to learn not scope spans of negation expressions, but negated predicates within the predicate-argument structure (Section 5). The re-mapping route takes us where we want to be, from the point of view of a practical application of negation-based inference: with access to negated predicate nodes. The end-to-end accuracy (overall, across three different genres) of 87% on blind test validates the creative way we propose to make use of a valuable and unique resource—despite its imperfections—by extracting the real value in it, while mitigating the effects of its various inconsistencies.

The results in Tables 2 and 3 show that we have achieved our primary objective: using BioScope to train a system which detects structured negation expressions in clinical text. Our approach to negation scope learning in the syntactic space is a two-step one—first, re-mapping the text-span annotations for negation scopes in BioScope to the syntactic space and then training a scope predicate predictor. We show that our transformation introduces only a small percentage of error and also that our predicted nodes can be transformed back to original span annotations with performance comparable to other negation scope span prediction systems trained on the same dataset. Notably, in clinical records, our system outperforms reported state-of-the-art results (column 8 of Table 3).

In a broader context, the work we report here indirectly argues that the method we propose to circumvent certain limitations of a corpus like BioScope can be applied to similar tasks (such as hedging, sentiment analysis, and variety of modalities, cf. Section 1), for which current annotation resources offer flat, and possibly inconsistent, annotations. In addition, we chose PAS as our syntactic framework for the reasons listed in Section 4, but our approach is not limited to PAS. Indeed, the claims, and methods, are presented to be applicable, and workable, in a more general syntactic framework.

Acknowledgments

This work was conducted while the first author was doing an internship at IBM Research at the TJ Watson Research Center in Yorktown Heights, NY, USA. We thank several anonymous reviewers for their constructive feedback.

References

Mordechai Averbuch, Tom Karson, Benjamin Ben-Ami, Oded Maimon, and Lior Rokach. 2004. Context-sensitive medical information retrieval. In *Proc. of the 11th World Congress on Medical Informatics (MEDINFO-2004)*, pages 1–8. Citeseer.

Miguel Ballesteros, Virginia Francisco, Alberto Díaz, Jesús Herrera, and Pablo Gervás. 2012. Inferring the scope of negation in biomedical documents. In *13th International Conference on Intelligent Text Processing and Computational Linguistics (CICLING 2012)*, New Delhi, 2012. Springer, Springer.

Wendy W Chapman, Will Bridewell, Paul Hanbury, Gregory F Cooper, and Bruce G Buchanan. 2001. A simple algorithm for identifying negated findings and diseases in discharge summaries. *Journal of biomedical informatics*, 34(5):301–310.

Md. Faisal Mahbub Chowdhury and Alberto Lavelli. 2013. Exploiting the scope of negations and heterogeneous features for relation extraction: A case study for drug-drug interaction extraction. In *Proceedings of the 2013 Conference of the North American Chapter of the Association for Computational Linguistics:*

Human Language Technologies, pages 765–771, Atlanta, Georgia, June. Association for Computational Linguistics.

Isaac G Councill, Ryan McDonald, and Leonid Velikovich. 2010. What's great and what's not: learning to classify the scope of negation for improved sentiment analysis. In *Proceedings of the workshop on negation and speculation in natural language processing*, pages 51–59. Association for Computational Linguistics.

Dina Demner-Fushman, Wendy W Chapman, and Clement J McDonald. 2009. What can natural language processing do for clinical decision support? *Journal of biomedical informatics*, 42(5):760–772.

Mona Diab, Lori Levin, Teruko Mitamura, Owen Rambow, Vinodkumar Prabhakaran, and Weiwei Guo. 2009. Committed belief annotation and tagging. In *Proceedings of the Third Linguistic Annotation Workshop*, pages 68–73, Suntec, Singapore, August. Association for Computational Linguistics.

Richárd Farkas, Veronika Vincze, György Szarvas, György Móra, and János Csirik, editors. 2010. *Proceedings of the Fourteenth Conference on Computational Natural Language Learning*. Association for Computational Linguistics, Uppsala, Sweden, July.

David Ferrucci, Eric Brown, Jennifer Chu-Carroll, James Fan, David Gondek, Aditya A Kalyanpur, Adam Lally, J William Murdock, Eric Nyberg, John Prager, et al. 2010. Building watson: An overview of the deepqa project. *AI magazine*, 31(3):59–79.

David A Ferrucci, Anthony Levas, Sugato Bagchi, David Gondek, and Erik T Mueller. 2013. Watson: Beyond jeopardy! *Artif. Intell.*, 199:93–105.

David A Ferrucci. 2012. Introduction to "this is watson". *IBM Journal of Research and Development*, 56(3.4):1:1–1:15.

Thorsten Joachims. 2006. Training Linear SVMs in Linear Time. In *Proceedings of the 12th ACM SIGKDD international conference on knowledge discovery and data mining*, pages 217–226. ACM.

Jin-Dong Kim, Tomoko Ohta, Sampo Pyysalo, Yoshinobu Kano, and Jun'ichi Tsujii. 2009. Overview of bionlp'09 shared task on event extraction. In *Proceedings of the Workshop on Current Trends in Biomedical Natural Language Processing: Shared Task*, BioNLP '09, pages 1–9, Stroudsburg, PA, USA. Association for Computational Linguistics.

Minsuk Lee, James Cimino, Hai Ran Zhu, Carl Sable, Vijay Shanker, John Ely, and Hong Yu. 2006. Beyond information retrievalmedical question answering. In *AMIA Annual Symposium Proceedings*, volume 2006, page 469. American Medical Informatics Association.

Michael C. McCord, J. William Murdock, and Branimir Boguraev. 2012. Deep parsing in Watson. *IBM Journal of Research and Development*, 56(3):3.

Michael C. McCord. 1990. Slot grammar: A system for simpler construction of practical natural language grammars. In R. Studer, editor, *Natural Language and Logic: Proc. of the International Scientific Symposium, Hamburg, FRG*, pages 118–145. Springer, Berlin, Heidelberg.

Stéphane M Meystre, Guergana K Savova, Karin C Kipper-Schuler, and John F Hurdle. 2008. Extracting information from textual documents in the electronic health record: a review of recent research. *Yearbook of medical informatics*, pages 128–144.

Roser Morante and Eduardo Blanco. 2012. * SEM 2012 shared task: Resolving the scope and focus of negation. In *Proceedings of the First Joint Conference on Lexical and Computational Semantics-Volume 1: Proceedings of the main conference and the shared task, and Volume 2: Proceedings of the Sixth International Workshop on Semantic Evaluation*, pages 265–274. Association for Computational Linguistics.

Roser Morante and Walter Daelemans. 2009. A metalearning approach to processing the scope of negation. In *Proceedings of the Thirteenth Conference on Computational Natural Language Learning*, pages 21–29. Association for Computational Linguistics.

Philip V. Ogren, Philipp G. Wetzler, and Steven Bethard. 2008. ClearTK: A UIMA toolkit for statistical natural language processing. In *Towards Enhanced Interoperability for Large HLT Systems: UIMA for NLP workshop at Language Resources and Evaluation Conference (LREC)*.

Vinodkumar Prabhakaran, Owen Rambow, and Mona Diab. 2010. Automatic committed belief tagging. In *COLING 2010: Posters*, pages 1014–1022, Beijing, China, August. COLING 2010 Organizing Committee.

Vinodkumar Prabhakaran, Michael Bloodgood, Mona Diab, Bonnie Dorr, Lori Levin, Christine D. Piatko, Owen Rambow, and Benjamin Van Durme. 2012a. Statistical Modality Tagging from Rule-based Annotations and Crowdsourcing. In *Proceedings of the Workshop on Extra-Propositional Aspects of Meaning in Computational Linguistics*, pages 57–64, Jeju, Republic of Korea, July. Association for Computational Linguistics.

Vinodkumar Prabhakaran, Owen Rambow, and Mona Diab. 2012b. Predicting Overt Display of Power in Written Dialogs. In *Human Language Technologies: The 2012 Annual Conference of the North American Chapter of the Association for Computational Linguistics*, Montreal, Canada, June. Association for Computational Linguistics.

Preethi Raghavan, Albert Lai, and Eric Fosler-Lussier. 2012. Learning to temporally order medical events in clinical text. In *Proceedings of the 50th Annual Meeting of the Association for Computational Linguistics (Volume 2: Short Papers)*, pages 70–74, Jeju Island, Korea, July. Association for Computational Linguistics.

Roser Saurí and James Pustejovsky. 2009. Factbank: a corpus annotated with event factuality. *Language Resources and Evaluation*, 43:227–268. 10.1007/s10579-009-9089-9.

Pontus Stenetorp, Sampo Pyysalo, Tomoko Ohta, Sophia Ananiadou, and Jun'ichi Tsujii. 2012. Bridging the gap between scope-based and event-based negation/speculation annotations: a bridge not too far. In *Proceedings of the Workshop on Extra-Propositional Aspects of Meaning in Computational Linguistics*, pages 47–56. Association for Computational Linguistics.

Kateryna Tymoshenko, Swapna Somasundaran, Vinodkumar Prabhakaran, and Vinay Shet. 2012. Relation mining in the biomedical domain using entity-level semantics. In *ECAI*, pages 780–785.

Özlem Uzuner, Imre Solti, and Eithon Cadag. 2010. Extracting medication information from clinical text. *Journal of the American Medical Informatics Association*, 17(5):514–518.

Erik Velldal, Lilja Øvrelid, Jonathon Read, and Stephan Oepen. 2012. Speculation and negation: Rules, rankers, and the role of syntax. *Computational linguistics*, 38(2):369–410.

Veronika Vincze, György Szarvas, Richárd Farkas, György Móra, and János Csirik. 2008. The BioScope corpus: biomedical texts annotated for uncertainty, negation and their scopes. *BMC bioinformatics*, 9(Suppl 11):S9.

Veronika Vincze, Gyorgy Szarvas, Gyorgy Mora, Tomoko Ohta, Richárd Farkas, et al. 2011. Linguistic scope-based and biological event-based speculation and negation annotations in the BioScope and Genia Event corpora. *Journal of Biomedical Semantics*, 2(Suppl 5):S8.

Michael Wiegand, Alexandra Balahur, Benjamin Roth, Dietrich Klakow, and Andrés Montoyo. 2010. A survey on the role of negation in sentiment analysis. In *Proceedings of the workshop on negation and speculation in natural language processing*, pages 60–68. Association for Computational Linguistics.

Bowei Zou, Guodong Zhou, and Qiaoming Zhu. 2013. Tree kernel-based negation and speculation scope detection with structured syntactic parse features. In *Proceedings of the 2013 Conference on Empirical Methods in Natural Language Processing*, pages 968–976, Seattle, Washington, USA, October. Association for Computational Linguistics.

A New Dataset and Evaluation for Belief/Factuality

Vinodkumar Prabhakaran[1], Tomas By[2], Julia Hirschberg[1], Owen Rambow[3]*, Samira Shaikh[4], Tomek Strzalkowski[4], Jennifer Tracey[5], Michael Arrigo[5], Rupayan Basu[6], Micah Clark[2], Adam Dalton[2], Mona Diab[7], Louise Guthrie[2], Anna Prokofieva[1], Stephanie Strassel[5], Gregory Werner[7], Janyce Wiebe[8], Yorick Wilks[2]

[1]Department of Computer Science, Columbia University, New York, NY, USA
[2]Florida Institute for Human and Machine Cognition (IHMC), FL, USA
[3]Center for Computational Learning Systems, Columbia University, New York, NY, USA
[4]State University of New York - University of Albany, NY, USA
[5]Linguistic Data Consortium (LDC), University of Pennsylvania, PA, USA
[6]Amazon.com Inc., CA, USA
[7]George Washington University, DC, USA
[8]University of Pittsburgh, PA, USA

*corresponding author; email address: rambow@ccls.columbia.edu

Abstract

The terms "belief" and "factuality" both refer to the intention of the writer to present the propositional content of an utterance as firmly believed by the writer, not firmly believed, or having some other status. This paper presents an ongoing annotation effort and an associated evaluation.

1 Introduction

This paper presents an ongoing project aimed at developing a community-wide evaluation of expressed belief, also known as "factuality". Belief and factuality are closely related to hedging, veridicality, and modality. The project has grown out of the DARPA DEFT project; participants include the Linguistic Data Consortium (LDC) and three performer sites: Columbia University/George Washington University, the Florida Institute for Human and Machine Cognition, and the University of Albany. The goal of our research project is not linguistic annotation, but the identification of meaning which is expressed in a non-linguistic manner. Such a meaning representation is useful for many applications; in our project we are specifically interested in knowledge base population. A different part of the DEFT program is concerned with the representation of propositional meaning, following the tradition of the ACE program in representing entities, relations and events (ERE) (Doddington et al., 2004). The work presented here is concerned with the attitude of agents towards propositional content: do the agents express a committed belief or a non-committed belief in the propositional content? Our work has several characteristics that set it apart from other work: we are interested in annotation which can be done fairly quickly; we are not interested in annotating linguistic elements (such as trigger words); and we are planning an integration with sentiment annotation.

The structure of the paper is as follows: we start out by situating our notion of "belief" with respect to other notions of extra-propositional meaning (Section 2); we then present our annotation in some detail, with a special comparison to FactBank (Saurí and Pustejovsky, 2012). While the goal of this paper is not to talk about computational systems that were run as part of the evaluation (different publications will be available for that purpose), we quickly summarize their main characteristics so that the evaluation results can be interpreted. We then turn to

*Proceedings of the Fourth Joint Conference on Lexical and Computational Semantics (*SEM 2015)*, pages 82–91,
Denver, Colorado, June 4–5, 2015.

the pilot evaluation we have performed, presenting first the evaluation with respect to propositions (Section 5) and then a qualitative evaluation. We conclude with a discussion of plans for the upcoming open evaluation, scheduled for December 2015.

2 Terminology and Related Work

In this section, we identify how we define different terms. Different papers may have different and conflicting definitions of these terms, but for lack of space we do not provide an overview over all definitions.

While at first the terms "belief" and "factuality" appear to relate to rather different things (a subjective state versus truth), in the NLP community they in fact refer to the same phenomenon, while having rather different connotations. The phenomenon is the communicative intention of a writer[1] to present propositional content as something that she firmly believes is true, weakly believes is true, or has some other attitude towards, namely a wish or a reported belief. The term "belief" here describes the cognitive state of the writer (Diab et al., 2009), and comes from artificial intelligence and cognitive science, as in the Belief-Desire-Intention model of Bratman (1999 1987). The term "factuality" describes the communicative intention of the writer (Saurí and Pustejovsky, 2012, p. 263) (our emphasis):

> The fact that an eventuality is depicted as holding or not does not mean that this is the case in the world, but that this is how it is characterized by its informant. Similarly, it does not mean that this is the real knowledge that informant has (his true cognitive state regarding that event) but what he *wants us to believe* it is.

We would like to emphasize that the terms "belief" and "factuality" do not refer to the underlying truth of propositions, only to the intention of the writer to present them as, in her view, true. Thus, we as researchers cannot determine what is true from an analysis of factuality (or of belief). The term "factuality" is often misunderstood in this respect, which is one of the reasons we prefer not to use it. In order to understand the relation between belief/factuality and truth, we need to distinguish two assumptions. First, we may assume that the writer is not lying (assumption of truthfulness). In this paper, we make this first assumption. Second, we could assume that the writer knows what is true (assumption of truth). In this paper, we do not make this second assumption. We discuss these two assumptions in turn.

We start with the assumption of truthfulness. In the quote above, Saurí and Pustejovsky (2012) (apart from distinguishing factuality from truth) also make the point that the writer's communicative intention of making the reader believe she has a specific belief state does not mean that she actually has that cognitive state, since she may be lying. Lying is clearly an important phenomenon that researchers have looked into (Mihalcea and Strapparava, 2009; Ott et al., 2011).[2] However, we (as linguists interested in understanding how language enables communication) feel that assuming the writer is truthful is a standard assumption about communication which we should in general make. This is because if we do not make this assumption, we cannot explain why communication is possible at all, since discourse participants would have no motivation to ever adopt another discourse participant's belief as their own. We therefore do claim that we can infer belief from utterances, while assuming that the writer is not lying, and knowing that this assumption may be false in certain cases.

We now turn to the second assumption, the assumption of truth. Even if we assume that the writer is not lying, the assumption of truth is not required for communication to succeed; this is because the writer may be wrong, and this has no effect on the communication. For example, Ptolemy successfully made many people believe that the sun rotates around the earth, as was his (presumably) honest communicative intention. Therefore, to us as researchers interested in describing how language

[1]For brevity, we will assume a female writer as the source of utterances in this paper. Everything we say applies equally to spoken and written communication, and equally to male and female communicators.

[2]Sarcasm and irony differ from lying in that the communicative intention and the cognitive state are aligned, but they do not align with the standard interpretation of the utterance. Here, the intention is that the reader recognizes that the form of the utterance does not literally express the cognitive state. We leave aside sarcasm and irony in this paper; for current computational work on sarcasm detection, see for example (González-Ibáñez et al., 2011).

is used to communicate, it does not matter that astronomers now believe that Ptolemy was wrong, it does not change our account of communication and it does not change the communication that happened two millennia ago. And since we do not need to make the assumption that the writer knows what she is talking about, we choose not to make this assumption. In the case of Ptolemy, we leave this determination – what is actually true – to astronomers. In other cases, we typically have models of trustworthiness: if a writer sends her spouse a text message saying she is hungry, the spouse has no reason to believe she is wrong. We leave this issue aside in this paper.

The term "hedge" refers to words or phrases that add ambiguity or uncertainty (Propositional Hedges) or show the speakers lack of commitment to a proposition (Relational Hedges). For example, *The ball is* **sort of** *blue* contains a Relational Hedge (*sort of*) and *I* **think** *the ball is blue* includes a propositional hedge (*think*). Propositional hedges indicate non-committed belief. There has been a major effort to annotate texts with hedging information (Farkas et al., 2010), with an open evaluation. While belief and hedging are closely related, we see the belief/factuality annotation as more general than hedging (since it does not only include non-committed belief), and also more semantic (since we are not identifying language use but underlying meaning).

The term "modality" is used in formal semantics as well as in descriptive linguistics. Many semanticists (e.g. (Kratzer, 1991; Kaufmann et al., 2006)) define modality as quantification over possible worlds. Modality can be of two types: epistemic, which qualifies the speaker's commitment, and deontic, which concerns freedom to act. Belief/factuality falls under epistemic modality. Another view of modality relates more to a speaker's attitude toward a proposition (e.g. (McShane et al., 2004; Baker et al., 2010; Prabhakaran et al., 2012)), which is closer to the way we model belief.

We interpret the term "veridical" as referring to a property of certain words (usually verbs), namely to mark the proposition expressed by their syntactic complement clause as firmly believed (committed belief) by the writer (Kiparsky and Kiparsky, 1970). Veridicality as a property of lexical or lexico-syntactic elements is thus a way of relating belief/factuality to linguistic means of expressing them, but we take the notion of belief/factuality as being the underlying notion.

3 Annotation

3.1 Annotation Manual

The purpose of this annotation is to capture the commitment of the writer's belief in the propositions expressed in the text. The annotation for this project marks beliefs held by the writer only. We exhaustively annotate all (clausal) propositions in each document with a four-way belief type distinction, with the following categories.

Committed belief (CB) – the writer strongly believes that the proposition is true. Examples:

(1) a. The sun will **rise** tomorrow.
b. I know John and Katie **went** to Paris last year.

Non-committed belief (NCB) – the writer believes that the proposition is possibly or probably true, but is not certain. Examples:

(2) a. It could **rain** tomorrow.
b. I think John and Katie **went** to Paris last year.

Reported belief (ROB) – the writer attributes belief (either committed or non-committed) to another person or group. Note that this label is only applied when the writer's own belief in the proposition is unclear. Examples:

(3) a. Channel 6 said it could **rain** tomorrow.
b. Sarah said that John and Katie **went** to Paris last year.

Non-belief propositions (NA) – the writer expressed some other cognitive attitude toward the proposition, such as desire or intention, or expressly states that s/he has no belief about the proposition (e.g., by asking a question). Examples:

(4) a. Is it going to **rain** tomorrow?
b. I hope John and Katie **went** to Paris last year.

We do not make any effort to evaluate the truth value of the propositions, only the expressed level of belief in them held by the writer. Thus a strongly held false belief would not appear any different from a strongly held true belief. Similarly, lying, sarcasm, irony, and other cases where the writer's internal belief may differ from the expressed belief are not captured. That is, we take all expressed beliefs at "face value". We also do not capture any cognitive attitudes expressed about a proposition other than belief. An NA tag signifies just that there is no belief expressed about the proposition; it does not signify that there is another cognitive attitude expressed (e.g., 4a). Similarly, a proposition tagged as CB may also have other cognitive attitudes expressed about them (e.g., in "John managed to go to Paris last week", the author is expressing CB towards the proposition *go*, but also the *success* modality (Prabhakaran et al., 2012)); we do not capture them.

Annotators are not required to identify the full text span of the proposition. Instead, we take advantage of the close relationship between the semantics of the proposition and the syntactic structure of the clause by marking only the head of the structural unit containing the proposition (propositional head). For each proposition, annotators mark a head word and tag it with one of the four belief types. Note that the syntactic head word (perhaps lemmatized) can serve as a convenient name for the proposition, so for the examples above, we can talk about the belief in the 'rain' proposition and in the 'go' proposition. When a sentence has a single clause containing only one proposition, there will be only one head word to identify (usually a verb, but see details below on identifying heads of propositions). Many sentences contain multiple propositions, and the annotation guidelines provide detailed instructions on identifying head words. Note that the (b) examples above contain an additional proposition which is not marked; a full markup for example (3b) is below.

(5) Sarah said/CB that John and Katie went/ROB to Paris last year.

This is equivalent to the following span-based annotation:

(6) [CB Sarah said [ROB that John and Katie went to Paris last year.]]

The general principles of head word selection for each proposition can be summarized as follows:

1. Annotate the lexical verb of the clause expressing the proposition, if there is one.
2. If the verb of the clause is a copula, annotate the head of the predicate that follows the copula (noun for NP, preposition for PP, etc.).
3. Deontic modal auxiliaries, which signal a complex proposition, are annotated in addition to the lexical verb, as a separate belief.

All annotations are applied to a single whitespace-delimited word. In cases where the head of a proposition is a multiword expression (MWE), the head of the MWE is selected. In cases of noun phrases where no head is apparent (e.g. *bok choy*), the last word of the MWE is selected.

3.2 Comparison with FactBank

As already explained (Section 2), we take the terms "belief" and "factuality" to refer to the same phenomenon underlyingly (with perhaps different emphases). Therefore, the FactBank annotation is basically compatible with ours. Our annotation is much simpler than that of FactBank in order to allow for a quicker annotation. We summarize the main points of simplification here.

- We have taken the source always to be the writer. As we will discuss in Section 7.1, we will adopt the FactBank annotation in the next iteration of our annotation.
- We do not distinguish between possible and probable; this distinction may be hard to annotate and not too valuable.
- We ignore negation. If present, we simply assume it is part of the proposition which is the target.

Werner et al. (2015) study the relation between belief and factuality in more detail. They provide an automatic way of mapping the annotations in FactBank to the 4-way distinction of speaker/writer's belief that we present in this paper.

3.3 Corpus and Annotation Results

The annotation effort for this phase of belief annotation for DEFT produced a training corpus of 852,836 words and an evaluation corpus of 100,037 words. All annotated data consisted of English text from discussion forum threads. The discussion forum threads were originally collected for the DARPA BOLT program, and were harvested from a wide variety of sites. Discussion forum sites were chosen for harvesting in BOLT based on human judgement that the site was likely to contain many threads discussing either current events or personal anecdotes. For details on the BOLT collection, see Garland et al. (2012). Threads longer than 1000 words were truncated to produce documents consisting of one or more consecutive posts from a single thread. Long threads may generate multiple documents consisting of non-overlapping sections of the same thread (e.g., document 1 contains posts 1-5, while document 2 contains posts 6-12, etc.). The distribution of the four belief types in the training and evaluation corpora can be seen in Table 1.

Annotations	CB	NCB	ROB	NA
	Training Corpus			
143240	79995 (56%)	3890 (3%)	7150 (5%)	52205 (36%)
	Evaluation Corpus			
17553	8730 (50%)	583 (3%)	941 (5%)	7299 (42%)

Table 1: Annotation Statistics

The source data pool, annotation procedures, and annotators were the same for both the training and evaluation datasets, with the exception of the fact that the evaluation annotations received a full second pass over the annotation by a senior annotator (not the same as the first pass annotator) to increase consistency and reduce annotator errors. The training annotations were produced with a single annotation pass, and quality control was conducted through a second pass by a senior annotator on a sample of approximately 15% of the data. Inter-annotator agreement on headword selection was 93% and agreement on belief type labeling was 84%. Overall observed agreement, combining headword selection and belief type label, was 78% (Kappa score .60). Agreement on belief type was least reliable on the categories of ROB and NCB, both of which were sometime erroneously marked as CB. Both of these categories, in addition to being less frequent in the corpus, have difficult edge cases in which the annotator must make a judgment based on the context of the document (for example, deciding whether the writer clearly shares a belief attributed to another person for ROB).

4 Evaluation Systems

We conducted a multi-site pilot evaluation for the task of identifying beliefs expressed in text. Three performer sites took part in this evaluation. In this section, we briefly describe the systems built at these performer sites. The first two systems are rule-based systems, whereas the third system is a supervised learning system. We limit the discussion of these systems to a high level, postponing the detailed system descriptions to separate future publications.

4.1 System A

System A is adapted from a Sentiment Slot Filling system which participated in the 2014 TAC KBP SSF Evaluation (Shaikh et al., 2014). This system uses the Stanford Parser to create a syntactic dependency structure for every sentence in a given document. Using the dependency tree, it extracts the belief targets, which are usually the subjects of the sentence. In addition, the system extracts belief relations – a unary or binary predicate – typically a verb, an adjective or a noun. The focus of this version of System A is to identify propositional heads that express belief of any type. Each relation so extracted was initially marked as CB. A few heuristics were then applied to distinguish CBs from NCBs - such as presence of hedge words (*maybe*, *guess*). In addition, a few heuristics were added to tag relations as NAs, for example when the predicates appear in a question. The current version of System A does not account for ROB tags.

4.2 System B

System B uses the dependency tree and part-of-speech tags from the Stanford NLP tools, together with a custom verb lexicon to recognize belief expressions. The tree is processed to convert objects and complements to a single format, and then transformed into one or more belief triples (subject, verb, object). The system maintains a database of nested belief context, as in 'X believes Y believes Z', but we did not notice many instances of this phenomenon in the data. Partly because our System B

	System A			System B			System C		
	Prec.	Rec.	F-meas.	Prec.	Rec.	F-meas.	Prec.	Rec.	F-meas.
CB	35.9	39.9	37.8	42.1	36.8	39.3	68.9	77.9	73.1
NCB	13.3	8.8	10.6	4.6	7.4	5.7	52.9	29.7	38.0
ROB	0.0	0.0	0.0	1.3	0.9	1.0	43.8	15.6	23.0
NA	40.3	5.9	10.2	35.8	4.8	8.4	80.1	62.0	69.9
Overall	35.5	22.5	27.6	34.4	20.6	25.8	72.0	66.4	69.1

Table 2: Results obtained for System A, System B, and System C on the final Evaluation dataset.

recognizes reported beliefs (ROB) independently of the distinction between committed/non-committed belief in the annotations, the heuristic rules (mainly based on the presence of modal auxiliaries) that we added for the purpose of classifying the beliefs (CB, NCB, ROB, NA) did not work reliably in all cases.

4.3 System C

System C uses a supervised learning approach to identify tokens denoting the heads of propositions that denote author's expressed beliefs. It approaches this problem as a 5-way (CB, NCB, ROB, NA, *nil*) multi-class classification task at the word level. System C is adapted from a previous system which uses an earlier, simpler definition and annotation of belief (Prabhakaran et al., 2010). The system uses lexical and syntactic features for this task, which are extracted using the part-of-speech tags and dependency parses obtained from the Stanford CoreNLP system. In addition to the features described in (Prabhakaran et al., 2010), System C uses a set of new features including features based on a dictionary of hedge-words (Prokofieva and Hirschberg, 2014). The hedge features improved the NCB F-measure by around 2.2 percentage points (an overall F-measure improvement of 0.25 percentage points) in experiments conducted on a separate development set. It uses a quadratic kernel SVM to build the model, which outperformed the linear kernel in experiments conducted on the development set.

5 Proposition-Oriented Evaluation

We now describe the results obtained on a proposition-oriented quantitative evaluation of these systems. We focus on a system's ability to correctly identify the propositional heads of each type of belief (CB, NCB, ROB, NA). Only the words denoting heads of propositions will get one of these tags, and hence the majority of words in our data will not have any tags. We expect the system to find the propositional heads and to correctly assign their belief tags.

We use the entire Evaluation dataset described in Section 3 for this evaluation (entirely unseen during the development of the systems). We report precision, recall and F-measure for each belief type. We also report their micro-averages as the overall result. We compute F-measure as the harmonic mean between precision and recall. The best results obtained by each system described in Section 4 are presented in Table 2.

For System A, four different configurations were run for the evaluation, in which the NCB and NA tagging was either enabled or disabled. (The current version does not account for ROB tags.) In Table 2, Columns 2-4, we show the performance of System A while all 3 tags (CB, NCB and NA) are enabled. The results of other three configurations are comparable. Any sentence where the belief target could not be located, either due to parsing error or due to missing coreference (as supplied by ERE), was discarded. This resulted in a relatively lower recall in the evaluation, but produced high precision in a target-driven pilot evaluation (Section 6). The results obtained by System B in the evaluation are shown in Table 2: Columns 5-7. The results of System B, when ignoring the belief categories (i.e., on identifying heads of propositions), were 83.6% precision and 50% recall. Table 2: Columns 8-10 shows results obtained by System C trained on 80% of the training dataset (the rest of the corpus was used as a development set).

The supervised learning approach obtained overall better performance than rule based approach in our evaluation. ROB and NCB were the most difficult classes to predict for all three systems (e.g., highest recall posted for ROB is only 15.6%). CB was relatively easier to predict. NA was difficult to predict using the rule based approach, but supervised learning approach obtained reasonable performance of 69.9 F-measure.

6 An Entity-Focused Evaluation: Preliminary Investigation

In this section, we describe an initial investigation towards an entity-focused evaluation. An entity-focused evaluation tests a different kind of question about beliefs: given an entity e, what beliefs does the writer have about e? This entity-focused evaluation draws its parallels from TAC KBP Sentiment Slot Filling Evaluation (SSF) task. In the SSF, the task is to determine a target entity given a source entity and a sentiment between them. The goal is to populate a knowledge base with information regarding entities and the sentiment relations between them. In the same vein, an entity-focused belief task would provide knowledge about the salient belief relations between entities. For this purpose, we needed to define what is meant by "having a belief about an entity" and agreed on the following preliminary rules. The rules are entirely syntactic. In the following examples, the target entity is Mary, and the statement after the arrow shows what the beliefs are about her (and what the level of commitment by the writer is).

Adjunct clause case 1. If the target entity is contained in a clause (lets call it the "core clause") but NOT in an adjunct clause which modifies the core clause, we omit the adjunct clause (even though the adjunct clause in some sense pertains to the core clause but by virtue of being an adjunct, it is omissable).

(7) While John was in/CB Paris, Mary left/CB Paul $\longrightarrow$ CB: Mary left Paul

Adjunct clause case 2. If the target is in an adjunct clause to a core clause where the target is not mentioned, we retain both the adjunct clause as a standalone belief, and the combination of the adjunct and core (i.e., we have two beliefs about the entity).

(8) John was happy/CB when Mary left/CB Paul $\longrightarrow$ CB: John was happy when Mary left Paul ; CB: Mary left Paul

We devised similar rules for complement clauses, we omit them here.

For the actual evaluation, we used files which also had been hand-annotated for ACE entities. However, we did not have a gold annotation for entity-focused belief, as this study is still contributing towards a definition of this notion. Only two systems participated, System A and System C. System A as described in Section 4.1 already takes the notion of entity into account. For System C, we used the parse to determine the span associated with the annotated headword, and counted a proposition whose span included an entity to be about that entity. In order to understand how these two ways of determining entity-focused belief relate to each other, we compared the two systems to each other. We obtained an F-measure of 52%. We also hand evaluated the positive claims of System C, obtaining an accuracy of 48% on the positive claims. The errors are due to parse errors, the presence of the entity in adjuncts which do not appear germane (contradicting adjunct clause case 2), the presence of irrelevant adjunct clauses (counter to adjunct clause case 1), and to a lack of clarity in the annotation standard. As an example of the lack of clarity, consider the following sentence from our evaluation corpus, with *two kids* as target entity:

(9) I didn't see these two kids (sic) names on the news

two kids is a possessor of the direct object, and fell into the span of the annotated *see* for System C, but System A deemed the 'see' belief not to be about it. We conclude that this purely syntactic definition of "belief about an entity" is not satisfactory. The definition of "belief about an entity" remains an open question and we return to it in Section 7.3.

7 Plans for Next Round

7.1 Adding the Source

Currently, we are only annotating and evaluating the writer's beliefs. Beliefs attributed by the writer to other sources are marked ROB. We intend to annotate the source for all beliefs, using the method of nested attribution pioneered by MPQA (Wiebe et al., 2005) and adopted by FactBank (Saurí and Pustejovsky, 2012). Consider the following sentence.

(10) John believes Mary knows that the clock was stolen

In the nested attribution approach, according to the writer, according to John, Mary firmly believes (CB) the 'steal' proposition. According to the writer, John firmly believes the 'know' proposition and the 'steal' proposition (as indicated by the veridical verb *know*). The writer herself firmly believes (CB) the 'believe' proposition, does not express an opinion on the 'know' proposition (ROB), and also firmly believes (CB) the 'steal' proposition (again, the reader infers this from the use of *know*). We intend to annotate all these levels of belief.

7.2 Defining the Target Proposition

In our work to date, we have assumed that the target of a belief is a proposition, and we have represented the proposition by the syntactic head word of the clause which describes the proposition (which is equivalent to a text span under syntactic projection). We are investigating extending this in several manners. First, we are considering including the heads of event noun phrases (*the sudden collapse of the building*). Second, we are looking at using a semantic representation for the proposition (as opposed the syntactic head of the text passage describing the proposition). We do not propose to develop our own semantic representation, but instead we will look to using existing relation and event representations based on the ACE program (Doddington et al., 2004). These have the advantage that there are off-the-shelf computational tools available for detecting ACE relations and events; they have the disadvantage that they do not cover all propositions we may be interested in. An alternative would be the use of a shallower semantic representation such as PropBank (Kingsbury et al., 2002), FrameNet (Baker et al., 1998), or AMR (Banarescu et al., 2013).

7.3 Entities as Targets

In Section 6, we discussed an initial evaluation of a belief being about an entity. In this section we discuss further guidelines for identifying belief targets, i.e., when one can say that someone's belief is about a certain entity.

In general, the notion of belief "aboutness" is fairly fuzzy and it may be difficult to circumscribe precisely without some additional constraints. Suppose then that one of the ultimate objectives of belief extraction is to populate a knowledge base with beliefs held about specific entities: individuals, groups, artifacts, etc., which adds this constraint that the extracted belief is knowledge-base-worthy, or reportable. Some initial guidelines may go as suggested below. The objective is to provide guidance for a human assessor — not to propose a solution. We should note that these guidelines generally transcend any syntactic or structural considerations and appeal directly to the annotators' judgment. Furthermore, we note that these guidelines are not about effects relating to information structure – in one sense of "being about", the same sentence may be referred to as being "about" different things in different contexts. We are aiming for a lexical-semantic, not a pragmatic notion of aboutness.

A belief whose target is proposition p is **about** an entity T if one of the following clauses holds:

1. p describes a property of T, where the property is considered semi-permanent but not necessarily limited to physical or mental characteristics (e.g., red, long, brainy) and may also include behavioral properties (smart, slow) as well as characteristics bestowed on by others (beloved).

2. T is an agent of p, i.e., T is said to be performing some activity, physical or mental: drive a car, send a letter, etc.

3. T is directly involved in (or affected by) p but is not an agent: this includes situations where T's involvement may be passive but is nonetheless required for p to be performed, e.g., receive a letter, win a prize, etc.

We make no claim that the above list is exhaustive or that there would not be exceptions to these rules. For this reason we may also attempt to describe conditions under which a belief is not about T. For example: a belief target p is not about entity T even though T may be mentioned within the scope of p if:

4. T appears uninvolved in p and is apparently unaffected by its execution, e.g., reading about, waiting for, etc.

We intend to explore whether we can define this notion of belief aboutness sufficiently well to obtain good inter-annotator agreement.

7.4 Combining with Sentiment

We are planning on working on an annotation and an evaluation that combines belief with sentiment. The motivation for this is that belief and sentiment are similar types of meaning: they are attitudes towards propositions or entities which are expressed directly or indirectly. The similarity can also be seen in the fact that FactBank took the notion of nested source from MPQA, which is a sentiment-annotated corpus. Furthermore, many lexical items express both a belief and a sentiment at once:

(11) I hope Bertha enjoys the oysters

Here, the writer expresses a positive sentiment towards the 'enjoy' proposition, and at the same time she is expressing a lack of certainty (NCB) in the 'enjoy' proposition.

7.5 Adding Spanish and Chinese

We will be extending our annotation (including some of the extensions mentioned above) to Spanish and Chinese.

8 Conclusion

We have presented an ongoing annotation effort related to belief/factuality and an initial evaluation based on that annotation effort. To our knowledge, the annotated corpus is by far the largest corpus annotated in terms of belief/factuality. We have presented several proposed extensions to the annotation. The linguistic resources described in this paper will be published in the LDC catalog, making them available to the broader research community. The materials will be used in an open evaluation in late 2015 or early 2016. The evaluation will cover both belief/factuality and sentiment.

Acknowledgments

This paper is based upon work supported by the DARPA DEFT Program. The views expressed are those of the authors and do not reflect the official policy or position of the Department of Defense or the U.S. Government. We thank several anonymous reviewers for their constructive feedback.

References

Collin F. Baker, J. Fillmore, and John B. Lowe. 1998. The Berkeley FrameNet project. In *36th Meeting of the Association for Computational Linguistics and 17th International Conference on Computational Linguistics (COLING-ACL'98)*, pages 86–90, Montréal.

Kathryn Baker, Michael Bloodgood, Bonnie J. Dorr, Nathaniel W. Filardo, Lori S. Levin, and Christine D. Piatko. 2010. A modality lexicon and its use in automatic tagging. In *LREC*.

Laura Banarescu, Claire Bonial, Shu Cai, Madalina Georgescu, Kira Griffitt, Ulf Hermjakob, Kevin Knight, Philipp Koehn, Martha Palmer, and Nathan Schneider. 2013. Abstract meaning representation for sembanking. In *Proceedings of the 7th Linguistic Annotation Workshop and Interoperability with Discourse*, pages 178–186, Sofia, Bulgaria, August. Association for Computational Linguistics.

Michael E. Bratman. 1999 [1987]. *Intention, Plans, and Practical Reason*. CSLI Publications.

Mona Diab, Lori Levin, Teruko Mitamura, Owen Rambow, Vinodkumar Prabhakaran, and Weiwei Guo. 2009. Committed belief annotation and tagging. In *Proceedings of the Third Linguistic Annotation Workshop*, pages 68–73, Suntec, Singapore, August. Association for Computational Linguistics.

George Doddington, Alexis Mitchell, Mark Przybocki, Lance Ramshaw, Stephanie Strassel, and Ralph Weischedel. 2004. The automatic content extraction (ace) program–tasks, data, and evaluation. In *Proceedings of the Fourth International Conference on Language Resources and Evaluation (LREC'04)*, pages 837–840.

Richárd Farkas, Veronika Vincze, György Móra, János Csirik, and György Szarvas. 2010. The conll-2010 shared task: Learning to detect hedges and their scope in natural language text. In *Proceedings of the Fourteenth Conference on Computational Natural Language Learning*, pages 1–12, Uppsala, Sweden, July. Association for Computational Linguistics.

Roberto González-Ibáñez, Smaranda Muresan, and Nina Wacholder. 2011. Identifying sarcasm in twitter: A closer look. In *Proceedings of the 49th Annual Meeting of the Association for Computational Linguistics: Human Language Technologies*, pages 581–586, Portland, Oregon, USA, June. Association for Computational Linguistics.

Stefan Kaufmann, Cleo Condoravdi, and Valentina Harizanov, 2006. *Formal Approaches to Modality*, pages 72–106. Mouton de Gruyter.

Paul Kingsbury, Martha Palmer, and Mitch Marcus. 2002. Adding semantic annotation to the Penn TreeBank. In *Proceedings of the Human Language Technology Conference*, San Diego, CA.

Paul Kiparsky and Carol Kiparsky. 1970. Facts. In Manfred Bierwisch and Karl Erich Heidolph, editors, *Progress in Linguistics*, pages 143–173. Mouton, The Hague, Paris.

Angelika Kratzer. 1991. Modality. In Arnim von Stechow and Dieter Wunderlich, editors, *Semantics: An International Handbook of Contemporary Research*. Walter de Gruyter, Berlin.

Marjorie McShane, Sergei Nirenburg, and Ron Zacharsky. 2004. Mood and modality: Out of the theory and into the fray. *Natural Language Engineering*, 19(1):57–89.

Rada Mihalcea and Carlo Strapparava. 2009. The lie detector: Explorations in the automatic recognition of deceptive language. In *Proceedings of the ACL-IJCNLP 2009 Conference Short Papers*, pages 309–312, Suntec, Singapore, August. Association for Computational Linguistics.

Myle Ott, Yejin Choi, Claire Cardie, and Jeffrey T. Hancock. 2011. Finding deceptive opinion spam by any stretch of the imagination. In *Proceedings of the 49th Annual Meeting of the Association for Computational Linguistics: Human Language Technologies*, pages 309–319, Portland, Oregon, USA, June. Association for Computational Linguistics.

Vinodkumar Prabhakaran, Owen Rambow, and Mona Diab. 2010. Automatic committed belief tagging. In *Coling 2010: Posters*, pages 1014–1022, Beijing, China, August. Coling 2010 Organizing Committee.

Vinodkumar Prabhakaran, Michael Bloodgood, Mona Diab, Bonnie Dorr, Lori Levin, Christine D. Piatko, Owen Rambow, and Benjamin Van Durme. 2012. Statistical modality tagging from rule-based annotations and crowdsourcing. In *Proceedings of the Workshop on Extra-Propositional Aspects of Meaning in Computational Linguistics*, pages 57–64, Jeju, Republic of Korea, July. Association for Computational Linguistics.

Anna Prokofieva and Julia Hirschberg. 2014. Hedging and speaker commitment. In *5th Intl. Workshop on Emotion, Social Signals, Sentiment & Linked Open Data*, Reykjavik, Iceland.

Roser Saurí and James Pustejovsky. 2012. Are you sure that this happened? assessing the factuality degree of events in text. *Computational Linguistics*, 38(2):261–299.

Samira Shaikh, Rob Giarrusso, Veena Ravishankar, and Tomek Strzalkowski. 2014. The SUNY Albany Sentiment Slot Filling System. In *Proceedings of the 2014 TAC KBP Sentiment Slot Filling Evaluation*, Gaithersburg, Maryland, USA. NIST.

Gregory J. Werner, Vinodkumar Prabhakaran, Mona Diab, and Owen Rambow. 2015. Committed belief tagging on the factbank and lu corpora: A comparative study. In *Proceedings of the Workshop on Extra-Propositional Aspects of Meaning in Computational Linguistics*, Denver, USA, June. Association for Computational Linguistics.

Janyce Wiebe, Theresa Wilson, and Claire Cardie. 2005. Annotating expressions of opinions and emotions in language ann. *Language Resources and Evaluation*, 39(2/3):164–210.

Non-Orthogonal Explicit Semantic Analysis

Nitish Aggarwal **Kartik Asooja** **Georgeta Bordea** **Paul Buitelaar**
Insight Centre for Data Analytics
National University of Ireland
Galway, Ireland
firstname.lastname@insight-centre.org

Abstract

Explicit Semantic Analysis (ESA) utilizes the Wikipedia knowledge base to represent the semantics of a word by a vector where every dimension refers to an explicitly defined concept like a Wikipedia article. ESA inherently assumes that Wikipedia concepts are orthogonal to each other, therefore, it considers that two words are related only if they co-occur in the same articles. However, two words can be related to each other even if they appear separately in related articles rather than co-occurring in the same articles. This leads to a need for extending the ESA model to consider the relatedness between the explicit concepts (i.e. Wikipedia articles in Wikipedia based implementation) for computing textual relatedness. In this paper, we present Non-Orthogonal ESA (NESA) which represents more fine grained semantics of a word as a vector of explicit concept dimensions, where every such concept dimension further constitutes a semantic vector built in another vector space. Thus, NESA considers the concept correlations in computing the relatedness between two words. We explore different approaches to compute the concept correlation weights, and compare these approaches with other existing methods. Furthermore, we evaluate our model NESA on several word relatedness benchmarks showing that it outperforms the state of the art methods.

1 Introduction

Significance of quantifying relatedness between two natural language texts has been shown in various tasks which deal with information retrieval (IR), natural language processing (NLP), or other related fields. The semantics of a word can be obtained from existing lexical resources like WordNet and FrameNet. However, such lexical resources require domain expertise for defining the hierarchical structure, which makes their creation very expensive. Therefore, distributional semantic models (DSMs) have achieved much attention as they utilize available document collections like Wikipedia, and do not depend upon human expertise (Harris, 1954). DSMs represent the semantics of a word by transforming it to a high dimensional distributional vector in a predefined concept space. Many models have been proposed that derive this concept space by using explicit concepts or implicit concepts. Explicit Semantic Analysis (ESA) (Gabrilovich and Markovitch, 2007) utilizes the concepts which are explicitly derived under human cognition like Wikipedia concepts (articles). However, Latent Semantic Analysis (LSA) derives a latent concept space by performing dimensionality reduction (Landauer et al., 1998).

Gabrilovich and Markovitch (2007) introduced ESA model in which Wikipedia and Open Directory Project were used to obtain the explicit concepts, however, Wikipedia has been a popular choice in further ESA implementations (Polajnar et al., 2013; Gottron et al., 2011; Aggarwal et al., 2014). ESA represents the semantics of a word with a high dimensional vector over the Wikipedia concepts. The tf-idf weight of the word with the textual content under a Wikipedia concept reflects the magnitude

*Proceedings of the Fourth Joint Conference on Lexical and Computational Semantics (*SEM 2015)*, pages 92–100,
Denver, Colorado, June 4–5, 2015.

Table 1: Top 5 Wikipedia concepts for "football" and "soccer" in the ESA vector

#	football	soccer
1	FIFA	History of soccer in the United States
2	Football	Soccer in the United States
3	History of association football	United States Soccer Federation
4	Football in England	North American Soccer League (196884)
5	Association football	United Soccer Leagues

of the corresponding vector dimension. To obtain the semantic relatedness between two words, it computes the vector dot product between their vectors. ESA considers the dimensions as orthogonal to each other. For instance, the synonyms like "soccer" and "football" are highly related, however, they may not co-occur together in many Wikipedia articles. Table 1 shows that the top 5 Wikipedia concepts retrieved for "football" and "soccer" do not share any concept, however, the concepts may exhibit relatedness to each other. Consequently, ESA model assumes that words can be related only if they co-occur in the same articles. However, two words can also be related even if they do not share the same articles at all, but appear in the related ones. LSA resolves the orthogonality issue to some extent by building latent concept space in an unsupervised way (Landauer et al., 1998). However, the resulting latent concepts are not as clearly interpretable as the human-labeled concepts in the ESA model. Previous studies (Gabrilovich and Markovitch, 2007; Cimiano et al., 2009; Hassan and Mihalcea, 2011) show that ESA performs better than LSA for computing text relatedness. Therefore, it is important to consider the relatedness between dimensions in the ESA model, rather than considering them orthogonal, and also without losing the explicit property of ESA model at the same time.

In this paper, we present Non-Orthogonal ESA (NESA) model, an extension to ESA, which also uses relatedness between the explicit concepts for computing semantic relatedness between texts. The concepts in ESA model are clearly interpretable and they refer to the title of Wikipedia articles. This characteristic provides an opportunity to investigate different concept relatedness measures, such as relatedness between articles' content (document relatedness) or relatedness between corresponding Wikipedia titles. In order to investigate the performance of these concept relatedness measures, we evaluate them on an entity relatedness benchmark called KORE (Hoffart et al., 2012) as Wikipedia article title generally refers to an entity.

We then apply the different approaches for computing concept relatedness in our model NESA to compute text relatedness. We evaluate NESA on several word relatedness benchmarks to verify whether considering non-orthogonality in ESA model improves its performance.

2 Related Work

2.1 Text Relatedness

In recent years, there have been a variety of efforts to develop semantic relatedness measures. Classical approaches assess the relatedness scores by using existing knowledge bases or corpus statistics. Lexical resources such as WordNet or Roget thesaurus (Jarmasz and Szpakowicz, 2004) are used as knowledge bases to compute the relatedness scores between two words. Most of these approaches make use of the hierarchical structure present in the lexical resources. For instance, Hirst and St-Onge (1998), Leacock and Chodorow (1998), and Wu and Palmer (1994) utilize the edges that define taxonomic relations between words; Banerjee and Pedersen (2002) computes the scores by obtaining the overlap between glosses associated with the words; and some of the other approaches (Resnik, 1995; Lin, 1998) use corpus evidence with the taxonomic structure of WordNet. These approaches are limited to perform only for the lexical entries and thus do not work with non-dictionary words. Moreover, these measures rely on the manually constructed lexical resources and they are not portable to multiple languages due to unavailability of lexical resources in multiple languages.

Corpus-based methods such as LSA (Landauer et al., 1998), Latent Dirichlet Allocation (LDA) (Blei et al., 2003), and ESA (Gabrilovich and Markovitch, 2007) employ statistical models to build the semantic profile of a word. LSA and LDA generate unsupervised topics from a textual corpus, and represent the semantics of a word by its distribution over these topics. LSA performs singular value decomposition (SVD) to obtain a latent concept space. On the contrary, ESA directly uses supervised topics such as Wikipedia concepts that are built manually, and considers that every concept is orthogonal to each other. Polajnar at el. (2013) proposed an approach to improve ESA by considering the concept relatedness using word overlap in Wikipedia articles' content. Radinsky at el. (2011) introduced Temporal Semantic Analysis (TSA) also considers the concept relatedness in ESA model, which is computed by using their temporal distribution over the NewYork Times news archives from the last 100 years. Although, these approaches consider relatedness between explicit concepts (Polajnar et al., 2013; Radinsky et al., 2011) and improve the accuracy, however, either they define a weak concept relatedness measure or require an external corpus statistics. Our approach takes inspiration from them and uses more advanced concept relatedness measures that rely on the same corpus statistics, which is used to build the ESA model.

2.2 Concept Relatedness

As NESA model requires a concept relatedness measure to overcome orthogonality, we address here the existing methods of computing it (Strube and Ponzetto, 2006; Witten and Milne, 2008; Polajnar et al., 2013). Most of these approaches rely on Wikipedia and its derived knowledge bases such as DBpedia[1], YAGO[2] and FreeBase[3]. These knowledge bases provide immense amount of information about millions of concepts or entities which can be utilized for computing concept relatedness. Strube and Ponzetto (2006) proposed WikiRelate that counts the edges between two concepts in Wikipedia link structure, and also considers the depth of a concept in the Wikipedia category structure. Witten and Milne (2008) applied Google distance metric (Cilibrasi and Vitanyi, 2007) on incoming links in Wikipedia. Hoffart at el. (2012) utilized the textual content associated with the Wikipedia concepts. It observes the partial overlap between the concepts (key-phrases) appearing in the article content. The above mentioned approaches mainly exploit the article content or Wikipedia link structure for computing concept relatedness. In this paper, we also utilize the distributional information of the title and hyperlinks for computing concept relatedness.

[1]http://dbpedia.org/About

[2]http://yago-knowledge.org/

[3]https://www.freebase.com/

3 Non-Orthogonal Explicit Semantic Analysis

To compute text relatedness, NESA uses relatedness between the dimensions of the distributional vectors to overcome the orthogonality in ESA model. In addition to represent the words as distributional vectors, where each dimension is associated with a Wikipedia concept as in ESA model, NESA also utilizes a square matrix $C_{n,n}$ (n is the total number of dimensions) containing the correlation weights between the dimensions. Thus, to obtain the relatedness score between the words *w1* and *w2*, NESA formulates the measure as follows:

$$rel_{NESA}(w1, w2) = \mathbf{w1}^T_{1,n}.C_{n,n}.\mathbf{w2}_{n,1} \quad (1)$$

where $\mathbf{w1}_{n,1}$ and $\mathbf{w2}_{n,1}$ are the corresponding distributional vectors consisting of n dimensions. Every concept dimension can be further semantically interpreted as a distributional vector in some other vector space of m dimensions. This transformation allows the computation of the correlation weights between the concept dimensions. Thus, a transformation matrix $E_{m,n}$ can be built, where each column corresponds to a transformation vector for each concept dimension. Using the matrix $E_{m,n}$, we can compute the matrix $C_{n,n}$ by multiplying $E_{m,n}$ with its transpose as in equation 2. In the next section, we discuss the different approaches used for computing $C_{n,n}$ containing the relatedness between the concept dimensions .

$$C_{n,n} = E^T_{n,m}.E_{m,n} \quad (2)$$

4 Computing Concept Relatedness

NESA requires the relatedness scores between Wikipedia concepts (articles), therefore we present the different approaches for computing $C_{n,n}$ matrix using $E_{m,n}$. Every Wikipedia article consists of different fields to represent the semantics of the concept dimensions, such as Wikipedia title, textual description and hyperlinks. We utilize this information to implement four different concept relatedness measures: VSM-Text, VSM-Hyperlinks, ESA-WikiTitle, and DiSER. These approaches represent the semantics of a concept with a distributional vector of m dimensions. All such vectors combined as column vectors for n concept dimensions form the matrix $E_{m,n}$.

4.1 VSM-Text

This approach is based on plain Vector Space Model (VSM) for text. It calculates the relatedness scores between concepts by taking word overlap between their corresponding Wikipedia article content. The concept is transformed to a column vector mx1, where m is the total number of unique words in the Wikipedia corpus. The magnitude of each dimension is calculated on the basis of the number of occurrences of the different words in the associated Wikipedia article content.

4.2 VSM-Hyperlink

Similar to the VSM-Text, this approach calculates the concept relatedness by taking the overlap between the hyperlinks present in their corresponding Wikipedia articles' content. The concept is transformed to a column vector mx1, where m is the total number of hyperlinks in the whole Wikipedia. The magnitude of each dimension is calculated on the basis of the number of occurrences of the different hyperlinks in the associated Wikipedia article content.

4.3 ESA-WikiTitle

One intuitive way of obtaining concept relatedness scores is by using ESA itself for calculating the relatedness between the concepts. We use the associated Wikipedia article title for this purpose. ESA represents the semantics of a word with a high dimensional vector over the Wikipedia concepts. Therefore, each concept dimension is transformed into a column vector of mx1, where m is the total number of Wikipedia concepts. The magnitude of each dimension is computed by using the term frequency (tf) and inverse document frequency (idf) for the terms appearing in the Wikipedia article title over the Wikipedia corpus (Gabrilovich and Markovitch, 2007).

4.4 DiSER

Distributional Semantics for Entity Relatedness (DiSER) (Aggarwal and Buitelaar, 2014) is a model for computing relatedness scores between entities. DiSER considers every Wikipedia concept as an entity. Therefore, it can be used for computing concept relatedness matrix $C_{n,n}$, as required by the NESA model. In contrast to text relatedness measures based on DSMs such as ESA, which do not distinguish between entity and text, DiSER differentiate between entity and its surface forms by using unique hyperlinks referring to entities in Wikipedia for encoding entities while building DSMs. It uses the distributional information of such hyperlinks only over the whole Wikipedia corpus for representing a concept by a high dimensional distributional vector. Therefore, each concept dimension is transformed into a column vector of mx1, where m is the total number of Wikipedia concepts. The magnitude of each dimension is computed by using the concept frequency (cf) and inverse document frequency (idf) for an concept in the Wikipedia corpus. The concept frequency (cf) is a slight variation of term frequency. It computes the frequency of a concept appearing as hyperlink in the Wikipedia articles. To obtain the DiSER based relatedness scores between Wikipedia concepts, we use Entity Relatedness Graph (EnRG)[4] (Aggarwal et al., 2015), which is a focused related entities explorer based on DiSER scores.

5 Evaluation of Concept Relatedness Measures

In this section, we evaluate the different approaches defined for computing concept relatedness measures in the previous section. For our evaluation, we use the snapshot of English Wikipedia from 1st October, 2013. This snapshot consists of 13,872,614 articles,

[4]EnRG demo: http://enrg.insight-centre.org

in which 5,934,022 are Wikipedia redirects. We filtered out all the namespace[5] pages by using the articles' titles as they have specific namespace patterns. There are 3,571,206 namespace pages in this snapshot. We remove all those articles which contain less than 100 unique words or less than 5 hyperlinks; such articles are too specific and may generate some noise. We perform further filtering by removing all the articles if their titles are numbers like "19", dates like "June 1", or if the title starts with "list". We finally obtain a total of 3,635,833 Wikipedia articles for our experiment. We implement all the concept relatedness measures by using these obtained Wikipedia articles.

VSM-Text represents the semantics of a concept with a column vector of mx1, where m is the total number of unique words appear in Wikipedia. Wikipedia contains more than 2.5 billion unique words, therefore, to reduce the matrix size, we use only 5 million most frequent words. ESA-WikiTitle represents the semantics of a concept with a column vector of mx1, where m is 3,635,833 in our implementation. In order to obtain the hyperlinks for VSM-Hyperlink and DiSER, we retain only those text segments which have manually defined links provided by Wikipedia volunteers. However, the volunteers may not create the link for every surface form appearing in the article content. For instance, "Apple" occurs 213 times in "Steve Jobs" Wikipedia page in our corpus, but only 7 out of these 213 are linked to the "Apple Inc." Wikipedia page. The term frequency of "Apple" is calculated without considering the partial string matches, for example, we do not count if "apple" appears as a substring of any annotated text segment like "Apple Store" or "Apple Lisa". To obtain the actual frequency of every hyperlink for computing the magnitude of the dimension, we apply "one sense per discourse" heuristic (Gale et al., 1992), which assumes that a term tends to have the same meaning in the same discourse. We link every additional un-linked occurrence of the text segment with the same hyperlink appearing most of the times for the same segment in the article. The total number of hyperlinks possible in our corpus would be equal to the total number of Wikipedia articles i.e. 3,635,833.

5.1 Dataset

In order to evaluate the concept relatedness measures, we performed our experiments on the gold standard benchmark dataset KORE (Hoffart et al., 2012). The KORE dataset consists of 21 seed Wikipedia concepts selected from the YAGO knowledge base[6]. Every seed concept has a ranked list of 20 related Wikipedia concepts. In order to build this dataset, 20 concept candidates are selected and ranked by human evaluators on crowdsourcing platforms to give the relative comparison between two candidates against the corresponding seed Wikipedia concept. For instance, human evaluators provide their judgement if "Mark Zuckerberg" is more related to "Facebook" than "Sean Parker". With the answers for such binary questions, a ranked list is prepared for every seed Wikipedia concept. The KORE dataset[7] consists of 21 seed candidates, thus forming 420 concept pairs with their relatedness scores assigned by 15 human evaluators.

5.2 Experiment

We compare the concept relatedness measures described in section 4 against other existing methods. Hoffart at el. (2012) proposed KORE and KPCS which use the article content to compute the concept relatedness. They use Mutual Information (MI-weight) to capture the importance of the hyperlink for a Wikipedia concept. To evaluate the concept relatedness measures using KORE dataset, we compute the concept relatedness scores for all the concept pairs and rank the list of 20 candidates for each seed Wikipedia concept. We calculated Spearman Rank correlation between the gold standard dataset and the results obtained from VSM-Text, VSM-Hyperlink, ESA-WikiTitle and DiSER.

5.3 Results and Discussion

Experimental results are shown in Table 2. We compare our results with the other existing methods of computing concept relatedness: WLM, KORE, and KPCS. WLM is the Wikipedia Link-based approach by Witten and Milne (2008). KPCS and

[5]http://en.wikipedia.org/wiki/Wikipedia:Namespace

[6]http://datahub.io/dataset/yago

[7]http://www.mpi-inf.mpg.de/yago-naga/aida

Table 2: Spearman rank correlation of concept relatedness measures with gold standard

Concept Relatedness Measures	Spearman Rank Correlation with human
VSM-Text	0.510
VSM-Hyperlink	0.637
ESA	0.661
DiSER	**0.781**
WLM	0.610
KPCS	0.698
KORE	0.673

KORE are the approaches proposed in (Hoffart et al., 2012), where KPCS is the cosine similarity on MI-weighted keyphrases while KORE represents the keyphrase overlap relatedness. These keyphrases can be the text segment with hyperlinks in the article content. Therefore, KPCS is a similar approach to VSM-Hyperlink, besides KPCS assigns MI-weights to capture the generality and specificity of concept in the Wikipedia article. Many concepts in the gold standard dataset are defined by ambiguous surface forms such as "NeXT" and "Nice", or they have ambiguous text segments in their surface forms like "Jobs" in "Steve Jobs" and "Guitar" in the "Guitar Hero" video game. Therefore, the effect of using only hyperlinks can be observed with the remarkable difference between the results obtained by ESA and DiSER. DiSER improves the accuracy over ESA by 20%. These scores illustrate that ESA fails in generating the appropriate semantic profiles for ambiguous terms. VSM-Text does not capture the semantics of Wikipedia concepts as the textual description in Wikipedia article also contains generic terms which are not enough to specify the precisely semantics of Wikipedia concepts. Therefore, VSM-Hyperlink achieved noticeable improvement over VSM-Text as VSM-Hyperlink builds the semantic profile by using hyperlinks in the article content. These hyperlinks are created by Wikipedia volunteers, therefore, it can be assumed that the text segments which are linked to other Wikipedia article, are more important than un-linked ones. However, KPCS and KORE achieved significantly higher accuracy in comparison to VSM-Hyperlink, which indicates that generality and specificity of hyperlinks in the article content are very influential features for concept relatedness measures.

6 Evaluation of NESA for Word Relatedness

In this section, we evaluate NESA for word relatedness. We experiment by using different concept relatedness measures as explained in section 4 for building the $C_{n,n}$ in NESA model as shown in equations 1 and 2. We use the same filtered Wikipedia articles as used for evaluating the concept relatedness measures in the previous section.

6.1 Dataset

We use 6 different word relatedness benchmarks to evaluate NESA.

WN353 consists of 353 word pairs annotated by 13-15 human experts on a scale of 0-10. 0 refers to un-related and 10 stands for highly related or identical. This dataset mainly contains generic words like "money", "drink", "movie", etc.. It also contains named entities such as "Jerusalem", "Palestinian" and "Israel", which makes this dataset more challenging for approaches that use only the lexical resources.

WN353Rel and WN353Sim datasets are the subsets of WN353. As WN353 contains similar and related word pairs, Agirre at el. (2009) refine the WN353 gold standard by splitting it in two parts: related word pairs and similar word pairs. The notion of similarity and relatedness are defined as follow: two words are similar if they are connected through the taxonomic relations like synonym or hyponym in lexical resources, while two words can be considered related if they are connected through other relations such as meronym and holonym. For instance, "football" and "soccer" are two similar words while "computer" and "software" can be considered as related. Finally, WN353Rel and WN353Sim contain 252 and 203 word pairs respectively.

MC30 is the dataset build by Miller and Charles (1991) that contains the selected word pairs of WN353. The relatedness scores of these words are

Table 3: Spearman rank correlation of relatedness measures with gold standard datasets

#	**WN353**	**WN353Rel**	**WN353Sim**	**MC30**	**RG65**	**MT287**
H&S	0.347	0.142	0.497	0.811	0.813	0.278
L&C	0.302	0.172	0.412	0.793	0.823	0.284
Lesk	0.337	0.125	0.511	0.583	0.5466	0.271
W&P	0.316	0.131	0.461	0.784	0.807	0.331
Resnik	0.353	0.184	0.535	0.693	0.731	0.234
J&C	0.317	0.089	0.442	0.820	0.804	0.296
Lin	0.348	0.154	0.483	0.750	0.788	0.286
Roget	0.415	- -	- -	**0.856**	0.804	- -
SSA	0.629	- -	- -	0.810	0.830	- -
Polajnar et al.	0.664	- -	- -	- -	- -	- -
ESA	0.660	0.643	0.663	0.765	0.826	0.507
NESA (VSM-Text)	0.666	0.648	0.669	0.768	0.827	0.509
NESA (VSM-Hyperlink)	0.670	0.649	0.672	0.768	0.828	0.516
NESA (ESA-WikiTitle)	0.681	0.652	0.684	0.774	0.830	0.541
NESA (DiSER)	**0.696**	**0.663**	**0.719**	0.784	**0.839**	**0.572**

provided by 38 human experts on a scale of 0-4.

RG65 is a collection of 65 non-technical word pairs. These word pairs are annotated by 51 human experts (see for more detail (Rubenstein and Goodenough, 1965)).

MT287 is a relatively newer dataset that contains 287 word pairs. This dataset is prepared mainly to study the effect of temporal distribution (Radinsky et al., 2011) of a word over several years. The relatedness scores of the word pairs are obtained from 15-20 mechanical turkers.

6.2 Experiment

We compare the NESA model with other state of the art methods of calculating word relatedness: Explicit Semantic Analysis (ESA), Salient Semantic Analysis (SSA), and several WordNet-based similarity measures. Hassan and Mihalcea (2011) reported SSA performance on WN353, MC30 and RG65 datasets as shown in table 3. The WordNet-based similarity measures are implemented using WS4J (WordNet Similarity for Java)[8] library built on WordNet 3.0.

[8]https://code.google.com/p/ws4j/

6.3 Results and Discussion

Table 3 shows the results of the NESA model with different concept relatedness approaches and other state of the art methods of calculating word relatedness. The knowledge-based methods that use lexical resources like WordNet or Roget thesaurus (Jarmasz and Szpakowicz, 2004), achieve higher accuracy if the words in benchmark datasets are available in the knowledge bases. For instance, WordNet-based measures (H&S (Hirst and St-Onge, 1998), L&C (Leacock and Chodorow, 1998), Lesk (Banerjee and Pedersen, 2002), W&P (Wu and Palmer, 1994), Resnik (Resnik, 1995) J&C (Jiang and Conrath, 1997), Lin (Lin, 1998)) and Roget thesaurus-based measure (Jarmasz and Szpakowicz, 2004) achieved higher accuracy on MC30 and RG65 datasets. However, these approaches may not fit well for the datasets that contain non-dictionary words, therefore, the accuracy of knowledge-based measures decrease significantly on other datasets. Corpus-based measures ESA and SSA achieved higher scores than knowledge-based methods on WN353, WN353Rel, WN353Sim and MT287 datasets. Moreover, corpus-based methods performed comparable to knowledge-based methods on MC30 and RG65. Most of the knowledge-based measures use the taxonomic relations for computing word relatedness. Therefore, these measures obtained poor results on WN353Rel in contrast to WN353Sim dataset. However, corpus-based measures performed well for both type of relations i.e. similarity and relatedness.

The NESA model combined with any concept relatedness measure outperforms ESA for all the word relatedness benchmark datasets. It shows that considering non-orthogonality between explicit concepts in ESA model improves the accuracy. NESA-VSM-Hyperlink performs better than NESA-VSM-Text implying that considering only the hyperlinks from the article content works better than taking the overlap of whole content. NESA-ESA-WikiTitle and NESA-DiSER achieved higher scores than both NESA-VSM-Text and NESA-VSM-Hyperlink. It shows that the distributional representation of the article title captures the semantic information better than considering only the corresponding article content. Another interesting thing to note is that the correlation scores obtained by NESA model with the four concept relatedness measures follow the same order in table 3 as of the correlation scores obtained in evaluating concept relatedness shown in table 2. It represents the consistency of proposed concept relatedness measures in two different experiment settings. NESA-DiSER achieved the highest correlation scores in all the word relatedness benchmark datasets.

7 Conclusion

We presented Non-Orthogonal ESA which introduces the relatedness between the explicit concepts in the ESA model for computing semantic relatedness, without compromising with the explicit property of the ESA concept space. We showed that the word relatedness results vary with the different concept relatedness measures. NESA outperformed all state of the art methods, in particular, NESA-DiSER achieved the highest correlation with the gold standard. We also evaluated the different concept relatedness measures using benchmark dataset KORE, in which DiSER outperformed all others.

8 Acknowledgements

This work has been funded by a research grant from Science Foundation Ireland (SFI) under Grant Number SFI/12/RC/2289 (INSIGHT).

References

Nitish Aggarwal and Paul Buitelaar. 2014. Wikipedia-based distributional semantics for entity relatedness. In *2014 AAAI Fall Symposium Series*.

Nitish Aggarwal, Kartik Asooja, and Paul Buitelaar. 2014. Exploring esa to improve word relatedness. *Lexical and Computational Semantics (* SEM 2014)*, 51.

Nitish Aggarwal, Kartik Asooja, Housam Ziad, and Paul Buitelaar. 2015. Who are the american vegans related to brad pitt? exploring related entities. In *24th International World Wide Web Conference (WWW 2015), Florence, Italy*.

Eneko Agirre, Enrique Alfonseca, Keith Hall, Jana Kravalova, Marius Paşca, and Aitor Soroa. 2009. A study on similarity and relatedness using distributional and wordnet-based approaches. In *Proceedings of Human Language Technologies: The 2009 Annual Conference of the North American Chapter of the Association for Computational Linguistics*, pages 19–27.

Satanjeev Banerjee and Ted Pedersen. 2002. An adapted lesk algorithm for word sense disambiguation using wordnet. In *Computational linguistics and intelligent text processing*, pages 136–145. Springer.

David M. Blei, Andrew Y. Ng, and Michael I. Jordan. 2003. Latent dirichlet allocation. *J. Mach. Learn. Res.*, 3:993–1022.

Rudi L Cilibrasi and Paul MB Vitanyi. 2007. The google similarity distance. *Knowledge and Data Engineering, IEEE Transactions on*, 19(3):370–383.

Philipp Cimiano, Antje Schultz, Sergej Sizov, Philipp Sorg, and Steffen Staab. 2009. Explicit versus latent concept models for cross-language information retrieval. In *IJCAI*, volume 9, pages 1513–1518.

Evgeniy Gabrilovich and Shaul Markovitch. 2007. Computing semantic relatedness using wikipedia-based explicit semantic analysis. In *Proceedings of the 20th IJCAI*, pages 1606–1611.

William A Gale, Kenneth W Church, and David Yarowsky. 1992. One sense per discourse. In *Proceedings of the workshop on Speech and Natural Language*, pages 233–237. ACL.

Thomas Gottron, Maik Anderka, and Benno Stein. 2011. Insights into explicit semantic analysis. In *Proceedings of the 20th CIKM*, pages 1961–1964. ACM.

Zellig Harris. 1954. Distributional structure. In *Word 10 (23)*, pages 146–162.

Samer Hassan and Rada Mihalcea. 2011. Semantic relatedness using salient semantic analysis. In *AAAI*.

Graeme Hirst and David St-Onge. 1998. Lexical chains as representations of context for the detection and correction of malapropisms. *WordNet: An electronic lexical database*, 305:305–332.

Johannes Hoffart, Stephan Seufert, Dat Ba Nguyen, Martin Theobald, and Gerhard Weikum. 2012. Kore: Keyphrase overlap relatedness for entity disambiguation. In *Proceedings of the 21st ACM international conference on Information and knowledge management*, pages 545–554. ACM.

Mario Jarmasz and Stan Szpakowicz. 2004. Rogets thesaurus and semantic similarity1. *Recent Advances in Natural Language Processing III: Selected Papers from RANLP*, 2003:111.

Jay J Jiang and David W Conrath. 1997. Semantic similarity based on corpus statistics and lexical taxonomy. *arXiv preprint cmp-lg/9709008*.

T K Landauer, P. W. Foltz, and D Laham. 1998. An introduction to latent semantic analysis. *Discourse Processes*, 25:259–284.

Claudia Leacock and Martin Chodorow. 1998. Combining local context and wordnet similarity for word sense identification. *WordNet: An electronic lexical database*, 49(2):265–283.

Dekang Lin. 1998. An information-theoretic definition of similarity. In *ICML*, volume 98, pages 296–304.

George A Miller and Walter G Charles. 1991. Contextual correlates of semantic similarity. *Language and cognitive processes*, 6(1):1–28.

Tamara Polajnar, Nitish Aggarwal, Kartik Asooja, and Paul Buitelaar. 2013. Improving esa with document similarity. In *Advances in Information Retrieval*, pages 582–593. Springer.

Kira Radinsky, Eugene Agichtein, Evgeniy Gabrilovich, and Shaul Markovitch. 2011. A word at a time: computing word relatedness using temporal semantic analysis. In *20th WWW*, pages 337–346.

Philip Resnik. 1995. Using information content to evaluate semantic similarity in a taxonomy. *arXiv preprint cmp-lg/9511007*.

Herbert Rubenstein and John B Goodenough. 1965. Contextual correlates of synonymy. *Communications of the ACM*, 8(10):627–633.

Michael Strube and Simone Paolo Ponzetto. 2006. Wikirelate! computing semantic relatedness using wikipedia. In *AAAI*, volume 6, pages 1419–1424.

I Witten and David Milne. 2008. An effective, low-cost measure of semantic relatedness obtained from wikipedia links. In *Proceeding of AAAI Workshop on Wikipedia and Artificial Intelligence: an Evolving Synergy, AAAI Press, Chicago, USA*, pages 25–30.

Zhibiao Wu and Martha Palmer. 1994. Verbs semantics and lexical selection. In *Proceedings of the 32nd annual meeting on ACL*, pages 133–138. ACL.

Combining Mention Context and Hyperlinks from Wikipedia for Named Entity Disambiguation

Ander Barrena
IXA NLP Group
UPV/EHU
Donostia, Basque Country
ander.barrena@ehu.eus

Aitor Soroa
IXA NLP Group
UPV/EHU
Donostia, Basque Country
a.soroa@ehu.eus

Eneko Agirre
IXA NLP Group
UPV/EHU
Donostia, Basque Country
e.agirre@ehu.eus

Abstract

Named entity disambiguation is the task of linking entity mentions to their intended referent, as represented in a Knowledge Base, usually derived from Wikipedia. In this paper, we combine local mention context and global hyperlink structure from Wikipedia in a probabilistic framework. We test our method in eight datasets, improving the state-of-the-art results in five. Our results show that the two models of context, namely, words in the context and hyperlink pathways to other entities in the context, are complementary. Our results are not tuned to any of the datasets, showing that it is robust to out-of-domain scenarios, and that further improvements are possible.

1 Introduction

Linking mentions occurring in documents to a knowledge base is the main goal of Entity Linking or Named Entity Disambiguation (NED). This problem has attracted a great number of papers in the NLP and IR communities, and a large number of techniques, including local context and global inference (Ratinov et al., 2011). We propose to use a probabilistic framework that combines entity popularity, name popularity, local mention context and global hyperlink structure, relying on information in Wikipedia alone. Entity and name popularity are useful disambiguation clues in the absence of any context. The local mention context provides direct clues (in the form of words in context) to disambiguate each mention separately. The hyperlink structure of Wikipedia provides a global coherence measure for all entities mentioned in the same context.

The advantages of our method with respect to other alternatives are as follows: (1) It does not involve a large number of methods and classifier combination. (2) The method learns the parameters directly from Wikipedia so no additional hand-labeled data and training is needed. (3) We combine the global hyperlink structure of Wikipedia with a local bag-of-words probabilistic model in an intuitive and complementary way. (4) The absence of training allows for robust results in out-of-domain scenarios.

The evaluation of NED is fragmented, with several popular shared tasks, such as TAC-KBP[1], ERD[2] or NEEL[3]. Other evaluation datasets include AIDA and KORE50[4], which are very common in NED evaluation. Note that each dataset poses different problems. For instance AIDA is composed of news, and systems need to disambiguate all occurring mentions. TAC includes news and discussion forums, and focuses on a large number of mentions for a handful of challenging strings. KORE includes short sentences with very ambiguous mentions. Unfortunately, there is no standard dataset, and many contributions in this area report results in just one or two datasets. We report our results on eight datasets, improving the state-of-the-art results on five.

2 Resources

The knowledge used by our Bayesian network comes from Wikipedia. We extract three informa-

[1] http://www.nist.gov/tac/2014/KBP/
[2] http://web-ngram.research.microsoft.com/erd2014/
[3] http://www.scc.lancs.ac.uk/microposts2015/challenge/index.html
[4] http://www.mpi-inf.mpg.de/departments/databases-and-information-systems/research/yago-naga/aida/downloads/

*Proceedings of the Fourth Joint Conference on Lexical and Computational Semantics (*SEM 2015)*, pages 101–105,
Denver, Colorado, June 4–5, 2015.

tion resources to perform the disambiguation: a dictionary, textual contexts and a graph.

The dictionary is an association between strings and Wikipedia articles. We construct the dictionary using article titles, redirections, disambiguation pages, and anchor text. If the mention links to a disambiguation page, it is associated with all possible articles the disambiguation page points to. Each association between a string and article is scored with the prior probability, estimated as the number of times that the mention occurs in the anchor text of an article divided by the total number of occurrences of the mention. We choose candidate entities for disambiguation by just assigning all entities linked to the mention in the dictionary.

In addition we build a graph using the Wikipedia link structure, where entities are nodes and edges are anchor links among entities from Wikipedia. We used the third-party dictionary and graph described in (Agirre et al., 2015), which is publicly available[5].

Finally, we extract textual contexts for all the possible candidate entities from a Wikipedia dump. We collect all the anchors including a link to each entity in Wikipedia, and extract a context of 50 words around the anchor link.

3 A Generative Bayesian Network

Given a mention s occurring in context c, our system ranks each of the candidate entities e. Figure 1 shows the dependencies among the different variables. Note that context probability is given by two different resources.

Candidate entities are ranked combining evidences from 4 different probability distributions, which we call entity knowledge $P(e)$, name knowledge $P(s|e)$, context knowledge $P(c_{\text{bow}}|e)$ and graph knowledge $P(c_{\text{grf}}|e)$ respectively.

Entity knowledge $P(e)$ represents the probability of generating entity e, and is estimated as follows:

$$P(e) = \frac{Count(e) + 1}{|M| + N}$$

where $Count(e)$ describes the entity popularity, e.g., the number of times the entity e is referenced within Wikipedia, $|M|$ is the number of entity mentions and N is the total number of entities

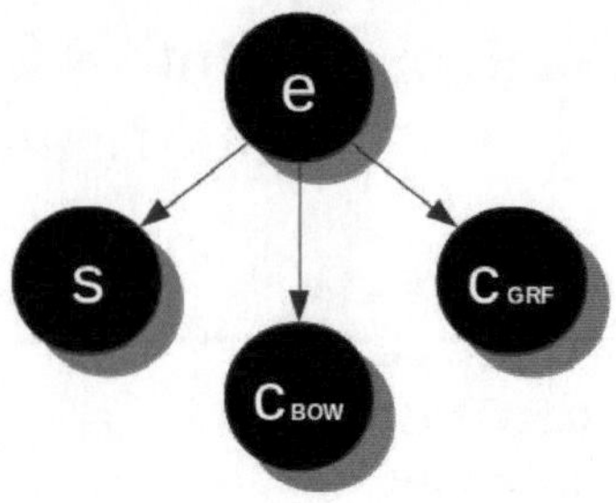

Figure 1: Dependencies among variables in a Bayesian network. The network gives as a result this formula: $P(s, c_{\text{bow}}, c_{\text{grf}}, e) = P(e)P(s|e)P(c_{\text{bow}}|e)P(c_{\text{grf}}|e)$.

in Wikipedia. As can be seen, the estimation is smoothed using the *add-one* method.

Name knowledge $P(s|e)$ represents the probability of generating a particular string s given the entity e, and is estimated as follows:

$$P(s|e) = \frac{Count(e, s) + 1}{Count(e) + S}$$

where $Count(e, s)$ is the number of times mention s is used to refer entity e and S is the number of different possible names used to refer to e.

The context knowledge is modeled in two different ways. In the bag-of-words model, $P(c_{\text{bow}}|e)$ represents the probability of generating context $c = \{w_1, w_2, \ldots, w_n\}$ given the entity e, and is estimated as follows:

$$P(c_{\text{bow}}|e) = P_{\text{e}}(w_1)P_{\text{e}}(w_2)...P_{\text{e}}(w_n)$$

where $P_{\text{e}}(w)$ is estimated as:

$$P_{\text{e}}(w) = \lambda P'_{\text{e}}(w) + (1 - \lambda)P_w(w)$$

$P'_{\text{e}}(w)$ is the maximum likelihood estimation of each word w in the context of e entity. Context words are smoothed by $P_w(w)$ that is the likelihood of words in the whole Wikipedia. λ parameter is set to 0.9 according to development experiments done in Aida development set (also known as Aida test-a).

The graph knowledge is estimated using personalized Pagerank. We used the probabilities returned by UKB[6] (Agirre et al., 2015). This software returns $P(e|c_{\text{grf}})$[7] the probability of visiting a candidate entity when performing a random walk on the

[5] http://ixa2.si.ehu.eus/ukb/ukb-wiki.tar.bz2

[6] http://ixa2.si.ehu.es/ukb/

[7] Note that, contrary to us, the results in (Agirre et al., 2015) multiply the Pagerank probability with the prior.

Wikipedia graph starting in the entity mentions in the context. In order to introduce it in the generative model, we must first convert it to $P(c_{\text{grf}}|e)$. We use Bayes' formula to estimate the probability:

$$P(c_{\text{grf}}|e) = P(e|c_{\text{grf}})P(c_{\text{grf}})/P(e)$$

Finally, the *Full Model* combines all evidences to find the entity that maximizes the following formula:

$$e = \arg\max_e P(s, c_{\text{bow}}, c_{\text{grf}}, e) = \\ \arg\max_e P(e)P(s|e)P(c_{\text{bow}}|e)P(c_{\text{grf}}|e)$$

4 Experiments

We tested our algorithms on a wide range of datasets: AIDA CoNLL-YAGO test-b (Hoffart et al., 2011), KORE50 (Hoffart et al., 2012) and six TAC-KBP[8] datasets corresponding to six years of the competition (Aida, Kore and Tac hereafter). No corpus was used for training the parameters of the system, apart from Wikipedia, as explained in the previous sections.

We used gold-standard mentions and we evaluated only those mentions linked to a Wikipedia entity (ignoring so-called NIL cases). Depending on the dataset, we used the customary evaluation measure: micro-accuracy (Aida, Kore, Tac09 and Tac10) or Bcubed+ (Tac11, Tac12, Tac13 and Tac14)[9].

Each gold standard uses a different Wikipedia version: 2010 for Aida and Kore, 2008 for Tac. We use the Wikipedia dump from 25-5-2011 to build our resources, as this is close to the versions used at the time. We mapped gold-standard entities to 2011 Wikipedia automatically, using redirects in the 2011 Wikipedia. This mapping could cause a small degradation of our results.

4.1 Results

The top 4 rows in table 1 show the performance of the different combinations among probabilities. The remaining row shows the best results reported to date on those datasets (see caption for details).

The results suggest that each probability contributes to the final score of the *Full Model*, shown on row 4, showing that both context models are complementary between each other[10]. The only exception is Tac13, where the bow model is best.

Our system obtains very good results in all datasets, excelling in Tac09-10-11-12-13, where it beats the state-of-the-art. The figures obtained by the *Full Model* on Aida, Kore and Tac14 are close to the best results. Note that the table shows the results of the system reporting the best values for each dataset, that is, our system is compared not to one single system but to all those systems. For example, (Hoffart et al., 2012) reported lower figures for Kore, 64.58. Regarding the results for TAC-KBP, the full task includes linking to the Knowledge Base and detecting and clustering NIL mentions. In order to make results comparable to those for in Aida and Kore, the table reports the results for mentions which are linked to the Knowledge Base, that is, results where NIL mentions are discarded.

5 Adjusting the model to the data

We experimented with weighting the probabilities to adapt the *Full Model* mentioned above to a specific scenario. For the *Weighted Full Model*, we introduce the α, β, γ and δ parameters[11] as follows:

$$e = \arg\max_e P(s, c_{\text{bow}}, c_{\text{grf}}, e) = \\ \arg\max_e P(e)^{\alpha}P(s|e)^{\beta}P(c_{\text{bow}}|e)^{\gamma}P(c_{\text{grf}}|e)^{\delta}$$

Weighting may change the optimal configuration for λ, we thus optimized all parameters on the development set of Aida, yielding $\lambda = 0.8$, $\alpha = 0.2$, $\beta = 0.1$, $\gamma = 0.6$ and $\delta = 0.1$ performing a exhaustive grid search. The step size used in this experiment is 0.1. The parameters yielded high results for development, up to 82.88.

Table 2 summarizes the results of the *Weighted Full Model* for Aida, showing that model reaches 83.61 points, close to the best micro accuracy reported by (Houlsby and Ciaramita, 2014) and above those reported by (Hoffart et al., 2011; Moro et al., 2014). The values of (Hoffart et al., 2011) and (Moro et al., 2014) for Aida are, respectively,

[8] `http://www.nist.gov/tac/publications/index.html`

[9] Note that Tac14 results correspond to the so-called Diagnostic Entity Linking task.

[10] The results of our combination involving the UKB software are not comparable to those reported by (Agirre et al., 2015), due to the different formulation of the probability distribution which involves the prior.

[11] $\alpha + \beta + \gamma + \delta = 1$

Test	Aida	Kore	Tac09	Tac10	Tac11	Tac12	Tac13	Tac14
$P(e)P(s\|e)$	67.51	36.11	67.46	76.76	68.09	46.34	68.20	62.51
$P(e)P(s\|e)P(c_{\text{bow}}\|e)$	75.41	60.42	78.39	85.29*	76.24	57.80	**76.34***	71.62
$P(e)P(s\|e)P(c_{\text{grf}}\|e)$	76.97	54.86	79.64*	83.63*	79.55	69.93*	71.67	71.56
$P(e)P(s\|e)P(c_{\text{bow}}\|e)P(c_{\text{grf}}\|e)$	**82.45**	**70.14**	**82.15***	**85.49***	**81.53***	**71.94***	74.92*	**76.34**
Best (state-of-the-art)	84.89	71.50	79.00	80.60	80.10	68.50	71.80	79.60

Table 1: Bold marks the best value among probability combinations, and * those results that overcome the best value reported in the state-of-the-art: (Houlsby and Ciaramita, 2014) for Aida, (Moro et al., 2014) for Kore, (Han and Sun, 2011) for Tac09 and see TAC-KBP proceedings for the rest[8].

Test	Aida
$P(e)P(s\|e)P(c_{\text{bow}}\|e)P(c_{\text{grf}}\|e)$	82.45
$P(e)^{\alpha}P(s\|e)^{\beta}P(c_{\text{bow}}\|e)^{\gamma}P(c_{\text{grf}}\|e)^{\delta}$	83.61
(Hoffart et al., 2011)	82.54
(Houlsby and Ciaramita, 2014)	84.89
(Moro et al., 2014)	82.10

Table 2: Micro accuracy results for Aida introducing the *Weighted Full Model* in row 2.

82.54[12] and 82.10. Unfortunately the parameter distribution seems to depend on the test dataset, as the same parameters failed to improve the results on the other datasets.

6 Related Work

The use of Wikipedia for named entity disambiguation is a common approach in this area. In the related field of Wikification, (Ratinov et al., 2011) introduced the supervised combination of a large number of global and local similarity measures. They learn weights for each of those measures training a supervised classifier on Wikipedia. Our approach is different in that we just combine four intuitive methods, without having to learn weights for them. Unfortunately they don't report results for NED.

(Moro et al., 2014) present a complex graph-based approach for NED and Word Sense Disambiguation which works on BabelNet, a complex combination of several resources including, among others, Wikipedia, WordNet and Wiktionary. Our results are stronger over Aida, but not on the smaller Kore.

(Hoffart et al., 2011) presents a robust method based on entity popularity and similarity measures, which are used to build a mention/entity graph. They include external knowledge from Yago, and train a classifier on the train part of Aida, obtaining results comparable to ours. Given that we do not train on in-domain training corpora, we think our system is more robust.

The use of probabilistic models using Wikipedia for NED was introduced in (Han and Sun, 2011). In this paper, we extend the model with a global model which takes the hyperlink structure of Wikipedia into account.

(Houlsby and Ciaramita, 2014) presents a probabilistic method using topic models, where topics are associated to Wikipedia articles. They present strong results, but they need to initialize the sampler on another NED system, Tagme (Ferragina and Scaiella, 2012). In some sense they also combine the knowledge in the graph with that of a local algorithm (Tagme), so their work is complementary to ours. They only provide results on AIDA, and it is thus not possible to see whether they are as robust as our algorithm.

7 Conclusions and future work

Bayesian networks provide a principled method to combine knowledge sources. In this paper we combine popularity, name knowledge and two methods to model context: bag-of-words context, and hyperlink graph. The combination outperforms the state-of-the-art in five out of eight datasets, showing the robustness of the system in different domain

[12]Note that values by (Hoffart et al., 2011) were reported on a subset of Aida. The micro accuracy results reported in our table correspond to the latest best model from the Aida web site: `http://www.mpi-inf.mpg.de/departments/databases-and-information-systems/research/yago-naga/aida/`.

and dataset types. Our results also show that in all but one dataset the combination outperforms individual models, indicating that bag-or-word context and graph context are complementary. We show that results can be further improved when tuning the weights on in-domain development corpora.

Given that Bayesian networks can be further extended, we are exploring to introduce additional models of context into a Markov Random Field algorithm. Our current model assumes that the two models of context (bag or words and graph) are independent given e, and we would like to explore alternatives to relax this assumption. We would also like to explore whether more sophisticated smoothing techniques could improve our probability estimates.

Acknowledgments

We thank the reviewers for their suggestions. This work was partially funded by MINECO (CHIST-ERA READERS project – PCIN-2013-002-C02-01, and SKaTeR project – TIN2012-38584-C06-02), and the European Commission (QTLEAP – FP7-ICT-2013.4.1-610516). The IXA group is funded by the Basque Government (A type Research Group). Ander Barrena enjoys an PhD scholarship from the Basque Government.

References

E. Agirre, A. Barrena, and A. Soroa. 2015. Studying the Wikipedia Hyperlink Graph for Relatedness and Disambiguation. *ArXiv e-prints*, March.

Paolo Ferragina and Ugo Scaiella. 2012. Fast and accurate annotation of short texts with wikipedia pages. *IEEE Software*, 29(1):70–75.

X. Han and L. Sun. 2011. A Generative Entity-mention Model for Linking Entities with Knowledge Base. In *Proceedings of the 49th Annual Meeting of the Association for Computational Linguistics: Human Language Technologies*, volume 1, pages 945–954.

J. Hoffart, M.A. Yosef, I. Bordino, H. Fürstenau, M. Pinkal, M. Spaniol, B. Taneva, S. Thater, and G. Weikum. 2011. Robust Disambiguation of Named Entities in Text. In *Conference on Empirical Methods in Natural Language Processing, Edinburgh, Scotland, United Kingdom 2011*, pages 782–792.

Johannes Hoffart, Stephan Seufert, Dat Ba Nguyen, Martin Theobald, and Gerhard Weikum. 2012. Kore: Keyphrase overlap relatedness for entity disambiguation. In *Proceedings of the 21st ACM international conference on Information and knowledge management*, page 545554.

Neil Houlsby and Massimiliano Ciaramita. 2014. A scalable gibbs sampler for probabilistic entity linking. In Maarten de Rijke, Tom Kenter, ArjenP. de Vries, ChengXiang Zhai, Franciska de Jong, Kira Radinsky, and Katja Hofmann, editors, *Advances in Information Retrieval*, volume 8416 of *Lecture Notes in Computer Science*, pages 335–346. Springer International Publishing.

Andrea Moro, Alessandro Raganato, and Roberto Navigli. 2014. Entity linking meets word sense disambiguation: a unied approach. *Transactions of the Association of Computational Linguistics*, 2:231–244, May.

L.A. Ratinov, D. Roth, D. Downey, and M. Anderson. 2011. Local and Global Algorithms for Disambiguation to Wikipedia. In *The 49th Annual Meeting of the Association for Computational Linguistics: Human Language Technologies, Proceedings of the Conference, 19-24 June, 2011, Portland, Oregon, USA*, pages 1375–1384. The Association for Computer Linguistics.

Collective Document Classification with Implicit Inter-document Semantic Relationships

Clinton Burford, Steven Bird and **Timothy Baldwin**
Department of Computing and Information Systems
The University of Melbourne, VIC 3010, Australia
clint@burford.co sbird@unimelb.edu.au tb@ldwin.net

Abstract

This paper addresses the question of how document classifiers can exploit implicit information about document similarity to improve document classifier accuracy. We infer document similarity using simple n-gram overlap, and demonstrate that this improves overall document classification performance over two datasets. As part of this, we find that collective classification based on simple iterative classifiers outperforms the more complex and computationally-intensive dual classifier approach.

1 Introduction

In machine learning, there is a rich tradition of research into the two tasks of: (1) "point-wise" classification, where each instance is represented as an independent instance, and the predictive model attempts to learn a decision boundary to capture instances of a given class; and (2) graphical learning and inference, where instances are connected in a graph, and learning/inference take place relative to the graph structure connecting those instances, based primarily on either conditional dependence (i.e. one event is dependent on the outcome of another) or "homophily" (i.e. the tendency for connected instances to share various properties).[1] Various joint models that combine the two have also been proposed, although in natural language processing at least, these have focused largely on conditional dependence, in the form of models such as hidden Markov models (Rabiner and Juang, 1986) and conditional random fields (Lafferty et al., 2001), where independent properties of words, e.g., are combined with conditional dependencies based on their context of use to jointly predict the senses of all words in a given sentence (Ciaramita and Johnson, 2003; Johannsen et al., 2014).

This paper explores the utility of homophily within joint models for document-level semantic classification, focusing specifically on tasks which are not associated with any explicit graph structure. That is, we examine whether *implicit* semantic document links can improve the results of a point-wise (content-based) classification approach.

Explicit inter-document links have been variously shown to improve document classifier performance, based on information sources including hyperlinks in web documents (Slattery and Craven, 1998; Oh et al., 2000; Yang et al., 2002), direct name-references in congressional debates (Thomas et al., 2006; Burfoot et al., 2011; Stoyanov and Eisner, 2012), citations in scientific papers (Giles et al., 1998; Lu and Getoor, 2003; McDowell et al., 2007), and user mentions or retweets in social media (Jiang et al., 2011; Tan et al., 2011). However, document collections often don't contain explicit inter-document links, limiting the practical usefulness of such methods. In this paper, we seek to expand the reach of research which incorporates linking information, in inducing implicit linking information between documents, and demonstrating that the resultant (noisy) network structure improves document classification accuracy.

The intuition underlying this work is that some types of documents have features which are either absent or ambiguous in training data, but which have

[1] In some tasks, it can also indicate heterophily, i.e. the tendency for connected instances to have contrasting properties, as we shall see for one of our two dataset.

*Proceedings of the Fourth Joint Conference on Lexical and Computational Semantics (*SEM 2015)*, pages 106–116,
Denver, Colorado, June 4–5, 2015.

the special characteristic of indicating relationships between the labels of documents. Most often, an inter-document relationship indicates that two documents have the same label, but depending of the task, it may also indicate that they have different labels. In either case, classifiers gain an advantage if they can consider these features as well as conventional content-based features.

The major contribution of this paper is in showing that document classification accuracy can be improved over a range of datasets using automatically-induced implicit semantic inter-document links, using collective classification. We are the first to achieve this using a general-purpose setup, as applied to a range of datasets. Our results are achieved using n-gram overlap features for both the CONVOTE and BITTERLEMONS corpora, without the use of annotations for explicit semantic inter-document relationships. A second contribution of this work is the finding that simple iterative classifiers outperform more complex dual classifiers when using implicit inter-document links. This finding contradicts earlier work using *explicit* document links, where the dual classifier approach has generally been found to perform best (Thomas et al., 2006; Burfoot et al., 2011). While the work presented here is conceptually quite simple, the findings are significant and potentially open the door to accuracy improvements on a range of document-level semantic tasks.

2 Related Work

Previous work has dealt with the question of collective document classification using implicit inter-document relationships in two basic ways:

1. **proximity**: use a spatial or temporal dimension of the domain to relate documents (Agrawal et al., 2003; Goldberg et al., 2007; McDowell et al., 2009; Somasundaran et al., 2009).

2. **similarity**: relate documents via some notion of their content-based similarity (Blum and Chawla, 2001; Joachims, 2003; Takamura et al., 2007; Sindhwani and Melville, 2008; Jurgens, 2013)

The work using similarity-based links is the closest to ours but is also strongly differentiated because it focuses on transductive semi-supervised classification. That task begins with the premise that only a small amount of labelled training data is available, so content-only classification is likely to be inaccurate. By contrast, the supervised techniques in this paper deal with large amounts of labelled training data and relatively high content-only performance – 76% for CONVOTE and 87% for BITTERLEMONS. It is reasonable to assume that the types of similarity-based relationships derived for transductive semi-supervised classification would be ineffective in a supervised context.

This conclusion is supported by an experiment that shows that the vocabularies of document pairs tend to overlap to similar degrees regardless of document class (Pang and Lee, 2005).

3 Corpora

We experiment with two corpora in this research: CONVOTE and BITTERLEMONS. These two are selected on the grounds that they satisfy two intuitive criteria about types of text collections that may contain features that are not useful for content-only classification, but which may indicate relationships between pairs of documents: (1) the corpora both use an unconstrained prose vocabulary, which increases the likelihood that authors will use distinctive words or sequences of words that are not frequent enough to be useful in training, but which can be used to semantically relate pairs of documents (c.f. newswire articles); and (2) the majority of the text content in both corpora is clearly relevant to the dimension of classification, i.e. there is minimal use of "boilerplate" or "background" material, so the pool from which to select task-relevant content to form inter-document semantic relationships is larger.

3.1 CONVOTE

CONVOTE (Thomas et al., 2006) consists of US congressional speeches relating to a specific bill or resolution, and the ultimate vote of each speaker ("for" or "against"). The document classifier uses the text of each speech to predict the vote of the speaker. Three modifications are made to the corpus: (1) speeches by the same speaker are concatenated, to more naturally represent the requirement that each speaker only has one vote; (2) we drop

	Total
Tokens	1.2M
Speeches	1699
Debates	53
Average speakers/speeches per debate	32
Average tokens per speech	735
Proportion of FOR speeches	49%

Table 1: Corpus statistics for CONVOTE.

	Total
Tokens	0.5M
Articles	594
Topics	149
Average articles per topic	4
Average tokens per article	843
Percentage of ISRAELI speeches	50%

Table 2: Corpus statistics for BITTERLEMONS.

the fixed train, test, development set assignments from the original dataset, and instead evaluate using leave-one-out cross-validation over the 53 debates contained in the dataset, to allow for a more statistically robust evaluation; and (3) we discard the manually annotated inter-document relationships based on references to speaker names, because implicit relationships are the focus of this work.

Table 1 gives statistics for our rendering of CONVOTE. The identical figures for the average number of speeches and speakers per debate reflect the fact that each speaker now contributes only one unified speech.

3.2 BITTERLEMONS

BITTERLEMONS (Lin et al., 2006) is a collection of articles on the Israeli–Arab conflict harvested from the Bitterlemons website.[2] In each weekly issue, the editors contribute an article giving their perspectives on some aspect of the conflict, and two guest authors contribute articles, one from an Israeli perspective and the other from a Palestinian perspective. Sometimes these guest contributions take the form of an interview, in which case we remove the questions (from the editors) and retain only the answers.

The statistics in Table 2 give a picture of the size and structure of BITTERLEMONS.

In accordance with Lin et al. (2006), we experiment with heldout evaluation, with all articles contributed by the editors placed in the training set and those contributed by the guests in the test set. This allows the task to be framed as "perspective" classification, rather than author attribution, i.e. we are focused on the content of the contributions rather than stylistic or biographical features that may identify one editor or the other.

4 Implicit Inter-document Similarity

To implement the hypothesis that documents that use the same rare word or sequence of words are more likely to carry the same label, we calculate a cosine similarity metric between every pairing of documents in a given corpus, using an idf-weighted term vector used to represent document d_i. The idf weighting serves to emphasise terms that are rare within the corpus, and de-emphasise terms that are common. To further enhance this effect, we represent terms by existence-based rather than frequency-based features.

An example of a (tokenised) high-idf sentence pair from CONVOTE is (with the speaker, party affiliation and vote shown in each case, and the high-idf token underlined):

(1) the president s top counselor dan bartlett said this week that there is no magic <u>wand</u> to reduce gas prices . [CROWLEY, JOE (D); AGAINST]

(2) mr. chairman , yesterday the president said , i wish i could simply wave a magic <u>wand</u> and lower gas prices tomorrow. [EMANUEL, RAHM (D); AGAINST]

An example for BITTERLEMONS is:

(3) Even if we /wanted/ to <u>succumb</u> to Israeli pressure, it is impossible to make a Palestinian teach his child that Jaffa or Haifa or Palestine

[2] http:/www.bitterlemons.org/

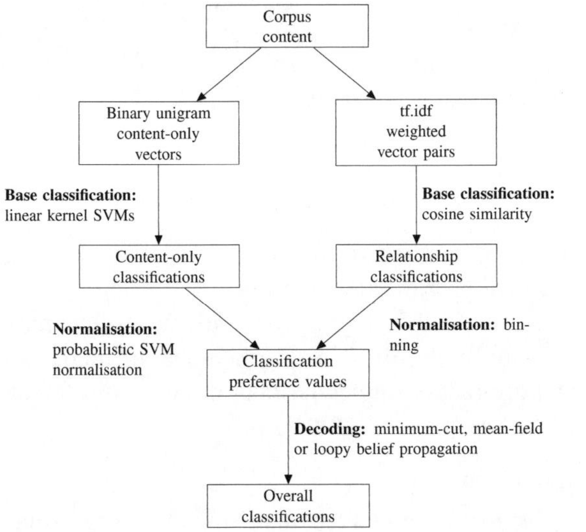

Figure 1: Dual classifier with similarity-based links.

before 1948 was not his land. [AHMAD HARB (GUEST); PALESTINIAN]

(4) This is being neglected and Sharon is having his way in brutalizing the Palestinian people in the hope that they will <u>succumb</u> and abandon their rights. [HAIDAR ABDEL SHAFI (GUEST); PALESTINIAN]

For other examples and more justification of this methodology, see Burford (2013).

5 Collective Classification

Two standard approaches to collective classification are: (1) the dual classifier approach; and (2) the iterative classifier approach. We briefly review these approaches below, but refer the reader to Sen et al. (2008), McDowell et al. (2009) and Burford (2013) for a more detailed methodological discussion.

5.1 Dual Classifier Approach

The dual classifier approach is made up of three steps, as depicted in Figure 1:

1. **Base classification:** Produce base classifications using (1) a **content-only classifier**; and (2) a **relationship classifier**. The content-only classifier makes a binary prediction: FOR and AGAINST for CONVOTE, and ISRAELI or PALESTINIAN for BITTERLEMONS. The relationship classifier indicates the preference that each document pair be SAME or not ($\overline{\text{SAME}}$).

2. **Normalisation:** Normalise the scores, producing values for the classification preference functions, ψ_i, which can be input into a collective classification algorithm.

3. **Decoding:** Produce final classifications by optimally decoding the content-only and relationship level preferences using a collective classification algorithm.

5.1.1 Base classification

For our content-only base classifier, we use the same bag-of-words SVM with binary (existence-based) unigram features as (Thomas et al., 2006). This classifier has been shown to be the best bag-of-words model for BITTERLEMONS (Beigman Klebanov et al., 2010). As our relationship base classifier, we use the cosine similarity scores described above, calculated using n-grams of several different lengths.

5.1.2 Normalisation

We use probabilistic SVM normalisation to convert the signed decision-plane distance output by the content-only classifier into the probability that the instance is in the positive class (Platt, 1999).

For the relationship classifier, the technique used to convert the cosine similarity score into a classification preference needs to fit complex criteria. Preliminary experiments suggested that while the very highest similarity scores are good indicators of SAME relationships, classifier precision drops quickly as recall increases. To avoid polluting the classification graph with large numbers of low-quality links, the normalisation method should incorporate a threshold that discards a significant proportion of the test set pairs. We adopt the following binning technique to convert the cosine similarity score into a probability that the two instances are

SAME:

$$\psi_{ij}(l,l) = \begin{cases} 0.9 & s(i,j) \geq b_1; \\ 0.8 & b_2 \leq s(i,j) < b_1; \\ 0.7 & b_3 \leq s(i,j) < b_2; \\ 0.6 & b_4 \leq s(i,j) < b_3; \\ 0.5 & s(i,j) < b_4; \end{cases}$$

where $\psi_{ij}(l,l)$ represents the SAME preference (i.e. the probability of i and j having the same label); the values for b_1, b_2, b_3, and b_4 are derived by sorting the relationships in the training data by similarity score, and separating them into intervals holding a proportion of SAME pairs equivalent to the nominated probability. This approach is similar to unsupervised discretisation (Kotsiantis and Kanellopoulos, 2006), except the intervals are arranged so that the output categories have a probabilistic interpretation.

5.1.3 Decoding

Decoding is carried out using three techniques: (1) loopy belief propagation (McDowell et al., 2009); (2) mean-field; and (3) minimum-cut.

Loopy Belief Propagation

Loopy belief propagation is a message passing algorithm that can be expressed as:

$$m_{i \to j}(l) = \alpha \sum_{l' \in L} \left(\psi_i(l')\psi_{ij}(l', l) \prod_{k \in N_i \cap D^U \setminus \{j\}} m_{k \to i}(l') \right)$$

$$b_i(l) = \alpha \psi_i(l) \prod_{k \in N_i \cap D^U} m_{k \to i}(l)$$

where $m_{i \to j}$ is a message sent by document d_i to document d_j, and α is a normalization constant that ensures that each message and each set of marginal probabilities sum to 1. The message flow from d_i to d_j communicates the belief of d_i about the label of d_j. The algorithm proceeds by making each node communicate with its neighbours until the messages stabilise. The marginal probability is then derived by calculating $b_i(l)$.

Loopy belief propagation was used in early collective classification work (Taskar et al., 2002) and has remained popular since (Sen et al., 2008; McDowell et al., 2009; Stoyanov and Eisner, 2012).

Mean-field

Mean-field is an alternative message passing algorithm, that can be expressed as:

$$b_i(l) = \alpha \psi_i(l) \prod_{j \in N_i \cap D} \prod_{l' \in L} \psi_{ij}^{b_i(l')}(l', l)$$

and is re-computed for each document until the marginal probabilities stabilise.

Loopy belief propagation and mean-field have both been justified as variational methods for Markov random fields (Jordan et al., 1999; Weiss, 2001; Yedidia et al., 2005).

Minimum Cut

The minimum-cut technique involves formulating a binary collective classification task as a flow graph and finding solutions using standard methods for solving minimum-cut (maximum-flow) problems.

We use the method described by Blum and Chawla (2001) in an in-sample setting, which is equivalent to finding the optimal solution for the cost function for labellings:

$$cost(Y) = \sum_{d_i \in D} w_i(Y_i) + \sum_{(d_i, d_j) \in E: Y_i \neq Y_j} w^r(d_i, d_j)$$

5.1.4 Tuning

The relative weights given to the content-only and relational classifiers can be tuned as follows (for CONVOTE, without loss of generality):

$$\psi'_i(\text{FOR}) = \psi_i(\text{FOR}) + \frac{\min(0,\gamma)(\psi_i(\text{FOR}) - \psi_i(\text{AGAINST}))}{2}$$

$$\psi'_{ij}(\text{FOR}, \text{FOR}) = \psi_{ij}(\text{FOR}, \text{FOR}) - \frac{\max(0,\gamma)(\psi_{ij}(\text{FOR},\text{FOR}) - \psi_{ij}(\text{FOR},\text{AGAINST}))}{2}$$

where ψ'_i and ψ'_{ij} refer to the dampened versions of the content-only and relationship preference functions, respectively, γ is the dampening parameter $\in [-1, 1]$, $\psi'_i(\text{AGAINST}) = 1 - \psi'_i(\text{FOR})$, $\psi'_{ij}(\text{AGAINST}, \text{AGAINST}) = \psi'_{ij}(\text{FOR}, \text{FOR})$, and $\psi'_{ij}(\text{FOR}, \text{AGAINST}) = \psi'_{ij}(\text{AGAINST}, \text{FOR}) = 1 - \psi'_{ij}(\text{FOR}, \text{FOR})$.

This approach works by reducing the difference between the preferences for the two classes (FOR or AGAINST) by an amount that is proportional to the

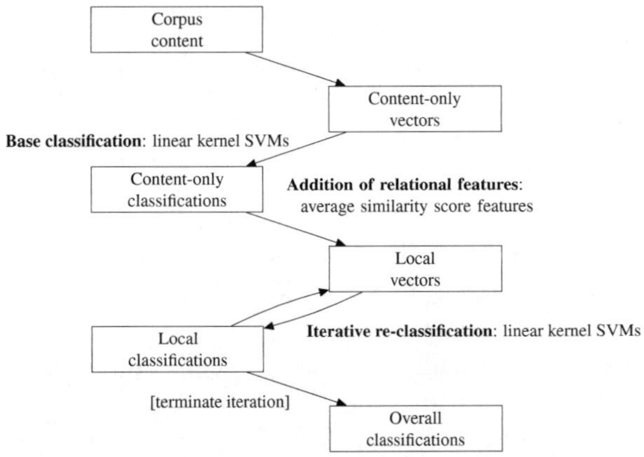

Figure 2: Iterative classifier approach with similarity-based relational features.

absolute value of the dampening parameter. If the dampening parameter is < 0, only the content-only preferences will be dampened (giving more relative weight to relationship preferences). If the dampening parameter is > 0, only the relationship preferences will be dampened (giving more relative weight to the content-only preferences).

For CONVOTE, the training fold is adapted for tuning by use of 52-fold cross-validation, where each of the 52 debates in the training fold is classified using all of the other debates as training data. BITTERLEMONS does not have internal structure within the training set, so it cannot be adapted in this way. Instead, we use leave-one-out cross-validation over the training set. Unfortunately this approach carries the risk of producing base classifications that are unrealistically accurate, because the training set is composed of articles by only two authors.

5.2 Iterative Classifier Approach

The iterative classifier approach has three major components, as depicted in Figure 2:

1. **Base classification**. Produce base classifications using a content-only classifier. As with the dual classifier approach, the content-only classifier will give the preference that each instance be classified with FOR or AGAINST for CONVOTE, and ISRAELI or PALESTINIAN for BITTERLEMONS.
2. **Addition of relational features**. Produce local vectors by adding relational features to the vectors previously used for content-only classification.
3. **Iterative re-classification**. Use a local classifier to classify the new feature vectors. Update the relational features after each iteration to reflect new class assignments. Repeat until class assignments stabilise or a threshold number of iterations is met.

5.2.1 Base Classification

Once again, content-only classification for the iterative classifier is performed using a bag-of-words SVM with binary unigram features.

5.2.2 Relational Features

Let, f^s be an average similarity score:

$$f^s(i,l) = \frac{\sum_{d_j \in D \setminus \{d_i\}} s(i,j)\delta_{Y_j,l}}{\sum_{d_j \in D \setminus \{d_i\}} \delta_{Y_j,l}} \quad (5)$$

where δ is the Kronecker delta. Put in words, f^s is the average of the similarity scores for the pairings of the given instance with each of the instances that have the label l.

We derive relational features for the iterative classifier from the average similarity score as follows:

$$f^{as}(i,l) = \begin{cases} 1 & f^s(i,l) > f^s(i,l'); \\ 0 & \text{otherwise.} \end{cases}$$

This means that the feature $f^{as}(i,l)$ is set to 1 iff the average similarity of document d_i to instances with label l is greater than its average similarity to instances with label l'. In training, document labels are used when counting negative and positive instances to determine the values for f^{as}. In evaluation, the classes assigned in the previous iteration are used.

6 Experiments

We assess the accuracy of the dual classifier and iterative classifier approaches described above over CONVOTE and BITTERLEMONS in terms of classification accuracy, micro-averaging across the 53 folds of cross-validation in the case of CONVOTE. When quoted, statistical significance has been determined

Type	Description	n-gram size				
		1	2	3	4	5
Baseline	Majority	51.44	51.44	51.44	51.44	51.44
Baseline	Content-only	76.40	76.40	76.40	76.40	76.40
Dual	Cosine similarity, min-cut	75.22	77.22⋆	76.52	77.28⋆	77.46⋆
Dual	Cosine similarity, loopy belief	75.10	74.99	75.10	75.46	76.16
Dual	Cosine similarity, mean-field	75.10	74.99	75.10	75.46	76.63
Iterative	Average similarity score	77.99⋆	78.10⋆	78.81⋆	**79.05**⋆	78.16⋆

Table 3: Collective classification performance on CONVOTE (⋆ signifies a statistically significant improvement over the content-only baseline, $p < 0.05$).

Type	Description	n-gram size				
		1	2	3	4	5
Baseline	Majority	49.83	49.83	49.83	49.83	49.83
Baseline	Content-only	86.53	86.53	86.53	86.53	86.53
Dual	Cosine similarity, min-cut	87.88	88.55⋆	88.89⋆	89.90⋆	90.57⋆
Dual	Cosine similarity, loopy belief	87.54	86.87	87.88	87.88	88.55
Dual	Cosine similarity, mean-field	87.54	86.87	87.88	87.88	88.55
Iterative	Average similarity score	87.54	89.90⋆	**90.91**⋆	**90.91**⋆	89.90⋆

Table 4: Collective classification performance on BITTERLEMONS (⋆ signifies a statistically significant improvement over the content-only baseline, $p < 0.05$).

using approximate randomisation with $p < 0.05$ (Nooreen, 1989).

Two baseline scores are shown in the tables for collective classification results: (1) "Majority" gives the performance of the simplest possible classifier, which classifies every instance with the label that is most frequent in training data; and (2) "Content-only" gives the performance of the bag-of-words linear-kernel SVM used to perform base classification.

6.1 Collective Classifier Performance

Table 3 shows the overall collective classifier performance on CONVOTE. The best performer is the iterative classifier with 4-grams, with an accuracy of 79.05%. This is a statistically significant 2.65% absolute gain over the content-only baseline. The iterative classifier is the best performer in general, obtaining the next four best results with statistically significant absolute gains of 2.41%, 1.76%, 1.70% and 1.59% for 3-grams, 5-grams, 2-grams and 1-grams respectively.

The dual classifier with minimum-cut is the next best performer, with a best score of 77.45% for 5-grams, a statistically significant absolute gain of 1.06%. 4-grams and 2-grams also provide statistically significant gains, but 3-grams and 1-grams do not.

For loopy-belief and mean-field the story is less positive. None of the variations gives a statistically significant improvement over the content-only baseline. The best performer is mean-field with 5-grams, with a score of 76.63, a 0.23% absolute improvement over the baseline.

Table 4 shows overall collective classifier performance on BITTERLEMONS. As with CONVOTE, the best performer is the iterative classifier. 4-grams and 3-grams are the top-performing variants, obtaining a score of 90.91%, a statistically significant 4.38% absolute gain over the content-only baseline. 2-grams and 5-grams are the next best, with a statistically significant 3.37% absolute gain over the content-only baseline. 1-grams are the only iterative classifier variant that do not yield a statistically significant improvement over the content-only baseline.

The dual classifier results for BITTERLEMONS

warrant special comment. As mentioned in Section 5.1.4, leave-one-out tuning with the BITTERLEMONS training corpus is compromised. The aim of cross-validation on the training set is to gain a picture of likely performance on the test set. Unfortunately, BITTERLEMONS is not homogeneous: articles in each class in the training set are contributed by just one author, whereas articles in the test set are contributed by different authors. Tuning on BITTERLEMONS failed because leave-one-out on the training set produced 100% accuracy, presumably because there are features specific to the two authors that make classification easy. This meant that the ideal dampening parameter was found to be exactly 1, i.e. collective classification was unnecessary, because the expected performance on the test set was 100%.

As with CONVOTE, none of the loopy belief or mean-field variants provide statistically significant improvements over the content-only baseline. The best performers are mean-field and loopy belief with 5-grams, with a score of 88.55%, a 2.02% absolute improvement over the baseline.

6.2 Dual Classifier Dampening Response

We next examine the dampening response of the dual classifier methods, by presenting six graphs showing the performance of the three different decoding algorithms on the two test corpora. This analysis helps to establish a picture of the limitations of the dual classifier approach in comparison with the iterative classifier approach.

Each of the graphs in this section shows the effect of a varying dampening factor on classification accuracy. In each graph only a small portion of the $[-1, 1]$ range supported by the dampening parameter is shown. The reason for this is visible on many of the graphs: performance is fixed at or near 50% until the dampening parameter is close to 1. This indicates that the probabilities of the content-only classifier and relationship classifier are badly mismatched: performance only becomes reasonable after the relationship preferences have been massively reduced in strength relative to the content-only preferences.

Figure 3 shows performance on CONVOTE for minimum-cut, loopy belief, and mean-field respectively. The trend is the same in each: performance is flat until a sudden jump-up, leading to steady improvement up to a peak, shortly before the maximum dampening value of 1. At 1, the relationship preferences are entirely dampened and performance is the same as the content-only baseline.

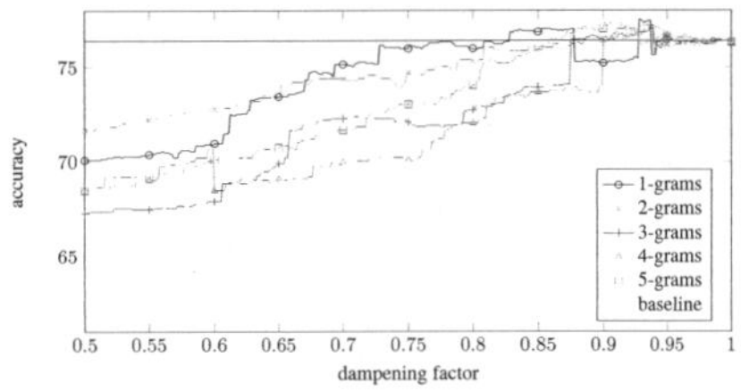

(a) Min-cut

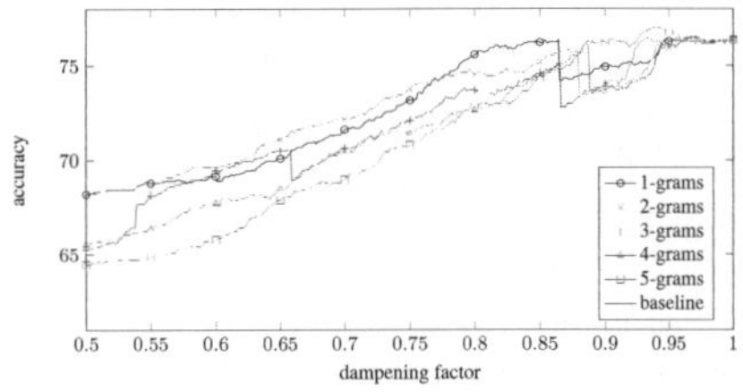

(b) Loopy belief

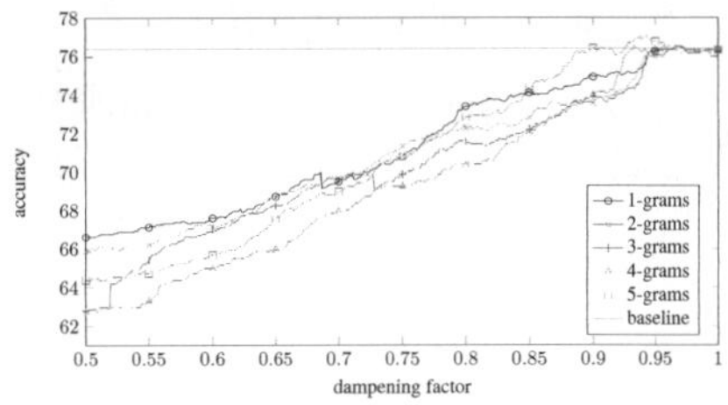

(c) Mean-field

Figure 3: The impact of the dampening factor on dual classifier performance for CONVOTE.

For minimum-cut, 1-grams provide the highest peak accuracy with close to 78% at dampening factor 0.93. Each of the other n-gram orders jumps above the 76.40% baseline at close to this point, with 5-grams providing the most sustained period of high performance from dampening factor 0.85 through to almost 1.

Performance is worse for loopy belief and mean-field. Only 5-grams do better than the baseline, between approximately 0.92 and 0.95 dampening factor for both algorithms.

Figure 4 shows performance on BITTERLEMONS

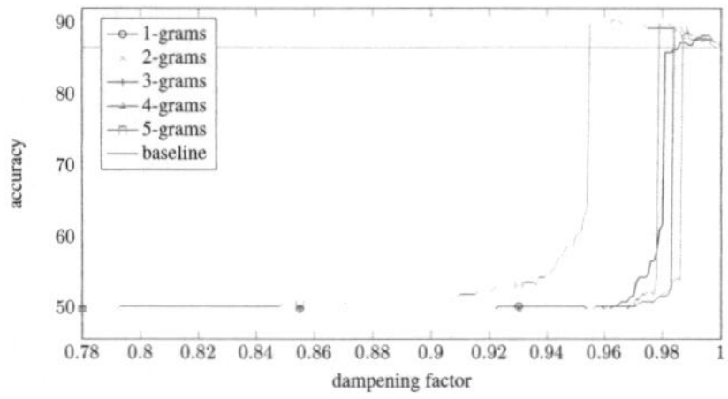

(a) Min-cut

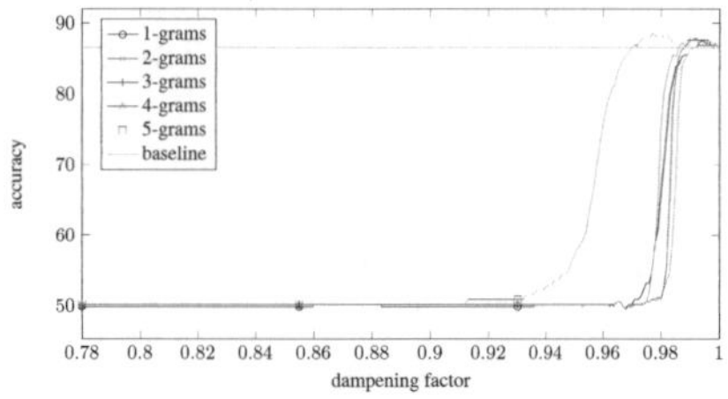

(b) Loopy belief

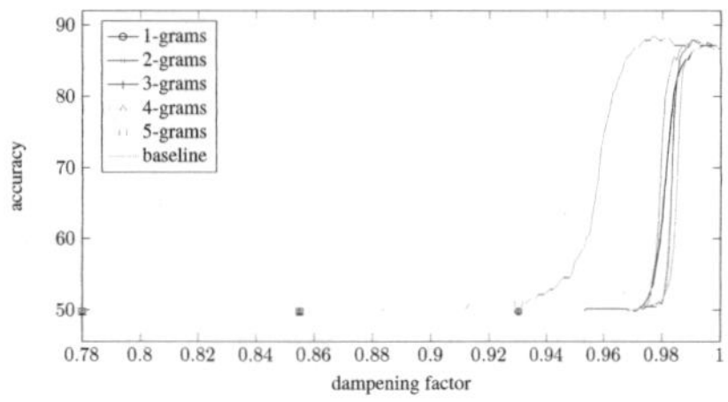

(c) Mean-field

Figure 4: The impact of the dampening factor on dual classifier performance for BITTERLEMONS.

for minimum-cut, loopy belief, and mean-field respectively. The trend is the same: after a period of flat performance, scores steadily improve as the dampening factor is increased, reaching a peak shortly before the maximum dampening value of 1.

For minimum-cut, 5-grams give the best performance with a peak of 90.57% accuracy at dampening factor 0.95. 4-grams do the next best, followed by 3-grams, 2-grams and 1-grams. Each algorithm rises to a sudden peak and then trails off as it approaches maximum dampening. Loopy belief and mean-field give almost identical performance. Both show the same peak-and-trail-off shape as with minimum-cut but the performance gain is smaller, with 5-grams obtaining a best score of 88.55%.

7 Conclusion and Future Work

The collective classification experiments in this paper demonstrate that useful inter-document semantic relationships can be accurately predicted using features based on *matching sequences of words*, i.e. semantic relationships between pairs of documents that can be detected based on the mutual use of particular n-grams. These semantic relationships can be used to build collective classifiers that outperform standard content-based classifiers.

Iterative classifiers do better than dual classifiers at collective classification using similarity-based relationships. Their superiority goes beyond measures of performance: iterative classifiers are simpler to implement, and more efficient. The key advantage of the iterative classifier seems to lie in its ability to sum up relationship information in a single average similarity score.

Future work should consider the combination of the methods investigated in this paper with more advanced content-only approaches. For dual classifiers and iterative classifiers, it would be also interesting to explore whether alternative base classifiers can provide better performance. For example, confidence-weighted linear classification has been shown to be highly effective on non-collective document classification tasks, and could be easily adapted for use in a dual classifier or iterative classifier (Dredze et al., 2008). Finally, there is significant scope to apply the techniques in this paper to other collective classification tasks and to unambiguously define the types of content for which collective document classification with implicit inter-document relationships can be expected to provide performance gains.

Acknowledgements

This research was supported in part by the Australian Research Council.

References

Rakesh Agrawal, Sridhar Rajagopalan, Ramakrishnan Srikant, and Yirong Xu. 2003. Mining newsgroups using networks arising from social behavior. In *Proceedings of the 12th International Conference on World Wide Web*, pages 529–535, Budapest, Hungary.

Beata Beigman Klebanov, Eyal Beigman, and Daniel Diermeier. 2010. Vocabulary choice as an indicator of perspective. In *Proceedings of the 48th Annual Meeting of the Association for Computational Linguistics: Short papers*, pages 253–257, Uppsala, Sweden.

Avrim Blum and Shuchi Chawla. 2001. Learning from labeled and unlabeled data using graph mincuts. In *Proceedings of the 18th International Conference on Machine Learning*, pages 19–26, Williamstown, USA.

Clinton Burfoot, Steven Bird, and Timothy Baldwin. 2011. Collective classification of congressional floor-debate transcripts. In *Proceedings of the 49th Annual Meeting of the Association for Computational Linguistics: Human Language Technologies*, pages 1506–1515, Portland, USA.

Clinton Burford. 2013. *Collective Document Classification Using Explicit and Implicit Inter-document Relationships*. Ph.D. thesis, The University of Melbourne.

Massimiliano Ciaramita and Mark Johnson. 2003. Supersense tagging of unknown nouns in WordNet. In *Proceedings of the 2003 Conference on Empirical Methods in Natural Language Processing*, pages 168–175, Sapporo, Japan.

Mark Dredze, Koby Crammer, and Fernando Pereira. 2008. Confidence-weighted linear classification. In *Proceedings of the 25th International Conference on Machine Learning*, pages 264–271, Helsinki, Finland.

C. Lee Giles, Kurt D. Bollacker, and Steve Lawrence. 1998. Citeseer: an automatic citation indexing system. In *Proceedings of the 3rd ACM Conference on Digital libraries*, pages 89–98, Pittsburgh, USA.

Andrew B. Goldberg, Xiaojin Zhu, and Stephen Wright. 2007. Dissimilarity in graph-based semi-supervised classification. *Journal of Machine Learning Research*, 2:155–162.

Long Jiang, Mo Yu, Ming Zhou, Xiaohua Liu, and Tiejun Zhao. 2011. Target-dependent Twitter sentiment classification. In *Proceedings of the 49th Annual Meeting of the Association for Computational Linguistics: Human Language Technologies*, pages 151–160, Portland, USA.

Thorsten Joachims. 2003. Transductive learning via spectral graph partitioning. In *Proceedings of the International Conference on Machine Learning*, pages 290–297, Washington, USA.

Anders Johannsen, Dirk Hovy, Héctor Martínez Alonso, Barbara Plank, and Anders Søgaard. 2014. More or less supervised supersense tagging of twitter. In *Proceedings of the Third Joint Conference on Lexical and Computational Semantics (*SEM 2014)*, pages 1–11, Dublin, Ireland.

Michael Jordan, Zoubin Ghahramani, Tommi Jaakkola, Lawrence Saul, and David Heckerman. 1999. An introduction to variational methods for graphical models. *Machine Learning*, 37:183–233.

David Jurgens. 2013. That's what friends are for: Inferring location in online social media platforms based on social relationships. In *Proceedings of the 7th International Conference on Weblogs and Social Media (ICWSM 2013)*, pages 273–282, Dublin, Ireland.

Sotiris Kotsiantis and Dimitris Kanellopoulos. 2006. Discretization techniques: A recent survey. In *GESTS International Transactions on Computer Science and Engineering*, volume 32, pages 47–58.

John D. Lafferty, Andrew McCallum, and Fernando C. N. Pereira. 2001. Conditional random fields: Probabilistic models for segmenting and labeling sequence data. In *Proceedings of the 18th International Conference on Machine Learning*, pages 282–289, Williamstown, USA.

Wei-Hao Lin, Theresa Wilson, Janyce Wiebe, and Alexander Hauptmann. 2006. Which side are you on? Identifying perspectives at the document and sentence levels. In *Proceedings of the 10th Conference on Computational Natural Language Learning*, pages 109–116, New York, USA.

Qing Lu and Lise Getoor. 2003. Link-based classification. In *Proceedings of the 20th International Conference on Machine Learning*, pages 496–503, Washington, USA.

Luke McDowell, Kalyan Moy Gupta, and David W. Aha. 2007. Case-based collective classification. In *Proceedings of the 20th International Florida Artificial Intelligence Research Society Conference*, pages 399–404, Key West, USA.

Luke K McDowell, Kalyan Moy Gupta, and David W Aha. 2009. Cautious collective classification. *Journal of Machine Learning Research*, 10:2777–2836.

Eric W. Nooreen. 1989. *Computer Intensive Methods for Testing Hypothesis*. Wiley and Sons Inc., New York, USA.

Hyo-Jung Oh, Sung Hyon Myaeng, and Mann-Ho Lee. 2000. A practical hypertext categorization method using links and incrementally available class information. In *Proceedings of the 23rd Annual International ACM SIGIR Conference on Research and Development in Information Retrieval*, pages 264–271, Athens, Greece.

Bo Pang and Lillian Lee. 2005. Seeing stars: Exploiting class relationships for sentiment categorization with respect to rating scales. In *Proceedings of the 43rd Annual Meeting of the Association for Computational Linguistics*, pages 115–124, Ann Arbor, USA.

John C. Platt. 1999. Probabilistic outputs for support vector machines and comparisons to regularized likelihood methods. In Alexander Smola, Peter Bartlett, and Bernhard Schölkopf, editors, *Advances in Large Margin Classifiers*, pages 61–74. MIT Press, Cambridge, USA.

Lawrence R. Rabiner and Biing-Hwang Juang. 1986. An introduction to hidden markov models. *ASSP Magazine, IEEE*, 3(1):4–16.

Prithviraj Sen, Galileo Mark Namata, Mustafa Bilgic, Lise Getoor, Brian Gallagher, and Tina Eliassi-Rad. 2008. Collective classification in network data. *AI Magazine*, 29(3):93–106.

Vikas Sindhwani and Prem Melville. 2008. Document-word co-regularization for semi-supervised sentiment analysis. In *Proceedings of the 2008 IEEE International Conference on Data Mining*, pages 1025–1030, Washington, USA.

Seán Slattery and Mark Craven. 1998. Combining statistical and relational methods for learning in hypertext domains. In *Proceedings of Inductive Logic Programming, 8th International Workshop*, pages 38–52, Madison, USA.

Swapna Somasundaran, Galileo Namata, Lise Getoor, and Janyce Wiebe. 2009. Opinion graphs for polarity and discourse classification. In *Proceedings of the 2009 Workshop on Graph-based Methods for Natural Language Processing*, pages 66–74, Singapore.

Veselin Stoyanov and Jason Eisner. 2012. Minimum-risk training of approximate CRF-based NLP systems. In *Proceedings of the 2012 Conference of the North American Chapter of the Association for Computational Linguistics: Human Language Technologies*, pages 120–130, Montréal, Canada.

Hiroya Takamura, Takashi Inui, and Manabu Okumura. 2007. Extracting semantic orientations of phrases from dictionary. In *Human Language Technologies 2007: The Conference of the North American Chapter of the Association for Computational Linguistics*, pages 292–299, Rochester, USA.

Chenhao Tan, Lillian Lee, Jie Tang, Long Jiang, Ming Zhou, and Ping Li. 2011. User-level sentiment analysis incorporating social networks. In *Proceedings of the 17th ACM SIGKDD International Conference on Knowledge Discovery and Data Mining*, pages 1397–1405, San Diego, USA.

Ben Taskar, Pieter Abbeel, and Daphne Koller. 2002. Discriminative probabilistic models for relational data. In *Proceedings of the 18th Conference on Uncertainty in Artificial Intelligence*, pages 485–492, Alberta, Canada.

Matt Thomas, Bo Pang, and Lillian Lee. 2006. Get out the vote: Determining support or opposition from congressional floor-debate transcripts. In *Proceedings of the 2006 Conference on Empirical Methods in Natural Language Processing*, pages 327–335, Sydney, Australia.

Yair Weiss. 2001. Comparing the mean field method and belief propagation for approximate inference in MRFs. In Manfred Opper and David Saad, editors, *Advanced mean field methods: theory and practice*, pages 229–239. MIT Press, Cambridge, USA.

Yiming Yang, Seán Slattery, and Rayid Ghani. 2002. A study of approaches to hypertext categorization. *Journal of Intelligent Information Systems*, 18(2-3):219–241.

Jonathan Yedidia, William Freeman, and Yair Weiss. 2005. Constructing free-energy approximations and generalized belief propagation algorithms. *IEEE Transactions on Information Theory*, 51:2282–2312.

SGRank: Combining Statistical and Graphical Methods to Improve the State of the Art in Unsupervised Keyphrase Extraction

Soheil Danesh
University of Colorado Boulder
soheildb@gmail.com

Tamara Sumner
University of Colorado Boulder
tamara.sumner@colorado.edu

James H. Martin
University of Colorado Boulder
james.martin@colorado.edu

Abstract

Keyphrase extraction is a fundamental technique in natural language processing. It enables documents to be mapped to a concise set of phrases that can be used for indexing, clustering, ontology building, auto-tagging and other information organization schemes. Two major families of unsupervised keyphrase extraction algorithms may be characterized as statistical and graph-based. We present a hybrid statistical-graphical algorithm that capitalizes on the heuristics of both families of algorithms and is able to outperform the state of the art in unsupervised keyphrase extraction on several datasets.

1 Introduction

Keyphrase extraction algorithms aim to extract, from within the document phrases and words that best represent the document's main topics. Being able to accurately determine what a document is about allows computers to cluster together documents that share topics (Hammouda et al., 2005), better answer search queries (Qiu et al., 2012), and generate short document summaries (D'Avanzo et al., 2004). Furthermore, keyphrase extraction can be used to facilitate the automatic construction of concept maps (Leake et al., 2003) or ontologies (Fortuna et al., 2006) which enable better understanding of the interconnections and relations between different topics. Keyphrase extraction is also used in content-based recommender systems which help users in discovering information relevant to their previously expressed interests (Lops et al., 2011). The aforementioned techniques are all important tools in the organization and understanding of the ever expanding repositories of textual information available online in the form of research papers, news articles, blog posts, etc. and keyphrase extraction is central to all of them. Therefore it could be said that keyphrase extraction is a fundamental NLP task, improvements in which could cascade into improvements in higher-level applications that build upon it.

In this work we have focused on unsupervised keyphrase extraction approaches as not only they are useful in domains where training data is hard to procure but even in the presence of ample training data word weights calculated using unsupervised methods can be used as one of several features in supervised keyphrase extraction algorithms. Therefore increases in the accuracy of unsupervised methods can propagate into the results of supervised algorithms as well.

There are two prominent families of unsupervised keyphrase extraction algorithms. The older of these two is clustered around the tf-idf term weighting metric where word statistics such as frequency of occurrence in the document or rareness in the corpus are used to distinguish potential keyphrases. The more recently developed of the two families has been built on the foundation of the TextRank algorithm (Mihalcea & Tarau, 2004). In algorithms of this family a graphical representation of the text is constructed with words as nodes and edges reflecting co-occurrence relations. This graph is then used to run node ranking algorithms such as PageRank (Page

*Proceedings of the Fourth Joint Conference on Lexical and Computational Semantics (*SEM 2015)*, pages 117–126,
Denver, Colorado, June 4–5, 2015.

et al., 1999) that assign weights to the node-words reflecting their semantic importance to the text.

Although some overlap between these two families of algorithms has occurred in works that incorporate statistical heuristics into graph-based methods this overlap is small and most methods do not utilize the full set of statistical heuristics. Our aim has been to 1) Construct a keyphrase extraction algorithm based on optimal statistical features and 2) Combine it with a graph-based algorithm for further improvements. The advantage of graph-based methods is that they take into account term co-occurrence patterns that are not generally utilized by statistical methods which take a bag of n-grams approach to document representation.

2 Related Works

In this section we focus mainly on related unsupervised keyphrase extraction algorithms. One of the most prominent of these algorithms has been the term frequency-inverse document frequency (tf-idf) term weighting function (Salton et al, 1975). Given a corpus of documents the tf-idf weight of term t in document d is mathematically expressed as *tf-idf(t,d)=tf(t,d)*idf(t)* where *tf(t,d)* is the frequency of term t in document d and *idf(t)=log(N/df(t))* where *N* is the total number of documents in the corpus and *df(t)* is the number of documents in the corpus that contain term t (Jones, 1972). The term frequency heuristic is based on the intuition that terms which occur more often in a document are more likely to be important to its meaning. The idf function captures the rareness heuristic, that is, words which occur in many documents in the corpus are unlikely to be important to the meaning of any specific one.

Tf-idf is simple yet relatively accurate therefore many variations of it have been used by other algorithms. One of the most successful of these is KP-Miner (El-Beltagy & Rafea , 2010) which to the best of our knowledge represents the state of the art in unsupervised keyphrase extraction. KP-Miner operates on n-grams and uses a modified version of tf-idf where the document frequency for n-grams with n greater than one is assumed to be one. We will explain the intuition behind this modification later as we have adopted it in our algorithm as well. KP-Miner's initial candidates are comprised of the longest n-grams that do not contain a stop word or punctuation mark, occur for the first time within the first 400 words of the document and have a term frequency above a minimum threshold determined by document length. KP-Miner also boosts the weights of multi-word candidates in proportion to the ratio of the frequencies of single word candidates to all candidates. In a reranking step, the tf-idf of each term is recalculated based on the number of times it is subsumed by other candidates in the top 15 candidates list. Another tf-idf based unsupervised system is KX-FBK (Pianta & Tonelli, 2010) which uses some of the same heuristics as KP-Miner but with different formulations and was shown to underperform in comparison in the Semeval 2010 keyphrase extraction task.

An approach fundamentally different from tf-idf and its family of algorithms is TextRank. It is based on the intuition that 1) keywords in a document are more semantically interrelated as they are generally about related topics and 2) that semantic relatedness can be estimated using co-occurrence relations. Therefore in TextRank a graphical representation of the text is constructed in which edges connect words co-occurring in a window of a certain length. The PageRank algorithm is then applied to this network of words to distinguish the important ones which are then reassembled into phrases wherever they occur next to each other in the text.

TopicRank (Bougouin et al., 2013) which to the best of our knowledge is the state of the art in graph-based keyphrase extraction, is an enhancement of TextRank. Here, nodes represent topics which consist of sets of candidate terms clustered around shared sub-terms. In (Liang et al., 2009) Chinese search engine query logs are used to extract candidate terms which are used as nodes in the graph. Edges are weighted based on co-occurrence count. Also candidate terms which are longer or whose first occurrence is in the title or first paragraph have boosted edge weights. SingleRank (Wan & Xiao, 2008) also uses co-occurrence counts as edge weights. It ranks noun phrases in the text based on the sum of their word weights. ExpandRank (Wan & Xiao, 2008) builds upon SingleRank by incorporating neighboring documents but without significant performance improvements (Hasan & NG, 2010).

3 Method

Our algorithm processes an input document in four stages. In the first stage we extract all possible n-grams from the input text and eliminate those that are highly unlikely to be keyphrases, for instance n-grams containing punctuation marks. In the second stage the remaining n-grams are ranked based on a modified version of tf-idf. In the third stage the top ranking candidates from stage two are reranked based on additional statistical heuristics such as position of first occurrence and term length. In the fourth and final stage the ranking produced in stage three is incorporated into a graph-based algorithm which produces the final ranking of keyphrase candidates.

3.1 Eliminating Unlikely Candidates

In the first stage all possible n-grams in the text for n from 1 to 6 are produced. Those n-grams considered highly unlikely to be keyphrases are eliminated from the candidates list. These include n-grams containing stop words, punctuation marks or words whose part of speech tag is anything different than noun, adjective or verb. Furthermore n-grams whose frequency of occurrence in the text falls below a minimum threshold are also eliminated. In the current work this threshold is determined based on document length and is 0 for short documents, 2 for medium-length documents and 3 for long documents where short is defined as containing less than 1500 words, medium as between 1500 to 4000 and long as any document with more than 4000 words.

3.2 Initial Ranking of All Candidates

In the second stage n-grams not eliminated in the first stage are ranked based on a modified version of tf-idf as used in KP-Miner. The modification involves changing the document frequency count in idf calculation such that for n-grams with n > 1 document frequency is always considered to be one. In other words we assume that all multi-word candidates occur in one document only. This is because while rareness is a reliable indication of semantic importance in the case of single words, it does not offer the same accuracy when it comes to multi-words. In many cases relatively common single words can combine into rare multi-words without much semantic importance. For example, in the Semeval test dataset of 100 full-length academic papers, to be described later in the evaluation section, the n-grams *control has*, *rule satisfies* and *become known* all have a document frequency of 1. On the other hand phrases chosen by humans as keyphrases such as *Query expansion* which occurs in 9 documents and as a keyphrase in 4 or *language models* which occurs in 12 document and again in 4 of them as key, have relatively high document frequency counts. These examples demonstrate how including the actual document frequency counts in idf calculation could be disadvantageous for distinguishing multi-word keyphrases.

3.3 Reranking Top Candidates

At the end of stage two we have an initial ranking of our candidates based on their tf-idf scores. In the third stage we rerank the top T candidates from stage two based on additional heuristics. These heuristics are position of first occurrence, term length and subsumption count. In the current work T is set to 100 based on experiments on a small development set of 40 documents from the Semeval trial set.

The position of first occurrence heuristic has performed consistently well in previous keyphrase extraction experiments. Medelyan and Witten (2008) use a linear decay function of the position of first occurrence as a feature in their supervised algorithm. It has also been utilized in unsupervised methods. In KP-Miner a constant position threshold is used where n-grams whose first occurrence is beyond it are eliminated from the candidate list. KX-FBK uses the linear decay function raised to the power of two. We introduce a novel encoding of this heuristic in the form of a logarithmic decay function, which as we will show in the discussion section outperforms all aforementioned variations. We define the Position of First Occurrence factor (PFO) according to the following formula:

$$PFO(t,d) = \log\left(\frac{cutoffPosition}{p(t,d)}\right) \quad (1)$$

where *p(t,d)* is the position of term t's first occurrence in document d. In the current work *cutoffPosition* is set to 3000 as it performed best in experiments on the development set.

Regarding term length, we hypothesize that among words with a high likelihood of being a keyphrase, in this case the top 100 candidates from stage two, the addition of a word to an n-gram is likely to construct a more semantically specific phrase geared towards signifying a specific topic or subject e.g. *web* versus *semantic web*. Therefore longer n-grams are generally more likely to be keyphrases. Accordingly, we boost term t's weight by its term length, TL(t) where length is the number of space separated words in t.

Finally, we recalculate a term's tf-idf weight by reducing its term frequency by its subsumption count among the top 100 candidates. Term t is said to be subsumed by term t_s when t_s contains t.

The following formula shows how the statistical weight for term t in document d is calculated:

$$w_s(t,d) = \left(tf(t,d) - subSumCount(t,d)\right) * idf(t) * PFO(t,d) * TL(t) \quad (2)$$

Where *subSumCount(t,d)* is the sum of term frequencies of all terms included in the top T list that subsume t.

3.4 Graph-based Ranking

In the fourth and final stage of our algorithm we use terms with positive weights after stage three as nodes in a graphical representation of the text. An edge is placed between two nodes if they co-occur within a window of width d. Whereas d is usually small, generally less than 20 words in most graph-based algorithms, we have chosen a large window of 1500 and instead attenuate the edge weight based on the average log decayed distance between all co-occurrences of the term pair as show in equation 3 below

$$w_d(t_i,t_j) = \frac{\sum_{i=1}^{tf(t_i)} \sum_{j=1}^{tf(t_j)} \log\left(\frac{winSize}{|pos_i - pos_j|}\right)}{numCo\text{-}occurrences(t_i,t_j)} \quad (3)$$

where *winSize* is the co-occurrence window size set to 1500 in the current work based on F-measure performance on the development set, pos_i and pos_j are the respective positions of occurrences of terms t_i and t_j and *numCo-occurrences*(t_i,t_j) is the number of co-occurrences of the terms within the window of 1500.

Furthermore, we incorporate term weights calculated using statistical features in the previous stages into the graphical representation of the text. We hypothesize that term weights calculated using statistical features may serve as a first estimate of a term's keyphraseness, i.e. likelihood of being a keyphrase. The PageRank algorithm simulates a random walker on the graph. Each node's eventual PageRank score reflects the portion of time the walker spends on that node (Langville & Meyer, 2011). To make sure terms with higher statistical weights are visited more often we would want higher transition probabilities between them but lower transition probabilities between terms with lower weights. Therefore we use the product of the term pair's weights as a factor into the weight of the edge between them in the graph. The weight of the edge between terms t_i and t_j is calculated using the following equation:

$$w_e(t_i,t_j) = w_d(t_i,t_j) * w_s(t_i) * w_s(t_j) \quad (4)$$

where, as previously defined in equation 3, w_d is the distance based portion of the edge weight while $w_s(t_i)*w_s(t_j)$ takes the terms' statistical properties into account.

For each node we normalize edge weights by dividing each outgoing edge weight by sum of outgoing edge weights for that node. This results in a slightly modified formula for PageRank compared to the one used in TextRank, where edges are uniform weight, as shown below.

$$S(V_i) = (1-d) + d * \sum_{j \epsilon In(V_i)} \frac{w_e(j,i) * S(V_i)}{\sum_{k \epsilon Out(V_j)} w_e(j,k)} \quad (5)$$

where $S(V_i)$ is the PageRank score of node V_i, d is the damping factor usually set to 0.15 and $In(V_i)$ and $Out(V_i)$ are the sets of edges where node V_i is the destination or the source respectively. PageRank consists of iteratively calculating the scores for each node until convergence where scores do not change significantly between iterations. The converged-on PageRank score for each node is our algorithm's final output and determines the rankings of the candidate terms.

4 Evaluation

We evaluate our keyphrase extraction algorithm by comparing it to two state-of-the-art algorithms, KP-Miner and TextRank, on three datasets: The Semeval 2010 keyphrase extraction shared task dataset, the Inspec dataset of ACM abstracts and the Krapivin dataset of full length papers. To obtain results for KP-Miner we have used an executable kindly shared with us by the system's author. For TextRank we have built on an existing open source implementation. The comparisons between the algorithms are done using the precision and recall at k metric where the top k terms returned by each algorithm are used to measure precision and recall. Here k ranges from 1 to 15. We also calculate the F-measure for k = 5, 10 and 15. In the following section we describe each dataset in detail and report the results achieved by each algorithm on each dataset.

The Semeval and Inspec datasets have also been used by Bougouin et al. (2013) for evaluating their implementation of TextRank along with more advanced graph-based algorithms SingleRank and TopicRank. We have used these results for further comparisons between our method and advanced graph-based algorithms as reported in section 4.4.

4.1 Semeval Dataset

The Semeval dataset was used in the Semeval 2010 keyphrase extraction shared task (Kim et al., 2010). To the best of our knowledge this shared task is the largest recent comparison of keyphrase extraction algorithms and an algorithm's performance on this dataset is a relatively good indication of where it stands compared to others in the field. The Semeval dataset consists of 284 full length ACM articles divided into a test set of size 100, training set of size 144 and trial set of size 40 which we used as the development set for parameter tuning. Each article has two sets of human assigned keyphrases: the author-assigned and reader-assigned ones. The gold standard used in our experiments is the combined set of author and reader assigned keyphrases which is the same as was done in the Semeval shared task. The table below provides a statistical overview of this dataset's documents.

100 docs	Document Length	Number of Keyphrases	Keyphrase Length
Max.	14171	29	8
Avg.	7979	15.13	2.14
Min.	4060	9	1

Table 1. Semeval test set statistics.

We have compared our algorithm with KP-Miner and TextRank using only the 100 documents in the test set. The following diagram shows the average precision and recall achieved by each algorithm. As was done in the Semeval task, comparisons are done between once stemmed human assigned keyphrases and ranked candidates returned by each algorithm.

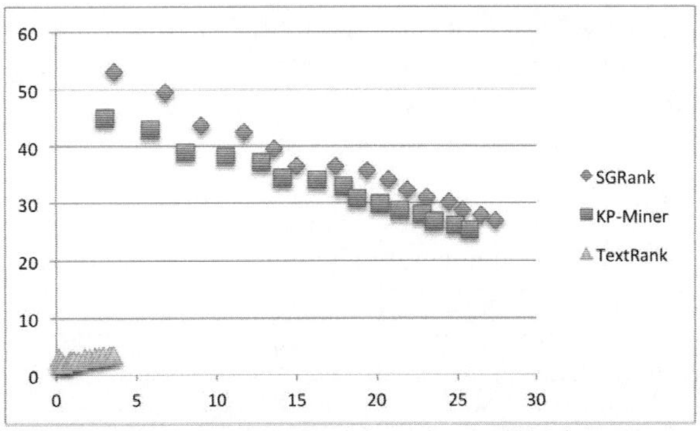

Figure 1. Semeval precision(y), recall(x) k < 16

The following table shows the achieved F-measure for each algorithm at k=5, 10 and 15. It also contains the corresponding percentage improvement at each k. The statistical significance of each improvement is measured using a 2-sided paired t-test. Improvements are in **bold** font where they are statistically significant at $p < 0.05$.

K =	5	10	15
SGRank	20.25	26.07	27.20
KPMiner Improvement	19.01 6.5%	24.06 **8.3%**	25.54 **6.4%**
Textrank Improvement	1.25 **1509%**	2.46 **960%**	3.47 **683%**

Table 2. Semeval F-measures and improvements.

As can be seen from the above results our method outperforms KP-Miner in both precision and recall for all k and achieves statistically significant improvements in the F-measure over KP-Miner for k=10 and 15. These results are noteworthy considering that in the Semeval keyphrase extraction shared task KP-Miner was the best performing unsupervised algorithm, and the second best overall out of 19 systems, outperforming prominent supervised algorithms such as Maui (Medelyan et al., 2009). TextRank seems to generally underperform on longer documents and has performed poorly on the Semeval dataset.

4.2 Inspec Dataset

The Inspec dataset is comprised of 2000 ACM abstracts divided into test, training and validation sets containing 500, 1000 and 500 abstracts respectively. We follow the same approach as taken by Mihalcea and Tarau (2004). We use only the 500 documents in the test set. The following table provides a statistical overview of this document set.

500 docs	Document Length	Number of Keyphrases	Keyphrase Length
Max.	338	31	9
Avg.	121.8	9.8	2.3
Min.	23	2	1

Table 3. Inspec dataset statistics.

Figure 2 shows the average precision and recall for all three algorithms for k from 1 to 15. Table 4 shows the F-measure improvements made by our method over the two other algorithms for k=5, 10 and 15. As these results show, on this dataset of relatively short documents, TextRank outperforms KP-Miner for k>2. Our algorithm achieves higher precision and recall than both KP-Miner and TextRank for all k with statistically significant gains in the F-measure for k=5, 10 and 15.

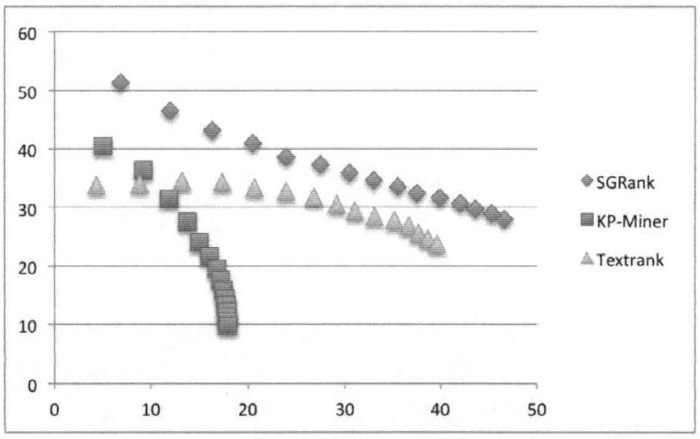

Figure 2. Inspec precision(y), recall(x) k < 16

K =	5	10	15
SGRank	29.16	33.95	33.66
KPMiner Improvement	18.45 **59.7%**	15.89 **118%**	12.73 **175%**
TextRank Improvement	25.53 **15.4%**	30.6 **13.3%**	29.7 **17.7%**

Table 4. Inspec F-measures and improvements.

4.3 Krapivin Dataset

The Krapivin dataset consists of 2000 full length ACM papers. This dataset has been prepared by Krapivin et al. (2009). Each article has author-assigned and editor-corrected keyphrases that we use as the gold standard in our evaluation. Our experiments are done on a 400-document subset of this dataset. The table below provides a statistical characterization of these 400 documents.

400 docs	Document Length	Number of Keyphrases	Keyphrase Length
Max.	16721	24	6
Avg.	7934	6.38	2.1
Min.	3892	1	1

Table 5. Krapivin dataset statistics.

On this dataset keyphrases and candidate terms have been stemmed once before comparison. Similar to the previously mentioned experiments we have measured the precision and recall of all three algorithms for k from 1 to 15 as shown in figure 3. Table 6 contains the F-measures for all three algorithms at k=5, 10 and 15 along with the improvements made by our algorithm. Similar to the Semeval dataset TextRank performs very poorly on this dataset of longer documents. KP-Miner performs much better but both methods are outperformed by our method on all k with statistical significance as shown in Table 6.

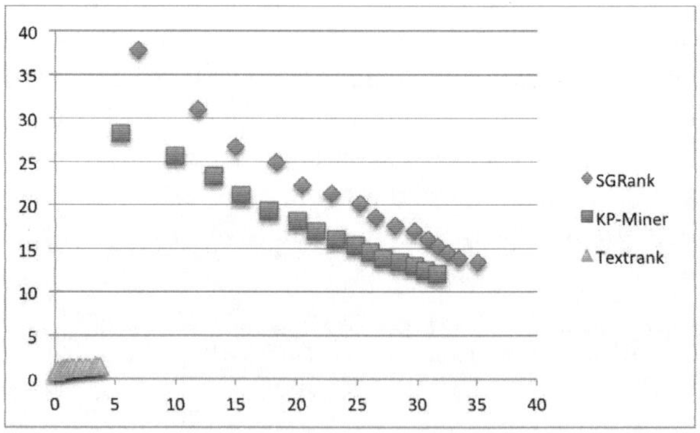

Figure 3. Krapivin precision(y), recall(x) k < 16

K =	5	10	15
SGRank	21.2	21.6	19.4
KPMiner Improvement	18.43 **15.%**	18.65 **16.1%**	17.4 **11.7%**
Textrank Improvement	1.02 **1974%**	1.61 **1240%**	2.1 **823%**

Table 6. Krapivin F-measures and improvements.

4.4 Advanced Graph-based Methods

As mentioned previously Bougouin et al. (2013) introduce TopicRank and use F-measure at k=10 to compare against TextRank and another advanced graph-ranking method SingleRank. They use the Semeval and Inspec datasets for comparison providing us with an opportunity to compare our performance with those of TextRank and the two more advanced graph-based algorithms. Table 7 contains the F-measures at k=10 for our algorithm, SGRank, and all aforementioned algorithms. Note that the particular implementation of TextRank used in this paper performs worse than ours on the Inspec dataset but better for the Semeval dataset.

F at k=10	Inspec	Semeval	Average
SGRank	33.95	26.4	30.1
TextRank	12.7	5.6	9.1
SingleRank	35.2	3.7	19.4
TopicRank	27.9	12.1	20

Table 7. Comparison with Advanced Graph-based methods F-measures at K=10.

As seen in Table 7 our algorithm's average performance is considerably better than all of the advanced graph-based algorithms.

5 Discussion

As shown in the preceding results our algorithm outperforms all other methods in all the used datasets. The only exception is SingleRank which marginally outperforms our method on the Inspec dataset but performs very poorly on the Semeval dataset, as seen in Table 7. Also worth noting is KP-Miner's relatively poor performance on the shorter documents of the Inspec dataset. This could potentially be due to the fact that KP-Miner only considers terms as candidates which occur on their own in the text i.e. surrounded by punctuation marks or stop words. In shorter documents it is more likely that fewer keyphrases would occur in such conditions in the text, causing them to be eliminated early on by KP-Miner. Our algorithm however considers all n-grams without requiring that they occur on their own. This allows us to consider more candidates and avoid a performance reduction in shorter documents. However, there is an advantage to eliminating terms that never occur on their own. Many keyphrases are multi-words. In some cases smaller parts of keyphrases tend to occur in high frequencies, as they are related to the topic of the document and are sometimes used in place of the keyphrase, and therefore achieve high rankings. We call such frequent sub-phrases keyphrase fragments. For example document C-1 in the Semeval test set includes two keyphrases *grid service discovery* and *web service* leading to a highly ranked keyphrase fragment *service*. High ranking keyphrase fragments are detrimental to the algorithm's performance. One way to counteract them is based on the observation that they rarely occur on their own as they usually appear as part of larger phrases. This is the motivation behind KP-Miner's elimination of candidates that do not occur on their own. Therefore, to consider all candidates, while countering the keyphrase fragments problem, we calculate the subsumption count over a much larger portion of the ranked terms compared to KP-Miner. This larger list will include more terms which keyphrase fragments are a part of, causing greater reductions in the fragments' rankings. The number of top candidates used in KP-Miner to calculated subsumption is set equal to an input parameter that determines the number of keyphrases to be returned to the user. In the current work and the Semeval shared task this parameter is 15. In other words KP-Miner calculates the subsumption count over the top 15 terms whereas we calculate it over the top 100 terms. To test the effectiveness of this strategy we reduced our subsumption threshold to 15. This change led to a 9% decrease in the F-Measure at k=15 on the Semeval dataset, 4.7% decrease on the Inspec and 1.5% decrease in the Krapivin dataset. Note that for the rest of the Discussion section percentage changes are those of the F-measure at k=15. Our algorithm's high performance on both short and long documents indicates the viability of considering all n-grams as candidates and mitigating the effect of keyphrase fragments by counting subsumption over more top ranking terms.

Another novel aspect of our algorithm is its formulation of the position of first occurrence heuristic as described by the PFO function in equation 1. We compare our approach with two other unsupervised algorithms that utilize this heuristic: KP-Miner and KX-FBK. The method used in KP-Miner is a hard cutoff threshold where candidates whose first occurrence is beyond 400 words into the document are eliminated. KX-FBK uses the following decay function:

$$PFO_{kx}(t,d) = \left(\frac{document\ length - p(t,d)}{document\ length}\right)^2 \quad (6)$$

We tested our system with our PFO function replaced by those of KP-Miner and KX-FBK on the Semeval, Inspec and Krapivin datasets. Replacement with KX-FBK's PFO led to respective reductions in the F-Measure at k=15 of 6.5%, 9.5% and 15.1%. Replacement with KP-Miner's PFO led to a 10.9% reduction in Semeval but no reduction in Inspeq and a 2.9% improvement in Krapivin. We also replaced our PFO function with the linear decay function used by Medelyan and Witten (2008). This function is the same as equation 9 but without the exponent. This led to a 1.4% reduction in Semeval, 0.7% reduction in Inspec and a 2.9% reduction in Krapivin. These results show that our encoding of the PFO heuristic as a logarithmic decay function leads to overall gains in accuracy although it underperforms slightly compared to KP-Miner's PFO on the Krapivin dataset which points to further room for improvement. One possible future direction would be to design functions that adjust the *cutoffPosition* in equation 1 based on document length as some sensitivity to this was observed in our experimentations. We also replaced our term length factor, TL in equation 2, with KP-miner's boosting function for multi-words. This caused a 3.2% reduction in Semeval, 5.1% reduction in Inspec and 2.3% reduction in Krapivin.

Our algorithm uses graph-based methods on top of statistical features to capture keyphrases not distinguishable using statistical heuristics. To test the effectiveness of this addition we eliminated the graph-based reranking stage. This caused a 1.1% reduction in Semeval, 4% reduction in Inspec and a 4.3% reduction in Krapivin which demonstrates that our approach of combining statistical and graph-based features leads to overall improvements in performance. Our method also introduces a novel distance-based edge weighting formula to the graph-based family of algorithms. Most graph-based algorithms place edges where terms co-occur within a window of a few words. This is equivalent to a sudden drop in the estimation of semantic relatedness at the edge of the window. We however choose a much larger window of 1500 and gradually reduce the edge weight with increasing distance between the terms according to equation 3. To measure the effectiveness of this approach we compared it with a window of 100 words with no positional decay, i.e. w_d in equation 4 is set to one for terms occurring within the window of 100 and zero otherwise. This caused a 2.2% drop in the Semeval dataset i.e. it performed lower than with no graphical reranking at all. In Krapivin it caused a 2.4% drop in performance and a 0.4% drop in the Inspec dataset. For further comparison we replaced w_d with the *dist* function used in TopicRank which is the sum of inverse distances between all occurrences of a term pair. This caused a 1.4% reduction in Semeval, no difference in Krapivin and a 0.3% reduction in Inspec. These results demonstrate the effectiveness of our novel distance based edge weighting function.

An interesting point is that both our positional functions, PFO and w_d are logarithmic decays. This hints at a logarithmic decrease in semantic importance or relatedness with increased distance which is the same as how the idf function relates a word's semantic importance to its document frequency. Our initial hypothesis for the success of logarithmic decay functions is that both positional and document frequency heuristics are governed by the law of diminishing returns. That is, the distinguishing power of each heuristic decreases as the inputs increase. Taking the document frequency heuristic (df) as an example, we know that rareness, i.e. small dfs, indicate higher semantic importance. Therefore, in a corpus of 1000 documents, a word with a df of 1 is much more likely to be a keyphrase than a word with a df of 20, as reflected in their idf scores. However as the df increases the same difference in df's does not imply the same difference in probability of being a keyphrase e.g. we intuitively know that based on rareness alone, our estimate of the difference in the probability of being a keyphrase for a pair of terms with df's 980 and 1000 would be much less reliable compared to a pair with df's 1 and 20, even though the difference in the df pairs are the same. The same logic applies to the position of first occurrence and distance based semantic relatedness heuristics. Incorporating this diminishing returns property into the mathematical formulation of the heuristic calls for a function with a decreasing absolute value slope i.e. with a second derivative with the opposite sign of the first, to reflect our decreasing confidence in the heuristic as values increase. This rules out linear functions. Although other functions such as reciprocals fulfill this property, judging based on the success of idf and our positional decay functions it seems that logarithmic decay does better at modeling the intrinsic rate of this diminishing distinguishing power of the heuristic, perhaps due to its slower decline. Why this is and whether better decay functions can be designed or tuned to specific domains is a future direction we plan to explore. It is also worth noting that unlike most graph-based algorithms whose performances are completely dependent on a POS tag filter, SGRank suffers relatively slight reductions in F-measure at 15 without the POS tag filter: 3.6% on Semeval, and 2.6% in Krapivin and 24.5% on Inspec.

Feature Tested	Datasets Average F at 15	Datasets Average Change	S.	I.	K.
None	26.7	0	27.2	33.6	19.4
Subsume Top 15	25.3	-5.6%	24.7	32	16.4
kx-fbk PFO	24.1	-10.3%	25.4	30.4	16.4
kp-miner PFO	25.95	-2.6%	24.2	33.6	19.9
kp-miner multi-word boosting	25.74	-3.5%	26.3	31.9	18.9
edge weight =1 if d<100	26.3	-1.6%	26.6	33.5	18.9
topicRa-nk edge weighting	26.5	-0.56%	26.8	31.9	18.9
no POS-tagging	23.5	-10.2%	26.2	25.4	18.9
no graph-based	25.9	-3.1%	26.9	32.2	18.5

Table 8. Effects of individual features on performance. Columns S., I. and K. contain F-measures (k=15) for the Semeval, Inspec and Krapivin datasets respectively.

Table 8 contains a summary of how the elimination or replacement of different features affects the performance of our algorithm, as discussed previously. It contains the F-measure at k = 15, averaged across all datasets, for the full algorithm along with variations of it produced by changing different features.

6 Conclusion and Future Directions

We introduce an unsupervised keyphrase extraction algorithm that combines statistical and graph-based heuristics and is able to improve upon the state of the art, with statistical significance, on several datasets. Among other features, our algorithm uses a novel variation of the subsumption heuristic. We also demonstrate the suitability of log decay functions for mathematically expressing heuristics that are based on phrase distance such as the position of first occurrence and the weighting of graph edges based on the average distance of phrase occurrences. Another way of looking at the presented algorithm is as a term weighting scheme. Therefore an interesting future direction would be to investigate whether replacing traditional term weighting schemes, e.g. tf-idf, in areas such as information retrieval, document clustering and supervised algorithms where tf-idf is used as a feature would cause any improvements in performance.

7 References

Bougouin A., F. Boudin, and B. Daille. 2013, October. Topicrank: Graph-based topic ranking for keyphrase extraction. In *International Joint Conference on Natural Language Processing (IJCNLP),* pages 543-551.

D'Avanzo F., B. Magnini, and A.Vallin. 2004. Keyphrase extraction for summarization purposes: The LAKE system at DUC-2004. In *Proceedings of the 2004 document understanding conference.*

El-Beltagy S. and A. Rafea. 2009. KP-Miner: A keyphrase extraction system for English and Arabic documents. In *Information Systems, 34*(1), pages 132-144.

Samhaa R. El-Beltagy and Ahmed Rafea. 2010. Kp-miner: Participation in semeval-2. In *Proceedings of the 5th international workshop on semantic evaluation*, pages 190-193.

Fortuna B., M. Grobelnik, and D. Mladenić. 2006. Semi-automatic data-driven ontology construction system. In *Proceedings of the 9th international multi-conference information society,* pages 223–226.

Hammouda K., D. Matute, and M. Kamel. 2005. Corephrase: Keyphrase extraction for document clustering. In *Machine Learning and Data Mining in Pattern Recognition*, pages 265-274.

Hasan, K. S., & Ng, V. 2010. Conundrums in unsupervised keyphrase extraction: making sense of the state-of-the-art. In *Proceedings of the 23rd International Conference on Computational Linguistics: Posters* (pp. 365-373). Association for Computational Linguistics.

Hulth A. 2003. Improved automatic keyword extraction given more linguistic knowledge. In *Proceedings of the 2003 conference on Empirical methods in natural language processing*, pages 216-223.

Jones K.. 1972. A statistical interpretation of term specificity and its application in retrieval. *Journal of documentation*, *28*(1), Pages 11-21.

Kim S., O. Medelyan, M. Kan, and T. Baldwin. 2010. Semeval-2010 task 5: Automatic keyphrase extraction from scientific articles. In *Proceedings of the 5th International Workshop on Semantic Evaluation* , pages 21-26.

Krapivin M., A. Autaeu & M. Marchese. 2009. Large dataset for keyphrases extraction. Technical Report DISI-09-055.

Langville, A. N., & Meyer, C. D. 2011. *Google's PageRank and beyond: the science of search engine rankings*. Princeton University Press.

Leake D., A. Maguitman, and T. Reichherzer. 2003. Topic Extraction and Extension to Support Concept Mapping. In *FLAIRS Conference*, pages 325-329.

Liang, W., Huang, C., Li, M., & Lu, B. L. 2009. Extracting Keyphrases from Chinese News Articles Using TextRank and Query Log Knowledge. In *PACLIC*

Lops P., M. Gemmis, and G. Semeraro. 2011. Content-based recommender systems: State of the art and trends. In *Recommender systems handbook*, pages 73-105.

Medelyan, O., & Witten, I. H. 2008. Domain Independent Automatic Keyphrase Indexing with Small Training Sets. *Journal of the American Society for Information Science and Technology*, *59*(7), 1026-1040.

Medelyan, O., Frank, E., & Witten, I. H. (2009). Human-competitive tagging using automatic keyphrase extraction. In *Proceedings of the 2009 Conference on Empirical Methods in Natural Language Processing: Volume 3-Volume 3* (pp. 1318-1327). Association for Computational Linguistics.

Mihalcea R. and P. Tarau. 2004. Textrank: Bringing order into texts. In *Proceedings of International Conference on Empirical Methods in Natural Language Processing*, pages 404–411

Page, L., Brin, S., Motwani, R., & Winograd, T. 1999. The PageRank citation ranking: Bringing order to the web.

Pianta, E., & Tonelli, S. 2010. KX: A flexible system for keyphrase extraction. In *Proceedings of the 5th international workshop on semantic evaluation* (pp. 170-173). Association for Computational Linguistics.

Qiu M., Y. Li, and Jing Jiang. 2012. Query-oriented keyphrase extraction. In *Information Retrieval Technology*, pages 64-75.

Salton, G., A. Wong, and C. Yang. 1975. A vector space model for automatic indexing. In *Communications of the ACM*, *18*(11), pages 613-620.

Xiaojun Wan and Jianguo Xiao. 2008. Single Document Keyphrase Extraction Using Neighborhood Knowledge. *In Proceedings of the 23rd National Conference on Artificial Intelligence* - Volume 2 , pages 855–860. AAAI Press.

Towards Semantic Language Classification: Inducing and Clustering Semantic Association Networks from Europarl

Steffen Eger[1], **Niko Schenk**[2] **and Alexander Mehler**[1]
[1]Text Technology Lab
[2]Applied Computational Linguistics Lab
Goethe University Frankfurt am Main
{steeger,nschenk,amehler}@em.uni-frankfurt.de

Abstract

We induce semantic association networks from translation relations in parallel corpora. The resulting semantic spaces are encoded in a single reference language, which ensures cross-language comparability. As our main contribution, we cluster the obtained (cross-lingually comparable) lexical semantic spaces. We find that, in our sample of languages, lexical semantic spaces largely coincide with genealogical relations. To our knowledge, this constitutes the first large-scale quantitative lexical semantic typology that is completely unsupervised, bottom-up, and data-driven. Our results may be important for the decision which multilingual resources to integrate in a semantic evaluation task.

1 Introduction

There has been a recent surge of interest in integrating multilingual resources in natural language processing (NLP). For example, Snyder et al. (2008) show that jointly considering morphological segmentations across languages improves performance compared to the monolingual baseline. Bhargava and Kondrak (2011) and Bhargava and Kondrak (2012) demonstrate that string transduction can benefit from supplemental information provided in other languages. Analogously, in lexical semantics, Navigli and Ponzetto (2012) explore semantic relations from Wikipedia in different languages to induce a huge integrated lexical semantic network.

In this paper, we also focus on multilingual resources in lexical semantics. But rather than *integrating* them, we investigate their *(dis-)similarities*. More precisely, we cluster (classify) languages based on their semantic relations between lexical units. The outcome of our classification may have direct consequences for approaches that integrate diverse multilingual resources. For example, from a linguistic point of view, it might be argued that integrating very heterogeneous/dissimilar semantic resources is *harmful*, e.g., in a monolingual semantic similarity task, because semantically unrelated languages might contribute semantic relations unavailable in the language for which semantic similarity is computed. Alternatively, from a statistical point of view, it might be argued that integrating heterogeneous/dissimilar resources is *beneficial* due to their higher degree of uncorrelatedness. In any case, either of these implications necessitates knowledge of a typology of lexical semantics.

In order to address this question, we provide a translation-based model of lexical semantic spaces. Our approach is to generate association networks in which the weight of a link between two words depends on their degree of partial synonymy. To measure synonymy, we rely on translation data that is input to a statistical alignment toolkit. We define the degree of synonymy of two words to be proportional to the number of common translations in a reference language, weighted by the probability of translation. By pivoting on the reference language, we represent semantic associations among words in different languages by means of the synonymy relations of their translations in the *same target language*. This approach ensures cross-language comparability of semantic spaces: Greek and Bulgarian are compared, for example, by means of the synonymy relations

*Proceedings of the Fourth Joint Conference on Lexical and Computational Semantics (*SEM 2015)*, pages 127–136,
Denver, Colorado, June 4–5, 2015.

that are retained when translating them into the same pivot language (e.g., English).

This approach does not only address proximities of pairs of words shared among languages (e.g., MEAT and BEEF, MOUTH and DOOR, CHILD and FRUIT – cf. Vanhove et al. (2008)). By averaging over word pairs, it also allows for calculating *semantic distances* between pairs of languages.

The *Sapir-Whorf Hypothesis* (SWH) (Whorf, 1956) already predicts that semantic relations are not universal. Though we are agnostic about the assumptions underlying the SWH, it nevertheless gives an evaluation criterion for our experiment: if the SWH is true, we expect a clustering of translation-based semantic spaces along the genealogical relationships of the languages involved. However, genealogy is certainly not the sole principle potentially underlying a typology of lexical semantics. For example, Cooper (2008) finds that French is semantically closer to Basque, a putatively non-Indoeuropean language, than to German. To the best of our knowledge, a large-scale quantitative typological analysis of lexical semantics is lacking thus far and we intend to make first steps towards this target.

The paper is structured as follows. Section 2 outlines related work. Section 3 presents our formal model and Section 4 details our experiments on clustering semantic spaces across selected languages of the European Union. We conclude in Section 5.

2 Related work

A field related to our research is *semantic relatedness*, in which the task is to determine the degree of semantic similarity between pairs of words, such as *tiger* and *cat*, *sex* and *love*, etc. Classically, semantic word networks such as WordNet (Fellbaum, 1998) or EuroWordNet (Vossen, 1998) have been used to address this problem (Jiang and Conrath, 1997), and, more recently, taxonomies and knowledge bases such as Wikipedia (Strube and Ponzetto, 2006). Hassan and Mihalcea (2009) define the task of *cross-lingual semantic relatedness*, in which the goal is to determine the semantic similarity between words from different languages, and Navigli and Ponzetto (2012) have combined WordNet with Wikipedia to construct a multi-layer semantic network in which computation of cross-lingual semantic relatedness may be performed. Most recently, neural network-based distributed semantic representations focusing on cross-language similarities between words and larger textual units have become popular (Chandar A P et al. (2014), Hermann and Blunsom (2014), Mikolov et al. (2013)).

There have been (a) few different computational approaches to *semantic language classification*. Mehler et al. (2011) test whether languages are genealogically separable via topological properties of semantic (concept) graphs derived from Wikipedia. This approach is top-down in that it assumes that the genealogical tree is the desired output of the classification. Cooper (2008) computes semantic distances between languages based on the curvature of translation histograms in bilingual dictionaries. While this results in some interesting findings as indicated, the approach is not applied to language classification, but focuses on computing semantically similar languages for a given query language. Vanhove et al. (2008) construct so-called semantic proximity networks based on monolingual dictionaries, and envision to use them for semantic typologies. They do not apply their methodology to the multilingual setup, however, which a typology necessitates.

Orthographic, phonetic and *syntactic* similarity of languages have received considerably more attention than *semantic* similarity, as we focus on. Classical approaches in determining orthographic/phonetic relatedness of languages are based on lexico-statistical comparisons of items in standardized word lists (Campbell, 2003; Rama and Borin, 2015), such as the Swadesh lists (Swadesh, 1955). Rama and Borin (2015) study the impact of different string similarity measures on orthographic language classification. Ciobanu and Dinu (2014) measure orthographic similarity between Romanian and related languages. They also indicate applications of (knowledge of) similarity values between languages, such as serving as a guide for machine translation (Scannell, 2006). Koehn (2005) produces a genealogical clustering of the languages in Europarl based on ease of translation, as measured in BLEU scores, between any two languages (which, putatively, yields a syntactic similarity indication). This results in an imperfect reproduction of the ge-

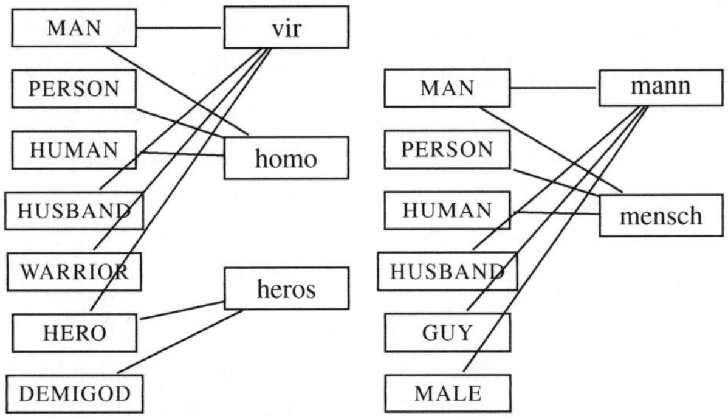

(a) English-Latin (b) English-German

Figure 1: Excerpts of bilingual dictionaries as bipartite graphs with links between words if and only if one is a translation of the other. Data from www.latin-dictionary.net and dict.leo.org.

nealogical language tree for the languages involved.

3 Model

We start with motivating our approach by example of bilingual *dictionaries* before we formally generalize it in terms of probabilistic translation relations. Bilingual dictionaries, or the bipartite graphs that represent them (cf. Figure 1), induce lexical semantic association networks in any of the languages involved by *placing a link between two words of the same language if and only if they share a common translation in the other language* (cf. Figure 2).

Since translations provide partially synonymous expression in the target language, the latter links can be seen to denote semantic relatedness (in terms of synonymy) of the interlinked words. Further, the more distant two words in such a lexical semantic association network, the lower the degree of their partial synonymy: the longer the path from one word to another, the higher the loss of relatedness among them (cf. Eger and Sejane (2010)).

Note that association networks derived from bilingual dictionaries represent semantic similarities of words of the source language R subject to semantic relations of their translations in the target language L. The reason is that whether or not a link is established between two words α and β in R depends on associations of their translations present in L. To illustrate this, consider the association networks outlined in Figure 2, induced from the bilingual dictionaries outlined in Figure 1, which match between R = English and L = Latin and L = German, respectively. When L is classical Latin, the semantic field centered around (the English word) MAN is partially different from the semantic field around MAN when L is German. For example, under L = Latin, MAN is directly linked with HERO and WARRIOR (indirectly with DEMIGOD) – these semantic associations are not present when German is the language L.

By fixing R and varying L, we can create different lexical semantic association networks, each encoded in language R, and each representing the semantic relations of L.[1] Analyzing and contrasting such networks may then allow for clustering languages due to shared lexical semantic associations.

As mentioned above, we generalize the model outlined so far to the situation of probabilistic translation relationships derived from corpus data, rather than from bilingual dictionaries. Working on corpus data has both advantages and disadvantages compared to using human compiled and edited dictionaries. On the one hand,

- the translation relations induced from corpus data are *noisy* since their estimation is partially inaccurate due to limitations of alignment toolkits such as GIZA++ (Och and Ney, 2003) as employed by us. Implications of this inaccuracy are outlined below.
- By using unannotated corpora, we cannot straightforwardly distinguish between cases of polysemy and homonymy. The problem is that homonymy should (ideally) not contribute to generating lexical semantic association networks as considered here. However, homonymy is apparently a rather rare phenomenon, while polysemy, which we expect to underlie the structure of our networks, is abundant (cf. Löbner (2002)).

On the other hand,

- classical dictionaries can be very heterogeneous in their scope and denomination of translation links between words (see, e.g., Cooper (2008)), making the respective editors of the bilingual dictionaries distorting variables.

[1] Each network represents the semantic relations of *both* languages R and L, but since we keep R fixed and vary L, each association network inherits the same properties from R.

- Corpus data allows for inducing probabilities of translation relations of words, which indicate weighted links more accurately than ranked assignments provided by classical dictionaries.
- Corpus data allows for dealing with real language use by means of comparable excerpts of natural language data.

Network generation Assume that we are given different natural languages $L_1, \ldots, L_M, R$ and bilingual translation relations that map from language L_k to language R, for all $1 \leq k \leq M$. We call the language R *reference language*.[2] In our work, we assume that the translation relations are probabilistic. That is, we assume that there exist probabilistic 'operators' P_k that indicate the probabilities – denoted by $P_k[\alpha|z]$ – by which a word z of language L_k translates into a word α of language R. Our motivation is to induce M different lexical semantic networks that represent the lexical semantic spaces of the languages $L_1, \ldots, L_M$, each encoded in language R, which finally allows for comparing the semantic spaces of the M different source languages. To this end, we define the weighted graphs $G_k = (V_k, W_k)$, where the nodes V_k of G_k are given by the vocabulary R^{voc} of language R, i.e. $V_k = R^{\text{voc}}$. We define the weight of an edge $(\alpha, \beta) \in (R^{\text{voc}})^2$ as

$$W_k(\alpha,\beta) = \sum_{z \in L_k^{\text{voc}}} P_k[\alpha|z] P_k[\beta|z] p[z], \quad (1)$$

where $p[z]$ denotes the (corpus) probability of word $z \in L_k^{\text{voc}}$. Since each G_k is spanned using the same subset of the vocabulary of the reference language R, we call it the *L_k(-based) network version of R.*

Eq. (1) can be motivated by postulating that W_k is a joint probability. In this case we can write

$$\begin{aligned} W_k(\alpha,\beta) &= \sum_{z \in L_k^{\text{voc}}} W_k(\alpha,\beta,z) = \sum_{z \in L_k^{\text{voc}}} W_k(\alpha,\beta|z) W_k(z) \\ &\approx \sum_{z \in L_k^{\text{voc}}} W_k(\alpha|z) W_k(\beta|z) W_k(z), \end{aligned} \quad (2)$$

where the first equality is marginalization ('summing out over the possible states of the world'), and the third step is an approximation which would be accurate if α and β were conditionally independent given z. By inserting the conditional probabilities $P_k[\alpha|z]$, $P_k[\beta|z]$ (whose existence we assumed above) and the corpus probability $p[z]$ into Eq. (2), we obtain Eq. (1). Note that in the special case of a bilingual dictionary of L_k and R, where $P_k[\alpha|z]$ can be defined as 1 or 0 depending on whether α is a translation of z or not,[3] $W_k(\alpha,\beta)$ is proportional to the *number of words z (in language L_k) whose translation is both α and β*; i.e., assuming that $p[z]$ is a constant in this setup, Eq. (1) simplifies to:

$$W_k(\alpha,\beta) \propto \sum_{z \in L_k^{\text{voc}} : z \text{ translates into } \alpha \text{ and } \beta} 1.$$

Clearly, the more common translations two words have in the target language, the closer their semantic similarity should be, all else being equal.[4] Eq. (1) generalizes this interpretation by non-uniformly 'prioritizing' the translations of z.

Network analysis In order to compare the network versions $G_1, \ldots, G_M$ of language R that are output by network generation, we first define the vector representation of node v^k in graph $G_k = (V_k, W_k)$ as the probability vector of ending up in any of the nodes of G_k when a random surfer starts from v^k and surfs on the graph G_k according to the normalized weight matrix $\mathbf{W}_k = [W_k(\alpha,\beta)]_{(\alpha,\beta)\in V_k \times V_k}$. Note that the higher $W_k(\alpha,\beta)$, the higher the likelihood that the surfer takes the transition from α to β. More precisely, we let the meaning $[\![v^k]\!]$ of node v^k in graph G_k be the vector $\mathbf{v}^k$ that results as the limit of the iterative process (see, e.g., Brin and Page (1998), Gaume and Mathieu (2008), Kok and Brockett (2010)),

$$\mathbf{v}_{N+1}^k = d\mathbf{v}_N^k \mathbf{A}^{(k)} + (1-d)\mathbf{v}_0^k,$$

where each $\mathbf{v}_N^k$, for $N \geq 0$, is a $1 \times |R^{\text{voc}}|$ vector, $\mathbf{A}^{(k)}$ is obtained from $\mathbf{W}_k$ by normalizing all rows such that $\mathbf{A}^{(k)}$ is row-stochastic, and d is a damping factor that describes preference for the starting vector $\mathbf{v}_0^k$, which is a vector of zeros except for index

[2] Alternative names for the concept we have in mind might, e.g., be *pivot language*, *tertium comparationis* or *interlingua*.

[3] More correctly, one could define $P_k[\alpha|z] = \frac{1}{f_z}$, whenever α is a translation of z, and $P_k[\alpha|z] = 0$, otherwise, where f_z is the number of translations of word z. This would lead to an analogous interpretation as the given one.

[4] This reasoning ignores cases of homonymy, which weaken the semantic argument. See our discussion above.

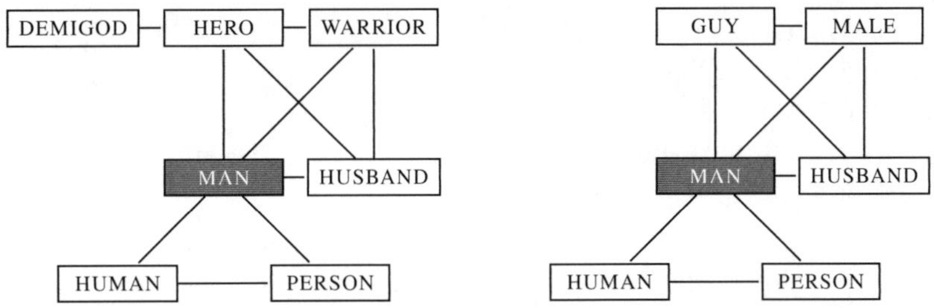

Figure 2: Lexical semantic association networks derived from bilingual dictionaries, given in Figure 1, by linking two English words if and only if they have a common translation in Latin (left) or German (right). The node for MAN is highlighted in both networks.

position of word v^k, where $\mathbf{v}_0^k$ has value 1.[5] Subsequently, we can contrast words v and w (or, rather, their meanings) in the same network version of reference language R, by considering, for instance, the cosine similarity or vector distance of their associated vectors. More generally, we can contrast the lexical semantic meanings $\mathbf{v}^k$ and $\mathbf{w}^j$ of any two language R words v and w, across two languages L_k and L_j, by, e.g., evaluating,

$$\mathbf{v}^k \cdot \mathbf{w}^j \quad \text{(scalar product, cosine similarity)}$$

or

$$||\mathbf{v}^k - \mathbf{w}^j|| \quad \text{(vector distance)}.$$

Finally, the lexical semantic distance or similarity between two *languages* L_k and L_j can be determined by simple averaging,

$$D(L_k, L_j) = \frac{1}{|R^{\text{voc}}|} \sum_{v \in R^{\text{voc}}} S(\mathbf{v}^k, \mathbf{v}^j), \qquad (3)$$

where S is a distance or similarity function.

Discussion We mentioned above that toolkits like GIZA++ cannot perfectly estimate translation relationships between words in different languages. Thus, we have to face situations of 'noisily' weighted links between words in the same network version of reference language R. Typically, a higher chance of mismatch occurs in the case of bigrams. To illustrate, consider the French phrase *êtres chers* ('beings loved'/'loved ones'). Here, GIZA++ typically assigns positive weight mass to $P_{\text{fr}}[\text{LOVE}|\text{être}]$ although, from a point of view of a classical dictionary, translating *être* into *love* is clearly problematic. Since it is likely that, e.g., $P_{\text{fr}}[\text{HUMAN}|\text{être}]$ and $P_{\text{fr}}[\text{BEING}|\text{être}]$ will also be positive, we can expect weighted links in the French network version of English between HUMAN and LOVE as well as between BEING and LOVE. Thus, besides 'true' semantic relations, our approach also captures, though unintentionally, co-occurrence relations.

4 Experiments

We evaluate our method by means of the Europarl corpus (Koehn, 2005). Europarl documents the proceedings of the European parliament in the 21 official languages of the European Union. This provides us with sentence-aligned multi-texts in which each tuple of sentences expresses the same underlying meaning.[6] Using GIZA++, this allows us to estimate the conditional translation probabilities $P[A|B]$ for any two words A, B from any two languages in the Europarl corpus. In our experiment, we focus on the approx. 400,000 sentences for which translations in all 21 languages are available. To process this data, we set all words of all sentences to lower-case. Ideally, we would have lemmatized all texts, but did not do so because of the unavailability of lemmatizers for some of the languages. Therefore, we decided to lemmatize only words in the reference language and kept full-forms for all source languages.[7] We choose

[5] We always set d to 0.8 in our experiments.

[6] In a tuple of sentences, one sentence is the source of which all the other sentences are translations.

[7] Lemmatization tools and models are taken from the TreeTagger (Schmid, 1994) home page www.cis.uni-muenchen.de/~schmid/tools/TreeTagger

English as the reference language.[8] In all languages, we omitted all words whose corpus frequency is less than 50 and excluded the 100 most frequent (mostly function) words.[9] In the reference language, we also ignored all words whose characters do not belong to the standard English character set.

Figure 3 shows subgraphs centered around the seed word WOMAN in five network versions of English. All subgraphs are constructed using the Europarl data. Apparently, the network versions of English diverge from each other. For instance, the semantic association between WOMAN and WIFE appears to be strongest in the French and in the Spanish version of English, while in the Finnish version there does not even exist a link between these nodes. In contrast, the weight of the link between WOMAN and LESBIAN is highest in the Czech version of English, while that between WOMAN and GIRL is strongest in the Finnish version. All in all, the wiring and the thickness of links clearly differ across language networks, indicating that the languages differ in terms of semantic relations of their translations.

Table 1 shows network statistics of the graphs G_k. All network versions of English consist of exactly 5,021 English (lemmatized) words. The networks show a high cluster value, indicating that neighbors of a word are probably interlinked (i.e., semantically related) (cf. Watts and Strogatz (1998)). Average path lengths and diameters are low, that is, distances between words are short, as is typically observed for semantic networks (cf. Steyvers and Tenenbaum (2005)). The density of the networks (measured by the ratio of existing links and the upper bound of theoretically possible links) varies substantially for the language networks. For instance, in the Hungarian network version of English, only 2.56% of the possible links are realized, while in the Dutch version, 8.45% are present. This observation may hint at the 'degree of analyticity' of a language: the more word forms per lemma there are in a language, the less likely they are linked by means of Eq. (1).

[8]Due to the limited availability of lemmatizers, not all languages could have served as a reference language. Although we posit that the choice of reference language has no (or minimal) impact upon the resulting language classification as outlined below, this would need to be experimentally verified in follow-up work.

[9]The threshold of 50 serves to reduce computational effort.

	# nodes	CV	GD	D	density (%)
cs	5,021	0.39	1.96	4	4.51
da	5,021	0.43	1.95	5	5.35
nl	5,021	0.50	1.85	4	8.45 (9.22)
et	5,021	0.37	1.98	5	3.81 (4.57)
fi	5,021	0.35	1.99	4	3.28 (6.63)
fr	5,021	0.44	1.91	4	6.37 (8.23)
de	5,021	0.43	1.96	5	5.03 (5.81)
el	5,021	0.36	2.00	5	3.79
hu	5,021	0.33	2.07	5	2.56
it	5,021	0.45	1.87	4	7.41 (9.53)
lv	5,021	0.41	1.94	4	5.29
lt	5,021	0.41	1.94	4	5.08
pl	5,021	0.39	1.94	4	4.84 (6.56)
pt	5,021	0.40	1.97	4	4.74
ro	5,021	0.39	2.00	5	4.22
sk	5,021	0.36	1.99	5	3.73 (5.23)
sl	5,021	0.38	1.97	4	4.13
es	5,021	0.40	1.98	5	4.67 (5.80)
sv	5,021	0.43	1.94	5	5.69

Table 1: Number of nodes, cluster value (CV), geodesic distance (GD), diameter (D) and density of different network versions of English. Links are binarized depending on whether their weights are positive or not. In brackets: values of lemmatized versions of L_k.

Note that since the density of a network may have substantial impact on random surfer processes as applied by us, and since analyticity is a morphological rather than a semantic phenomenon, it may be possible that the classification results reported below are in fact due to syntagmatic relations – in contrast to our hypothesis about their semantic, paradigmatic nature. We address this issue below.

Semantic similarity Before proceeding to our main task, the clustering of semantic spaces, we measure how strongly our semantic association networks capture semantics. To this end, we compute the correlation coefficient between the semantic similarity scores of the word pairs in the WordSimilarity-353 (Finkelstein et al., 2001) English word relatedness dataset and the similarity scores, for the same word pairs, obtained by our method. The WordSimilarity-353 dataset consists of 353 word pairs annotated by the average of 13 human experts, each on a scale from 0 (unrelated) to 10 (very closely related or identical). We evaluated only on those word pairs for which each word in the pair is contained in our set of 5,021 English words, which amounted to 172 word pairs. To be more

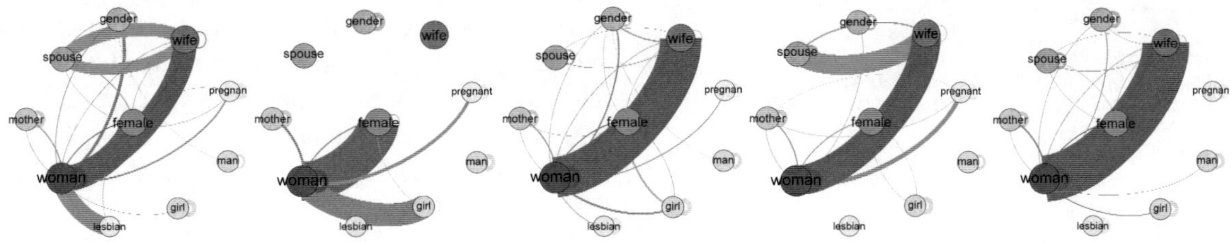

Figure 3: From left to right: Czech, Finnish, French, German, and Spanish networks. Thickness of edges indicates weights of links. Links with weights below a fixed threshold are ignored for better graphical presentation.

precise on the computation of semantic relatedness, for each word pair (u, v) in the WordSimilarity-353 dataset, we computed the semantic similarity of the word pair in the language L_k version of English by considering the cosine similarity of $\mathbf{u}^k$ and $\mathbf{v}^k$, that is, by means of the semantic meanings of u and v generated by the random surfer process on network G_k. Doing so for each language L_k gives 20 different correlation coefficients, one for each network version of English, shown in Table 2.

it	0.34678	⋮	⋮
pt	0.32249	sl	0.25720
es	0.31990	bg	0.25372
ro	0.31204	hu	0.24910
nl	0.30885	et	0.24212
da	0.30715	lt	0.24207

Table 2: Sample Pearson correlation coefficients between human gold standard and our approach for different network versions of English.

We first note that the correlation coefficients differ between network versions of English, where the Italian version exhibits the highest correlation with the (English) human reference, and the Lithuanian version the lowest. Note that Hassan and Mihalcea (2009) obtain a correlation coefficient of 0.55 on the whole WordSimilarity-353 dataset, which is considerably higher than our best score of 0.34. However, first note that our networks, which consist of 5,021 lexical units, are quite small compared to the data sizes that other studies rely on, which makes a comparison highly unfair. Secondly, one has to see that we compute the semantic relatedness of English words *from the semantic point of view of two languages:* the reference language and the respective source language (e.g., the Italian version of English), which, by our very postulate, differs from the semantics of the reference language. According to Table 2, the semantics of English is apparently better represented by the semantics of Italian, Portuguese, Spanish, Romanian, and Dutch, than, e.g., by the one of Bulgarian, Hungarian, Estonian, and Lithuanian – at least subject to the translations provided by the Europarl corpus.[10]

Clustering of semantic spaces Finally, we cluster semantic spaces by comparing the network versions of the English reference language. To determine the semantic distance between two languages L_k and L_j, we plug in each pair of languages in Eq. (3) with $S(\mathbf{v}^k, \mathbf{v}^j)$ as vector distance – thus obtaining a symmetric 20×20 distance matrix. Figures 4 and 5 show the results when feeding this distance matrix as input to k-means clustering (a centroid based clustering approach) and to hierarchical clustering using default parameters. As can be seen, both clustering methods arrange the languages on the basis of their semantic spaces along genealogical relationships. For instance, both clustering algorithms group Danish, Swedish, Dutch and German (Germanic), Portuguese, Spanish, French, Italian, Romanian (Romance), Bulgarian, Czech, Polish, Slovak, Slovene (Slavic), Finnish, Hungarian, Estonian (Finno-Ugric), and Latvian, Lithuanian (Baltic). Greek, which is genealogically isolated in our selection of languages, is in our classification associated with the Romance languages, but constitutes an outlier in this group. All in all, the clustering appears highly non-random and almost a

[10] Table 2 also suggests that the Romance languages are semantically closer to English in our data than, e.g., the Germanic, which may be considered a deviation from, e.g., genealogical language similarity.

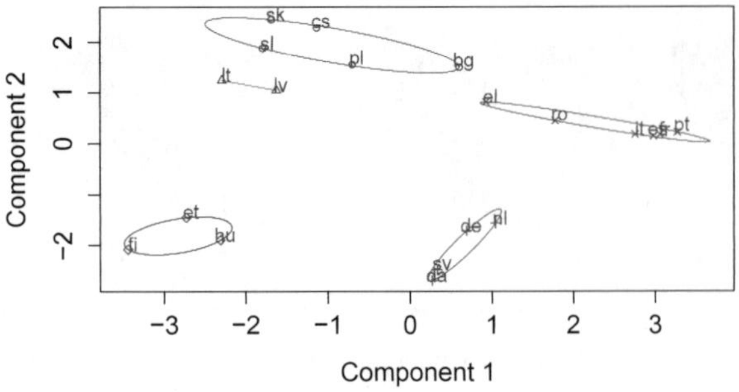

Figure 4: k-means cluster analysis of the 20 Europarl languages. Optimal number of clusters $k = 5$ determined by sum of squared error analysis.

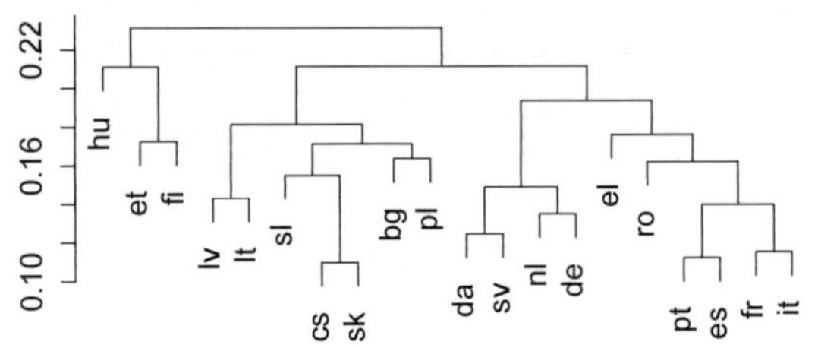

Figure 5: Dendrogram of hierarchical clustering of the 20 non-lemmatized Europarl languages.

perfect match of what is genealogically expected.

To address the question of whether morphological principles are the driving force behind the clustering of the semantic spaces generated here, we lemmatized the reference language English and all source languages L_k for which lemmatizers were freely available in order to conduct the same classification procedure. This included 10 languages: Bulgarian, Dutch, Estonian, Finnish, French, German, Italian, Polish, Slovak, and Spanish. This procedure leads to an assimilation of density values in the graphs G_k as shown in Table 1: for the 10 languages, the relative standard deviation in network density decreases by about 23%. However, the optimal groupings of the languages do not change in that k-means clustering determines the five groups Spanish, French, Italian; Bulgarian, Slovak, Polish; German, Dutch; Finnish; Estonian, *irrespective of whether the named ten languages are lemmatized or not.*[11]

Integrated networks Lastly, we address the derivative question raised in the introduction, viz., whether the integration of heterogeneous/dissimilar multilingual resources may be harmful or beneficial. To this end, we consider *integrated networks* $G^{(S)}$ in which the weight of a link $(\alpha, \beta) \in E^{(S)}$ is given as the *average* (arithmetic mean) link weight of all link weights in the networks for a selection of languages S. Using our optimal number of $k = 5$ clusters (and the clusters themselves) derived above, we thus let S range over the union of all the languages in the $2^k - 1$ possible subsets of clusters.[12] For each so resulting network $G^{(S)}$, we determine semantic similarity between any pair of words exactly as above and then compute correlation with the WordSimilarity-353 dataset. Results are given in Table 3. The numbers appear to support the hypothesis that, in the given monolingual semantic similarity task for English, integrating semantically similar languages (and, putatively, languages whose semantic similarity to English itself is closer) leads to better results than integrating heterogeneous languages. For example, the average network consisting of the Romance languages has a roughly 2% higher correlation than the network consisting of all languages. Interestingly, however, the very best combination result is achieved when we integrate the Romance, Germanic and the three non-Indoeuropean languages Finnish, Hungarian and Estonian.

R+G+F	0.34402	⋮	⋮
R+G	0.34376	S+B	0.27496
R+F	0.33743	S	0.27462
R	0.33719	B+F	0.27424
⋮	⋮	F	0.26074
R+G+F+B+S	0.31670	B	0.25904

Table 3: Sample Pearson correlation coefficients between human gold standard and our approach for different integrated network versions. Language cluster abbreviations: **R**omance (it, fr, pt, es, ro, el), **G**ermanic (sv, nl, de, da), **S**lavic (bg, cz, pl, sk, sl), **B**altic (lv, lt), **F**inno-Ugric (fi, hu, et).

[11]The clustering based on 10 languages slightly differs in that Finnish and Estonian are assigned to distinct clusters.

[12]Ideally, we would have let S range over all possible $2^n - 1$ nonempty subsets of n languages, but this would have required $2^{20} - 1 > 1$ million comparisons.

5 Conclusion

We have encoded lexical semantic spaces of different languages by means of the same pivot language in order to make the languages comparable. To this end, we introduced association networks in which links between words in the reference language depend on translations from the respective source language, weighted by probability of translation. Our methodology is closely related to analogous approaches in the paraphrasing community which interlink paraphrases by means of their translations in other languages (e.g., Bannard and Callison-Burch (2005), Kok and Brockett (2010)), but our application scenario is different and we also describe a principled manner to generate *weighted links* between lexical units from multilingual data. Using random walks to represent similarities among words in the association networks, we finally derived similarity values for pairs of languages. This allowed us to perform several cluster analyses to group the 20 source languages. Interestingly, in our data sample, semantic language classification appears to be almost perfectly correlated with genealogical relationships between languages. To the best of our knowledge, our translation-based lexical semantic classification is the first large-scale quantitative approach to establishing a lexical semantic typology that is completely unsupervised, 'bottom-up', and data-driven.[13]

In future work, we intend to delineate specific lexical semantic fields in which particular languages differ, which can easily be accomplished within our approach. Also, it must be investigated whether our association networks can capture semantic similarity in a competitive manner once they are scaled up appropriately. Finally, applying our methodology to a much larger set of languages is highly desirable.

References

Colin Bannard and Chris Callison-Burch. 2005. Paraphrasing with Bilingual Parallel Corpora. In *Proceedings of the 43rd Annual Meeting on Association for Computational Linguistics*, ACL '05, pages 597–604, Stroudsburg, PA, USA. Association for Computational Linguistics.

Aditya Bhargava and Grzegorz Kondrak. 2011. How Do You Pronounce Your Name?: Improving G2P with Transliterations. In *Proceedings of the 49th Annual Meeting of the Association for Computational Linguistics: Human Language Technologies - Volume 1*, HLT '11, pages 399–408, Stroudsburg, PA, USA. Association for Computational Linguistics.

Aditya Bhargava and Grzegorz Kondrak. 2012. Leveraging Supplemental Representations for Sequential Transduction. In *HLT-NAACL*, pages 396–406. The Association for Computational Linguistics.

Sergey Brin and Lawrence Page. 1998. The Anatomy of a Large-scale Hypertextual Web Search Engine. *Comput. Netw. ISDN Syst.*, 30(1-7):107–117, April.

Lyle Campbell. 2003. How to show Languages are related: Methods for Distant Genetic Relationship. In *The Handbook of Historical Linguistics*. Blackwell.

Sarath Chandar A P, Stanislas Lauly, Hugo Larochelle, Mitesh Khapra, Balaraman Ravindran, Vikas C Raykar, and Amrita Saha. 2014. An Autoencoder Approach to Learning Bilingual Word Representations. In Z. Ghahramani, M. Welling, C. Cortes, N.D. Lawrence, and K.Q. Weinberger, editors, *Advances in Neural Information Processing Systems 27*, pages 1853–1861. Curran Associates, Inc.

Alina Maria Ciobanu and Liviu P. Dinu. 2014. An Etymological Approach to Cross-Language Orthographic Similarity. Application on Romanian. In *Proceedings of the 2014 Conference on Empirical Methods in Natural Language Processing, EMNLP 2014, October 25-29, 2014, Doha, Qatar, A meeting of SIGDAT, a Special Interest Group of the ACL*, pages 1047–1058.

Martin C. Cooper. 2008. Measuring the Semantic Distance between Languages from a Statistical Analysis of Bilingual Dictionaries. *Journal of Quantitative Linguistics*, 15(1):1–33.

Steffen Eger and Ineta Sejane. 2010. Computing Semantic Similarity from Bilingual Dictionaries. In *Proceedings of the 10th International Conference on the Statistical Analysis of Textual Data (JADT-2010)*, pages 1217–1225, Rome, Italy, June. JADT-2010.

Steffen Eger. 2012. Lexical Semantic Typologies from Bilingual Corpora — A Framework. In **SEM 2012: The First Joint Conference on Lexical and Computational Semantics – Volume 1: Proceedings of the main conference and the shared task, and Volume 2: Proceedings of the Sixth International Workshop on Semantic Evaluation (SemEval 2012)*, pages 90–94. Association for Computational Linguistics.

Christiane Fellbaum, editor. 1998. *WordNet: An Electronic Lexical Database*. MIT Press.

[13]But see also the first author's preliminary investigations on semantic language classification in Sejane and Eger (2013), based on freely available (low-quality) bilingual dictionaries, and Eger (2012).

Lev Finkelstein, Gabrilovich Evgenly, Matias Yossi, Rivlin Ehud, Solan Zach, Wolfman Gadi, and Ruppin Eytan. 2001. Placing Search in Context: The Concept Revisited. In *Proceedings of the Tenth International World Wide Web Conference*.

Bruno Gaume and Fabien Mathieu. 2008. PageRank Induced Topology for Real-World Networks. *Complex Systems*, page (on line).

Samer Hassan and Rada Mihalcea. 2009. Cross-lingual Semantic Relatedness Using Encyclopedic Knowledge. In *EMNLP*, pages 1192–1201. ACL.

Karl Moritz Hermann and Phil Blunsom. 2014. Multilingual Models for Compositional Distributed Semantics. *CoRR*, abs/1404.4641.

Jay J. Jiang and David .W. Conrath. 1997. Semantic Similarity Based on Corpus Statistics and Lexical Taxonomy. In *Proc. of the Int'l. Conf. on Research in Computational Linguistics*, pages 19–33.

Philipp Koehn. 2005. Europarl: A Parallel Corpus for Statistical Machine Translation. In *Conference Proceedings: The Tenth Machine Translation Summit*, pages 79–86, Phuket, Thailand. AAMT, AAMT.

Stanley Kok and Chris Brockett. 2010. Hitting the Right Paraphrases in Good Time. In *HLT-NAACL*, pages 145–153. The Association for Computational Linguistics.

Sebastian Löbner. 2002. *Understanding Semantics*. Oxford University Press, New York.

Alexander Mehler, Olga Pustylnikov, and Nils Diewald. 2011. Geography of social ontologies: Testing a variant of the Sapir-Whorf Hypothesis in the context of Wikipedia. *Computer Speech & Language*, 25(3):716–740.

Tomas Mikolov, Kai Chen, Greg Corrado, and Jeffrey Dean. 2013. Efficient estimation of word representations in vector space. *CoRR*, abs/1301.3781.

Roberto Navigli and Simone Paolo Ponzetto. 2012. BabelNet: The Automatic Construction, Evaluation and Application of a Wide-coverage Multilingual Semantic Network. *Artificial Intelligence*, 193(0):217 – 250.

Franz Josef Och and Hermann Ney. 2003. A Systematic Comparison of Various Statistical Alignment Models. *Comput. Linguist.*, 29(1):19–51, March.

Taraka Rama and Lars Borin. 2015. Comparative evaluation of string similarity measures for automatic language classification. In *Sequences in Language and Text*. De Gruyter Mouton.

Kevin Scannell. 2006. Machine translation for closely related languages. In *Proceedings of the Workshop on Strategies for Developing Machine Translation for Minority Languages*, pages 103–107.

Helmut Schmid. 1994. Probabilistic Part-of-Speech Tagging Using Decision Trees. In *International Conference on New Methods in Language Processing*, pages 44–49, Manchester, UK.

Ineta Sejane and Steffen Eger. 2013. Semantic typologies by means of network analysis of bilingual dictionaries. In Lars Borin and Anju Saxena, editors, *Approaches to Measuring Linguistic Differences*, pages 447–474. De Gruyter.

Benjamin Snyder, Tahira Naseem, Jacob Eisenstein, and Regina Barzilay. 2008. Unsupervised Multilingual Learning for POS Tagging. In *EMNLP*, pages 1041–1050. ACL.

Mark Steyvers and Josh Tenenbaum. 2005. The Large-Scale Structure of Semantic Networks: Statistical Analyses and a Model of Semantic Growth. *Cognitive Science*, 29(1):41–78.

Michael Strube and Simone P. Ponzetto. 2006. WikiRelate! Computing Semantic Relatedness using Wikipedia. In *Proceedings of the National Conference on Artificial Intelligence*, volume 21, page 1419. Menlo Park, CA; Cambridge, MA; London; AAAI Press; MIT Press; 1999.

Morris Swadesh. 1955. Towards Greater Accuracy in Lexicostatistic Dating. *International Journal of American Linguistics*, 21:121–137.

Martine Vanhove, Bruno Gaume, and Karine Duvignau. 2008. Semantic Associations and Confluences in Paradigmatic Networks. In *From Polysemy to Semantic Change: Towards a Typology of Lexical Semantic Associations*, pages 233–264. John Benjamins.

Piek Vossen, editor. 1998. *EuroWordNet: A Multilingual Database with Lexical Semantic Networks*. Kluwer Academic Publishers, Norwell, MA, USA.

Duncan. J. Watts and Steven H. Strogatz. 1998. Collective dynamics of 'small-world' networks. *Nature*, 393(6684):409–10.

Benjamin Whorf. 1956. *Language, Thought, and Reality: Selected Writings of Benjamin Lee Whorf*. MIT Press, Cambridge.

Ideological Perspective Detection Using Semantic Features

Heba Elfardy
Columbia University
New York, NY
heba@cs.columbia.edu

Mona Diab
George Washington University
Washington, DC
mtdiab@gwu.edu

Chris Callison-Burch
University of Pennsylvania
Philadelphia, PA
ccb@cis.upenn.edu

Abstract

In this paper, we propose the use of word sense disambiguation and latent semantic features to automatically identify a person's perspective from his/her written text. We run an Amazon Mechanical Turk experiment where we ask Turkers to answer a set of constrained and open-ended political questions drawn from the American National Election Studies (ANES). We then extract the proposed features from the answers to the open-ended questions and use them to predict the answer to one of the constrained questions, namely, their preferred Presidential Candidate. In addition to this newly created dataset, we also evaluate our proposed approach on a second standard dataset of "Ideological-Debates". This latter dataset contains topics from four domains: Abortion, Creationism, Gun Rights and Gay-Rights. Experimental results show that using word sense disambiguation and latent-semantics, whether separately or combined, beats the majority and random baselines on the cross-validation and held-out-test sets for both the ANES and the four domains of the "Ideological Debates" datasets. Moreover combining both feature sets outperforms a stronger unigram-only classification system.

1 Introduction

With the pervasiveness of social media and online discussion fora, there has been a significant increase in documented political and ideological discussions. Automatically predicting the perspective or stance of users in such media is a challenging research problem that has a wide variety of applications including recommendation systems, targeted advertising, political polling, product reviews and even predicting possible future events. Ideology refers to the beliefs that influence an individual's goals, expectations and views of the world (Van Dijk, 1998; Ahmed and Xing, 2010). The ideological perspective of a person is often expressed in his/her choice of discussed topics. People with opposing perspectives will choose to make different topics more salient. (Entman, 1993).

From a social-science viewpoint, the notion of "perspective" is related to the concept of "framing". Framing involves making some topics (or some aspects of the discussed topics) more prominent in order to promote the views and interpretations of the writer (communicator). The communicator makes these framing decisions either consciously or unconsciously (Entman, 1993). These decisions are often expressed in the lexical choice. For example, a person who holds anti-abortion views, is more likely to use the terms "life" and "kill" whereas a person who is pro a woman having an option to go for an abortion will often stress on "choice".

From a computational viewpoint, work on perspective-detection is closely related to subjectivity and sentiment analysis. One's perspective normally influences his/her sentiment towards different topics or targets. Conversely identifying the sentiment of a person towards multiple targets can serve as a cue for identifying his/her perspective. The main difference between perspective and sentiment is that unlike sentiment that is more transient, perspective is often more deeply seated and less likely

*Proceedings of the Fourth Joint Conference on Lexical and Computational Semantics (*SEM 2015)*, pages 137–146,
Denver, Colorado, June 4–5, 2015.

to change. Most of the current perspective-detection work focuses on "Ideological Perspective" by trying to predict a person's stance on controversial topics such as the Palestinian-Israeli conflict, abortion, gay-rights, gun-rights, etc.

In this paper, we are interested in identifying the "Ideological Perspective" of a person using semantic features derived from his/her written text. We use two different sets of semantic features to train several supervised systems that predict different aspects of a person's ideological stance toward specific topics.

We explore the use of Word Sense Disambiguation from the high dimensional space and Latent Semantic models from the low dimensional space on two datasets. We find that explicitly modeling the lexical and contextual semantics to predict a person's perspective outperforms a strong-baseline system trained on standard unigram features.

2 Related Work

Current computational linguistics research on automatic perspective detection uses both supervised and unsupervised techniques. The main task handled by supervised approaches is to perform document (or post) level perspective (or stance) classification, whether binary or multiclass labeling. Unsupervised approaches on the other hand, mainly try to cluster users in a discussion. One of the early works on binary perspective identification is that of Lin et al. (2006) which uses articles from the Bitter-Lemons website –a website that discusses the Palestinian-Israeli conflict from each side's point of view– to train a system for performing automatic perspective detection on the sentence and document levels. On the website, an Israeli editor and a Palestinian editor, together with invited guests, contribute articles to the website on a weekly basis. Lin et al. (2006) use bag-of-words features. They run different experiments where they vary the training and test sets between: (a) editors' articles and (b) guests' articles. The accuracies of the different experimental conditions vary between 86% and 99%. As one might expect the highest accuracy (99%) is that of the system that is trained and tested on the editors' articles. For this system, the classifier is not only capturing the perspective but also the editors' writing styles. In Klebanov et al. (2010), the authors tackle the same problem of binary-perspective detection and experiment with four corpora; Bitter-Lemons, Bitter-Lemons-International, Partial-Birth-Abortion and Death-Penalty. They show that using term-frequencies does not improve over using binary bag-of-words features and that using only the best 1-4.9% features is sufficient to achieve high accuracy. They achieve the highest accuracy (97%) on the Partial-Birth-Abortion dataset and the lowest accuracy (73%) on the Death-Penalty dataset.

Hasan and Ng (2012) also tackle the problem of binary perspective detection but using Integer Linear Programming (ILP) to perform joint inference over the predictions made by a post-stance classifier and several topic-stance classifiers. The authors use n-grams, sentence-type and opinion-dependencies as features to train their classifiers. They collect debate posts discussing Abortion and Gun-Rights and achieve an $F_{\beta=1}$ score of 61.1% on the Abortion dataset and 57.8% on the Gun-Rights dataset. In Hasan and Ng (2013), they extend their previous work by incorporating two soft-constraints that treat the task of post-stance classification as a sequence-labeling problem and ensure that the topic-stance of each author is consistent across all posts.

Somasundaran and Wiebe (2010) employ the notion of *"arguing"* to identify a person's stance (supporting or opposing) towards a topic. Arguing can be indicated by using either positive lexical cues such as *"actually"* or negative ones such as *"certainly not"*. They construct an arguing lexicon and use it to derive features for their classifier. They experiment with both arguing and sentiment features on four datasets; Abortion, Creationism, Gun-Rights and Gay-Rights. They show that combining arguing and sentiment features outperforms a unigram baseline on Abortion, Gay-Rights and Gun-Rights datasets while the unigram system performs best on the Creationism dataset.

A closely related work is that of Al Khatib et al. (2012). In this work, the authors use a set of Arabic and English Wikipedia articles about Arab and Israeli public figures to explore the differences in point of view between the Arabic and English articles about each figure. They assign a point-of-view score to each article in each language, and use these scores to train a classifier to predict the difference in

		Obama	Romney	Neither
PCC	Train	62.9	25.3	11.8
	Test	67.6	18.5	13.9

Table 1: Class Distribution of Presidential Candidate Choice (PCC) in the ANES dataset

point of view between each article-pair.

For unsupervised approaches, two of the most recent works are those of Abu-Jbara et al. (2012) and Dasigi et al. (2012). In Abu-Jbara et al. (2012), the authors perform subgroup detection by clustering authors according to their sentiment towards topics, Named-Entities as well as other discussants. Dasigi et al. (2012) extend the previous work by introducing the notion of implicit attitude which models the similarity between the topics discussed by a pair of people. They note that people that share the same opinion tend to discuss similar topics, thereby their texts tend to have a high semantic similarity. By adding implicit attitude, namely by explicitly modeling latent sentential semantics, they achieve an $F_{\beta=1}$ score improvement of 3.83% and 2.12% on "Wikipedia-Discussions" and "Online-Debates" datasets, respectively.

Yano et al. (2010) study the linguistic cues for bias in political blogs. The authors draw sentences from American political blogs and annotate them for bias on Amazon Mechanical Turk. They explore whether the Turkers' decisions are influenced by their perspectives, for example whether a self proclaimed liberal Turker is more likely to view sentences written by a conservative as biased and vice versa.

3 Datasets

We use two datasets to evaluate our approach.

3.1 ANES Dataset

We create this dataset by drawing a set of questions from the American National Election Studies (ANES) survey questions.[1] ANES conducts various surveys in order to provide better explanations and analysis of the outcomes of USA Presidential elections. While the officially administered ANES survey contains both constrained multiple choice questions and open-ended (free form essay style) questions, the answers to the open-ended questions, which are more interesting from an NLP perspective, are not made publicly available in order to protect the privacy of respondents. In this work, we run an Amazon Mechanical Turk annotation experiment where we ask Amazon Mechanical Turk annotators (aka Turkers) to answer a large set of constrained and open-ended questions drawn from ANES.[2] The constrained questions may be considered a form of self labeling indicating the respondent/Turker's background or perspective on specific issues. All Turkers participating in the experiment were required to be from the US. Moreover, we added seven quality-control questions with a correct (and obvious) answer in order to identify spam Turkers. All submissions that rendered more than one of these questions wrong were automatically rejected.

		Pro	Against
Train	Abortion	55.3	44.7
	Creationism	35.8	64.2
	Gay-Rights	64	36
	Gun-Rights	74	26
Test	Abortion	50.4	49.6
	Creationism	27.9	72.1
	Gay-Rights	63.6	36.4
	Gun-Rights	57.5	42.5

Table 2: Class Distribution across the four domains of the Online Debates Dataset

The first set of questions that required constrained answers, such as multiple choice or binary responses as true or false can be binned into the following categories:

- Background Questions: A person's age, gender, educational level, income, marital-status, social-status, how often he/she follows the news, what news sources he/she follows, etc.;
- Opinion of Political Parties: Democratic and Republican parties and their respective public figure representatives;
- Opinion on major economic and political problems facing the USA;

[1] electionstudies.org/studypages/2010_2012EGSS/2010_2012EGSS

[2] Please contact the authors to obtain the dataset

Q1	I approve of Obama's and the Democrats' position on abortion and gay marriage and their tendency to favor programs that help the poor and working class. They seem more compassionate and more socially progressive.
Q2	Neither Obama nor the Democrats seems able to get a hold on spending, the deficit or help the economy and unemployment. They seem to spend too much time criticizing their opponents rather than work toward viable solutions and seem to distort facts against the other party more.
Q3	I think Mitt Romney and the republicans in general would do a better job at lowering the deficit and stimulating the economy and reducing unemployment. I also agree with their position of less government involvement in some areas.
Q4	I dislike Mitt Romney's plans to eliminate funding for Planned Parenthood and the republicans stand on social issues such as abortion and gay rights, especially gay marriage. I feel Republicans have been taken over by the religious right and are socially regressive.

Table 3: Sample answers provided by one Turker to the first four essay questions in the ANES dataset.

- Ideology Questions: Importance of religion, political-party-affiliation, presidential candidate choice, etc.;
- Opinion on contentious issues: Such as Race (White, Black, Asian and Hispanic Americans), same-sex marriage, gun-control, universal healthcare, etc.

The second set of questions ask about a person's opinion of certain ideological topics. The responses are not constrained in any manner.

Since our main objective is to study whether a person's perspective can be automatically identified using NLP techniques applied to his/her written text, we choose to predict the answer to one of the constrained ideological questions, "Presidential Candidate Choice" (PCC), based on the answers to the following open ended questions: (Table 1 shows the distribution of PCC in the training and test sets)

- **Q1**: Is there something that would make you vote for a Democratic presidential candidate?
- **Q2**: Is there something that would make you vote against a Democratic presidential candidate?
- **Q3**: Is there something that would make you vote for a Republican presidential candidate?
- **Q4**: Is there something that would make you vote against a Republican presidential candidate?
- **Q5**: If you said there is something you like about the Democratic Party: What is that?
- **Q6**: If you said there is something you dislike about the Democratic Party: What is that?
- **Q7**: If you said there is something you like about the Republican Party: What is that?
- **Q8**: If you said there is something you dislike about the Republican Party: What is that?
- **Q9**: What has been the most important issue to you personally in this election?
- **Q10**: What has been the second most important issue to you personally in this election?
- **Q11**: What do you think is the most important political problem facing the United States today?
- **Q12**: What do you think is the second most important political problem facing the United States today?
- **Q13**: What do you think the terrorists were trying to accomplish by September 11th attacks?

Table 3 shows the answers provided by a Turker to the first four of these questions.

In order to simulate user generated content where people are not providing answers to a predefined set of questions but are rather discussing current events or topics, we decide to combine the answers to all of these questions in one document per Turker and use this combined resulting document to derive features (as opposed to deriving features from the answer to each question separately). In order to reduce ambiguity, we perform a quasi co-reference resolution step on pronouns. Prior to combining the answers to all 13 questions, we perform a "pronoun-rewriting" step where we replace the sentence initial pronouns with the topic the question is about. For example, for Q3, *"Is there something that would make you vote for a Republican presidential candidate?"*, and the answer provided is *"They are against voting rights for illegal immigrants. They want to balance the budget and find a way to slowly reduce the national*

Domain	Stance	Post
Abortion	Pro	So abortion is okay in areas where more people like it than don't?
Abortion	Against	your exact words "But successful abortion carries a 100% rate of risk of death to the child" no duh, that's the whole point of abortion, is to KILL THE BABY. well actually that's MURDER
Creationism	Pro	You cant make nothing out of nothing!!!
Creationism	Against	It is only belief. No one has any real evidence.
Gay-Rights	Pro	This post is almost insulting in its complete lack of evidence or even a reasoned argument. Merely dismissing the other side is not an argument
Gay-Rights	Against	Compared to children with a father and a mother married to each other and getting along with each other, the answer is yes. Compared to children living in an orphanage, it's hard to say.
Gun-Rights	Pro	An assault weapon ban violates the second amendment
Gun-Rights	Against	Dude. Are you home all the time? Is this secured? Do you have a lot of fire extinguishers?

Table 4: Sample posts from "Ideological Debates" dataset.

	Train					Test				
	Posts	Tokens	Token/Post	Types	Types/Post	Posts	Tokens	Tokens/Post	Types	Types/Post
ANES	965	437,080	453	14,410	15	108	61,414	569	5,487	51
Abortion	1,036	154,929	150	10,192	10	115	18,299	159	2,734	24
Creationism	1,108	217,262	196	13,466	12	122	10,756	88	2,160	18
Gay-Rights	1,858	312,900	168	16,742	9	206	17,400	84	2,842	14
Gun-Rights	963	146,886	153	10,969	11	106	7,142	67	1,588	15

Table 5: Statistics of the training and test sets for both the ANES and the four domains of the Ideological-Debates datasets.

debt.", we replace "They" with "Republicans".

3.2 Ideological Debates Dataset

This dataset was collected by Somasundaran and Wiebe (2010) . It contains debate posts from six domains; (a) Abortion, (b) Creationism, (c) Gay-Rights, (d) Gun-Rights, (e) Healthcare and (f) Existence of God. Each domain represents an ideological topic with two possible perspectives, pro and against. Similar to the work of (Somasundaran and Wiebe, 2010), we use the first four domains to evaluate our approach. Table 2 shows the class distribution in each of these four domains while table 4 lists some sample posts. It should be noted that our results are not comparable to those obtained by (Somasundaran and Wiebe, 2010), since they used a subset of the posts in each domain and the split was not publicized.

Table 5 shows the size of the training and test data in the ANES and Ideological-Debates datasets.

4 Approach

Our goal is to determine whether semantic features help in identifying a person's ideological perspective as determined by his/her answer to the PCC constrained question in the "ANES" dataset and his/her stance towards the ideological-topics discussed in the "Ideological-Debates" dataset independently.

4.1 Preprocessing

We apply basic preprocessing to the text by separating punctuation and numbers from words. All punctuation and numbers are then ignored when training the classifier for all of our systems including the unigram baseline. The intuition behind this is that punctuation and numbers do not capture the perspective of a person but rather the writing style. Moreover, by ignoring them, we avoid overfitting the training data.

4.2 Word Sense Disambiguation (WSD)

We use WN-Sense-Relate (Patwardhan et al., 2005) to perform word sense disambiguation. Sense-Relate uses WordNet (Miller, 1995) to tag each word with the part-of-speech and sense-id. The only parts of speech that are handled by WN-Sense-Relate are adjectives (a), adverbs (r), verbs (v) and nouns (n). In addition to the part-of-speech and sense-id, WN-Sense-Relate also identifies and tags compounds. The word sense tagging process can be either contextual or can rely on the most frequent sense. We experiment with both variants.

4.2.1 Contextual WSD (WSD-CXT)

In this variant of WSD, in addition to tagging compounds, we contextually disambiguate each word and tag it with its sense-id and part-of-speech. We use the default setting of SenseRelate which employs a modified version of the Lesk algorithm (Banerjee and Pedersen, 2002) to perform the disambiguation. This version of the Lesk algorithm measures the similarity between the WordNet gloss of each sense of the target word and those of its surrounding context words in the text. It then chooses the sense whose gloss is most similar to the surrounding words. We use a window of size three which uses one word before and one word after the target word.

ex.
"*The Democratic Party supports women 's equality , including equal pay , access to health care and other issues .*"
becomes:
"*the#ND democratic_party#n#1 supports#n#10 women#n#1 's#ND equality#n#1 including#v#3 equal#a#1 pay#v#1 access#n#2 to#ND health_care#n#1 and#ND other#a#1 issues#n#7*"[3]

We then use the tagged-words to retrieve the Synonym-Set (Synset) of this sense of the word using WN-QueryData (Pedersen et al., 2004). We assign each Synset an ID and whenever any of the words in the retrieved Synset is seen in the input text, we replace it with this Synset-ID.

For example, the Synset of "*issues#n#7*" is identified as "*issue#n#7, consequence#n#1, effect#n#1, outcome#n#2, result#n#1, event#n#4, issue#n#7, upshot#n#1*". We assign this Synset a unique ID, for example "*Synset-100*", and any occurrence of any of "*issue#n#7, consequence#n#1, effect#n#1, outcome#n#2, result#n#1, event#n#4, issue#n#7, and upshot#n#1*" is replaced by "*Synset-100*".

[3]#ND indicates a non-defined word

4.2.2 Most Frequent Sense WSD (WSD-MFS)

In this variant of WSD, instead of performing the disambiguation contextually, we rely on the most frequent sense. Using this scheme, "*issues*" is tagged as "*issues#n#1*" whose Synset is "*issue#n#1*", while "*support*" is tagged as "*support#v#1*" whose Synset is *support#v#1', back_up#v#1*.

4.3 Latent Semantics

The next set of features relies on "Latent Semantics" which maps text from a high-dimensional space such as unigrams to a low-dimensional one such as topics. Most of these models assign a semantic profile to each given sentence (or document) by considering the observed words and assuming that each given document has a distribution over "K" topics. We apply (1) Latent Dirichlet Allocation (LDA) (Blei et al., 2003) as implemented in MALLET toolkit (McCallum, 2002), and (2) Weighted Textual Matrix Factorization (WTMF) (Guo and Diab, 2012) to each post. In addition to observed words, WTMF also models missing ones namely explicitly modeling what the post is not about. WTMF defines missing words as the whole vocabulary of the training data minus the ones observed in the given document.

4.3.1 Number of Topics

We vary the number of topics (K) between 100 and 500 (with a step-size of 100) and use the best "K" for each dataset. We define the best K, for each of LDA and WTMF, as the one that yields the best cross-validation results when combined with unigram features. The best K value for LDA is 400 for PCC and Abortion, 500 for Creationism, 300 for Gay-Rights and 100 for Gun-Rights. For WTMF, the best K is 500 for PCC, and Gun-Rights and 100 for Abortion, Creationism and Gay-Rights.

	PCC $F_{\beta=1}$ score
Train	74.65
Test	74.81
All	74.69

Table 6: Performance of human annotators in predicting "PCC" of a person from his/her responses to ANES essay questions.

4.3.2 Training Data

We collected our training data for topic modeling from Facebook comments of renowned American politicians such as Joe-Biden, Chris-Christie, George W. Bush, Michelle-Obama, etc. We trained LDA and WTMF using a subset of 100,000 comments (corresponding to ~5,000,000 tokens and ~265,000 types.

4.4 Classifier Training

Using WEKA toolkit (Hall et al., 2009) and the derived features, we train Sequential Minimal Optimization (SMO) SVM classifiers (Platt, 1998) for each of "ANES" and the four domains of "Ideological-Debates" datasets. We use a normalized quadratic kernel, set the parameter C to 100 and apply a 10-fold cross validation on the training sets.

5 Experiments

5.1 Baselines

We compare our approach to three baselines;

- **Majority Baseline *(MAJ-BL)***: which assigns all posts to the most frequent class-label;
- **Random Baseline *(RAND-BL)***: which randomly chooses the class-label;
- **Unigram Baseline *(UNI-BL)***: a strong baseline that uses standard unigram features.

In addition to these three baselines, we do a human-evaluation for the ANES dataset in order to assess the difficulty of the task and in order to get an upper-bound on how well we can do in predicting PCC. We run an Amazon Mechanical Turk experiment where we ask Turkers to read each post (constructed by combining the answers to the open-ended questions of each record) and ask them to guess the PCC of the person who wrote that text along with the reason for their answer. We found

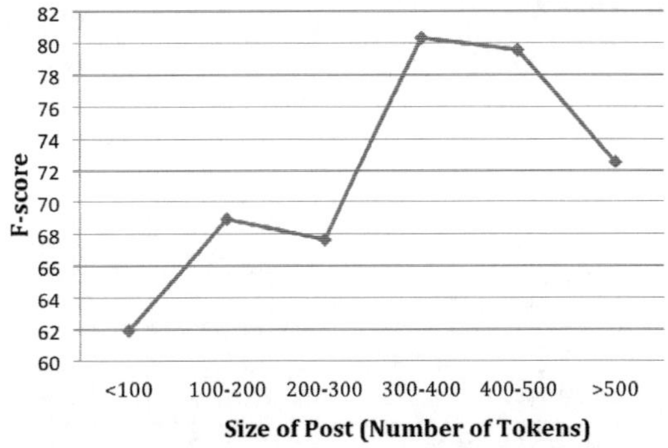

Figure 1: $F_{\beta=1}$ score of human judgments in predicting "PCC" from the answers to the essay questions in the ANES dataset across different post-sizes

that Turkers were able to predict the PCC with an average $F_{\beta=1}$ score of ~75% on both the cross-validation and test-sets. We also found that the task is particularly difficult for very short (< 100 words) documents. Table 6 and Figure 1 show the results of this qualitative assessment.

5.2 Experimental Setup

We first evaluate each variant of the proposed features separately and then we combine the latent-semantics features with unigram-features and the two variants of WSD.

Tables 7 and 8 show the cross-validation results on the training data and the results on the held-out test sets respectively.

6 Discussion

6.1 Cross Validation Results

For the cross-validation results, all configurations of the proposed features outperform the majority and random baselines. Moreover using WSD-MFS, either separately or combined with LDA or WTMF, outperforms the unigram-baseline. Overall WSD-MFS performs better than WSD-CXT, except on the Abortion dataset.

For Latent-Semantics, even though using either of LDA or WTMF separately, without unigram-features, does not outperform the unigram baseline, combining each of them with unigrams outperforms the unigram-only setup. When combined with unigram or WSD features, WTMF outperforms LDA on PCC, Creationism and Gun-Rights while LDA out-

	PCC	Abortion	Creationism	Gay-Rights	Gun-Rights
MAJ-BL	48.6	39.4	50.2	50	63
RAND-BL	36.7	47.6	50	52.9	52.6
UNI-BL	66.3	63.1	58.7	67.1	72.7
WTMF	62.9	56.9	57.1	57.1	72.6
LDA	62.4	57.4	58.7	63.6	71
Unigram+WTMF	68.8	62.7	62	67.2	**75.7**
Unigram+LDA	66.6	64.5	60	67.4	72.9
WSD-CXT	65.8	64.8	59.4	69.6	73.8
WSD-MFS	67.5	64	61.1	**69.7**	75
WSD-CXT + WTMF	68	64.1	61.6	68.1	74.8
WSD-CXT + LDA	65	64.3	59.3	69.1	73.8
WSD-MFS + WTMF	**69.2**	64.7	**62.7**	67.6	**75.7**
WSD-MFS + LDA	67.3	**65.1**	62.1	69.5	75

Table 7: 10-fold cross-validation results (measured in $F_{\beta=1}$ score) of using WSD and Latent-Semantics against the baselines.

	PCC	Abortion	Creationism	Gay-Rights	Gun-Rights
MAJ-BL	54.5	33.8	60.5	49.4	42
RAND-BL	46.6	47.3	54.9	41.9	45.5
UNI-BL	68	54.3	67.1	52.4	48.1
WTMF	69.1	58.1	60.1	49.2	43.7
LDA	60.4	55.3	58.7	**58.1**	**62.4**
Unigram+WTMF	68.9	54.2	**71.2**	56.8	58.7
Unigram+LDA	68	58.9	70.7	56.4	48.1
WSD-CXT	66.8	52.8	66.2	53.4	44.1
WSD-MFS	64.2	54.6	69.8	56.3	46.2
WSD-CXT + WTMF	66.1	52.9	71	55.1	53.7
WSD-CXT + LDA	67.6	57	68.5	55.6	46.2
WSD-MFS + WTMF	**71.6**	55.7	69.1	56.7	52.7
WSD-MFS + LDA	65.3	**62.6**	69.6	56.4	44.1

Table 8: Held-out test-set results (measured in $F_{\beta=1}$ score) of using WSD and Latent-Semantics against the baselines.

performs WTMF on the other two datasets. Combining WSD-MFS with LDA for Abortion and Gay-Rights and with WTMF for PCC, Creationism and Gun-Rights yields the best (or close to the best) results.

6.2 Held-out Test-Sets Results

Unlike the cross-validation results, using latent-semantics features separately improves over the unigram baseline for four out of the five datasets and in some cases adding unigrams to latent-semantics features actually hurts the performance. This suggests that latent-semantics are less likely to overfit the training data.

Table 9 shows examples of the posts that were misclassified by the majority and unigram baselines and correctly classified by the best semantic model for each dataset.

6.3 General Observations

We investigated the data to identify the different challenges faced when trying to identify a person's

Domain	Stance	Post
Abortion	Against	Yes, all innocent life. But that depends on how you define innocent life.
Creationism	Pro	There's a definite difference between micro-evolution and macro-evolution in the sense that with the moths and the finches, there are minor changes that happen. It's kind of like a pendulum. It swings far to the right and to the left, but in the end, it's right in the center again, if you understand me correctly.
Gay-Rights	Against	Not necessarily the question of whether or not same-sex couples' marriages specifically are recognized by the government. As for my personal views on the issue I honestly think the best solution is for the government to simply call all civil unions precisely what they are: civil unions. Leave it to individuals and churches to determine the definition of "marriage."
Gun-Rights	Against	I agree that gun ownership should be strictly controlled. Put a gun in the hands of a crackpot and there's going to be a problem.

Table 9: Examples of the posts that were misclassified by the unigram baseline and were correctly classified by the right semantic model.

perspective and found the following:

1. In ANES dataset, due to the structure of the questions, some Turkers were trying to be objective which makes it difficult even for a human evaluator to identify the political leaning of the person who wrote the text. The example in Table 3 illustrates such a case where it is not easy to detect the PCC of the Turker from the provided answers.
2. The use of sarcasm, which can be easily detected by human evaluators but not by an automated system. For example, in Abortion dataset, a participant who does not oppose abortion wrote *"Why should people use reason and logic to discover right and wrong when a priest can decide for them?"*
3. Misspelled words such as writing *"Romeny"* instead of *"Romney"*
4. In each domain of the Ideological Debates dataset, the posts were collected from different discussion fora pertaining to the domain of interest. For example, in the Abortion dataset, posts were collected from "Can Catholics Vote For Pro-Choice Politicians", "Should South Dakota pass the Abortion Ban", "Should abortion be legal" and other fora. For some of the posts, the participants provided very short answers such as *"Once they take the booth who they vote for is supposed to be secret."* which makes it almost impossible to identify their stance without knowing the exact question the forum posed.

7 Conclusion

In this paper, we explore the use of semantic features to perform automatic detection of ideological-perspective from written text. Using Word Sense Disambiguation and Latent Semantics features, we trained several SVM classifiers that predict different aspects of the ideological-perspective of a person. We evaluated the presented approach on two datasets. The first of which comprises answers to questions about American politics collected from an Amazon Mechanical Turk experiment while the second one consists of four subsets of a standard dataset, discussing Abortion, Creationism, Gay-Rights and Gun-Rights. Results show that using the proposed features outperforms a system that relies on standard unigram features on all datasets. On the cross-validation sets, combining word sense disambiguation with latent semantics performs best while on the held-out test sets, the best configuration various across the different domains.

We plan to explore other methods for performing word sense disambiguation in addition to using semantic-role-labeling and modeling sarcasm.

8 Acknowledgment

We thank the three anonymous reviewers for their useful comments and suggestions.

This research is funded by DARPA DEFT program with a subcontract from Columbia University and a Google Faculty Research Award to Diab.

References

Amjad Abu-Jbara, Mona Diab, Pradeep Dasigi, and Dragomir Radev. 2012. Subgroup detection in ideological discussions. In *Proceedings of the 50th Annual Meeting of the Association for Computational Linguistics: Long Papers-Volume 1*, pages 399–409. Association for Computational Linguistics.

Amr Ahmed and Eric P Xing. 2010. Staying informed: supervised and semi-supervised multi-view topical analysis of ideological perspective. In *Proceedings of the 2010 Conference on Empirical Methods in Natural Language Processing*, pages 1140–1150. Association for Computational Linguistics.

Khalid Al Khatib, Hinrich Schütze, and Cathleen Kantner. 2012. Automatic detection of point of view differences in wikipedia. In *COLING*, pages 33–50.

Satanjeev Banerjee and Ted Pedersen. 2002. An adapted lesk algorithm for word sense disambiguation using wordnet. In *Computational linguistics and intelligent text processing*, pages 136–145. Springer.

David M Blei, Andrew Y Ng, and Michael I Jordan. 2003. Latent dirichlet allocation. *the Journal of machine Learning research*, 3:993–1022.

Pradeep Dasigi, Weiwei Guo, and Mona Diab. 2012. Genre independent subgroup detection in online discussion threads: a pilot study of implicit attitude using latent textual semantics. In *Proceedings of the 50th Annual Meeting of the Association for Computational Linguistics: Short Papers-Volume 2*, pages 65–69. Association for Computational Linguistics.

Robert M Entman. 1993. Framing: Toward clarification of a fractured paradigm. *Journal of communication*, 43(4):51–58.

Weiwei Guo and Mona Diab. 2012. Modeling sentences in the latent space. In *Proceedings of the 50th Annual Meeting of the Association for Computational Linguistics: Long Papers-Volume 1*, pages 864–872. Association for Computational Linguistics.

Mark Hall, Eibe Frank, Geoffrey Holmes, Bernhard Pfahringer, Peter Reutemann, and Ian H Witten. 2009. The weka data mining software: an update. *ACM SIGKDD Explorations Newsletter*, 11(1):10–18.

Kazi Saidul Hasan and Vincent Ng. 2012. Predicting stance in ideological debate with rich linguistic knowledge. In *Proceedings of the 24th International Conference on Computational Linguistics*.

Kazi Saidul Hasan and Vincent Ng. 2013. Extra-linguistic constraints on stance recognition in ideological debates. In *Proceedings of the 51st Annual Meeting of the Association for Computational Linguistics*. Association for Computational Linguistics.

Beata Beigman Klebanov, Eyal Beigman, and Daniel Diermeier. 2010. Vocabulary choice as an indicator of perspective. In *ACL*, pages 253–257. Association for Computational Linguistics.

Wei-Hao Lin, Theresa Wilson, Janyce Wiebe, and Alexander Hauptmann. 2006. Which side are you on?: identifying perspectives at the document and sentence levels. In *Proceedings of the Tenth Conference on Computational Natural Language Learning*, pages 109–116. Association for Computational Linguistics.

Andrew Kachites McCallum. 2002. Mallet: A machine learning for language toolkit. http://mallet.cs.umass.edu.

George A Miller. 1995. Wordnet: a lexical database for english. *Communications of the ACM*, 38(11):39–41.

Siddharth Patwardhan, Satanjeev Banerjee, and Ted Pedersen. 2005. Senserelate:: Targetword: a generalized framework for word sense disambiguation. In *Proceedings of the ACL 2005 on Interactive poster and demonstration sessions*, pages 73–76. Association for Computational Linguistics.

Ted Pedersen, Siddharth Patwardhan, and Jason Michelizzi. 2004. Wordnet:: Similarity: measuring the relatedness of concepts. In *Demonstration Papers at HLT-NAACL 2004*. Association for Computational Linguistics.

John C. Platt. 1998. Sequential minimal optimization: A fast algorithm for training support vector machines. *Technical Report MSR-TR-98-14, Microsoft Research.*

Swapna Somasundaran and Janyce Wiebe. 2010. Recognizing stances in ideological online debates. In *Proceedings of the NAACL HLT 2010 Workshop on Computational Approaches to Analysis and Generation of Emotion in Text*, pages 116–124. Association for Computational Linguistics.

Teun A Van Dijk. 1998. *Ideology: A multidisciplinary approach*. Sage.

Tae Yano, Philip Resnik, and Noah A Smith. 2010. Shedding (a thousand points of) light on biased language. In *Proceedings of the NAACL HLT 2010 Workshop on Creating Speech and Language Data with Amazon's Mechanical Turk*, pages 152–158. Association for Computational Linguistics.

Mapping Different Rhetorical Relation Annotations: A Proposal

Farah Benamara Zitoune
IRIT, Toulouse University
Université Paul Sabatier
Toulouse, France
benamara@irit.fr

Maite Taboada
Department of Linguistics
Simon Fraser University
Vancouver, Canada
mtaboada@sfu.ca

Abstract

Annotation efforts have resulted in the availability of a number of corpora with rhetorical relation information. The corpora, unfortunately, are annotated under different theoretical approaches and have different hierarchies of relations. In addition, new sets of rhetorical relations have been proposed to account for language variation. The types of relations, however, tend to overlap or be related in specific ways. We believe that differences across approaches are minimal, and a unified set of relations that works across languages is possible. This paper details a new taxonomy of relations organized in four top level-classes with a total of 26 relations. We propose a mapping between existing annotations and show that our taxonomy is robust across theories, and can be applied to multiple languages.

1 Motivation

The annotation of discourse relations in language can be broadly characterized as falling under two main approaches: the *lexically grounded approach* and an approach that aims at *complete discourse coverage*. Perhaps the best example of the first approach is the Penn Discourse Treebank (Prasad et al., 2008). The annotation starts with specific lexical items, most of them conjunctions, and includes two arguments for each conjunction. This leads to partial discourse coverage, as there is no guarantee that the entire text is annotated, since parts of the text not related through a conjunction are excluded. On the positive side, such annotations tend to be reliable. PDTB-style annotations have been carried out in a variety of languages (Arabic, Chinese, Czech, Danish, Dutch, French, Hindi and Turkish), and in some cases the taxonomy of relations had to be modified, by adding or merging relations (Prasad et al., 2014).

Complete discourse coverage requires annotation of the entire text, with most of the propositions in the text integrated in a structure. It includes work from two theoretical perspectives, either intentionally driven, such as RST (Mann and Thompson, 1988) or semantically driven, such as SDRT (Asher and Lascarides, 2003). RST proposes a tree-based representation, with relations between adjacent segments, and emphasizes a differential status for discourse components (the nucleus vs. satellite distinction). Annotated resources exist in Basque, Dutch, German, English, Portuguese and Spanish. Captured in a graph-based representation, with long-distance attachments, SDRT proposes relations between abstract objects using a relatively small set of relations. Corpora following SDRT exist in Arabic, French and English.

Manually annotated resources have contributed to a number of applications, most notably discourse segmentation into elementary discourse units, identification of explicit and implicit relations for the purpose of discourse parsing, and development of end-to-end discourse parsers (Hernault et al., 2010; Feng and Hirst, 2014; Joty et al., 2015). These parsers have been successfully deployed in NLP applications including machine translation, sentiment analysis and automatic summarization (Thione et al., 2004; Heerschop et al., 2011; Hardmeier, 2013).

Each approach has its own hierarchy of discourse relations, but relations tend to overlap or be re-

*Proceedings of the Fourth Joint Conference on Lexical and Computational Semantics (*SEM 2015)*, pages 147–152,
Denver, Colorado, June 4–5, 2015.

lated in a few specific ways. We suggest there are four general ways of mapping relations across approaches: (1) *Specialization*, where a relation R in one approach can correspond to several relations in another approach, (2) *Generalization*, in which several relations in one approach correspond to one relation in another approach, (3) *Omission* involves a relation defined in one approach, but not taken into account in another. Finally, in (4), *Definition*, relations have similar names, but different definitions.

We propose here a unified hierarchy of discourse relations. Our proposal has several motivations. First of all, with the wide availability of annotated corpora, it would be beneficial to have a system for mapping relations across approaches. In particular for classification tasks such as discourse parsing, access to larger amounts of data is likely to yield better results. Secondly, and from a more theoretical point of view, we would like to propose that differences across approaches are minimal, and a unified set of relations is possible. This would facilitate the work of discourse analysts and would also result in better annotation efforts. Third, a unified set of discourse relations would allow us to compile a list of discourse markers and other signals for those relations, which would also benefit discourse annotation. Finally, this is a first step towards multilingual discourse analysis. Many studies have compared the use of discourse markers across languages, and how they differ in translation (Degand, 2009; Zufferey and Degand, 2014). We would like to contribute to that area of study by unifying and integrating the types of relations that markers can signal.

Merging different discourse relation taxonomies involves, in our view, different steps, having to do with: (1) segmentation, (2) unifying the set of relations, (3) proposing possible signals, (4) unifying discourse structures, and (5) providing a language for merging annotations. We focus here on step (2). For proposals for steps (4) and (5), see Venant et al. (2013), and Chiarcos (2014), respectively.

2 Methodology

Our first focus are the two theories that we are most familiar with, RST and SDRT. We next plan to find correspondences between our unified RST-SDRT hierarchy and the PDTB taxonomy.

The first step consists of grouping relations in top-level classes. Our goal is to minimize the number of top-level classes and, at the same time, reduce the number at the fine-grained level, avoiding the proliferation of relations seen in the RST Discourse Tree-Bank (Carlson et al., 2003).

Two main criteria were used in creating the hierarchy. First of all, the proposed hierarchy should be stable enough for language variation. By this we mean that the main classes at the top level should remain constant. We believe that there is little cross-linguistic variation when it comes to the higher-level classification of discourse relations. The second, related criterion in our organization, is that the hierarchy has to be open to modification at the low level. This is where previous research has observed variation due to language and genre.

Definitions of relations are based on three further criteria. First of all, we do not define relations on the basis of the status of their arguments. The nucleus-satellite distinction in RST is not relevant for our basic definition of relations. Secondly, we focus on the effect that a relation has on meaning, and not on how it is lexically triggered by a discourse marker or lexical device. Finally, we provide intentional effects when needed. Our taxonomy is both intentionally and semantically driven, motivated by our desire to find a balance between RST and SDRT.

Our starting points are the set of RST definitions from the RST website[1] and the definitions provided within the RST-DT (Carlson et al., 2003). For SDRT, we considered the relations defined in the SDRT literature (Asher and Lascarides, 2003), plus the adaptations created when annotating data in different projects: Discor (Reese et al., 2007), Annodis (Afantenos et al., 2012), plus the classification proposed for Arabic (Keskes et al., 2014).

3 Towards a unified hierarchy

We built a hierarchy with four top-level classes: TEMPORAL, STRUCTURAL, THEMATIC and CAUSAL-ARGUMENTATIVE, organized in three levels with a total of 26 relations. We have taken into account all SDRT, PDTB, RST-DT and RST relations, with the exception of the following relations from the RST-DT: Topic Change (topic-shift,

[1] `http://www.sfu.ca/rst/`

topic-drift), Textual Organization and Topic-Comment (problem-solution, question-answer, statement-response, topic-comment, comment-topic, rhetorical-question). We believe that some of those relations structure topics, but are not necessarily discourse relations. Table 1 summarizes the inventory of the proposed relations at each level.

3.1 Temporal class

A class of relations indicating relations which set events in terms of time or a similar frame is a component of most hierarchies. In some classifications, this group includes relations of background or framing, but we prefer an exclusively temporal class.

Arguments in the temporal class need to share the same topic, and the relations always express co-temporal constraints, i.e., temporal ordering between the main eventualities e_1 and e_2 introduced respectively in their arguments. The class includes three relations: SEQUENCE, INVERTED SEQUENCE and SYNCHRONOUS.

3.2 Thematic class

Thematic is a broad class which includes relations among the content of the propositions. They structure and organize information in the discourse, and can be divided into three different subclasses:

(1) ELABORATION. A group of discourse relations that connect utterances describing the same state of affairs. Further classified into: PARTITIVE, GENERALITY, OBJECT, SUMMARY, RESTATEMENT, and MEANS. For most purposes, the further specificity is not necessary, and in some cases it may be difficult to distinguish among the subclasses. We believe, however, that these more specific relations may be useful when analyzing certain genres, or for particular applications.

(2) FRAMING. This class includes relations that provide a framework for understanding the content of the situation described in the discourse segment. It includes two relations: FRAME and BACKGROUND. FRAME holds when a is a frame and b is in the scope of that frame, generally when a is at the beginning of a sentence. Several cases are possible: temporal, spatial or domain frames. This relation has no direct equivalence in RST. BACKGROUND is equivalent to the RST relations Background and Circumstance. It is used to capture a specific spatio-temporal structure, to accommodate presuppositions in discourse, or to set the stage of a story.

(3) ATTRIBUTION. Attribution relates a communicative agent in the first argument and the content of a communicative act introduced in the second. Both the RST-DT and SDRT take Attribution as a discourse relation. PDTB, on the other hand, treats it as orthogonal to discourse annotation. In our case, we follow Asher et al.'s (2006) position on reportative constructions in discourse, who consider that the treatment of these verbs is necessary for a correct analysis of the semantics and discourse structure of stories in news corpora. We agree, however, with the PDTB, that it is not a fully-fledged relation, with the same intentional effects, but we do believe that it should be annotated.

3.3 Structuring class

This class contains relations of textual organization at a high level, which organize the structure of the information in terms of themes or topics (but are rhetorical, not relations of topic management). ALTERNATION holds when there is a disjunction between a and b. PARALLEL occurs when a and b have similar semantic and syntactic structures, and it requires a and b to share a common theme. It has the same semantics as List in RST-DT. CONTINUATION holds between two segments when they both elaborate or provide background to the same segment. It also occurs in cases where there is no clear rhetorical relation between the segments. Equivalent to the RST-DT relation Elaboration-additional and to Continuation in SDRT.

3.4 Causal-argumentative class

This class contains two broad classes, one causal and one argumentative. We see them as related to each other, as conjunctions and other discourse markers can be present to indicate a causal relation or be more abstract in an argumentative use (e.g., *I'm only saying this because I care.*).

3.4.1 Causal

We distinguish between CAUSE/RESULT and PURPOSE. Within the first sub-class, REASON holds when the main eventuality of the second argument is understood as the cause of the eventuality in the first argument. RESULT relates a cause to its effect: the

TEMPORAL	SEQUENCE, INVERTED SEQUENCE, SYNCHRONOUS
THEMATIC	ELABORATION → Partitive, Generality, Object, Summary, Restatement, Means
	FRAMING → Frame, Background
	ATTRIBUTION
STRUCTURING	ALTERNATION, PARALLEL, CONTINUATION
CAUSAL-ARGUMENTATIVE	CAUSAL Cause/Result → Reason, Result, General Condition Purpose
	ARGUMENTATIVE Support → Motivation, Evidence/Justification, Evaluation/Interpretation Opposition → Contrast, Concession, Antithesis

Table 1: Inventory of proposed relations in the unified hierarchy

main eventuality of *a* caused the eventuality given by *b*. GENERAL CONDITION holds when the first segment is a hypothesis and the second the consequence. PURPOSE holds when the second segment (*b*) describes the aim, the goal or the purpose of the event described in the first segment (*a*). Most often, it can be paraphrased as "*a* in order to *b*."

3.4.2 Argumentative

This class includes the SUPPORT and OPPOSITION sub-classes, which are used to advance an argument. SUPPORT mainly captures justification, explanation (not causal), evaluation and evidence. OPPOSITION groups relations where the segments have similar semantic structures, but contrasting themes, i.e., sentence topics, or when one constituent negates a default consequence of the other.

4 Mapping RST and SDRT annotations

To test the stability of our proposed hierarchy across both theoretical and language variations, we mapped it to annotations in three corpora: the RST-DT English corpus (Carlson et al., 2003), the SDRT Annodis French corpus (Afantenos et al., 2012), and the RST Spanish Treebank (RST-ST) (da Cunha et al., 2011). The taxonomies in these corpora respectively contain 78, 17 and 28 relations. The total number of annotated information in terms of frequency of relations is 18,255 for RST-DT, 3,345 for Annodis, and 3,115 for RST-ST. Tables 2, 3, 4, and 5 provide frequency of our relations in each of the three corpora above in the four main classes. The distribution of our four classes across the corpora is respectively 3.61%, 25.55%, 47.80%, and 23.08%. The proportions are quite similar to the original distribution in each corpus, taking into account the slightly different structures of each taxonomy.

	RST-DT	Annodis	RST-ST
Seq.	224	350	74
Sync.	160		
Inv. Seq.	59	27	
Total TEMPORAL: **894**			

Table 2: Temporal class mapping

	RST-DT	Annodis	RST-ST	Total
Alter.	21	18	9	48
Paral.	1,211	59		1,270
Conti.	4,144	682	171	4,997
Total STRUCTURING: **6,315**				

Table 3: Structuring class mapping

Most mappings were relatively straightforward, except for some relations that can be either *missing* or *too specific*. The first case concerns the relations FRAME, PARALLEL and ATTRIBUTION that were not annotated in the RST-ST, as well as the relation FRAME for RST-DT. The second case is the most frequent and occurs when at least two relations having specific semantics or intentional effects need to be merged to find their corresponding instances in a given corpus. For example, the Temporal relations SEQUENCE and SYNCHRONOUS in Annodis were annotated using the same Narration relation. The SDRT Elaboration captures most of our ELABORATION relations (except for OBJECT). On the other hand, the RST-ST corpus considers only one Temporal relation, namely Sequence, and RST-ST Elaboration includes OBJECT, PARTITIVE, and GENERALITY. Another interesting case concerns the Support relations MOTIVATION and EVIDENCE/JUSTIFICATION. SDRT does not distinguish between the causal and the epistemic use of causal relations and considers only two causal relations, Explanation and Result. This is why we counted SDRT causal relations only in the Causal/Result sub-class (this is marked by (*) and (+) in Table 5). Finally, the RST-DT multinuclear relations Cause-result and Consequence are similar and can correspond to either REASON or RESULT. We only counted them in the total column (see † in Table 5).

	RST-DT	Annodis	RST-ST	Total
Obj.	2,698	525	1,444	6,995
Part.	176	614		
Gen.	884			
Sum.	83		8	
Rest.	140		22	
Means	226		175	
Frame		225		225
Backg.	937	157	344	1,438
Attr.	3,070	74		3,144
Total THEMATIC: **11,802**				

Table 4: Thematic class mapping

	RST-DT	Annodis	RST-ST	Total
Reason	52	128 (+)	77	1245†
Result	159	162 (*)	193	
Cond.	285	20	53	406
Excep.	43		5	
Purp.	568	94	127	789
Motiv.	206	cf. (*)	28	234
Evid.	780	cf. (+)	98	878
Eval.	600	75	99	774
Cont.	352	143	58	1,378
Conc.	293		50	
Antith.	402		80	
Total CAUS.ARG.: **5,704**				

Table 5: Causal-Argumentative class mapping

5 Discussion and conclusions

We have presented a unified taxonomy for discourse relations which can be used to map existing annotations, and to annotate new corpora. We believe our taxonomy is robust across theoretical approaches, and can be applied to multiple languages.

A number of issues are outstanding, the first with regard to segmentation. Different corpora have followed different segmentation methodologies, sometimes impacting the types of relations present in the taxonomy, as is the case with the multiple subtypes of Elaboration relations in the RST-DT corpus. Our intention is to provide coarse and fine-grained segmentation options, so that either can be adopted, depending on the goals of the research.

More crucial to the task of unifying annotations is the issue of the structure of the discourse. RST, RST-DT and RST-ST all take trees as the fundamental structure. SDRT, however, postulates graphs as the basic structure. On the other hand, mapping to a lexically-grounded approach, like that in the PDTB, is certainly possible. We believe that mapping and predicting relations can be a theory-independent task, and that the rich annotations in PDTB are useful for tasks such as discourse parsing.

Two further practical aspects remain unresolved. First, relations with no correspondence across taxonomies need to be considered. One solution is to ignore them and then predict a partial structure for some texts. The second issue is the task of manual annotation. As we have pointed out, in cases where one original taxonomy is more detailed, mapping relations from that taxonomy onto an existing corpus may require further annotation. If annotation is undertaken, then that could solve our first practical problem, because then there is an opportunity to annotate some of the relations with no mapping.

Finally, an excellent test of the usefulness of the taxonomy would be to carry out experiments in discourse parsing. We would like to merge annotated corpora, and test whether the larger size of the training data improves the results of a discourse parser.

Acknowledgments

We thank Nicholas Asher for his useful comments. This work is conjointly supported by the Natural Sciences and Engineering Research Council of Canada and the ERC grant 269427 (STAC).

References

Stergos Afantenos, Nicholas Asher, Farah Benamara, Myriam Bras, Cecile Fabre, Mai Ho-Dac, Anne

Le Draoulec, Philippe Muller, Marie-Paule Pery-Woodley, Laurent Prevot, Josette Rebeyrolles, Ludovic Tanguy, Marianne Vergez-Couret, and Laure Vieu. 2012. An empirical resource for discovering cognitive principles of discourse organisation: The ANNODIS corpus. In *Proceedings of the Eighth International Conference on Language Resources and Evaluation (LREC 2012)*.

Nicholas Asher and Alex Lascarides. 2003. *Logics of Conversation*. Cambridge University Press.

Nicholas Asher, Julie Hunter, Pascal Denis, and Brian Reese. 2006. Evidentiality and intensionality: Two uses of reportative constructions in discourse. In *Workshop on Constraints in Discourse*.

Lynn Carlson, Daniel Marcu, and Mary Ellen Okurowski. 2003. Building a discourse-tagged corpus in the framework of rhetorical structure theory. In Jan van Kuppevelt and Ronnie Smith, editors, *Current Directions in Discourse and Dialogue*, pages 85–112. Kluwer.

Christian Chiarcos. 2014. Towards interoperable discourse annotation. discourse features in the ontologies of linguistic annotation. In *Proceedings of the Ninth International Conference on Language Resources and Evaluation (LREC'14)*.

Iria da Cunha, Juan-Manuel Torres-Moreno, and Gerardo Sierra. 2011. On the Development of the RST Spanish Treebank. In *Proceedings of the 5th Linguistic Annotation Workshop*, pages 1–10.

Liesbeth Degand. 2009. Describing polysemous discourse markers: What does translation add to the picture? In Stef Slembrouch, Miriam Taverniers, and Mieke Van Herreweghe, editors, *From will to well. Studies in Linguistics offered to Anne-Marie Simon-Vandenbergen*. Academia Press, Gent.

Vanessa Wei Feng and Graeme Hirst. 2014. A linear-time bottom-up discourse parser with constraints and post-editing. In *Proceedings of the 52nd Annual Meeting of the Association for Computational Linguistics*, pages 511–521.

Christian Hardmeier. 2013. Discourse in statistical machine translation: A survey and a case study. *Discours*, 11.

Bas Heerschop, Frank Goossen, Alexander Hogenboom, Flavius Frasincar, Uzay Kaymak, and Franciska de Jong. 2011. Polarity analysis of texts using discourse structure. In *Proceedings of the 20th ACM international conference on Information and knowledge management*, pages 1061–1070.

Hugo Hernault, Helmut Prendinger, David A. duVerle, and Mitsuru Ishizuka. 2010. HILDA: A discourse parser using Support Vector Machine classification. *Dialogue and Discourse*, 1(3).

Shafiq Joty, Giuseppe Carenini, and Raymond Ng. 2015. CODRA: A novel discriminative framework for rhetorical analysis. *Computational Linguistics*, page in press.

Iskandar Keskes, Farah Benamara, and Lamia Belguith Hadrich. 2014. Learning Explicit and Implicit Arabic Discourse Relations. *Journal of King Saud University Computer and Information Sciences: Special Issue on Arabic NLP: Current State and Future Challenges*.

William C. Mann and Sandra A. Thompson. 1988. Rhetorical structure theory: Toward a functional theory of text organization. *Text*, 8(3):243–281.

Rashmi Prasad, Nikhil Dinesh, Alan Lee, Eleni Miltsakaki, Livio Robaldo, Aravind Joshi, and Bonnie Webber. 2008. The Penn Discourse Treebank 2.0. In *6th International Conference on Language Resources and Evaluation (LREC)*.

Rashmi Prasad, Bonnie Webber, and Aravind Joshi. 2014. Reflections on the penn discourse treebank, comparable corpora, and complementary annotation. *Computational Linguistics*, 40(4):921–950.

B. Reese, J. Hunter, P. Denis, N. Asher, and J. Baldridge. 2007. Reference manual for the analysis and annotation of rhetorical structure. Technical report, Department of Linguistics, The University of Texas, Austin.

Gian Lorenzo Thione, Martin Van den Berg, Livia Polanyi, and Chris Culy. 2004. Hybrid text summarization: Combining external relevance measures with structural analysis. In Stan Szpakowicz Marie-Francine Moens, editor, *Text Summarization Branches Out: Proceedings of the ACL-04 Workshop*.

Antoine Venant, Nicholas Asher, Philippe Muller, Pascal Denis, and Stergos Afantenos. 2013. Expressivity and comparison of models of discourse structure. In *Proceedings of the SIGDIAL 2013 Conference*, Metz, France, August.

Sandrine Zufferey and Liesbeth Degand. 2014. Annotating the meaning of discourse connectives in multilingual corpora. *Corpus Linguistics and Linguistic Theory*, page in press.

Dissecting the Practical Lexical Function Model for Compositional Distributional Semantics

Abhijeet Gupta, Jason Utt and **Sebastian Padó**
Institut für Maschinelle Sprachverarbeitung
Universität Stuttgart
`[guptaat|uttjn|pado]@ims.uni-stuttgart.de`

Abstract

The Practical Lexical Function model (PLF) is a recently proposed compositional distributional semantic model which provides an elegant account of composition, striking a balance between expressiveness and robustness and performing at the state-of-the-art. In this paper, we identify an inconsistency in PLF between the objective function at training and the prediction at testing which leads to an over-counting of the predicate's contribution to the meaning of the phrase. We investigate two possible solutions of which one (the exclusion of simple lexical vector at test time) improves performance significantly on two out of the three composition datasets.

1 Introduction

Compositional distributional semantic models (CDSMs) make an important theoretical contribution, explaining the meaning of a phrase by the meanings of its parts. They have also found application in psycholinguistics (Lenci, 2011), in sentiment analysis (Socher et al., 2012), and in machine translation (Kalchbrenner and Blunsom, 2013).

A first generation of CDSMs represented all words as vectors and combined them by component-wise operations (Mitchell and Lapata, 2010). Given the conceptual limitations of this simple approach, numerous models were subsequently proposed which represent the meaning of predicates as higher-order algebraic objects such as matrices and tensors (Baroni and Zamparelli, 2010; Guevara, 2010; Coecke et al., 2010). For example, one-place predicates such as adjectives or intransitive verbs can be modeled as matrices (order-2 tensors), and two-place predicates, e.g., transitive verbs, as order-3 tensors, and so forth. While such tensors enable mathematically elegant accounts of composition, their large degrees of freedom lead to severe sparsity issues when they are learned from corpora.

The recently proposed Practical Lexical Function model (PLF; Paperno et al., 2014) represents a compromise between these two extremes by restricting itself to vectors and matrices, effectively reducing sparsity while retaining state-of-the-art performance across multiple datasets. It does away with tensors by ignoring interactions among the arguments of predicates p. Instead, each argument position arg is modeled as a matrix $\overset{\Box_{arg}}{p}$ that is applied to a vector for the argument's meaning, $\vec{a}$. The meaning of the phrase is then defined as the sum of the lexical meaning of the predicate, $\vec{p}$, and the contributions of each argument (see Fig. 1). The matrices can be learned in a supervised manner with regression from pairs of corpus-extracted vectors for arguments and phrases.

In this paper, we identify an inconsistency between the training and testing phases of the PLF. More specifically, we show that its composition procedure leads to over-counting of the contribution of the predicate. We propose two remedies to harmonize the training and prediction phases – by excluding the predicate meaning from either training or testing. In an evaluation of the standard PLF and our variants on three datasets, we find that modifying the training phase fails, but that modifying testing phase improves performance on two out of three datasets. We analyze this effect in terms of a bias-variance tradeoff.

*Proceedings of the Fourth Joint Conference on Lexical and Computational Semantics (*SEM 2015)*, pages 153–158,
Denver, Colorado, June 4–5, 2015.

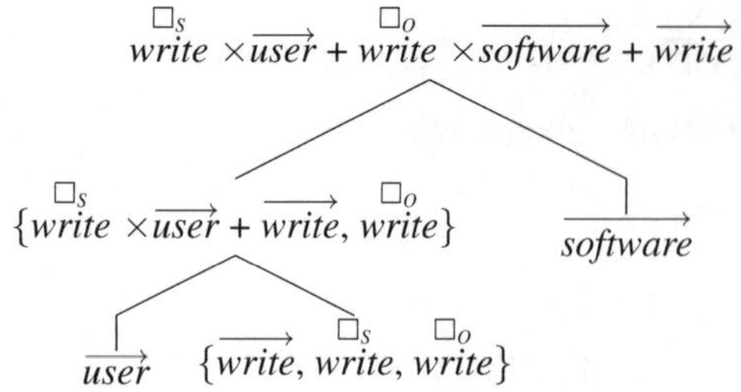

Figure 1: Practical Lexical Function model derivation for the noun-verb-noun phrase *"user writes software"*.

2 Debugging the PLF model

2.1 An Inconsistency

We have identified an inconsistency in the PLF model as a result of which the predicted vector for a phrase systematically differs from the corpus-observed vector of the phrase. We will illustrate it on a minimal example, the phrase "*dogs sleep*".

Training Phase. The training of PLF creates three representations: (1), a lexical vector for the noun ($\overrightarrow{n}$); (2), the lexical vector for the verb ($\overrightarrow{v}$); and (3), a matrix for the subject argument position of the verb ($\overset{\square_S}{v}$). While (1) and (2) can be acquired directly from the corpus, (3) involves optimization, since the matrix (3) is supposed to account for the verb's disambiguating effect on all its subjects. PLF proposes to learn matrices via regression problems such as the following (Guevara, 2010), where $subj(v)$ comprises the subjects seen with the verb v:[1]

$$\overset{\square_S}{v} := \underset{M}{\operatorname{argmin}} \sum_{n \in subj(v)} \|M \times \overrightarrow{n} - \overrightarrow{n\,v}\|^2 \quad (1)$$

That is, the verb's subject matrix is learned as the matrix which, multiplied with a subject noun vector, best predicts the noun-verb phrase vector. If we assume that the verb of our example (*sleep*) is only seen with a single noun in the corpus, namely its subject *dog*, Eq. (1) has a particularly simple solution where the matrix can perfectly predict the phrase vector:

$$\overset{\square_S}{sleep} \times \overrightarrow{dog} = \overrightarrow{dog\ sleep} \quad (2)$$

[1]All matrices are learned using least-squares regression and, for the sake of simplicity, we ignore regularization. Adjective matrices are obtained in the same fashion.

Testing Phase. PLF predicts the phrase meaning $\mathcal{P}$ for our example as predicate plus argument meaning:

$$\mathcal{P}(dog\ sleeps) = \overrightarrow{sleep} + \overset{\square_S}{sleep} \times \overrightarrow{dog} \quad (3)$$

Intuitively, what we would expect as the result of this computation to be $\overrightarrow{dog\ sleeps}$ — the empirically observed vector for the noun-verb phrase. However, substituting Eq. (2) into Eq. (3), we instead obtain:

$$\mathcal{P}(dog\ sleeps) = \overrightarrow{sleep} + \overrightarrow{dog\ sleeps} \quad (4)$$

The predicted phrase meaning does not correspond to the empirical phrase vector because in PLF, the verb contributes twice to the phrase meaning.

Discussion. This issue remains pertinent beyond the minimal example presented above. The reason is a discrepancy between the training and test setups: The argument matrices in PLF are learned so as to predict the *complete* phrase vector when multiplied with an argument (compare Eq. (1)).[2] This objective is inconsistent with the way phrase vectors are predicted at test time. The addition of the predicate's lexical vector thus amounts to a **systematic over-counting** of the predicate's lexical contribution.

2.2 Two Ways to Remedy the Inconsistency

The above description gives direct rise to two simple strategies to harmonize training and test procedures.

Adapting the Training Phase. One strategy is to adapt the training objective from Eq. (1). Recognizing that the predicate vector is added in by Eq. (3) at test time, we can attempt to learn a matrix that predicts not the phrase vector, but the *difference* between the phrase vector and the predicate vector. That means, the matrices capture only the disambiguating contribution of argument positions such as subject:

$$\overset{\square_S}{v} = \underset{M}{\operatorname{argmin}} \sum_{n \in subj(v)} \|M \times \overrightarrow{n} - (\overrightarrow{n\,v} - \overrightarrow{v})\|^2 \quad (5)$$

Adapting the Testing Phase. Another strategy is to adapt the phrase meaning prediction at test time by simply leaving out the predicate vector. For subject-verb combinations, we predict $\mathcal{P}(n\ v) = \overset{\square_S}{v} \times \overrightarrow{n}$.

[2]A formal, more general argument can be made based on the error term $\vec{\epsilon} = \overset{\square_{arg}}{v} \times \overrightarrow{n} - \overrightarrow{n\,v}$ which is minimized in training.

verb in context	landmark in context	similarity
private landlord ***charge*** *annual rent*	*private landlord* ***accuse*** *annual rent*	low
private landlord ***charge*** *annual rent*	*private landlord* ***bill*** *annual rent*	high
armed police ***charge*** *unemployed person*	*armed police* ***accuse*** *unemployed person*	high
armed police ***charge*** *unemployed person*	*armed police* ***bill*** *unemployed person*	low

Table 1: Example of experimental items in the ANVAN data sets (target verb: *charge*).

For transitive sentences (cf. Figure 1), we predict $\mathcal{P}(n\ v\ n) = \overset{\square_S}{v} \times \overrightarrow{n} + \overset{\square_O}{v} \times \overrightarrow{n}$ (the sum of the subject and the object contributions), and analogously for other constructions.

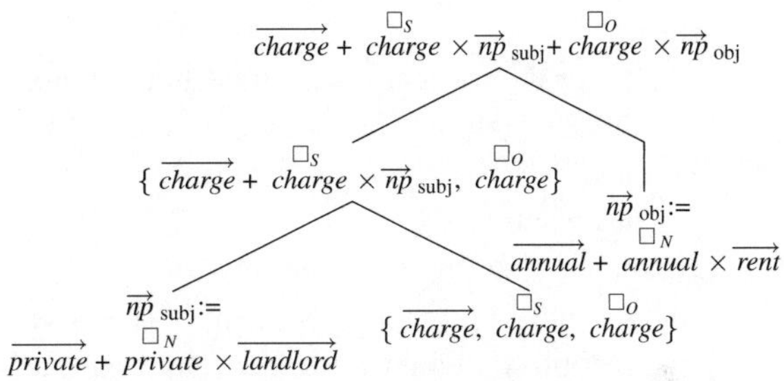

Figure 2: PLF Derivation for ANVAN phrase *"private landlord charge yearly rent"*.

3 Experimental Setup

Evaluation Datasets. We evaluate the modifications from the last section on three standard benchmarks for CDSMs: ANVAN-1 (Kartsaklis et al., 2013), ANVAN-2 (Grefenstette, 2013) (Paperno et al.'s term) and NVN (Grefenstette and Sadrzadeh, 2011) (our term).

As the abbreviations indicate, the two ANVAN datasets contain transitive verbs whose NP arguments are modified by arguments; the NVN dataset contains only bare noun arguments. All three datasets are built around ambiguous target verbs that are combined with two disambiguating contexts (subjects plus objects) and two landmark verbs in a balanced design (cf. Table 1). Each context matches one of the landmark verbs, but not the other. Annotators were asked to rate the similarity between the target verb in context and the landmark on a Likert scale.

Corpus and Co-Occurrences. We followed the specifications by Paperno et al. (2014) as closely as possible to replicate the original PLF results. As corpora, we used ukWAC, English Wikipedia, and the BNC. We extracted a square co-occurrence matrix for the 30K most frequent content words using a 3-word window and applied the PPMI transformation. Subsequently, the matrix was reduced to 300 dimensions with SVD. In the same manner, we built a co-occurrence matrix for all corpus bigrams for relevant adjectives and verbs from the experimental materials, applying a frequency threshold of 5.

Composition Models and Evaluation. We build matrix representations for adjectives and subject and object positions of verbs using the DISSECT toolkit (Dinu et al., 2013). In addition to the standard PLF model, which we see as a baseline, we implement both proposals from Section 2.2. On the NVN dataset, both training and test modification can apply only to the verb (cf. Figure 1), which gives us two conditions. On the ANVAN datasets (cf. Figure 2), the changes can be applied to the verb, to the adjectives, or to both, for a total of six conditions.

Our evaluation measure is the nonparametric Spearman correlations between each annotator's similarity rating and the cosine between the predicted sentence vectors containing the ambiguous and landmark verb, respectively.

4 Evaluation

Main Results. The main results are shown in Table 2. Our PLF re-implementation in the first column almost replicates the results reported by Paperno et al. (2014) for ANVAN1 and ANVAN2 (20 and 36, respectively). On NVN, no results for the PLF were previously reported. Our result (35.4) is substantially above the result of 21.0 reported by Greffenstette and Sadrzadeh (2011) for their categorial model. This supports our general focus on the PLF as an interesting target for analysis.

Dataset	PLF	Training phase modifications			Test phase modifications		
		Sub Adj	Sub Verb	Sub Both	No Adj	No Verb	No Both
ANVAN1	20.6	18.7	-0.3	3.8	19.2	20.7	**22.1***
ANVAN2	35.2	32.8	13.8	17.0	33.8	**35.7**	35.4
NVN	35.4	–	25.5	–	–	**40.6****	–

Table 2: Experimental results (Spearman's ρ) on three dataset. Significant improvements over the PLF results are indicated with stars (*: p<0.05, **: p<0.01), – denotes non-applicability of parameter.

The results for the training phase modification are overwhelmingly negative. There is a minor degradation when the adjective is subtracted at training time, and major degradation when the verb is subtracted. We will come back to this result below.

In contrast, we obtain improvements when we modify the test phase, when we either leave out the verb or both the verb and the adjective in the composition. For two out of the three datasets, the respective best models perform statistically significantly better than the PLF as determined by a bootstrap resampling test (Efron and Tibshirani, 1993): ANVAN1 (+1.5%, p<0.05) and NVN (+5.2%, p<0.01). The improvement for ANVAN2 (+0.5%) is not large enough to reach significance.

Discussion. These results leave us with two main questions: (a), why does the modification at training time fail so completely; and (b), can we develop a better understanding of the kind of improvement that the modification at test time introduces?

Regarding question (a), we believe that the difference between the phrase vector and the predicate vector that we are training the matrix to predict in Eq. (5) is, in practice, a very brittle representation. The reason is that typically the phrase nv is much less frequent than v, and therefore $\overrightarrow{nv} - \overrightarrow{v} \approx -\overrightarrow{v}$ (cf. Figure 3). Consequently, the matrix attempts to predict the verb vector from the noun – not only a very hard problem, but one that does not help solve the task at hand.

To answer question (b), we perform a mixed effects linear regression analysis (Hedeker, 2005) on the three datasets, concentrating on a comparison of the standard PLF and the best respective test phase modification. We follow the intuition that the frequency and ambiguity of the target verbs should influence the quality of the prediction both in the PLF and in the modified model, and that it might be informative to look at differences in these effects. To this effect, we construct a mixed-effects model which predicts, for each experimental item (cf. Table 1), the *absolute rank difference* between the item's rank in the gold standard ratings and the item's rank in the model prediction. Thus, high values of the output variable denote items which are difficult to predict, while low values of the output variable denote items which are easy to predict. As fixed effects, we include the target verbs' logarithmized corpus frequencies (*logf*), their ambiguities, measured as the number of WordNet top nodes subsuming their synsets (*ambig*), the presence of the test phase modification (NoVerb for ANVAN2 and NVN, NoBoth for ANVAN1; *ModTest*) as well as interaction terms between ModTest and the two other predictors. We also include the identity of the target verb as random effect.

	ANVAN1	ANVAN2	NVN
logf	-359***	-182 n.s.	-96***
ambig	118***	8 n.s.	6***
ModTest	438***	-2606***	-1413***
ModTest:logf	-53**	165***	94***
ModTest:ambig	20*	32***	8***

Table 3: Coefficients of Linear Mixed Effects Model. *: p<0.05; **: p<0.01; ***: p<0.001. See text for details.

The results are shown in Table 3. There are considerable differences between the datasets, but the overall patterns are nevertheless comparable. Notably, frequency has a negative effect on rank difference. In other words, more frequent verbs are easier to predict. Conversely, the ambiguity of the target verb has a positive effect on rank difference, that is, higher ambiguity makes predictions more difficult. Both of these effects are very strong on ANVAN1 and NVN

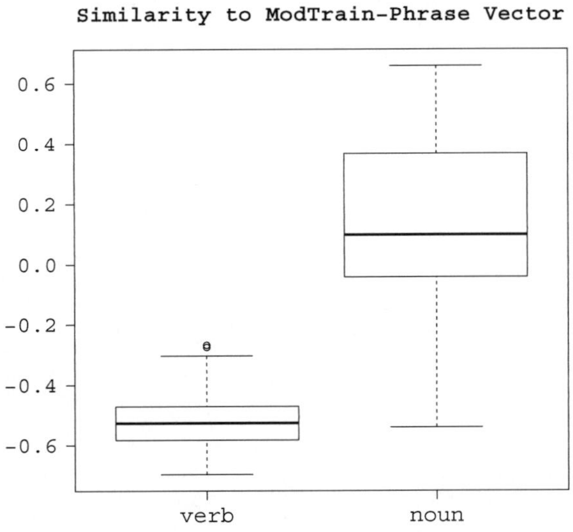

Figure 3: Similarities between the training-time modified phrase vector (subject-verb & verb-object) and the respective word vectors in the NVN dataset. The low values and smaller variance in verb similarities shows the information encoded by the modified phrase vector aligns better with the verb's (or predicate's) information than that of the noun (argument).

and not significant on ANVAN2, which appears to be a more controlled dataset. Taken together, the models still seem to struggle with ambiguous and infrequent target verbs.

The coefficients that we obtain for ModTest look puzzling at first glance: we obtain a negative coefficient (i.e., an overall improvement) only for ANVAN2 and NVN while the coefficient is positive for ANVAN1. For ANVAN1, the improvement is brought about by the interaction with the frequency variable: when the test phase is modified, the (beneficial) effect of frequency becomes much stronger, that is, the predictions for high-frequency verbs improve. In contrast, the effect of frequency becomes weaker for the test phase modification on ANVAN2 and NVN. What is true for all three datasets is that the effect of ambiguity gets stronger when the test phase is modified: ambiguous verbs become significantly more difficult to model.

On the basis of this analysis, we believe that this difference between the standard PLF and our test phase modification can be understood as a classical bias-variance tradeoff: the addition of the predicate meaning in the standard PLF reduces variance, ensuring that the phrase meaning stays close to the predicate meaning prior even for matrices that are difficult to learn, e.g., due to sparse data or high ambiguity. At the same time, this dilutes the disambiguating effect of composition. In our modified scheme, the situation is reversed: the composed representations vary more freely, which benefits well-learned matrices but leads to worse predictions for poorly learned ones.

5 Conclusion

In this paper, we have presented an analysis of the recent Practical Lexical Function (PLF) model in compositional distributional semantics. We have shown that the PLF contains an inconsistency between the objective function at training time and the definition of compositional phase construction at testing time. We have argued that either training or testing needs to be modified to harmonize the two. Our empirical evaluation found that testing phase modification is indeed effective (by reducing bias in the predictions), while the training phase modification is not (by relying on brittle representations). In the spirit of the bias-variance analysis, future work is to experiment with weighting schemes to optimize the relative contributions of predicate and arguments.

Acknowledgments

We gratefully acknowledge funding of our research by the DFG (SFB 732, Project D10).

References

Marco Baroni and Roberto Zamparelli. 2010. Nouns are vectors, adjectives are matrices: Representing adjective-noun constructions in semantic space. In *Proceedings of the 2010 Conference on Empirical Methods in Natural Language Processing*, pages 1183–1193.

Bob Coecke, Mehrnoosh Sadrzadeh, and Stephen Clark. 2010. Mathematical foundations for a compositional distributional model of meaning. *Linguistic Analysis*, 36:345–386.

Georgiana Dinu, Nghia The Pham, and Marco Baroni. 2013. DISSECT - DIStributional SEmantics Composition Toolkit. In *Proceedings of the 51st Annual Meeting of the Association for Computational Linguistics: System Demonstrations*, pages 31–36, Sofia, Bulgaria.

Bradley Efron and Robert J. Tibshirani. 1993. *An Introduction to the Bootstrap*. Chapman and Hall, New York.

Edward Grefenstette and Mehrnoosh Sadrzadeh. 2011. Experimental support for a categorical compositional distributional model of meaning. In *Proceedings of the 2011 Conference on Empirical Methods in Natural Language Processing*, pages 1394–1404, Edinburgh, Scotland, UK.

Edward Grefenstette. 2013. *Category-Theoretic Quantitative Compositional Distributional Models of Natural Language Semantics*. Ph.D. thesis.

Emiliano Guevara. 2010. A regression model of adjective-noun compositionality in distributional semantics. In *Proceedings of the 2010 Workshop on GEometrical Models of Natural Language Semantics*, pages 33–37, Uppsala, Sweden, July. Association for Computational Linguistics.

Donald Hedeker. 2005. Generalized linear mixed models. In *Encyclopedia of Statistics in Behavioral Science*. Wiley, New York.

Nal Kalchbrenner and Phil Blunsom. 2013. Recurrent continuous translation models. In *Proceedings of the Conference on Empirical Methods in Natural Language Processing*, pages 1700–1709, Melbourne, Australia.

Dimitri Kartsaklis, Mehrnoosh Sadrzadeh, and Stephen Pulman. 2013. Separating disambiguation from composition in distributional semantics. In *Proceedings of the Seventeenth Conference on Computational Natural Language Learning*, pages 114–123, Sofia, Bulgaria.

Alessandro Lenci. 2011. Composing and updating verb argument expectations: A distributional semantic model. In *Proceedings of the 2nd Workshop on Cognitive Modeling and Computational Linguistics*, pages 58–66, Portland, OR.

Jeff Mitchell and Mirella Lapata. 2010. Composition in distributional models of semantics. *Cognitive Science*, 34(8):1388–1429.

Denis Paperno, Nghia The Pham, and Marco Baroni. 2014. A practical and linguistically-motivated approach to compositional distributional semantics. In *Proceedings of the 52nd Annual Meeting of the Association for Computational Linguistics*, pages 90–99, Baltimore, Maryland.

Richard Socher, Brody Huval, Christopher D. Manning, and Andrew Y. Ng. 2012. Semantic compositionality through recursive matrix-vector spaces. In *Proceedings of the 2012 Joint Conference on Empirical Methods in Natural Language Processing and Computational Natural Language Learning*, EMNLP-CoNLL '12, pages 1201–1211, Stroudsburg, PA, USA. Association for Computational Linguistics.

Event Extraction as Frame-Semantic Parsing

Alex Judea and **Michael Strube**
Heidelberg Institute for Theoretical Studies gGmbH
Schloss-Wolfsbrunnenweg 35
69118 Heidelberg, Germany
(alex.judea|michael.strube)@h-its.org

Abstract

Based on the hypothesis that frame-semantic parsing and event extraction are structurally identical tasks, we retrain SEMAFOR, a state-of-the-art frame-semantic parsing system to predict event triggers and arguments. We describe how we change SEMAFOR to be better suited for the new task and show that it performs comparable to one of the best systems in event extraction. We also describe a bias in one of its models and propose a feature factorization which is better suited for this model.

1 Introduction

Event Extraction is a task in information extraction where mentions of predefined events are extracted from texts. We follow the task definition of the Automatic Content Extraction (ACE) program of 2005. It defines 33 event types, organized in eight categories. Each event type has associated *roles*, e.g., ATTACK has the roles *attacker*, *target*, and *instrument*, whereas DIE has the roles *agent*, *victim*, and *instrument*. The roles *place* and *time* are shared by all event types.

ACE events occur only within sentences. Each event is indicated by a word, the *trigger*. The roles associated with the respective event type are filled by zero or more *arguments*. Most arguments are mentions of entities, e.g. persons, locations, or organizations. Some arguments are mentions of points in time, amounts of money, etc. Arguments may be shared by multiple events and may play different roles in each of them.

Figure 1 illustrates an example. The sentence contains two events, DIE and ATTACK, triggered by "died" and "fired", respectively. For DIE, the roles *victim*, *instrument*, and *place* are filled with the arguments "cameraman", "American tank", and "Baghdad", respectively. For ATTACK, the role *target* has two arguments, namely "cameraman" and "Palestine hotel", the roles *instrument*, and *place* have the arguments, "American tank", and "Baghdad", respectively. Three arguments are shared. One of them, "cameraman", plays different roles in the events, namely *victim* of DIE and *target* of ATTACK.

Frame-semantic parsing is the task of extracting semantic predicate-argument structures from texts. It is built on the theory of frame semantics and FrameNet (Fillmore et al., 2003; Das et al., 2014). As in event extraction, frames occur within sentences and have triggers and roles (called lexical units and frame elements).

Our hypothesis is that the two tasks are structurally identical. From a computational point of view, they differ only in feature types. We can use the same approach and infrastructure to tackle both. Based on this hypothesis, we retrain a frame-semantic parsing system, SEMAFOR, for event extraction.

We describe differences between frame-semantic parsing and event extraction and the adaptions needed to better prepare SEMAFOR for the new task. We also describe a bias in the trigger classification model which affects frame-semantic parsing as well as event extraction and propose a new factorization of features which is better suited for this

*Proceedings of the Fourth Joint Conference on Lexical and Computational Semantics (*SEM 2015)*, pages 159–164,
Denver, Colorado, June 4–5, 2015.

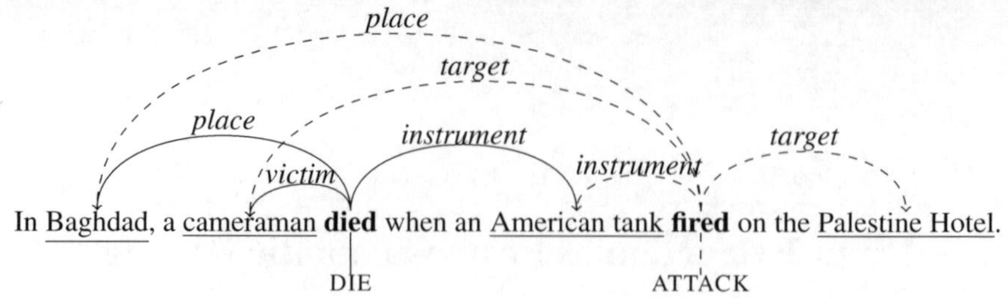

Figure 1: A sentence with two event instances, a DIE event triggered by the word "died", and an ATTACK event triggered by "fired". Three arguments are shared by both events.

model. Finally, we evaluate the retrained system on the ACE 2005 data (Walker et al., 2006).

2 Related Work

Many approaches to event extraction do not cross sentence boundaries, e.g. Grishman et al. (2005), Ahn (2006), Lu and Roth (2012), Li et al. (2013) and Li et al. (2014). Only few approaches, like Ji and Grishman (2008) and Liao and Grishman (2010) go beyond sentences and even beyond documents in order to exploit richer context for the extraction of events.

While early systems usually predict triggers and arguments independently, more recent work employs joint inference, i.e., predicts triggers and arguments (or only arguments) jointly, e.g., Lu and Roth (2012), Li et al. (2013), and Li et al. (2014).

3 Approach

We make use of SEMAFOR, a state-of-the-art frame-semantic parsing system (Das et al., 2010)[1]. We retrain it to predict ACE events, i.e., triggers with event types and arguments for their roles, and make adaptions to better prepare it for event extraction. We call the new system SEMAFOR$_{\mathrm{E}}$.

3.1 Trigger Classification

In order to classify triggers (single or multiple tokens), the original SEMAFOR uses a log-linear model. To cope with unknown triggers the model includes a latent variable iterating over triggers seen in training (called *hidden units*). At inference time, hidden units serve as prototypes for unknown words. The model is defined as

$$e_i = \operatorname*{argmax}_{e \in E_i} \sum_{l \in L_e} p_\theta(e, l \mid t_i, x). \quad (1)$$

e_i is the best event type for trigger t_i according to the model. E_i is the set of observed event types for t_i. L_e is the set of triggers observed during training for event e. All $l \in L_e$ are called hidden units. $p_\theta(e, l \mid t_i, x)$ gives the probability of e and a hidden unit l given the trigger t_i and a sentence x. This probability is modeled as

$$p_\theta(e, l \mid t_i, x) = \frac{1}{Z} \exp \theta^\top g(e, l, t_i, x). \quad (2)$$

This is a conditional log-linear model with a normalization constant Z, weights θ, and a vector-valued feature function g.

The model is biased towards classes with many hidden units. In order to illustrate this, imagine there is only one feature which does not depend on hidden units, e.g., if there is a named entity in the sentence. During inference, the sum in Equation 1 is computed. As a constant, Z is ignored during inference. The named entity feature would be active for every hidden unit, having the same weight in every iteration, because features are always evaluated inside the sum. Then, the sum is not meaningful anymore, because the event with the most hidden units wins. This bias affects both, frame-semantic parsing and event extraction.

In order to weaken the bias we propose to separate features which actually depend on hidden units, e.g., because they capture lexical similarity to some of them, from features which do not, like the named entity feature. Then, inference is performed as

$$\begin{aligned} e_i = \operatorname*{argmax}_{e \in E_i} & \sum_{l \in L_e} \exp \theta^\top g'(e, l, t_i, x) \\ & + \exp \theta^\top g^\star(e, t_i, x). \end{aligned} \quad (3)$$

g' is a function for features depending on hidden units, $g^\star$ is a function for the remaining features. In this way, activation frequencies of features become meaningful. However, the model is still biased towards events with many hidden units. This is problematic, because the distribution of triggers over events is diverse and arbitrary. The number of hidden units does not necessarily correlate with occurrence probabilities of events. On the other

[1] http://www.ark.cs.cmu.edu/SEMAFOR/; we use version 2.1, without semi-supervised extensions or dual decomposition.

hand, the idea of known triggers being prototypes for events is appealing, therefore we did not change this part of the model.

3.2 Argument Classification

The argument model predicts the best argument A_i for every role r_k of an event e_i given a set of spans S. In our experiments, spans are extents of gold mentions, including the empty span. The argument-role mapping is defined as

$$A_i(r_k) = \operatorname*{argmax}_{s \in S} p_\psi(s \mid r_k, e_i, t_i, x). \quad (4)$$

Again, a conditional log-linear model with weights ψ, a normalization constant Z, and a feature function h is used to model p_ψ:

$$p_\psi = \frac{1}{Z} \exp \psi^\top h(s, r_k, e_i, t_i, x). \quad (5)$$

3.3 Adaptions

Based on our hypothesis that event extraction is structurally identical to frame-semantic parsing, we retrain SEMAFOR to predict ACE events. While the structure of the tasks may be identical, their behavior is not. It does not suffice to convert the ACE data to the right format and retrain the model.

There are two important differences between frame-semantic parsing and event extraction. First, in frame-semantic parsing, there is no 'null class' for triggers. A trigger may indicate multiple frames, but it always invokes one of them. In event extraction, we have potential triggers, which may or may not invoke events. Second, most event arguments are defined based on entity types. ACE distinguishes between the entity types person, organization, geopolitical entity, location, facility, vehicle, and weapon. For frame-semantic parsing, no such restriction in entity type exists. Thus, we need to introduce entity type features to tackle argument classification for event extraction. Such features are also useful for the trigger model.

One way to allow potential triggers to be classified as non-triggers is to introduce a null class to the event types. Each trigger in the training data also becomes a trigger of the null class (or *null event*). If a null event is triggered, we filter it out. Note that having a class with so many triggers biases our model towards it (Section 3.1). A less biased way would be to introduce a 'null version' of every event type, having the same triggers. However, we would have to predict twice as much classes (66 instead of 33). Having only one null class better exploits the limited training data. Furthermore, biasing SEMAFOR$_\text{E}$ towards null events is acceptable because there are considerably more null events than events.

Allowing all triggers from the training data in prediction hurts performance, mainly due to triggers which coincide with high-frequency words like "be". In order to prune the trigger set we compute a score for each trigger, catching its distribution among events and non-events: $s(t) = f_e/(f_e+f_n)d$. f_e is the frequency of t as an event trigger, f_n is the frequency of t in non-events, and d is the number of events t is a trigger of. The measure prefers triggers which are frequently triggers for only a few events. We filter all triggers with $s < 0.01$[2].

Finally, we changed the learning algorithm from the maximum entropy to the perceptron framework. This was done because the perceptron gives better performance for SEMAFOR$_\text{E}$ and is considerably faster, e.g., the argument model can be trained in a few seconds instead of several hours. The new models have a simpler form because we do not have to compute probabilities anymore. The new trigger model is defined as

$$\begin{aligned} e_i = \operatorname*{argmax}_{e \in E_i} & \sum_{l \in L_e} \theta^\top g'(e, l, t_i, x) \\ & + \theta^\top g^\star(e, t_i, x). \end{aligned} \quad (6)$$

The new argument model is defined as

$$A_i(r_k) = \operatorname*{argmax}_{s \in S} \psi^\top h(s, r_k, e_i, t_i, x). \quad (7)$$

Weights θ and ψ are learned using a variant of the averaged perceptron (Collins, 2002), where we store feature vectors only after each pass through the training data.

3.4 Features

For the trigger model, SEMAFOR's features include lemmas (of trigger tokens and of the head governor), dependencies of the head, if the head is equal to or has semantic relations with any hidden unit, as well

[2]The threshold was determined on development data.

as the type of these relations[3]. Additionally, we include unigrams and bigrams around the trigger in a window of two. Following Li et al. (2013), we also look at the mention nearest to the trigger. We include its entity type and its string representation as features.

Potential triggers are compared to hidden units by semantic relations. We extend this by incorporating measures of semantic similarity. We compare tokens in the actual sentence with tokens of all sentences the actual hidden unit appeared in (in the training data) and with tokens of all sentences all hidden units of the actual frame appeared in. The comparison is made in terms of cosine similarity.

SEMAFOR's features for the argument model characterize the actual span (its length, tokens, and head dependencies), the voice and string representation of the trigger, and the dependency path between span and trigger heads. Additionally, we include the token before the argument and its part-of-speech, and all tokens and parts-of-speech between argument and trigger as features. Following Li et al. (2013), we also use as features the type of the entity the actual span represents, if it is the only mention of its entity type, or the nearest to the trigger.

4 Experiments

We trained SEMAFOR_E on the English ACE 2005 data. We followed Li et al. (2014) and removed the two smallest and most informal parts of the data, namely 'conversational telephone speech' and 'Usenet newsgroups'. From the remaining 511 documents, 351 are used for training, 80 for development, and 80 for testing.

We follow standard evaluation procedures for triggers and events (Ji and Grishman, 2008). A trigger is correct, if its span and event type match a reference trigger. An argument is correct, if its span, event type, and role match a reference argument.

Table 1 summarizes results for SEMAFOR_E and a state-of-the-art system for event extraction (Li et al., 2013). To make a fair comparison, we report the numbers of their pipeline version, i.e., predicting trigger and arguments sequentially, as we do. Both systems use gold mentions and gold entity types. For SEMAFOR_E, we excluded all nested mentions of the same type: From "said [president [Obama]]", the inner span would be excluded.

SEMAFOR_E's recall is comparable to Li et al. (2013). However, their system gives a higher precision for both subtasks. We believe that the higher precision of their argument model comes from the higher precision of their trigger model. Similarly, the lower precision of SEMAFOR_E's argument model is due to the lower precision of its trigger model. Because of this, SEMAFOR_E is a few F_1 points below Li et al. (2013).

We note that there is only a minor drop in performance when comparing numbers for the development and test sets. This indicates that SEMAFOR_E's performance is robust.

The biggest error source for trigger classification is missing triggers. The second biggest error source is confusion of events with null events. Consider the following example: "Saba hasn't delivered yet". SEMAFOR_E predicted a null event for the trigger "delivered" instead of the right BE-BORN event. The context it had to analyze did not suffice to overcome its bias towards null events. Even for humans it seems hard to infer the right event type here. One would need to know that "Saba" refers to a pregnant woman, which could be inferred from the document. However, the sentence alone does not provide enough information.

The biggest error source for argument classification is error propagation from the trigger model. The second major error source is the local prediction of arguments. It seems better to predict triggers and arguments jointly in order to weaken error propagation (Li et al., 2013; Li et al., 2014). For example, SEMAFOR_E finds a START-ORG event for the trigger "set up" in the following sentence: "At the site, equipment has been set up to test conventional explosives [...]". In such cases, the model would need to know that the argument "equipment" cannot fill the *org* role of START-ORG because it is no organization. Inferring triggers and arguments jointly would enable SEMAFOR_E to better prevent such errors.

5 Conclusions and Future Work

Based on the hypothesis that frame-semantic parsing and event extraction are structurally identical, we retrained a state-of-the-art frame-semantic pars-

[3]Semantic relations come from WordNet (Fellbaum, 1998)

	Triggers			Arguments		
	P	R	F_1	P	R	F_1
SEMAFOR_E dev	65.8	57.8	61.6	57.0	32.4	41.3
SEMAFOR_E test	62.6	56.8	60.0	53.5	33.3	41.0
Li et al. (2013)	74.5	59.1	65.9	65.4	33.1	43.9

Table 1: Evaluation results for SEMAFOR_E on the development and test sets compared to a state-of-the-art system.

ing system for event extraction. We presented the adaptions in prediction classes and features needed to make the system better suited for the more restrictive task of event extraction. We also described a bias in the trigger classification model and proposed a feature factorization which is better suited for this model. As the evaluation shows, the retrained system can rival the state-of-the-art in event extraction.

For future work, we plan to incorporate mention detection into SEMAFOR_E . SEMAFOR's segmentation approach is not suited for event extraction because it produces too many argument candidates. Furthermore, error analysis and evaluation suggest that we need to predict triggers and arguments jointly. We also plan to go beyond sentences and search for larger contexts which may be relevant for event extraction. These changes may also be beneficial for frame-semantic parsing.

Acknowledgments

This work has been funded by the Klaus Tschira Foundation, Heidelberg, Germany. The first author has been supported by a HITS Ph.D. scholarship. We would like to thank our colleagues Sebastian Martschat, Daraksha Parveen, Nafise Moosavi, Yufang Hou and Mohsen Mesgar who commented on earlier drafts of this paper.

References

David Ahn. 2006. The stages of event extraction. In *Proceedings of the Workshop on Annotating and Reasoning about Time and Events,* Sydney, Australia, 23 July 2006, pages 1–8.

Michael Collins. 2002. Discriminative training methods for Hidden Markov Models: Theory and experiments with perceptron algorithms. In *Proceedings of the 2002 Conference on Empirical Methods in Natural Language Processing,* Philadelphia, Penn., 6–7 July 2002, pages 1–8.

Dipanjan Das, Nathan Schneider, Desai Chen, and Noah A. Smith. 2010. Probabilistic frame-semantic parsing. In *Proceedings of Human Language Technologies 2010: The Conference of the North American Chapter of the Association for Computational Linguistics,* Los Angeles, Cal., 2–4 June 2010, pages 948–956.

Dipanjan Das, Desai Chen, André F. T. Martins, Nathan Schneider, and Noah A. Smith. 2014. Frame-semantic parsing. *Computational Linguistics*, 40(1):9–56.

Christiane Fellbaum, editor. 1998. *WordNet: An Electronic Lexical Database.* MIT Press, Cambridge, Mass.

Charles J. Fillmore, Christopher R. Johnson, and Miriam R. L. Petruck. 2003. Background to FrameNet. *International Journal of Lexicography*, 16(3):235–250.

Ralph Grishman, David Westbrook, and Adam Meyers. 2005. NYU's English ACE 2005 system description. Technical report, Department of Computer Science, New York University, New York, N.Y.

Heng Ji and Ralph Grishman. 2008. Refining event extraction through cross-document inference. In *Proceedings of the 46th Annual Meeting of the Association for Computational Linguistics: Human Language Technologies,* Columbus, Ohio, 15–20 June 2008, pages 254–262.

Qi Li, Heng Ji, and Liang Huang. 2013. Joint event extraction via structured prediction with global features. In *Proceedings of the 51st Annual Meeting of the Association for Computational Linguistics (Volume 1: Long Papers),* Sofia, Bulgaria, 4–9 August 2013, pages 73–82.

Qi Li, Heng Ji, Yu Heng, and Sujian Li. 2014. Constructing information networks using one single model. In *Proceedings of the 2014 Conference on Empirical Methods in Natural Language Processing,* Doha, Qatar, 25–29 October 2014, pages 1846–1851.

Shasha Liao and Ralph Grishman. 2010. Using document level cross-event inference to improve event extraction. In *Proceedings of the 48th Annual Meeting of the Association for Computational Linguistics,* Uppsala, Sweden, 11–16 July 2010, pages 789–797.

Wei Lu and Dan Roth. 2012. Automatic event extraction with structured preference modeling. In *Proceedings of the 50th Annual Meeting of the Association for Computational Linguistics (Volume 1: Long Papers)*, Jeju Island, Korea, 8–14 July 2012, pages 835–844.

Christopher Walker, Stephanie Strassel, Julie Medero, and Maeda Kazuaki. 2006. ACE 2005 multilingual training corpus. LDC2006T06, Philadelphia, Penn.: Linguistic Data Consortium.

Competence in lexical semantics

András Kornai
Institute for Computer Science
Hungarian Academy of Sciences
Kende u. 13-17
1111 Budapest, Hungary
andras@kornai.com

Judit Ács
Dept of Automation and
Applied Informatics, BUTE
Magyar Tudósok krt. 2
1117 Budapest, Hungary
judit@aut.bme.hu

Márton Makrai
Institute for Linguistics
Hungarian Academy of Sciences
Benczúr u. 33
1068 Budapest, Hungary
makrai@nytud.hu

Dávid Nemeskey
Faculty of Informatics
Eötvös Loránd University
Pázmány Péter sétány 1/C
1117 Budapest, Hungary
nemeskeyd@gmail.com

Katalin Pajkossy
Department of Algebra
BUTE
Egry J. u. 1
1111 Budapest, Hungary
pajkossy@math.bme.hu

Gábor Recski
Institute for Linguistics
Hungarian Academy of Sciences
Benczúr u. 33
1068 Budapest, Hungary
recski@mokk.bme.hu

Abstract

We investigate from the competence standpoint two recent models of lexical semantics, algebraic conceptual representations and continuous vector models.

Characterizing what it means for a speaker to be competent in lexical semantics remains perhaps the most significant stumbling block in reconciling the two main threads of semantics, Chomsky's cognitivism and Montague's formalism. As Partee (1979) already notes (see also Partee 2013), linguists assume that people know their language and that their brain is finite, while Montague assumed that words are characterized by intensions, formal objects that require an infinite amount of information to specify.

In this paper we investigate two recent models of lexical semantics that rely exclusively on finite information objects: algebraic conceptual representations (ACR) (Wierzbicka, 1985; Kornai, 2010; Gordon et al., 2011), and continuous vector space (CVS) models which assign to each word a point in finite-dimensional Euclidean space (Bengio et al., 2003; Turian et al., 2010; Pennington et al., 2014). After a brief introduction to the philosophical background of these and similar models, we address the hard questions of competence, starting with learnability in Section 2; the ability of finite networks or vectors to replicate traditional notions of lexical relatedness such as synonymy, antonymy, ambiguity, polysemy, etc. in Section 3; the interface to compositional semantics in Section 4; and language-specificity and universality in Section 5. Our survey of the literature is far from exhaustive: both ACR and CVS have deep roots, with significant precursors going back at least to Quillian (1968) and Osgood et al. (1975) respectively, but we put the emphasis on the computational experiments we ran (source code and lexica available at `github.com/kornai/4lang`).

1 Background

In the eyes of many, Quine (1951) has demolished the traditional analytic/synthetic distinction, relegating nearly all pre-Fregean accounts of word meaning from Aristotle to Locke to the dustbin of history. The opposing view, articulated clearly in Grice and Strawson (1956), is based on the empirical observation that people make the call rather uniformly over novel examples, an argument whose import is evident from the (at the time, still nascent) cognitive perspective. Today, we may agree with Putnam (1976):

> 'Bachelor' may be synonymous with 'unmarried man' but that cuts no philosophic ice. 'Chair' may be synonymous with 'moveable seat for one with back' but that bakes no philosophic bread and washes no philosophic windows. It is the belief that there are synonymies and analyticities of a deeper nature - synonymies and analyticities that cannot be discovered by the lexicographer or the linguist but only by the philosopher - that is incorrect.

*Proceedings of the Fourth Joint Conference on Lexical and Computational Semantics (*SEM 2015)*, pages 165–175,
Denver, Colorado, June 4–5, 2015.

Fortunately, one philosopher's trash may just turn out to be another linguist's treasure. What Putnam has demonstrated is that "a speaker can, by all reasonable standards, be in command of a word like *water* without being able to command the intension that would represent the word in possible worlds semantics" (Partee, 1979). Computational systems of Knowledge Representation, starting with the Teachable Word Comprehender of Quillian (1968), and culminating in the Deep Lexical Semantics of Hobbs (2008), carried on this tradition of analyzing word meaning in terms of 'essential' or 'analytic' components.

A particularly important step in this direction is the emergence of modern, computationally oriented lexicographic work beginning with Collins-COBUILD (Sinclair, 1987), the Longman Dictionary of Contemporary English (LDOCE) (Boguraev and Briscoe, 1989), WordNet (Miller, 1995), FrameNet (Fillmore and Atkins, 1998), and VerbNet (Kipper et al., 2000). Both the network- and the vector-based approach build on these efforts, but through very different routes.

Traditional network theories of Knowledge Representation tend to concentrate on nominal features such as the IS_A links (called hypernyms in WordNet) and treat the representation of verbs somewhat haphazardly. The first systems with a well-defined model of predication are the Conceptual Dependency model of Schank (1972), the Natural Syntax Metalanguage (NSM) of Wierzbicka (1985), and a more elaborate deep lexical semantics system that is still under construction by Hobbs and his coworkers (Hobbs, 2008; Gordon et al., 2011). What we call algebraic conceptual representation (ACR) is any such theory encoded with colored directed edges between the basic conceptual units. The algebraic approach provides a better fit with functional programming than the more declarative, automata-theoretic approach (Huet and Razet, 2008), and makes it possible to encode verbal subcategorization (case frame) information that is at the heart of FrameNet and VerbNet in addition to the standardly used nominal features (Kornai, 2010).

Continuous vector space (CVS) is also not a single model but a rich family of models, generally based on what Baroni (2013) calls the *distributional hypothesis*, that semantically similar items have similar distribution. This idea, going back at least to Firth (1957) is not at all trivial to defend, and not just because defining 'semantically similar' is a challenging task: as we shall see, there are significant design choices involved in defining similarity of vectors as well. To the extent CVS representations are primarily used in artificial neural net models, it may be helpful to consider the state of a network being described by the vector whose nth coordinate gives the activation level of the nth neuron. Under this conception, the meaning of a word is simply the activation pattern of the brain when the word is produced or perceived. Such vectors have very large (10^{10}) dimension so dimension reduction is called for, but direct correlation between brain activation patterns and the distribution of words has actually been detected (Mitchell et al., 2008).

2 Learnability

The key distinguishing feature between 'explanatory' or competence models and 'descriptive' or performance models is that the former, but not the latter, come complete with a learning algorithm (Chomsky, 1965). Although there is a wealth of data on children's acquisition of lexical entries (McKeown and Curtis, 1987), neither cognitive nor formal semantics have come close to formulating a robust theory of acquisition, and for intensions, infinite information objects encoding the meaning in the formal theory, it is not at all clear whether such a learning algorithm is even possible.

2.1 The basic vocabulary

The idea that there is a small set of conceptual primitives for building semantic representations has a long history both in linguistics and AI as well as in language teaching. The more theory-oriented systems, such as Conceptual Dependency and NSM assume only a few dozen primitives, but have a disquieting tendency to add new elements as time goes by (Andrews, 2015). In contrast, the systems intended for teaching and communication, such as Basic English (Ogden, 1944) start with at least a thousand primitives, and assume that these need to be further supplemented by technical terms from various domains. Since the obvious learning algorithm based on any such reductive system is one where the primitives are assumed universal (and possibly innate, see Section 5), and the rest is learned by reduction to the primitives, we performed a series of 'ceiling' experiments aiming at a determination of how big the universal/innate component of the lexicon must be. A trivial lower bound is given by the current size of the NSM inventory, 65 (Andrews, 2015), but as long as we don't have the complete lexicon of at least one language defined in NSM terms the reductivity of the system remains in doubt.

For English, a Germanic language, the first provably reductive system is the Longman Defining Vocabulary (LDV), some 2,200 items, which provide a sufficient basis for defining all entries in LDOCE (using English syntax in the definitions). Our work started with a superset of the LDV that was obtained by adding the most frequent words according to the Google unigram count (Brants and Franz, 2006) and the BNC, as well as the most frequent words from a Slavic, a Finnougric, and a Romance language (Polish, Hungarian, and Latin), and Whitney (1885) to form the `4lang` conceptual dictionary, with the long-term design goal of eventually providing reductive definitions for the vocabularies of all Old World languages. Ács et al. (2013) describes how bindings in other languages can be created automatically and compares the reductive method to the familiar term- and document-frequency based searches for core vocabulary.

This superset of LDV, called '4lang' in Table 1 below, can be considered a directed graph whose nodes are the disambiguated concepts (with exponents in four languages) and whose edges run from each definiendum to every concept that appears in its definition. Such a graph can have many cycles. Our main interest is with selecting a defining set which has the property that each word, including those that appear in the definitions, can be defined in terms of members of this set. Every word that is a true primitive (has no definition, e.g. the basic terms of the Schank and NSM systems) must be included in the defining set, and to these we must add at least one vertex from every directed cycle. Thus, the problem of finding a defining set is equivalent to finding a *feedback vertex set,* (FVS) a problem already proven NP-complete in Karp (1972). Since we cannot run an exhaustive search, we use a heuristic algorithm which searches for a defining set by gradually eliminating low-frequency nodes whose outgoing arcs lead to not yet eliminated nodes, and make no claim that the results in Table 1 are optimal, just that they are typical of the reduction that can be obtained by modest computation. We defer discussion of the last line to Section 4, but note that the first line already implies that a defining set of 1,008 concepts will cover all senses of the high frequency items in the major Western branches of IE, and to cover the first (primary) sense of each word in LDOCE 361 words suffice.

Dictionary	#words	FVS
4lang (all senses)	31,192	1,008
4lang (first senses)	3,127	361
LDOCE (all senses)	79,414	1,061
LDOCE (first senses)	34,284	376
CED (all senses)	154,061	6,490
CED (first senses)	80,495	3,435
`en.wiktionary` (all senses)	369,281	2,504
`en.wiktionary` (first senses)	304,029	1,845
formal	2,754	129

Table 1: Properties of four different dictionaries

While a feedback vertex set is guaranteed to exist for any digraph (if all else fails, the entire set of vertices will do), it is not guaranteed that there exists one that is considerably smaller than the entire graph. (For random digraphs in general see Dutta and Subramanian 2010, for highly symmetrical lattices see Zhou 2013 ms.) In random digraphs under relatively mild conditions on the proportion of edges relative to nodes, Łuczak and Seierstad (2009) show that a strong component essentially the size of the entire graph will exist. Fortunately, digraphs built on definitions are not at all behaving in a random fashion, the strongly connected components are relatively small, as Table 1 makes evident. For example, in the English Wiktionary, 369,281 definitions can be reduced to a core set of 2,504 defining words, and in CED we can find a defining set of 6,490 words, even though these dictionaries, unlike LDOCE, were not built using an explicit defining set. Since LDOCE pioneered the idea of actively limiting the defining vocabulary, it is no great surprise that it has a small feedback vertex set, though everyday users of the LDV may be somewhat surprised that less than half (1,061 items) of the full defining set (over 2,200 items) are needed.

We also experimented with an early (pre-COBUILD) version of the Collins English Dictionary (CED), as this is more representative of the traditional type of dictionaries which didn't rely on a defining vocabulary. In 154,061 definitions, 65,891 words are used, but only 15,464 of these are not headwords in LDOCE. These words appear in less than 10% of Collins definitions, meaning that using LDOCE as an intermediary the LDV is already sufficient for defining over 90% of the CED word senses. An example of a CED defining word missing not just from LDV but the entire LDOCE would be *aigrette* ‘a long plume worn on hats or as a headdress, esp. one of long egret feathers’.

This number could be improved to about 93% by detail parsing of the CED definitions. For example, *aigrette* actually appears as crossreference in the definition of *egret*, and deleting the cross-reference would not alter the sense of *egret* being defined. The remaining cases would require better morphological parsing of latinate terms than we currently have access to: for now, many definitions cannot be automatically simplified because the system is unaware that e.g. *nitrobacterium* is the singular of *nitrobacteria*. Manually spot-checking 2% of the remaining CED words used in definitions found over 75% latinate technical terms, but no instances of undefinable non-technical senses that would require extending the LDV. This is not that every sense of every nontechnical word of English is listed in LDOCE, but inspecting even more comprehensive dictionaries such as the Concise Oxford Dictionary or Webster's 3rd makes it clear that their definitions use largely words which are themselves covered by LDOCE. Thus, if we see a definition such as *naphtha* ‘kinds of inflammable oil got by dry distillation of organic substances as coal, shale, or petroleum’ we can be nearly certain that words like *inflammable* which are not part of the LDV will nevertheless be definable in terms of it, in this case as ‘materials or substances that will start to burn very easily’.

The reduction itself is not a trivial task, in that a simplified definition of *naphtha* such as ‘kinds of oils that will start to burn very easily and are produced by dry distillation ...’ can eliminate *inflammable* only if we notice that the ‘oil’ in the definition of *naphtha* is the ‘material or substance’ in the definition of *inflammable*. Similarly, we have to understand that ‘got’ was used in the sense *obtained* or *produced*, that *dry distillation* is a single concept ‘the heating of solid materials to produce gaseous products’ that is not built compositionally from *dry* and *distillation* in spite of being written as two separate words, and so forth. Automated detection and resolution of these and similar issues remain challenging NLP tasks, but from a competence perspective it is sufficient to note that manual substitution is performed effortlessly and near-uniformly by native speakers.

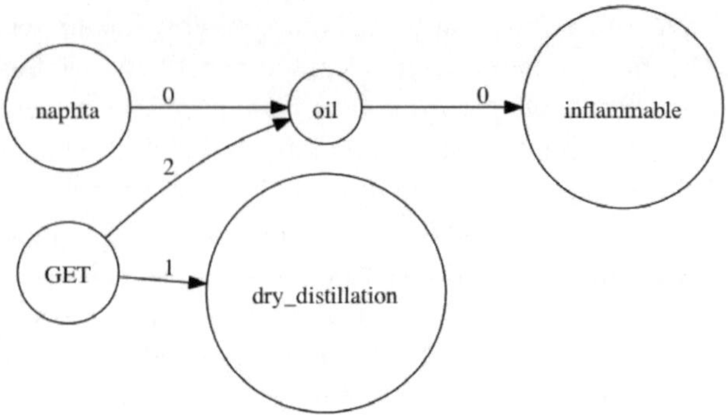

Figure 1: Original definition of `naphtha`

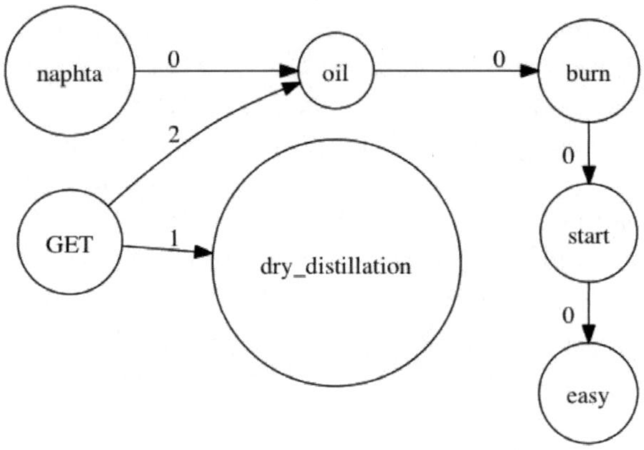

Figure 2: Reduced definition of `naphtha`

2.2 Learnability in CVS semantics

The reductive theory of vocabulary acquisition is a highly idealized one, for surely children don't learn the meaning of *sharp* by their parents telling them it means ‘having a thin cutting edge or point’. Yet it is clear that computers that lack a sensory system that would deliver intense signals upon encountering sharp objects can nevertheless acquire something of the meaning by pure deduction (assuming also that they are programmed to know that cutting one's body will CAUSE PAIN) and further, the dominant portion of the vocabulary is not connected to direct sensory signals but is learned from context (see Chapter 6 of McKeown and Curtis 1987).

This brings us to CVS semantics, where learning theory is idealized in a very different way, by assuming that the learner has access to very large corpora, gigaword and beyond. We must agree with Miller and Chomsky (1963) that in real life a child exposed to a word every second would require over 30 years to hear gigaword amounts, but we take this to be a reflection of the weak inferencing ability of current statistical models, for there is nothing in the argument that says that models that are more efficient in extracting regularities can't learn these from orders of magnitude less data, especially as children are known to acquire words based on a single exposure. For now, such *one shot learning* remains something of an ideal, in that CVS systems prune infrequent words (Collobert et al., 2011; Mikolov et al., 2013a; Luong et al., 2013), but it is clear that both CVS and ACR have the beginnings of a feasible theory of learning, while the classical theory of meaning postulates offers nothing of the sort, not even for the handful of lexical items (tense and aspect markers in particular, see Dowty 1979) where the underlying logic has the resources to express these.

3 Lexical relatedness

Ordinary dictionary definitions can be mined to recover the conceptual entailments that are at the heart of lexical semantic competence. Whatever naphtha is, knowing that it is inflammable is sufficient for knowing that it will start to burn easily. It is a major NLP challenge to make this deduction (Dagan et al. 2006), but ACR can store the information trivially and make the inference by spreading activation.

We implemented one variant of the ACR theory of word meaning by a network of Eilenberg machines (Eilenberg, 1974) corresponding to elements of the reduced vocabulary. Eilenberg machines are a simple generalization of the better known finite state automata (FSA) and transducers (FSTs) that have become standard since Koskenniemi (1983) in describing the rule-governed aspects of the lexicon, morphotactics and morphophonology (Huet and Razet, 2008; Kornai, 2010). The methods we use for defining word senses (concepts) are long familiar from Knowledge Representation. We assume the reader is familiar with the knowledge representation literature (for a summary, see Brachman and Levesque 2004), and describe only those parts of the system that differ from the mainstream assumptions. In particular, we collapse attribution, unary predication, and `IS_A` links in a single link type '0' (as in Figs. 1-2 above) and have only two other kinds of links to distinguish the arguments of transitive verbs, '1' corresponding to subject/agent; and '2' to object/patient. The treatment of other link types, be they construed as grammatical functions or as deep cases or even thematic slots, is deferred to Section 4.

By creating graphs for all LDOCE headwords based on dependency parses of their definitions (the 'literal' network of Table 1) using the unlexicalized version of the Stanford Dependency Parser (Klein and Manning, 2003), we obtained measures of lexical relatedness by defining various similarity metrics over pairs of such graphs. The intuition underlying all these metrics is that two words are semantically similar if their definitions overlap in (i) the concepts present in their definitions (e.g. the definition of both *train* and *car* will make reference to the concept *vehicle*) and (ii) the binary relations they take part in (e.g. both *street* and *park* are `IN` *town*). While such a measure of semantic similarity builds more on manual labor (already performed by the lexicographers) than those gained from state-of-the-art CVS systems, recently the results from the 'literal' network have been used in a competitive system for measuring semantic textual similarity (Recski and Ács, 2015). In Section 4 we discuss the 'formal' network of Table 1 built directly on the concept formulae. By spectral dimension reduction of the incidence matrix of this network we can create an embedding that yields results on world similarity tasks comparable to those obtained from corpus-based embeddings (Makrai et al., 2013).

CVS models can be explicitly tested on their ability to recover synonymy by searching for the nearest word in the sample (Mikolov et al., 2013b); antonymy by reversing the sign of the vector (Zweig, 2014); and in general for all kinds of analogical statements such as *king is to queen as man is to woman* by vector addition and subtraction (Mikolov et al., 2013c); not to speak of cross-language paraphrase/translation (Schwenk et al., 2012), long viewed a key intermediary step toward explaining competence in a foreign language.

Currently, CVS systems are clearly in the lead on such tasks, and it is not clear what, if anything, can be salvaged from the truth-conditional approach to these matters. At the same time, the CVS approach to quantifiers is not mature, and ACR theories support generics only. These may look like backward steps, but keep in mind that our goal in competence modeling is to characterize everyday knowledge, shared by all competent speakers of the language, while quantifier and modal scope ambiguities are something that ordinary speakers begin to appreciate only after considerable schooling in these matters, with significant differences between the naive (preschool) and the learned adult systems (É. Kiss et al., 2013). On the traditional account, only subsumption (IS_A or '0') links can be easily recovered from the meaning postulates, the cognitively central similarity (as opposed to exact synonymy) relations receive no treatment whatsoever, since similarity of meaning postulates is undefined.

4 Lexical lookup

The interaction with compositional semantics is a key issue for any competence theory of lexical semantics. In the classical formal system, this is handled by a mechanism of *lexical lookup* that substitutes the meaning postulates at the terminal nodes of the derivation tree, at the price of introducing some lexical redundancy rule that creates the intensional meaning of each word, including the evidently non-intensional ones, based on the meaning postulates that encode the extensional meaning. (Ch. 19.2 of Jacobson (2014) sketches an alternative treatment, which keeps intensionality for the intended set of cases.) While there are considerable technical difficulties of formula manipulation involved, this is really one area where the classical theory shines as a competence theory – we cannot even imagine to create a learning algorithm that would cover the meaning of infinitely many complex expressions unless we had some means of combining the meanings of the lexical entries.

CVS semantics offers several ways of combining lexical entries, the simplest being simply adding the vectors together (Mitchell and Lapata, 2008), but the use of linear transformations (Lazaridou et al., 2013) and tensor products (Smolensky, 1990) has also been contemplated. Currently, an approach that combines the vectors of the parts to form the vector of the whole by recurrent neural nets appears to work best (Socher et al., 2013), but this is still an area of intense research and it would be premature to declare this method the winner. Here we concentrate on ACR, investigating the issue of the inventory of graph edge colors on the same core vocabulary as discussed above. The key technical problem is to bring the variety of links between verbs and their arguments under control: as Woods (1975) already notes, the naive ACR theories are characterized by a profusion of link types (graph edge colors).

We created a version of ACR that is limited to three link types. Both the usual network representations (digraphs, as in Figs. 1 and 2 above) and a more algebraic model composed of extended finite state automata (Eilenberg machines) are produced by parsing formulas defined by a formal grammar summarized in Figure 3. For ease of reading, in unary predication (e.g. `mouse` $\xrightarrow{0}$ `rodent`) we permit both prefix and suffix order, but with different kinds of parens `mouse[rodent]` and `rodent(mouse)`; and we use infix notation (`cow MAKE milk`) for transitives (`cow` $\xleftarrow{1}$ `MAKE` $\xrightarrow{2}$ `milk`, link types '1' and '2').

The right column of Figure 3 shows the digraph obtained from parsing the formula on the right hand hand side of the grammar rules. There are no '3' or higher links, as ditransitives like *x give y to z* are decomposed at the semantic level into unary and binary atoms, in this case `CAUSE` and `HAVE`, 'x cause (z have y)', see Kornai (2012) for further details. A digraph representing the whole lexicon was built in two steps: first, every clause in definitions was manually translated to a formula (which in turns is automatically translated into a digraph), then the digraphs were connected by unifying nodes that have the same label and no outgoing edges.

The amount of manual labor involved was considerably lessened by the method of Section 3 that

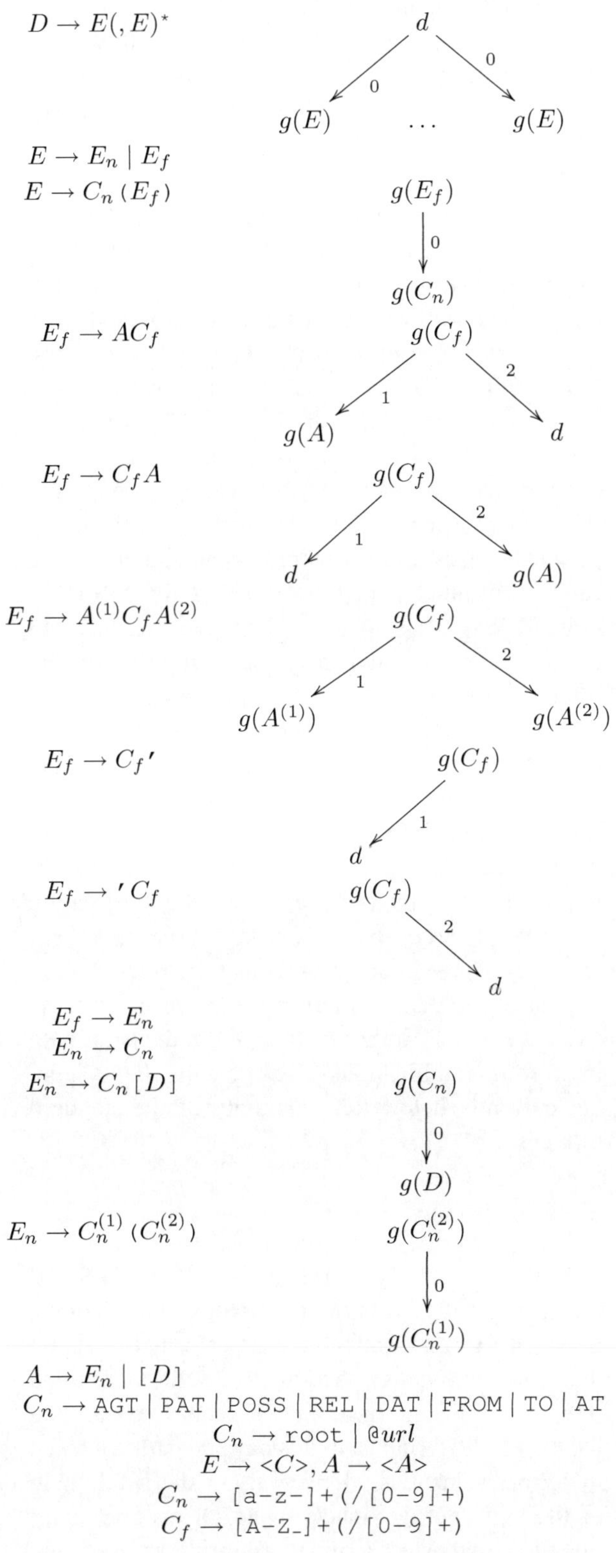

Figure 3: The syntax of the definitions

finds the feedback vertex set, in that once such a set is given, the rest could be built automatically. This gives us a means of investigating the prevalence of what would become different deep cases (colors, link types) in other KR systems. Deep cases are distinguishers that mediate between the purely semantic (theta) link types and the surface case/adposition system. We have kept our system of deep cases rather standard, both in the sense of representing a common core among the many proposals starting with Gruber (1965) and Fillmore (1968) and in the sense of aiming at universality, a subject we defer to the next section. The names and frequency of use in the core vocabulary are given in Table 2. The results are indicative of a primary (agent/patient, what we denote '1'/'2'), a secondary (DAT/REL/POSS), and a tertiary (locative) layer in deep cases – how these are mapped on language-specific (surface) cases will be discussed in Section 5.

freq	**abbreviation**	**comment**
487	AGT	agent
388	PAT	patient
34	DAT	dative
82	REL	root or adpositional object
70	POSS	default for relational nouns
20	TO	target of action
15	FROM	source of action
3	AT	location of action

Table 2: Deep cases

To avoid problems with multiple word senses and with constructional meaning (as in *dry distillation* or *dry martini*) we defined each entry in this formal language (keeping different word senses such as `light/739` 'the opposite of *dark*' and `light/1381` 'the opposite of *heavy*' distinct by disambiguation indexes) and built a graph directly on the resulting conceptual network rather than the original LDOCE definitions. The feedback vertex set algorithm `uroboros.py` determined that a core set of 129 concepts are sufficient to define the others in the entire concept dictionary, and thus for the entire LDOCE or similar dictionaries such as CED or Webster's 3rd. This upper bound is so close to the NSM lower bound of 65 that a blow-by-blow comparison would be justified.

5 Universality

The final issue one needs to investigate in assessing the potential of any purported competence theory is that of universality versus language particularity. For CVS theories, this is rather easy: we have one system of representation, finite dimensional vector spaces, which admits no typological variation, let alone language-specific mechanisms – one size fits all. As linguists, we see considerable variation among the surface, and possibly even among the deeper aspects of case linking (Smith, 1996), but as computational modelers we lack, as of yet, a better understanding of what corresponds to such mechanisms within CVS semantics.

ACR systems are considerably more transparent in this regard, and the kind of questions that we would want to pose as linguists have direct reflexes in the formal system. Many of the original theories of conceptual representation were English-particular, sometimes to the point of being as naive as the medieval theories of universal language (Eco, 1995). The most notable exception is NSM, clearly developed with the native languages of Australia in mind, and often exercised on Russian, Polish, and other IE examples as well. Here we follow the spirit of GFRG (Ranta, 2011) in assuming a common abstract syntax for all languages. For case grammar this requires some abstraction, for example English NPs must also get case marked (an idea also present in the 'Case Theory' of Government-Binding and related theories of transformational grammar). The main difference between English and the overtly case-marking languages such as Russian or Latin is that in English we compute the cases from prepositions and word order (position relative to the verb) rather than from overt morphological marking as standard. This way, the lexical entries can be kept highly abstract, and for the most part, universal. Thus the verb *go* will have a source and a goal. For every language there is a `langspec` component of the lexicon which stores e.g. for English the information that source is expressed by the preposition *from* and destination by *to*. For Hungarian the `langspec` file stores the information that source can be linked by delative, elative, and ablative; goal by illative, sublative, or terminative. Once this kind of language-specific variation is factored out, the `go` entry becomes `before AT src, after AT goal`. The same technique is used to encode both lexical entries and constructions in the sense of Berkeley Construction Grammar (CxG, see Goldberg 1995).

Whether two constructions (in the same language or two different languages) have to be coded by different deep cases is measured very badly, if at all, by the standard test suits used e.g. in paraphrase detection or question answering, and we would need to invest serious effort in building new test suites. For example, the system sketched above uses the same deep case, `REL`, for linking objects that are surface marked by quirky case and for arguments of predicate nominals. Another example is the dative/experiencer/beneficent family. Whether the experiencer cases familiar from Korean and elsewhere can be subsumed under the standard dative role (Fillmore, 1968) is an open question, but one that can at least be formulated in ACR. Currently we distinguish the dative `DAT` from possessive marking `POSS`, generally not considered a true case but quite prevalent in this function language after language: consider English *(the) root of a tree,* or Polish *korzen drzewa*. This is in contrast to the less frequent cases like *(an excellent) occasion for martyrdom* marked by obliques (here the preposition *for*). What these nouns (*occasion, condition, reason, need*) have in common is that the related word is goal of the definiendum in some sense. In these cases we use `TO` rather than `POSS`, a decision with interesting ramifications elsewhere in the system, but currently below the sensitivity of the standard test sets.

6 Conclusion

It is not particularly surprising that both CVS and ACR, originally designed as performance theories, fare considerably better in the performance realm than Montagovian semantics, especially as detailed intensional lexica have never been crafted, and Dowty (1979) remains, to this day, the path not taken in formal semantics. It is only on the subdomain of the logic puzzles involving Booleans and quantification that Montagovian solutions showed any promise, and these, with the exception of elementary negation, do not even appear in more down to earth evaluation sets such as (Weston et al., 2015). The surprising conclusion of our work is that standard Montagovian semantics also falls short in the competence realm, where the formal theory has long been promoted as offering psychological reality.

We have compared CVS and ACR theories of lexical semantics to the classical approach based on meaning postulates by the usual criteria for competence theories. In Section 2 we have seen that both ACR and CVS are better in terms of learnability than the standard formal theory, and it is worth noting that the number of ACR primitives, 129 in the version implemented here, is less than the dimensions of the best performing CVS embeddings, 150-300 after data compression by PCA or similar methods. In Section 3 we have seen that lexical relatedness tasks also favor ACR and CVS over the meaning postulate approach (for a critical overview of meaning postulates in model-theoretic semantics see Zimmermann 1999), and in Section 4 we have seen that compositionality poses no problems for ACR. How compositional semantics is handled in CVS semantics remains to be seen, but the problem is not a dearth of plausible mechanisms, but rather an overabundance of these.

Acknowledgments

The `4lang` conceptual dictionary is the work of many people over the years. The name is no longer quite justified, in that natural language bindings, automatically generated and thus not entirely free of errors and omissions, now exist for 50 languages (Ács et al., 2013), many of them outside the Indoeuropean and Finnougric families originally targeted. More important, formal definitions of the concepts that rely on less than a dozen theoretical primitives (including the three link types) and only 129 core concepts, are now available for all the concepts. So far, only the theoretical underpinnings of this formal system have been fully described in English (Kornai, 2010; Kornai, 2012), with many details presented only in Hungarian (Kornai and Makrai, 2013), but the formal definitions, and the parser that can build both graphs and Eilenberg machines from these, are now available as part of the `kornai/4lang` github repository. These formal definitions were written primarily by Makrai, with notable contributions by Recski and Nemeskey.

The system has been used as an experimental platform for a variety of purposes, including quantitative analysis of deep cases by Makrai, who developed the current version of the deep case system with Nemeskey (Makrai, 2015); for defining lexical relatedness (Makrai et al., 2013; Recski and Ács, 2015); and in this paper, for finding the definitional core, the feedback vertex set.

Ács wrote the first version of the feedback vertex set finder which was adapted to our data by Ács and Pajkossy, who also took part in the computational experiments, including preprocessing the data, adapting the vertex set finder, and running the experiments. Recski created the pipeline in the `http://github/kornai/4lang` repository that builds formal definitions from English dictionary entries. Kornai advised and wrote the paper.

We are grateful to Attila Zséder (HAS Linguistics Institute) for writing the original parser for the formal language of definitions and to András Gyárfás (HAS Rényi Institute) for help with feedback vertex sets. Work supported by OTKA grant #82333.

References

Judit Ács, Katalin Pajkossy, and András Kornai. 2013. Building basic vocabulary across 40 languages. In *Proceedings of the Sixth Workshop on Building and Using Comparable Corpora*, pages 52–58, Sofia, Bulgaria, August. ACL.

Avery Andrews. 2015. Reconciling NSM and formal semantics. *ms*, pages v2, jan 2015.

Marco Baroni. 2013. Composition in distributional semantics. *Language and Linguistics Compass*, 7(10):511–522.

Yoshua Bengio, Réjean Ducharme, Pascal Vincent, and Christian Janvin. 2003. A neural probabilistic language model. *Journal of Machine Learning Research*, 3:1137–1155.

Branimir K. Boguraev and Edward J. Briscoe. 1989. *Computational Lexicography for Natural Language Processing*. Longman.

R.J. Brachman and H. Levesque. 2004. *Knowledge Representation and reasoning*. Morgan Kaufman Elsevier, Los Altos, CA.

Thorsten Brants and Alex Franz. 2006. *Web 1T 5-gram Version 1*. Linguistic Data Consortium, Philadelphia.

Noam Chomsky. 1965. *Aspects of the Theory of Syntax*. MIT Press.

R. Collobert, J. Weston, L. Bottou, M. Karlen, K. Kavukcuoglu, and P. Kuksa. 2011. Natural language processing (almost) from scratch. *Journal of Machine Learning Research (JMLR)*.

Ido Dagan, Oren Glickman, and Bernardo Magnini. 2006. The PASCAL recognising textual entailment challenge. In *Machine Learning Challenges. Evaluating Predictive Uncertainty, Visual Object Classification, and Recognising Tectual Entailment*, volume 3944 of *LNCS*, pages 177–190. Springer.

David Dowty. 1979. *Word Meaning and Montague Grammar*. Reidel, Dordrecht.

Kunal Dutta and C. R. Subramanian. 2010. Induced acyclic subgraphs in random digraphs: Improved bounds. In *Discrete Mathematics and Theoretical Computer Science*, pages 159–174.

Katalin É. Kiss, Mátyás Gerőcs, and Tamás Zétényi. 2013. Preschoolers interpretation of doubly quantified sentences. *Acta Linguistica Hungarica*, 60:143–171.

Umberto Eco. 1995. *The Search for the Perfect Language*. Blackwell, Oxford.

Samuel Eilenberg. 1974. *Automata, Languages, and Machines*, volume A. Academic Press.

Charles Fillmore and Sue Atkins. 1998. Framenet and lexicographic relevance. In *Proceedings of the First International Conference on Language Resources and Evaluation*, Granada, Spain.

Charles Fillmore. 1968. The case for case. In E. Bach and R. Harms, editors, *Universals in Linguistic Theory*, pages 1–90. Holt and Rinehart, New York.

John R. Firth. 1957. A synopsis of linguistic theory. In *Studies in linguistic analysis*, pages 1–32. Blackwell.

Adele E. Goldberg. 1995. *Constructions: A Construction Grammar Approach to Argument Structure*. University of Chicago Press.

Andrew S. Gordon, Jerry R. Hobbs, and Michael T. Cox. 2011. Anthropomorphic self-models for metareasoning agents. In Michael T. Cox and Anita Raja, editors, *Metareasoning: Thinking about Thinking*, pages 295–305. MIT Press.

Paul Grice and Peter Strawson. 1956. In defense of a dogma. *The Philosophical Review*, 65:148–152.

Jeffrey Steven Gruber. 1965. *Studies in lexical relations*. Ph.D. thesis, Massachusetts Institute of Technology.

J.R. Hobbs. 2008. Deep lexical semantics. *Lecture Notes in Computer Science*, 4919:183.

Gérard Huet and Benoît Razet. 2008. Computing with relational machines. In *Tutorial at ICON, Dec 2008*.

Pauline Jacobson. 2014. *Compositional Semantics*. Oxford University Press.

Richard M. Karp. 1972. Reducibility among combinatorial problems. In R. Miller and J.W. Thatcher, editors, *Complexity of Computer Computations*, pages 85–104. Plenum Press, New York.

Karin Kipper, Hoa Trang Dang, and Martha Palmer. 2000. Class based construction of a verb lexicon. In *AAAI-2000 Seventeenth National Conference on Artificial Intelligence*, Austin, TX.

Dan Klein and Christopher D Manning. 2003. Accurate unlexicalized parsing. In *Proceedings of the 41st Annual Meeting on Association for Computational Linguistics-Volume 1*, pages 423–430.

András Kornai and Márton Makrai. 2013. A 4lang fogalmi szótár. In Attila Tanács and Veronika Vincze, editors, *IX. Magyar Számítógépes Nyelvészeti Konferencia*, pages 62–70.

András Kornai. 2010. The algebra of lexical semantics. In Christian Ebert, Gerhard Jäger, and Jens Michaelis, editors, *Proceedings of the 11th Mathematics of Language Workshop*, LNAI 6149, pages 174–199. Springer.

András Kornai. 2012. Eliminating ditransitives. In Ph. de Groote and M-J Nederhof, editors, *Revised and Selected Papers from the 15th and 16th Formal Grammar Conferences*, LNCS 7395, pages 243–261. Springer.

Kimmo Koskenniemi. 1983. Two-level model for morphological analysis. In *Proceedings of IJCAI-83*, pages 683–685.

Angeliki Lazaridou, Marco Marelli, Roberto Zamparelli, and Marco Baroni. 2013. Compositional-ly derived representations of morphologically complex words in distributional semantics. In *ACL (1)*, pages 1517–1526.

Tomasz Łuczak and Taral Guldahl Seierstad. 2009. The critical behavior of random digraphs. *Random Structures and Algorithms*, 35:271–293.

Thang Luong, Richard Socher, and Christopher D. Manning. 2013. Better word representations with recursive neural networks for morphology. In *CoNLL*, pages 104–113.

Márton Makrai, Dávid Márk Nemeskey, and András Kornai. 2013. Applicative structure in vector space models. In *Proceedings of the Workshop on Continuous Vector Space Models and their Compositionality*, pages 59–63, Sofia, Bulgaria, August. ACL.

Márton Makrai. 2015. Deep cases in the 4lang conceptlexicon. In Attila Tancs, Viktor Varga, and Veronika Vincze, editors, *X. Magyar Szmtgpes Nyelvszeti Konferencia (MSZNY 2014)*, pages 50–57 (in Hungarian), 387 (English abstract).

Margaret G. McKeown and Mary E. Curtis. 1987. *The nature of vocabulary acquisition*. Lawrence Erlbaum Associates.

Tomas Mikolov, Kai Chen, Greg Corrado, and Jeffrey Dean. 2013a. Efficient estimation of word representations in vector space. In Y. Bengio and Y. LeCun, editors, *Proc. ICLR 2013*.

Tomas Mikolov, Ilya Sutskever, Kai Chen, Greg S Corrado, and Jeff Dean. 2013b. Distributed representations of words and phrases and their compositionality. In C.J.C. Burges, L. Bottou, M. Welling, Z. Ghahramani, and K.Q. Weinberger, editors, *Advances in Neural Information Processing Systems 26*, pages 3111–3119. Curran Associates, Inc.

Tomas Mikolov, Wen-tau Yih, and Zweig Geoffrey. 2013c. Linguistic regularities in continuous space word representations. In *Proceedings of NAACL-HLT-2013*, pages 746–751.

George A. Miller and Noam Chomsky. 1963. Finitary models of language users. In R.D. Luce, R.R. Bush, and E. Galanter, editors, *Handbook of Mathematical Psychology*, pages 419–491. Wiley.

George A. Miller. 1995. Wordnet: a lexical database for English. *Communications of the ACM*, 38(11):39–41.

Jeff Mitchell and Mirella Lapata. 2008. Vector-based models of semantic composition. In *Proceedings of ACL-08: HLT*, pages 236–244, Columbus, Ohio. Association for Computational Linguistics.

T. M. Mitchell, S.V. Shinkareva, A. Carlson, K.M. Chang, V.L. Malave, R.A. Mason, and M.A. Just. 2008. Predicting human brain activity associated with the meanings of nouns. *Science*, 320(5880):1191.

C.K. Ogden. 1944. *Basic English: A General Introduction with Rules and Grammar.* Psyche miniatures: General Series. Kegan Paul, Trench, Trubner.

Charles E. Osgood, William S. May, and Murray S. Miron. 1975. *Cross Cultural Universals of Affective Meaning.* University of Illinois Press.

Barbara H. Partee. 1979. Semantics mathematics or psychology? In R. Bauerl, U. Egli, and A. von Stechow, editors, *Semantics from Different Points of View*, pages 1–14. Springer-Verlag, Berlin.

Barbara Partee. 2013. Changing perspectives on the 'mathematics or psychology' question. In *Philosophy Wkshp on "Semantics Mathematics or Psychology?"*.

Jeffrey Pennington, Richard Socher, and Christopher Manning. 2014. Glove: Global vectors for word representation. In *Conference on Empirical Methods in Natural Language Processing (EMNLP 2014)*.

H. Putnam. 1976. Two dogmas revisited. *printed in his (1983) Realism and Reason, Philosophical Papers*, 3.

M. Ross Quillian. 1968. Word concepts: A theory and simulation of some basic semantic capabilities. *Behavioral Science*, 12:410–430.

Willard van Orman Quine. 1951. Two dogmas of empiricism. *The Philosophical Review*, 60:20–43.

Aarne Ranta. 2011. *Grammatical Framework: Programming with Multilingual Grammars.* CSLI Publications, Stanford.

Gábor Recski and Judit Ács. 2015. MathLingBudapest: Concept networks for semantic similarity. In *Proceedings of the 9th International Workshop on Semantic Evaluation (SemEval 2015)*, Denver, CO, June. ACL.

Roger C. Schank. 1972. Conceptual dependency: A theory of natural language understanding. *Cognitive Psychology*, 3(4):552–631.

Holger Schwenk, Anthony Rousseau, and Mohammed Attik. 2012. Large, pruned or continuous space language models on a gpu for statistical machine translation. In *Proceedings of the NAACL-HLT 2012 Workshop: Will We Ever Really Replace the N-gram Model? On the Future of Language Modeling for HLT*, pages 11–19. Association for Computational Linguistics.

John M. Sinclair. 1987. *Looking up: an account of the COBUILD project in lexical computing.* Collins ELT.

Henry Smith. 1996. *Restrictiveness in Case Theory.* Cambridge University Press.

Paul Smolensky. 1990. Tensor product variable binding and the representation of symbolic structures in connectionist systems. *Artificial intelligence*, 46(1):159–216.

R. Socher, M. Ganjoo, H. Sridhar, O. Bastani, C. D. Manning, and A. Y. Ng. 2013. Zero-shot learning through cross-modal transfer. In *International Conference on Learning Representations (ICLR)*.

Joseph Turian, Lev Ratinov, and Yoshua Bengio. 2010. Word representations: a simple and general method for semi-supervised learning. In *Proceedings of the 48th Annual Meeting of the Association for Computational Linguistics*, pages 384–394. Association for Computational Linguistics.

Jason Weston, Antoine Bordes, Sumit Chopra, and Tomas Mikolov. 2015. Towards ai-complete question answering: A set of prerequisite toy tasks. *arXiv:1502.05698*.

William Dwight Whitney. 1885. The roots of the Sanskrit language. *Transactions of the American Philological Association (1869-1896)*, 16:5–29.

Anna Wierzbicka. 1985. *Lexicography and conceptual analysis.* Karoma, Ann Arbor.

William A. Woods. 1975. What's in a link: Foundations for semantic networks. *Representation and Understanding: Studies in Cognitive Science*, pages 35–82.

Hai-Jun Zhou. 2013. Spin glass approach to the feedback vertex set problem. *ms, arxiv.org/pdf/1307.6948v2.pdf.*

Thomas E. Zimmermann. 1999. Meaning postulates and the model-theoretic approach to natural language semantics. *Linguistics and Philosophy*, 22:529–561.

Geoffrey Zweig. 2014. Explicit representation of antonymy in language modeling. Technical report, Microsoft Research.

Extending a Single-Document Summarizer to Multi-Document: a Hierarchical Approach

Luís Marujo[1,2,3], **Ricardo Ribeiro**[1,4], **David Martins de Matos**[1,2],
João P. Neto[1,2], **Anatole Gershman**[3], **and Jaime Carbonell**[3]
[1]INESC-ID Lisboa, [2]IST/ULisboa, [4]ISCTE-IUL, Lisboa, Portugal
[3]School of Computer Science, CMU, Pittsburgh, USA
{lmarujo,anatoleg,jgc}@cs.cmu.edu
{ricardo.ribeiro,david.matos,joao.neto}@inesc-id.pt

Abstract

The increasing amount of online content motivated the development of multi-document summarization methods. In this work, we explore straightforward approaches to extend single-document summarization methods to multi-document summarization. The proposed methods are based on the hierarchical combination of single-document summaries, and achieves state of the art results.

1 Introduction

The use of the Internet to fulfill generic information needs motivated pioneer multi-document summarization efforts as NewsInEssence (Radev et al., 2005) or Newsblaster (McKeown et al., 2002), online since 2001. In general, multi-document summarization approaches have to address two different problems: passage selection and information ordering. Current multi-document systems adopt, for passage selection, approaches similar to the ones used in single-document summarization, and use the chronological order of the documents for information ordering (Christensen et al., 2013). The problem is that most approaches fail to generate summaries that cover generic topics which comprehend different, equally important, subtopics.

We propose to extend a state-of-the-art single-document summarization method, KP-CENTRALITY (Ribeiro et al., 2013), capable of focusing on diverse important topics while ignoring unimportant ones, to perform multi-document summarization. We explore two hierarchical strategies to perform this extension.

This document is organized as follows: Sect. 2 addresses the related work; Sect. 3 presents our multi-document summarization appproach; experimental results close the paper.

2 Related Work

Most of the current work in automatic summarization focuses on extractive summarization. The most popular baselines for multi-document summarization fall into one of the following general models: Centrality-based (Radev et al., 2004; Erkan and Radev, 2004; Wang et al., 2008; Ribeiro and de Matos, 2011), Maximal Marginal Relevance (MMR) (Carbonell and Goldstein, 1998; Guo and Sanner, 2010; Sanner et al., 2011; Lim et al., 2012), and Coverage-base methods (Lin and Hovy, 2000; Sipos et al., 2012). Additionally, methods such as KP-CENTRALITY (Ribeiro et al., 2013), which is centrality and coverage-based, follow more than one paradigm. In general, Centrality-based models are used to produce generic summaries, while the MMR family generates query-oriented ones. Coverage-base models produce summaries driven by words, topics or events.

Centrality-as-relevance methods base the detection of the most salient passages on the identification of the central passages of the input source(s). One of the main representatives of this family is *Passage-to-Centroid Similarity-based Centrality*. Centroid-based methods build on the idea of a pseudo-passage that represents the central topic of the input source—the *centroid*—selecting as passages to be included in the summary the ones that are close to the centroid. Another approach to centrality estimation is to com-

*Proceedings of the Fourth Joint Conference on Lexical and Computational Semantics (*SEM 2015)*, pages 176–181,
Denver, Colorado, June 4–5, 2015.

pare each candidate passage to every other passage and select the ones with higher scores (the ones that are closer to every other passage): the *Pair-wise Passage Similarity-based Centrality*.

MMR (Carbonell and Goldstein, 1998) is a query driven relevance model based on the following mathematical model:

$$\arg\max_{S_i} \left[\lambda(Sim_1(S_i, Q)) - (1-\lambda)(\max_{S_j} Sim_2(S_i, S_j))\right]$$

where $Sim1$ and $Sim2$ are similarity metrics that do not have to be different; S_i are the yet unselected passages and S_j are the previously selected ones; Q is the required query to apply the model; and, λ is a parameter that allows to configure the result to be from a standard relevance-ranked list ($\lambda = 1$) to a maximal diversity ranking ($\lambda = 0$).

Coverage-based summarization defines a set of concepts that need to occur in the sentences selected for the summaries. The concepts are events (Filatova and Hatzivassiloglou, 2004), topics (Lin and Hovy, 2000), salient words (Lin and Bilmes, 2010; Sipos et al., 2012), and word n-grams (Gillick et al., 2008; Almeida and Martins, 2013).

3 Multi-Document Summarization

Our multi-document approach is built upon a centrality and coverage-based single-document summarization method, KP-CENTRALITY (Ribeiro et al., 2013). This method, through the use of key phrases, is easily adaptable and has been shown to be robust in the presence of noisy input. This is an important aspect considering that using as input several documents frequently increases the amount of unimportant content).

When adapting a single-document summarization method to perform multi-document summarization, a possible strategy is to combine the summaries of each document. To iteratively combine the summaries, we explore two different approaches: single-layer hierarchical and waterfall. Given that the summarization method also uses as input a set of key phrases, we extract from each input document the required set of key phrases, join the extracted sets, and rank the key phrases using their frequency. To generate each summary, we use the top key phrases, excluding the ones that do not occur in the input document.

3.1 Single-Document Summarization Method

To retrieve the most important sentences of an information source, we used the KP-CENTRALITY method (Ribeiro et al., 2013). We chose this model for its adaptability to different types of information sources (e.g., text, audio and video), while supporting privacy (Marujo et al., 2014), and offering state-of-art performance. It is based on the notion of combining key phrases with support sets. A support set is a group of the most semantically related passages. These semantic passages are chosen using heuristics based on the passage order method (Ribeiro and de Matos, 2011). This type of heuristics uses the structure of the input document (source) to partition the candidate passages to be included in the support set in two subsets: the ones closer to the passage associated with the support set under construction and the ones further apart. These heuristics use a permutation, $d_1^i, d_2^i, \cdots, d_{N-1}^i$, of the distances of the passages s_k to the passage p_i, related to the support set under construction, with $d_k^i = dist(s_k, p_i)$, $1 \leq k \leq N-1$, where N is the number of passages, corresponding to the order of occurrence of passages s_k in the input source. The metric that is normally used is the cosine distance.

The KP-Centrality method consists of two steps. First, it extracts key phrases using a supervised approach (Marujo et al., 2012) and combines them with a bag-of-words model in a compact matrix representation, given by:

$$\begin{bmatrix} w(t_1,p_1) \ldots w(t_1,p_N)\; w(t_1,k_1) \ldots w(t_1,k_M) \\ \vdots \qquad\qquad\qquad\qquad\qquad \vdots \\ w(t_T,p_1) \ldots w(t_T,p_N)\; w(t_T,k_1) \ldots w(t_T,k_M) \end{bmatrix}, \tag{1}$$

where w is a function of the number of occurrences of term t_i in passage p_j or key phrase k_l, T is the number of terms and M is the number of key phrases. Then, using a segmented information source $I \triangleq p_1, p_2, \ldots, p_N$, a support set S_i is computed for each passage p_i using:

$$S_i \triangleq \{s \in I \cup K : sim(s, q_i) > \varepsilon_i \wedge s \neq q_i\}, \tag{2}$$

for $i = 1, \ldots, N + M$. Passages are ranked excluding the key phrases K (*artificial passages*) according to:

$$\arg\max_{s \in (\cup_{i=1}^{n} S_i) - K} \left|\{S_i : s \in S_i\}\right|. \tag{3}$$

3.2 Single-Layer Hierarchical

In this model, we use KP-CENTRALITY to generate, for each news document, an intermediate summary with the same size of the output summary for the input documents. An aggregated summary is obtained by concatenating the chronologically ordered intermediate summaries. The output summary is again generated by applying KP-CENTRALITY to the aggregated summary as Figure 1 shows.

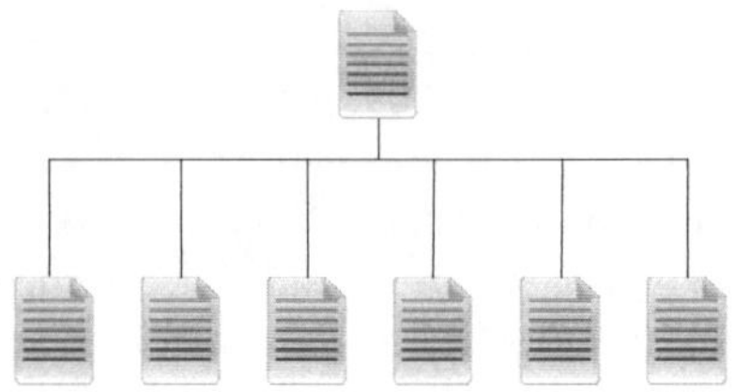

Figure 1: Single-layer architecture.

3.3 Waterfall

This model differs from the previous one in the merging process. The underlying merging of the documents follows a cascaded process: it starts by merging the intermediate summaries, with the same size of the output summary, of the first two documents, according to their chronological order. This document is then summarized and merged with the summary of following document. We iterate this process through all the documents until the most recent one as Figure 2 illustrates.

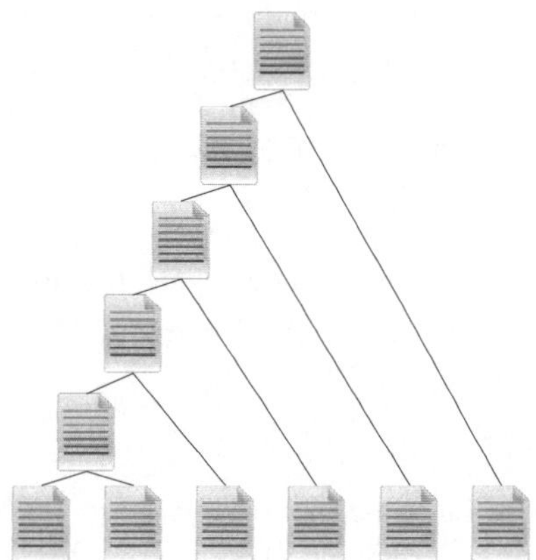

Figure 2: Waterfall architecture.

4 Experimental Results

We compare the performance of our methods against other representative models, namely MEAD, MMR, Expected n-call@k (Lim et al., 2012), and the Portfolio Theory (Wang and Zhu, 2009). MEAD is a centroid-based method and one of the most popular centrality-based methods. MMR is one of the most used query-based methods. Expected n-call@k adapts and extends MMR as a probabilistic model (Probabilistic Latent MMR). The Portfolio Theory also extends MMR based on the idea of ranking under uncertainty. As baseline, we used the straightforward idea of combining all input documents into a single one, and then submit the document to the single-document summarization method. Considering that most coverage-based systems explore event information, we opted for not including them in this comparative analysis.

To assess the informativeness of the summaries generated by our methods, we used ROUGE-1 and ROUGE-2 (Lin, 2004) on DUC 2007 and TAC 2009 datasets. The main summarization task in DUC 2007[1] is the generation of 250-word summaries of 45 clusters of 25 newswire documents (from the AQUAINT corpus) and 4 human reference summaries. The TAC 2009 Summarization task[2] has 44 topic clusters. Each topic has 2 sets of 10 news documents obtained from the AQUAINT 2 corpus.There are 4 human 100-word reference summaries for each set, where the reference summaries for the first set are query-oriented, and for the second set are update summaries. In this work, we used the first set of reference summaries. We evaluate the different models by generating summaries with 250 words. We only present the best results.

The used features include the bag-of-words model representation of the sentences (TF-IDF), the key phrases and the query (obtained from the topics descriptions). Including the query is a new extension to the KP-CENTRALITY method, which, in general, improved the results. We experimented with different numbers of key phrases, obtaining the best results with 40 key phrases. To compare and rank the sentences, we use several distance metrics, namely: Frac133 (generic Minkowski distance,

[1] http://www-nlpir.nist.gov/projects/duc/duc2007/tasks.html
[2] http://www.nist.gov/tac/2009/Summarization/

Distance	Model	DUC 2007 R1	DUC 2007 R2	TAC 2009 R1	TAC 2009 R2
frac133	baseline	0.3565	0.0744	0.4706	0.1268
cosine	baseline	0.3406	0.0670	0.4746	0.1391
frac133	waterfall	0.3569	0.0765	0.4943	0.1441
frac133	single-layer	**0.3775**	0.0882	0.4983	0.1526
cosine	waterfall	0.3701	**0.0904**	**0.5137**	**0.1693**
cosine	single-layer	0.3707	0.0822	0.4993	0.1590
frac133	single-layer (shuffle)	0.3689	0.0807	0.5060	0.1483
cosine	waterfall (shuffle)	0.3626	0.0844	0.5107	0.1630
	MEAD	0.3282	0.0765	0.4153	0.0845
	MMR	0.3269	0.0780	0.3917	0.0801
	E.n-call@k	0.3209	0.0701	0.3873	0.0699
	Portfolio	0.3595	0.0792	0.4292	0.0758
	LexRank	0.2881	0.0534	0.3845	0.0623

Table 1: ROUGE-1 (R1) and ROUGE-2 (R2) scores.

with $N = 1.(3)$), Euclidean, Chebyshev, Manhattan, Minkowski, the Jensen-Shannon Divergence, and the cosine similarity. Table 1 shows that the best results were obtained by the proposed hierarchical models, in both datasets. Overal, the best performing distance metric for our centrality-based method was the cosine similarity and the best strategy for combining the information was the waterfall approach, namely, in terms of ROUGE-2. In DUC 2007, frac133 using the single-layer method achieved the best ROUGE-1 score, although the difference for cosine is hardly noticeable. Single-layer with frac133 shows a performance improvement of 0.0180 ROUGE-1 points (relative performance improvement of 5.0%) over the best of the other systems, Portfolio, in DUC 2007, and of 0.0845 ROUGE-1 points (19.7% relative performance improvement) in TAC 2009. In terms of ROUGE-2, the waterfall method using cosine achieved an improvement of 0.0112 (relative performance improvement of 14.1%) over Portfolio, in DUC 2007, and of 0.0848 (relative performance improvement of 100.4%) over MEAD, the best performing of the reference systems using this metric, in TAC 2009. Note that our baseline obtained results similar to the best reference system in DUC 2007 and better results than all reference systems in TAC 2009 (0.0454 ROUGE-1 points corresponding to a 10.6% relative performance improvement; 0.0546 ROUGE-2 points corresponding to a 64.6% relative performance improvement). The better results obtained on the TAC 2009 dataset are due to the small size of the reference summaries and to the fact that the documents sets to be summarized contain topics with higher diversity of subtopics.

The shuffle results included in Table 1 are averages of 10 trials. They are lower than the other obtained using the documents organized in chronological order. This suggests that the order of the input documents is important to the summarization methods.

Figure 3 shows an example of summary produced by our multi-document method. The figure also includes the respective reference summary for comparison.

5 Conclusions and Future Work

In this work, we explore two different approaches to extend a single-document summarization method to multi-document summarization: single-layer hierarchical and waterfall.

Experimental results show that the proposed approaches perform better than previous state-of-the-art methods on standard datasets used to evaluate this task. In general, the best performing approach is the waterfall approach using the cosine similarity. In fact, this configuration achieves the best results on the TAC 2009 dataset, considering both ROUGE-1

Generated Summary:

President Bill Clinton said Friday he will appeal a federal judge's ruling that struck down a law giving the president the power to veto specific items in bills passed by Congress. The law, passed by Congress last year, allowed the president for the first time to veto particular items in spending bills and certain limited tax provisions passed by Congress. Clinton said the funding that Congress has added to the bill is excessive and threatened to veto some items by using the line-item veto power. The White House said that the president used his authority to cancel projects that were not requested in the budget and would not substantially improve the quality of life of military service members. Judge Thomas Hogan ruled that the law – which gives the president the power to strike items from tax and spending measures without vetoing the entire bill – violates the traditional balance of powers between the various branches of government "The Line-Item Veto Act is unconstitutional because it impermissibly disrupts the balance of powers among the three branches of government," said Thomas Hogan." In its appeal, the Justice Department argues that the new challengers also do not have standing to challenge the law, and that in any case the law is in line with the historic relationship between Congress and the president.

Reference summary:

Congress passed a law authorizing the line item veto (LIV) in 1996 accepting arguments that the measure would help preserve the integrity of federal spending by allowing the president to strike unnecessary spending and tax items from legislation thus encouraging the government to live within its means. It was considered in line with the historic relationship between Congress and the president and would provide a tool for eliminating wasteful pork barrel spending while enlivening debate over the best use of funds. It was argued that the LIV would represent presidential exercise of spending authority delegated by Congress. President Clinton exercised the LIV on 82 items in 1997 saving $1.9 billion in spending projected over five years. The affected items were projects for specific localities, many in the area of military construction, which had been added to the president's budget by Congress. The first court ruling on the LIV act was in U.S. District Court when in February 1998 it was ruled unconstitutional on the grounds that it violated the separation of powers. The Department of Justice appealed that decision and in June 1998 the Supreme Court ruled the LIV act unconstitutional but on the grounds that it violated Article I, 7, Clause 2 (The "presentment clause") of the Constitution that establishes the process by which a bill becomes law. President Clinton expressed his deep disappointment.

Figure 3: Example of summary produced by our summarizer and the reference summary Topic D0730G of DUC 2007

and ROUGE-2 metrics, and, although not achieving the best results in the DUC 2007 dataset, in terms of ROUGE-1, it also achieves a performance improvement over Portfolio of 0.0106 ROUGE-1 points (relative performance improvement of 3%).

In future work, we aim to adapt the proposed multi-document summarization method to perform abstractive summarization.

Acknowledgments

This work has been partially supported by national funds through Fundação para a Ciência e a Tecnologia (FCT) with reference UID/CEC/50021/2013, the grant numbers SFRH/BD/33769/2009 and CMUP-EPB/TIC/0026/2013. The authors would also like to thank Eduard Hovy, Isabel Trancoso, Ricardo Baeza-Yates, and the anonymous reviewers for fruitful comments.

References

Miguel Almeida and Andre Martins. 2013. Fast and robust compressive summarization with dual decomposition and multi-task learning. In *Proceedings of the 51st Annual Meeting of the Association for Computational Linguistics*, pages 196–206, Sofia, Bulgaria, August. ACL.

Jaime Carbonell and Jade Goldstein. 1998. The use of mmr, diversity-based reranking for reordering documents and producing summaries. In *Proceedings of the 21st Annual International ACM SIGIR Conference on Research and Development in Information Retrieval*, pages 335–336. ACM.

Janara Christensen, Mausam, Stephen Soderland, and Oren Etzioni. 2013. Towards coherent multi-document summarization. In *Proceedings of the North American Chapter of the Association for Computational Linguistics*. ACL.

Güneş Erkan and Dragomir R. Radev. 2004. LexRank: Graph-based Centrality as Salience in Text Summarization. *Journal of Artificial Intelligence Research*, 22:457–479.

Elena Filatova and Vasileios Hatzivassiloglou. 2004. Event-based extractive summarization. In *Proc. of ACL Workshop on Summarization*, pages 104–111.

Dan Gillick, Benoit Favre, and Dilek Hakkani-Tur. 2008. The icsi summarization system at tac 2008. In *Proceedings of the Text Understanding Conference*.

Shengbo Guo and Scott Sanner. 2010. Probabilistic latent maximal marginal relevance. In *Proc. of the 33rd International ACM SIGIR Conference on Research and Development in Information Retrieval*, pages 833–834. ACM.

Kar Wai Lim, Scott Sanner, and Shengbo Guo. 2012. On the Math. Relationship Between Expected N-call@K and the Relevance vs. Diversity Trade-off. In *Proc. of the 35th International ACM SIGIR Conference on Research and Development in Information Retrieval*, pages 1117–1118. ACM.

Hui Lin and Jeff Bilmes. 2010. Multi-document summarization via budgeted maximization of submodular functions. In *Proceedings of the North American Chapter of the Association for Computational Linguistics*, pages 912–920. ACL.

Chin-Yew Lin and Eduard Hovy. 2000. The automated acquisition of topic signatures for text summarization. In *Proceedings of the 18th Conference on Computational Linguistics - Volume 1*, pages 495–501. ACL.

Chin-Yew Lin. 2004. ROUGE: A Package for Automatic Evaluation of Summaries. In *Text Summ. Branches Out: Proc. of the ACL-04 Workshop*.

Luís Marujo, Anatole Gershman, Jaime Carbonell, Robert Frederking, and Joã P. Neto. 2012. Supervised topical key phrase extraction of news stories using crowdsourcing, light filtering and co-reference normalization. In *Proceedings of the Eight International Conference on Language Resources and Evaluation (LREC'12)*. ELRA.

Luís Marujo, José Portêlo, David Martins de Matos, João P Neto, Anatole Gershman, Jaime Carbonell, Isabel Trancoso, and Bhiksha Raj. 2014. Privacy-preserving important passage retrieval. In *ACM SIGIR PIR workshop*.

Kathleen R. McKeown, Regina Barzilay, David Evans, Vasileios Hatzivassiloglou, Judith L. Klavans, Ani Nenkova, Carl Sable, Barry Schiffman, and Sergey Sigelman. 2002. Tracking and Summarizing News on a Daily Basis with Columbia's Newsblaster. In *HLT*.

Dragomir R. Radev, Hongyan Jing, Małgorzata Styś, and Daniel Tam. 2004. Centroid-based summarization of multiple documents. *Information Processing and Management*, 40.

Dragomir R. Radev, Jahna Otterbacher, Adam Winkel, and Sasha Blair-Goldensohn. 2005. NewsInEssence: Summarizing Online News Topics. *Communications of the ACM*, 48(10):95–98.

Ricardo Ribeiro and David Martins de Matos. 2011. Revisiting Centrality-as-Relevance: Support Sets and Similarity as Geometric Proximity. *JAIR*, 42:275–308.

Ricardo Ribeiro, Luís Marujo, David Martins de Matos, João P. Neto, Anatole Gershman, and Jaime Carbonell. 2013. Self reinforcement for important passage retrieval. In *Proceedings of the 36th International ACM SIGIR Conference on Research and Development in Information Retrieval*, pages 845–848. ACM.

Scott Sanner, Shengbo Guo, Thore Graepel, Sadegh Kharazmi, and Sarvnaz Karimi. 2011. Diverse retrieval via greedy optimization of expected 1-call@k in a latent subtopic relevance model. In *Proc. of the 20th ACM International Conference on Information and Knowledge Management*, pages 1977–1980. ACM.

Ruben Sipos, Adith Swaminathan, Pannaga Shivaswamy, and Thorsten Joachims. 2012. Temporal corpus summarization using submodular word coverage. In *Proc. of the 21st ACM International Conference on Information and Knowledge Management*. ACM.

Jun Wang and Jianhan Zhu. 2009. Portfolio theory of information retrieval. In *Proceedings of the 32Nd International ACM SIGIR Conference on Research and Development in Information Retrieval*, pages 115–122.

Dingding Wang, Tao Li, Shenghuo Zhu, and Chris Ding. 2008. Multi-document summarization via sentence-level semantic analysis and symmetric matrix factorization. In *Proc. of the 31st Annual International ACM SIGIR Conference on Research and Development in Information Retrieval*, pages 307–314. ACM.

Reading Between the Lines: Overcoming Data Sparsity for Accurate Classification of Lexical Relationships

Silvia Necşulescu
Universitat Pompeu Fabra
Barcelona, Spain
silvia.necsulescu@upf.edu

Sara Mendes
Universidade de Lisboa
Lisboa, Portugal
sara.mendes@clul.ul.pt

David Jurgens
McGill University
Montreal, Canada
jurgens@cs.mcgill.ca

Núria Bel
Universitat Pompeu Fabra
Barcelona, Spain
nuria.bel@upf.edu

Roberto Navigli
Università "La Sapienza"
Rome, Italy
navigli@di.uniroma1.it

Abstract

The lexical semantic relationships between word pairs are key features for many NLP tasks. Most approaches for automatically classifying related word pairs are hindered by data sparsity because of their need to observe two words co-occurring in order to detect the lexical relation holding between them. Even when mining very large corpora, not every related word pair co-occurs. Using novel representations based on graphs and word embeddings, we present two systems that are able to predict relations between words, even when these are never found in the same sentence in a given corpus. In two experiments, we demonstrate superior performance of both approaches over the state of the art, achieving significant gains in recall.

1 Introduction

Resources containing lexical-semantic relations such as *hypernymy* or *meronymy* have proven useful in many NLP tasks. While resources such as WordNet (Miller, 1995) contain many general relations and subsequently have seen widespread adoption, developing this type of rich resource for new languages or for new domains is prohibitively costly and time-consuming. Therefore, automated approaches are needed and, in order to create such a lexical-semantic database, a first step is to develop accurate techniques for classifying the type of lexical-semantic relationship between two words.

Approaches to classifying the relationship between a word pair have typically relied on the assumption that contexts where word pairs co-occur will yield information on the semantic relation (if any) between them. Given a set of example word pairs having some relation, relation-specific patterns may be automatically acquired from the contexts in which these example pairs co-occur (Turney, 2008b; Mintz et al., 2009). Comparing these relation-specific patterns with those seen with other word pairs measures *relational similarity*, i.e., how similar is the relation holding between two word pairs. However, any classification system based on patterns of co-occurrence is limited to only those words co-occurring in the data considered; due to the Zipfian distribution of words, even in a very large corpus there are always semantically related word pairs that do not co-occur. As a result, these pattern-based approaches have a strict upper-bound limit on the number of instances that they can classify. As an alternative to requiring co-occurrence, other works have classified the relation of a word pair using *lexical similarity*, i.e., the similarity of the concepts themselves. Given two word pairs, (w_1, w_2) and (w_3, w_4), if w_1 is lexically similar to w_3 and w_2 to w_4 (i.e., are pair-wise similar) then the pairs are said to have the same semantic relation. These two sources of information are used as two independent units: *relational similarity* is calculated using co-occurrence information; *lexical similarity* is calculated using distributional information (Snow et al., 2004; Séaghdha and Copestake, 2009; Herdadelen and Baroni, 2009), and ultimately these scores are combined. Experimental evidence has shown that relational similarity cannot necessarily be revealed through lexical similarity (Turney, 2006b; Turney, 2008a), and therefore, the issue of how to collect in-

*Proceedings of the Fourth Joint Conference on Lexical and Computational Semantics (*SEM 2015)*, pages 182–192,
Denver, Colorado, June 4–5, 2015.

formation for word pairs that do not co-occur is still an open problem.

We propose two new approaches to representing word pairs in order to accurately classify them as instances of lexical-semantic relations – even when the pair members do not co-occur. The first approach creates a word pair representation based on a graph representation of the corpus created with dependency relations. The graph encodes the distributional behavior of each word in the pair and consequently, patterns of co-occurrence expressing each target relation are extracted from it as relational information. The second approach uses word embeddings which have been shown to preserve linear regularities among words and pairs of words, therefore, encoding lexical and relational similarities (Baroni et al., 2014), a necessary property for our task. In two experiments comparing with state-of-the-art pattern-based and embedding-based classifiers (Turney, 2008b; Zhila et al., 2013), we demonstrate that our approaches achieve higher accuracy with significantly increased recall.

2 Related work

Initial approaches to the extraction of lexical-semantic relations have relied on hand-crafted lexico-syntactic patterns to identify instances of semantic relations (Hearst, 1992; Widdows and Dorow, 2002; Berland and Charniak, 1999). These manually designed patterns are explicit constructions expressing a target semantic relation such as the pattern *X is a Y* for the relation of *hypernymy*. However, these approaches are limited because a relation may be expressed in many ways, depending on the domain, author, and writing style, which may not match the originally identified patterns. Moreover, the identification of high-quality patterns is costly and time-consuming, and must be repeated for each new relation type, domain and language. To overcome these limitations, techniques have been developed for the automatic acquisition of meaningful patterns of co-occurrence cueing a single target relation (Snow et al., 2004; Girju et al., 2006; Davidov and Rappoport, 2006).

More recent work focuses on methods for the classification of word pairs as instances of several relations at once, based on their relational similarity. This similarity is calculated using a vectorial representation for each pair, created by relying on co-occurrence contexts (Turney, 2008b; Séaghdha and Copestake, 2009; Mintz et al., 2009). These representations are very sparse due to the scarce contexts where the members of many word pairs co-occur. Moreover, many semantically related word pairs do not co-occur in corpus.

For overcoming these issues, relational similarity was combined with lexical similarity calculated based on the distributional information of words (Cederberg and Widdows, 2003; Snow et al., 2004; Turney, 2006a; Séaghdha and Copestake, 2009; Herdadelen and Baroni, 2009). However, (Turney, 2006b; Turney, 2008a) showed that relational similarity cannot be improved using the distributional similarity of words. In contrast with the previous approaches that took into account lexical and relational information as a linear combination of lexical and relational similarity scores, the present work focuses on introducing word pair representations that merge and jointly represent types of information: lexical and relational. In this way, we aim to reduce vector sparseness and to increase the classification recall.

As a first approach, we use a graph to model the distributional behavior of words. Other researchers used graph-based approaches to model corpus information for the extraction of co-hyponyms (Widdows and Dorow, 2002), hypernyms (Navigli and Velardi, 2010) or synonyms (Minkov and Cohen, 2012), or for inducing word senses (Di Marco and Navigli, 2013). Navigli and Velardi (2010) have the most similar representation to ours, creating a graph that models only definitional sentences. In contrast, our objective is to create a general representation of the whole corpus that can be used for classifying instances of several lexical semantic relations. The second approach presented in this paper, relies on word embeddings to create word pair representations. Extensive experiments have leveraged word embeddings to find general semantic relations (Mikolov et al., 2013a; Mikolov et al., 2013b; Mikolov et al., 2013c; Levy and Goldberg, 2014b). Nevertheless, only one work has applied word embeddings for classifying instances of a lexical semantic relation, specifically the relation *hyponymy-hypernymy* (Fu et al., 2014). This relation is more complex than other semantic relations tested and therefore, it is reflected in more than one offset, depending on the domain of each instance. The present work uses a machine learning approach to discover meaningful information for the semantic relations encoded in the dimensions of the embeddings.

3 Task description

The goal of this work is to classify word pairs as instances of lexical-semantic relations. Given a set of target semantic relations $R = \{r_1, \ldots, r_n\}$, and a set of word pairs $W = \{(x,y)_1, \ldots, (x,y)_n\}$, the task is to label each word pair $(x,y)_i$ with the relation $r_j \in R$ holding between its members and outputting a set of tuples $((x,y)_i, r_j)$. For this task, we propose two novel representations of word pairs (described next), which are each used to train a classifier. Following, in Section 3.1 and Section 3.2 we describe each representation and then, in Section 3.3, we describe the common classification setup used with both representations.

3.1 Graph-based Representation Model

The present section introduces a novel word pair representation model based on patterns of co-occurrence contexts, and on a graph-based corpus representation created with dependency relations. A word pair is represented as a vector of features set up with the most meaningful patterns of context and filled in with information extracted from the graph representation of the corpus. We refer to systems trained with these graph-based representations as **Gra**ph-based **C**lassification syst**E**m (GraCE).

The novelty of this system stands in the graph-based representation. Its main advantage is that all the dependency relations of a target word, extracted from different sentences, are incident edges to its corresponding node in the graph. Thus, words that never co-occur in the same context in corpus, are linked in the graph through bridging words: words that appear in a dependency relation with each member of the pair but in different sentences. With this representation we address the data sparsity issue, aiming to overcome the reported major bottleneck of previous approaches: low recall because information can only be gathered from co-occurrences in the same sentence of two related words.

Word pair representations are created in three steps:

(1). Corpus representation: the input corpus is represented as a graph;

(2). Feature selection: the input corpus is used to extract meaningful patterns of co-occurrence for each semantic relation r_i starting from an initial set of examples E;

(3). Word pair representation: the information acquired in **(1)** and **(2)** is used to create vectorial representations of target word pairs.

Next, we present an example of how the graph representation of the corpus addresses the sparsity problem in distributional data and formally introduce each step of the GraCE algorithm.

Example To illustrate the benefit of acquiring information about a word pair from the graph instead of using co-occurrence information, let us consider that, given the sentences (S1) and (S2) below, we want to classify the pair *(chisel, tool)* as an instance of the relation of hypernymy.

(S1) The students learned how to handle screwdrivers, hammers and other tools.

(S2) The carpenter handles the new chisel.

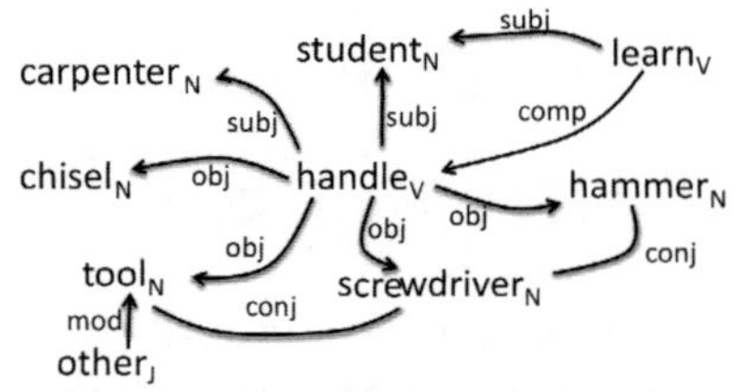

Figure 1: Dependency multigraph built from a two sentence corpus using GraCE. See text for details.

The word pair *(chisel, tool)* has a relation of hypernymy but its members do not co-occur in the same sentence. However, both words occur as objects of the verb *to handle* in different sentences, just like other hypernym word pairs such as *(hammer, tool)* and *(screwdriver, tool)* which do co-occur in the same sentence. This shows that *handle* is one of the contexts shared between these semantically related words that provide information regarding a possible semantic relatedness between them. Leveraging only the information provided by each sentence, as existing pattern-based approaches do, no evidence is acquired regarding the semantic relation holding between *chisel* and *tool*. GraCE combines the dependency relations seen in each sentence in the graph shown in Figure 1. In this graph, *chisel* and *tool* are connected by a path passing through the bridging word *handle* which shows that both *chisel* and *tool* could co-occur in a sentence as objects of the verb *to handle*, although they do not in the example two-sentence corpus.

Corpus representation The goal of the first step is to generate a graph connecting semantically associated words using observed dependency relations.

Formally, the corpus is represented as a graph $\mathbb{G} = (V, E)$, where V is a set of POS-tagged lemmas in a corpus and E is the set of dependency relations connecting two lemmas from V in the corpus. From each parsed sentence of the corpus, a set of dependency relations linking the words in it is produced: $D = \{d_1 \ldots, d_{|D|}\}$, where $d = (w_i, dep, w_j)$ and w_i, w_j and dep denote POS-tagged lemmas and a dependency relation, respectively. The graph $\mathbb{G}$ is created using all the dependency relations from D.

The output of this step is a multigraph, where two words are connected by the set of edges containing all the dependency relations holding between them in the corpus.

Feature Selection The goal of the second step is to collect features associated with each relation r from the parsed input corpus. Similarly to the work of Snow et al. (2004), our features are *patterns of co-occurrence contexts* created with dependency paths. For acquiring patterns of co-occurrence contexts for each relation r, we use the set of labeled examples E, assuming that all the contexts in which a word pair $(x, y)_i \in E$ co-occurs provide information about the relation r holding between its members. All the dependency paths between x and y up to three edges are extracted from the dependency graph of each sentence where $(x, y)_i$ co-occur.[1] For example, $((hammer_N, tool_N), hyper)$ is an instance of the relation of hypernymy. In the dependency graph of sentence (S1), the words $hammer_N$ (hyponym) and $tool_N$ (hypernym) are connected by the dependency path $hammer_N \xleftarrow{\text{obj}} handle_V \xrightarrow{\text{obj}} tool_N$. This path is converted into a *pattern of co-occurrence contexts* by replacing the seeds in the path with their parts of speech as follows: $N \xleftarrow{\text{obj}} handle_V \xrightarrow{\text{obj}} N$. Table 1 illustrates several examples of pattern of co-occurrence contexts.

attribute	$X_N \xrightarrow{\text{prep\_such\_as}^{-1}} tool_N \xrightarrow{\text{mod}} Y_J$
co-hyponymy	$X_N \xrightarrow{\text{obj}^{-1}} use_V \xrightarrow{\text{obj}} Y_N$
action	$X_N \xrightarrow{\text{obj}^{-1}} use_V \xrightarrow{\text{conj}} Y_V$
hypernymy	$X_N \xrightarrow{\text{prep\_such\_as}^{-1}} tool_N \xrightarrow{\text{conj}} Y_N$
meronymy	$X_N \xrightarrow{\text{nn}^{-1}} blade_N \xrightarrow{\text{conj}} Y_N$

Table 1: Examples of relation features

For the word pairs vectorial representation, the top 5000 most meaningful patterns are considered in the final set of patterns $\mathbb{P}$ to form a feature space.[2] In order to rank the patterns, the *tf-idf score* is calculated for each pattern with respect to each lexical semantic relation. Here, $tf - idf$ is defined as $max_j(\frac{log(uniq(p_i,r_j)+1)*|R|}{|R_p|})$, where p_i is a pattern of co-occurrence, $uniq(p_i, r_j)$ is the number of unique instances of the relation r_j occurring in the pattern p_i and $|R_p|$ is the number of relations r_j whose example instances are seen occurring in the pattern p_i. Each pattern is then associated with the highest *tf-idf* score obtained across all relations.

Word pair representations Using the graph model $\mathbb{G}$ and the set of contextual patterns automatically acquired $\mathbb{P}$, each word pair (x, y) is represented as a binary distribution over each pattern from $\mathbb{P}$. Rather than using the input corpus to identify contexts of occurrence for the word pair (x, y) and match those with the acquired patterns, GraCE uses paths connecting x and y in $\mathbb{G}$. All the paths between x and y up to three edges are extracted from $\mathbb{G}$. These paths are then matched against the feature patterns from $\mathbb{P}$ and the word pair (x, y) is represented as a binary vector encoding non-zero values for all the features matching the pair's paths extracted from $\mathbb{G}$, and zero otherwise.[3] Because the graph contains combinations of multiple dependency relations, extracted from various sentences, paths not observed in the corpus can be found in the graph.

[1] Paths with more than three edges commonly connect semantically-unrelated portions of a sentence and therefore are not beneficial for the purposes of relation classification.

[2] Initial experiments tested different amounts of patterns using held out data and the best results were obtained with the top 5000 patterns.

[3] Binary weights are used because the feature values are derived observing paths in the graph, which is a generalization of the corpus; because not all paths in the graph are observed in the corpus, weighting based on path frequency would encounter the same data sparsity issue that the graph is intended to overcome.

3.2 Word Embeddings Representations

The present section introduces two word pair representations based on word embeddings. We refer to a system based on embeddings as **W**ord **E**mbeddings **C**lassification syst**E**m (WECE). An embedding is a low-dimensional vectorial representation of a word, where the dimensions are latent continuous features and vector components are set to maximize the probability of the contexts in which the target word tends to appear. Since similar words occur in similar contexts the word embeddings learn similar vectors for similar words. Moreover, the vector offset of two word embeddings reflect the relation holding between them. For instance, Mikolov et al. (2013c) give the example that $v(king) - v(man) \approx v(queen) - v(women)$, where $v(x)$ is the embedding of the word x, indicating the vectors are encoding information on the words' semantic roles.

For learning word embeddings, we used the Skip-gram model, improved with techniques of negative sampling and subsampling of frequent words, which achieved the best results for detecting semantically similar words (Mikolov et al., 2013a; Mikolov et al., 2013b). Moreover, for a fair comparison with the GraCE system, developed with dependency relations, we also tested the results obtained with a dependency-based Skip-gram model (Levy and Goldberg, 2014a). Words occurring only once in corpus are filtered out and 200-dimensional vectors are learned.

Two embedding-based representations are considered for a relation: $WECE_{offset}$ leverages the offset of the word embeddings, while $WECE_{concat}$ concatenates the embeddings, both described next.

$\mathbf{WECE_{offset}}$ Representation Mikolov et al. (2013c) shows that the vectorial representation of words provided by word embeddings captures syntactic and semantic regularities and that each relationship is characterized by a relation specific vector offset. Word pairs with similar offsets can be interpreted as word pairs with the same semantic relation. Therefore, given a target word pair (x, y), the vectorial representation is calculated from the difference between its vectors, i.e., $v((x, y)) = v(x) - v(y)$. Note that this operation is dependent on the order of the arguments and is therefore potentially able to capture asymmetric relationships.

$\mathbf{WECE_{concat}}$ Representation A novel word pair representation is proposed to test if the information encoded directly in the embeddings reflects the semantic relation of the word pair.

A word pair is represented by concatenating the vectorial representation of its members. Formally, given a word pair (x, y), whose members vectorial representations are $v(x) = (x_1, x_2, \ldots, x_n)$, and $v(y) = (y_1, y_2, \ldots, y_n)$ respectively, the vectorial representation of (x, y) is defined as the concatenation of $v(x)$ and $v(y)$: $v((x, y)) = (x_1, x_2, \ldots, x_n, y_1, y_2, \ldots, y_n)$ Consequently the length of $v((x, y))$ is $2n$, where n is the dimension of the embedding space.

3.3 Relation Classification

For both representations, a supervised classifier is trained. Given a set of tuples $E = ((x, y)_i, r_i)$ of example instances for each relation $r_i \in R$, a support vector machine (SVM) multi-class classifier with a radial basis function kernel (Platt, 1999) is trained using WEKA (Hall et al., 2009) to classify each word pair based on its representation provided by a graph-based representation model (Section 3.1) or a word embeddings representation model (Section 3.2) for N different lexical relations. The SVM classifier generates a distribution over relation labels and the highest weighted label is selected as the relation holding between the members of the word pair.

4 Experiments

While several datasets have been created for detecting semantic relations between two words in context (Hendrickx et al., 2010; Segura-Bedmar et al., 2013), in our work we focus on the classification of word pairs as instances of lexical-semantic relations out of context. The performance of the GraCE and WECE systems is tested across two datasets, focusing on their ability to classify instances of specific lexical-semantic relations as well as to provide insights into the systems' generalization capabilities.

4.1 Experimental Setup

Corpora Many pattern-based systems increase the size of the input corpus in an attempt to overcome data sparsity and to achieve a better recall. Therefore, in our experiments, we train our systems using two corpora of different sizes: the British National Corpus (BNC), a 100 million-word corpus, and a Wikipedia dump created from 5 million pages and containing 1.5 billion words. The size difference allows us to measure the potential impact of increased word co-occurrence on recall. Both corpora were initially parsed with the Stanford dependency parser in the *collapsed dependency* format (Manning et al., 2014).

Embbedings $\text{WECE}_{\text{offset}}$ and $\text{WECE}_{\text{concat}}$ are implemented based on a bag-of-words (BoW) (Mikolov et al., 2013a) and based on dependency relations (Dep) (Levy and Goldberg, 2014a).

Evaluation We compare each system by reporting precision (P), recall (R) and F1 measure (F).

4.2 Comparison Systems

The two proposed models are compared with two state-of-the-art systems and one baseline system.

PAIRCLASS The PairClass algorithm (Turney, 2008b) provides a state-of-the-art pattern-based approach for extracting and classifying the relationship between word pairs and has performed well for many relation types. Using a set of seed pairs (x, y) for each relation, PairClass acquires a set of lexical patterns using the template *[0 to 1 words] x [0 to 3 words] y [0 to 1 words]*. Using the initial set of lexical patterns extracted from a corpus, additional patterns are generated by optionally generalizing each word to its part of speech. For N seed pairs, the most frequent kN patterns are retained. We follow Turney (2008b) and set $k = 20$. The patterns retained are then used as features to train an SVM classifier over the set of possible relation types.

DS_{Zhila} & DS_{Levy} Word embeddings have previously been shown to accurately measure relational similarity; Zhila et al. (2013) demonstrate state-of-the-art performance on SemEval-2012 Task 2 (Jurgens et al., 2012) which measures word pair similarity within a particular semantic relation (i.e., which pairs are most prototypical of a semantic relation). This approach can easily be extended to the classification setting: Given a target word pair (x, y), the similarity is computed between (x, y) and each word pair $(x, y)_i$ of a target relation r. The average of these similarity measurements was taken as the final score for each relation r.[4] Finally, the word pair is classified as an instance of the relation with the highest associated score. Two types of embeddings are used, (a) the word embeddings produced using the method of Mikolov et al. (2011), which was originally used in Zhila et al. (2013) and (b) the embeddings using the method of Levy and Goldberg (2014a), which include dependency parsing information. We refer to these as DS_{Zhila} and DS_{Levy}, respectively. The inclusion of this system enables comparing the performance impact of using an SVM classifier with our embedding-based pair representations versus classifying instances by comparing the embeddings themselves. We note a DS system represents a minimally-supervised system whose features are produced in an unsupervised way (i.e., through the embedding process) and are therefore not necessarily tuned for the task of relation classification; however, such embeddings have previously been shown to yield state-of-the-art performance in other semantic relation tasks (Baroni et al., 2014) and therefore the DS systems are intended to identify potential benefits when adding feature selection by means of the SVM in WECE systems.

BASELINE The purported benefit of the GraCE model is that the graph enables identifying syntactic features between pair members that are never observed in the corpus, which increases the number of instances that can be classified without sacrificing accuracy. Therefore, to quantify the effect of the graph, we include a baseline system, denoted BL, that uses an identical setup to GraCE but where the feature vector for a word pair is created only from the dependency path features that were observed in the corpus (as opposed to the graph). Unlike the GraCE model which has binary weighting (due to the graph properties), the baseline model's feature values correspond to the frequencies with which patterns occur; following common practice, the values are log-normalized.

4.3 Experiment 1

Both of the proposed approaches rest on the hypothesis that the graph or embeddings can enable accurate pair classification, even when pairs never co-

[4] Additional experiments showed that using alternate ways of measuring similarity, such as using the maximum similarity for any instance of r, attained similar results.

Domain	#Co-hypo	#Hyper	#Mero
Animals	8038 (92.4%)	3039 (97.2%)	386 (89.1%)
Plants	18972 (95.5%)	1185 (97.4%)	330 (82.4%)
Vehicles	530 (82.6%)	189 (97.9%)	455 (100%)

Table 2: Distribution of K&H dataset, with the % of instances which occur in the corpora.

	BNC			Wikipedia		
	P	R	F	P	R	F
$PairClass$	76.9	4.6	8.7	77.0	11.7	20.4
BL	82.6	7.7	14.2	89.4	16.2	27.5
$GraCE$	90.7	43.8	59.0	94.0	75.5	83.7
DS_{Zhila}	31.6	15.7	21.0	32.8	22.6	26.8
DS_{Levy}	18.7	11.4	14.2	27.7	15.6	20.0
$WECE^{BoW}_{offset}$	96.0	59.1	73.1	96.8	87.7	92.0
$WECE^{BoW}_{concat}$	**97.4**	60.0	74.2	**97.6**	**89.3**	**93.2**
$WECE^{Dep}_{offset}$	87.9	63.1	73.5	95.4	86.1	90.5
$WECE^{Dep}_{concat}$	93.1	**64.7**	**76.4**	96.7	88.4	92.4

Table 3: Aggregated results obtained for the in-domain setup with the K&H dataset. Detailed results are presented in the Appendix A.

occur in text. Therefore, in the first experiment, we test whether the recall of classification systems is improved when the word pair representation encodes information about lexical and relational similarity. As an evaluation dataset, we expand on the dataset of Kozareva and Hovy (2010) (K&H), which was collected from hyponym-hypernym instances from WordNet (Miller, 1995) spanning three topical domains: *animals*, *plants* and *vehicles*. Because our systems are capable of classifying instances with more than one relation at once, we enhance this dataset with instances of two more relation types: co-hyponymy and meronymy. Co-hyponyms are extracted directly from the K&H dataset: two words are co-hyponyms if they have the same direct ancestor.[5] To avoid including generic nouns, such as "migrator" in the "animal" domain, only leaf nodes are considered. The meronym instances are extracted directly from WordNet. The final dataset excludes multi-word expressions, which were not easily handled by any of the tested systems. The total number of instances considered in our experiments is presented in Table 2.

Results Table 3 presents the average of the results obtained by the systems when tested *in-domain* in a 10-fold cross-validation setup. For the *in-domain* setup, only instances from one domain are used for training and testing.

As expected, all the systems gain recall with a larger corpus, like Wikipedia, showing that the recall depends on the size of that corpus when a system acquires its distributional information directly from the input corpus and thus is dependent on the word pairs co-occurring. Indeed, in the BNC, only 19.4% of the K&H instances never co-occur, while in Wikipedia –a corpus 15 times larger than BNC– the number of co-occurrences rises only to 30.7%, demonstrating the challenge of classifying such pairs. Therefore, the real upper-bound limit for these types of systems is the amount of word pairs co-occurring in the same sentence in the corpus. The recall achieved by GraCE overcomes this limitation of pattern-based systems: 40% and 78.7% of the instances that never co-occur in BNC and in Wikipedia, respectively, are correctly classified by GraCE. This ability causes GraCE to improve the BL performance by 8.1 points in precision and 36.1 points in recall on BNC and 4.6 points in precision and 59.3 in recall on Wikipedia. Given that the BL system is constructed identically to GraCE but without using a graph, these results demonstrate the performance benefit of joining the distributional information of a corpus into a graph-based corpus representation.

Analyzing the false negatives of the GraCE classifier, we observe that even relying on a graph-based corpus representation to extract the distributional information of a word pair, many errors are still caused by the sparsity of their vectorial representation. For the word pairs that do not co-occur in the same sentence, the GraCE vector representations of correctly-classified pairs have a median of eight non-zero features, indicating that the graph was beneficial for still providing evidence of a relationship; in contast, incorrectly-classified pairs had a median of only three non-zero features, suggesting that data sparisity is still major contributor to classification error.

By combining all the distributional information into a denser vector, WECE systems are able to improve upon GraCE's results by an average of 2.9 points in precision and 17.9 points in recall. WECE results see an increase by 62 points in precision and 46 in recall over DS_{Zhila} which used the same em-

[5] y is a direct ancestor of x if there is no other word z which is hypernym of x and hyponym of y.

beddings, highlighting the importance of the SVM classifier for learning which features of the embeddings reflect the lexical relation. Although embeddings have been argued to reflect the semantic or syntactic relations between two words (Mikolov et al., 2013c), our results suggest that additional machine learning (as done with $\text{WECE}_{\text{offset}}$) is needed to identify which dimensions of the embeddings accurately correspond to specific relationships. Between the WECE systems, $\text{WECE}_{\text{concat}}$ achieves slightly better results on the K&H dataset.

4.4 Experiment 2

In the first experiment, the proposed systems were compared to test the importance of having a representation that includes information about lexical and relational similarities for the classifier to generalize and to gain recall. Therefore, as further validation, a second experiment is carried out, where the systems have to classify word pairs from a different domain than the domains in the training set. The objective is to assess the importance of the domain-aware training instances for the classification.

The K&H dataset contains only instances from three domains and is imbalanced between the number of instances across domains and relation types. Therefore, our second experiment tests each method on the BLESS dataset (Baroni and Lenci, 2011), which spans 17 topical domains and includes five relation types, the three in K&H and (a) attributes of concepts, a relation holding between nouns and adjectives, and (b) actions performed by/to concepts a relation holding between nouns and verbs. In total, the BLESS dataset contains 14400 positive instances and an equal number of negative instances. This experiment measures the generalizability of each system and tests the capabilities of the systems for lexical-semantic relation types other than taxonomic relations.

Domain-aware training instances To show the importance of the domain-aware training instances, the average results of the systems obtained for the *in-domain* setup across the BLESS dataset are compared with the average results obtained when the systems are trained *out-of-domain*. For the *out-of-domain* setup, one domain is left out from the training set and used for testing. The experiment was repeated for each domain and the average results are presented in Table 4. In this experiment, the systems are tested over the BNC corpus to show the capabilities of the systems to classify *out-of-domain* in a more reduced corpus.

	In-domain			Out-of-domain		
	P	R	F	P	R	F
$PairClass$	66.8	35.6	46.4	78.9	43.2	55.8
BL	79.5	51.6	62.6	71.7	40.0	51.4
$GraCE$	87.7	85.0	86.3	66.2	36.3	46.9
DS_{Zhila}	62.1	47.4	53.7	50.7	46.9	48.7
DS_{Levy}	53.0	49.2	51.0	51.1	47.5	49.2
$WECE^{BoW}_{offset}$	**90.0**	90.9	**90.4**	68.0	**66.9**	67.5
$WECE^{BoW}_{concat}$	89.9	**91.0**	**90.4**	**83.8**	57.0	67.8
$WECE^{Dep}_{offset}$	85.3	86.5	85.9	68.7	62.3	65.4
$WECE^{Dep}_{concat}$	85.9	87.0	86.5	78.2	63.8	**70.3**

Table 4: Aggregated results obtained when systems are tested with the BLESS dataset over BNC.

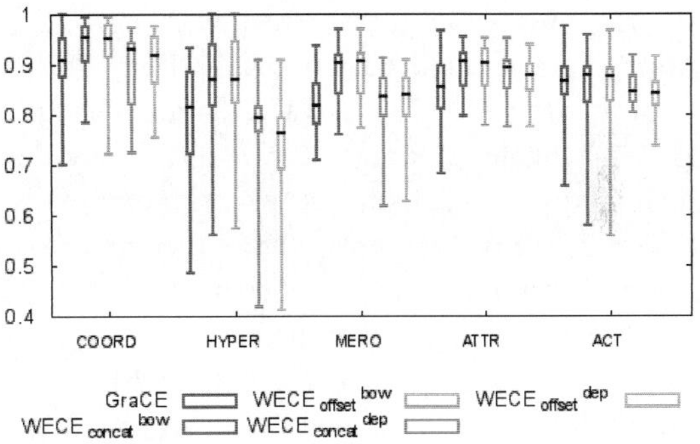

Figure 2: F1 scores distribution across domains for each proposed system and relation type over BNC corpus.

Results When no examples from a domain are provided, a general significant decrease in performance is observed. The GraCE performance decreases 39.4 points in F1, while the WECE systems decrease 20.55 points in average.

The results obtained show that when the instances to be classified are less homogeneous, i.e. when the instances belong to different domains, none of the systems can achieve the level of performance reported for the in-domain setup. These were the expected results for the GraCE system due to the lexical features that it uses and which are domain dependent. However, the WECE systems are also affected by this lack of domain-aware training instances. $\text{WECE}_{\text{concat}}$ results decrease because similar embeddings are associated with similar words.

When two words belong to two different topical domains, their embeddings are less similar and, therefore, the SVM system cannot learn distinctive features for each lexical-semantic relation.

In-domain results per relation type In this work we are interested in creating a general approach for the classification of any lexical semantic relation instances. Figure 2 shows the box and whisker plot of the results obtained per relation type across domains in the in-domain setup over the BNC corpus.

Discussion The results confirm that the proposed systems achieve satisfactory results across all the relations, the median of the results being around 90 points in F1. The most accurate system is $WECE^{bow}$, which supports the assertion by Levy and Goldberg (2014a) that bag-of-word embeddings should offer superior performance to dependency-based embeddings on task involving semantic relations. Carrying out an error analysis, the lowest results of the WECE systems are obtained in the domains with the fewest training instances, making apparent that word embedding systems are dependent on the number of training instances. For these domains, GraCE achieves better results.

5 Conclusions

In this paper we have presented two systems for classifying the lexical-semantic relation of a word pair. Both are designed to address the challenge of data sparsity, i.e., classifying word pairs whose members never co-occur, in order to improve classification recall. The two main contributions are the word pair vectorial representations, one based on a graph-based corpus representation and the other one based on word embeddings. We have demonstrated that by including information about lexical and relational similarity in the word pair vectorial representation, the recall of our systems increases, overcoming the upper-bound limit of state-of-the-art systems. Furthermore, we show that our systems are able to classify target word pairs into multiple lexical semantic relation types, beyond the traditional taxonomic types. In future work, we plan to analyze the properties of the instances that can be classified with the GraCE system but not with the WECE systems.

Acknowledgments

The authors gratefully acknowledge the support of the CLARA project (EU-7FP-ITN-238405), the SKATER project (Ministerio de Economia y Competitividad, TIN2012-38584-C06-05) and of the MultiJEDI ERC Starting Grant no. 259234.

Appendix

A Full Classifier Results

		BNC			Wikipedia		
		P	R	F	P	R	F
PairClass	C	84.1	3.6	6.9	92.4	9.3	16.8
	H	79.7	10.1	17.9	75.6	26.1	38.8
	M	38.6	8.5	14.0	23.9	15.5	18.8
	*	76.9	4.6	8.7	77.0	11.7	20.4
BL	C	84.4	5.6	10.4	88.8	13.8	23.9
	H	82.4	20.1	32.3	92.7	31.9	47.5
	M	69.4	12.8	21.6	77.3	14.5	24.4
	*	82.6	7.7	14.2	89.4	16.2	27.5
GraCE	C	90.9	43.7	59.0	94.2	78.7	85.7
	H	90.5	48.9	63.5	93.2	67.8	78.5
	M	87.5	26.3	40.4	91.8	28.7	43.7
	*	90.7	43.8	59.0	94.0	75.5	83.7
DS	C	97.2	8.0	14.8	95.5	11.5	20.5
	H	28.2	58.6	38.1	29.1	85.4	43.4
	M	8.4	36.4	13.7	8.5	48.0	14.5
	*	31.6	15.7	21.0	32.8	22.6	26.8
DS^{Dep}	C	82.0	2.6	5.0	84.0	5.2	9.8
	H	20.7	62.7	31.1	21.8	80.7	34.4
	M	5.1	26.1	8.6	11.3	43.6	17.9
	*	18.7	11.4	14.2	27.7	15.6	20.0
$WECE^{Bow}_{offset}$	C	95.9	60.4	74.1	96.6	89.7	93.0
	H	98.1	56.5	71.7	98.9	85.3	91.6
	M	88.6	38.3	53.5	90.8	51.2	65.4
	*	96.0	59.1	73.1	96.8	87.7	92.0
$WECE^{Bow}_{concat}$	C	98.2	60.6	74.9	98.5	89.8	93.9
	H	96.0	60.1	73.9	97.1	91.3	94.1
	M	81.1	45.9	58.7	77.9	68.6	72.9
	*	97.4	60.0	74.2	97.6	89.3	93.2
$WECE^{Dep}_{offset}$	C	87.0	66.5	75.4	95.1	88.1	91.5
	H	96.6	51.9	67.5	98.1	84.3	90.7
	M	83.1	26.4	40.1	88.2	44.7	59.3
	*	87.9	63.1	73.5	95.4	86.1	90.5
$WECE^{Dep}_{concat}$	C	94.0	66.7	78.0	98.0	89.2	93.4
	H	93.1	60.2	73.1	95.5	90.3	92.8
	M	67.0	35.8	46.7	69.5	62.0	65.6
	*	93.1	64.7	76.4	96.7	88.4	92.4

Table 5: Detailed results for each relation tested, coordination (C), hypernymy (H) and meronymy (M), and the aggregated results (*) obtained with K&H dataset over BNC and Wikipedia.

References

Marco Baroni and Alessandro Lenci. 2011. How we BLESSed distributional semantic evaluation. In *Proceedings of the Workshop on Geometrical Models of Natural Language Semantics*, pages 1–10.

Marco Baroni, Georgiana Dinu, and Germán Kruszewski. 2014. Don't count, predict! a systematic comparison of context-counting vs. context-predicting semantic vectors. In *Proceedings of ACL*.

Matthew Berland and Eugene Charniak. 1999. Finding parts in very large corpora. In *Proceedings of ACL*, pages 57–64.

Scott Cederberg and Dominic Widdows. 2003. Using LSA and noun coordination information to improve the precision and recall of automatic hyponymy extraction. In *Proceedings of CoNLL*, pages 111–118.

Dmitry Davidov and Ari Rappoport. 2006. Efficient unsupervised discovery of word categories using symmetric patterns and high frequency words. In *Proceedings of COLING-ACL*, pages 297–304.

Antonio Di Marco and Roberto Navigli. 2013. Clustering and Diversifying Web Search Results with Graph-Based Word Sense Induction. *Computational Linguistics*, 39(3):709–754.

Ruiji Fu, Jiang Guo, Bing Qin, Wanxiang Che, Haifeng Wang, and Ting Liu. 2014. Learning semantic hierarchies via word embeddings. In *Proceedings of ACL*, volume 1.

Roxana Girju, Adriana Badulescu, and Dan I. Moldovan. 2006. Automatic discovery of part-whole relations. *Computational Linguistics*, 32(1):83–135.

Mark Hall, Eibe Frank, Geoffrey Holmes, Bernhard Pfahringer, Peter Reutemann, and Ian H. Witten. 2009. The WEKA data mining software: an update. *SIGKDD Explorations Newsletter*, 11(1):10–18.

Marti A. Hearst. 1992. Automatic acquisition of hyponyms from large text corpora. In *Proceedings of COLING*, pages 539–545.

Iris Hendrickx, Su Nam Kim, Zornitsa Kozareva, Preslav Nakov, Diarmuid Ó Séaghdha, Sebastian Padó, Marco Pennacchiotti, Lorenza Romano, and Stan Szpakowicz. 2010. SemEval-2010 Task 8: Multi-Way Classification of Semantic Relations between Pairs of Nominals. In *Proceedings of the 5th International Workshop on Semantic Evaluation*, pages 33–38.

Amaç Herdadelen and Marco Baroni. 2009. Bagpack: A general framework to represent semantic relations. In *Proceedings of the Workshop on Geometrical Models of Natural Language Semantics*, pages 33–40.

David Jurgens, Peter D Turney, Saif M Mohammad, and Keith J Holyoak. 2012. Semeval-2012 Task 2: Measuring degrees of relational similarity. In *Proceedings of the Sixth International Workshop on Semantic Evaluation*, pages 356–364.

Zornitsa Kozareva and Eduard H. Hovy. 2010. A semi-supervised method to learn and construct taxonomies using the web. In *Proceedings of EMNLP*, pages 1110–1118.

Omer Levy and Yoav Goldberg. 2014a. Dependency-based word embeddings. In *Proceedings of ACL*.

Omer Levy and Yoav Goldberg. 2014b. Linguistic regularities in sparse and explicit word representations. In *Proceedings of CoNLL*.

Christopher D Manning, Mihai Surdeanu, John Bauer, Jenny Finkel, Steven J Bethard, and David McClosky. 2014. The Stanford CoreNLP natural language processing toolkit. In *Proceedings of 52nd Annual Meeting of the Association for Computational Linguistics: System Demonstrations*, pages 55–60.

Tomas Mikolov, Anoop Deoras, Daniel Povey, Lukas Burget, and Jan Cernocky. 2011. Strategies for training large scale neural network language models. In *Proceedings of the 2011 IEEE Workshop on Automatic Speech Recognition and Understanding (ASRU)*, pages 196–201.

Tomas Mikolov, Kai Chen, Greg Corrado, and Jeffrey Dean. 2013a. Efficient estimation of word representations in vector space. *Proceedings of Workshop at ICLR*.

Tomas Mikolov, Ilya Sutskever, Kai Chen, Greg S Corrado, and Jeff Dean. 2013b. Distributed representations of words and phrases and their compositionality. In *Proceedings of NIPS*, pages 3111–3119.

Tomas Mikolov, Wen-tau Yih, and Geoffrey Zweig. 2013c. Linguistic regularities in continuous space word representations. In *Proceedings of HLT-NAACL*, pages 746–751.

George A. Miller. 1995. Wordnet: A lexical database for english. *Communications of the ACM*, 38:39–41.

Einat Minkov and William W. Cohen. 2012. Graph based similarity measures for synonym extraction from parsed text. In *Proceedings of the Workshop on Graph-based Methods for Natural Language Processing*, pages 20–24.

Mike Mintz, Steven Bills, Rion Snow, and Dan Jurafsky. 2009. Distant supervision for relation extraction without labeled data. In *Proceedings of ACL-CONLL*, pages 1003–1011.

Roberto Navigli and Paola Velardi. 2010. Learning word-class lattices for definition and hypernym extraction. In *Proceedings of ACL*, pages 1318–1327.

John C. Platt. 1999. Fast training of support vector machines using sequential minimal optimization. In Bernhard Schölkopf, Christopher J. C. Burges, and

Alexander J. Smola, editors, *Advances in kernel methods*, pages 185–208. MIT Press, Cambridge, MA, USA.

Diarmuid O Séaghdha and Ann Copestake. 2009. Using lexical and relational similarity to classify semantic relations. In *Proceedings of EACL*, pages 621–629.

Isabel Segura-Bedmar, Paloma Martınez, and Marıa Herrero-Zazo. 2013. Semeval-2013 task 9: Extraction of drug-drug interactions from biomedical texts. In *Proceedings of the 7th International Workshop on Semantic Evaluation*.

Rion Snow, Daniel Jurafsky, and Andrew Y. Ng. 2004. Learning syntactic patterns for automatic hypernym discovery. In *Proceedings of NIPS*.

Peter D. Turney. 2006a. Expressing implicit semantic relations without supervision. In *Proceedings of COLING-ACL*, pages 313–320.

Peter D Turney. 2006b. Similarity of semantic relations. *Computational Linguistics*, 32(3):379–416.

Peter D Turney. 2008a. The latent relation mapping engine: Algorithm and experiments. *Journal of Artificial Intelligence Research (JAIR)*, 33:615–655.

Peter D. Turney. 2008b. A uniform approach to analogies, synonyms, antonyms, and associations. In *Proceedings of COLING*, pages 905–912.

Dominic Widdows and Beate Dorow. 2002. A graph model for unsupervised lexical acquisition. In *Proceedings of COLING*.

Alisa Zhila, Wen-tau Yih, Christopher Meek, Geoffrey Zweig, and Tomas Mikolov. 2013. Combining heterogeneous models for measuring relational similarity. In *Proceedings of HLT-NAACL*, pages 1000–1009.

Multi-Level Alignments As An Extensible Representation Basis for Textual Entailment Algorithms

Tae-Gil Noh (noh@cl.uni-heidelberg.de)[1], **Sebastian Padó** (pado@ims.uni-stuttgart.de)[2], **Vered Shwartz** (vered1986@gmail.com)[3], **Ido Dagan** (dagan@cs.biu.ac.il)[3], **Vivi Nastase** (nastase@fbk.eu)[4], **Kathrin Eichler** (kathrin.eichler@dfki.de)[5], **Lili Kotlerman** (lili.dav@gmail.com)[3], and **Meni Adler** (meni.adler@gmail.com)[3]

[1]Institute of Computational Linguistics, Heidelberg University, Germany
[2]Institute of Natural Language Processing, Stuttgart University, Germany
[3]Department of Computer Science, Bar-Ilan University, Israel
[4]Human Language Technologies, Fondazione Bruno Kessler, Italy
[5]Language Technology Lab, DFKI GmbH, Germany

Abstract

A major problem in research on Textual Entailment (TE) is the high implementation effort for TE systems. Recently, interoperable standards for annotation and preprocessing have been proposed. In contrast, the algorithmic level remains unstandardized, which makes component re-use in this area very difficult in practice. In this paper, we introduce *multi-level alignments* as a central, powerful representation for TE algorithms that encourages modular, reusable, multilingual algorithm development. We demonstrate that a pilot open-source implementation of multi-level alignment with minimal features competes with state-of-the-art open-source TE engines in three languages.

1 Introduction

A key challenge of Natural Language Processing is to determine what conclusions can be drawn from a natural language text, a task known as *Textual Entailment* (TE, Dagan and Glickman 2004). The ability to recognize TE helps dealing with surface variability in tasks like Question Answering (Harabagiu and Hickl, 2006), Intelligent Tutoring (Nielsen et al., 2009), or Text Exploration (Berant et al., 2012). Open source implementations a number of TE algorithms have become available over the last years, including BIUTEE (Stern and Dagan, 2012) and EDITS (Kouylekov and Negri, 2010), which has made it much easier for end users to utilize TE engines.

At the same time, the situation is still more difficult for researchers and developers. Even though recently a common platform for TE has been proposed (Padó et al., 2015) that standardizes important aspects like annotation types, preprocessing, and knowledge resources, it largely ignores the algorithmic level. In fact, TE algorithms themselves are generally not designed to be extensible or interoperable. Therefore, changes to the algorithms – like adding support for a new language or for new analysis aspect – are often very involved, if not impossible. This often forces the next generation of TE researchers to develop and implement their own core algorithms from scratch.

In this paper, we address this problem by proposing a schema for TE algorithms that revolves around a central representation layer called *multi-level alignment* geared towards encoding the relevant information for deciding entailment. The use of multi-level alignments encourages a modular, extensible development of TE algorithms that can be partitioned into "alignment producers" and "alignment consumers". This enables for future researchers and developers to change analysis components or add new ones in a straightforward manner.

We also present evaluation results for a very simple TE algorithm based on multi-level alignments for English, German and Italian. It utilizes a minimal set of analyzers and four basic language-independent features. It can thus be regarded as a baseline of the performance achievable with this approach. The results can already compete with the best open-source engines available for each of the languages.

2 TE with Multi-Level Alignments

The quality of the word alignment between a Text (T) and a Hypothesis (H) has been used very early as a simple feature to decide about TE. When it was found

*Proceedings of the Fourth Joint Conference on Lexical and Computational Semantics (*SEM 2015)*, pages 193–198,
Denver, Colorado, June 4–5, 2015.

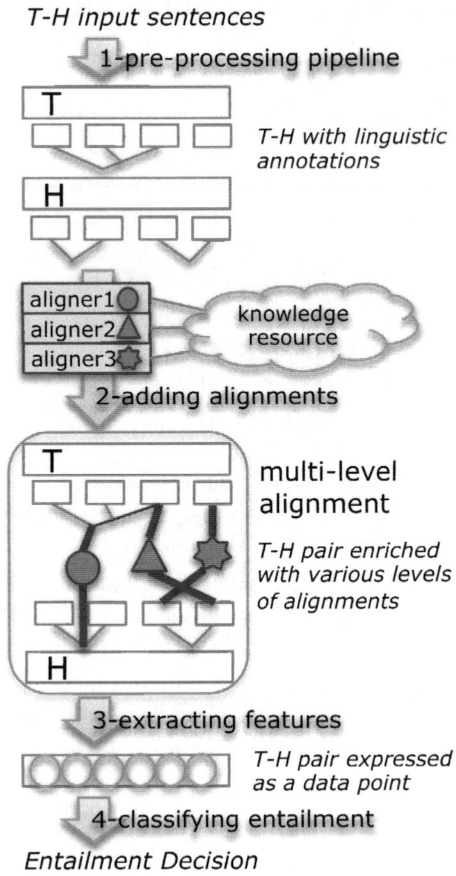

Figure 1: Dataflow for TE algorithms based on multi level alignment

that alignment strength can be misleading (MacCartney et al., 2006), alignment was understood as an intermediate step whose outcome is a set of correspondences between parts of T and H that can be used to define (mis-)match features. Alignments can be established at the word level, phrase level (MacCartney et al., 2008), or dependency level (Dinu and Wang, 2009). Dagan et al. (2013) generalized this practical use to an architectural principle: They showed that various TE algorithms can be mapped onto a universal alignment-based schema with six steps: preprocessing, enrichment, candidate alignment generation, alignment selection, and classification.

Proposal. Our proposal is similar to, but simpler than, Dagan et al.'s. Figure 1 shows the data flow.

First, the text and the hypothesis are linguistically pre-processed. Then, the annotated T-H pair becomes the input for various independent aligners, which have access to knowledge resources and can compute any evidence for or against entailment that can be represented as a weighted alignment between any linguistic levels of H and T. Note that this includes many analyses not normally treated as alignment, e.g. match or mismatch in negation or modality between parts of T and H. The union of all alignments forms the central data structure, the *Multi-Level Alignments*.

The next step is feature extraction. Features can be extracted on the basis of individual alignments, or from sets of alignments. We assume that the features form a vector describing the T-H pair, and that the last step is supervised entailment classification.

Discussion. The main difference to Dagan et al.'s schema is that we intentionally leave out the step of *alignment selection* which explicitly selects a single alignment for each part of H or T, typically the globally most probable one. Our decision to forgo selection is grounded in our design of multi-level alignments as a repository that supports coexistence of information from different sources. This has the following benefits: (a) aligners become decoupled in that adding a new aligner does not have a direct impact on other aligners; (b) alignments produced by different aligners can have different semantics, e.g. positive (match) or negative (mismatch); (c) interactions between alignments can still be captured by defining features in the feature extraction step.

In this manner, multi-level alignments serve as an abstraction layer that encourages the development of TE algorithms composed of small, self-contained modules that solve specialized tasks in TE recognition. Each of these modules consists of two parts: an aligner, and a set of feature extractors. A priori, each module can be defined independently; to introduce interactions with other modules, it should be sufficient to extend the feature extractors.

The practical benefit for the developer is that even relatively complex TE algorithms use a small set of well-defined interfaces, which makes them easy to manage, even at the implementation level. The startup cost is getting acquainted with the common data structure of multi-level alignments. We believe that developers are willing to pay this cost, especially when this provides them with a platform that supports multilingual pre-processing and resources.

3 Implementation and Evaluation

We describe an implementation of a pilot TE algorithm based on the Multi-Level Alignment approach and its evaluation in three languages (EN, DE, IT). The system is available as open-source.[1]

3.1 Technical Foundations

We implement the algorithm within an open source TE development platform (Padó et al., 2015). The platform provides various multilingual pre-processing pipelines and knowledge resources such as WordNet, VerbOcean, etc., under a shared API. For pre-processing, we use TreeTagger-based pipelines for all three languages.

Another important service provided by the platform is the ability of storing a wide range of linguistic annotations in a common, language-independent data representation. The platform uses UIMA CAS (Ferrucci and Lally, 2004) as the data container, adopts the DKPro type system (de Castilho and Gurevych, 2014), and defines annotation types which can be extended in a controlled manner. We used this capability to define a multilingual Multi-Level Alignment layer with little implementation effort.

3.2 A Minimal Set of Aligners

The pilot algorithm restricts itself to three aligners. All three are fully language-independent, even if two use language-specific knowledge resources.

Lexical Aligner. The lexical aligner adds an alignment link for a pair of lemmas in T and H if it finds some kind of semantic relationships between them in a set of lexical resources. The link is directed, labeled (by the semantic relation, e.g. "synonym", "antonym") and weighted, with the weight indicating the strength of the relationship. Note that this aligner can on its own already produce alignment links with inconsistent semantics (positive and negative). For English, WordNet and VerbOcean were used as lexical resources. Italian WordNet was used for Italian, and GermaNet and German DerivBase (Zeller et al., 2013) were used as lexical resources for German.

Paraphrase Aligner. The paraphrase aligner concentrates on surface forms rather than lemmas and can align sequences of them rather than just individual tokens. It uses paraphrase tables, e.g. extracted from parallel corpora (Bannard and Callison-Burch, 2005). The alignment process is similar to the lexical aligner: any two sequences of tokens in T and H are aligned if the pair is listed in the resource. The alignment links created by this aligner instantiate only one relation ("paraphrase") but report the strength of the relation via the translation probability. We used the paraphrase tables provided by the METEOR MT evaluation package (Denkowski and Lavie, 2014), which are available for numerous languages.

Lemma Identity Aligner. This aligner does not use any resources. It simply aligns identical lemmas between T and H and plays an important role in practice to deal with named entities.

3.3 A Minimal Feature Set

Similar to the aligners, we concentrate on a small set of four features in the pilot algorithm. Again, the features are completely language independent, even at the implementation level. This is possible because the linguistic annotations and the alignments, use a language-independent type system (cf. Section 3.1).

All current features measure some form of *coverage* on the Hypothesis, i.e. the percentage of H that can be explained by T. The underlying hypothesis is that a higher coverage of H corresponds to a higher chance of entailment. Since parts-of-speech arguably differ in the importance of being covered, we compute coverage for four sets of words separately: (a), for all words; (b), for content words; (c), for verbs; (d), for proper names (according to the POS tagger). The features are defined on the union of all produced alignments: i.e., two words count as aligned if they were aligned by any aligner. Clearly, this is an overly simplistic (albeit surprisingly effective) strategy. It can be considered a baseline for our approach that can be extended with many features that suggest themselves from the literature.

4 Experimental Evaluation

Evaluation 1: RTE-3. RTE-3 was the third instance of the yearly benchmarking workshops of the Textual Entailment community (Giampiccolo et al.,

[1] As a part of Excitement Open Platform for Textual Entailment. `https://github.com/hltfbk/EOP-1.2.1/wiki/AlignmentEDAP1`

	English	German	Italian
MultiAlign	**67.0**	**64.5**	**65.4**
BIUTEE	**67.0**	-	-
TIE	65.2	63.1	-
EDITS	63.6	-	62.6
RTE3 median	61.8		

Table 1: Accuracy evaluation on the RTE3 dataset

	English	German	Italian
MultiAlign	69.2	**72.4**	**69.5**
BIUTEE	**71.3**	-	-
TIE	67.3	**72.4**	-
EDITS	66.6	-	65.6

Table 2: F_1 evaluation on application data

2007). The English dataset created for RTE-3 consists of 800 training and 800 testing T-H pairs. Later, the RTE-3 dataset was translated into both German and Italian (Magnini et al., 2014). It is the only Textual Entailment dataset in multiple languages with the same content. The task is binary TE recognition, with baseline of 50% accuracy (balanced classes).

We trained and tested our Multi-Level Alignment approach (*MultiAlign*) on the RTE-3 dataset separately for each language. We compare against the other RTE systems from the platform by Padó et al. (2015), namely BIUTEE (Stern and Dagan, 2012), EDITS (Kouylekov and Negri, 2010), and TIE (Wang and Zhang, 2009). Each system is configured with its best known configurations. The pilot system supports all three languages, while others support one (BIUTEE) or two languages (EDITS, TIE).

The results are shown in Table 1. The pilot system performs well in all three languages. It ties with BIUTEE on English and it outperforms TIE and EDITS in their respective results on German and Italian. This is particularly notable since all three systems have gone through several years of development, while *MultiAlign* is only a pilot implementation.

Evaluation 2: T-H pairs from Application Data. We perform the second evaluation on real-world application data from two application datasets: an entailment graph dataset (for English and Italian), and an e-mail categorization dataset (for German). Entailment graph building is the task of constructing graphs that hierarchically structure the statements from a collection (Berant et al., 2012) for the application of Text Exploration. In TE-based e-mail categorization, the goal is to assign the right category to an email with TE, using the email as T and a category description as H. (Eichler et al., 2014).

Due to space constraints, we cannot evaluate these applications end-to-end. Instead, we focus on the respective first step, the binary decision of entailment for individual T-H pairs. This task corresponds to RTE-3, and the main difference to Evaluation 1 is that these pairs come from real-world interactions and were produced by native speakers. All T-H pairs are sampled from application gold data which were manually constructed on the basis of anonymized customer interactions (Eichler et al. (2014) for German; Kotlerman et al. (2015) for English and Italian[2]). The sets are fairly large (5300 pairs for English, 1700 for Italian, 1274 for German), and were sampled to be balanced. We report F_1 for comparability with non-balanced setups (our random baseline is F_1=50).

Table 2 shows our evaluation results. *MultiAlign* system beats EDITS for Italian (+4), and ties with TIE for German. On English, BIUTEE still outperforms *MultiAlign* (-2). Thus, *MultiAlign* also performs acceptably on real-world data.

In sum, we find that *MultiAlign* is already competitive with state-of-the-art open-source TE engines on three languages. *MultiAlign* is not only much less complex, but it is also a single system covering all three languages, without any language-specific optimizations. We interpret this as a positive sign for the future of the Multi-Level Alignment approach.

Visualization. The platform also supports visualization of individual Text-Hypothesis pairs, showing the alignments that were created by the system as well as the features computed on the basis of the alignments. The visualization was built on the basis of the BRAT library.[3]

Figure 2 shows an example for the Text *The judges made an assessment of Peter's credibility* and the Hypothesis *The judges assessed if Peter was credible*. The top line shows the final prediction, Entailment, and the confidence (75%). The main part shows the Text and the Hypothesis below each other, connected

[2]Both datasets are publicly available.

[3]`http://brat.nlplab.org/index.html`

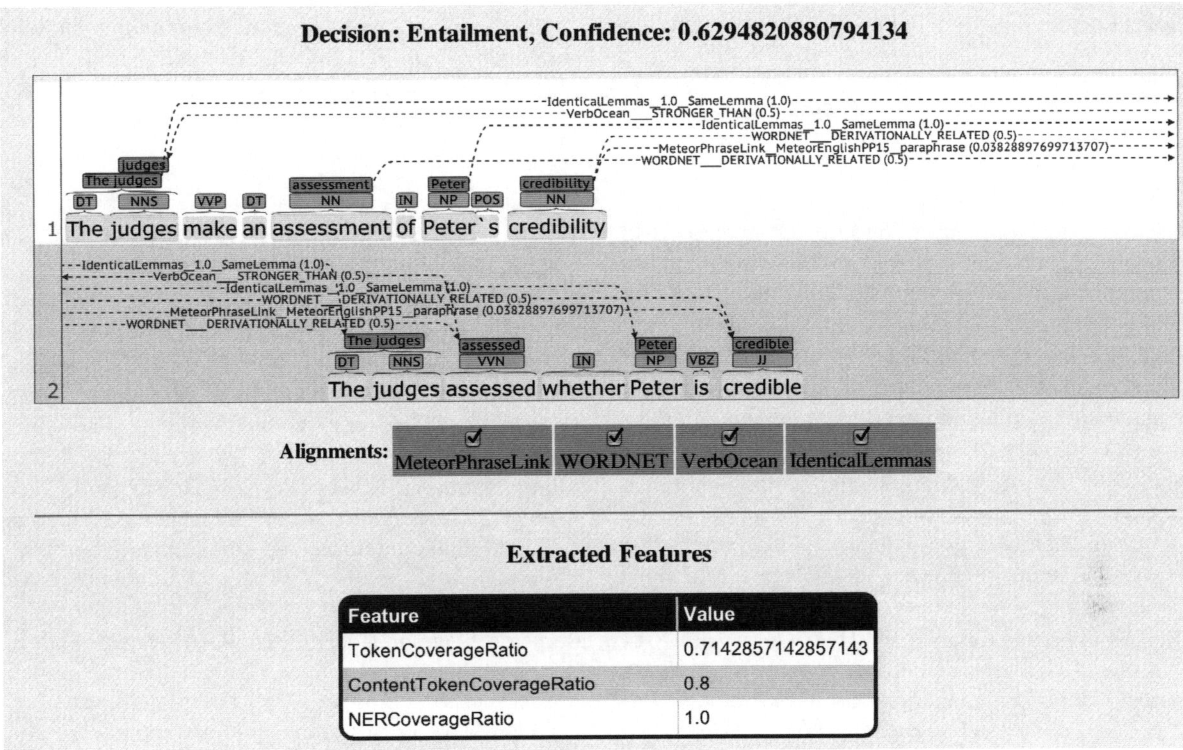

Figure 2: Screenshot of the Multi-Level Alignment Visualizer

by alignment links that are labeled with their source and their score. Note that the alignments can link individual words (*assessment* and *assess* are aligned through a derivational link from WordNet) but also phrases (The two occurrences of *The judges* in Text and Hypothesis are linked by virtue of being identical lemmas).

The three features currently used by the English system are are shown below. As can be seen, they aggregate very simple statistics about the alignments: 5 of 7 tokens in the hypothesis are covered, 4 out of 5 content words, and the one proper name is also aligned. This situation motivates nicely the use of those features: a relatively low alignment coverage on all tokens is still compatible with entailment as long as the crucial tokens are aligned.

This visualization enables end users to quickly take in the justification behind the system's decision. Developers can inspect alignments and features for plausibility and detect possible bugs and assess the limitations of aligners and their underlying resources. For example, the current example shows a wrong link produced by the VerbOcean resource between the noun *judges* in the Text and the verb *assessed* in the Hypothesis. The reason is that the noun *judges* is mistaken for an inflected form of the verb *to judge* which indeed stands in a *Stronger-than* relationship to *to assess*.

5 Conclusion

This paper proposed the use of *multi-level alignments*, a rich data structure allowing multiple alignments to co-exist. We argued that multi-level alignments are a suitable basis for developing Textual Entailment algorithms by virtue of providing a beneficial abstraction layer that supports extensible and modular entailment algorithms. A pilot TE algorithm developed in this schema showed performance comparable to much more sophisticated state-of-the-art open-source TE engines and is available as open source software.

Acknowledgments

This work was partially supported by the EC-funded project EXCITEMENT (FP7ICT-287923).

References

Colin Bannard and Chris Callison-Burch. 2005. Paraphrasing with bilingual parallel corpora. In *Proceedings of the 43rd Annual Meeting of the Association for Computational Linguistics*, pages 597–604, Ann Arbor, MI.

Jonathan Berant, Ido Dagan, and Jacob Goldberger. 2012. Learning entailment relations by global graph structure optimization. *Computational Linguistics*, 38(1):73–111.

Ido Dagan and Oren Glickman. 2004. Probabilistic textual entailment: Generic applied modeling of language variability. In *PASCAL workshop on Learning Methods for Text Understanding and Mining*, Grenoble, France.

Ido Dagan, Dan Roth, Mark Sammons, and Fabio Massimo Zanzotto. 2013. *Recognizing Textual Entailment: Models and Applications*. Number 17 in Synthesis Lectures on Human Language Technologies. Morgan & Claypool.

Richard Eckart de Castilho and Iryna Gurevych. 2014. A broad-coverage collection of portable NLP components for building shareable analysis pipelines. In *Proceedings of the Workshop on Open Infrastructures and Analysis Frameworks for HLT at COLING 2014*, pages 1–11, Dublin, Ireland, August.

Michael Denkowski and Alon Lavie. 2014. Meteor universal: Language specific translation evaluation for any target language. In *Proceedings of the Ninth Workshop on Statistical Machine Translation*, pages 376–380, Baltimore, MD.

Georgiana Dinu and Rui Wang. 2009. Inference rules and their application to recognizing textual entailment. In *Proceedings of the 12th Conference of the European Chapter of the ACL*, pages 211–219, Athens, Greece.

Kathrin Eichler, Aleksandra Gabryszak, and Günter Neumann. 2014. An analysis of textual inference in German customer emails. In *Proceedings of the Third Joint Conference on Lexical and Computational Semantics*, pages 69–74, Dublin, Ireland.

David Ferrucci and Adam Lally. 2004. UIMA: An architectural approach to unstructured information processing in the corporate research environment. *Natural Language Engineering*, 10(3–4):327–348.

Danilo Giampiccolo, Bernardo Magnini, Ido Dagan, and Bill Dolan. 2007. The third PASCAL recognising textual entailment challenge. In *Proceedings of the ACL-PASCAL Workshop on Textual Entailment and Paraphrasing*, pages 1–9, Prague, Czech Republic.

Sanda Harabagiu and Andrew Hickl. 2006. Methods for using textual entailment in open-domain question answering. In *Proceedings of the 21st International Conference on Computational Linguistics and 44th Annual Meeting of the Association for Computational Linguistics*, pages 905–912, Sydney, Australia.

Lili Kotlerman, Ido Dagan, Bernardo Magnini, and Luisa Bentivogli. 2015. Textual entailment graphs. *Natural Language Engineering*.

Milen Kouylekov and Matteo Negri. 2010. An open-source package for recognizing textual entailment. In *Proceedings of the ACL 2010 System Demonstrations*, pages 42–47, Uppsala, Sweden.

Bill MacCartney, Trond Grenager, Marie-Catherine de Marneffe, Daniel Cer, and Christopher D Manning. 2006. Learning to recognize features of valid textual entailments. In *Proceedings of the Human Language Technology Conference of the NAACL*, pages 41–48, New York City, USA.

Bill MacCartney, Michel Galley, and Christopher D Manning. 2008. A phrase-based alignment model for natural language inference. In *Proceedings of the Conference on Empirical Methods in Natural Language Processing*, pages 802–811, Honolulu, Hawaii.

Bernardo Magnini, Roberto Zanoli, Ido Dagan, Kathrin Eichler, Günter Neumann, Tae-Gil Noh, Sebastian Padó, Asher Stern, and Omer Levy. 2014. The EXCITEMENT open platform for textual inferences. In *Proceedings of the ACL 2014 System Demonstrations*, pages 43–48, Baltimore, MD.

Rodney D Nielsen, Wayne Ward, and James H Martin. 2009. Recognizing entailment in intelligent tutoring systems. *Journal of Natural Language Engineering*, 15(4):479–501.

Sebastian Padó, Tae-Gil Noh, Asher Stern, Rui Wang, and Roberto Zanoli. 2015. Design and realization of a modular architecture for textual entailment. *Journal of Natural Language Engineering*, 21(2):167–200.

Asher Stern and Ido Dagan. 2012. BIUTEE: A modular open-source system for recognizing textual entailment. In *Proceedings of the ACL 2012 System Demonstrations*, pages 73–78, Jeju Island, Korea.

Rui Wang and Yi Zhang. 2009. Recognizing textual relatedness with predicate-argument structures. In *Proceedings of the Conference on Empirical Methods in Natural Language Processing*, pages 784–792, Singapore.

Britta Zeller, Jan Šnajder, and Sebastian Padó. 2013. DErivBase: Inducing and evaluating a derivational morphology resource for German. In *Proceedings of ACL*, pages 1201–1211, Sofia, Bulgaria.

Leveraging Preposition Ambiguity to Assess Compositional Distributional Models of Semantics

Samuel Ritter* Princeton University

Cotie Long Indiana University

Denis Paperno University of Trento

Marco Baroni University of Trento

Matthew Botvinick Princeton University

Adele Goldberg Princeton University

Abstract

Complex interactions among the meanings of words are important factors in the function that maps word meanings to phrase meanings. Recently, compositional distributional semantics models (CDSM) have been designed with the goal of emulating these complex interactions; however, experimental results on the effectiveness of CDSM have been difficult to interpret because the current metrics for assessing them do not control for the confound of lexical information. We present a new method for assessing the degree to which CDSM capture semantic interactions that dissociates the influences of lexical and compositional information. We then provide a dataset for performing this type of assessment and use it to evaluate six compositional models using both co-occurrence based and neural language model input vectors. Results show that neural language input vectors are consistently superior to co-occurrence based vectors, that several CDSM capture substantial compositional information, and that, surprisingly, vector addition matches and is in many cases superior to purpose-built paramaterized models.

1 Introduction

Consider the meanings of the following phrases: "red apple," "red hair," and "red state." The meaning of the word "red" in each of these examples interacts with the meaning of the noun it modifies, applying a different color to the first two and a political affiliation to the third. This is an example of a common phenomenon in natural language in which the meaning of a whole expression is not derived from a simple concatenation of its parts, but is composed by interactions among their meanings.

Cognitive and computer scientists have pointed out this complexity and proposed various models for accommodating it (Kintsch, 2001; Mitchell and Lapata, 2010; Socher et al., 2013). A dominant modeling approach seeks to learn functions that combine word representations derived from the distributional structure of large natural language corpora (Deerwester et al., 1990; Landauer and Dumais, 1997). Because the word representations to be combined and the compositional functions are generated based on the distributions of words in corpora, these models have been dubbed compositional distributional semantic models, or CDSM (Marelli et al., 2014). CDSM produce fixed-dimensional vector representations of arbitrary sentences and phrases, and the foundational principle of these models is, stated simply, that semantically similar phrases should have vector representations that are close together in the vector space.

1.1 CDSM Assessment

Past studies have tested how well CDSM adhere to this principle by comparing the vector similarity of pairs of sentences with similarity ratings given by humans. Many of these studies used datasets in which the amount of lexical overlap between the sentence pairs is not carefully controlled, e.g., the datasets of Dolan and Brockett (2005) and Agirre

*Please address correspondence to the first author at swritter@princeton.edu

*Proceedings of the Fourth Joint Conference on Lexical and Computational Semantics (*SEM 2015)*, pages 199–204, Denver, Colorado, June 4–5, 2015.

et al. (2014). One such study obtained the influential result that on such a dataset, simple composition models such as vector addition perform comparably to a state-of-the-art composition model (Blacoe and Lapata, 2012). The success of these simplistic models led to the conjecture that these data sets fail to assess critical aspects of language (Baroni et al., 2014a) and leaves open the question of whether CDSM would outperform simplistic models in a setting in which lexical cues are uninformative.

In the present study, we develop a method for removing the confound of lexical cues from CDSM assessment. The method is to create a set of sentences where each sentence fits into a semantic category and where a sentence's semantic category cannot be determined based on any individual word in the sentence. CDSM are then challenged to create a vector space in which the representations for sentences in a given category cluster together, even though the individual word vectors do not cluster together. This clustering can be tested by training a simple linear classifier on the CDSM representations, then testing it on representations for held out sentences.

Here, we build a suitable test set by leveraging the lexical ambiguity inherent in locative expressions. Locative expressions are phrases that describe a spatial relationship between two objects using two nouns joined by a preposition; for example, "The magnet is on the refrigerator", which describes the relationship of adhesion to a vertical surface. Crucially, the spatial relationship between the two nouns in a locative expression is undetermined by the spatial preposition, and can only be determined based on semantic interactions among the prepositions and the two nouns (Herskovits, 1985).

For example, while "The magnet is on the refrigerator" describes the spatial relationship of adhesion to a vertical surface, "The apple is on the refrigerator" describes support by a horizontal surface. In order to classify a new sentence, e.g., "The magnet is on the papers", into the correct category of support by a horizontal surface, the CDSM vectors for the three sentences must encode the fact that "The magnet is on the papers" shares a common spatial relationship with "The apple is on the refrigerator" and not with "The magnet is on the refrigerator", even though the latter pair of sentences share more words than the former.

Given this dissociation between lexical overlap and spatial relationship, we were able to construct a dataset wherein lexical information is uninformative, and models must rely on compositionality to score well in classification.

1.2 Relation to Past Work

This approach to CDSM assessment is similar to a previous method wherein polysemous verbs are paired with disambiguating nouns in transitive or intransitive verb phrases. These phrases are then matched with "landmark" verbs that are either similar or not similar in meaning to the full phrase. CDSM are then challenged to create representations of the phrases from which classifiers can determine whether or not a phrase is similar to its landmark verb (Kintsch, 2001; Mitchell and Lapata, 2008; Mitchell and Lapata, 2010; Grefenstette and Sadrzadeh, 2011). Another notable CDSM assessment task involves matching a phrase with a word with a similar meaning, for example, matching a short dictionary definition with the word it defines (Kartsaklis et al., 2012; Turney, 2014).

While these methods are applicable only to simple phrases that can be mapped reasonably to a single word, the present method can, in principle, be applied to any type of phrase. This allowed us to build a dataset that extends the current landmark word and word matching datasets in at least two important ways. First, it includes function words, specifically prepositions. Second, it requires the characterization of interactions among three words in each expression, whereas previous datasets had two words per expression, or subsets of the words did not interact in complex ways.

Other important approaches to CDSM assessment include rating the similarity of sentence pairs, determining whether two sentences are paraphrases (Dolan and Brockett, 2005), classifying the entailment relationship between two sentences (Marelli et al., 2014), classifying the relationship between two entities named in a sentence (Hendrickx et al., 2009), and classifying the valence of the sentiment expressed in a sentence (Socher et al., 2013). These methods have primarily been aimed at assessing CDSM on the full array of constructions inherent in naturally generated language, while our method aims to isolate a specific construction of interest.

Category	Example
Adhesion to Vertical Surface	"There is a magnet on the refrigerator."
Support by Horizontal Surface	"There is an apple on the refrigerator."
Support from Above	"There is an apple on the branch."
Full Containment	"There is an apple in the refrigerator."
Partial Containment	"There is an apple in the water."

Table 1: Categories and Example Sentences

2 The Dataset

A list of all of the spatial categories with examples is given in Table 1. The authors chose the set of categories to produce the desired dissociation between lexical meaning and phrase category, taking inspiration from the observations of Herskovits (1985). To produce a dataset of expressions fitting these categories, the first and second authors - both native English speakers - generated a large set of locative expressions, intending each expression for a specific category. Then all of the expressions were independently rated by the first two authors, and any expression for which the ratings disagreed were excluded from the dataset. In order to achieve a balanced category size, the second author then created additional sentences intended for underrepresented categories. All additional sentences were stripped of labels and rated independently by the first author. If the first and second authors' categorizations did not match, the sentence was not added to the dataset.

The dataset contains 500 sentences in total with 100 sentences per category. There is a large amount of lexical variety in the set, with 242 distinct words occurring in noun position one and 213 occurring in noun position two. The dataset is publicly available for download at www.princeton.edu/~swritter.

3 Evaluation Setup

Classification among the five categories was performed using a naive Bayes classifier. Two of the categories contained "in" as the preposition in all sentences while the other three contained "on" in all sentences. To be certain that the held out sentences on which the classifier was tested did not contain even a single category-informative noun, we operationally defined informativeness and relegated all sentences with an informative noun to the training set. A noun was deemed informative if it both occurred more than once in the entire data set and it occurred more frequently in one category than in any other. This criterion yielded a set of 80 sentences with no informative nouns, and a set of 420 sentences with at least one informative noun. By this method, we ensured that no component of the models' classification accuracy on the test set is due to the recognition of individual nouns.

In addition to the CDSM, we included two non-distributional models for comparison. The first, referred to as word overlap, consists of a binary feature vector containing one feature per vocabulary item. This model's performance provides an upper-bound on the performance that a model can achieve given only the distribution of word tokens in the training set. The second model, inspired by Srikumar and Roth (2013), contains binary features for Wordnet hypernyms (up to 4 levels) of each sense of the noun and a binary feature for each preposition. This model's score provides an indication of the amount of task-relevant information contained in the taxonomic features of individual words.

We compared CDSM to a further control that consisted of the concatenation of the word vectors. The concatenated vectors contain a complete representation of all of the individual word information, so that any performance the CDSM can achieve above the concatenation score can be attributed to semantic interaction information contained in the parameters of the CDSM.[1]

[1]One other experiment we considered was to test the models on the dataset phrases with prepositions removed. However, LF and PLF are undefined for such an input, and the element-wise models trivially perform better with the preposition included because the preposition is the only word that is not stripped of informativeness by design of the task. As such, we excluded this experiment from this report.

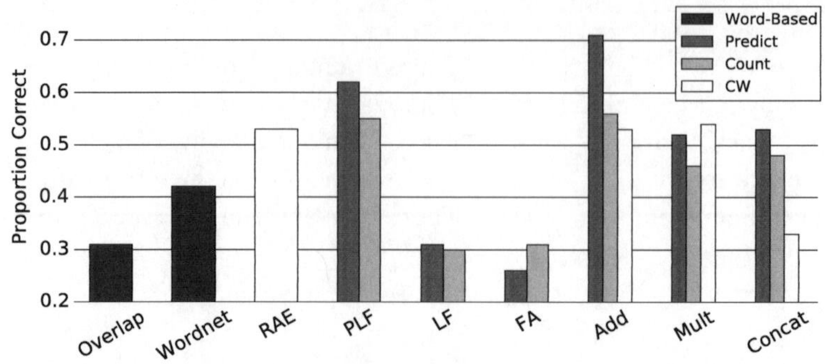

Figure 1: Naive Bayes accuracy scores for count and predict variants of several CDSM. Chance performance on this task was 0.2. Overlap refers to the word overlap baseline. CW refers to the vectors from Collobert and Weston (2008)

3.1 Compositional Distributional Models

We compared six models that are currently prominent in the CDSM literature: addition, multiplication (Mitchell and Lapata, 2008), lexical function (LF) (Coecke et al., 2010), practical lexical function (PLF) (Paperno et al., 2014), full additive (FA) (Guevara, 2010; Zanzotto et al., 2010), and the recursive auto-encoder (RAE) (Socher et al., 2011).

The training data for LF, PLF, and FA was the UKWAC+Wikipedia+BNC 2.8 billion word corpus. In training LF, we followed Grefenstette et al. (2013), employing a two-step training regime using corpus-extracted vectors for noun–preposition–noun combinations to estimate matrices of corresponding prepositional phrases, which were in turn used to estimate a three-way tensor of each preposition. For PLF and FA, we learned separate matrices for combining prepositions with each of the two nouns in the construction, using corpus-based vectors of prepositional phrases for training preposition–noun combination. For training composition of the head noun with the prepositional phrase, we used corpus-extracted noun+preposition (for lexical matrices in PLF) or attributive adjective+noun (for attributive construction in FA) vectors. Phrase vectors for training were built as DISSECT 'peripheral' spaces from phrase cooccurrence data in the count models. In the predict models, phrase vectors were learned along with word vectors in one pass, feeding all phrases of the relevant type as single tokens.

The RAE vectors were computed using Socher et al.'s implementation which is trained on a 150K sentence subset of the NYT and AP sections of the Gigaword corpus.

For all compositional models, we used as input two varieties of word level representations: co-occurrence based (Turney et al., 2010) and neural language model (Mikolov et al., 2013). Following Baroni et al. (2014b), we will refer to these variants as *count* and *predict* models respectively. Both word models were trained on the same corpus as those used to train the compositional models. Count was based on a 5 word window weighted with positive PMI and was reduced to 300 dimensions via SVD, while predict was based on a 5 word window using Mikolov's continuous bag of words approach with negative sampling (Mikolov et al., 2013). These parameters were based on their strong performance in the systematic evaluation by Baroni et al. (2014b). Socher et al.'s RAE implementation composes neural language model vectors described by Collobert and Weston (2008) and supplied by Turian et al. (2010). For comparison with the RAE, we report results for addition, multiplication, and concatenation of these same embeddings.

4 Results

The naive Bayes accuracy scores for all models are displayed in Figure 1. Addition, PLF, and the RAE each substantially outperformed concatenation, indicating that these models' vectors contain information about the semantic interactions between phrase constituents. Addition scored higher than PLF, while the RAE achieved comparable performance to its additive counterpart. In all cases except FA in which predict and count vectors were compared, predict achieved a higher score. This last result shows that the superiority of predict vectors documented by Baroni et al. (2014b) extends to their use in compositional models.

All of the models performed well above chance accuracy of 0.2. The Wordnet based model achieved accuracy substantially above word overlap using hypernym information, indicating that although each noun is uninformative, its membership in higher level semantic categories is informative. All of the distributional models outperform the non-distributional models, except for LF and FA, which also fail to outperform concatenations of their input vectors. One explanation for the poor performance of LF and FA is that the 2.8B word corpus used to train them did not have sufficient relevant information to specify their large sets of parameters. This explanation is supported by the fact that PLF, a model designed as a parameter-reduced version of LF, performs well.

5 Discussion

The most important finding of this study is that, even on a test painstakingly designed to exclusively assess composition, vector addition matches or outperforms sophisticated CDSM. This finding implies that the structure of distributional vector spaces admits the effective use of addition for modeling complex interactions between meanings. This suggests that future work should be concerned with understanding the properties of distributional vector spaces that make this possible, as well as with understanding how these properties can be leveraged by sophisticated models.

A further contribution of this work is that it serves as a proof-of-concept for a new method for dissociating the influences of lexical and compositional influences on CDSM performance. Future work can extend this approach by finding alternatives to locative expressions in order to test a wider variety of constructions. More immediately, future work may improve the locative expressions dataset by using crowdsourcing to obtain naive participant ratings to corroborate the expert ratings and to increase the size of the dataset.

Acknowledgments

Denis Paperno and Marco Baroni were supported by ERC 2011 Starting Independent Research Grant n. 283554 (COMPOSES). Samuel Ritter and Matthew Botvinick were supported by Intelligence Advanced Research Projects Activity (IARPA) Grant n. 102-01.

References

Eneko Agirre, Carmen Baneab, Claire Cardiec, Daniel Cerd, Mona Diabe, Aitor Gonzalez-Agirre, Weiwei Guof, Rada Mihalceab, German Rigaua, and Janyce Wiebeg. 2014. Semeval-2014 task 10: Multilingual semantic textual similarity. *SemEval 2014*, page 81.

Marco Baroni, Raffaela Bernardi, and Roberto Zamparelli. 2014a. Frege in space: A program of compositional distributional semantics. *Linguistic Issues in Language Technology*, 9.

Marco Baroni, Georgiana Dinu, and Germán Kruszewski. 2014b. Dont count, predict! a systematic comparison of context-counting vs. context-predicting semantic vectors. In *Proceedings of the 52nd Annual Meeting of the Association for Computational Linguistics*, volume 1.

William Blacoe and Mirella Lapata. 2012. A comparison of vector-based representations for semantic composition. In *EMNLP*, pages 546–556.

Bob Coecke, Mehrnoosh Sadrzadeh, and Stephen Clark. 2010. Mathematical foundations for a compositional distributional model of meaning. *arXiv preprint arXiv:1003.4394*.

Ronan Collobert and Jason Weston. 2008. A unified architecture for natural language processing: Deep neural networks with multitask learning. In *Proceedings of the 25th international conference on Machine learning*, pages 160–167. ACM.

Scott C. Deerwester, Susan T Dumais, Thomas K. Landauer, George W. Furnas, and Richard A. Harshman. 1990. Indexing by latent semantic analysis. *JASIS*, 41(6):391–407.

William B Dolan and Chris Brockett. 2005. Automatically constructing a corpus of sentential paraphrases. In *Proc. of IWP*.

Edward Grefenstette and Mehrnoosh Sadrzadeh. 2011. Experimental support for a categorical compositional distributional model of meaning. In *EMNLP*, pages 1394–1404.

Edward Grefenstette, Georgiana Dinu, Yao-Zhong Zhang, Mehrnoosh Sadrzadeh, and Marco Baroni. 2013. Multi-step regression learning for compositional distributional semantics. In *Proceedings of IWCS*, pages 131–142, Potsdam, Germany.

Emiliano Guevara. 2010. A regression model of adjective-noun compositionality in distributional semantics. In *Proceedings of the 2010 Workshop on Geometrical Models of Natural Language Semantics*, pages 33–37.

Iris Hendrickx, Su Nam Kim, Zornitsa Kozareva, Preslav Nakov, Diarmuid Ó Séaghdha, Sebastian Padó, Marco Pennacchiotti, Lorenza Romano, and Stan Szpakowicz. 2009. Semeval-2010 task 8: Multi-way classification of semantic relations between pairs of nominals. In *Proceedings of the Workshop on Semantic Evaluations: Recent Achievements and Future Directions*, pages 94–99. Association for Computational Linguistics.

Annette Herskovits. 1985. Semantics and pragmatics of locative expressions*. *Cognitive Science*, 9(3):341–378.

Dimitri Kartsaklis, Mehrnoosh Sadrzadeh, and Stephen Pulman. 2012. A unified sentence space for categorical distributional-compositional semantics: Theory and experiments. In *In Proceedings of COLING: Posters*. Citeseer.

Walter Kintsch. 2001. Predication. *Cognitive Science*, 25(2):173–202.

Thomas K Landauer and Susan T Dumais. 1997. A solution to plato's problem: The latent semantic analysis theory of acquisition, induction, and representation of knowledge. *Psychological review*, 104(2):211.

Marco Marelli, Luisa Bentivogli, Marco Baroni, Raffaella Bernardi, Stefano Menini, and Roberto Zamparelli. 2014. Semeval-2014 task 1: Evaluation of compositional distributional semantic models on full sentences through semantic relatedness and textual entailment. *SemEval-2014*.

Tomas Mikolov, Kai Chen, Greg Corrado, and Jeffrey Dean. 2013. Efficient estimation of word representations in vector space. *arXiv preprint arXiv:1301.3781*.

Jeff Mitchell and Mirella Lapata. 2008. Vector-based models of semantic composition. In *ACL*, pages 236–244. Citeseer.

Jeff Mitchell and Mirella Lapata. 2010. Composition in distributional models of semantics. *Cognitive science*, 34(8):1388–1429.

Denis Paperno, Nghia The Pham, and Marco Baroni. 2014. A practical and linguistically-motivated approach to compositional distributional semantics. In *Proceedings of the 52nd Annual Meeting of the Association for Computational Linguistics (Volume 1: Long Papers)*, pages 90–99, Baltimore, Maryland, June.

Richard Socher, Eric H. Huang, Jeffrey Pennington, Andrew Y. Ng, and Christopher D. Manning. 2011. Dynamic Pooling and Unfolding Recursive Autoencoders for Paraphrase Detection. In *Advances in Neural Information Processing Systems 24*.

Richard Socher, Alex Perelygin, Jean Y Wu, Jason Chuang, Christopher D Manning, Andrew Y Ng, and Christopher Potts. 2013. Recursive deep models for semantic compositionality over a sentiment treebank. In *EMNLP*, pages 1631–1642. Citeseer.

V. Srikumar and D. Roth. 2013. Modeling semantic relations expressed by prepositions. In *Transactions of the Association for Computational Linguistics*, volume 1, pages 231–242.

Joseph Turian, Lev Ratinov, and Yoshua Bengio. 2010. Word representations: a simple and general method for semi-supervised learning. In *Proceedings of the 48th Annual Meeting of the Association for Computational Linguistics*, pages 384–394. Association for Computational Linguistics.

Peter D Turney, Patrick Pantel, et al. 2010. From frequency to meaning: Vector space models of semantics. *Journal of artificial intelligence research*, 37(1):141–188.

Peter D Turney. 2014. Semantic composition and decomposition: From recognition to generation. *arXiv preprint arXiv:1405.7908*.

Fabio Massimo Zanzotto, Ioannis Korkontzelos, Francesca Fallucchi, and Suresh Manandhar. 2010. Estimating linear models for compositional distributional semantics. In *Proceedings of the 23rd International Conference on Computational Linguistics*, pages 1263–1271.

Learning to predict script events from domain-specific text

Rachel Rudinger[1], **Vera Demberg**[3], **Ashutosh Modi**[3],
Benjamin Van Durme[1,2], **Manfred Pinkal**[3]
Center for Language and Speech Processing[1]
Human Language Technology Center of Excellence[2]
Johns Hopkins University, Baltimore, MD USA
MMCI Cluster of Excellence[3]
Saarland University, Saarbrücken, Germany
rudinger@jhu.edu, {vera,pinkal}@coli.uni-saarland.de,
amodi@mmci.uni-saarland.de, vandurme@cs.jhu.edu

Abstract

The automatic induction of scripts (Schank and Abelson, 1977) has been the focus of many recent works. In this paper, we employ a variety of these methods to learn Schank and Abelson's canonical *restaurant script*, using a novel dataset of restaurant narratives we have compiled from a website called "Dinners from Hell." Our models learn *narrative chains*, script-like structures that we evaluate with the "narrative cloze" task (Chambers and Jurafsky, 2008).

1 Introduction

A well-known theory from the intersection of psychology and artificial intelligence posits that humans organize certain kinds of general knowledge in the form of *scripts*, or common sequences of events (Schank and Abelson, 1977). Though many early AI systems employed hand-encoded scripts, more recent work has attempted to induce scripts with automatic and scalable techniques. In particular, several related techniques approach the problem of script induction as one of learning *narrative chains* from text corpora (Chambers and Jurafsky, 2008; Chambers and Jurafsky, 2009; Jans et al., 2012; Pichotta and Mooney, 2014). These statistical approaches have focused on open-domain script acquisition, in which a large number of scripts may be learned, but the acquisition of any particular set of scripts is not guaranteed. For many specialized applications, however, knowledge of a few relevant scripts may be more useful than knowledge of many irrelevant scripts. With this scenario in mind, we attempt to learn the famous "restaurant script" (Schank and Abelson, 1977) by applying the aforementioned narrative chain learning methods to a specialized corpus of dinner narratives we compile from the website "Dinners from Hell." Our results suggest that applying these techniques to a domain-specific dataset may be reasonable way to learn domain-specific scripts.

2 Background

Previous work in the automatic induction of scripts or script-like structures has taken a number of different approaches. Regneri et al. (2010) attempt to learn the structure of specific scripts by eliciting event sequence descriptions (ESDs) from humans to which they apply multiple sequence alignment (MSA) to yield one global structure per script. (Orr et al. (2014) learn similar structures in a probabilistic framework with Hidden Markov Models.) Although Regneri et al. (2010), like us, are concerned with learning pre-specified scripts, our approach is different in that we apply unsupervised techniques to scenario-specific collections of natural, pre-existing texts.

Note that while the applicability of our approach to script learning may appear limited to domains for which a corpus conveniently already exists, previous work demonstrates the feasibility of assembling such a corpus by automatically retrieving relevant documents from a larger collection. For example, Chambers and Jurafsky (2011) use information retrieval techniques to gather a small number of bombing-related documents from the Gigaword corpus, which they successfully use to learn a MUC-style (Sundheim, 1991) information extraction tem-

*Proceedings of the Fourth Joint Conference on Lexical and Computational Semantics (*SEM 2015)*, pages 205–210,
Denver, Colorado, June 4–5, 2015.

plate for bombing events.

Following the work of Church and Hanks (1990) in learning word associations via mutual information, and the DIRT system introduced by Lin and Pantel (2001), Chambers and Jurafsky (2008) propose a PMI-based system for learning script-like structures called *narrative chains*. Several follow-up papers introduce variations and improvements on this original model for learning narrative chains (Chambers and Jurafsky, 2009; Jans et al., 2012; Pichotta and Mooney, 2014). It is from this body of work that we borrow techniques to apply to the Dinners from Hell dataset.

As defined by Chambers and Jurafsky (2008), a narrative chain is "a partially ordered set of narrative events that share a common actor," where a *narrative event* is "a tuple of an event (most simply a verb) and its participants, represented as typed dependencies." To learn narrative chains from text, Chambers and Jurafsky extract chains of narrative events linked by a common coreferent within a document. For example, the sentence "John drove to the store where he bought some ice cream." would generate two narrative events corresponding to the protagonist John: (DRIVE, *nsubj*) followed by (BUY, *nsubj*). Over these extracted chains of narrative events, pointwise mutual information (PMI) is computed between all pairs of events. These PMI scores are then used to predict missing events from such chains, i.e. the *narrative cloze* evaluation.

Jans et al. (2012) expand on this approach, introducing an ordered PMI model, a bigram probability model, skip n-gram counting methods, coreference chain selection, and an alternative scoring metric (recall at 50). Their bigram probability model outperforms the original PMI model on the narrative cloze task under many conditions. Pichotta and Mooney (2014) introduce an extended notion of narrative event that includes information about subjects and objects. They also introduce a competitive "unigram model" as a baseline for the narrative cloze task.

To learn the restaurant script from our dataset, we implement the models of Chambers and Jurafsky (2008) and Jans et al. (2012), as well as the unigram baseline of Pichotta and Mooney (2014). To evaluate our success in learning the restaurant script, we perform a modified version of the narrative cloze task, predicting only verbs that we annotate as "restaurant script-relevant" and comparing the performance of each model. Note that these annotations are not used for training.

3 Methods

This section provides an overview of each of the different methods and parameter settings we employ to learn narrative chains from the Dinners from Hell corpus, starting with the original model (Chambers and Jurafsky, 2008) and extending to the modifications of Jans et al. (2012). As part of this work, we are releasing a program called NaChos, our integrated Python implementation of each of the methods for learning narrative chains described in this section.[1]

3.1 Counting methods for PMI

Formally, a narrative event, $e := (v, d)$, is a verb, v, paired with a typed dependency (De Marneffe et al., 2006), d, defining the role a "protagonist" (coreference mention) plays in an event (verb). The main computational component of learning narrative chains in Chambers and Jurafsky's model is to learn the pointwise mutual information for any pair of narrative events:

$$pmi(e_1, e_2) := \log \frac{C(e_1, e_2)}{C(e_1, *)C(*, e_2)} \qquad (1)$$

where $C(e_1, e_2)$ is the number of times that narrative events e_1 and e_2 "co-occur" and

$$C(e, *) := \sum_{e'} C(e, e') \qquad (2)$$

Chambers and Jurafsky define $C(e_1, e_2)$ as "the number of times the two events e_1 and e_2 had a coreferring entity filling the values of the dependencies d_1 and d_2." This is a symmetric value with respect to e_1 and e_2.

We implement the following counting variants:

Skip N-gram By default, $C(e_1, e_2)$ is incremented if e_1 and e_2 occur anywhere within the same chain of events derived from a single coreference chain (**skip-all**); we also implement an option to restrict the distance between e_1 and e_2 to 0 though 5 intervening events (**skip-0** through **skip-5**). (Jans et al., 2012)

[1] www.clsp.jhu.edu/people/rachel-rudinger

Coreference Chain Length The original model counts co-occurrences in **all** coreference chains; we include Jans et al. (2012)'s option to count over only the **longest** chains in each document, or to count only over chains of length 5 or greater (**long**).

Count Threshold Because PMI favors low-count events, we add an option to set $C(e_1, e_2)$ to zero for any e_1, e_2 for which $C(e_1, e_2)$ is below some threshold, T, up to 5.

3.2 Predictive Models for Narrative Cloze

In order to perform the narrative cloze task, we need a model for predicting the missing narrative event, e, from a chain of observed narrative events, $e_1 \ldots e_n$, at insertion point k. The original model, proposed by Chambers and Jurafsky (2008), predicts the event that maximizes **unordered pmi**,

$$\hat{e} = \arg\max_{e \in V} \sum_{i=1}^{n} pmi(e, e_i) \quad (3)$$

where V is the set of all observed events (the vocabulary) and $C(e_1, e_2)$ is symmetric. Two additional models are introduced by Jans et al. (2012) and we use them here, as well. First, the **ordered pmi** model,

$$\hat{e} = \arg\max_{e \in V} \sum_{i=1}^{k} pmi(e_i, e) + \sum_{i=k+1}^{n} pmi(e, e_i) \quad (4)$$

where $C(e_1, e_2)$ is asymmetric, i.e., $C(e_1, e_2)$ counts only cases in which e_1 occurs *before* e_2. Second, the **bigram probability** model:

$$\hat{e} = \arg\max_{e \in V} \prod_{i=1}^{k} p(e|e_i) \prod_{i=k+1}^{n} p(e_i|e) \quad (5)$$

where $p(e_2|e_1) = \frac{C(e_1,e_2)}{C(e_1,*)}$ and $C(e_1, e_2)$ is asymmetric.

Discounting For each model, we add an option for discounting the computed scores. In the case of the two PMI-based models, we use the discount score described in Pantel and Ravichandran (2004) and used by Chambers and Jurafsky (2008). For the bigram probability model, this PMI discount score would be inappropriate, so we instead use absolute discounting.

Document Threshold We include a document threshold parameter, D, that ensures that, in any narrative cloze test, any event e that was observed during training in fewer than D distinct documents will receive a worse score (i.e. be ranked behind) any event e' whose count meets the document threshold.

4 Dataset: Dinners From Hell

The source of our data for this experiment is a blog called "Dinners From Hell"[2] where readers submit stories about their terrible restaurant experiences. For an example story, see Figure 1. To process the raw data, we stripped all HTML and other non-story content from each file and processed the remaining text with the Stanford CoreNLP pipeline version 3.3.1 (Manning et al., 2014). Of the 237 stories obtained, we manually filtered out 94 stories that were "off-topic" (e.g., letters to the webmaster, dinners not at restaurants), leaving a total of 143 stories. The average story length is 352 words.

4.1 Annotation

For the purposes of evaluation only, we hired four undergraduates to annotate every non-copular verb in each story as either corresponding to an event "related to the experience of eating in a restaurant" (e.g., *ordered* a steak), "unrelated to the experience of eating in a restaurant" (e.g., *answered* the phone), or uncertain. We used the WebAnno platform for annotation (Yimam et al., 2013).

A total of 8,202 verb (tokens) were annotated, each by three annotators. 70.3% of verbs annotated achieved 3-way agreement; 99.4% had at least 2-way agreement. After merging the annotations (simple majority vote), 30.7% of verbs were labeled as restaurant-script-related, 68.6% were labeled as restaurant-script-unrelated, and the remaining 0.7% as uncertain.

Corresponding to the 8,202 annotated verb tokens, there are 1,481 narrative events at the type level. 580 of these narrative event types were annotated as script-relevant in at least one token instance.

[2] www.dinnersfromhell.com

"A long time ago when I was still in college, my family decided to take me out for pizza on my birthday. We decided to try the new location for a favorite pizza chain of ours. It was all adults and there were about 8 of us, so we **ordered** 3 large pizzas. We **got** to chatting and soon realized that the pizzas should've been ready quite a bit ago, so we **called** the waitress over and she went to check on our pizzas. She did not come back. We **waited** about another 10 minutes, then called over another waitress, who went to check on our pizzas and waitress. It now been over an hour. About 10 minutes later, my Dad goes up to the check-out and asks the girl there to send the manager to our table. A few minutes later the manager comes out. He **explains** to us that our pizzas got stuck in the oven and burned. They were out of large pizza dough bread, so they were making us 6 medium pizzas for the price of 3 large pizzas. We had so many [pizzas] on our table we barely had [room] to eat! Luckily my family is pretty easy going so we just **laughed** about the whole thing. We did **tell** the manager that it would have been nice if someone, anyone, had **said** something earlier to us, instead of just disappearing, and he agreed. He even said it was his responsibility, but that he had been busy trying to fix what caused the pizzas to jam up in the oven. He went so far as to **give** us 1/2 off our bill, which was really nice. It was definitely a memorable birthday!"

Figure 1: Example story from Dinners from Hell corpus. Bold words indicate events in the "we" coreference chain (the longest chain). Boxed words (blue) indicate best narrative chain of length three (see Section 5.2); underlined words (orange) are corresponding subjects and bracketed words (green) are corresponding objects.

MODEL	AVGRNK	MRR	R@50
unigram model (baseline)	298.13	0.062	0.50
1. unordered pmi; avgrnk	**276.88**	**0.063**	0.36
2. unordered pmi; mrr	376.25	0.058	0.33
3. unordered pmi; R@50	400.36	0.050	0.50
4. ordered pmi; avgrnk	**284.68**	0.061	0.32
5. ordered pmi; mrr	381.44	0.054	0.25
6. ordered pmi; R@50	401.69	0.047	0.50
7. bigram; avgrnk	**281.07**	**0.077**	0.38
8. bigram; mrr	378.06	**0.066**	0.30
9. bigram; R@50	**271.78**	**0.084**	0.43
10. bigram disc; avgrnk	**283.01**	**0.077**	0.38
11. bigram disc; mrr	378.10	**0.067**	0.30
12. bigram disc; R@50	**271.62**	**0.089**	0.43

Figure 2: Narrative cloze evaluation. Shaded blue cells indicate which scoring metric that row's parameter settings have been optimized to. Bold numbers indicate a result that beats the baseline. Row 12 representes the best model performance overall.

ROW	SKIP	T	D	COREF	PMI DISC	ABS DISC
1	0	1	3	all	yes	N/A
2	1	3	5	long	no	N/A
3	1	5	4	longest	yes	N/A
4	0	1	3	all	yes	N/A
5	3	5	5	long	no	N/A
6	0	3	4	longest	yes	N/A
7	all	1	3	all	N/A	no
8	3	5	5	long	N/A	no
9	all	1	5	all	N/A	no
10	all	1	3	all	N/A	yes
11	3	5	5	long	N/A	yes
12	all	1	5	all	N/A	yes

Figure 3: Parameter settings corresponding to each model in Fig 2.

5 Evaluation

5.1 Narrative Cloze

We evaluate the various models on the narrative cloze task. What is different about our version of the narrative cloze task here is that we limit the cloze tests to only "interesting" events, i.e., those that have been identified as relevant to the restaurant script by our annotators (see Section 4.1).

Because our dataset is small (143 documents), we perform leave-one-out testing at the document level, training on 133 folds total. (Ten documents are excluded for a development set.) For each fold of training, we extract all of the narrative chains (mapped directly from coreference chains) in the held out test document. For each test chain, we generate one narrative cloze test per "script-relevant" event in that chain. For example, if a chain contains ten events, three of which are "script-relevant," then three cloze tests will be generated, each containing nine "observed" events. Chains with fewer than two events are excluded. In this way, we generate a total of 2,273 cloze tests.

Scoring We employ three different scoring metrics: average rank (Chambers and Jurafsky, 2008), mean reciprocal rank, and recall at 50 (Jans et al., 2012).

Baseline The baseline we use for the narrative cloze task is to rank events by frequency. This is the "unigram model" employed by Pichotta and Mooney (2014), a competitive baseline on this task.

For each model and scoring metric, we perform a complete grid search over all possible parameter settings to find the best-scoring combination on a cloze tests from a set-aside development set of ten documents. The parameter space is defined as the Cartesian product of each of the following possible parameter values: skip-n (all,0-5), coreference chain length (all, long, longest), count threshold (T=1-5), document threshold (D=1-5), and discounting (yes/no). Bigram probability with and without discounting are treated as two separate models.

Figure 2 reports the results of the narrative cloze evalutation. Each of the four models (unordered pmi, ordered pmi, bigram, and bigram with discounting) outperform the baseline on the average rank metric when the parameters are optimized for that metric. Both bigram models beat the baseline on mean reciprocal rank not only for MRR-optimized parameter settings, but for the average-rank- and recall-at-50-optimized settings. None of the parameter settings are able to ouperform the baseline on recall at 50, though both PMI models tie the baseline. Overall, the model that performs the best is the bigram probability model with discounting (row 12 of Figure 2) which has the following parameter settings: skip-all, coref-all, T=1, and D=5.

The fact that several model settings outperform an informed baseline on average rank and mean reciprocal rank indicates that these methods may in general be applicable to smaller, domain specific corpora. Furthermore, it is apparent from the results that the bigram probability models perform better overall than PMI-based models, a finding also reported in Jans et al. (2012). This replication is futher evidence that these methods do in fact transfer.

5.2 Qualitative Example

To get a qualitative sense of the narrative events these models are learning to associate from this data, we use the conditional probabilities learned in the bigram model (Fig 2, row 12) to select the highest probability narrative chain of length three out of the 12 possible events in the "we" coreference chain in Figure 1 (bolded). The three events selected are boxed and highlighted in blue. The bigram model selects the "deciding" event (selecting restaurant) and the "having" event (having pizza), both reasonable components of the restaurant script. The third event selected is "having room," which is not part of the restaurant script. This mistake illustrates a weakness of the narrative chains model; without considering the verb's object, the model is unable to distinguish "have pizza" from "have room." Incorporating object information in future experiments, as in Pichotta and Mooney (2014), might resolve this issue, although it could introduce sparsity problems.

6 Conclusion

In this work, we describe the collection and annotation of a corpus of natural descriptions of restaurant visits from the website "Dinners from Hell." We use this dataset in an attempt to learn the restaurant script, using a variety of related methods for learning narrative chains and evaluating on the narrative cloze task. Our results suggest that it may be possible in general to use these methods on domain-specific corpora in order to learn particular scripts from a pre-specified domain, although further experiments in other domains would help bolster this conclusion. In principle, a domain-specific corpus need not come from a website like Dinners from Hell; it could instead be sub-sampled from a larger corpus, retrieved from the web, or directly elicited. Our domain-specific approach to script learning is potentially useful for specialized NLP applications that require knowledge of only a particular set of scripts.

One feature of the Dinners from Hell corpus that bears further inspection in future work is the fact that its stories contain many violations of the restaurant script. A question to investigate is whether these violations impact how the restaurant script is learned. Other avenues for future work include incorporating object information into event representations and applying domain adaptation techniques in order to leverage larger general-domain corpora.

Acknowledgments

This research was sponsored in part by the NSF under grant 0530118 (PIRE) and with additional support from the Allen Institute for Artificial Intelligence (AI2). The authors would also like to thank Michaela Regneri, Annemarie Friedrich, Stefan Thater, Alexis Palmer, Andrea Horbach, Diana Steffen, Asad Sayeed, and Frank Ferraro for their insightful contributions.

References

Nathanael Chambers and Dan Jurafsky. 2008. Unsupervised learning of narrative event chains. In *Proceedings of ACL-08: HLT*, pages 789–797, Columbus, Ohio. Association for Computational Linguistics.

Nathanael Chambers and Dan Jurafsky. 2009. Unsupervised learning of narrative schemas and their participants. In *Proceedings of the Joint Conference of the 47th Annual Meeting of the ACL and the 4th International Joint Conference on Natural Language Processing of the AFNLP*, pages 602–610, Suntec, Singapore. Association for Computational Linguistics.

Nathanael Chambers and Dan Jurafsky. 2011. Template-based information extraction without the templates. In *Proceedings of the 49th Annual Meeting of the Association for Computational Linguistics: Human Language Technologies*, pages 976–986, Portland, Oregon, USA. Association for Computational Linguistics.

Kenneth Ward Church and Patrick Hanks. 1990. Word association norms, mutual information, and lexicography. *Computational linguistics*, 16(1):22–29.

Marie-Catherine De Marneffe, Bill MacCartney, Christopher D Manning, et al. 2006. Generating typed dependency parses from phrase structure parses. In *Proceedings of LREC*, volume 6, pages 449–454.

Bram Jans, Steven Bethard, Ivan Vulić, and Marie-Francine Moens. 2012. Skip n-grams and ranking functions for predicting script events. In *Proceedings of the 13th Conference of the European Chapter of the Association for Computational Linguistics*, pages 336–344, Avignon, France. Association for Computational Linguistics.

Dekang Lin and Patrick Pantel. 2001. Dirt - discovery of inference rules from text. In *Proceedings of the seventh ACM SIGKDD international conference on Knowledge discovery and data mining*, pages 323–328. ACM.

Christopher D. Manning, Mihai Surdeanu, John Bauer, Jenny Finkel, Steven J. Bethard, and David McClosky. 2014. The Stanford CoreNLP natural language processing toolkit. In *Proceedings of 52nd Annual Meeting of the Association for Computational Linguistics: System Demonstrations*, pages 55–60.

J Walker Orr, Prasad Tadepalli, Janardhan Rao Doppa, Xiaoli Fern, and Thomas G Dietterich. 2014. Learning scripts as hidden markov models. In *Twenty-Eighth AAAI Conference on Artificial Intelligence*.

Patrick Pantel and Deepak Ravichandran. 2004. Automatically labeling semantic classes. In Daniel Marcu Susan Dumais and Salim Roukos, editors, *HLT-NAACL 2004: Main Proceedings*, pages 321–328, Boston, Massachusetts, USA. Association for Computational Linguistics.

Karl Pichotta and Raymond Mooney. 2014. Statistical script learning with multi-argument events. In *Proceedings of the 14th Conference of the European Chapter of the Association for Computational Linguistics*, pages 220–229, Gothenburg, Sweden. Association for Computational Linguistics.

Michaela Regneri, Alexander Koller, and Manfred Pinkal. 2010. Learning script knowledge with web experiments. In *Proceedings of the 48th Annual Meeting of the Association for Computational Linguistics*, pages 979–988, Uppsala, Sweden. Association for Computational Linguistics.

Roger Schank and Robert Abelson. 1977. *Scripts, plans, goals and understanding: An inquiry into human knowledge structures*. Lawrence Erlbaum Associates, Hillsdale, NJ.

Beth M. Sundheim. 1991. Third message understanding evaluation and conference (muc-3): Phase 1 status report. In *Proceedings of the Message Understanding Conference*.

Seid Muhie Yimam, Iryna Gurevych, Richard Eckart de Castilho, and Chris Biemann. 2013. Webanno: A flexible, web-based and visually supported system for distributed annotations. In *Proceedings of the 51st Annual Meeting of the Association for Computational Linguistics: System Demonstrations*, pages 1–6, Sofia, Bulgaria. Association for Computational Linguistics.

Combining Open Source Annotators for Entity Linking through Weighted Voting

Pablo Ruiz and **Thierry Poibeau**
LATTICE Lab
CNRS, École Normale Supérieure, U Paris 3 Sorbonne Nouvelle
1, rue Maurice Arnoux, 92120 Montrouge, France
{pablo.ruiz.fabo,thierry.poibeau}@ens.fr

Abstract

An English entity linking (EL) workflow is presented, which combines the annotations of five public open source EL services. The annotations are combined through a weighted voting scheme inspired by the ROVER method, which had not been previously tested on EL outputs. The combined results improved over each individual system's results, as evaluated on four different golden sets.

1 Introduction

The Entity Linking (EL) literature has shown that the quality of EL systems' results varies widely depending on characteristic of the corpora they are applied to, or on the types of entities we need to link (Cornolti et al., 2013, Usbeck et al., 2015). For instance, a system that links to a wide set of entity types can be less accurate at basic types like *Person, Location, Organization* than systems specializing in those basic types.

A way to make up for the uneven performance of entity linking methods across corpora would be mixing different annotators' results, so that the annotators' strengths complement each other. This paper presents a method to combine the outputs of five open source entity linking systems, in order to obtain improved results. The method involves a weighted voting scheme that had not been previously applied to EL, and improves annotation results across four test-corpora.

The structure of the paper is as follows: Section 2 presents related work. Section 3 describes the combined entity linking system. Section 4 provides an evaluation of the system's results and a discussion.

2 Related Work

General surveys on EL can be found in (Cornolti et al., 2013) and (Rao et al., 2013). Besides the EL literature, work on combining NLP annotators is particularly relevant for the present article.

The goal of combining different NLP systems is obtaining combined results that are better than the results of each individual system. Fiscus (1997) created the ROVER method, with weighted voting to improve speech recognition outputs. ROVER was found to improve parsing results by De la Clergerie et al. (2008). In Named Entity Recognition (NER), Rizzo et al. (2014) improved results combining systems via different machine learning algorithms.

In entity linking, the potential benefits of combining annotations have been explored before. Rizzo and Troncy (2012) describe the NERD system, which combines entity linkers. However, we are not aware of a system that, like ours, makes an automatic choice among the systems' conflicting annotations, based on an estimate of each annotation's quality. Our approach to choose among conflicting annotations is inspired by the ROVER method, which had not been previously attempted for EL to our knowledge. A further difference in our system is that the set of linkers we combine is public and open-source.

*Proceedings of the Fourth Joint Conference on Lexical and Computational Semantics (*SEM 2015)*, pages 211–215,
Denver, Colorado, June 4–5, 2015.

3 Combining Annotators

Our workflow performs English EL to Wikipedia, combining the outputs of the following EL systems: Tagme 2[1] (Ferragina and Scaiella, 2010), DBpedia Spotlight[2] (Mendes et al. 2011), Wikipedia Miner[3] (Milne and Witten, 2008a), AIDA[4] (Hoffart et al., 2011) and Babelfy[5] (Moro et al. 2014). A description of the different systems can be found in (Usbeck et al., 2015). The systems rely on a variety on algorithms and it can be expected that their results will complement each other.

3.1 Obtaining Individual Annotator Outputs

First of all, a client requests the annotations for a text from each linker's web-service, using the services' default settings except for the confidence threshold,[6] which is configured in our workflow.

We obtained optimal thresholds for each system (Column t in Tables 1 and 2) with the BAT Framework[7] (Cornolti et al., 2013). The BAT Framework allows calling several entity linking tools and compares their results using different annotation confidence thresholds, with a view to finding the thresholds that yield best results according to several evaluation measures.

Annotations are filtered out if their confidence is below the thresholds obtained in the way just described. The remaining annotations proceed to the annotation-voting step.

3.2 Pre-ranking Annotators

Our annotation voting exploits annotators' precision on an annotated reference set in order to weight the annotations produced by each annotator (details in 3.3 below). It is not viable to create a reference set for each new corpus that we need to perform entity linking on. To help overcome this issue, we adopt the following approach: We have ranked the annotators for precision on two reference sets: AIDA/CONLL Test B (Hoffart et al., 2011), and IITB (Kulkarni et al., 2009). The IITB dataset contains annotations for category *Others*, i.e. entities that are not a person, organization or location, whereas AIDA/CONLL B does not contain such annotations. The proportion of annotations in a corpus that fall into the *Others* category is a strong predictor of annotators' performance on that corpus, according to a study on how different dataset features correlate with annotators' results, available on the GERBIL platform[8] (Usbeck et al., 2015). Taking this into account, in order to annotate a new corpus, if annotations for the *Others* category are needed for that new corpus, the annotator ranking for the IITB corpus will be used in order to weight the new corpus' annotations, since IITB is the only one among our two reference sets that contains annotations for *Others*, and an annotator performing well on IITB is likely to perform well when annotations for *Others* are needed. If, conversely, annotations for the *Others* category are not needed, the annotator ranking for the AIDA/CONLL B reference corpus is used in order to weight the new corpus' annotations.

3.3 Annotation Voting Scheme

The voting scheme is in Figure 1. Each annotation is formalized as a pairing between a mention m (a span of characters in the text) and a Wikipedia entity e. For each annotation $<m, e>$, Ω_m is the set of annotations whose mentions overlap[9] with m. The set Ω_m is divided into disjoint subsets, each of which contains annotations linking to a different entity. Each subset L is voted by $vote(L)$: For each annotation o in L, N is the number of annotators we combine (i.e. 5), $r_{o,anr}$, is the rank of annotator anr, which produced annotation o, and P_{anr} is anr's precision on the ranking reference corpus (see 3.2 above). Finally, parameter α influences the distance between the annotations' votes based on their annotators' rank, and was set at 1.75 based on the best results on both ranking reference corpora.

[1] http://tagme.di.unipi.it/tagme_help.html

[2] https://github.com/dbpedia-spotlight/dbpedia-spotlight/wiki

[3] http://wikipedia-miner.cms.waikato.ac.nz/

[4] https://github.com/yago-naga/aida

[5] http://babelfy.org/download.jsp

[6] The public deployments were used, but for AIDA, which was set up locally: Source v2.1.1, Data 2010-08-17v7. In AIDA, the tech=GRAPH option was used (non-default, but recommended by AIDA's authors for benchmarking).

[7] https://github.com/marcocor/bat-framework

[8] See *Annotator - Dataset feature correlations* at http://gerbil.aksw.org/gerbil/overview

[9] Assume two mentions (p1, e1) and (p2, e2), where p1 and p2 are the mentions' first character indices, and e1 and e2 are the mentions' last character indices. The mentions overlap iff $((p1 = p2) \wedge (e1 = e2)) \vee ((p1 = p2) \wedge (e1 < e2)) \vee ((p1 = p2) \wedge (e2 < e1)) \vee ((e1 = e2) \wedge (p1 < p2)) \vee ((e1 = e2) \wedge (p2 < p1)) \vee ((p1 < p2) \wedge (p2 < e1)) \vee ((p2 < p1) \wedge (p1 < e2))$.

for each set Ω_m of overlapping annotations:

for $L \in \Omega_m$:

$$vote(L) = \frac{\sum_{o \in L} \left(N - \left(r_{o,anr} - \alpha\right)\right) \cdot P_{o,anr}}{N}$$

if $\max_{L \in \Omega_m} (vote(L)) > P_{max}$: select $\operatorname{argmax}_{L \in \Omega_m}(vote(L))$

Figure 1: Entity voting scheme.

The entity for the subset L which obtains the highest vote among Ω_m's subsets is selected if its vote is higher than P_{max}, i.e. the maximum precision for all annotators on the ranking corpus.[10] Once an entity has been selected for a set of overlapping mentions, the mention itself needs to be selected. Best results were obtained when the most common mention in the set was selected. In case of ties, the longest mention among the most common ones was selected (e.g. if two mentions occur twice each in the set, select the longer one).

4 Evaluation and Results

4.1 Evaluation Method

Datasets: The workflow was tested on four golden sets. First, the two datasets that had also been used as reference sets in order to obtain the weights to vote annotations with (see Section 3.2). These two datasets were AIDA/CONLL B (231 documents with 4485 annotations; 1039 characters avg., news and sports topics) and IITB (103 documents with 11245 annotations; 3879 characters avg., topics from news, science and others). In order to test whether the annotator weights obtained from those two corpora can improve results when applied to annotator combination on other corpora, we tested on two additional datasets: MSNBC (Cucerzan, 2007), with 20 documents and 658 annotations (3316 characters avg., news topics) and AQUAINT (Milne and Witten, 2008b), with 50 documents and 727 annotations (1415 characters avg., news topics).

The AQUAINT dataset contains annotations for common noun entities (besides Person, Location, Organization). For this reason, according to the procedure described in 3.2 above, its annotations were weighted according to annotators' ranking on the IITB corpus, which also contains common-noun annotations. The MSNBC dataset does not contain common-noun annotations, so the annotator ranking for the AIDA/CONLL test-set was used in order to combine annotations in MSNBC.

Measures: The EL literature has stressed the importance of evaluating systems on more than one measure. We tested the workflow on strong annotation match (SAM) and entity match (ENT) (Cornolti et al., 2013). SAM requires an annotation's position to exactly match the reference, besides requiring the entity annotated to match the reference entity. ENT ignores positions and only evaluates whether the entity proposed by the system matches the reference.

Mapping files: Evaluating EL to Wikipedia requires making sure that we consider the same set of target entities for each EL system, since the versions of Wikipedia deployed within each system may differ. A mapping between current Wikipedia titles for the golden set annotations and non-canonical forms for these titles was created (including e.g. older titles redirecting to the new ones), and applied to golden and system sets before evaluation.[11]

Tools: Evaluation was carried out with the *neleval* tool[12] from the TAC-KBP Entity Discovery and Linking task (Ji et al., 2014). The tool implements several EL-relevant metrics, accepting a common delimited format for golden sets and results across corpora. The tool's significance testing function via randomized permutation/bootstrap methods was also applied to our results.

4.2 Results and Discussion

Results are provided in Table 1 (SAM measure) and Table 2 (ENT measure). Note that, to promote transparency, individual system annotations, combined results, reference annotations and mapping files are available on a website.[13] Each table shows micro-averaged precision, recall and F1 on the four golden sets, for each individual system, plus results for the combined workflow in the last row. The optimal confidence thresholds for each annotator are also indicated where applicable.

[10] See Table 1 and Table 2 below for P_{max} values in the ranking reference corpora: P_{max} is the maximum (excluding row *Combined*) in columns AIDA/CONLL B and IITB.

[11] The mapping was created based on *fetch_map* from the conll03_nel_eval tool by Hachey et al. (2013), https://github.com/wikilinks/conll03_nel_eval

[12] https://github.com/wikilinks/neleval/wiki

[13] https://sites.google.com/site/entitylinking1/

Corpus	AIDA/CONLL B				IITB				MSNBC				AQUAINT			
System	*t*	P	R	F1	*t*	P	R	F1	*t*	P	R	F1	*t*	P	R	F1
Tagme	0.219	54.8	53.9	54.4	0.086	41.1	42.6	41.8	0.188	44.7	42.4	*43.5*	0.188	39.9	46.5	43.0
Spotlight	0.086	28.1	38.8	32.6	0.016	41.0	48.2	44.3	0.063	21.8	28.1	24.6	0.055	15.6	45.3	23.2
W Miner	0.57	45.3	50.3	47.7	0.25	55.2	44.4	*49.2*	0.664	42.3	38.2	40.2	0.57	34.8	57.6	*43.4*
AIDA	0.0	76.7	46.7	*58.1*	0.0	50.2	5.6	10.0	0.0	63.6	23.8	34.7	0.0	50.3	27.7	35.7
Babelfy	dna	34.7	34.0	34.3	dna	46.8	14.9	22.7	dna	31.8	28.8	31.1	dna	22.6	31.5	26.3
Combined	dna	64.8	61.7	***61.9**	dna	59.3	44.7	***50.0**	dna	54.3	43.4	***48.2**	dna	34.1	64.1	**44.5**

Table 1: **Strong annotation match (SAM).** Optimal confidence thresholds (*t*), Micro-averaged Precision, Recall, F1 for each annotator and combined system. Babelfy and the combined system use no confidence thresholds (dna).

Corpus	AIDA/CONLL B				IITB				MSNBC				AQUAINT			
System	*t*	P	R	F1	*T*	P	R	F1	*t*	P	R	F1	*t*	P	R	F1
Tagme	0.234	58.2	67.9	62.7	0.102	47.6	45.7	46.7	0.328	66.8	49.9	57.1	0.198	63.8	55.4	59.3
Spotlight	0.094	30.8	40.1	34.8	0.008	36.6	51.8	42.9	0.063	21.6	27.5	24.2	0.055	26.2	49.8	34.3
W Miner	0.477	46.9	57.3	51.6	0.195	61.3	43.3	*50.6*	0.664	50.1	52.8	51.4	0.523	59.9	62.5	*61.1*
AIDA	0.0	79.7	79.7	***79.7**	0.0	61.4	11.72	19.7	0.0	74.6	56.3	*64.2*	0.0	67.8	37.3	48.1
Babelfy	dna	35.6	37.9	36.7	dna	48.4	16.3	24.4	dna	36.5	37.5	37.0	dna	39.1	37.8	38.3
Combined	dna	65.0	78.5	*71.1*	dna	60.7	44.6	***51.4**	dna	66.7	62.3	**64.4**	dna	58.4	67.3	***62.5**

Table 2: **Entity match (ENT).** Optimal confidence thresholds (*t*), Micro-averaged Precision, Recall, F1 in for each annotator and combined system. Babelfy and the combined system use no confidence thresholds (dna).

The annotator rankings and weights with which annotations were weighted in our voting scheme (Figure 1) can be read off the *P* column for the ranking reference corpora (AIDA/CONLL or IITB). For instance, results for MSNBC were combined using the ranking from AIDA/CONLL. In terms of Figure 1, this means that MSBC annotations (for the SAM measure) were weighted with the following values, in format (Annotator, Rank, Weight): (AIDA, 0, 0.767), (Tagme, 1, 0.548), (Wikipedia Miner, 2, 0.453), (Babelfy, 3, 0.347), (Spotlight, 4, 0.281). The P_{max} value that each annotation's vote is compared to in MSNBC is 0.767.

In the tables, the best F1 score in each corpus is marked in bold, and the second-best F1 is in italics. The combined workflow obtains the best score in all cases, except ENT scores on AIDA/CONLL B. For the SAM measure, the improvements range between 0.8 points and 4.7 points of F1. For the ENT measure, improvements range between 0.2 and 1.4 points of F1. The differences are statistically significant in the majority of cases (scores with a star). Significance ($p < 0.05$) was assessed with the random permutation method in the *neleval* tool[12].

The combined workflow was able to improve over the best individual system regardless of which this system was: Tagme, Wikipedia Miner or AIDA. In some cases, the improvements over the best individual system's F1 take place because of markedly increased recall in the combined system compared to the best individual system's recall, without a major decrease in precision in the combined system (see AQUAINT results for ENT). The opposite pattern of improvement is also attested: In the MSNBC results for SAM, it is the increased precision of the combined workflow that makes its F1 improve over the best individual system's F1.

Regarding the significant drop in F1 in the combined system vs. the best individual system (AIDA) in the ENT results for the AIDA/CONLL B corpus, note that, in this case, the difference between AIDA's individual results and the results for the second-best individual system was much higher (17.2 points of F1) than anywhere else in the rest of tests performed. When such a large difference exists between the best individual system and the rest, an alternative type of voting may be needed in order to improve results over the best individual system.

5 Conclusion and Future Work

A workflow that combines the outputs of public open source entity linking (EL) systems via weighted voting was presented. The simple voting scheme generally improved F1 scores over the best individual system's F1, as assessed by the strong annotation match and entity match measures. Besides some enhancements to the voting scheme, interesting future work could be comparing this simple scheme's results with a more complex combination method, e.g. involving supervised learning based on available corpora annotated for entity linking (with mention–entity pairings).

Acknowledgements

Pablo Ruiz was supported through a PhD scholarship from Région Île de France.

References

Marco Cornolti, Paolo Ferragina, and Massimiliano Ciaramita. (2013). A framework for benchmarking entity-annotation systems. In *Proc. of WWW*, 249–260.

Silviu Cucerzan. (2007). Large-scale named entity disambiguation based on Wikipedia data. In *Proc. EMNLP and CNLL*, 708–716.

Éric V. De La Clergerie, Olivier Hamon, Djamel Mostefa, Christelle Ayache, Patrick Paroubek, and Anne Vilnat. (2008). Passage: from French parser evaluation to large sized treebank. In *Proc. of LREC 2008*, 3570–3576.

Paolo Ferragina and Ugo Scaiella. (2010). Tagme: on-the-fly annotation of short text fragments (by wikipedia entities). In *Proc. of CIKM'10*, 1625–1628.

Jonathan G. Fiscus. (1997). A post-processing system to yield reduced word error rates: Recognizer output voting error reduction (ROVER). In *Proc. of the IEEE Workshop on Automatic Speech Recognition and Understanding, 1997*, 347–354.

Ben Hachey, Joel Nothman, and Will Radford. (2014). Cheap and easy entity evaluation. In *Proc. ACL*, 464–469.

Johannes Hoffart, Mohamed Amir Yosef, Ilaria Bordino, Hagen Fürstenau, Manfred Pinkal, Marc Spaniol, Bilyana Taneva, Stefan Thater, and Gerhard Weikum. (2011). Robust disambiguation of named entities in text. In *Proc. of EMNLP*, 782–792.

Heng Ji, Joel Nothman and Ben Hachey. (2014). Overview of TAC-KBP2014 Entity Discovery and Linking Tasks. In *Proc. Text Analysis Conference*.

Sayali Kulkarni, Amit Singh, Ganesh Ramakrishnan, and Soumen Chakrabarti. (2009). Collective annotation of Wikipedia entities in web text. In *Proc. ACM SIGKDD*, 457–466.

Pablo N. Mendes, Max Jakob, Andrés García-Silva, and Christian Bizer. (2011). DBpedia spotlight: shedding light on the web of documents. In *Proc. of the 7th Int. Conf. on Semantic Systems, I-SEMANTICS'11*, 1–8.

David Milne and Ian H. Witten. (2008a). An effective, low-cost measure of semantic relatedness obtained from Wikipedia links. In *Proc. of AAAI Workshop on Wikipedia and Artificial Intelligence: an Evolving Synergy,* 25–30.

David Milne and Ian H. Witten. (2008b). Learning to link with Wikipedia. In *Proc. CIKM*, 509–518.

Andrea Moro, Alessandro Raganato, and Roberto Navigli. (2014). Entity Linking meets Word Sense Disambiguation: A Unified Approach. *Transactions of the ACL*, 2, 231–244.

Delip Rao, Paul McNamee, and Mark Dredze. (2013). Entity linking: Finding extracted entities in a knowledge base. In *Multi-source, Multilingual Information Extraction and Summarization*, 93–115. Springer.

Giuseppe Rizzo and Raphaël Troncy. (2012). NERD: a framework for unifying named entity recognition and disambiguation extraction tools. In *Proc. of the Demonstrations at EACL'12*, 73–76.

Giuseppe Rizzo, Marieke van Erp, and Raphaël Troncy. (2014). Benchmarking the Extraction and Disambiguation of Named Entities on the Semantic Web. In *Proc. of LREC 2014*, 4593–4600.

Ricardo Usbeck, Michael Röder, Axel-Cyrille Ngonga, Ciro Baron, Andrea Both, Martin Brümmer, Diego Ceccarelli, Marco Cornolti, Didier Cherix, Bernd Eickmann, Paolo Ferragina, Christiane Lemke, Andrea Moro, Roberto Navigli, Francesco Piccino, Giuseppe Rizzo, Harald Sack, René Speck, Raphaël Troncy, Jörg Waitelonis, and Lars Wesemann. (2015). GERBIL–General Entity Annotator Benchmarking Framework. In *Proc. of WWW*.

Automatic Generation of a Lexical Resource to support Semantic Role Labeling in Portuguese

Magali Sanches Duran
Center for Computational Linguistics (NILC)
São Paulo University (USP)
São Carlos-SP, Brazil
magali.duran@uol.com.br

Sandra Aluísio
Center for Computational Linguistics (NILC)
São Paulo University (USP)
São Carlos-SP, Brazil
sandra@icmc.usp.br

Abstract

This paper reports an approach to automatically generate a lexical resource to support incremental semantic role labeling annotation in Portuguese. The data come from the corpus Propbank-Br (Propbank of Brazilian Portuguese) and from the lexical resource of English Propbank, as both share the same structure. In order to enable the strategy, we added extra annotation to Propbank-Br. This approach is part of a previous decision to invert the process of implementing a Propbank project, by first annotating a core corpus and only then generating a lexical resource to enable further annotation tasks. The reasoning behind such inversion is to explore the task empirically before distributing the annotation task and to provide simultaneously: 1) a first training corpus for SRL in Brazilian Portuguese and 2) annotated examples to compose a lexical resource to support SRL. The main contribution of this paper is to point out to what extent linguistic effort may be reduced, thereby speeding up the construction of a lexical resource to support SRL for less resourced languages. The corpus Propbank-Br, with the extra annotation described herein, is publicly available.

1 Introduction

The task of semantic role labeling (SRL) consists of identifying a predicate (a verb or a predicate noun) and its arguments, assigning to each argument the semantic roles it play in the argumental structure (Palmer et al. 2010). For example, in the sentence *"Parents complain to education department about schools constantly switching uniforms",* there are two predicates: "complain" and "switching". The argumental structure of "complain" is: "Parents" (agent), "to the education department" (recipient), "about schools constantly switching uniforms" (theme). The argumental structure of "switching" is: "schools" (agent); "constantly" (time/frequency); "uniforms" (theme).

There is no consensus regarding an ideal set of semantic role labels and, for this reason, the first difficult decision in a project of SRL is to choose which set to adopt. No matter which set is used, it is not always easy to decide which label to assign to each argument during the annotation task. In order to facilitate such decision, some projects of SRL developed lexical resources that predict the set of semantic roles required by each predicate. Some of such resources define semantic roles for verb classes, as Verbnet (Kipper et al. 2006); others for semantic frames, as Framenet (Baker et al. 1998); others define semantic roles for verb senses, as Propbank (Palmer et al. 2005) or for predicate nouns, as Nombank (Meyers et al, 2004).

The more detailed and clear is the lexical resource, the easier the decision about which role label to assign during a manual annotation task. This is very important, because when we ease SRL annotation, we increase the likelihood of obtaining a high inter-annotator agreement and, consequently, the likelihood of obtaining a good precision for machine learning classifiers for the task.

*Proceedings of the Fourth Joint Conference on Lexical and Computational Semantics (*SEM 2015)*, pages 216–221,
Denver, Colorado, June 4–5, 2015.

Among the lexical resources available for SRL in English, we consider that of Propbank[1] the best one for supporting a distributed task of SRL annotation. From hereafter, we will refer to such lexical resource simply as Propbank, regardless the fact that Propbank encompass both the lexical resource and the annotated corpus.

Propbank does not require any linguistic expertise from the annotators and, instead of using role labels as "agent" and "patient", it uses a small set of numbered arguments, like Arg0 (for agents, causers or experiencers) and Arg1 (for patients and themes), which are described differently for each verb sense. For example, the verb sense "give.01" predicts an Arg0: "giver", an Arg1: "thing given" and an Arg2: "entity given to". This kind of description renders the roles very clear for annotators, regardless their background on semantic role labels.

Propbank has 5649[2] frame files, which are files containing (a) simple and complex predicates associated to a given verb; (b) a coarse distinction of the verb senses; (c) the set of semantic roles of each sense of a verb (rolesets) and (d) several annotated examples to show how the semantic roles may occur in real texts.

In practice, the annotator consults this kind of lexical resource while performing the annotation task. In the frame file of the verb being annotated, he looks for the sense that best suits the instance of annotation in question. Once identified the verb sense, the annotator needs to identify the constituents that play the semantic roles predicted for that verb sense, assigning them the respective role labels.

In short, the lexical resource of verbal frame files works as a repository of knowledge for SRL, accessible during the annotation task, that reduces the learning curve of SRL and facilitates the assignment of annotation tasks to several annotators. Provided that every instance receives a double-blind annotation, the quality of the annotation may be controlled through inter-annotator agreement. Instances with disagreement may be discarded or receive linguists' adjudication. This kind of lexical resource, therefore, is an essential part of the infrastructure to produce large training corpus for SRL classifiers.

It is not a simple task to construct a lexical resource, equivalent to Propbank, to support SRL in another language. Everyone that consults regularly the Unified Verb-Index[3], the system that gives access to Propbank's frame files, may observe that Propbank has been improved over the years, incorporating evidence provided by continuous annotation experience. In a project with limited budget and time, it is natural to think about reusing existing resources in order to maximize the results. In this paper, we report the strategies used to build a lexical resource to support SRL in Portuguese (hereafter referred as Verbo-Brasil), profiting from the English resource developed within the Propbank project and of annotated instances of the corpus Propbank-Br (Duran and Aluísio, 2012).

The remainder of this paper is organized as follows. Section 2 explains the strategies used in minimizing the efforts towards the construction of frame files; Section 3 briefly addresses an extrinsic evaluation of Verbo-Brasil obtained from a particular SRL annotation task. Finally, in Section 4, we present our conclusions and future work.

2 Methodology

Initially, we intended to construct Verbo-Brasil by manually creating frame files for the 1000 most frequent verbs in Portuguese, using the editor of frame files Cornerstone (Choi et. al. 2010), developed within the Propbank project. We envisaged, from the beginning, the possibility of reusing annotated instances of the corpus Propbank-Br, described in the Subsection 2.1, as examples to illustrate verb senses. However, when we started the task, we realized it was possible to automatically construct frame files, reducing the effort required for the task. Automatization entailed the use of two strategies. The first strategy constituted the creation of frame files using the existing data from both the corpus of the earlier version of Propbank-Br and the lexical repository of the English Propbank plus some new data, which was incorporated for this purpose in an updated version of Propbank-Br; this strategy is described in the Subsection 2.2. In the second strategy, described in Subsection 2.3, we duplicated the structure of the framefiles from

[1] http://verbs.colorado.edu/~mpalmer/projects/ace.html

[2] As informed in the site of the Verb-Index, updated on 08/01/2013.

[3] http://verbs.colorado.edu/verb-index/

the English Propbank to Propbank-Br for every verb which, in English, possessed a single sense.

2.1 The corpus Propbank-Br

The corpus Propbank-Br (Duran and Aluisio, 2012) was annotated by a sole linguist, aiming to provide a training corpus for SRL. During this process, we investigated to which extent the Propbank guidelines were reusable for undertaking an analogous approach to SRL in Portuguese. We ascertained the need of some adjustments in the guidelines in order to deal with differences between the Portuguese and English languages, as well as the differences between the parser outputs of the respective treebanks. As there was no lexical resource to support the annotation task, the sense distinction was made simultaneously to the annotation task, taking as base the guidelines of Propbank [4] [5].

The annotation was over the Brazilian portion of Bosque corpus (Afonso et. al. 2002), containing 4213 sentences. Bosque corpus is a treebank annotated by the parser Palavras (Bick, 2000) and revised by linguists. The sentences produced 6142 instances for annotation. Two SRL classifiers were trained on the resulting corpus. One of them (Alva-Manchego and Rosa, 2012) adopted a semi-supervised approach and obtained an F-Measure of 82.3%; the other (Fonseca and Rosa, 2013) adopted a neural architecture to label semantic arguments, disregarding the syntactic layer of annotation, and obtained an F-Measure of 62.82%.

2.2 Reusing existing data from Propbank-Br and English Propbank

To enable this strategy, it was necessary to add previously some extra data in the corpus Propbank-Br, a manual task that was by far quicker than constructing the frame files from scratch. First, we defined which fields of the frame file could be filled in with information from English Propbank, which ones could be filled in with information from Propbank-Br and which fields would require new information, not available in any one of the existing resources. The idea was to add the extra information required to the corpus Propbank-Br. Aiming this, we created six "word tags" in corpus Propbank-Br, using the same annotation tool used to annotate the original corpus (SALTO – Burchardt et al. 2006), as may be seen in Fig.1.

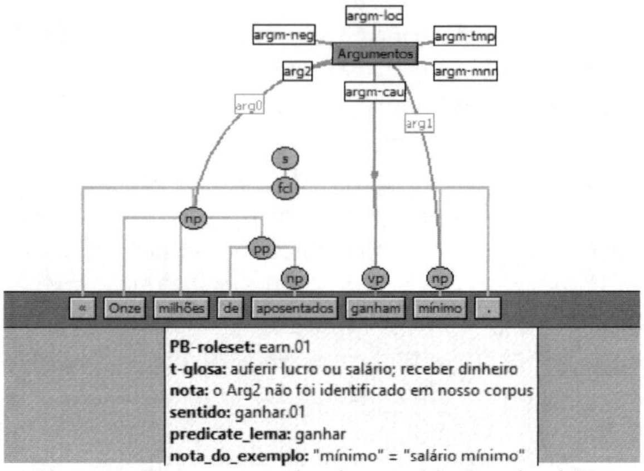

Figure 1. Extra annotation inserted in Propbank-Br.

The word tags are:

(1) *PB-roleset*: an equivalent roleset-id in Propbank, was used as field key to bring, from Propbank, the semantic roles, the semantic roles description, the related Verbnet classes and the Verbnet roles to the framefiles (Fig. 2);
(2) *t-glosa*: field that was filled in only in the first occurrence of a verb sense; it contains a brief description or a synonym of this sense of the verb to distinguish it from the other possible senses.
(3) *Nota* (note): field used for observations regarding a roleset contained within a verb's framefile when further clarification is thought to be helpful to the annotator;
(4) *Predicate_lemma*: field, filled in only in the first occurrence of a verb sense, containing the verb lemma or the name of a complex predicate (phrasal verb) when applicable;
(5) *Sentido* (sense): field that indicates which verb sense is the one being used in the sentence in question, also referred as roleset id, and is filled in for all instances. Once classified, the sentences can be subsequently added as examples of their respec-

[4]http://verbs.colorado.edu/~mpalmer/projects/ace/PBguidelines.pdf
[5] http://verbs.colorado.edu/~mpalmer/projects/ace/ FramingGuidelines.pdf

tive verb sense within the appropriate frame file;

(6) *Nota_do_exemplo* (example note): field used to convey information about a given example.

Predicate: earn

Roleset id: earn.01 , *wages*, **vncls:** 13.5.1-1, **framnet:**

Roles:

Arg0: *earner* (vnrole: 13.5.1-1-Agent)
Arg1: *wages* (vnrole: 13.5.1-1-Theme)
Arg2: *benefactive* (vnrole: 13.5.1-1-Beneficiary)
Arg3: *source* (vnrole: 13.5.1-1-Source)

Figure 2. Data brought from Propbank using the roleset id as field key.

Once we had created the word tags in the corpus, we undertook the annotation task to fill in them, as showed in the Fig.1. The greater the number of senses of a verb (polysemy), the greater was the difficulty to elect an English equivalent in English Propbank to fill in the word tag "PB_roleset". We realized that highly polysemous verbs would demand special attention in the next phase of the process, that is, during the revision of frame files automatically generated.

The annotation task provided the identification of 1453 verb senses in Portuguese for 1060 verb lemmas (an average of 1.37 senses per lemma). From the 1060 verb lemmas annotated in the corpus, 80% present only one sense, 13% present two senses; 3% present three senses and 4% present four or more senses. Only 109 of the 1453 senses identified in Portuguese did not have an equivalent verb sense in English identified in Propbank. Consequently, as the frame files of such 109 verbs could not obtain the fields brought from Propbank automatically, they required manual edition.

Using the XML frame file structure of Propbank, we defined the automatic generation of frame files, combining data from Propbank-Br and from Propbank, as shown in Fig.3. In the frame file structure, we used the field called "framnet" (aimed to store mappings to Framenet) for the information brought from the word tag "PB-roleset", that is, the equivalent roleset id in the English Propbank. The Propbank roleset id was the field key to access and bring data from the respective English frame file.

```
<predicate lemma="ganhar">

    <roleset     framnet="earn.01" id="ganhar.01"
                 name="auferir lucro ou salário; receber dinheiro"
                 source=""
                 vncls="13.5.1">
        <roles>
            <role descr="earner" f="" n="0">
                <vnrole vncls="13.5.1" vntheta="agent"/>
            </role>
            <role descr="wages" f="" n="1">
                <vnrole vncls="13.5.1" vntheta="theme"/>
            </role>
            <role descr="benefactive" f="" n="2">
                <vnrole vncls="13.5.1" vntheta="beneficiary"/>
            </role>
            <role descr="source" f="" n="3">
                <vnrole vncls="13.5.1" vntheta="source"/>
            </role>

        <note/>
```

Figure 3. Frame file combining data from Propbank-Br and data brought from Propbank

The strategy succeeded, and we achieved 1060 frame files with 1453 verb senses and 6142 annotated examples. After the generation, we began the revision of frame files with the most frequent verbs, translating the description of semantic roles, as may be seen in Fig.4. Currently, 541 frame files are fully revised.

Predicate: *ganhar*

Roleset id: ganhar.01, **auferir lucro ou salário; receber dinheiro,**
vncls: 13.5.1-1, **Propbank:** earn.01

Ganhar.01: Arg2 não foi identificado em nosso corpus de português

Roles:

Arg0: *ganhador* (vnrole: 13.5.1-1-Agent)
Arg1: *salário* (vnrole: 13.5.1-1-Theme)
Arg2: *beneficiário* (vnrole: 13.5.1-1-Beneficiary)
Arg3: *fonte* (vnrole: 13.5.1-1-Source)

Example:

Onze milhões de aposentados ganham mínimo.

Arg0: Onze milhões de aposentados
Rel: ganham
Arg1: mínimo

Example:

As crianças que ganham mesada dos pais aprendem a poupar desde cedo.

Arg0: As crianças (que)
Rel: ganham
Arg1: mesada
Arg3: dos pais

Figure 4. Frame file that combines information from corpus Propbank-Br and from Propbank's equivalent roleset.

2.3 Extension of the lexical resource using monosemous verbs

During the task of filling in the word tags in the corpus Propbank-Br, we observed that verbs presenting a unique sense (monosemous verbs) were the easiest to link to an English verb sense in Propbank and almost always the equivalent verb sense was the unique sense of the respective frame file. This led us to hypothetize that monosemous verbs in Portuguese, would probably correspond to monosemous verbs in English and vice-versa, whenever an equivalent verb exists.

On that basis, we decided to extend our resource taking as the start point the frame files that have a single verb sense in English Propbank. We identified 3737 English frame files that met such condition. We then translated only the verb lemmas of such frame files. Translation was executed automatically using Google translator and revised manually. We chose Google translator because we needed to translate at once 3737 out-of-context verb lemmas in a quickly and uncomplicated manner. It would be ideal if Google translator returned the word class of the results, thus allowing us to filter the verbs (we would only have obtained such result if we had translated the verbs one-by-one).

For several verbs, the automatic translation provided no output. Among the output words in Portuguese, there were several nouns, many of which do not correspond to any verb in Portuguese (eg. "to hangar", "to shark", "to tassle"). We then revised the translation, providing better equivalents when necessary and marking an "N" for those translated lexical items that were not verbs in Portuguese. After eliminating: (1) repetitions of translated verbs (two or more verbs translated into a same verb in Portuguese) and (2) verbs that we already had in our database, we obtained 1538 new verbs to extend our resource.

The next step was to duplicate the respective English frame files, using the name of the verb in Portuguese to substitute the name of the English verb in the fields "roleset id" and "predicate lemma". Subsequently, we replaced the example sentences in English by ones in Portuguese, extracted from corpus PLN-Br (Bruckschen et al., 2008). Lastly, to complete these new frame files, we are now annotating the examples with semantic role labels. Cornerstone frame files editor is being used for this task.

3 Evaluation

The two strategies we reported to automatically generate Portuguese frame files gave us 2598 framefiles. The 541 frame files already revised correspond to the verbs with frequency above 1000 in the corpus PLN-Br, which include the most polysemous verbs in Portuguese. Such verbs were target of a double-blind annotation task of 8345 instances extracted from the same corpus. The annotation task has just been accomplished and will be fully reported in a later date; the Kappa inter annotator agreement (Carletta, 1996) for verb sense identification was 0.93.

This annotation task gave us feedback to evaluate and improve the respective frame files. Among the actions taken during the annotation task we can cite: adding new senses identified in the corpus; merging or splitting senses for verbs that presented low inter-annotator agreement; including new examples to better illustrate a verb sense.

4 Concluding Remarks and Future work

The approach we adopted to build a Propbank-like lexical resource to support SRL in Brazilian Portuguese may be of use for other researchers working on under-represented languages and with a limited budget.

The 541 already revised frame files were used in a double-blind annotation SRL task that obtained a Kappa inter-annotator agreement for sense distinction of 0.93.

In the future, we plan to use Verbnet classes, an information brought from the equivalent verb sense in Propbank, to find in Verbnet-Br (Scarton et al., 2014) verb senses that are not in Verbo-Brasil.

As soon as we accomplish the revision of the frame files, we will make Verbo-Brasil publicly available. The new version of the corpus Propbank-Br, with the extra annotation described in this paper is now available for download at nilc.icmc.usp.br/portlex/index.php/en/downloadsingl.

Acknowledgments

Part of the results presented in this paper were obtained through research activity in the project entitled "Semantic Processing of Texts in Brazilian Portuguese", sponsored by Samsung Eletrônica da Amazônia Ltda, under the terms of Brazilian federal law number 8.248/91. We also thank financial support from FAPESP and CAPES, process number 151/2013 (Portal de Min@s project).

References

Afonso S. ; Bick, E. ; Haber, E. ; Santos, D. (2002) Floresta sintá(c)tica: a treebank for Portuguese. *Proceedings of LREC 2002*.

Alva Manchego, F. E.; Rosa, J. L. G. (2012). Semantic Role Labeling for Brazilian Portuguese: A Benchmark. In IBERAMIA 2012, *Lecture Notes in Artificial Intelligence*, v. 7637 p. 481–490. Springer.

Baker, C.F.; Fillmore, C. J.; Lowe. J. B. (1998).The Berkeley FrameNet Project. *Proceedings of Computational Linguistics 1998 Conference*.

Bick, E. (2000). *The Parsing System Palavras Automatic Grammatical Analysis of Portuguese in a Constraint Grammar Framework*. Aarhus, Denmark, Aarhus University Press.

Bruckschen, M., Muniz, F., Souza, J. G. C., Fuchs, J. T., Infante, K., Muniz, M., Gonçalves, P. N., Vieira, R.; Aluísio, S. M. (2008) "Anotação Linguística em XML do Corpus PLN-BR". *NILC-TR-09-08*, 39 p.

Burchardt, A.; Erk, K.; Frank, A.; Kowalski, A.; Pado, S. (2006) SALTO - A Versatile Multi-Level Annotation Tool. *Proceedings of LREC 2006*.

Carletta, Jean. (1996) Assessing agreement on classification tasks: The kappa statistic. *Computational Linguistics*, 22(2), pp. 249–254.

Choi, J. D.; Bonial, C.; Palmer, M. (2010) Propbank Frameset Annotation Guidelines Using a Dedicated Editor, Cornerstone. *Proceedings of LREC-2010*.

Duran, M. S.; Aluísio, S. M. (2012). Propbank-Br: a Brazilian Treebank annotated with semantic role labels. *Proceedings of LREC 2012*, pp. 1862-1867.

Fonseca, E. R.; Rosa, J. L. G. (2013) A Two-Step Convolutional Neural Network Approach for Semantic Role Labeling. Proceedings of IJCNN 2013 International Joint Conference on Neural Networks.

Kipper,K.; Korhonen, Anna; Ryant, N.; Palmer, M. (2006). Extensive Classifications of English verbs. *Proceedings of the 12th EURALEX International Congress*. Turin, Italy.

Meyers, A.; Reeves, R.; Macleod, C.; Szekely, R.; Zielinska, V.; Young, B.; Grishman, R. (2004), The NomBank Project: An Interim Report. *Proceedings. of HLT-EACL Workshop: Frontiers in Corpus Annotation*.

Palmer, M.; Gildea, D.; Kingsbury, P. (2005). The Proposition Bank: An Annotated Corpus of Semantic Roles. *Computational Linguistics*, 31:1, pp. 71-105.

Palmer, M.; Gildea, D.; Xue, N. (2010). Semantic Role Labeling. *Synthesis Lectures on Human Language Technology Series*, ed. Graeme Hirst, Mogan & Claypoole.

Scarton, C. ; Duran, M. S.; Aluísio, S. M. (2014) Using Cross-linguistic Knowledge to Build VerbNet-Style Lexicons: Results for a (Brazilian) Portuguese VerbNet. *Proceedings of the International Conference on Computational Processing of Portuguese* (PROPOR 2014). Heidelberg: Springer Verlag, 2014. v. 1. p. 153-164.

Can Selectional Preferences Help Automatic Semantic Role Labeling?

Shumin Wu
Department of Computer Science
University of Colorado Boulder
shumin@colorado.edu

Martha Palmer
Department of Linguistics
University of Colorado Boulder
mpalmer@colorado.edu

Abstract

We describe a topic model based approach for selectional preference. Using the topic features generated by an LDA model on the extracted predicate-arguments over the Chinese Gigaword corpus, we show improvement to our state-of-the-art Chinese SRL system by 2.34 F1 points on arguments of nominal predicates, 0.40 F1 point on arguments of verb predicates, and 0.66 F1 point overall. More over, similar gains were achieved on out-of-genre test data, as well as on English SRL using the same technique.

1 Introduction

It's long been theorized that selectional preferences (SP)/semantic constraints can improve automatic semantic role labeling (SRL). And while there have been several publications showing positive effects of SP, the evaluations have been dominated by pseudo-disambiguation. Zapirain et al. (2013) demonstrated end-to-end SRL improvement on arguments of English verb predicates by using a combination of lexical resources and distributional similarity based SP. However, the margin of improvement is a modest 0.4 F1 point (on WSJ) over a baseline system with performance over 4 F1 points lower than the top system in CoNLL-2005 (Carreras and Màrquez, 2005). These results may not be convincing enough to motivate the incorporation of SP when building an SRL system. One reason for the small improvement may be that arguments of a verb predicate are highly constrained by the underlying syntactic parse, and SP features that could disambiguate between role types are often negated by parse errors. With the recent extension of PropBank SRL to nominal and adjective predicates, preposition relationships, light-verb constructions, and abstract meaning representation (Bonial et al., 2014; Banarescu et al., 2013), it may be time to revisit SP for SRL. We hypothesize that SP will provide a greater benefit to nominal SRL, especially on a language with lower parsing accuracy.

In this paper, we apply SP to Chinese SRL (which has few morphological clues that impacts parsing accuracy) for arguments of both verb and nominal predicates using Chinese Gigaword. Our hypothesis, that SP will provide a greater benefit for nominal predicates than for verbal predicates, is verified by our results. We achieve a 2.34 F1 point improvement to our Chinese SRL system on arguments of nominal predicates, 0.40 F1 point on arguments of verb predicates, and 0.66 F1 point overall.

2 Previous Work on Selectional Preference

Inducing selectional preferences from corpus data was first proposed by Resnik (1997) for sense disambiguation. He generalized seen words using the WordNet (Fellbaum, 1998) hierarchy. Gildea and Jurafsky (2002) applied SP to automatic SRL by clustering extracted verb-direct object pairs, resulting in modest improvements. This syntactic signature based selectional preference technique has also been successfully extended and applied to unsupervised SRL by Lang and Lapata (2011) (using split-merge role clustering), as well as Titov and Klementiev (2012) (using a distance-dependent Chinese Restaurant Process prior for role clustering). Zapirain et al. (2013) improved the end-to-end perfor-

*Proceedings of the Fourth Joint Conference on Lexical and Computational Semantics (*SEM 2015)*, pages 222–227,
Denver, Colorado, June 4–5, 2015.

mance of an English PropBank SRL system by 0.4 F1 points using a variety of word similarity measures, from WordNet hierarchy distance to distributional similarity measures.

Ritter and Etzioni (2010) reasoned that the set of hidden variables modeled by latent Dirichlet allocation (LDA) naturally represents the semantic structure of a document collection, and the topics generated can be viewed as the latent set of classes that store preferences. The work utilizes LinkLDA, a variant of the standard LDA that models two sets of distributions for each topic simultaneously, with the resulting topics encoding the mutual constraints of a pair of arguments for the same predicate. Séaghdha and Korhonen (2014) also proposed SP w/ the LDA variants ROOTH-LDA and LEX-LDA.

There has also been work on Chinese selectional preferences, both lexical resource (HowNet) based and corpus based (Jia et al., 2011; Jia et al., 2013). The authors found the LDA corpus based SP improved over the HowNet based SP on pseudo-disambiguation. All of these results encouraged us to also attempt an LDA based approach to SP.

3 Selectional Preference for SRL

3.1 SP Representation

Some of the most discriminative SP models used by Zapirain et al. (2013) relied on distributional similarity computed over dependency relationships (provided by Lin (1998)). For example, in "*John lent Mary the book.*", we would extract *John-nsubj*, *Mary-iobj*, *book-dobj* for the predicate *lend*. While this has proven to be of higher quality than pure word co-occurrence based similarity, it may not be optimal for semantic-based processing. With nominal SRL, a large portion of the arguments (around 50% in Chinese PropBank) are not the direct syntactic dependents of the predicate: in figure 1, because of a light verb-like construction, all the arguments of 欢迎/*welcome* are the syntactic dependents of 表示/*express*. To address this, we directly extract SP of the predicates by running our SRL system over the unannotated corpus. For our example, we would extract *John-Arg0*, *Mary-Arg2*, *book-Arg1* for *lend*.

3.2 SP with LDA-based Topic Model

Our approach to modeling selectional preferences (SP) follows a relatively straightforward application of LDA to a set of predicate-argument instances derived from a corpus. In the standard LDA model, a document d is represented by a bag of words and is drawn from a multi-nominal Dirichlet θ_d over topics. The resulting model is a probability distribution of each word amongst the topics.

For the SRL application, we treat each extracted argument (represented by the $(label, headword)$ pair) as a "word", and the collection of arguments for all instances of a particular predicate as a "document". The generated topics would then contain arguments sharing a similar set of predicates. With this definition, we allow different role labels to share the same topic (though it does not encode role constraints quite like LinkLDA, ROOTH-LDA, etc). For prepositional phrases, we used the dependent of the preposition as the head word since the preposition can often be omitted in Chinese.

3.3 SRL Filtering

Building selectional preferences by means of using the output of an SRL system is unlikely to improve the same SRL system unless one filters out the lower quality labels (in earlier experiments where we performed no filtering, this was indeed the case). We ran SRL on the unannotated corpus using a logistic regression model and filtered out the low probability output. To balance between precision and recall, we set a hard 0.5 probability cutoff and discounted the occurrences of the rest using the label probability.

Since we can extract higher quality SP from the output of a better performing SRL system, we can iteratively improve our SRL system by re-extracting SP using a retrained (SP enhanced) SRL system. We arrived at diminishing returns after one additional iteration (of training SRL, extracting SP, and retraining SRL w/ new SP).

4 SRL Implementation

Our Chinese SRL system follows the standard (English) approach where the SRL task is posed as a multi-class classification problem requiring the identification of argument candidates for each predicate and their argument types using a set of lexical

A0			AM-tmp				A1				Sup	V
[香港	长官	董建华]	[今天]	[对	美国	基金会	发表 的	经济		报告]	[表示]	欢迎
Hong Kong	official	Dong Jianhua	today	toward	US	foundation	post	economic		report	express	welcome

[AM-tmp Today], [A0 Hong Kong official Dong Jianhua] [V ***welcomed***] [A1 the economic report released by the US foundation].

Figure 1: Chinese nominal predicate translated to English verb predicate

and syntactic features (predicate word, constituent head, path, syntactic frame, etc). While the top SRL systems from CoNLL-2005[1] and some subsequent systems use multiple parses for structural inference, we instead implement a 2-stage argument label classification system on a single input parse: the argument set found by the first classifier is used as an additional feature for the second classifier (to identify missing or duplicate argument label types).

4.1 Selectional Preference

The LDA topic model produces a probability distribution of words (represented here by the ($label$, $headword$) pair) over topics. For the SRL task, argument candidates with topic distributions similar to those of the arguments found in the training set are likely to be permissible. Ideally, we would use these distributions directly. Since our SRL system was designed to accept lexical (binary) features only (for training/decoding performance), we pared the distribution down to at most 3 topics for each $label$ type and excluded words that do not have high affinity to a few topics (sum of the probability of the top 3 topics $< 50\%$) to prevent diluting the discriminative power of the topic feature. We used the resulting list of ($label$, $topic\_id$) pairs for each word as the selectional preference feature for each encountered constituent in the Chinese SRL system.

During the normal LDA inference stage, using the learned topic model, a predicate instance ("document") will be assigned a probability distribution over topics based on its arguments, and each argument will be assigned a specific topic (or topic distribution). This could further constrain an argument's selectional preference within the context of the predicate instance and other arguments. For our system, we experimented with performing inference on the argument label set extracted from the first stage classifier and using the constrained argument topic distribution for the second stage classifier. However, we observed no improvement, likely because there are only a few arguments for each predicate instance.

[1]We use CoNLL-2005 instead of CoNLL-2009 for comparison because our SRL system is based on constituent parses.

5 Experiment

5.1 Setup

Our Chinese SRL system is trained on Chinese TreeBank 5.1 and Chinese PropBank 1.0. We used the standard: sections 81-885 for training, sections 41-80 for development, and sections 1-40, 900-931 for testing. We generated the training parses (with 10 fold cross-validation) and the test parses using the Berkeley parser[2] (5 split-merge cycles). The parser F1 score on the test sections is 82.73 as measured by ParseEval (Black et al., 1991).

We prepared the Chinese Gigaword[3] corpus with the Stanford Chinese Word Segmenter[4]. We performed LDA topic modeling using PLDA+ (Liu et al., 2011) and the recommended $\alpha = 50/topic\_cnt$, $\beta = 0.01$ values. We chose 2000 topics (tuned on the SRL performance of the development set rather than any topic based metrics). Table 1 lists some of the found topics (with the most frequent, relatively interesting, and least frequent headword, label pairs) using Chinese Gigaword.

5.2 Performance

As table 2 shows, the addition of the *SP* feature improved nominal SRL by 2.34 F1 points. Verb SRL improved by 0.40 F1 point and overall SRL improved by 0.66 F1 point. These F1 differences were all found to be statistically significant[5] ($p \leq 0.05$).

We also tested the system on Sinorama magazine and other out-of-genre sections (broadcast conversation, broadcast news, web blog) in Chinese Prop-

[2]code.google.com/p/berkeleyparser/

[3]LDC2011T13

[4]nlp.stanford.edu/software/segmenter.shtml

[5]$SIGF$ (www.nlpado.de/%7esebastian/software/sigf.shtml), using stratified approximate randomization test (Yeh, 2000)

topic	headword:argument_label pairs
emergency response	破坏/damage:Arg1 阻止/stop:Arg1 制造/fabricate:Arg1 寻找/search:Arg1 自杀/suicide:Arg1 ... 灭火/extinguish:Arg1 敲诈/blackmail:Arg1 挣脱/break_free:Arg1 东山再起/comeback:Arg1
government agency	海关/custom:Arg0 联合会/union:Arg0 务部/work_department:Arg0 旅游局/travel_department:Arg0 统计局/census:Arg0 ... 部会/ministries:Arg0 边检站/checkpoint:Arg0 财政局/finance_bureau:Arg0
law & order	警方/police:Arg0 嫌犯/suspect:Arg1 男子/male:Arg1 到案/court_appearance:Arg1 公安/public_safety:Arg0 ... 巷/alley:Argm-loc 嘉义市/Chiayi_City:Argm-loc 哥伦比亚人/Columbian:Arg1
path	道路/road:Arg1 路/path:Arg1 大道/avenue:Arg1 ... 红地毯/red_carpet:Arg1 钢丝/steel_wire:Arg1 独木桥/plank_bridge:Arg1 ... 迷宫/maze:Arg1 侧门/side_entrance:Arg1 险棋/risky_move:Arg1
competition	比赛/competition:Arg1 决赛/final:Arg1 联赛/league_comp:Arg1 ... 考试/exam:Arg1 大选/election:Arg1 世乒赛/world_pingpong_match:Arg1 ... 加赛/playoff:Arg1 分团/sub-group:Arg0
moral & ethics	精神/spirit:Arg1 传统/tradition:Arg1 作风/style:Arg1 文明/civil:Arg1 ... 校风/school_spirit:Arg1 同舟共济/share_hard_time:Arg1 ... 幸福观/happy_outlook:Arg1 博爱/universal_love:Arg1

Table 1: Topics in Chinese Gigaword

system	nominal			verb	all
	p	r	f1	f1	f1
baseline	64.71	48.20	55.25	75.53	72.08
SP_{LDA}	65.70	**51.27**	**57.59**	**75.93**	**72.74**

Table 2: Chinese PropBank 1.0 results

sections	system	p	r	f1
Sinorama nominal	baseline	37.58	25.10	30.10
	SP_{LDA}	39.72	27.36	32.40
verb	baseline	67.13	50.37	57.55
	SP_{LDA}	67.56	50.59	57.86
4051-4411 (verb)	baseline	62.01	50.74	55.81
	SP_{LDA}	62.70	51.03	56.27

Table 3: Chinese PropBank 3.0 out-of-genre results

Bank 3.0. Only Sinorama has nominal SRL annotations. As table 3 shows, even though the absolute performance is much lower, SP improved the precision and recall in all cases, the nominal SRL score on Sinorama by 2.30 F1 points, and verb SRL score by 0.31-0.46 F1 point. Again, these F1 differences were statistically significant.

5.2.1 Comparison

Direct performance comparison with previous Chinese SRL systems is a bit difficult: Xue (2008), Zhuang and Zong (2010) trained the syntactic parsers with an additional 250K word broadcast news corpus found in Chinese TreeBank 6.0, while Sun (2010) only reported results using gold POS tags but no additional gold parses. However, as table 4 shows, for verb predicates, our system bests Xue's (2008) system by 4-7 F1 points with less parser training data and when tested with (but was not retrained to take full advantage of) gold POS tags besting Sun's (2010) system by 0.53 F1 point. For nominal predicates, our system bests Xue's (2008) system, by 1.9 F1 points on arguments of nominal predicates (since we have an integrated SRL system, the results are obtained by training both verb and nominal predicates, then using only the nominal classifier to classify the nominal predicates).

5.2.2 English SRL

We applied the same techniques to English SRL using the English Gigaword[7] corpus. We used 800 topics (w/ lemmatized headwords) tuning on the

[6]Verb results are from SRL systems trained on verbs only. Table 2 results are from SRL systems trained on all predicates.

[7]LDC2003T05

type	system	p	r	f1
verb	Xue 2008	76.8	62.5	68.9
	w/ gold POS	79.5	65.6	71.9
	Sun 2010 (gold POS)	81.03	**72.38**	76.46
	SP_{LDA}	82.74	70.96	76.40
	w/ gold POS	**82.81**	71.93	**76.99**
nominal	Xue 2008	62.9	53.1	57.6
	SP_{LDA}	**67.30**	**53.31**	**59.50**

Table 4: Chinese SRL comparison[6]

system	p	r	f1	$error_{\Delta}$
SwiRL	79.7	70.9	75.0	
Zapirain 2013	80.0	71.3	**75.4**	-1.60%
baseline	82.59	77.27	79.84	
SP_{LDA}	82.96	77.52	**80.15**	-1.54%

Table 5: English SRL comparison (CoNLL-2005 WSJ)

CoNLL-2005 development set. Compared to Zapirain et al. (2013) (table 5), our SP approach had a smaller (but still statistically significant) absolute F1 gain, with most of the gain coming from core argument type improvements. But with a much higher performing baseline system (one of the highest reported results using a single input parse per sentence), the error reduction rate is comparable.

6 Conclusion

We presented a LDA topic model based selectional preference approach to improving automatic SRL. Using SP extracted from a 63.6M sentence Chinese Gigaword corpus, we were able to improve on the results of an already competitive Chinese SRL system by 2.34 F1 points on nominal predicates, 0.40 F1 point on verb predicates, and 0.66 F1 point on the standard test set. More over, we obtained comparable improvement on out-of-genre data and demonstrated our technique is also applicable to English SRL. Given the margin of improvement on nominal SRL, which is not as well constrained by syntax as verb SRL, there are reasons to speculate the proposed technique could be applicable to other predicate type extensions of PropBank SRL.

As our first attempt at automatically deriving Chinese selectional preference, there is a lot of room for future improvement. Notably, these include techniques used for English SP such as computing similarity based on lexical resources (for Chinese - HowNet (Dong et al., 2010)), distributional similarity, latent word language model (Deschacht and Moens, 2009), different variants of LDA topic models, as well as taking advantages of argument constraints in parallel corpora to extract higher quality SP.

Acknowledgement

We gratefully acknowledge the support of the National Science Foundation CISE-IISRI-0910992, Richer Representations for Machine Translation, DARPA FA8750-09-C-0179 (via BBN) Machine Reading: Ontology Induction: Semlink+, and DARPA HR0011-11-C-0145 (via LDC) BOLT. This work utilized the Janus supercomputer, which is supported by the National Science Foundation (award number CNS-0821794) and the University of Colorado Boulder. The Janus supercomputer is a joint effort of the University of Colorado Boulder, the University of Colorado Denver and the National Center for Atmospheric Research. Any opinions, findings, and conclusions or recommendations expressed in this material are those of the authors and do not necessarily reflect the views of the National Science Foundation.

References

Laura Banarescu, Claire Bonial, Shu Cai, Madalina Georgescu, Kira Griffitt, Ulf Hermjakob, Kevin Knight, Philipp Koehn, Martha Palmer, and Nathan Schneider, 2013. *Proceedings of the 7th Linguistic Annotation Workshop and Interoperability with Discourse*, chapter Abstract Meaning Representation for Sembanking, pages 178–186. Association for Computational Linguistics.

E. Black, S. Abney, S. Flickenger, C. Gdaniec, C. Grishman, P. Harrison, D. Hindle, R. Ingria, F. Jelinek, J. Klavans, M. Liberman, M. Marcus, S. Roukos, B. Santorini, and T. Strzalkowski. 1991. Procedure for quantitatively comparing the syntactic coverage of english grammars. In *Proceedings of the Workshop on Speech and Natural Language*, HLT '91, pages 306–311, Stroudsburg, PA, USA. Association for Computational Linguistics.

Claire Bonial, Julia Bonn, Kathryn Conger, Jena D. Hwang, and Martha Palmer. 2014. Propbank: Semantics of new predicate types. In *Proceedings of the Ninth International Conference on Language Resources and Evaluation (LREC'14)*, Reykjavik, Iceland, may.

Xavier Carreras and Lluís Màrquez. 2005. Introduction to the conll-2005 shared task: Semantic role labeling. In *Proceedings of the Ninth Conference on Computational Natural Language Learning*, CONLL '05, pages 152–164, Stroudsburg, PA, USA. Association for Computational Linguistics.

Koen Deschacht and Marie-Francine Moens. 2009. Semi-supervised semantic role labeling using the latent words language model. In *Proceedings of the 2009 Conference on Empirical Methods in Natural Language Processing: Volume 1 - Volume 1*, EMNLP '09, pages 21–29, Stroudsburg, PA, USA. Association for Computational Linguistics.

Zhendong Dong, Qiang Dong, and Changling Hao. 2010. Hownet and its computation of meaning. In *Proceedings of the 23rd International Conference on Computational Linguistics: Demonstrations*, COLING '10, pages 53–56, Stroudsburg, PA, USA. Association for Computational Linguistics.

Christiane Fellbaum. 1998. *WordNet: An Electronic Lexical Database*. MIT Press.

Daniel Gildea and Daniel Jurafsky. 2002. Automatic labeling of semantic roles. *Computational Linguistics*, 28(3):245–288.

Yuxiang Jia, Hongying Zan, and Ming Fan. 2011. Inducing chinese selectional preference based on hownet. In *Proceedings of the Seventh International Conference on Computational Intelligence and Security*, CIS2011, pages 1146–1149.

Yuxiang Jia, Hongying Zan, Ming Fan, , Shiwen Yu, and Zhimin Wang. 2013. Computational models for chinese selectional preferences induction. *International Journal of Advanced Intelligence*, 5(1):110–119, July.

Joel Lang and Mirella Lapata. 2011. Unsupervised semantic role induction via split-merge clustering. In *Proceedings of the 49th Annual Meeting of the Association for Computational Linguistics: Human Language Technologies*, Portland, Oregon, USA, June. Association for Computational Linguistics.

Dekang Lin. 1998. Automatic retrieval and clustering of similar words. In *Proceedings of ACL 1998*, ACL '98, pages 768–774, Stroudsburg, PA, USA. Association for Computational Linguistics.

Zhiyuan Liu, Yuzhou Zhang, Edward Y. Chang, and Maosong Sun. 2011. Plda+: Parallel latent dirichlet allocation with data placement and pipeline processing. *ACM Trans. Intell. Syst. Technol.*, 2(3):26:1–26:18, May.

Philip Resnik. 1997. Selectional preference and sense disambiguation. In *Proceedings of ACL SIGLEX Workshop on Tagging Text with Lexical Semantics*, pages 52–57, Washington, D.C. ACL.

Alan Ritter and Oren Etzioni. 2010. A latent dirichlet allocation method for selectional preferences. In *In Proceedings of the 48th Annual Meeting of the Association for Computational Linguistics (ACL)*.

Diarmuid Séaghdha and Anna Korhonen. 2014. Probabilistic distributional semantics with latent variable models. *Computational Linguistics*, 40(3):587–631, September.

Weiwei Sun. 2010. Semantics-driven shallow parsing for chinese semantic role labeling. In *Proceedings of the ACL 2010 Conference Short Papers*, ACLShort '10, pages 103–108, Stroudsburg, PA, USA. Association for Computational Linguistics.

Ivan Titov and Alexandre Klementiev. 2012. A Bayesian approach to unsupervised semantic role induction. In *Proceedings of the Conference of the European Chapter of the Association for Computational Linguistics*, Avignon, France, April.

Nianwen Xue. 2008. Labeling chinese predicates with semantic roles. *Computational Linguistics*, 34(2):225–255.

Alexander Yeh. 2000. More accurate tests for the statistical significance of result differences. In *Proceedings of the 18th Conference on Computational Linguistics - Volume 2*, COLING '00, pages 947–953, Stroudsburg, PA, USA. Association for Computational Linguistics.

Beñat Zapirain, Eneko Agirre, Lluís Màrquez, and Mihai Surdeanu. 2013. Selectional preferences for semantic role classification. In *Computational Linguistics*, pages 631–663.

Tao Zhuang and Chengqing Zong. 2010. Joint inference for bilingual semantic role labeling. In *Proceedings of EMNLP 2010*, pages 304–314, Cambridge, MA, October. Association for Computational Linguistics.

Implicit Entity Recognition in Clinical Documents

Sujan Perera*, Pablo Mendes†, Amit Sheth*, Krishnaprasad Thirunarayan*, Adarsh Alex*, Christopher Heid¶, Greg Mott¶

*Kno.e.sis Center, Wright State University, Dayton, OH, USA
†IBM Research, San Jose, CA, USA
¶Boonshoft School of Medicine, Wright State University, Dayton, OH, USA
sujan@knoesis.org, pnmendes@us.ibm.com, amit@knoesis.org, tkprasad@knoesis.org
adarsh@knoesis.org, caheid2@gmail.com, mott11@wright.edu

Abstract

With the increasing automation of health care information processing, it has become crucial to extract meaningful information from textual notes in electronic medical records. One of the key challenges is to extract and normalize entity mentions. State-of-the-art approaches have focused on the recognition of entities that are explicitly mentioned in a sentence. However, clinical documents often contain phrases that indicate the entities but do not contain their names. We term those *implicit entity mentions* and introduce the problem of implicit entity recognition (IER) in clinical documents. We propose a solution to IER that leverages entity definitions from a knowledge base to create entity models, projects sentences to the entity models and identifies implicit entity mentions by evaluating semantic similarity between sentences and entity models. The evaluation with 857 sentences selected for 8 different entities shows that our algorithm outperforms the most closely related unsupervised solution. The similarity value calculated by our algorithm proved to be an effective feature in a supervised learning setting, helping it to improve over the baselines, and achieving F1 scores of .81 and .73 for different classes of implicit mentions. Our gold standard annotations are made available to encourage further research in the area of IER.

1 Introduction

Consider the following sentence, extracted from a clinical document: *"Patient has shortness of breath with reaccumulation of fluid in extremities."* It states that the patient has 'shortness of breath' and 'edema'. The former is explicitly mentioned, while the latter is implied by the semantics of the phrase *'reaccumulation of fluid in extremities'*. We term such occurrences *implicit entity mentions*.

While implicit entity mentions are common in many domains, resolving them is particularly valuable in the clinical domain. Clinical documents are rich in information content that plays a central role in understanding patients' health status and improving the quality of the delivered services. It is a common practice to employ computer assisted coding (CAC) solutions to assist expert "coders" in determining the unique identifier (e.g., ICD9 or ICD10) for each medical condition or combination of conditions. These identifiers are important to unambiguously represent the medical conditions, to prepare the post-discharge plan, and to perform secondary data analysis tasks. A human coder reading the sentence *'Patient has shortness of breath with reaccumulation of fluid in extremities'* would generate the corresponding codes for entities 'shortness of breath' and 'edema'. However, the solutions developed to perform entity recognition in clinical documents (Aronson, 2006) (Friedman et al., 1994) (Savova et al., 2010) (Friedman et al., 2004) (Fu and Ananiadou, 2014) (Pradhan et al., 2015) do not recognize the presence of entity 'edema' in this sentence.

Implicit entity mentions are a common occurrence in clinical documents as they are often typed during a patient visit in a way that is natural in spoken language and meant for consumption by the professionals with similar backgrounds. An analysis with 300 documents in our corpus showed that 35% of the 'edema' mentions and 40% of the 'shortness of breath' mentions are implicit.

Recognizing implicit mentions is particularly

*Proceedings of the Fourth Joint Conference on Lexical and Computational Semantics (*SEM 2015)*, pages 228–238,
Denver, Colorado, June 4–5, 2015.

challenging since, besides the fact that they lack the entity name, they can be embedded with negations. For example, the semantics of the sentence *'The patients' respiration become unlabored'* implies that the patient does not have 'shortness of breath'. Identification of the negated mentions of entities in clinical documents is crucial as they provide valuable insights into the patients' health status.

We propose an unsupervised solution to the IER problem that leverages knowledge embedded in entity definitions obtained for each entity from the Unified Medical Language System (UMLS) (Bodenreider, 2004). UMLS provides a standard vocabulary for the clinical domain. Our solution: a) Creates an entity model from these definitions, b) Identifies the sentences in input text that may contain implicit entity mentions, c) Projects these sentences onto our entity model, and d) Classifies the sentences to distinguish between those containing implicit entity mentions or negated implicit mentions, by calculating the semantic similarity between the entity model and the projected sentences.

The contributions of this work are as follows:

1. We introduce the problem of implicit entity recognition (IER) in clinical documents.
2. We propose an unsupervised solution to IER that outperforms the most relevant unsupervised baseline and improves the results of a supervised baseline.
3. We create a gold standard corpus annotated for IER in the clinical domain and make it available to encourage research in this area.

2 Related Work

To the best of our knowledge, this is the first work to address the problem of Implicit Entity Recognition (IER) in clinical documents. However, there is a large body of research that is relevant to the problem, including Named Entity Recognition (NER), Entity Linking (EL), Coreference Resolution, Paraphrase Recognition, and Textual Entailment Recognition.

Much like IER, both NER and EL have the objective of binding a natural language expression to a semantic identifier. However, related work in NER and EL expect the proper name (explicit mention) of entities and assume the presence of noun phrases (Collins and Singer, 1999) (Bunescu and Pasca, 2006). The solutions developed for NER leverage regularities on morphological and syntactical features that are unlikely to hold in the case of IER. The most successful NER approaches use word-level features (such as capitalization, prefixes/suffixes, and punctuation), list lookup features (such as gazetteers, lexicons, or dictionaries), as well as corpus-level features (such as multiple occurrences, syntax, and frequency) (Nadeau and Sekine, 2007) that are not exhibited by the phrases with implicit entity mentions.

Many approaches couple NER with a follow up EL step (Hachey et al., 2013) in order to assign an unique entity identifiers to mentions. Therefore, the inadequacy of NER techniques will limit the capability of recognizing implicit entity mentions by a solution developed for EL. Moreover, state-of-the-art EL approaches include a 'candidate mapping' step that uses entity names to narrow down the space of possible entity identifiers, which is also a limiting factor in the IER case. Finally, neither NER nor EL deal with the negated mentions of entities.

Coreference resolution (CR) focuses on grouping multiple mentions of the same entity with different surface forms. The solutions to CR focus on mapping explicit mentions of entity names to other pronouns and noun phrases referring to the same entity (Ng, 2010) (Durrett and Klein, 2013). In IER implicit mentions occur without co-referring corresponding entity. Hence, they must be resolved without dependencies on co-referents.

In contrast to NER, EL, and CR problems and their solutions, IER addresses instances where neither explicit mention of an entity nor noun phrases or any of the above mentioned features are guaranteed to appear in the text but still have a reference to a known entity. Hence, IER solutions require treatment for implied meaning of the phrases beyond its syntactic features.

Since our solution to IER establishes a relationship between entity definitions and the input text, the tasks of paraphrase recognition (Barzilay and Elhadad, 2003) (Dolan et al., 2004) and textual entailment recognition (Giampiccolo et al., 2007) are related to our solution. However, these tasks are fundamentally different in two aspects: 1) Both paraphrase recognition and textual entailment recognition are defined at the sentence level, whereas text phrases considered for IER can exist as a sentence fragment or span across multiple sentences, and 2) The objective of IER is to find whether a given text phrase has a mention of an *entity*—as opposed to determining whether two sentences are similar or entail one another. However, our solution benefits from the lessons learned from both tasks.

The question answering solutions cope with the questions that describe the characteristics of a concept and expect that concept as the answer. This particular type of questions resembles implicit entity mentions. However, they assume that the questions are referring to some concept and the problem is to uncover which one, whereas the implicit entity mention problem requires us to first check whether a particular sentence/phrase has a mention of an entity at all. Furthermore, question answering systems benefit from the presence of pronouns, nouns, and noun phrases in the questions and the candidate answers to derive helpful syntactic and semantic features (Lally et al., 2012)(Wang, 2006), while phrases with implicit entity mentions may not contain such features.

The existing work on clinical document annotation focused on explicit entity mentions with contiguous phrases (Aronson, 2006) (Savova et al., 2010) (Friedman et al., 2004) (Fu and Ananiadou, 2014). Going one step beyond, the SemEval 2014 task 7 recognized the need for identifying discontiguous mentions of explicit entities (Pradhan et al., 2014). However, the recognition of implicit entities has yet to address by this community.

3 Implicit Entity Recognition (IER) in Clinical Documents

We define the Implicit Entity Recognition (IER) task in clinical documents as: given input text that does not have explicit mentions of target entities, find which target entities are implied (including implied negations) in the input text.

Negation detection is traditionally separated from the entity recognition task because negation indicating terms can be recognized separately from the phrases that contain explicit mention of an entity. In contrast, implicit mention can involve an antonym that fuses the entity indication with negated sense (e.g., *'patient denies shortness of breath'* vs *'patient is breathing comfortably'*). Hence, negation detection is considered as a sub-task of IER.

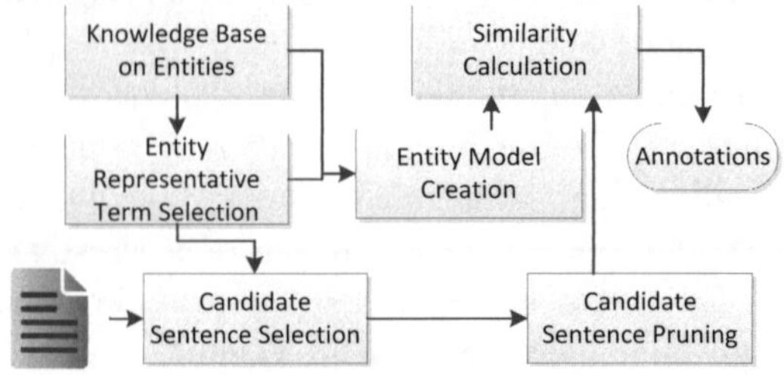

Figure 1: Components of the Proposed Solution

Typical entity recognition task considers the detection of the boundaries of the phrases with entities (i.e., segmentation) as a sub-task. We consider boundary detection of the implicit entity mentions as an optional step due to two reasons: 1) It is considered an optional step in biomedical entity recognition task (Tsai et al., 2006), and 2) The phrases with implicit entity mentions can be noncontiguous and span multiple sentences. Further, in some cases, even domain experts disagree on the precise phrase boundaries.

We define the IER as a classification task. Given an input text, classify it to one of the three categories: TP_e if the text has a mention of entity e, or $Tneg_e$ if the text has a negated mention of entity e, or TN_e if the entity e is not mentioned at all. As mentioned, the phrases with implicit entity mentions can span to multiple sentences. However, this work will focus only on implicit mentions exist within a sentence. Our unsupervised solution to this classification task: 1) Creates an *entity model* from the entity definitions, 2) Selects *candidate sentences* that may contain implicit entity mentions, 3) Projects the candidate sentences into entity model space, and 4) Calculates the semantic similarity between projected sentences and the *entity model*. Figure 1 shows the components of our solution which are discussed below in detail.

In order to facilitate these sub-tasks, our algorithm introduces the concept of an *entity representative term* for each entity and propose an automatic way to select these terms from entity definitions.

3.1 Entity Representative Term Selection

Entity representative term (ERT) selection finds a term with high *representative power* to an entity and plays an important role in defining it.

The *representative power* of a term t for entity e is defined based on two properties: its dominance among the definitions of entity e, and its ability to discriminate the mentions of entity e from other entities. This is formalized in eq. (1). Consider the entity 'appendicitis' as an example. It is defined as *'acute inflammation of appendix'*. Intuitively, both terms *inflammation* and *appendix* are candidates to explain the entity *appendicitis*. However, the term *appendix* has more potential to discriminate the implicit mentions of *appendicitis* than the term *inflammation*, because the term *inflammation* is used to describe many entities. Also, none of the definitions define *appendicitis* without using the term *appendix*; therefore, *appendix* is the dominant term, and consequently it has the most representative power for the entity 'appendicitis'.

We used a score inspired by the TF-IDF measure to capture this intuition. The IDF (inverse document frequency) value measures the specificity of a term in the definitions. The TF (term frequency) captures the dominance of a term. Hence the representative power of a term t for entity e (r_t) is defined as,

$$r_t = freq(t, \mathcal{Q}_e) * \log \frac{|E|}{|E_t|} \quad (1)$$

$\mathcal{Q}_e$ is the set of definitions of entity e, E is the set of all entities. $freq(t, \mathcal{Q}_e)$ is the frequency of term t in set $\mathcal{Q}_e$, $|E|$ is the size of the set E (3962 in our corpus), and the denominator $|E_t|$ calculates the number of entities defined using term t. We expand the ERT found for an entity with this technique by adding its synonyms obtained from WordNet.

We can define entity representative terms based on the definition of representative power.

Definition 3.1 (Entity Representative Term). Let $\mathcal{L}_e = \{t_1, t_2, ..., t_n\}$ be the set of terms in a definitions of an entity e. Let $\mathcal{R}_{\mathcal{L}_e} = \{r_{t_1}, r_{t_2}, ..., r_{t_n}\}$ be the representative power calculated for each term t_i in $\mathcal{L}_e$ for e. We select term t_m as the entity representative term of the entity e if its representative power is maximum, i.e., $r_{t_m} \geq r_{t_i}$ for all i where $1 \leq i \leq n$.

3.2 Entity Model Creation

Our algorithm creates an *entity indicator* from a definition of the entity. An entity indicator consists of terms that describe the entity. Consider the definition *'A disorder characterized by an uncomfortable sensation of difficulty breathing'* for 'shortness of breath', for which the selected ERT is *'breathing'*. The terms *uncomfortable*, *sensation*, *difficulty*, and *breathing* collectively describe the entity. Adding other terms in this definition to the entity indicator negatively affects the similarity calculation with the candidate sentences since they are less likely to appear in a candidate sentence. We exploited the neighborhood of the ERT in the definition to create the entity indicator and automatically selected the nouns, verbs, adjectives, and adverbs in the definition within a given window size to the left and to the right of the ERT. We used a window size of four in our experiments.

An entity can have multiple definitions each explaining it using diverse vocabulary. On average, an entity in our corpus had 3 definitions. We create an entity indicator from each definition of the entity, hence an entity has multiple indicators. We call the collection of indicators of an entity as its *entity model*. In other words, an entity model consists of multiple entity indicators that capture diverse and orthogonal ways an entity can be expressed in the text.

3.3 Candidate Sentence Selection

The sentences with ERT in an input text are identified as *candidate sentences* containing implicit mention of the corresponding entity. A sentence may contain multiple ERTs and consequently become a candidate sentence for multiple entities. This step reduces the complexity of the classification task as now a sentence has only a few target entities.

3.4 Candidate Sentence Pruning

In order to evaluate the similarity between any given candidate sentence and the entity model, we perform a projection of candidate sentences onto the same semantic space. We perform this by pruning the terms in candidate sentences that does not participate in forming the segment with implicit entity mentions. Candidate sentences are pruned by following the same steps followed to create the entity indicators from the entity definitions.

3.5 Semantic Similarity Calculation

As the last step, our solution calculates the similarity between the entity model and the pruned candidate sentence. The sentences with implicit entity mentions often use adjectives and adverbs to describe the entity and they may indicate the absence of the entities using antonyms or explicit negations. These two characteristics pose challenges to the applicability of existing text similarity algorithms such as MCS (Mihalcea et al., 2006) and matrixJcn (Fernando and Stevenson, 2008) which are proven to perform well among the unsupervised algorithms in paraphrase identification task (ACLWiki, 2014).

The existing text similarity algorithms largely benefit from the WordNet similarity measures. Most of these measures use the semantics of the hierarchical arrangement of the terms in WordNet. Unfortunately, adjectives and adverbs are not arranged in a hierarchy, and terms with different part of speech (POS) tags cannot be mapped to the same hierarchy. Hence, they are limited in calculating the similarity between terms of these categories. This limitation negatively affects the performance of IER as the entity models and pruned sentences often contain terms from these categories. Consider the following examples:

1. *Her breathing is still uncomfortable*$_{adjective}$.
2. *She is breathing comfortably*$_{adverb}$ *in room air.*
3. *His tip of the appendix was inflamed*$_{verb}$.

The first two examples use an adjective and an adverb to mention the entity 'shortness of breath' implicitly. The third example uses a verb to mention the entity 'appendicitis' implicitly instead of the noun *inflammation* that is used by its definition.

We have developed a text similarity measure overcoming these challenges and weigh the contributions of the words in the entity model to the similarity value based on their representative power.

Handling adjectives, adverbs and words with different POS tags: To get the best out of all WordNet similarity measures, we exploited the relationships between different forms of the terms in WordNet to find the noun form of the terms in the entity models and pruned sentences before calculating the similarity. We found the adjective for an adverb using relationship 'pertainym' and noun for an adjective or a verb using the relationship 'derivationally related form' in WordNet.

Handling negations: Negations are of two types: 1) Negations mentioned with explicit terms such as no, not, and deny, and 2) Negations indicated with antonyms (e.g., 2nd example in above list). We used the NegEx algorithm (Chapman et al., 2001) to address the first type of negations. To address the second type of negations, we exploited the antonym relationships in the WordNet.

The similarity between an entity model and the pruned candidate sentence is calculated by computing the similarities of their terms. The term similarity is computed by forming an ensemble using the standard WordNet similarity measures namely, WUP (Wu and Palmer, 1994), LCH (Leacock and Chodorow, 1998), Resnik (Resnik, 1995), LIN (Lin, 1998), JCN (Jiang and Conrath, 1997), as well as a predict vector-based measure Word2vec (Mikolov et al., 2013) and a morphology-based similarity metric Levenshtein[1] as:

$$sim(t_1, t_2) = max_{m \in M}(sim_m(t_1, t_2)) \quad (2)$$

where t_1 and t_2 are input terms and M is the set of above mentioned similarity measures. This ensemble-based similarity measure exploits orthogonal ways of comparing terms: semantic, statistical, and syntactic. An ensemble-based approach is preferable over picking one of them exclusively since they are complementary in nature, that is, each outperforms the other two in certain scenarios.

The similarity values calculated by WordNet similarity measures in $sim_m(t_1, t_2)$ are normalized to range between 0 and 1.

The similarity of a pruned candidate sentence to the entity model is calculated by calculating its similarity to each entity indicator in the entity model, and picking the maximum value as the final similarity value for the candidate sentence. The similarity between entity indicator e and pruned sentence s, $sim(e, s)$, is calculated by summing the similarities calculated for each term t_e in the entity indicator weighted by its representative power as defined

[1] http://en.wikipedia.org/wiki/Levenshtein_distance

in eq. (1). If t_e is an antonym for any term in s (t_s), it contributes negatively to the overall similarity value, else it contributes in linear portion of the maximum similarity value between t_e and some t_s (eqs. (4) and (5)). The overall similarity value is normalized based on the total representative power of all the terms t_es (eq. (1)) and ranges between -1 and +1.

Note that this formulation weighs the contribution of each term according to its importance in defining the entity. The higher similarity with a term that has higher representative power leads to higher overall similarity value, while the lower similarity with such terms leads to a lower total similarity value. The special treatment for antonyms takes care of the negated mentions of an entity.

$$sim(e, s) = \frac{\sum_{t_e \in e} f(t_e, s) * r_{t_e}}{\sum_{t_e \in e} r_{t_e}} \quad (3)$$

$$f(t_e, s) = \begin{cases} -1 & \alpha(t_e, s) == 0 \\ \max_{t_s \in s} \text{sim}(t_e, t_s) & \text{otherwise} \end{cases} \quad (4)$$

$$\alpha(t_e, s) = \prod_{t_s \in s} \begin{cases} 0 & \text{if } t_e \text{ is an antonym of } t_s \\ 1 & \text{otherwise} \end{cases} \quad (5)$$

Finally, the sentences are classified based on a configurable threshold values selected between -1 and +1.

4 Evaluation

We reannotated a sample of the corpus created for SemEval-2014 task 7 (Pradhan et al., 2014) to include implicit mention annotations and measured the performance of our proposed method in classifying entities annotated with *TP* and *Tneg* mentions[2].

4.1 Gold Standard Dataset

The SemEval-2014 task 7 corpus consists of 24,147 de-identified clinical notes. We used this corpus to create a gold standard for IER with the help of three domain experts. The gold standard consists of 857 sentences selected for eight entities. The creation of the gold standard is described below in detail.

Entity	*TP*	*Tneg*	*TN*
Shortness of breath	93	94	29
Edema	115	35	81
Syncope	96	92	24
Cholecystitis	78	36	4
Gastrointestinal gas	18	14	5
Colitis	12	11	0
Cellulitis	8	2	0
Fasciitis	7	3	0

Table 1: Candidate Sentence Statistics

We have annotated the corpus for explicit mentions of the entities using cTAKES (Savova et al., 2010) and ranked the entities based on their frequency. The domain experts on our team then selected a subset of these entities that they judged to be frequently mentioned implicitly in clinical documents. For example, the frequent entity 'shortness of breath' was selected but not 'chest pain' since the former is mentioned implicitly often but not the latter. We used four frequently implicitly mentioned entities as the primary focus of our evaluation. We refer to these as *primary entities* from here on (the first four entities in Table 1). To test the generalizability of our method, as well as to evaluate its robustness when lacking training data, we selected another four entities (the last four entities in Table 1). We then selected a random sample of candidate sentences for each of these entities based on their ERTs and winnowed it down further by manually selecting a subset that exhibits syntactic diversity. Ultimately, our corpus consisted of 120-200 sentences for each primary entity and additional 80 sentences selected from the other four entities.

Each candidate sentence was annotated as TP_e (contains a mention of entity e), $Tneg_e$ (contains a negated mention of entity e), or TN_e (does not contain a mention of entity e). Each sentence was annotated by two domain experts, and we used the third one to break the ties. The Cohens' kappa value for the annotation agreement was 0.58. While the annotators have good agreement on annotating sentences in category *TP*, they agreed less on the categories *Tneg* and *TN*. The latter categories are indeed difficult to distinguish. For example, annotators often argue whether *'patient breathing at a rate of 15-20'*

[2]We do not explicitly report performance on *TN* because our focus is to find sentences that contain entity mentions rather than those devoid of mentions.

means the negation of entity 'shortness of breath' (because that is a normal breathing pattern) or just lacks a mention of the entity. The final annotation label for a sentence is decided based on majority voting. Table 1 shows the statistics of the annotated candidate sentences. The prepared data set is available at `http://knoesis.org/researchers/sujan/data-sets.html`

4.2 Implicit Entity Recognition Performance

Since IER is a novel task, there are no baseline algorithms that can be directly applied such that it would yield a fair comparison with our algorithm. However, we deem some of the related algorithms to have good potential applicability for this task. Therefore, we included two strong algorithms from the closest related work as baseline solutions to the problem.

The first baseline is the well-known text similarity algorithm MCS (Mihalcea et al., 2006). MCS is one of the best performing unsupervised algorithms in paraphrase recognition task (ACLWiki, 2014). It uses an ensemble of statistical and semantic similarity measures, which is a preferable feature for the IER as opposed to one measure used by the matrixJcn (Fernando and Stevenson, 2008). Both MCS and our algorithm classify the candidate sentences based on threshold values selected experimentally.

To include also a supervised baseline, we trained an SVM (Cortes and Vapnik, 1995) one of the state-of-the-art learning algorithms, shown to perform remarkably well in a number of classification tasks. We trained separate SVMs for each primary entity, considering unigrams, bigrams, and trigrams as the features. It has been shown that SVM trained on ngrams performed well on text classification tasks (Pang et al., 2002) (Zhang and Lee, 2003). The SVMs trained with bigrams consistently produced the best results for the 4-fold cross validation. Therefore, our testing phase used the SVMs trained with the bigrams.

Preparation of training and testing datasets: We created training and testing datasets by splitting the dataset annotated for each primary entity as 70% (training) and 30% (testing). The training datasets were used to train the SVM models for each primary entity and to select the threshold values for both MCS and our algorithm.

The classification performance of each algorithm is studied in the *TP* and *Tneg* categories using precision, recall, and F-measure.

The precision (*PP*) and recall (*PR*) for category *TP* at threshold t are defined as:

$$PP_t = \frac{S_{TP}\ with\ sim \geq t}{all\ sentences\ with\ sim \geq t}$$
$$PR_t = \frac{S_{TP}\ with\ sim \geq t}{S_{TP}}$$

Similarly, *NP* and *NR* for *Tneg* are defined as:

$$NP_t = \frac{S_{Tneg}\ with\ sim < t}{all\ sentences\ with\ sim < t}$$
$$NR_t = \frac{S_{Tneg}\ with\ sim < t}{S_{Tneg}}$$

where S_{TP} and S_{Tneg} denote the sentences annotated with *TP* and *Tneg* respectively by domain experts and sim is the calculated similarity value for the pruned sentence.

Selecting threshold value: The threshold values for both MCS and our algorithm are selected based on their classification performance in the training dataset. The MCS algorithm produced the best F1 score for the *TP* category with a threshold value of 0.5, and for the *Tneg* category with a threshold value of 0.9, while our algorithm produced the best F1 for the *TP* category with 0.4 and for the *Tneg* category with 0.3. We examined threshold values that produce best F1 scores by the two algorithms by starting with 10% of the training data and gradually increasing the size of the training data. The threshold values with best F1 scores were stabilized after adding 30% of the training data. Hence, we could select the threshold values with just 50% of the training data.

4.3 Classification Performance

The first experiment evaluates the classification performance of our algorithm, MCS, and SVM.

Method	*PP*	*PR*	*PF1*	*NP*	*NR*	*NF1*
Our	0.66	0.87	0.75	**0.73**	0.73	**0.73**
MCS	0.50	**0.93**	0.65	0.31	**0.76**	0.44
SVM	**0.73**	0.82	**0.77**	0.66	0.67	0.67

Table 2: precision, recall, and F1 values for each algorithm (PF1 and NF1 indicate F1 scores for the *TP* and *Tneg* categories respectively). SVM outperforms our algorithm in the *TP* category, while our algorithm outperforms SVM on the *Tneg* category.

Our algorithm outperforms the other unsupervised solution MCS, but the SVM was able to leverage supervision to outperform our algorithm in the *TP* category in terms of F-measure ($PF1$ on Table 2). For example, the sentence *'he was placed on mechanical ventilation shortly after presentation'* is annotated as *TP* in the gold standard for the entity 'shortness of breath' since *'mechanical ventilation'* indicates the presence of 'shortness of breath'. This annotation requires domain knowledge that was not present in the entity definitions that we used to build entity models. However, with enough examples, the SVM was able to learn the importance of the bigram *'mechanical ventilation'* and classify it as *TP*.

For the *Tneg* category, however, our algorithm outperforms the SVM ($NF1$ on Table 2). This is due to the explicit treatment for the negated mentions by our algorithm to capture different variations of the negated mentions.

The MCS algorithm underperformed in both categories. We observed that this was mostly due to its limitations described in Section 3.5. The overall classification accuracy—the accuracy of classifying both *TP* and *Tneg* instances—of our algorithm, MCS, and SVM are 0.7, 0.4, and 0.7 respectively.

Method	*PP*	*PR*	*PF1*	*NP*	*NR*	*NF1*
SVM	0.73	0.82	0.77	0.66	0.67	0.67
SVM+MCS	0.73	0.82	0.77	0.66	0.66	0.66
SVM+Our	**0.77**	**0.85**	**0.81**	**0.72**	**0.75**	**0.73**

Table 3: Comparison of SVM results incorporating similarity values calculated by our algorithm and MCS as a feature. Our algorithm complements the SVM in both categories whereas MCS does not contribute to improve the classification.

The second experiment evaluates the impact of including the similarity scores calculated by MCS and our algorithm for each candidate sentence as a feature to the best performing SVM model. Table 3 shows that the inclusion of MCS scores as a feature did not help to improve the SVM results. In fact, it negatively affected the results for the *Tneg* category. Since the MCS showed low precision for the *Tneg* category in the previous experiment (Table 2), it is potentially introducing too much noise that the SVM is not able to linearly separate. However, the similarity value calculated by our algorithm improves the SVM classifiers. It increased the precision and recall values for both the *TP* and *Tneg* categories. This shows that the similarity value calculated by our algorithm can be used as an effective feature for a learning algorithm that is designed to solve the IER problem. The overall classification accuracy of SVM, SVM+MCS, and SVM+Our configurations are 0.7, 0.7, and 0.74 respectively.

We were interested in exploring how much labeled data would be needed for supervised solution to outperform our unsupervised score alone. We analyzed the behavior of the three configurations of the SVM with our unsupervised approach with different training set sizes. Figure 2 shows the F1 values obtained by gradually increasing the size of the training dataset[3], while testing on the same test set. The F1 value of our approach remains constant after 50% training data since it has already decided the threshold values. Figure 2 shows that the SVM trained with bigrams needs 76% of the training dataset to achieve the F1 value achieved by our unsupervised approach in the *TP* category, and it does not achieve the F1 achieved by our algorithm in *Tneg* category (note the crossing points of the line marked with 'X' and line marked with circles).

Figure 2 also shows that the similarity score calculated by our algorithm complements the SVM at each data point. After adding our similarity score to the SVM as a feature, it achieved the F1 achieved by our unsupervised algorithm with 50% of the training data in the *TP* category and with 90% of the training data in the *Tneg* category (note the crossing points of the line marked with 'X' and line marked with '+'). Also, SVM+Our configuration achieved the best F1 value for SVM with just 70% of the training data in the *TP* category and with just 50% of the training data in the *Tneg* category. This shows that our similarity score can be used as an effective feature to reduce manual labeling effort and to improve the supervised learning algorithms to solve the IER problem.

Finally, to evaluate the generalization ability of our algorithm and to demonstrate its usage in situations with a lack of training data, we applied it to a set of 80 sentences selected for four new entities (the last four entities in Table 1). Our algorithm produced the following results for these entities when we classify their sentences with the threshold values selected using the training dataset created for the primary entities.

$$PP = 0.72, PR = 0.77, PF1 = 0.74$$
$$NP = 0.78, NR = 0.83, NF1 = 0.80$$

[3]We draw these graphs considering training dataset size >50% for clarity.

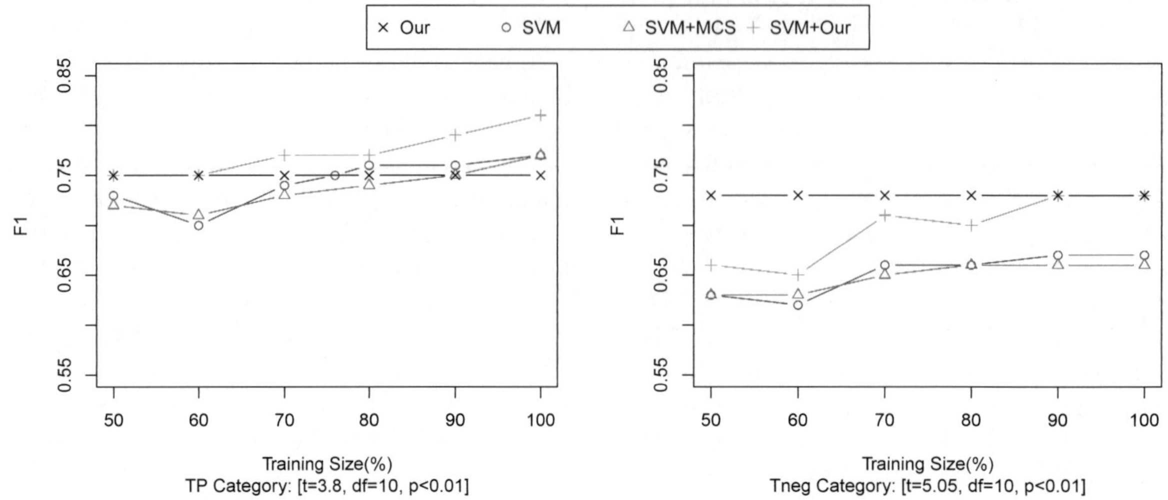

Figure 2: The variation of the F1 value in the *TP* (left) and *Tneg* (right) categories with varying sizes of training datasets. These graphs show that the SVM trained with bigrams needs 76% of the training data to achieve the F1 score of our unsupervised method in the *TP* category while it does not achieve the F1 score of our algorithm in the *Tneg* category. This also shows that the similarity value calculated by our algorithm complements the SVM trained with bigrams at each data point and helps it to beat or perform on par with our algorithm. The paired T-test values calculated for SVM and SVM+Our configurations show that this is not a random behavior (t- T-test value, df- degree of freedom, p- probability value).

Although negation detection with NegEx is not a contribution of our work, our algorithm enables its application to IER. This is not possible for MCS. NegEx requires two inputs: 1) The sentence, and 2) The term being considered for possible negation. MCS does not detect the key term in the sentence, hence it is not possible to apply NegEx with MCS. However, our algorithm starts with identifying the ERT which is considered for possible negation.

5 Limitations

The candidate sentence selection based on the ERT can be seen as a limitation of our approach since it does not select sentences with implicit entity mentions that do not use the selected ERT. However, we do not expect this limitation to have a major impact. We asked our domain experts to come up with sentences that contain implicit mentions of the entity 'shortness of breath' without using its ERT *'breathing'* or its synonyms (*'respiration'* and *'ventilation'*). According to them, the sentences *'the patient had **low oxygen saturation**'*, *'the patient was **gasping for air**'*, and *'patient was **air hunger**'* are such sentences (the emphasis indicates the phrases that imply 'shortness of breath'). However, we found only 113 occurrences of these phrases as opposed to 8990 occurrences of its ERTs in our corpus.

6 Conclusion and Future Work

We defined the problem of *implicit entity recognition* in clinical documents and proposed an unsupervised solution that recognizes the implicit mentions of entities using a model built from their definitions in a knowledge base. We showed that our algorithm outperforms the most relevant unsupervised method and it can be used as an effective feature for a supervised learning solution based on an SVM. The ability to capture the diverse ways in which an entity can be implicitly mentioned by exploiting their definitions with special treatment for two types of negations are the main strengths of our method.

In the future, we will explore the ability to detect the boundary of the phrases with implicit mentions, capture the sentences with implicit mentions without selected ERT, and investigate more intensive exploitation of domain knowledge for IER.

7 Acknowledgement

We acknowledge the medical students Logan Markins, Kara Joseph, and Robert Beaulieu of Wright State University for their assistance in creating the gold-standard corpus.

References

ACLWiki. 2014. Paraphrase identification (state of the art). http://aclweb.org/aclwiki/index.php?title=Paraphrase_Identification_(State_of_the_art). [Online; accessed 19-Dec-2014].

Alan R Aronson. 2006. Metamap: Mapping text to the umls metathesaurus. *Bethesda, MD: NLM, NIH, DHHS.*

Regina Barzilay and Noemie Elhadad. 2003. Sentence alignment for monolingual comparable corpora. In *Proceedings of the 2003 conference on Empirical methods in natural language processing*, pages 25–32. Association for Computational Linguistics.

Olivier Bodenreider. 2004. The unified medical language system (umls): integrating biomedical terminology. *Nucleic acids research*, 32(suppl 1):D267–D270.

Razvan C Bunescu and Marius Pasca. 2006. Using encyclopedic knowledge for named entity disambiguation. In *EACL*, volume 6, pages 9–16.

Wendy W Chapman, Will Bridewell, Paul Hanbury, Gregory F Cooper, and Bruce G Buchanan. 2001. A simple algorithm for identifying negated findings and diseases in discharge summaries. *Journal of biomedical informatics*, 34(5):301–310.

Michael Collins and Yoram Singer. 1999. Unsupervised models for named entity classification. In *Proceedings of the joint SIGDAT conference on empirical methods in natural language processing and very large corpora*, pages 100–110. Citeseer.

Corinna Cortes and Vladimir Vapnik. 1995. Support-vector networks. *Machine learning*, 20(3):273–297.

Bill Dolan, Chris Quirk, and Chris Brockett. 2004. Unsupervised construction of large paraphrase corpora: Exploiting massively parallel news sources. In *Proceedings of the 20th international conference on Computational Linguistics*, page 350. Association for Computational Linguistics.

Greg Durrett and Dan Klein. 2013. Easy victories and uphill battles in coreference resolution. In *EMNLP*, pages 1971–1982.

Samuel Fernando and Mark Stevenson. 2008. A semantic similarity approach to paraphrase detection. In *Proceedings of the 11th Annual Research Colloquium of the UK Special Interest Group for Computational Linguistics*, pages 45–52. Citeseer.

Carol Friedman, Philip O Alderson, John HM Austin, James J Cimino, and Stephen B Johnson. 1994. A general natural-language text processor for clinical radiology. *Journal of the American Medical Informatics Association*, 1(2):161–174.

Carol Friedman, Lyudmila Shagina, Yves Lussier, and George Hripcsak. 2004. Automated encoding of clinical documents based on natural language processing. *Journal of the American Medical Informatics Association*, 11(5):392–402.

Xiao Fu and Sophia Ananiadou. 2014. Improving the extraction of clinical concepts from clinical records. *Proceedings of BioTxtM14.*

Danilo Giampiccolo, Bernardo Magnini, Ido Dagan, and Bill Dolan. 2007. The third pascal recognizing textual entailment challenge. In *Proceedings of the ACL-PASCAL workshop on textual entailment and paraphrasing*, pages 1–9. Association for Computational Linguistics.

Ben Hachey, Will Radford, Joel Nothman, Matthew Honnibal, and James R. Curran. 2013. Evaluating entity linking with wikipedia. *Artif. Intell.*, 194:130–150, January.

Jay J Jiang and David W Conrath. 1997. Semantic similarity based on corpus statistics and lexical taxonomy. *arXiv preprint cmp-lg/9709008.*

Adam Lally, John M Prager, Michael C McCord, BK Boguraev, Siddharth Patwardhan, James Fan, Paul Fodor, and Jennifer Chu-Carroll. 2012. Question analysis: How watson reads a clue. *IBM Journal of Research and Development*, 56(3.4):2–1.

Claudia Leacock and Martin Chodorow. 1998. Combining local context and wordnet similarity for word sense identification. *WordNet: An electronic lexical database*, 49(2):265–283.

Dekang Lin. 1998. An information-theoretic definition of similarity. In *ICML*, volume 98, pages 296–304.

Rada Mihalcea, Courtney Corley, and Carlo Strapparava. 2006. Corpus-based and knowledge-based measures of text semantic similarity. In *AAAI*, volume 6, pages 775–780.

Tomas Mikolov, Kai Chen, Greg Corrado, and Jeffrey Dean. 2013. Efficient estimation of word representations in vector space. *arXiv preprint arXiv:1301.3781.*

David Nadeau and Satoshi Sekine. 2007. A survey of named entity recognition and classification. *Lingvisticae Investigationes*, 30(1):3–26.

Vincent Ng. 2010. Supervised noun phrase coreference research: The first fifteen years. In *Proceedings of the 48th Annual Meeting of the Association for Computational Linguistics*, ACL '10, pages 1396–1411, Stroudsburg, PA, USA. Association for Computational Linguistics.

Bo Pang, Lillian Lee, and Shivakumar Vaithyanathan. 2002. Thumbs up?: sentiment classification using machine learning techniques. In *Proceedings of the ACL-02 conference on Empirical methods in natural language processing-Volume 10*, pages 79–86. Association for Computational Linguistics.

Sameer Pradhan, Noémie Elhadad, Wendy Chapman, Suresh Manandhar, and Guergana Savova. 2014. Semeval-2014 task 7: Analysis of clinical text. *SemEval 2014*, 199(99):54.

Sameer Pradhan, Noémie Elhadad, Brett R South, David Martinez, Lee Christensen, Amy Vogel, Hanna Suominen, Wendy W Chapman, and Guergana Savova. 2015. Evaluating the state of the art in disorder recognition and normalization of the clinical narrative. *Journal of the American Medical Informatics Association*, 22(1):143–154.

Philip Resnik. 1995. Using information content to evaluate semantic similarity in a taxonomy. In *Proceedings of the 14th International Joint Conference on Artificial Intelligence - Volume 1*, IJCAI'95, pages 448–453, San Francisco, CA, USA. Morgan Kaufmann Publishers Inc.

Guergana K Savova, James J Masanz, Philip V Ogren, Jiaping Zheng, Sunghwan Sohn, Karin C Kipper-Schuler, and Christopher G Chute. 2010. Mayo clinical text analysis and knowledge extraction system (ctakes): architecture, component evaluation and applications. *Journal of the American Medical Informatics Association*, 17(5):507–513.

Richard Tzong-Han Tsai, Shih-Hung Wu, Wen-Chi Chou, Yu-Chun Lin, Ding He, Jieh Hsiang, Ting-Yi Sung, and Wen-Lian Hsu. 2006. Various criteria in the evaluation of biomedical named entity recognition. *BMC bioinformatics*, 7(1):92.

Mengqiu Wang. 2006. A survey of answer extraction techniques in factoid question answering. *Computational Linguistics*, 1(1).

Zhibiao Wu and Martha Palmer. 1994. Verbs semantics and lexical selection. In *Proceedings of the 32Nd Annual Meeting on Association for Computational Linguistics*, ACL '94, pages 133–138, Stroudsburg, PA, USA. Association for Computational Linguistics.

Dell Zhang and Wee Sun Lee. 2003. Question classification using support vector machines. In *Proceedings of the 26th annual international ACM SIGIR conference on Research and development in informaion retrieval*, pages 26–32. ACM.

A Distant Supervision Approach to Semantic Role Labeling

Peter Exner **Marcus Klang** **Pierre Nugues**

Lund University
Department of Computer Science
Lund, Sweden
{Peter.Exner, Marcus.Klang, Pierre.Nugues}@cs.lth.se

Abstract

Semantic role labeling has become a key module for many language processing applications such as question answering, information extraction, sentiment analysis, and machine translation. To build an unrestricted semantic role labeler, the first step is to develop a comprehensive proposition bank. However, creating such a bank is a costly enterprise, which has only been achieved for a handful of languages.

In this paper, we describe a technique to build proposition banks for new languages using distant supervision. Starting from PropBank in English and loosely parallel corpora such as versions of Wikipedia in different languages, we carried out a mapping of semantic propositions we extracted from English to syntactic structures in Swedish using named entities.

We trained a semantic parser on the generated Swedish propositions and we report the results we obtained. Using the CoNLL 2009 evaluation script, we could reach the scores of 52.25 for labeled propositions and 62.44 for the unlabeled ones. We believe our approach can be applied to train semantic role labelers for other resource-scarce languages.

1 Introduction

Semantic role labeling has become a key module for many language processing applications and its importance is growing in fields like question answering (Shen and Lapata, 2007), information extraction (Christensen et al., 2010), sentiment analysis (Johansson and Moschitti, 2011), and machine translation (Liu and Gildea, 2010; Wu et al., 2011). To build an unrestricted semantic role labeler, the first step is to develop a comprehensive proposition bank. However, building proposition banks is a costly enterprise and as a consequence of that, they only exist for a handful of languages such as English, Chinese, German, or Spanish.

In this paper, we describe a technique to create proposition banks for new languages using distant supervision. Our approach builds on the transfer of semantic information through named entities. Starting from an existing proposition bank, PropBank in English (Palmer et al., 2005), and loosely parallel corpora such as versions of Wikipedia in different languages, we carried out a mapping of the semantic propositions we extracted from English to syntactic structures in the target language.

We parsed the English edition of Wikipedia up to the predicate–argument structures using a semantic role labeler (Björkelund et al., 2010a) and the Swedish Wikipedia using a dependency parser (Nivre et al., 2006). We extracted all the named entities we found in the propositions and we disambiguated them using the Wikidata nomenclature[1]. Using recurring entities, we aligned sentences in the two languages; we transferred the semantic annotation from English sentences to Swedish sentences; and we could identify 2,333 predicate–argument frames in Swedish.

Finally, we used the resulting corpus to train a semantic role labeler for Swedish that enabled us to evaluate the validity of our approach. Beyond Swedish, we believe it can apply to any resource-

[1] http://www.wikidata.org

*Proceedings of the Fourth Joint Conference on Lexical and Computational Semantics (*SEM 2015)*, pages 239–248,
Denver, Colorado, June 4–5, 2015.

scarce language.

2 Previous Work

The techniques we applied in this paper are similar to those used in the extraction of relations between entity mentions in a sentence, where relational facts are often expressed in the form of triples, such as: (Seoul, CapitalOf, South Korea). While supervised and unsupervised techniques have been applied to the extraction of such relations, they both suffer from drawbacks. Supervised learning relies on labor-intensive, hand-annotated corpora, while unsupervised approaches have lower precision and recall levels.

Distant supervision is an alternative to these approaches that was introduced by Craven and Kumlien (1999). They used a knowledge base of existing biological relations, automatically identified sentences containing these relations, and trained a classifier to recognize the relations. Distant supervision has been successfully transferred to other fields. Mintz et al. (2009) describe a method for creating training data and relation classifiers without a hand-labeled corpus. The authors used Freebase and its binary relations between entities, such as (/location/location/contains, Belgium, Nijlen). They extracted entity pairs from the sentences of a text and matched them to those found in Freebase. Using the entity pairs, the relations, and the corresponding sentence text, they could train a relation extractor.

Padó and Lapata (2009) used parallel corpora and constituent-based models to automatically project FrameNet annotations from English to German. Hoffmann et al. (2010) introduced Wikipedia infoboxes in relation extraction, where the authors trained a classifier to predict the infobox schema of an article prior to the extraction step. They used relation-specific lexicons created from a web crawl to train individual extractors for 5,025 relations and, rather than running all these extractors on every article and sentence, they first predicted the schema of an article and then executed the set of corresponding extractors. Early work in distant supervision assumed that an entity pair expresses a unique explicit relation type. Surdeanu et al. (2012) describe an extended model, where each entity pair may link multiple instances to multiple relations. Ritter et al. (2013) used a latent-variable approach to model information gaps present in either the knowledge base or the corresponding text.

As far as we know, all the work on relation extraction focused on the detection of specific semantic relations between entities. In this paper, we describe an extension and a generalization of it that potentially covers all the relations tied to a predicate and results in the systematic extraction of the semantic propositions observed in a corpus.

Similarly to Mintz et al. (2009), we used an external resource of relational facts and we matched the entity pairs in the relations to a Swedish text corpus. However, our approach substantially differs from theirs by the form of the external resource, which is a parsed corpus. To our best knowledge, there is no Swedish repository of relational facts between entities in existence. Instead, we semantically parsed an English corpus, in our case the English edition of Wikipedia, and we matched, article by article, the resulting semantic structures to sentences in the Swedish edition of Wikipedia. Using the generated Swedish semantic structures, we could train a semantic role labeler.

3 Extending Semantic Role Labeling

In our approach, we employ distantly supervised techniques by combining semantic role labeling (SRL) with entity linking. SRL goes beyond the extraction of n-ary relations and captures a semantic meaning of relations in the form of predicates–argument structures. Since SRL extracts relations between a predicate and its arguments, it can be considered as a form of relation extraction which involves a deeper analysis.

However, the semantic units produced by classical semantic role labeling are still shallow, as they do not resolve coreference or disambiguate named entities. In this work, we selected the propositions, where the arguments corresponded to named entities and we resolved these entities in unique identifiers. This results in a limited set of extended propositions that we think are closer to the spirit of logical forms and can apply in a cross-lingual setting.

Input	Explanation	# cand.	Output
helsingborg c	*Railway station in Helsingborg*	1	wikidata:Q3062731
kärna	*Medieval tower in Helsingborg*	27	wikidata:Q1779457
berga	*District in Helsingborg*	33	wikidata:Q25411

Table 1: Entries in the detection dictionary, all related to the city of Helsingborg in Sweden, with their unique Wikidata Q-number and a short explanation in italics.

4 Named Entity Linking

Named entity linking (or disambiguation) (NED) is the core step of distant supervision to anchor the parallel sentences and propositions. NED usually consists of two steps: first, extract the entity mentions, usually noun phrases, and if a mention corresponds to a proper noun – a named entity –, link it to a unique identifier.

For the English part, we used Wikifier (Ratinov et al., 2011) to disambiguate entities. There was no similar disambiguator for Swedish and those described for English are not directly adaptable because they require resources that do not exist for this language. We created a disambiguator targeted to Swedish: NEDforia. NEDforia uses a Wikipedia dump as input and automatically collects a list of named entities from the corpus. It then extracts the links and contexts of these entities to build disambiguation models. Given an input text, NEDforia recognizes and disambiguates the named entities, and annotates them with their corresponding Wikidata number.

4.1 Entity Detection

We created a dictionary of entities from Wikipedia using the combination of a POS tagger (Östling, 2013), language-dependent uppercase rules, and two entity databases: Freebase (Bollacker et al., 2008) and YAGO2 (Hoffart et al., 2010). Table 1 shows three dictionary entries, where an entry consists of a normalized form and the output is a list of Wikidata candidates in the form of Q-numbers. The output can be the native Wikipedia page, if a Wikidata mapping could not be found, as for "wikipedia.sv:Processorkärna" ("wikipedia.en:Multi-core_processor" in the English Wikipedia).

The entity detection module identifies the strings in the corpus representing named entities. It tokenizes the text and uses the longest match to find the sequences of tokens that can be associated to a list of entity candidates in the dictionary.

4.2 Disambiguation

We disambiguated the entities in a list of candidates using a binary classifier. We trained this classifier with a set of resolved links that we retrieved from the Swedish Wikipedia articles. As in Bunescu and Paşca (2006), we extracted all the manually created mention–entity pairs, encoded as `[[target|label]]` in the Wikipedia markup, and we marked them as positive instances. We created the negative instances with the other mention–candidate pairs that we generated with our dictionary.

As classifier, we used the L2-regularized logistic regression (dual) from LIBLINEAR (Fan et al., 2008) with three features and we ranked the candidates according to the classifier output. The features are the popularity, commonness (Milne and Witten, 2008), and context. The popularity is the probability that a candidate is linked to an entity. We estimate it through the count of unique inbound links to the candidate article (Table 2). The commonness is the probability the sequence of tokens could be the candidate: $P(\text{candidate}|\text{sequence of tokens})$. We compute it from the target–label pairs (Table 3). The context is the count of unique words extracted from the two sentences before the input string that we intersect with the words found in the candidate's article.

Entity	Occupation	Popularity
Göran Persson	Skåne politician	4
Göran Persson	Musician	5
Göran Persson	Prime minister	257

Table 2: The popularity of some entities.

Entity	Mention	Common.
Scandinavian Airlines	SAS	90.4%
Special Air Service	SAS	5.4%
SAS System	SAS	0.4%
Cable News Network	CNN	99.2%
Cable News Network Int.	CNN	0.8%

Table 3: The commonness of some entities.

5 Distant Supervision to Extract Semantic Propositions

The distant supervision module consists of three parts:

1. The first one parses the Swedish Wikipedia up to the syntactic layer and carries out a named entity disambiguation.
2. The second part carries out a semantic parsing of the English Wikipedia and applies a named entity disambiguation.
3. The third part identifies the propositions having identical named entities in both languages using the Wikidata Q-number and aligns them.

5.1 Semantic and Syntactic Parsing

As first step, we parsed the English edition of Wikipedia up to the predicate–argument structures using the Mate-Tools dependency parser and semantic role labeler (Björkelund et al., 2010a) and the Swedish Wikipedia using MaltParser (Nivre et al., 2006). To carry out these parsing tasks, we used a Hadoop-based architecture, Koshik (Exner and Nugues, 2014), that we ran on a cluster of 12 machines.

5.2 Named Entity Disambiguation

The named entity disambiguation links strings to unique Wikidata and is instrumental to the proposition alignment. For the two English-Swedish equivalent sentences:

> Cologne is located on both sides of the Rhine River

and

> Köln ligger på båda sidorna av floden Rhen,

Wikifier, on the English version, identifies *Cologne* and *Rhine river* as named entities and links them respectively to the `en.wikipedia.org/wiki/Cologne` and `en.wikipedia.org/wiki/Rhine` pages, while NEDforia, on the Swedish text, produces a ranked list of entity candidates for the words *Köln* and *Rhen* shown in Table 4. We assign the named entities to the top candidates, Q365 for *Köln* 'Cologne' and Q584 for *Rhen* 'Rhine.' We import the resulting annotated Wikipedia into Koshik, where we map the document titles and anchor targets to Q-numbers.

Words	Entities	English pages
Köln	Q365	Cologne
	Q54096	University of Cologne
	Q104770	1. FC Köln
	Q7927	Cologne (region)
	Q157741	Cologne Bonn Airport
	...	...
Rhen	Q584	Rhine
	Q10650601	No English page

Table 4: The ranked entity candidates matching the words *Köln* 'Cologne' and *Rhen* 'Rhine.' The entities are identified by their Wikidata Q-numbers.

5.3 Alignment of Parallel Sentences

We ran the alignment of loosely parallel sentences using MapReduce (Dean and Ghemawat, 2008) jobs. Both the English and Swedish articles are sequentially read by mappers. For each sentence, the mappers build and emit key-value pairs. The mappers create keys from the entity Q-numbers in each sentence and we use the sentences as values.

The shuffle-and-sort mechanism in Hadoop ensures that, for a given key, each reducer receives all the sentences. In this process, the sentences are aligned by their Q-numbers and given as a group to the reducers with each call. The reducers process each group of aligned sentences and annotate the Swedish sentence by linking the entities by their Q-numbers and by inferring the semantic roles from the aligned English sentences. The annotated Swedish sentences are then emitted from the reducers. For each newly formed Swedish predicate, we select the most frequent alignments to form the final Swedish predicate–argument frames. Figure 1 shows this alignment process.

We believe that by only using pairs of corresponding articles in different language editions and, hence, by restraining cross-article supervision using the unique identifiers given by Wikipedia, we can decrease the number of false negatives. We based this conviction on the observation that many Swedish Wikipedia articles are loosely translated from their corresponding English article and therefore express the same facts or relations.

5.4 Semantic Annotation Transfer

Figure 2 shows the parsing results for the sentences *Cologne is located on both sides of the Rhine River* and *Köln ligger på båda sidorna av floden Rhen* in terms of predicate–argument structures for English, and functions for Swedish. We identify the named entities in the two languages and we align the predicates and arguments. We obtain the complete argument spans by projecting the yield from the argument token. If the argument token is dominated by a preposition, the preposition token is used as the root token for the projection.

5.4.1 Forming Swedish Predicates

During the alignment of English and Swedish sentences, we collect token-level mappings between sentences. The mappings keep a record of how many times an English predicate is aligned with a Swedish verb. For each Swedish verb, we then select the most frequent English predicate it is aligned with. We create a new Swedish frame by using the lemmatized form of the verb and attaching the sense of the English predicate. We use the sentences representing the most frequent mappings to generate our final corpus of Swedish propositions. Table 6 shows how two Swedish frames, *vinna.01* and *vinna.03*, are created by selecting the most frequent mappings. Table 7 shows the ten most frequent Swedish frames created using this process.

6 A Swedish Corpus of Propositions

We processed more than 4 million English Wikipedia articles and almost 3 million Swedish Wikipedia pages from which we could align over 17,000 English sentences with over 16,000 Swedish sentences. This resulted into 19,000 supervisions and the generation of a corpus of Swedish propositions. Table 5 shows an overview of the statistics of this distant supervision process.

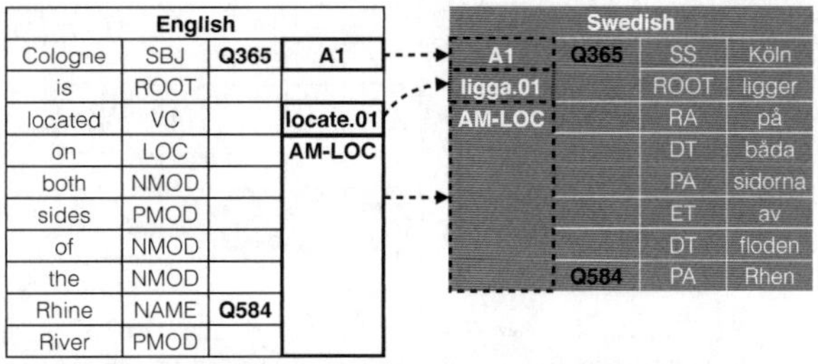

Figure 2: Transfer of the predicate–argument structure from an English sentence to a corresponding Swedish sentence. The sentences are aligned by the two entities that they both share: Cologne (**Q365**) and the Rhine River (**Q584**). The argument roles are transferred using the Q-number entity links. The Swedish predicate is formed using the lemma of the verb token, that is the syntactical parent of the arguments.

Type	Count
English articles	4,152,283
Swedish articles	2,792,089
Supervising sentences (English)	17,115
Supervised sentences (Swedish)	16,636
Number of supervisions	19,121

Table 5: An overview of distant supervision statistics.

The generated corpus consists of over 4,000 sentences, a subset of the 16,000 Swedish sentences used in the supervision process. These 4,000 sentences participate in the most frequent English to Swedish mappings, as detailed in Sect 5.4.1. Table 8 shows an overview of the corpus statistics.

Table 7 shows the ten most frequent mappings and we can see that all of them form meaningful Swedish frames. We can with caution state that our method of selecting the most frequent mapping works surprisingly well. However, if we examine Table 6, we observe some drawbacks to this approach. Although some unlikely mappings, such as pay.01 are filtered out, defeat.01 and prevail.01 could be used to form new Swedish predicates with different senses of the verb *vinna* 'win'. In addition, the predicates, help.01, take.01, and scoring.01, might participate as auxiliary verbs or otherwise form propositions

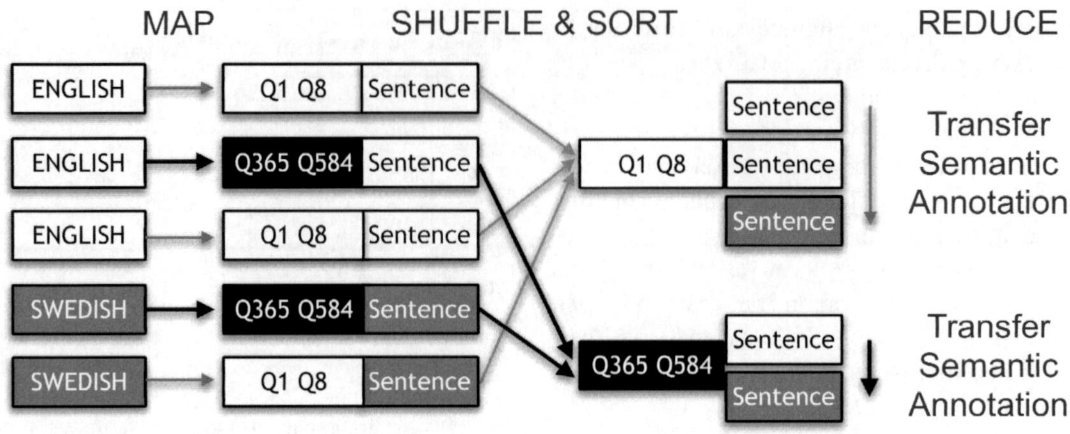

Figure 1: Automatic parallel alignment of sentences through MapReduce. The *Map* phase creates a key-value pair consisting of list of entities and a sentence. The *Shuffle & Sort* mechanism groups the key-value pairs by the list of entities, effectively aligning sentences across the languages. The *Reduce* phase steps through the list of aligned sentences and transfers semantic annotation from a language to another. Figure 2 shows this latter process.

English predicate	Count	Swedish predicate
win.01	**125**	**vinna.01**
defeat.01	24	–
beat.03	**10**	**vinna.03**
help.01	4	–
take.01	4	–
scoring.01	2	–
pay.01	1	–
prevail.01	1	–

Table 6: Selecting the most frequent English to Swedish mapping to form new Swedish predicates for the verb *vinna* 'win'. A bold typeface indicates a newly formed Swedish predicate. A dash indicates that a Swedish predicate for the verb *vinna* was not formed using the corresponding English predicate.

English predicate	Swedish predicate	Count
win.01	vinna.01	125
follow.01	följa.01	107
become.01	bli.01	93
play.01	spela.01	67
locate.01	ligga.01	55
move.01	flytta.01	55
find.01	förekomma.01	41
bear.02	föda.02	41
use.01	använda.01	39
release.01	släppa.01	37

Table 7: The ten most frequent Swedish frames and their mappings from English predicates.

having the same meaning as win.01. A more thorough investigation of the roles played by the entities, possibly in combination with the use of additional semantic information from Wikidata, would certainly aid in improving the extraction of Swedish predicates.

7 Semantic Role Labeling

To assess the usefulness of the proposition corpus, we trained a semantic role labeler on it and we compared its performance with that of a baseline parser. Some roles are frequently associated with grammatical functions, such as A0 and the subject in PropBank. We created the baseline using such association rules and we measured the gains brought by the corpus and a statistical training.

We split the generated corpus into a training, development, and test sets with a 60/20/20 ratio. We used the training and development sets for selecting features during training and we carried out a final evaluation on the test set.

7.1 Baseline Parser

The baseline parser creates a Swedish predicate from the lemma of each verbal token and assigns it the sense 01. Any token governed by the verbal token having a syntactic dependency function is identified as an argument. The Talbanken corpus (Teleman, 1974) serves as training set for the Swedish model of MaltParser. We used four of its grammatical functions: subject (SS), object (OO), temporal adjunct (TA), and location adjunct (RA) to create the roles A0, A1, AM-TMP (temporal), and AM-LOC (locative), respectively.

7.2 Training a Semantic Role Labeler

The SRL pipeline, modified from Björkelund et al. (2010b), consists of four steps: Predicate identification, predicate disambiguation, argument identification, and argument classification.

During predicate identification, a classifier determines if a verb is a predicate and identifies their possible sense. Predicates may have different senses together with a different set of arguments. As an example, the predicate open.01 describes *opening something*, for example, *opening a company branch or a bottle*. This differs from the predicate sense, open.02, having the meaning of *something beginning in a certain state*, such as *a stock opening at a certain price*.

The argument identification and classification steps identify the arguments corresponding to a predicate and label them with their roles.

7.3 Feature Selection

We considered a large number of features and we evaluated them both as single features and in pairs to model interactions. We used the same set as Johansson and Nugues (2008) and Björkelund et al. (2009), who provide a description of them. We used a greedy forward selection and greedy backward elimination procedure to select the features (Björkelund et al., 2010a). We ran the selection process in multiple iterations, until we reached a stable F1 score. Table 10 shows the list of single features we found for the different steps of semantic role labeling: Predicate identification, predicate disambiguation, argument identification, and argument classification.

Interestingly, the amount of features used in argument identification and classification, by far exceeds those used for predicate identification and disambiguation. This hints that, although our generated corpus only considers entities for argument roles, the diverse nature of entities creates a corpus in which arguments hold a wide variety of syntactical and lexical roles.

Property	Unfiltered Count	Filtered Count
Generated frames	2,333	457
Number of propositions	4,369	2,663
Number of sentences	4,152	2,562
Number of tokens	77,015	43,617

Table 8: An overview of corpus statistics.

7.4 The Effect of Singleton Predicate Filtering

We performed a secondary analysis of our generated corpus and we observed that a large number of predicates occurs in only one single sentence. In addition, these predicates were often the result of errors that had propagated through the parsing pipeline.

We filtered out the sentences having mentions of singleton predicates and we built a second corpus to determine what kind of influence it had on the quality of the semantic model. Table 8, right column, shows the statistics of this second corpus. Singleton predicates account for a large part of the corpus and removing them shrinks the number of sentences by almost a half and dramatically reduces the overall number of predicates.

7.5 Validation on the Test Set

Table 9 shows the final evaluation of the baseline parser and the semantic role labeler trained on the generated corpus using distant supervision. The baseline parser reached a labeled F1 score of 22.38%. Clearly, the indiscriminating choice of predicates made by the baseline parser gives a higher recall but a poor precision. The semantic role labeler, trained on our generated corpus, outperforms the baseline parser by a large margin with a labeled F1 score of 39.88%. Filtering the corpus for singleton mention predicates has a dramatic effect on the parsing quality, increasing the labeled F1 score to 52.25%. We especially note a F1 score of 62.44% in unlabeled proposition identification showing the validity of the approach.

Method	Labeled			Unlabeled		
	Precision	Recall	F1	Precision	Recall	F1
Baseline	15.74	38.73	22.38	25.10	**61.78**	35.70
Distant supervision (Unfiltered corpus)	46.99	34.65	39.88	67.06	49.45	56.92
Distant supervision (Filtered corpus)	**58.23**	**47.38**	**52.25**	**69.59**	56.62	**62.44**

Table 9: Summary of semantic role labeling results. The table shows precision, recall, and F1 scores for our baseline and distant supervision methods. Evaluation performed on test set.

Feature	PI	PD	AI	AC
ArgDeprel			•	•
ArgPOS			•	•
ArgWord			•	•
ChildDepSet		•		•
ChildPOSSet		•		•
ChildWordSet		•	•	
DepSubCat	•	•		
DeprelPath			•	•
LeftPOS				•
LeftSiblingPOS				•
LeftSiblingWord				•
LeftWord				•
POSPath			•	•
Position	•		•	•
PredLemma	•		•	•
PredLemmaSense				•
PredPOS		•	•	•
PredParentPOS	•	•	•	•
PredParentWord	•	•		•
PredWord	•			•
RightPOS			•	•
RightSiblingWord			•	
RightWord			•	•

Table 10: List of features used in the four stages of semantic role labeling. PI stands for predicate identification, PD for predicate disambiguations, AI for argument identification, and AC for argument classification.

8 Conclusion

By aligning English and Swedish sentences from two language editions of Wikipedia, we have shown how semantic annotation can be transferred to generate a corpus of Swedish propositions. We trained a semantic role labeler on the generated corpus and showed promising results in proposition identification.

We aligned the sentences using entities and frequency counts to select the most likely frames. While this relatively simple approach could be considered inadequate for other distant supervision applications, such as relation extraction, it worked surprisingly well in our case. We believe this can be attributed to the named entity disambiguation, which goes beyond a simple surface form comparison and uniquely identifies the entities used in the supervision. In addition, we believe that the implicit entity types that a set of named entities infer, constrain a sentence to a certain predicate and sense. This increases the likelihood that the Swedish aligned sentence contains a predicate which preserves the same semantics as the English verb of the source sentence. Furthermore, we go beyond infobox relations as we infer new predicates with different senses. Using infobox relations would have limited us to relations already described by the infobox ontology.

Since our technique builds on a repository of entities extracted from Wikipedia, one future improvement could be to exploit the semantic information residing in it, possible from other repositories such as DBpedia (Bizer et al., 2009) or YAGO2. Another possible improvement would be to increase the size of the generated corpus. We envision this being done either by applying a coreference solver to anaphoric mentions to increase the number of sentences that could be aligned or by synthetically generating sentences through the use of a semantic repository. An additional avenue of exploration lies in extending our work to other languages.

Acknowledgements

This research was supported by Vetenskapsrådet under grant 621-2010-4800, and the *Det digitaliserade samhället* and eSSENCE programs.

References

Christian Bizer, Jens Lehmann, Georgi Kobilarov, Sören Auer, Christian Becker, Richard Cyganiak, and Sebastian Hellmann. 2009. DBpedia—a crystallization point for the web of data. *Journal of Web Semantics*, pages 154–165.

Anders Björkelund, Love Hafdell, and Pierre Nugues. 2009. Multilingual semantic role labeling. In *Proceedings of The Thirteenth Conference on Computational Natural Language Learning (CoNLL-2009)*, pages 43–48, Boulder, June 4-5.

Anders Björkelund, Bernd Bohnet, Love Hafdell, and Pierre Nugues. 2010a. A high-performance syntactic and semantic dependency parser. In *Coling 2010: Demonstration Volume*, pages 33–36, Beijing, August 23-27. Coling 2010 Organizing Committee.

Anders Björkelund, Bernd Bohnet, Love Hafdell, and Pierre Nugues. 2010b. A high-performance syntactic and semantic dependency parser. In *COLING (Demos)*, pages 33–36. Demonstrations Volume.

Kurt Bollacker, Colin Evans, Praveen Paritosh, Tim Sturge, and Jamie Taylor. 2008. Freebase: A collaboratively created graph database for structuring human knowledge. In *Proceedings of the 2008 ACM SIGMOD International Conference on Management of Data*, SIGMOD '08, pages 1247–1250.

Razvan Bunescu and Marius Paşca. 2006. Using encyclopedic knowledge for named entity disambiguation. In *Proceedings of the 11th Conference of the European Chapter of the Association for Computational Linguistics*, pages 9–16, Trento, April. Association for Computational Linguistics.

Janara Christensen, Mausam, Stephen Soderland, and Oren Etzioni. 2010. Semantic role labeling for open information extraction. In *Proceedings of the NAACL HLT 2010 First International Workshop on Formalisms and Methodology for Learning by Reading*, FAM-LbR '10, pages 52–60.

Mark Craven and Johan Kumlien. 1999. Constructing biological knowledge bases by extracting information from text sources. In *Proceedings of the Seventh International Conference on Intelligent Systems for Molecular Biology (ISMB'99)*, pages 77–86.

Jeffrey Dean and Sanjay Ghemawat. 2008. MapReduce: simplified data processing on large clusters. *Communications of the ACM*, 51(1):107–113.

Peter Exner and Pierre Nugues. 2014. KOSHIK: A large-scale distributed computing framework for nlp. In *Proceedings of ICPRAM 2014 – The 3rd International Conference on Pattern Recognition Applications and Methods*, pages 464–470, Angers, March 6-8.

Rong-En Fan, Kai-Wei Chang, Cho-Jui Hsieh, Xiang-Rui Wang, and Chih-Jen Lin. 2008. LIBLINEAR: A library for large linear classification. *Journal of Machine Learning Research*, 9:1871–1874.

Johannes Hoffart, Fabian M. Suchanek, Klaus Berberich, and Gerhard Weikum. 2010. YAGO2: a spatially and temporally enhanced knowledge base from Wikipedia. Research Report MPI-I-2010-5-007, Max-Planck-Institut für Informatik, Stuhlsatzenhausweg 85, 66123 Saarbrücken, Germany, November.

Raphael Hoffmann, Congle Zhang, and Daniel S Weld. 2010. Learning 5000 relational extractors. In *Proceedings of the 48th Annual Meeting of the Association for Computational Linguistics*, pages 286–295.

Richard Johansson and Alessandro Moschitti. 2011. Extracting opinion expressions and their polarities: exploration of pipelines and joint models. In *Proceedings of the 49th Annual Meeting of the Association for Computational Linguistics: Human Language Technologies: short papers. Volume 2*, pages 101–106.

Richard Johansson and Pierre Nugues. 2008. Dependency-based syntactic–semantic analysis with PropBank and NomBank. In *Proceedings of CoNLL-2008: The Twelfth Conference on Computational Natural Language Learning*, pages 183–187, Manchester, August 16-17.

Ding Liu and Daniel Gildea. 2010. Semantic role features for machine translation. In *COLING '10 Proceedings of the 23rd International Conference on Computational Linguistics*, pages 716–724, Beijing, June.

David Milne and Ian H. Witten. 2008. Learning to link with wikipedia. In *Proceedings of the 17th ACM conference on Information and knowledge management*, CIKM '08, pages 509–518.

Mike Mintz, Steven Bills, Rion Snow, and Dan Jurafsky. 2009. Distant supervision for relation extraction without labeled data. In *Proceedings of the Joint Conference of the 47th Annual Meeting of the ACL and the 4th International Joint Conference on Natural Language Processing of the AFNLP: Volume 2-Volume 2*, pages 1003–1011.

Joakim Nivre, Johan Hall, and Jens Nilsson. 2006. MaltParser: A data-driven parser-generator for dependency parsing. In *Proceedings of the fifth international conference on Language Resources and Evaluation (LREC2006)*, pages 2216–2219, Genoa.

Robert Östling. 2013. Stagger: an open-source part of speech tagger for Swedish. *Northern European Journal of Language Technology*, 3:1–18.

Sebastian Padó and Mirella Lapata. 2009. Cross-lingual annotation projection for semantic roles. *Journal of Artificial Intelligence Research*, 36(1):307–340.

Martha Palmer, Daniel Gildea, and Paul Kingsbury. 2005. The Proposition Bank: an annotated corpus of semantic roles. *Computational Linguistics*, 31(1):71–105.

Lev Ratinov, Dan Roth, Doug Downey, and Mike Anderson. 2011. Local and global algorithms for disambiguation to wikipedia. In *Proceedings of the 49th Annual Meeting of the Association for Computational Linguistics: Human Language Technologies - Volume 1*, HLT '11, pages 1375–1384.

Alan Ritter, Luke Zettlemoyer, Oren Etzioni, et al. 2013. Modeling missing data in distant supervision for information extraction. *Transactions of the Association for Computational Linguistics*, 1:367–378.

Dan Shen and Mirella Lapata. 2007. Using semantic roles to improve question answering. In *Proceedings of the 2007 Joint Conference on Empirical Methods in Natural Language Processing and Computational Natural Language Learning*, pages 12–21, Prague, June.

Mihai Surdeanu, Julie Tibshirani, Ramesh Nallapati, and Christopher D Manning. 2012. Multi-instance multi-label learning for relation extraction. In *Proceedings of the 2012 Joint Conference on Empirical Methods in Natural Language Processing and Computational Natural Language Learning*, pages 455–465.

Ulf Teleman. 1974. *Manual för grammatisk beskrivning av talad och skriven svenska*. Studentlitteratur, Lund.

Dekai Wu, Pascale Fung, Marine Carpuat, Chi kiu Lo, Yongsheng Yang, and Zhaojun Wu. 2011. Lexical semantics for statistical machine translation. In Joseph Olive, Caitlin Christianson, and John McCary, editors, *Handbook of Natural Language Processing and Machine Translation: DARPA Global Autonomous Language Exploitation*, pages 236–252. Springer, Heidelberg.

Discovering Hypernymy Relations using Text Layout

Jean-Philippe Fauconnier
Institut de Recherche en
Informatique de Toulouse
118, Route de Narbonne
31062 Toulouse, France
faucon@irit.fr

Mouna Kamel
Institut de Recherche en
Informatique de Toulouse
118, Route de Narbonne
31062 Toulouse, France
kamel@irit.fr

Abstract

Hypernymy relation acquisition has been widely investigated, especially because taxonomies, which often constitute the backbone structure of semantic resources are structured using this type of relations. Although lots of approaches have been dedicated to this task, most of them analyze only the written text. However relations between not necessarily contiguous textual units can be expressed, thanks to typographical or dispositional markers. Such relations, which are out of reach of standard NLP tools, have been investigated in well specified layout contexts. Our aim is to improve the relation extraction task considering both the plain text and the layout. We are proposing here a method which combines layout, discourse and terminological analyses, and performs a structured prediction. We focused on textual structures which correspond to a well defined discourse structure and which often bear hypernymy relations. This type of structure encompasses titles and sub-titles, or enumerative structures. The results achieve a precision of about 60%.

1 Introduction

The hypernymy relation acquisition task is a widely studied problem, especially because taxonomies, which often constitute the backbone structure of semantic resources like ontologies, are structured using this type of relations. Although this task has been addressed in literature, most of the publications report analyses based on the written text only, usually at the phrase or sentence level. However, a written text is not merely a set of words or sentences. When producing a document, a writer may use various layout means, in addition to strictly linguistics devices such as syntactic arrangement or rhetorical forms. Relations between textual units that are not necessarily contiguous can thus be expressed thanks to typographical or dispositional markers. Such relations, which are out of reach of standard NLP tools, have been studied within some specific layout contexts. Our aim is to improve the relation extraction task by considering both the plain text and the layout. This means (1) identifying hierarchical structures within the text using only layout, (2) identifying relations carried by these structures, using both lexico-syntactic and layout features.

Such an approach is deemed novel for at least two reasons. It combines layout, discourse and terminological analyses to bridge the gap between the document layout and lexical resources. Moreover, it makes a structured prediction of the whole hierarchical structure according to the set of visual and discourse properties, rather than making decisions only based on parts of this structure, as usually performed.

The main strength of our approach is its applicability to different document formats as well to several domains. It should be highlighted that encyclopedic, technical or scientific documents, which are often analyzed for building semantic resources, are most of the time strongly structured. Our approach has been implemented for the French language, for which only few resources are currently available. In this paper we focus on specific textual

*Proceedings of the Fourth Joint Conference on Lexical and Computational Semantics (*SEM 2015)*, pages 249–258,
Denver, Colorado, June 4–5, 2015.

structures which share the same discourse properties and that are expected to bear hypernymy relations. They encompass for instance titles/sub-titles, or enumerative structures.

The paper is organized as follows. Some related works about hypernymy relation identification are reported in section 2. Section 3 presents the theoretical framework on which the proposed approach is based. Sections 4 and 5 respectively describe transitions from the text layout to its discourse representation and from this discourse structure to the terminological structure. Finally we draw conclusions and propose some perspectives.

2 Related works

The task of extracting hypernymy relations (it may also be denoted as generic/specific, taxonomic, is-a or instance-of relations) is critical for building semantic resources and for semantic content authoring. Several parameters concerning corpora may affect the methods used for this task: the natural language quality (carefully written or informal), the textual genre (scientific, technical documents, newspapers, etc.), technical properties (corpus size, format), the level of precision of the resource (thesaurus, lightweight or full-fledged ontology), the degree of structuring, etc. This task may be carried out by using the proper text and/or external pre-existing resources. Various methods for exploiting plain text exist using techniques such as regular expressions (also known as lexico-syntactic patterns) (Hearst, 1992), classification using supervised or unsupervised learning (Snow et al., 2004; Alfonseca and Manandhar, 2002), distributional analysis (Lenci and Benotto, 2012) or Formal Concepts Analysis (Cimiano et al., 2005). In the Information Retrieval area, the relevant terms are extracted from documents and organized into hierarchies (Sánchez and Moreno, 2005).

Works on the document structure and on the discourse relations that it conveys have been carried out by the NLP community. Among these are the Document Structure Theory (Power et al., 2003), and the DArt_{bio} system (Bateman et al., 2001). These approaches offer strong theoretical frameworks, but they were only implemented from a text generation point of view.

With regard to the relation extraction task using layout, two categories of approaches may be distinguished. The first one encompasses approaches exploiting documents written in a markup language. The semantics of these tags and their nested structure is used to build semantic resources. For instance, collection of XML documents have been analyzed to build ontologies (Kamel and Aussenac-Gilles, 2009), while collection of HTML or MediaWiki documents have been exploited to build taxonomies (Sumida and Torisawa, 2008).

The second category gathers approaches exploiting specific documents or parts of documents, for which the semantics of the layout is strictly defined. Let us mention dictionaries and thesaurus (Jannink and Wiederhold, 1999) or specific and well localized textual structures such as category field (Chernov et al., 2006; Suchanek et al., 2007) or infoboxes (Auer et al., 2007) from Wikipedia pages. In some cases, these specific textual structures are also expressed thanks to a markup language. All these works implement symbolic as well as machine learning techniques.

Our approach is similar to the one followed by Sumida and Torisawa (2008) which analyzes a structured text according to the following steps: (1) they represent the document structure from a limited set of tags (headings, bulleted lists, ordered lists and definition lists), (2) they link two tagged strings when the first one is in the scope of the second one, and (3) they use lexico-syntactic and layout features for selecting hypernymy relations, with the help of a machine learning algorithm. Some attempts have been made for improving these results (Oh et al., 2009; Yamada et al., 2009). However our work differs in two points: we aimed to be more generic by proposing a discourse structure of layout that can be inferred from different document formats, and we propose to find out the relation arguments (hypernym-hyponym term pairs) by analyzing propositional contents. Prior to describing the implemented processes, the underlying principles of our approach will be reported in the next section.

3 Underlying principles of our approach

We rely on principles of discourse theories and on knowledge models for respectively formalizing text layout and identifying hypernymy relations.

3.1 Discourse analysis of the layout

Several discourse theories exist. Their starting point lies in the idea that a text is not just a collection of sentences, but it also includes relations between all these sentences that ensure its coherence (Mann and Thompson, 1988; Asher and Lascarides, 2003). Discourse analysis aims at observing the discourse coherence from a rhetorical point of view (the intention of the author) or from a semantic point of view (the description of the world). A discourse analysis is a three step process: splitting the text into Discourse Units (DU), ensuring the attachment between DUs, and then labeling links between DUs with discourse relations. Discourse relations may be divided into two categories: nucleus-satellite (or subordinate) relations which link an important argument to an argument supporting background information, and multi-nuclear (or coordinate) relations which link arguments of equal importance. Most of discourse theories acknowledge that a discourse is hierarchically structured thanks to discourse relations.

Text layout supports a large part of semantics and participates to the coherence of the text; it thus contributes to the elaboration of the discourse. Therefore, we adapted the discourse analysis to treat the layout, according to the following principles:

- a DU corresponds to a visual unit (a bloc);
- two units sharing the same role (title, paragraph, etc.) and the same typographic and dispositional markers are linked with a multi-nuclear relation; otherwise, they are linked with a nuclear-satellite relation.

An example[1] of document from Wikipedia and the tree which results from the discourse analysis of its layout is given (Figure 1). In the following figures, we represent nucleus-satellite relations with solid lines and multi-nuclear relations with dashed lines.

[1]http://fr.wikipedia.org/wiki/Redécentralisation_d'Internet

We are currently interested in discourse structures displaying the following properties:

- n DUs are linked with multi-nuclear relations;
- one of these coordinated DU is linked to another DU with a nucleus-satellite relation.

Figure 2 gives a representation of such a discourse structure according to the Rhetorical Structure Theory (Mann and Thompson, 1988).

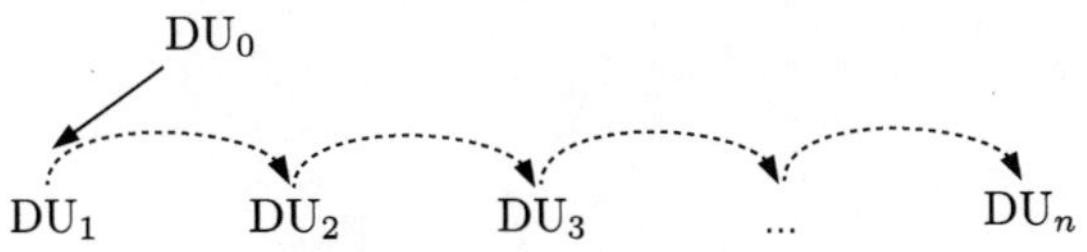

Figure 2: Rhetorical representation of the discourse structure of interest

Although there is only one explicit nucleus-satellite relation, this kind of structure involves n implicit nucleus-satellite relations (between DU_0 and DU_i ($2 \leq i \leq n$)). Indeed, from a discourse point of view, if a DU_j is subordinated to a DU_i, then all DU_k coordinated to DU_j, are subordinated to DU_i. As mentioned above, this kind of discourse structure encompasses textual structures such as titles/sub-titles and enumerative structures which are frequent in structured documents, and which often convey hypernymy relation. In that context, the hypernym is borne by the DU_0 and each DU_i ($1 \leq i \leq n$) bears at least one hyponym.

3.2 Knowledge models for hypernymy relation identification

Hypernymy relation identification is carried out in two stages: specifying if the relation is hypernymic and, if appropriate, identifying its arguments. The first stage relies on linguistic regularities denoting a hypernymy relation, regularities which are expressed thanks to lexical, syntactic, typographical and dispositional clues.

The second stage is based on a graph representation. Rather than independently identifying links between the hypernym and each potential hyponym, we take advantage from the fact that writers use the same syntactic and visual skills (recognized by a textual parallelism) for expressing knowledge units of equal rhetorical importance. Generally, these salient units are semantically linked and belong to a same lexical field.

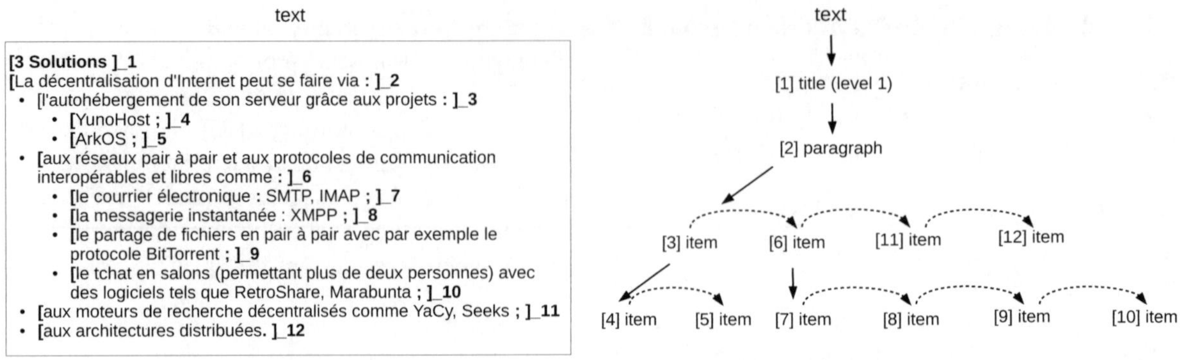

Figure 1: Example of a discourse analysis of text layout

Thus, we represent each discourse structure of interest bearing a hypernymy relation as a directed acyclic graph (DAG), where the nodes are terms and the edges are possible relations between them. This DAG is decomposed into layers, each layer i gathering nodes corresponding to terms of a given DU_i $(0 \leq i \leq n)$. Each node of a layer i $(0 \leq i \leq (n-1))$ is connected by directed edges to all nodes of the layer $i+1$. A root node is added on the top of the DAG. Figure 3 presents an example of this DAG.

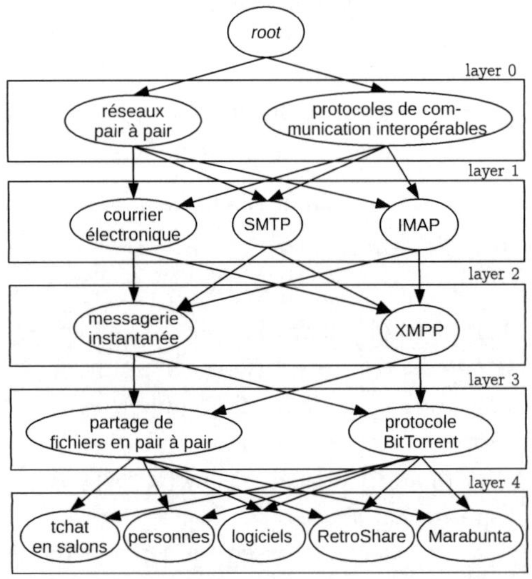

Figure 3: Example of a DAG

We weight the edges according to the inverse similarity of terms they link. Thus, the terms in the lower-cost path starting from the root and ending at the last layer are maximally cohesive. A flatter representation does not allow this structured prediction.

4 From text layout to its discourse representation

To elicit discourse structures from text layout, the system detects visuals units and labels them with their role (paragraph, title, footnote, etc.) in the text. Then, it links the labeled units using discourse relations (nucleus-satellite or multi-nuclear) in order to produce a discourse tree.

We are currently able to process two types of documents: documents written in a markup language and documents in PDF format. It is obvious that tags of markup languages both delimit blocs and give their role. Getting the visual structure is thus straightforward. Conversely, PDF documents do not benefit from such tags. So we used the LAPDF-Text tool (Ramakrishnan et al., 2012) which is based on a geometric analysis for detecting blocs, and we have implemented a machine learning method for labeling these blocs. The features include typographical markers (size of fonts, emphasis markers, etc.) and dispositional one (margins, position in page, etc.).

For labeling relations, we used an adapted version of the shift-reduce algorithm as (Marcu, 1999) did. We thus obtain a dependency tree representing the discourse structure of the text layout. We evaluate this process on a corpus of PDF documents (documents written in a markup language pose no problem). Results are good since we obtain an accuracy of 80.46% for labeling blocs, and an accuracy of 97.23% for labeling discourse relations (Fauconnier et al., 2014). The whole process has been implemented in the LaToe[2] tool.

[2] http://github.com/fauconnier/LaToe

Finally, the extraction of discourse structures of interest may be done easily by means of tree patterns (Levy and Andrew, 2006).

5 From layout discourse structure to terminological structure

We wish to elicit possible hypernymy relations from identified discourse structures of interest. This task involves a two-step process. The first step consists in specifying the nature of the relation borne by these structures. The second step aims at identifying the related terms (the relation arguments). These steps have been independently evaluated on an annotated corpus, while the whole system has been evaluated on another not annotated corpus. Corpora and evaluation protocols are described in the next section.

5.1 Corpora and evaluation protocols

The annotated corpus includes 166 French Wikipedia pages corresponding to urban and environmental planning. 745 discourse structures of interest were annotated by 3 annotators (2 students in Linguistics, and an expert in knowledge engineering) according to a guideline. The annotation task for each discourse structure of interest has consisted in annotating the nucleus-satellite relation as hypernymy or not, and when required, in annotating the terms involved in the relation. For the first stage, we have calculated a degree of inter-annotator agreement (Fleiss et al., 1979) and obtained a kappa of 0.54. The second stage was evaluated as a named entity recognition task (Tateisi et al., 2000) for which we have obtained an F-measure of 79.44. From this dataset, 80% of the discourse structures of interest were randomly chosen to constitute the development set, and the remaining 20% were used for the test set. The tasks described below were tuned on the development set using a k-10 cross-validation. The evaluation is done using the precision, the recall and the F-measure metrics.

A second evaluation for the entire system was led on two corpora respectively made of Wikipedia pages from two domains: *Transport* and *Computer Science*. For each domain, we have randomly selected 400 pages from a French Wikipedia Dump (2014-09-28). Since those copora are not manually annotated, we have only reported the precision.

5.2 Qualifying the nucleus-satellite relation

Hypernymy relations present lexical, syntactic, typographical and dispositional regularities in the text. The recognition of these relations is thus based on the analysis of these regularities within the two DUs explicitly linked by the nucleus-satellite relation. We consider this problem as a binary classification one: each discourse structure is assigned to either the *Hypernymy-Structure* class or the *nonHypernymy-Structure* class. The *Hypernymy-Structure* class encompasses discourse structures with a nucleus-satellite relation bearing a hypernymy, whereas the *nonHypernymy-Structure* one gathers all others discourse structures. In the example given in figure 1, the discourse structures constituted of DUs {3,4,5} and {6,7,8,9,10} would be classified as *Hypernymy-Structure*, while this constituted of DUs {2,3,6,11,12} would be assigned to the *nonHypernymy-Structure* class.

For this purpose, we applied feature functions (summarized in table 1) in order to map the two DUs linked by the explicit nucleus-satellite relation into a numerical vector which is submitted to a classifier. The feature functions were defined according to background knowledge and were selected on the basis of a Pearson's correlation.

Features	Description
POS	Unigrams of parts of speech
Position	Position of a token in a DU
Markers	Boolean indicating whether a token belongs to a predefined lexicon
Gram	Boolean indicating whether the last sentence of a DU shows a syntactic hole
Punc	Returns the last punctuation of a DU
NbToken	Number of tokens in a DU
NbSent	Number of sentences in a DU

Table 1: Main features for qualifying the relation

We have compared two types of classifiers: a linear one which generalizes well, but may produce more misclassifications when data distribution presents a large spread, and a non-linear one which may lead to a model separating well the training set but with an overfitting risk. We respectively used a Maximum Entropy classifier (MaxEnt) (Berger et al., 1996) and a Support Vector Machine (SVM) with a Gaussian kernel (Cortes and Vapnik, 1995).

The morphological and lexical information used were obtained from the French dependency parser Talismane (Urieli, 2013). For the classifiers, we have used the OpenNLP[3] library for the MaxEnt and the LIBSVM implementation of the SVM[4]. This task has been evaluated against a majority baseline which better reflects the reality because of the asymmetry of the relation distribution. Table 2 presents the results. The two supervised strategies outperform significantly the baseline (p-values<0.01)[5].

Strategies	Prec.	Rec.	F1
MaxEnt	**78.01**	84.78	81.25
SVM	74.77	**90.22**	81.77
Baseline	63.01	100.0	77.31

Table 2: Results for qualifying the relation

Regarding the F-measure metric, the difference between the MaxEnt and the SVM is not significant. We observe that the MaxEnt achieves the best precision, while the SVM reaches the best recall. These results are not surprising since the SVM decision boundary seems to be biased by outliers, thus increasing the false positive rate on unseen data.

5.3 Identifying the terms linked by the hypernymy relation

We have now to identify terms linked by the hypernymy relation. As previously mentioned we build a DAG reflecting all possible relations between terms of the DUs, to find the lower-cost path which represents the most cohesive sequence of terms.

If we consider the discourse structure constituted of DUs $\{6,7,8,9,10\}$ in figure 1, the retrieved path from the corresponding DAG (figure 3) would be ["protocoles de communication interopérables" (*interoperable communication protocols*), "courrier électronique" (*email*), "messagerie instantanée" (*instant messaging*), "partage de fichiers en pair à pair" (*peer-to-peer file sharing*), "tchat en salons" (*chat room*)]. Then, an example of hypernymy relation would be "courrier électronique" (*email*) is a kind of "protocoles de communication interopérables" (*interoperable communication protocols*).

[3] http://opennlp.apache.org/

[4] http://www.csie.ntu.edu.tw/~cjlin/libsvm/

[5] The p-values are calculated using a paired t-test.

The cost of an edge is defined using the following function:

$$\text{cost}(< T_i^j, T_{i+1}^k >) = 1 - p(y|T_i^j, T_{i+1}^k)$$

where T_i^j is the j-th term of DU_i. The probability assigned to the outcome y measures the likeliness that both terms are linked. This probability is conditioned by lexical and dispositional clues. Since it is expected that terms involved in the relation share the same lexical field, we also consider the cosine similarity between the term vectors. All those clues are mapped into a numerical vector using feature functions summarized in table 3.

Features	Description
POS_c	Context of a term (bigrams and unigrams of parts of speech)
POS_t	Parts of speech of a term
Role	Role of a DU
Visual	Boolean indicating whether a pair of terms share the same visual properties
Position_t	Value indicating a term position
Position_d	Position of a DU in the whole document
Coord	For a DU, presence of coordinated DUs
Sub	For a DU, presence of subordinated DUs
Level	Value indicating the level of a DU in the structure of document
Punc	Returns the last punctuation of a DU
NbToken	Number of tokens in a DU
NbSent	Number of sentences in a DU
COS	Cosine similarity for a pair of terms

Table 3: Main features for the terms recognition

We built two models based on supervised probabilistic classifiers since characteristics of links between a hypernym and a hyponym are different from those between two hyponyms. The first model considers only the edges between layer 0 and layer 1 (hypernym-hyponym link), whereas the second one is dedicated to the edges of remaining layers (hyponym-hyponym link).

For this step, we used ACABIT (Daille, 1996) and YaTeA (Aubin and Hamon, 2006) for extracting terms. The cosine similarity is based on a distributional model constructed with the word2vec tool (Mikolov et al., 2013) and the French corpus FrWac (Baroni et al., 2009). We have learned the models using a Maximum Entropy classifier.

For computing the lower-cost path, we use an A* search algorithm because it can handle large search space with an admissible heuristic. The estimated cost of a path P, a sequence of edges from the root to a given term, is defined by:

$$f(P) = g(P) + h(P)$$

The function $g(P)$ calculates the real cost along the path P and it is defined by:

$$g(P) = \sum_{<T_i^j, T_{i+1}^k> \in P} \text{cost}(< T_i^j, T_{i+1}^k >)$$

The heuristic $h(P)$ is a greedy function which picks a new path with the minimal cost over d layers and returns its cost:

$$h(P) = g(l_d(P))$$

The function $l_d(P)$ is defined recursively: $l_0(P)$ is the empty path. Assume $l_d(P)$ is defined and $T_{i_d}^{j_d}$ is the last node reached on the path formed by the concatenation of P and $l_d(P)$, then we define:

$$l_{d+1}(P) = l_d(P). < T_{i_d}^{j_d}, T_{i_d+1}^{m} >$$

where m is the index of the term with the lower cost edge and belonging to the layer $i_d + 1$:

$$m = \underset{k<|\text{layer } i_d+1|}{\text{argmin}} \text{cost}(< T_{i_d}^{j_d}, T_{i_d+1}^{k} >)$$

This heuristic is admissible by definition. We set d=3 because it is a good tradeoff between the number of operations and the number of iterations during the A* search.

In order to evaluate this task, we compare it to a baseline and two vector-based approaches. The baseline works on the assumption that two related terms belong to a same window of words; then it takes the last term of the layer 0 as hypernym, and the first term of each layer i ($1 \leq i \leq n$) as hyponym. The two other strategies use a cosine similarity (calculated with respectively 200- and 500-dimensional vectors) for the costs estimation. Table 4 presents the results.

The MaxEnt achieves the best F-measure and outperforms the others proposed strategies. The vector-based strategies present interesting precisions, which seems to confirm a correlation between the lexical cohesion of terms and their likelihood of being involved in a relation.

Strategies	Prec.	Rec.	F1
MaxEnt	78.98	69.09	**73.71**
w2v-200	66.52	30.10	41.45
w2v-500	83.71	30.10	44.28
Baseline	48.37	69.09	56.91

Table 4: Results for terms recognition

To lead additional evaluations we define the score of a path as the mean of its costs, and we select results using a list of threshold values: only the paths with a score lower than a given threshold are returned. Figure 4 shows the Precision-Recall curves using the whole list of threshold values.

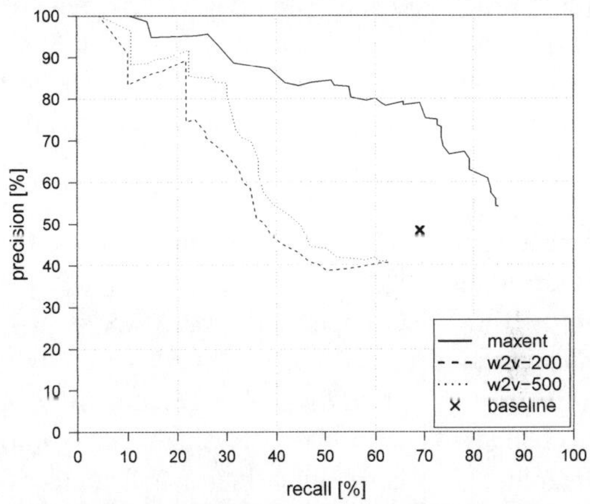

Figure 4: Comparison between the baseline, the vector-based strategies and the MaxEnt

5.4 Evaluation of the whole system

In this section, we report the results for the whole process applied on two corpora made of Wikipedia pages from two domains: *Transport* and *Computer Science*. For each of them, we applied a discourse analysis of the layout, and we extracted the hypernym-hyponym pairs. This extraction was done with a Maximum Entropy classifier which has shown a good precision for the two tasks described before. The retrieved pairs were ranked according to the score of the path they belong to. Finally, we

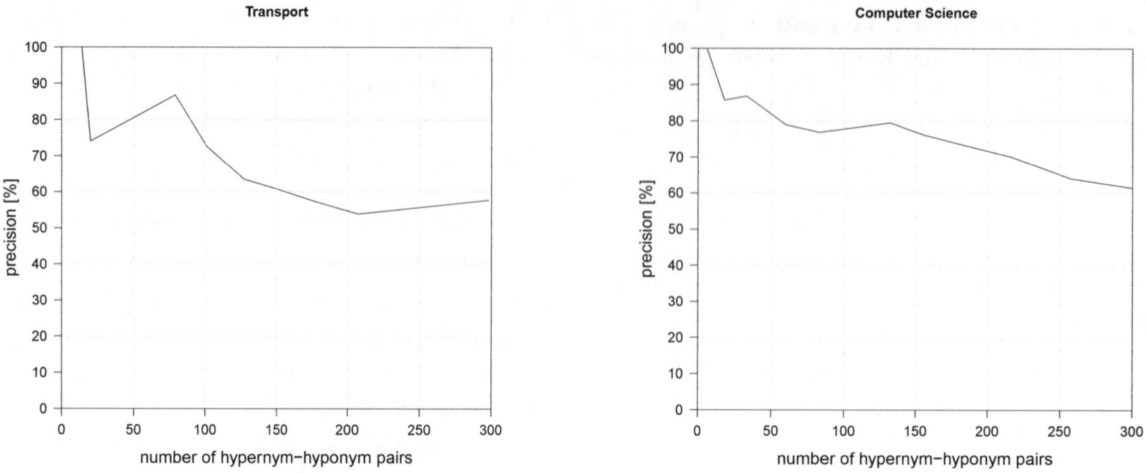

Figure 5: Precision curves for two domains of Wikipedia

manually checked the first 500 pairs. The curves in figure 5 indicate the precision. For the two domains, around 300 pairs were retrieved with a precision of about 60% for the highest threshold. Table 5 presents examples of extracted relations. The terms noted with a symbol '*' are considered as errors.

hypernyms	hyponyms
transporteurs frigorifiques (refrigerated transporters)	STEF, transporteur*, Groupe Delanchy, Norbert Dentressangle, Groupe Malherbe, Madrias
pôles d'échanges (interchange stations)	Gare de la Part Dieu, Centre intermodal d'échanges de Limoges, Union Station à Toronto
transmission (transmission)	Courte distance*, Moyenne distance*, Longue distance*

Table 5: Examples of extracted relations

We have identified the main sources of error. The most common arises from nested discourse structures. In this case, intermediate DUs often specify contexts, and therefore do not contain the searched hyponyms. This is the case in the last example of table 5 where the retrieved hyponyms for "transmission" (transmission) are "Courte distance" (*Short distance*), "Moyenne distance" (*Medium distance*) and "Longue distance" (*Long distance*).

Another error comes from a confusion between hypernymy and meronymy relations, which are both hierarchical. The fact that these two relations share the same linguistic properties may explain this confusion (Ittoo and Bouma, 2009). Furthermore we are still faced with classical linguistic problems which are out of the scope of this paper: anaphora, ellipse, coreference, etc.

Finally, we ignore cases where the hypernymy relation is reversed, i.e. when the hyponym is localized into the nucleus DU and its hypernym into a satellite DU. Clues that we use are not enough discriminating at this level.

6 Conclusion

In this paper we investigate a new way for extracting hypernymy relations, exploiting the text layout which expresses hierarchical relations and for which standard NLP tools are not suitable.

The system implements a two steps process: (1) a discourse analysis of the text layout, and (2) a hypernymy relation identification within specific discourse structures. We first evaluate each module independently (discourse analysis of the layout, identification of the nature of the relation, and identification of arguments of the relation), and we obtain accuracies of about 80% and 97% for the discourse analysis, and F-measures of about 81% and 73% for the relation extraction. We then evaluate the whole process and we obtain a precision of about 60%.

One way to improve this work is to extend this analysis to other hierarchical relations. We plan to investigate more advanced techniques offered by distributional semantic models in order to discriminate hypernymy relation from meronymy ones.

Another way is to extend the scope of investigation of the layout to take into account new discursive structures. Moreover, a subsequent step to this work is its large scale application on collections of structured web documents (such as Wikipedia pages) in order to build semantic resources and to share them with the community.

References

Enrique Alfonseca and Suresh Manandhar. 2002. Improving an ontology refinement method with hyponymy patterns. *cell*, 4081:0–0087.

N. Asher and A. Lascarides. 2003. *Logics of conversation*. Cambridge University Press.

Sophie Aubin and Thierry Hamon. 2006. Improving term extraction with terminological resources. In *Advances in Natural Language Processing*, pages 380–387. Springer.

Sören Auer, Christian Bizer, Georgi Kobilarov, Jens Lehmann, Richard Cyganiak, and Zachary Ives. 2007. Dbpedia: A nucleus for a web of open data. In *The semantic web*, pages 722–735. Springer.

Marco Baroni, Silvia Bernardini, Adriano Ferraresi, and Eros Zanchetta. 2009. The wacky wide web: a collection of very large linguistically processed web-crawled corpora. *Language resources and evaluation*, 43(3):209–226.

John Bateman, Thomas Kamps, Jörg Kleinz, and Klaus Reichenberger. 2001. Towards constructive text, diagram, and layout generation for information presentation. *Computational Linguistics*, 27(3):409–449.

Adam L Berger, Vincent J Della Pietra, and Stephen A Della Pietra. 1996. A maximum entropy approach to natural language processing. *Computational linguistics*, 22(1):39–71.

Sergey Chernov, Tereza Iofciu, Wolfgang Nejdl, and Xuan Zhou. 2006. Extracting semantics relationships between wikipedia categories. *SemWiki*, 206.

Philipp Cimiano, Andreas Hotho, and Steffen Staab. 2005. Learning concept hierarchies from text corpora using formal concept analysis. *J. Artif. Intell. Res.(JAIR)*, 24:305–339.

Corinna Cortes and Vladimir Vapnik. 1995. Support-vector networks. *Machine learning*, 20(3):273–297.

Béatrice Daille. 1996. Study and implementation of combined techniques for automatic extraction of terminology. *The balancing act: Combining symbolic and statistical approaches to language*, 1:49–66.

Jean-Philippe Fauconnier, Laurent Sorin, Mouna Kamel, Mustapha Mojahid, and Nathalie Aussenac-Gilles. 2014. Détection automatique de la structure organisationnelle de documents à partir de marqueurs visuels et lexicaux. In *Actes de la 21e Conférence sur le Traitement Automatique des Langues Naturelles (TALN 2014)*, pages 340–351.

Joseph L Fleiss, John C Nee, and J Richard Landis. 1979. Large sample variance of kappa in the case of different sets of raters. *Psychological Bulletin*, 86(5):974–977.

Marti A Hearst. 1992. Automatic acquisition of hyponyms from large text corpora. In *Proceedings of the 14th conference on Computational linguistics*, volume 2, pages 539–545. Association for Computational Linguistics.

Ashwin Ittoo and Gosse Bouma. 2009. Semantic selectional restrictions for disambiguating meronymy relations. In *proceedings of CLIN09: The 19th Computational Linguistics in the Netherlands meeting, to appear*.

Jan Jannink and Gio Wiederhold. 1999. Thesaurus entry extraction from an on-line dictionary. In *Proceedings of Fusion*, volume 99. Citeseer.

Mouna Kamel and Nathalie Aussenac-Gilles. 2009. How can document structure improve ontology learning? In *Workshop on Semantic Annotation and Knowledge Markup collocated with K-CAP*.

Alessandro Lenci and Giulia Benotto. 2012. Identifying hypernyms in distributional semantic spaces. In *Proceedings of the First Joint Conference on Lexical and Computational Semantics-Volume 1: Proceedings of the main conference and the shared task, and Volume 2: Proceedings of the Sixth International Workshop on Semantic Evaluation*, pages 75–79. Association for Computational Linguistics.

Roger Levy and Galen Andrew. 2006. Tregex and tsurgeon: tools for querying and manipulating tree data structures. In *Proceedings of the fifth international conference on Language Resources and Evaluation*, pages 2231–2234. Citeseer.

William C Mann and Sandra A Thompson. 1988. Rhetorical structure theory: Toward a functional theory of text organization. *Text*, 8(3):243–281.

Daniel Marcu. 1999. A decision-based approach to rhetorical parsing. In *Proceedings of the 37th annual meeting of the Association for Computational Linguistics on Computational Linguistics*, pages 365–372. Association for Computational Linguistics.

Tomas Mikolov, Kai Chen, Greg Corrado, and Jeffrey Dean. 2013. Efficient estimation of word representations in vector space. *arXiv preprint arXiv:1301.3781*.

Jong-Hoon Oh, Kiyotaka Uchimoto, and Kentaro Torisawa. 2009. Bilingual co-training for monolingual hyponymy-relation acquisition. In *Proceedings of the 47th Annual Meeting of the ACL and the 4th IJCNLP of the AFNL*, pages 432–440. Association for Computational Linguistics.

Richard Power, Donia Scott, and Nadjet Bouayad-Agha. 2003. Document structure. *Computational Linguistics*, 29(2):211–260.

Cartic Ramakrishnan, Abhishek Patnia, Eduard H Hovy, Gully APC Burns, et al. 2012. Layout-aware text extraction from full-text pdf of scientific articles. *Source code for biology and medicine*, 7(1):7.

David Sánchez and Antonio Moreno. 2005. Web-scale taxonomy learning. In *Proceedings of Workshop on Extending and Learning Lexical Ontologies using Machine Learning (ICML 2005)*, pages 53–60, Bonn, Germany.

Rion Snow, Daniel Jurafsky, and Andrew Y Ng. 2004. Learning syntactic patterns for automatic hypernym discovery. In *Advances in Neural Information Processing Systems*, volume 17.

Fabian M Suchanek, Gjergji Kasneci, and Gerhard Weikum. 2007. Yago: a core of semantic knowledge. In *Proceedings of the 16th international conference on World Wide Web*, pages 697–706. ACM.

Asuka Sumida and Kentaro Torisawa. 2008. Hacking wikipedia for hyponymy relation acquisition. In *IJCNLP*, volume 8, pages 883–888. Citeseer.

Yuka Tateisi, Tomoko Ohta, Nigel Collier, Chikashi Nobata, and Jun-ichi Tsujii. 2000. Building an annotated corpus in the molecular-biology domain. In *Proceedings of the COLING-2000 Workshop on Semantic Annotation and Intelligent Content*, pages 28–36. Association for Computational Linguistics.

Assaf Urieli. 2013. *Robust French syntax analysis: reconciling statistical methods and linguistic knowledge in the Talismane toolkit*. Ph.D. thesis, Université de Toulouse.

Ichiro Yamada, Kentaro Torisawa, Jun'ichi Kazama, Kow Kuroda, Masaki Murata, Stijn De Saeger, Francis Bond, and Asuka Sumida. 2009. Hypernym discovery based on distributional similarity and hierarchical structures. In *Proceedings of the 2009 Conference on Empirical Methods in Natural Language Processing: Volume 2-Volume 2*, pages 929–937. Association for Computational Linguistics.

The complexity of finding the maximum spanning DAG and other restrictions for DAG parsing of natural language

Natalie Schluter
Center for Language Technology
University of Copenhagen
Copenhagen, Denmark
natalie.elaine.schluter@jur.ku.dk

Abstract

Recently, there has been renewed interest in semantic dependency parsing, among which one of the paradigms focuses on parsing directed acyclic graphs (DAGs). Consideration of the decoding problem in natural language semantic dependency parsing as finding a maximum spanning DAG of a weighted directed graph carries many complexities. In particular, the computational complexity (and approximability) of the problem has not been addressed in the literature to date. This paper helps to fill this gap, showing that this general problem is APX-hard, and is NP-hard even under the planar restriction, in the graph-theoretic sense. On the other hand, we show that under the restriction of projectivity, the problem has a straightforward $O(n^3)$ algorithm. We also give some empirical evidence of the algorithmic importance of these graph restrictions, on data from the SemEval 2014 task 8 on Broad Coverage Semantic Dependency Parsing.

1 Introduction

Consideration of the decoding problem in natural language semantic dependency parsing as finding a maximum spanning DAG of a weighted directed graph carries many complexities that have not been addressed in the literature to date. Amongst these are the problem's computational complexity (and its approximability). The decoding problem for semantic dependency parsing was first introduced as the maximum spanning directed acyclic graph problem (MSDAG) by McDonald and Pereira (2006), where it is stated to be NP-hard.[1] The MSDAG problem asks for the highest weighted spanning sub-DAG of an input weighted digraph.

In this paper, we explain the APX-hardness of MSDAG, by relating it to the almost identical minimum weighted feedback arc set and maximum weighted acyclic subgraph problems. The proof of MSDAG's APX-hardness seems to discourage its use for decoding in semantic dependency parsing. However, unlike in syntactic dependency (tree) parse decoding, where projective decoding given by Eisner (1996)'s algorithm has a slightly higher computational complexity ($O(n^3)$) than the non-projective (Tarjan) maximum spanning tree algorithm ($O(n^2)$) (Tarjan, 1977; Chu and Liu, 1965; Edmonds, 1967; McDonald et al., 2005), finding the maximum spanning projective dependency DAG is tractable and can be found in time $O(n^3)$, contrary to its APX-hard non-projective counterpart.

Projective MSDAG has been referred to in the semantic dependency parsing literature as "*planar* MSDAG", which is an unfortunate mismatch with long-established graph theoretical terminology, that we need in this paper. As we discuss below, the planar MSDAG problem is in fact NP-hard, where "planar" is used in the graph theoretical sense. We generalise the definition of projectivity from tree models of syntax theory, which forbids crossing edges, to digraphs.

The projectivity restriction itself has not been linguistically motivated to date. However, an efficient

[1] McDonald and Pereira (2006) provide a reference to (Heckerman et al., 1995) for this fact. This fact is actually indirectly shown much earlier, as we discuss in Section 4.

*Proceedings of the Fourth Joint Conference on Lexical and Computational Semantics (*SEM 2015)*, pages 259–268,
Denver, Colorado, June 4–5, 2015.

exact algorithm for this restriction would pose a starting point for various relaxations of the definition (also known as *mild non-projectivity*) that reflect linguistic description of the data, as has been done for the Eisner algorithm (in for example (Bodirsky et al., 2005; Gómez-Rodríguez et al., 2011; Pitler et al., 2012; Pitler et al., 2013; Satta and Kuhlmann, 2013)). This projectivity restriction has been inherent in transition-based approaches to semantic dependency parsing (for example, in (Sagae and Tsujii, 2008; Titov et al., 2009)), without any study of the complexity nor proof of the power of the automaton models in recognising all projective DAGs. So, in terms of computational efficiency, we provide theoretical justification for the already used restriction of projectivity in DAG parsing, exhibiting a dynamic programming algorithm for this task, which runs in polynomial time.

Previous automaton approaches to DAG parsing can roughly be separated into two camps: one similar to (Sagae and Tsujii, 2008), which assumes projectivity of graphs in the data and parses without carrying out any transformation to relax the constraint of projectivity, and another similar to (Titov et al., 2009), which attempts (online) to find a re-ordering of the words in the sentence such that the resulting graph is projective. The latter approach assumes, as we will explain, precisely *outerplanarity* of the graphs, which, it turns out, is also NP-hard (Cf. §2 and §7). With respect to the data that we consider here, it turns out that the assumption of graph outerplanarity is well represented (almost all graphs among three data sets being outerplanar), whereas the percentage of projective graphs differs greatly from one dataset to another (from 57% to 84%, Cf. Section 5).

The projective MSDAG algorithm presented here is a first-order decoding algorithm, and empirical research on semantic parsing seems to have already gone beyond this (for example, in (Martins and Almeida, 2014)); moreover, first-order decoding using MSDAG in general seems not to be appropriate (Schluter, 2014), though the empirical work presented by Martins and Almeida (2014) on digraph decoding using a second order model suggests the relevance of higher-order DAG decoding in semantic dependency parsing. Manufacturing higher-order parsing algorithms in the sense of (McDonald and Satta, 2007; Carreras, 2007) from the tree decoding literature, based on the algorithm presented here is straightforward. And we believe that it is these latter algorithms, rather, that would provide the basis for empirical studies based on the generally theoretical research presented here.

2 Preliminaries

A graph is called *planar* if it can be drawn in the plane with no crossing edges. Each maximal region of the plane surrounded by edges of the planar graph drawn in the plane is called a *face*. There is one *outer* or *unbounded* face and some number of *inner* or *bounded* faces. If a connected planar graph can be written in the plane so that all vertices are on the outer face, then we call the graph *outerplanar*. A *connected component* of a graph is a maximal subgraph in which any two vertices are connected to each other by a path. A *digraph* is a directed graph (where edges have an orientation). A *DAG* is a digraph without any directed cycles. Consider the underlying undirected graph H of a digraph G. A *weakly connected component* of G is a maximal sub-digraph whose underlying undirected graph is a connected component of H.

Notation. We put $[i, j] := \{i, i+1, \ldots, j-1, j\}$, for $i \leq j$, and $[i] := [1, i]$.

In this paper, edge weights can be positive or negative and not zero, unless otherwise stated.

Hardness of approximability. APX is the class of all NP optimisation problems that can be solved in polynomial time with approximation ratio bounded by some constant. A problem is APX-hard if there is a PTAS-reduction from every problem in APX to that problem.[2] In this paper, we use a simpler type of PTAS-reduction called an L-reduction (linear reduction), which intuitively is a mapping between problems so that (approximate) solutions differ only by some constant factor. Any L-reduction is also a PTAS-reduction (but not vice versa).

Definition 1. *An L-reduction from problem A to problem B with respective cost functions c_A and*

[2] A discussion of PTAS-reductions is out of the scope of this paper. The definition of a PTAS-reduction can be found, for example, in (Wegener, 2005).

c_B *consists of a pair of polynomial-time computable functions* f *and* g *such that:*

- *if* $x \in A$ *then* $f(x) \in B$,
- *if* y *is a solution to* $f(x)$, *then* $g(y)$ *is a solution to* x,
- *there exists a positive constant* α *such that the optimal solution for* $f(x) \in B$ $(opt_B(f(x)))$ *is bounded by a factor* α *of the optimal solution for* $x \in A$ $(opt_A(x))$, *and*

$$opt_B(f(x)) \leq \alpha \cdot opt_A(x)$$

- *there exists a positive constant* β *bounding differences between solutions and optimal solutions*

$$|opt_A(x) - c_A(g(y))| \leq \beta \cdot |opt_B(f(x)) - c_B(y)|.$$

3 Generalising projectivity to DAGs

In statistical natural language syntactic or semantic dependency parsing decoding problems, the input is a sequence of n words, $W = \langle w_1, \ldots, w_n \rangle$, called the *sentence* and a further set of weighted asymmetric binary relations (directed edges) between these words (nodes). The task is to output a most likely connected and spanning digraph over those words, where the formal expressivity of the structure is defined with respect to the linguistic theory in question.

The order of words in the sentence is essential for the description of important restrictions of trees and DAGs for natural language. We therefore include the order in the sentence digraph structure, so $G_W = (V, E, \leq_W)$ is a *dependency digraph* for the sentence W, where V is the set of words tokens, E is the set of directed binary relations between words, and $\leq_W$ describes the order of the words in the sentence W ($\leq_W$ is the sentential order). For the remainder of this paper, when we talk about dependency digraphs (or *dependency DAGs* or *dependency trees*) the nodes of the underlying digraphs are associated with some fixed total order. Also we use the terms "word" and "node" synonymously in this context.

In linguistic terms, if (w_i, w_j) is an edge, then we say that w_i is a *head* of w_j and that w_j is a *dependent* of w_i. We can also write the edge (w_i, w_j) as $w_i \rightarrow w_j$. $w_i \xrightarrow{*} w_j$ is the *reflexive transitive closure* of the dependency relation.

A *dependency tree* then is just a connected dependency digraph in which every node has a unique head, except for a special node called the root, which has no head.

An interesting property yielding good coverage of some natural languages (for example, English) is that resulting dependency trees should be *projective*.

Definition 2. *A dependency tree* $T = (V, E, \leq_W)$ *is* projective *if for all edges* $(w_i, w_j) \in E$, *for all intervening words,* w_k *such that* $k \in [\min\{i,j\}, \max\{i,j\}]$, *we have* $w_i \xrightarrow{*} w_k$.

It turns out that the edges of a projective dependency tree can be written above the sentence (i.e., words written on a line segment in sentential order) without any crossing edges. This notion of avoiding crossing edges in "desirable" spanning DAGs has been considered in recent natural language parsing research, however the projectivity of edges as given in Definition 3 for dependency trees is no longer a sufficient condition to ensure this property in DAGs. As such, NLP researchers have adopted the unfortu nate term "planar". Rather than assign a new meaning to the term planar, we generalise the definition of projectivity using the notion of crossing edges so that it applies to dependency digraphs, adopting this definition for the remainder of the paper. We then provide the correct restriction of planar digraphs that projective digraphs correspond to.

Definition 3. *For a dependency digraph* $G_W = (V, E, \leq_W)$, *an edge* (w_i, w_j) *or* (w_j, w_i), *with* $i \leq j$ *is* projective *if and only if for all words* w_k *such that* $i < k < j$, *there are no edges* (w_l, w_k) *or* (w_k, w_l) *such that* $l < i$ *or* $l > j$.
G_W *is* projective *if and only if all its edges are projective.*

Since the definition of projectivity excludes crossing edges when nodes are laid out on a line segment (sentential order), we see that the underlying digraph of a projective digraph is outerplanar. Moreover, it is easy to prove that for any planar digraph with all nodes on its outer face, we can choose a first node and define an ordering $\leq_W$ on the nodes by following the order of nodes (in a fixed direction) along an outer face, skipping repeats, until the original node is met (recalling that one can find this outer face in linear time). So, there is a correspondence between the sets of projective digraphs and outerplanar digraphs.

Proposition 4. *For the projective digraph* $G_W = (V, E, \leq_W)$, (V, E) *is an outerplanar digraph. Also, every outerplanar digraph corresponds to some projective digraph with a sentential ordering defined by node traversal in a fixed direction along its outer face.*

On the other hand, given an outerplanar graph and some random sentential order, we of course do not necessarily have a projective digraph. In particular, an outerplanar drawing in the plane of a digraph does not necessarily have the specific desired order of vertices on its outer face. So, for example, finding the outerplanar MSDAG and the projective MSDAG are two *different* problems.

4 APX-hardness of MSDAG and its dual

In this section we give L-reductions from the APX-hard problems *maximum weighted directed acyclic subgraph* and its dual *minimum weighted feedback set* to MSDAG and its dual.

Minimum weighted feedback arc set. The dual problem of the MSDAG problem is almost identical with that of finding a minimum weighted feedback arc set. Given a directed graph, $G = (V, E)$, a *feedback arc set* (FAS) is a subset S of G's edges whose removal leaves a DAG (i.e., such that $(V, E(G)\backslash E(S))$ is a DAG). A *minimum feedback arc set* (MFAS) is the smallest among all possible feedback arc sets and a *minimum weighted feedback arc set* (MWFAS) is a feedback arc set of minimum weight. We call an MWFAS whose removal leaves a connected DAG a *nice MWFAS*. Finding a nice MWFAS is the dual of the MSDAG problem.

Already, the decision version of the FAS problem, which asks whether there is a feedback arc set of size k was listed as one of Karp's original 21 NP-complete problems (Karp, 1972), which shows the NP-hardness of the optimisation version. In fact, this optimisation problem is also shown to be APX-hard (Kann, 1992). The best approximation algorithm in the literature to date for this problem has an approximation guarantee of $O(\log n \log \log n)$ and the solution is NP-hard to approximate to within any factor smaller than $10\sqrt{5} - 21 \approx 1.36$ (Even et al., 1998).

An L-reduction from MWFAS to MSDAG for a weighted directed digraph G goes as follows. We first show that if the G has no edge cut consisting only of edges of negative weights, then the nice MWFAS is simply the MWFAS. Let D^* be an MSDAG for G. We show that the nice MWFAS $F := E(G) - E(D^*)$ must also form an MWFAS. Suppose otherwise, then there is some other F' of lower weight and such that $D' := (V(G), E(G) - F')$ is acyclic. So D' is disconnected and has at least two weakly connected components; we suppose without loss of generality that it has precisely two weakly connected components, C_1 and C_2. But then there must not be any positive weighted edge e in $E(G)$ between C_1 and C_2; otherwise we could remove that edge from F' to achieve an MWFAS of lower weight, since $C_1 \cup C_2 \cup \{e\}$ is still acyclic.

Now suppose that there is some edge cut consisting solely of edges of negative weight in G and therefore in D^*. Without loss of generality, we can suppose that there is only one such edge cut. Clearly, D^* contains at most one edge from this edge cut, the rest of them being in the nice MWFAS. An MWFAS would contain every negative weighted edge. So, the difference between a nice MWFAS and an MWFAS is just this one edge, for G. In particular, we have given an L-reduction from MWFAS to nice MWFAS, where the optimal solution for MWFAS is just the nice MWFAS with negative weighted edges removed (so both α and β from Definition 1 are equals to 1).

This shows the APX-hardness of the dual of the MSDAG problem, nice MWFAS.

Maximum weighted directed acyclic subgraph. An almost identical problem to MSDAG is the maximum weighted directed acyclic subgraph problem (MWDAS), which aims to find the (not necessarily spanning) DAG of highest weight. The decision version of the maximum directed acyclic subgraph problem (MDAS) problem which asks whether there is a directed acyclic subgraph on k edges can be solved by the decision version of the FAS problem, with $m - k$ as the parameter (where m is the number of edges in the input graph), and hence has long been shown to be NP-complete (Karp, 1972). By the same token, the optimisation problem has been shown to be APX-hard (Kann, 1992). The best approximation algorithm in the literature to date for this problem has an approximation guarantee of $\frac{1}{2} + \Omega\left(\frac{1}{\sqrt{d_{\max}}}\right)$ where $d_{\max}$ is the maximum vertex degree for the graph (Berger and Shor, 1997). Moreover, the solution is Unique Games-hard to approximate to within any factor smaller than $1/2$, which is a tight bound (Guruswami et al., 2008).

Again, if there are no edge cuts in the graph consisting only of negative weighted edges, then the MSDAG and MWDAS solutions are identical. Otherwise, the MWDAS is just the MSDAG without its negative weighted edges, by the discussion above L-reducing MWFAS to nice MWFAS.

We have therefore shown the following fact.

Theorem 5. *MSDAG and its dual, nice MWFAS, are APX-hard.*

5 Planarity, outerplanarity and projectivity of DAGs in English data

APX-hardness of the MSDAG problem not only means that the problem is essentially infeasible, but also that it theoretically cannot be very well approximated. However, with some structural assumptions, such as the planarity, outerplanarity or projectivity of the objective DAGS, either approximation algorithms with a good approximation guarantee or even feasible algorithms might be achievable. The authors are not aware of any specific theoretical linguistic evidence for the planarity or outerplanarity of semantic dependency DAGs. However, we consider the three datasets from SemEval 2014 task 8 on Broad Coverage Semantic Dependency Parsing (Oepen et al., 2014), referred to as PAS, DM and PCEDT, following the packing conversion into DAGs described in (Schluter et al., 2014), without the actual label packing or edge removal heuristic, finding that almost all DAGs are outerplanar (and therefore also planar). Moreover, the datasets consist of a majority of projective DAGs, with those graphs that are not projective having proportionally on average a large projective subgraph (respectively 0.555, 0.580,and 0.605 for the PAS, DM, and PCEDT datasets). This large projective proportion suggests future avenues for algorithms for mildly projective DAGs, based on the projective algorithm presented in this paper.

	PAS	DM	PCEDT
% projective	58.461	56.840	84.192
% outerplanar	97.796	99.160	95.390
% planar	99.997	100	99.904

Table 1: Percentage of projective, planar, and outerplanar DAGs in the data.

6 The NP-hardness of finding a planar or outerplanar MSDAG

By a similar discussion to that in Section 4 on the relationship between MWDAS and MSDAG, finding the both the maximum weighted planar or outerplanar spanning DAG of a directed weighted graph can simply be shown to be NP-hard, where "planar" (and "outerplanar") is used in the graph-theoretical sense (Garey and Johnson, 1979). To our knowledge, approximability of finding a maximum weighted planar or outerplanar acyclic *directed* subgraph is still an open problem. The NP-hardness of finding a maximum weighted outerplanar spanning DAG is somewhat discouraging. But the next section provides a polynomial algorithm if there is a restriction on the the order of nodes on the outer face of the output (which is just projective MSDAG).

7 Finding a projective MSDAG or digraph in $O(n^3)$ time

We now turn our attention to the projective MSDAG problem, which can be solved efficiently. Our algorithm employs bottom-up dynamic programming across spans of words, where a span consists of a segment of words of the input sentence $W = \langle w_1, w_2, \ldots, w_n \rangle$ along with any attributed edges, similarly to the CKY-algorithm for context-free language parsing (Cocke, 1969; Kasami, 1965; Younger, 1967) and projective maximum spanning tree algorithms (Eisner, 1996), though the proof of correctness is slightly more complex. Following this, we explain how to simplify the algorithm to the task of finding the maximum weighted spanning digraph of digraph within the same time complexity.

Let $G_W = (V, E, \leq_W)$ be a weighted dependency digraph over the input sentence $W =$

$\langle w_1, w_2, \ldots, w_n \rangle$ and we suppose without loss of generality that $|E| = n(n-1)$. An (i,j)-span (with $i \leq j$) for S is the subsequence of consecutive words $w_i, w_{i+1}, \ldots, w_{j-1}, w_j$. We construct an algorithm **proj-MSDAG** (Algorithm 1) which takes G_W as input and outputs a highest weighted projective spanning dependency DAG for G_W: a projective MSDAG for G_W. For simplicity, instead of G_W, we just write G.

We call a directed path from node i to node j, an $i-j$ path. The algorithm constructs the upper triangular square matrix $A = \{a_{i,j}\}$ $(i, j \in [n])$, from left to right and from the diagonal upwards, where component $a_{i,j}$ contains at most three different restrictions of optimal projective spanning DAGs for the (i,j) span along with their associated weights:

1. $a_{i,j}.G_1$ is a projective MSDAG of the spanning subgraph $G[i,j]$, and $a_{i,j}.w_1$ is its weight
2. $a_{i,j}.G_2$ is a maximum projective spanning DAG for which there is no $i-j$ path, and $a_{i,j}.w_2$ is its weight, and
3. $a_{i,j}.G_3$ is a maximum projective spanning DAG for which there is no $j-i$ path, and $a_{i,j}.w_3$ is its weight.

The solution to the problem is then $a_{1,n}.G_1$. The motivation for distinguishing between these three types of graphs is to allow restricted combinations of them which ensure that no cycles are introduced.

We claim that these three restrictions on projective MSDAGs for the span (i,j) can be constructed from those of shorter spans within (i,j) using the three following operations, (A1), (A2), and (A3) (Lemma 6).

(A1) Concatenate sub-DAGs $H_{a_{i,k}}$ and $H_{a_{k,j}}$ from among the graphs in the cells $a_{i,k}$ and $a_{k,j}$ respectively $(i < k < j)$, creating the graph

$$(\{w_i, \ldots, w_j\}, E(H_{a_{i,k}}) \cup E(H_{a_{k,j}})),$$

(A2) Concatenate a single edge $e \in \{(i,j),(j,i)\}$ with the sub-DAGs $H_{a_{i,k}}$ and $H_{a_{k,j}}$ from among the graphs in the cells $a_{i,k}$ and $a_{k,j}$ respectively $(i < k < j)$, creating the graph

$$(\{w_i, \ldots, w_j\}, \{e\} \cup E(H_{a_{i,k}}) \cup E(H_{a_{k,j}})),$$

(A3) Connect two sub-DAGs $H_{a_{i,k}}$ and $H_{a_{k+1,j}}$ from among the graphs in the cells $a_{i,k}$ and $a_{k+1,j}$ respectively $(i \leq k < j)$ with a single edge $e \in \{(i,j),(j,i)\}$, creating the graph

$$(\{w_i, \ldots, w_j\}, \{e\} \cup E(H_{a_{i,k}}) \cup E(H_{a_{k+1,j}})).$$

Lemma 6. *The projective DAGs $a_{i,j}.G_1, a_{i,j}.G_2$, and $a_{i,j}.G_3$ can be de-constructed, by reversing a single operation (A1), (A2) or (A3), to obtain two sub-DAGs D_1 and D_2 which span their vertices and where either*

- *D_1 is on vertices $\{w_i, \ldots, w_k\}$ and D_2 is on vertices $\{w_k, \ldots, w_j\}$, for $i < k < j$, or*
- *D_1 is on vertices $\{w_i, \ldots, w_k\}$ and D_2 is on vertices $\{w_{k+1}, \ldots, w_j\}$, for $i \leq k < j$.*

Furthermore, for $p \in [2]$ and $1 \leq a < b \leq n$, let $G[a,b]$ be the spanning subgraph of G on the vertices $\{w_a, w_{a+1}, \ldots, w_{b-1}, w_b\}$, let D_p be a DAG on the vertices $w_a, w_{a+1}, \ldots, w_{b-1}, w_b$.

1. *D_p is a projective MSDAG for $G[a,b]$, or*
2. *D_p is the a highest projective spanning DAG with no $a-b$ path for $G[a,b]$, or*
3. *D_p is the a highest projective spanning DAG with no $b-a$ path for $G[a,b]$.*

Proof. We separate the proof into two parts: Part 1 for the graph $a_{i,j}.G1$ and Part 2 for the graphs $a_{i,j}.G2$, and $a_{i,j}.G3$.

Part 1. Let us denote $a_{i,j}.G1$ by D for ease in notation. We denote by $E_D(u)$ the set of edges in $E(D)$ having u for some endpoint. Consider the word w_i. By D's connectivity, $E_D(w_i)$ is non-empty. Let e be the edge in $E_D(w_i)$ of longest span, and suppose without loss of generality in edge direction that $e = (w_i, w_k)$ for some $k \in \{i+1, \ldots, j\}$.

There are two cases to consider. Either $k < j$ in which case we can reverse (A1) (Case 1), or $k = j$ in which case we can reverse (A2) or (A3) (Case 2).

Consider first Case 1, where $k < j$. By D's projectivity and the fact that e has the longest span in $E_D(w_1)$, there are no edges with one endpoint among $w_i, \ldots, w_{k-1}$ and the other endpoint among $w_{k+1}, \ldots, w_j$. So we can partition D into two sub-DAGs $D[i,k]$, which is a spanning subgraph over the nodes $w_i,\ldots,w_k$ and $D[k,j]$, which is a spanning subgraph over the nodes $w_k,\ldots,w_j$. Both $D[i,k]$ and $D[k,j]$ are projective MSDAGs for $G[i,k]$ and $G[k,j]$ respectively, otherwise we can construct a projective MSDAG D' for G of higher weight than D, by taking the respective projective MSDAGs to form D'.

Otherwise, we have Case 2, with $k=j$. Note that there must not be any $w_j - w_i$ path in D (for acyclicity). We remove the edge (w_i, w_j) from D, the result of which is either connected or disconnected.

If $D - \{(w_i, w_j)\}$ is connected, it must be the maximum spanning DAG for G not containing any $w_j - w_i$ path. In the same manner as for the case where $k < j$, we can partition $D - \{(w_i, w_j)\}$ into two sub-DAGs $D[i,k]$, which is a spanning sub-DAG over the nodes $w_i,\ldots,w_k$ and $D[k,j]$, which is a spanning sub-DAG over the nodes $w_k,\ldots,w_j$, where either $D[i,k]$ does not have a $k-i$ path or $D[k,j]$ does not have a $j-k$ path. Clearly $D[i,k]$ and $D[k,j]$ are the maximum weighted projective spanning DAGs with this property for $G[i,k]$ and $G[k,j]$ respectively. This is the reversal of (A2).

Otherwise $D - \{(w_i, w_j)\}$ is disconnected into two weakly connected components $D[i,k]$ and $D[k+1,j]$, with $k \in [j-1]$, such that $D[i,k]$ is a projective MSDAG for $G[i,k]$ and $D[k+1,j]$ is a projective MSDAG for $G[k+1,j]$ (which is the reversal of (A3)).

Part 2. We prove, without loss of generality, the result for the graph $a_{i,j}.G_3$, the proof for the graph $a_{i,j}.G_2$ being symmetric. The proof follows almost exactly the one in Part 1, so we simply indicate the differences here. Again, for ease in notation, we denote $a_{i,j}.G_2$ by D, and carry out the same partition of D as in Part 1.

The difference for Case 1 is that either the resulting $D[i,k]$ must be a maximum weighted projective spanning DAG for $G[i,k]$ with no $k-i$ path, or $D[k,j]$ must be a maximum weighted projective spanning DAG for $G[k,j]$ with no $j-k$ path.

Case 2 is precisely the same if the result of removing the edge (w_i, w_j) is disconnected. If the result is connected, then the difference is that $D[i,k]$ must be a maximum projective weighted spanning DAG for $G[i,k]$ with no $k-i$ path, or $D[k,j]$ must be a maximum weighted projective spanning DAG for $G[k,j]$ with no $j-k$ path. □

Algorithm 1 uses the operations (A1), (A2) and (A3) to fill the matrix A. In Figure 1, we define three different subroutines corresponding to each of these operations, which take the matrix A, the span, and the forbidden direction for the edge of the span, if there is one (and the empty set otherwise). Clearly each of these runs in $O(n)$ time.

We observe that Lines 9 through 14 in Algorithm 1 dominate the time complexity, taking $O(n^3)$. Lemma 7 shows that Algorithm 1 fills the table cells with the correct projective MSDAG restrictions.

Lemma 7. *For $i \leq j$, Algorithm 1 fills matrix entry $a_{i,j}$ with:*

1. *a projective MSDAG for $G[i,j]$,*
2. *a projective MSDAG for $G[i,j]$ with no $i-j$ path, and*
3. *a projective MSDAG for $G[i,j]$ with no $j-i$ path.*

Proof. The proof is by induction on the span size. For the table cells $a_{i,i}$ for $i \in [n]$, we have $a_{i,i}.G_1 = a_{i,i}.G_2 = a_{i,i}.G_3 = (\{w_i\}, \emptyset)$; the graphs are all single nodes. For our base case, $a_{i,i+1}, i \in [n-1]$, we construct the cell contents as follows:

1. $a_{i,i+1}.G_1$ is the highest weighted edge among (w_i, w_{i+1}) and (w_{i+1}, w_i).
2. $a_{i,i+1}.G_2$ is (w_i, w_{i+1}) if this edge is in G.
3. $a_{i,i+1}.G_3$ is (w_{i+1}, w_i) if this edge is in G.

This is Lines 1 through 8 in Algorithm 1.

Suppose now that the entries $a_{i,k}$ and $a_{k,j}$ contain the appropriate graphs G_1, G_2 and G_3, for $i < k < j$. For each k ($i < k < j$), Lines 9 through 14 in Algorithm 1 construct the three graphs, $a_{i,j}.G_1(k)$, $a_{i,j}.G_2(k)$, and $a_{i,j}.G_3(k)$, as follows, which is possible according to Lemma 6:

1. $a_{i,j}.G_1(k)$ is a highest weighted projective dependency DAG for $G[i,j]$ that can be constructed from the graphs stored in $a_{i,k}$ and $a_{k,j}$.
2. $a_{i,j}.G_2(k)$ is a highest weighted projective dependency DAG for $G[i,j]$ that can be constructed from the graphs stored in $a_{i,k}$, $a_{i,k+1}$ and $a_{k,j}$, which avoids an $i-j$ path.

$$\texttt{A1}(G,A,i,j,\emptyset) = \operatorname*{arg\,max}_{\{H|H=(\{w_i,\ldots,w_j\},E(a_{i,k}.G_1)\cup E(a_{k,j}.G_1)),\ i<k<j\}} w(H)$$

$$\texttt{A1}(G,A,i,j,\rightarrow) = \operatorname*{arg\,max}_{\substack{\{H|H=(\{w_i,\ldots,w_j\},E(a_{i,k}.G_2)\cup E(a_{k,j}.G_1)),\ i<k<j\} \\ \cup\{H|H=(\{w_i,\ldots,w_j\},E(a_{i,k}.G_1)\cup E(a_{k,j}.G_2)),\ i<k<j\}}} w(H)$$

$$\texttt{A1}(G,A,i,j,\leftarrow) = \operatorname*{arg\,max}_{\substack{\{H|H=(\{w_i,\ldots,w_j\},E(a_{i,k}.G_3)\cup E(a_{k,j}.G_1)),\ i<k<j\} \\ \cup\{H|H=(\{w_i,\ldots,w_j\},E(a_{i,k}.G_1)\cup E(a_{k,j}.G_3)),\ i<k<j\}}} w(H)$$

$$\texttt{A2}(G,A,i,j,\emptyset) = \operatorname*{arg\,max}_{\{H|H=(\{w_i,\ldots,w_j\},\ \{(w_i,w_j)\}\cup E(a_{i,k}.G_1)\cup E(a_{k,j}.G_1)),\ i<k<j\}} w(H)$$

$$\texttt{A2}(G,A,i,j,\rightarrow) = \operatorname*{arg\,max}_{\substack{\{H|H=(\{w_i,\ldots,w_j\},\ \{(w_j,w_i)\}\cup E(a_{i,k}.G_2)\cup E(a_{k,j}.G_1)),\ i<k<j\} \\ \cup\{H|H=(\{w_i,\ldots,w_j\},\ \{(w_j,w_i)\}\cup E(a_{i,k}.G_1)\cup E(a_{k,j}.G_2)),\ i<k<j\}}} w(H)$$

$$\texttt{A2}(G,A,i,j,\leftarrow) = \operatorname*{arg\,max}_{\substack{\{H|H=(\{w_i,\ldots,w_j\},\ \{(w_i,w_j)\}\cup E(a_{i,k}.G_3)\cup E(a_{k,j}.G_1)),\ i<k<j\} \\ \cup\{H|H=(\{w_i,\ldots,w_j\},\ \{(w_i,w_j)\}\cup E(a_{i,k}.G_1)\cup E(a_{k,j}.G_3)),\ i<k<j\}}} w(H)$$

$$\texttt{A3}(G,A,i,j,\emptyset) = \operatorname*{arg\,max}_{\{H|H=(\{w_i,\ldots,w_j\},\ \{(w_i,w_j)\}\cup E(a_{i,k}.G_1)\cup E(a_{k+1,j}.G_1)),\ i\leq k<j\}} w(H)$$

$$\texttt{A3}(G,A,i,j,\rightarrow) = \operatorname*{arg\,max}_{\substack{\{H|H=(\{w_i,\ldots,w_j\},\ \{(w_j,w_i)\}\cup E(a_{i,k}.G_2)\cup E(a_{k+1,j}.G_1)),\ i\leq k<j\} \\ \cup\{H|H=(\{w_i,\ldots,w_j\},\ \{(w_j,w_i)\}\cup E(a_{i,k}.G_1)\cup E(a_{k+1,j}.G_2)),\ i\leq k<j\}}} w(H)$$

$$\texttt{A3}(G,A,i,j,\leftarrow) = \operatorname*{arg\,max}_{\substack{\{H|H=(\{w_i,\ldots,w_j\},\ \{(w_i,w_j)\}\cup E(a_{i,k}.G_3)\cup E(a_{k+1,j}.G_1)),\ i\leq k<j\} \\ \cup\{H|H=(\{w_i,\ldots,w_j\},\ \{(w_i,w_j)\}\cup E(a_{i,k}.G_1)\cup E(a_{k+1,j}.G_3)),\ i\leq k<j\}}} w(H)$$

Figure 1: Subroutines corresponding to the operations (A1), (A2), and (A3) as used by Algorithm 1.

Algorithm 1 $\texttt{proj-MSDAG}(G)$

for $i \leftarrow 1,\ldots,n$ **do**
  $a_{i,i}.G_1 \leftarrow a_{i,i}.G_2 \leftarrow a_{i,i}.G_3 = (\{i\},\emptyset)$
  if $i < n$ **then**
    $a_{i,i+1}.G_1 \leftarrow (\{w_i, w_{i+1}\}, \{\operatorname{arg\,max}_{e\in\{(w_i,w_{i+1}),(w_{i+1},w_i)\}} w(e)\})$
    $a_{i,i+1}.G_2 \leftarrow (\{w_i, w_{i+1}\}, \{(w_{i+1}, w_i)\})$
    $a_{i,i+1}.G_3 \leftarrow (\{w_i, w_{i+1}\}, \{(w_i, w_{i+1})\})$
  end if
end for
for $i \leftarrow 1,\ldots,n$ **do**
  for $j \leftarrow i-1,\ldots,1$ **do**
    $a_{i,j}.G_1 \leftarrow \operatorname{arg\,max}_{H\in\{\texttt{A1}(G,A,i,j,\emptyset),\texttt{A2}(G,A,i,j,\emptyset),\texttt{A3}(G,A,i,j,\emptyset)\}} w(H)$
    $a_{i,j}.G_2 \leftarrow \operatorname{arg\,max}_{H\in\{\texttt{A1}(G,A,i,j,\rightarrow),\texttt{A2}(G,A,i,j,\rightarrow),\texttt{A3}(G,A,i,j,\rightarrow)\}} w(H)$
    $a_{i,j}.G_3 \leftarrow \operatorname{arg\,max}_{H\in\{\texttt{A1}(G,A,i,j,\leftarrow),\texttt{A2}(G,A,i,j,\leftarrow),\texttt{A3}(G,A,i,j,\leftarrow)\}} w(H)$
  end for
end for
return $a_{1,n}.G_1$

3. $a_{i,j}.G_3(k)$ is a highest weighted projective dependency DAG for $G[i,j]$ that can be constructed from the graphs stored in $a_{i,k}$, $a_{i,k+1}$ and $a_{k,j}$, which avoids an $j-i$ path.

□

With Lemmata 6 and 7, the proof of correctness of the following theorem is complete.

Theorem 8. *There is an algorithm for finding a projective MSDAG of a weighted digraph in $O(n^3)$ time, where n is the number of word tokens of the input sentence.*

The proof of Theorem 8 can be simplified to adapt it to that of projective digraphs. We simply substitute the word "DAG" by "digraph", and disregard all graphs in table entries avoiding certain paths, since cycles are permitted: in the entry $a_{i,j}$, we need only construct and record the graph $a_{i,j}.G_1$. We have thus also shown the following fact.

Theorem 9. *There is an algorithm for finding a projective maximum weighted spanning digraph of a weighted digraph in $O(n^3)$ time, where n is the number of word tokens of the input sentence.*

8 Concluding Remarks

Understanding the complexity of the problem of finding a maximum spanning DAG as well as important restrictions provides a basis for both theoretical and empirical studies using restrictions or relaxations of the DAG parsing paradigm. We have provided the first direct discussion of this problem's complexity, showing that the problem is APX-hard as well as the first algorithm for the projective MSDAG problem proven to be exact and polynomial time. Additionally, we briefly discussed the complexity of finding a planar and outerplanar MSDAG, the approximability of which remains open.

References

Bonnie Berger and Peter W. Shor. 1997. Tight bounds for the maximum acyclic subgraph problem. *Journal of Algorithms*, 25:1–18.

Manuel Bodirsky, Marco Kuhlmann, and Mathias Möhl. 2005. Well-nested drawings as models of syntactic structure. In *Proc. of the Tenth Conference on FOrmal Grammar and Ninth Meeting on Mathematics of Language*.

Xavier Carreras. 2007. Experiments with a higher-order projective dependency parser. In *Proc. of CoNLL Shared Task Session of EMNLP-CoNLL*, pages 957–961, Prague, Czech Republic.

Y.J. Chu and T. H. Liu. 1965. On the shortest arborescence of a directed graph. *Science Sinica*, 14:1396–1400.

John Cocke. 1969. Programming languages and their compilers: Preliminary notes. Technical Report B0007F4UOA, Courant Institute of Mathematical Sciences, New York University.

Jack Edmonds. 1967. Optimum branchings. *J. Res. Nat. Bur. Standards*, 71B:233–240.

Jason Eisner. 1996. Three new probabilistic models for dependency parsing: An exploration. In *Proceedings of COLING-96)*, pages 340–345, Copenhagen, Denmark.

Guy Even, Joseph Naor, Baruch Schieber, and Madhu Sudan. 1998. Approximating minimum feedback sets and multicuts in directed graphs. *Algorithmica*, 20:151–174.

Michael R. Garey and David S. Johnson. 1979. *Computers and Intractability: A Guide to the Theory of NP-completeness*. Freeman & Co., San Francisco.

Carlos Gómez-Rodríguez, John Carroll, and David Weir. 2011. Dependency parsing schemata and mildly non-projective dependency parsing. *Computational Linguistics*, 37:541–586.

Venkatesan Guruswami, Rajsekar Manokaran, and Prasad Raghavendra. 2008. Beating the random ordering is hard: Inapproximability of maximum acyclic subgraph. In *Proc. of FOCS*.

D. Heckerman, D. Geiger, and D. M. Chickering. 1995. Learning bayesian networks: The combination of knowledge and statistical data. Technical report, Microsoft Research. MSR-TR-94-09.

Viggo Kann. 1992. *On the approximability on NP-complete Optimization Problems*. Ph.D. thesis, Department of Numerical Analysis and Computing Science, Royal Institute of Technology, Stockholm, Sweden.

Richard M. Karp. 1972. Reducibility among combinatorial problems. In *Complexity of Computer Computations, Proc. Sympos. IBM Thomas J. Watson Res. Center*, pages 85–103, New York, NY.

Tadao Kasami. 1965. An efficient recognition and syntax-analysis algorithm for context-free languages. Technical Report AFCRL-65-758, Air Force Cambridge Research Lab, Bedford, MA.

André F. T. Martins and Mariana S. C. Almeida. 2014. Priberam: A turbo semantic parser with second order features. In *Proc of SemEval*, Dublin, Ireland.

Ryan McDonald and Fernando Pereira. 2006. Online learning of approximate dependency parsing algorithms. In *Proc. of EACL*, pages 81–88.

Ryan McDonald and Giorgio Satta. 2007. On the complexity of non-projective data-driven dependency parsing. In *Proceedings of the Tenth International Conference on Parsing Technologies*, pages 121–132, Prague, Czech Republic, June.

Ryan McDonald, Fernando Pereira, Kiril Ribarov, and Jan Haji. 2005. Non-projective dependency parsing using spanning tree algorithms. In *Proc. of HLT-EMNLP*, pages 523–530, Vancouver, BC, Canada.

Stephan Oepen, Marco Kuhlmann, Yusuke Miyao, Daniel Zeman, Dan Flickinger, Jan Hajič, Angelina Ivanova, and Yi Zhang. 2014. Semeval 2014 task 8: Broad-coverage semantic dependency parsing. In *Proc. of SemEval*, pages 63–71, Dublin, Ireland.

Emily Pitler, Sampath Kannan, and Mitchell Marcus. 2012. Dynamic programming for higher order parsing of gap-minding trees. In *Proceedings of EMNLP/CoNLL*, pages 478–488, Jeju Island, Republic of Korea.

Emily Pitler, Sampath Kannan, and Mitchell Marcus. 2013. Finding optimal 1-endpoint-crossing trees. *Transactions of the Association for Computational Linguistics*.

Kenji Sagae and Jun'ichi Tsujii. 2008. Shift-reduce dependency dag parsing. In *22nd International Conference on Computational Linguistics (Coling 2008)*, Manchester, UK.

Giorgio Satta and Marco Kuhlmann. 2013. Efficient parsing for head-split dependency trees. *Trans. ACL*, pages 267–278.

Natalie Schluter, Anders Søgaard, Jakob Elming, Dirk Hovy, Barbara Plank, Hector Martinez Alonso, Anders Johanssen, and Sigrid Klerke. 2014. Copenhagen: Tree approximations of semantic parsing problems. In *Proceedings of SemEval*, Dublin, Ireland.

Natalie Schluter. 2014. On maximum spanning dag algorithms for semantic dag parsing. In *ACL 2014 Workshop on Semantic Parsing*.

Robert Tarjan. 1977. Finding optimum branchings. *Networks*, pages 25–35.

Ivan Titov, James Henderson, Paola Merlo, and Gabrielle Musillo. 2009. Online graph planarization for synchronous parsing of semantic and synactic dependencies. In *Proceedings of IJCAI 2009*, pages 1562–1567.

Ingo Wegener. 2005. *Complexity Theory*. Springer.

Daniel H. Younger. 1967. Recognition and parsing of context-free languages in time n^3. *Information and Control*, 10(2):189– 208.

Incremental Semantic Construction Using Normal Form CCG Derivation

Yoshihide Kato[1] and **Shigeki Matsubara**[2]
[1]Information & Communications, Nagoya University
[2]Graduate School of Information Science, Nagoya University
Furo-cho, Chikusa-ku, Nagoya, 464-8601 Japan
yoshihide@icts.nagoya-u.ac.jp

Abstract

This paper proposes a method of incrementally constructing semantic representations. Our method is based on Steedman's Combinatory Categorial Grammar (CCG), which has a transparent correspondence between the syntax and semantics. In our method, a derivation for a sentence is constructed in an incremental fashion and the corresponding semantic representation is derived synchronously. Our method uses normal form CCG derivation. This is the difference between our approach and previous ones. Previous approaches use most left-branching derivation called incremental derivation, but they cannot process coordinate structures incrementally. Our method overcomes this problem.

1 Introduction

By incremental interpretation, we mean that a sentence is analyzed from left to right, and a semantic representation is assigned to each initial fragment of the sentence. These properties enable NLP systems to analyze unfinished sentences. Moreover, incremental interpretation is useful for incremental dialogue systems (Allen et al., 2001; Aist et al., 2007; Purver et al., 2011; Peldszus and Schlangen, 2012). Furthermore, in the field of psycholinguistics, incremental interpretation has been explored as a human sentence processing model.

This paper proposes a method of constructing a semantic representation for each initial fragment of a sentence in an incremental fashion. The proposed method is based on Combinatory Categorial Grammar (CCG) (Steedman, 2000). CCG represents the syntactic process as a derivation which is a tree structure. Our method constructs a CCG derivation by applying operations used in incremental phrase structure parsing. Each intermediate data structure constructed by the operations represents partial information of some derivation. Our method obtains a semantic representation from the intermediate structure. Since the obtained semantic representations conform to the CCG semantic construction, we can expect that incremental semantic interpretation is realized by applying a CCG based semantic analysis such as (Bos, 2008).

This paper is organized as follows: Section 2 briefly explains Combinatory Categorial Grammar. Section 3 gives an overview of previous work of CCG-based incremental parsing and discusses its problem. Section 4 proposes our CCG-based method of incrementally constructing semantic representations. Section 5 reviews related work and Section 6 concludes this paper.

2 Combinatory Categorial Grammar

Combinatory Categorial Grammar (CCG) (Steedman, 2000) is a grammar formalism which has a transparent correspondence between the syntax and semantics. Syntactic information is represented using basic categories (e.g., $\mathtt{S}$, $\mathtt{NP}$) and complex categories. Complex categories are in the form of X/Y or $X\backslash Y$, where X and Y are categories. Intuitively, each category in the form of X/Y means that it receives a category Y from its right and returns a category X. In the case of the form $X\backslash Y$, the direction is to left. For example, the category of a transitive verb is $(\mathtt{S}\backslash\mathtt{NP})/\mathtt{NP}$, which receives an object $\mathtt{NP}$

*Proceedings of the Fourth Joint Conference on Lexical and Computational Semantics (*SEM 2015)*, pages 269–278,
Denver, Colorado, June 4–5, 2015.

Forward function application:	$X/Y : f$	$Y : a$	$\Rightarrow_{>}$	$X : fa$
Backward function application:	$Y : a$	$X\backslash Y : f$	$\Rightarrow_{<}$	$X : fa$
Forward function composition:	$X/Y : f$	$Y/Z : g$	$\Rightarrow_{>B}$	$X/Z : \lambda x.f(gx)$
Backward function composition:	$Y\backslash Z : g$	$X\backslash Y : f$	$\Rightarrow_{<B}$	$X\backslash Z : \lambda x.f(gx)$
Backward crossed substitution:	$Y/Z : g$	$(X\backslash Y)/Z : f$	$\Rightarrow_{<S_\times}$	$X/Z : \lambda x.fx(gx)$
Forward type-raising:	$X : a$		$\Rightarrow_{>T}$	$T/(T\backslash X) : \lambda f.fa$
Backward type-raising:	$X : a$		$\Rightarrow_{<T}$	$T\backslash(T/X) : \lambda f.fa$
Coordination:	$X : f$	$CONJ : b \quad X : g$	$\Rightarrow_{<\Phi>}$	$X : \lambda \ldots b(g \ldots)(f \ldots)$

Figure 1: CCG rules

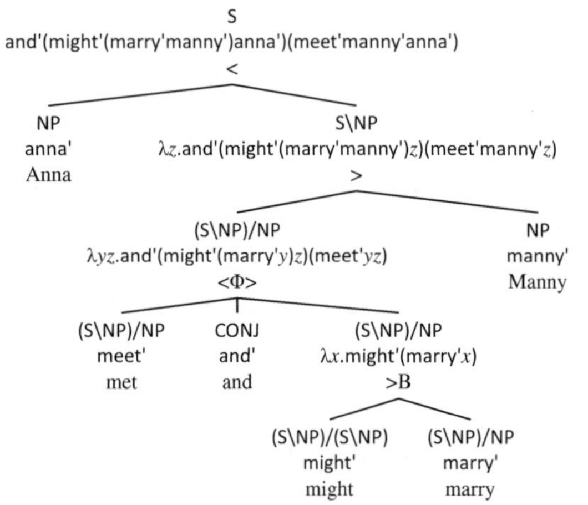

Figure 2: An example of CCG derivation.

from its right and returns a category S\NP. The category S\NP corresponds to a verb phrase. It receives a subject NP from its left and the result is a sentence S. Formally, categories are combined using CCG rules such as the ones shown in Figure 1. Each rule means that, when the elements of the left-hand side of the arrow are combined in this order, the result is the right-hand side. The symbol with which the arrow is subscripted designates its rule type. Each element consists of a syntactic category and a semantic representation which is separated by a colon. A semantic representation is a λ-term. Each combination of syntactic categories has a corresponding semantic composition of their semantic representations. Figure 2 shows an example of CCG derivation, which is taken from (Steedman, 2000).[1] Here, we write $\lambda x_1 x_2 \cdots x_n.M$ and $M_1 M_2 M_3 \cdots M_n$ to abbreviate λ-terms $(\lambda x_1.(\lambda x_2.(\cdots(\lambda x_n.M)\cdots)))$ and $((\cdots((M_1 M_2) M_3)\cdots) M_n)$, respectively. In this example, each node has three labels: a syntactic category, a semantic representation and the rule type which is used to derive this node. For each leaf node, a word is assigned instead of a rule type.

3 Incremental Parsing Based on CCG

Incremental parsing methods based on CCG have been proposed so far (Reitter et al., 2006; Hassan et al., 2008; Hefny et al., 2011). By using the property that CCG allows non-standard constituents, previous CCG-based incremental parsers assign a syntactic category to each initial fragment of an input sentence. The obtained derivations are most left-branching ones which are called *incremental derivations*. Figure 3 shows two examples of incremental derivations. In Figure 3(a), the fragment "Anna met" is a non-phrase, but it has a syntactic category S/NP.

However, Demberg (2012) has demonstrated that some kinds of sentences cannot have strictly left-branching derivations. This means that previous approaches have the case where the parser cannot assign any syntactic categories to an initial fragment. This also means that such initial fragments do not have any semantic representations.

A typical example is coordinate structure. In CCG, a coordinate structure is derived by combining conjuncts and a conjunction using coordination rule. This prevents the first conjunct from combining with its left constituent. As an example, let us consider the incremental derivation shown in Figure 3(b). Here, the word "met" is the first conjunct of "met and might marry" and cannot be combined with "Anna". If we assign the category S/NP to initial fragment "Anna met" as shown in Figure 3(a), the word "met" cannot be treated as a con-

[1]For simplicity, we use a symbol for a semantic representation of a word. Note that it is allowed to use complex semantic representations. For example, by assigning $\lambda px.\Diamond(px)$ ($\Diamond$ is possibility operator.) and $\lambda pq.p \wedge q$ to "might" and "and" respectively, we can obtain a modal logic formula $\Diamond(\text{marry'manny'anna'}) \wedge \text{meet'manny'anna'}$.

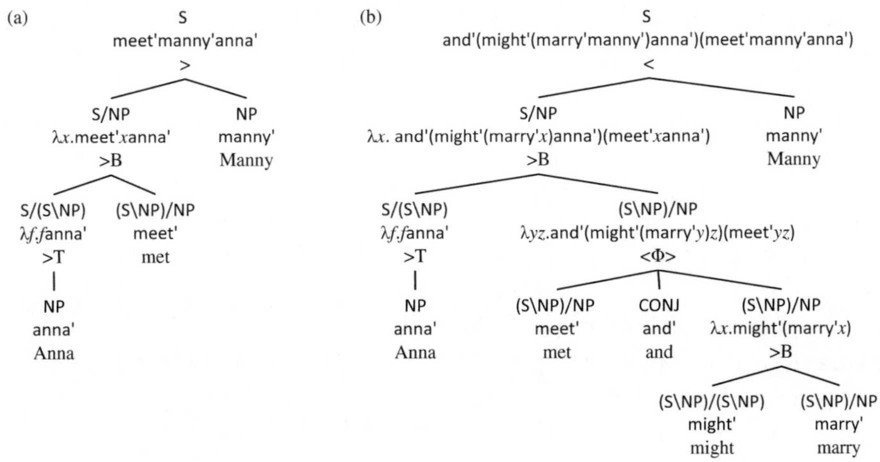

Figure 3: Incremental derivations.

junct. This example demonstrates that sentences including coordinate structures cannot be represented by any strictly left-branching derivations. That is, incremental derivation approaches cannot achieve a word-by-word incremental interpretation.

4 Incremental Semantic Construction Based on CCG

This section proposes a method of constructing semantic representations in an incremental fashion. To overcome the problem described in the previous section, our method adapts a different approach. Our method needs not to use incremental derivations. For each initial fragment of a sentence, our proposed method obtains a semantic representation from the normal form derivation. A normal form derivation is defined as the one which uses type-raising and function composition only if they are required.[2] We consider a derivation as a parse tree and construct it based on incremental phrase structure parsing. For each initial fragment of a sentence, incremental parsing can construct a partial parse tree which connects all words in the fragment. Our method obtains a semantic representation from the partial parse tree. In the constructed partial parse tree, some parts of the derivation are underspecified. Our method introduces variables to denote underspecified parts of the semantic representation. These variables are replaced with semantic representations as soon as they are determined. In the rest of this section, we first describe incremental parsing which is the basis of our method. Next, we explain how to obtain a semantic representation from a partial parse tree constructed by incremental parsing.

4.1 Incremental Construction of CCG Derivation

Our method considers a CCG derivation as a tree structure. We call this *parse tree*. Our method constructs a parse tree according to an incremental parsing formalism proposed in (Kato and Matsubara, 2009). This formalism extends the incremental parsing of (Collins and Roark, 2004) by introducing adjoining operation used in Tree Adjoining Grammar (Joshi, 1985). The incremental parsing assigns partial parse trees for any initial fragments of a sentence. Adjoining operation reduces local ambiguity caused by left-recursive structure, and improves the parsing accuracy (Kato and Matsubara, 2009). Furthermore, in the field of psycholinguistics, adjoining operation is introduced to a human sentence processing model (e.g., (Sturt and Lombardo, 2005; Mazzei et al., 2007; Demberg et al., 2013)).

4.1.1 A Formal Description of Incremental Parsing

This section gives a formal description of incremental parsing of (Kato and Matsubara, 2009). The

[2]Several variants of normal form have been presented. For example, see (Eisner, 1996) and (Hockenmaier and Bisk, 2010).

parsing grammar consists of three types of elements: *allowable tuples*, *allowable chains* and *auxiliary trees*. Each allowable tuple is a 3-tuple $\langle X, Y, Z \rangle$ which means that the grammar allows a node labelled with Z to follow a node labelled with Y under its parent labelled with X. Each allowable chain is a sequence of labels. This corresponds to a sequence of labels on a path from a node to its leftmost descendant leaf in a parse tree. Each auxiliary tree consists of two nodes: a root and a foot. The label of a root is the same as that of its foot.

A parse tree is constructed by applying two operations: *attaching* and *adjoining*. Attaching operation combines a partial parse tree and an allowable chain. The operation is defined as follows:

attaching: Let σ be a partial parse tree and c be an allowable chain. Let η be the attachment site of σ. $attach(\sigma, c)$ is the result of attaching c to η as the rightmost child (see Figure 4(a)).

Let X, Y and Z be the label of η, the label of the rightmost child of η and the label of the root of c. If a grammar does not have allowable tuple $\langle X, Y, Z \rangle$, $attach(\sigma, c)$ is not allowed by the grammar. Next, we give the definition of adjoining operation. Adjoining operation inserts an auxiliary tree into a partial parse tree. The operation is defined as follows:

adjoining: Let σ be a partial parse tree and a be an auxiliary tree. Let η be the adjunction site of σ. $adjoin(\sigma, a)$ is the result of splitting σ at η and combining the upper tree of σ with the root of a and the lower tree of σ with the foot of a (see Figure 4(b)). If the label of η is not the same as that of the foot of a, $adjoin(\sigma, a)$ is undefined.

Here, we give the definitions of attachment site and adjunction site. These sites are defined in order to construct a parse tree from left to right. We say that a node η is *complete* if η satisfies the following conditions:

- All children of η are instantiated and complete.[3]
- Adjoining operation is not applicable to η. By the term "applicable", we mean that the grammar has an auxiliary tree whose foot label is identical to that of η and adjoining operation has not been applied to η yet.

The attachment site of σ is defined as the node η satisfying the following conditions:

- Not all children of η are instantiated.
- All instantiated children of η are complete.

The adjunction site of σ is defined as the node η satisfying the following conditions:

- All children of η are instantiated and complete.
- Adjoining operation is applicable to η.

Finally, we introduce *nil-adjoining operation* which changes not a partial parse tree, but node states. When the operation is applied to a node, we deem that adjoining operation is applied to the node. This affects whether or not each node in the partial parse tree is complete. The symbol nil designates the operation.

4.1.2 Constructing CCG Derivations

First of all, we show an example of incremental constructing process of CCG derivations in our proposed method. See Figure 5. Attaching operation is represented as a solid arrow labelled with an allowable chain. Adjoining operation is represented as a dotted arrow labelled with an auxiliary tree. The subscript i of a node indicates that the node is instantiated at the point when i-th word w_i is consumed. The solid boxes mean that the nodes are complete. The dotted box represents that adjoining operation is applicable to the node. The symbol '*' means that the annotated node is introduced by adjoining operation (This node corresponds to the root of the auxiliary tree.). We call it *adjoined node*. Each node in a partial parse tree is labelled with a syntactic category and a rule type (or a word). No semantic representations are assigned. This is because each partial parse tree includes underspecified parts and it is impossible to determine their contents. This example

[3] In incremental phrase structure parsing, to identify whether or not all children are instantiated, (Collins and Roark, 2004) and (Kato and Matsubara, 2009) use a special symbol which means end of constituent. All children of η are instantiated if and only if the rightmost child of η is labelled with this special symbol. In CCG derivation, it can be identified by counting the number of children, since the number is uniquely determined by the rule type of η.

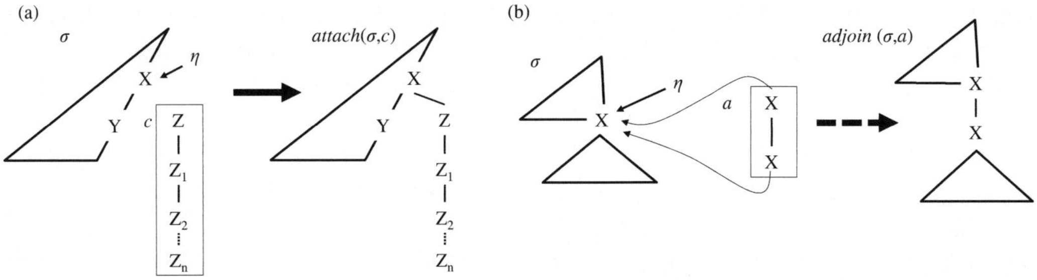

Figure 4: Attaching operation and adjoining operation.

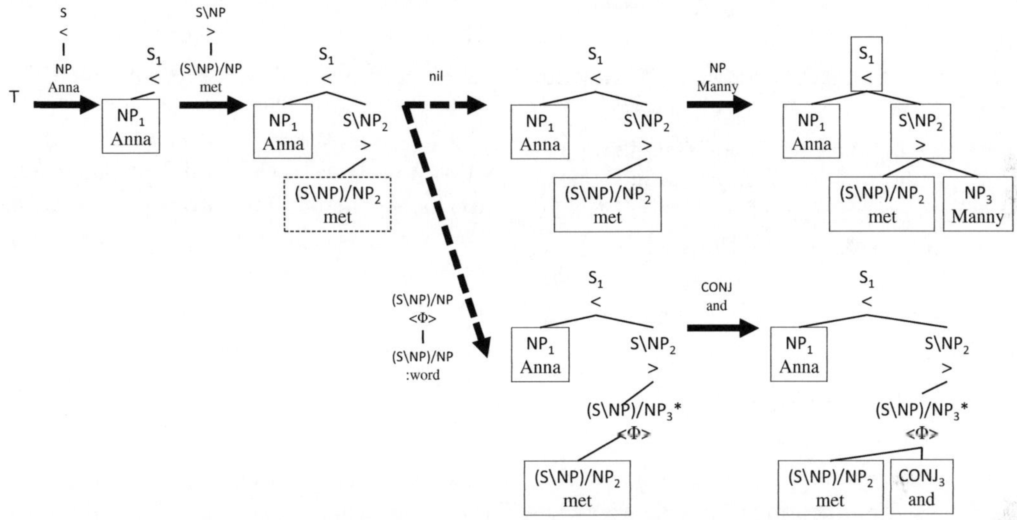

Figure 5: Incremental constructing process of CCG derivations.

demonstrates that each initial fragment has a partial parse tree, which connects all the words in the fragment.

Next, we consider the parsing grammar for CCG derivation. We do not need any allowable tuples, since the CCG rules determine the syntactic category of the node which follows a node. For example, when a parent node is labelled with category S and rule type $<$, and its leftmost child is labelled with category NP, the following node must be labelled with S\NP. The rule type is arbitrary. Of course, we can also define allowable tuples to restrict the rule type.

Each node of the allowable chains and the auxiliary trees is also labelled with a category and a rule type as shown in Figure 5. When an auxiliary tree a is adjoined to a partial parse tree at a node η, the label of η must be the same as that of the foot of a. That is, $cat(\eta) = cat(foot(a))$ and $rule(\eta) = rule(foot(a))$ hold. Here, we write $cat(\eta)$ and $rule(\eta)$ for the category and the rule type of a node η, respectively. $foot(a)$ is the foot node of an auxiliary tree a.

4.2 Incremental Semantic Construction

This section presents our incremental semantic construction procedure. For each initial fragment, our method derives a semantic representation from the partial parse tree obtained by the incremental constructing process. The semantic representation is composed as follows:

- Construct a function t_i which adds the information about the word w_i to the semantic representation s_{i-1} for $w_1 \cdots w_{n-1}$. The function is obtained from the nodes which are instantiated at the point when the word w_i is consumed.

- Apply the function t_i to the semantic representation s_{i-1}. That is, the semantic representation for $w_1 \cdots w_i$ is $s_i = t_i(s_{i-1})$.

We call the function t_i *semantic transition function* (or *transition function* for short). The key point is how to construct the semantic transition function for a word. In the following, we explain it.

To construct a semantic transition function t_i, our method assigns a pair $\langle \alpha, M \rangle$ to each node $\eta \in N_i(\sigma)$ where $N_i(\sigma)$ is the set of the nodes in a partial parse tree σ which are instantiated at the point when i-th word w_i is consumed. Here, α is a sequence of variables and M is a semantic representation. The variables in α occur in M and represent underspecified parts of the semantic representation M. The semantic representation M conveys information about the word w_i. The variables are expected to be specified in the order of α. A transition function is obtained from a pair.

4.2.1 Semantic Construction without Adjoining Operation

For ease of explanation, we first describe the construction of transition function in the case where adjoining operation is not used. Below, $arity(R)$ is the number of the elements of the left-hand side of rule R. $C_R[M_1, \ldots, M_n]$ is the result of combining semantic representations M_1, …, M_n using rule R where n must be equal to $arity(R)$. The procedure of constructing a transition function is as follows:

1. For the leaf node $\eta \in N_i(\sigma)$, if $cat(\eta) : M$ is a lexical entry for w_i, assign $\langle \varepsilon, M \rangle$ to η.

2. Let η be an inner node in $N_i(\sigma)$. Let $\langle \alpha, M \rangle$ be the pair assigned to the child of η. Assign $\langle \alpha x_2 \cdots x_n, C_{rule(\eta)}[M, x_2, \ldots, x_n] \rangle$ to η, where $n = arity(rule(\eta))$ and x_2,…,x_n are fresh variables.

3. Let $\langle \alpha, M \rangle$ be the pair assigned to the highest node in $N_i(\sigma)$. The semantic transition function t_i is defined as follows:

$$\lambda s\alpha.sM$$

   where s is a fresh variable.

By applying semantic transition functions, our method realizes incremental semantic construction. All semantic representations for initial fragments are in the form of $\lambda x\alpha'.M'$ where $x\alpha'$ is a sequence of variables designating underspecified parts in a semantic representation M' (x is the first variable.). By applying semantic transition function $\lambda s\alpha.sM$, we obtain the following semantic representation:

$$(\lambda s\alpha.sM)(\lambda x\alpha'.M') \twoheadrightarrow_\beta \lambda\alpha\alpha'.M'[x := M]$$

The result is in the same form. The underspecified part designated by the variable x is replaced with M which is specified by the word w_i.

As an example of our incremental semantic construction, let us consider a sentence "Anna met Manny." Figure 6 shows examples of semantic transition functions. The initial semantic representation is the identity function $\lambda x.x$. For the word "Anna", the transition function shown in Figure 6(a) is constructed. By applying this function to the initial semantic representation, we obtain the following semantic representation for the initial fragment "Anna":

$$(\lambda sy.s(y\mathsf{anna}'))(\lambda x.x) \twoheadrightarrow_\beta \lambda y.y\mathsf{anna}' \quad (1)$$

Next, by applying the semantic transition function for "met" which is shown in Figure 6(b) to the semantic representation (1), the following one is obtained for the initial fragment "Anna met":

$$(\lambda sy.s(\mathsf{meet}'y))(\lambda y.y\mathsf{anna}') \twoheadrightarrow_\beta \lambda y.\mathsf{meet}'y\mathsf{anna}' \quad (2)$$

This semantic representation captures the predicate-argument relation between anna' and meet'. Finally, by applying the semantic transition function $\lambda s.s\mathsf{manny}'$ to the semantic representation (2), we can obtain the following one:

$$\mathsf{meet}'\mathsf{manny}'\mathsf{anna}' \quad (3)$$

This semantic representation is the same as that of the normal form derivation.

4.2.2 Semantic Construction Using Adjoining Operation

In this section, we extend the transition function construction procedure to allow adjoining operation.

For $\eta \in N_i(\sigma)$ which is a node of an allowable chain, we modify steps 1 and 2 in the transition function construction procedure as follows:

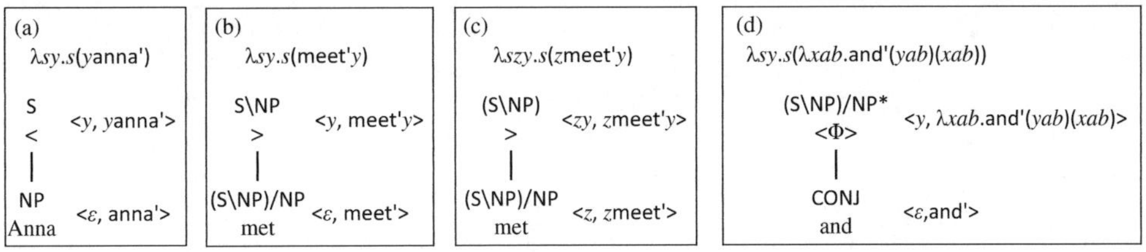

Figure 6: Examples of semantic transition function construction.

- Let $\langle \alpha, M \rangle$ be the pair assigned to η in the version without adjoining operation. If adjoining operation is applicable to η, assign the pair $\langle \alpha z, zM \rangle$ to η instead of $\langle \alpha, M \rangle$ where z is a fresh variable.

The variable z is utilized for updating a semantic representation when adjoining operation is applied to η. When nil-adjoining operation is applied to η, the variable z is replaced with the identity function $\lambda x.x$. That is, after applying $\lambda s.s(\lambda x.x)$ to the semantic representation s_{i-1}, the semantic transition function t_i is applied.

For an adjoined node $\eta \in N_i(\sigma)$, the modified procedure assigns a pair to η in the following way:

- Let $\langle \alpha, M \rangle$ be the pair assigned to the root node of the allowable chain which is attached under η. Let R be $rule(\eta)$ and n be $arity(R)$. If adjoining operation is applicable to η, assign the following pair to η:

  $$\langle \alpha y_3 \ldots y_n z, \lambda x.zC_R[x, M, y_3, \ldots y_n] \rangle$$

  Otherwise, assign the following pair to η:

  $$\langle \alpha y_3 \ldots y_n, \lambda x.C_R[x, M, y_3, \ldots y_n] \rangle$$

  Here, x, y_3,. . .,y_n and z are fresh variables.

The pair assignment for a node to which adjoining operation is applicable and the one for an adjoined node work cooperatively (see Figure 7). If adjoining operation is applicable to a node, a fresh variable z is introduced to the semantic representation. When adjoining operation is applied to the node, this variable is replaced with a function in the form of $\lambda x.C_R[x, M_2, \ldots]$ which receives a semantic representation of the first child and returns the result of semantic composition. Figure 6(c) shows an example of constructing the transition function where adjoining operation is applicable to the node $(\mathtt{S}\backslash\mathtt{NP})/\mathtt{NP}$. Figure 6(d) shows an example of constructing the transition function where the node $(\mathtt{S}\backslash\mathtt{NP})/\mathtt{NP}$ is an adjoined node.

Table 1: Incremental semantic construction of "Anna met and might marry Manny."

word	#	semantic representation
Anna	1	$\lambda y.y\mathsf{anna}'$
met	2	$\lambda zy.z\mathsf{meet}'y\mathsf{anna}'$
and	3	$\lambda yx.\mathsf{and}'(yx\mathsf{anna}')(\mathsf{meet}'x\mathsf{anna}')$
might	4	$\lambda yx.\mathsf{and}'(\mathsf{might}'(yx)\mathsf{anna}')(\mathsf{meet}'x\mathsf{anna}')$
marry	5	$\lambda x.\mathsf{and}'(\mathsf{might}'(\mathsf{marry}'x)\mathsf{anna}')(\mathsf{meet}'x\mathsf{anna}')$
Manny	6	$\mathsf{and}'(\mathsf{might}'(\mathsf{marry}'\mathsf{manny}')\mathsf{anna}')(\mathsf{meet}'\mathsf{manny}'\mathsf{anna}')$

The transition function is applied in the same way as the version without adjoining operation. Table 1 shows an example of the semantic representations constructed by our method.

As an example, let us consider the initial fragment "Anna met..." By applying the transition function shown in Figure 6(c) to the semantic representation (1), we obtain the semantic representation #2 shown in Table 1.

In the case where the next word is "Manny", nil-adjoining operation is applied to the node $(\mathtt{S}\backslash\mathtt{NP})/\mathtt{NP}$, that is, the function $\lambda s.s(\lambda x.x)$ is applied to #2. The result is identical to the semantic representation (2), therefore, we obtain the semantic representation (3) for "Anna met Manny".

Next, let us consider the case where the word "and" follows the initial fragment "Anna met." In this case, the derivation is constructed as shown in the lower side of Figure 5. The semantic transition function for the word "and" is constructed as shown in Figure 6(d). By applying the function to the semantic representation #2, we obtain the semantic representation #3. Furthermore, if the word sequence "might marry Manny" follows this initial

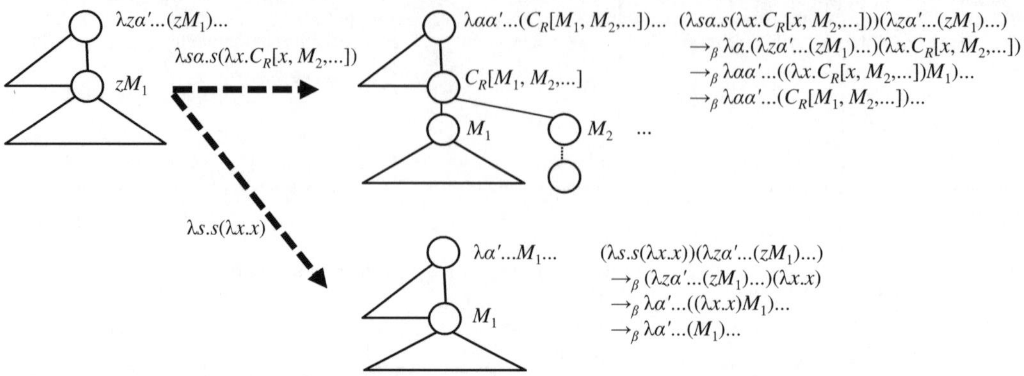

Figure 7: Updating a semantic representation by adjoining operation.

Table 2: Semantic representations assigned by incremental derivations.

word	semantic representation
Anna	anna′
met	—
and	—
might	—
marry	λx.and′(might′(marry′x)anna′)(meet′$x$anna′)
Manny	and′(might′(marry′manny′)anna′)(meet′manny′anna′)

fragment, the semantic representations #4, #5 and #6 are obtained in this order. This example demonstrates that our method can incrementally construct semantic representations for sentences including coordinate structures. In comparison with our incremental semantic construction, incremental derivation approaches have the case where no semantic representations are assigned to initial fragments. Table 2 shows semantic representations which are assigned using incremental derivations. There exist initial fragments which have no semantic representations as discussed in Section 3.[4]

5 Related Work

Our incremental semantic construction is based on the λ-calculus. There have been several methods of incremental semantic construction using the λ-calculus. Pulman (1985) has developed an incremental parser which uses context-free rules annotated with semantic representations. The parsing process proceeds on a word-by-word basis, but its intermediate structure is a stack, that is, the parser does not assign a fully-connected semantic representation to each initial fragment. Milward (1995) has proposed an incremental semantic construction method based on Categorial Grammar. The method uses two types of transition functions: state-application and state-prediction. Our semantic transition function is similar to these functions. However, our method is more general than that of Milward. Milward's method cannot produce CCG derivations, since it can deal with only function application.

There are other approaches to incremental semantic construction, which use different formalism. Purver et al. (2011) have developed a dialogue system based on Dynamic Syntax (DS) (Kempson et al., 2001), which provides an incremental framework of constructing semantic representations. Peldszus and Schlangen (2012) have proposed incremental semantic construction based on Robust Minimal Recursion Semantics (RMRS) (Copestake, 2007). Sayeed and Demberg (2012) have proposed incremental semantic construction for PLTAG (Demberg et al., 2013). It is unclear how to construct a wide coverage grammar (with semantic annotation) in these frameworks.[5] On the other hand, our method can use

[4]The initial fragment "Anna met" can have the semantic representation λx.meet′$x$anna′ as shown in Figure 3(a). However, the derivation which has this semantic representation is not a partial structure of incremental derivation shown in Figure 3(b). That is, the derivation is not consistent with that of "Anna met and might marry Manny."

[5]DS grammar induction method (Eshghi et al., 2013) was only applied to a small artificial corpus (200 sentences, max sentence length is 6.). Peldszus and Schlangen (2012) manually assigned semantic annotations to a small set of context-free rules (30 rules). Sayeed and Demberg (2012) only provided small examples.

CCG-based lexicon (e.g., (Bos, 2009)) directly. Although our method requires a set of allowable chains and auxiliary trees in addition to such a lexicon, we can easily extract it from CCGbank (Hockenmaier and Steedman, 2007) by using the method proposed in (Kato and Matsubara, 2009).

6 Conclusion

This paper proposed a CCG-based method of incrementally constructing semantic representations. Our approach is based on normal form derivations unlike previous ones. In this paper, we focused on the formal aspect of our method. We defined semantic transition function to obtain semantic representations for each initial fragment of an input sentence.

Another important issue is how to interpret intermediate semantic representations for initial fragments. To our knowledge, there is little work to this direction. In future work, we will explore a model-theoretic approach to this problem.

Acknowledgements

This research was partially supported by the Grant-in-Aid for Scientific Research (B) (No.26280082) of JSPS.

References

Gregory Aist, James Allen, Ellen Campana, Carlos G. Gallo, Scott Stoness, Mary Swift, and Michael K. Tanenhaus. 2007. Incremental understanding in human-computer dialogue and experimental evidence for advantages over nonincremental methods. In Ron Artstein and Laure View, editors, *Proceedings of the 11th Workshop on the Semantics and Pragmatics of Dialogue*, pages 149–154, Trento, Italy, June.

James Allen, George Ferguson, and Amanda Stent. 2001. An architecture for more realistic conversational systems. In *Proceedings of International Conference of Intelligent User Interfaces*, pages 1–8, Santa Fe, New Mexico, USA, January.

Johan Bos. 2008. Wide-coverage semantic analysis with Boxer. In *Semantics in Text Processing. STEP 2008 Conference Proceedings*, pages 277–286.

Johan Bos. 2009. Towards a large-scale formal semantic lexicon for text processing. In *Proceedings of the Biennal GSCL Conference From Form to Meaning: Processing Texts Automatically*, pages 3–14.

Michael Collins and Brian Roark. 2004. Incremental parsing with the perceptron algorithm. In *Proceedings of the 42nd Meeting of the Association for Computational Linguistics (ACL'04), Main Volume*, pages 111–118, Barcelona, Spain, July.

Ann Copestake. 2007. Semantic composition with (robust) minimal recursion semantics. In *Proceedings of the ACL 2007 Workshop on Deep Linguistic Processing*, pages 73–80, Prague, Czech Republic, June.

Vera Demberg, Frank Keller, and Alexander Koller. 2013. Incremental, predictive parsing with psycholinguistically motivated tree-adjoining grammar. *Computational Linguistics*, 39(4):1025–1066.

Vera Demberg. 2012. Incremental derivations in CCG. In *Proceedings of the 11th International Workshop on Tree Adjoining Grammars and Related Formalisms (TAG+ 11)*, pages 198–206.

Jason Eisner. 1996. Efficient normal-form parsing for combinatory categorial grammar. In *Proceedings of the 34th Annual Meeting of the Association for Computational Linguistics*, pages 79–86, Santa Cruz, California, USA, June.

Arash Eshghi, Matthew Purver, and Julian Hough. 2013. Probabilistic induction for an incremental semantic grammar. In *Proceedings of the 10th International Conference on Computational Semantics*, pages 107–118.

Hany Hassan, Khalil Sima'an, and Andy Way. 2008. A syntactic language model based on incremental CCG parsing. In *Spoken Language Technology Workshop, 2008. SLT 2008. IEEE*, pages 205–208.

Ahmed Hefny, Hany Hassan, and Mohamed Bahgat. 2011. Incremental combinatory categorial grammar and its derivations. In *Computational Linguistics and Intelligent Text Processing*, pages 96–108. Springer.

Julia Hockenmaier and Yonatan Bisk. 2010. Normal-form parsing for combinatory categorial grammars with generalized composition and type-raising. In *Proceedings of the 23rd International Conference on Computational Linguistics (Coling 2010)*, pages 465–473, Beijing, China, August.

Julia Hockenmaier and Mark Steedman. 2007. CCGbank: A corpus of CCG derivations and dependency structures extracted from the Penn Treebank. *Computational Linguistics*, 33(3):355–396.

Aravind K. Joshi. 1985. Tree adjoining grammars: How much context sensitivity is required to provide a reasonable structural description? In David R. Dowty, Lauri Karttunen, and Arnold M. Zwicky, editors, *Natural Language Parsing*, pages 206–250. Cambridge University Press.

Yoshihide Kato and Shigeki Matsubara. 2009. Incremental parsing with adjoining operation. *IEICE Transactions on Information and Systems*, E92-D(12):2306–2312.

Ruth Kempson, Wilfried Meyer-Viol, and Dov Gabbay. 2001. *Dynamic Syntax: the Flow of Language Understanding*. Blackwell.

Alessandro Mazzei, Vincenzo Lombardo, and Patrick Sturt. 2007. Dynamic TAG and lexical dependencies. *Research on Language and Computation*, 5(3):309–332, September.

David Milward. 1995. Incremental interpretation of categorial grammar. In *Proceedings of the Seventh Conference on European Chapter of the Association for Computational Linguistics*, pages 119–126.

Andreas Peldszus and David Schlangen. 2012. Incremental construction of robust but deep semantic representations for use in responsive dialogue systems. In *Proceedings of the Workshop on Advances in Discourse Analysis and its Computational Aspects*, pages 56–76.

Stephen G. Pulman. 1985. A parser that doesn't. In *Proceedings of the Second Conference on European Chapter of the Association for Computational Linguistics*, pages 128–135.

Matthew Purver, Arash Eshghi, and Julian Hough. 2011. Incremental semantic construction in a dialogue system. In *Proceedings of the Ninth International Conference on Computational Semantics*, pages 365–369. Association for Computational Linguistics.

David Reitter, Julia Hockenmaier, and Frank Keller. 2006. Priming effects in combinatory categorial grammar. In *Proceedings of the 2006 Conference on Empirical Methods in Natural Language Processing*, pages 308–316.

Asad Sayeed and Vera Demberg. 2012. Incremental neo-davidsonian semantic construction for TAG. In *Proceedings of 11th International Workshop on Tree-Adjoining Grammars and Related Formalisms*, pages 64–72.

Mark Steedman. 2000. *The Syntactic Process*. The MIT press.

Patrick Sturt and Vincenzo Lombardo. 2005. Processing coordinated structures: Incrementality and connectedness. *Cognitive Science*, 2(29):291–305.

Dependency-Based Semantic Role Labeling using Convolutional Neural Networks

William R. Foland Jr.
OKRobotGo, Ltd.
5345 Dunraven Circle
Golden, Co, 80403, USA
bill.foland@okrobotgo.com

James H. Martin
Department of Computer Science and
Institute of Cognitive Science
University of Colorado
Boulder, CO 80309
James.Martin@colorado.edu

Abstract

We describe a semantic role labeler with state-of-the-art performance and low computational requirements, which uses convolutional and time-domain neural networks. The system is designed to work with features derived from a dependency parser output. Various system options and architectural details are discussed. Incremental experiments were run to explore the benefits of adding increasingly more complex dependency-based features to the system; results are presented for both in-domain and out-of-domain datasets.

1 Introduction

Semantic role labeling (Gildea and Jurafsky [2002]), the task of identifying and classifying the semantic arguments of verbal and nominal predicates in text, represents one of the most complex NLP tasks to be addressed by supervised machine learning techniques. In the standard supervised approach to building SRL systems, collections of multiway classifiers are trained using annotated corpora such as PropBank (Palmer et al. [2005]). In this approach, classifiers are trained using features derived directly from the original source text, as well as from subsequent syntactic and semantic processing.

As reported in several shared tasks (Carreras and Màrquez [2004],Carreras and Màrquez [2005],Hajič et al. [2009]), SRL systems trained in this manner can achieve high performance. State-of-the-art systems employ classifiers such as support vector machines trained with large numbers of relatively complex combinations of features, often combined with re-ranking based on multiple syntactic analyses. Unfortunately, these approaches have a number of non-trivial limitations including the computational cost of the syntactic parsing and the sparse nature of the complex features on which they rely. This latter limitation is particularly critical since it leads to significant degradation in performance when the trained system is applied to texts from new domains.

However, recent results using multilayer neural networks and pre-trained word embeddings have demonstrated high performance using a much smaller number of minimalist features. The architecture described by Collobert et al. [2011] combines time delay convolutional neural networks (Waibel et al. [1989]) and pre-trained word embeddings for a number of NLP tasks. They develop four components and compare their performance to previous benchmarks, one of which is an SRL system which uses features derived from a phrase-structure parse as input, based on the CoNLL 2005 shared task (Carreras and Màrquez [2005]).

The work described here adopts the basic architecture from Collobert et al. [2011] and explores issues related to the use of this architecture in the context of the CoNLL 2009 shared task. In particular, we present Daisy, a system that (1) employs features derived from dependency parse as input, (2) assigns semantic roles to both verbal and nominal predicates, and (3) automatically assigns word senses to the predicates as described in the CoNLL 2009 shared task (Hajič et al. [2009]).

The following sections will describe the architecture of the Daisy system, present state-of-the-art performance on the CoNLL 2009 shared task, and ex-

*Proceedings of the Fourth Joint Conference on Lexical and Computational Semantics (*SEM 2015)*, pages 279–288,
Denver, Colorado, June 4–5, 2015.

plore the utility of features derived from dependency parses, including a version of the traditional SRL syntactic path feature.

2 Experimental Setup

The CoNLL 2009 shared task consists of identifying the sense and semantic arguments for each given argument-bearing token (predicate). In addition to the words themselves, the training data provides the part of speech, syntactic head, and syntactic dependency relation to the head for each word in the sentence. Table 1 shows an example sentence and its representation in the dataset. The PDEPREL and PHEAD features are the head word and dependency relation predicted automatically by a dependency parser. In the example sentence, there are two predicates identified for labeling: *announce*, and *close*. The system should output two arguments for *announce*: *results*:A1 (Object), and *after*:AM-TEMP (Temporal Marker). Similarly, *market*:A1 should be output for the predicate *close*. In addition to role identification, the word sense for each predicate is output, in the example, the expected sense for *announce* is 01, and for *close* is 02.

The training, validation, and evaluation datasets are annotated sentences from the Wall Street Journal. An additional out of domain dataset mostly from the Brown corpus was also supplied. A comprehensive F1 score was generated for both role labels and sense predictions using the provided eval09.pl perl script.

3 Semantic Role Labeling System

The general block diagrams for the Daisy SRL system are shown in Figure 1. The input to the system is a list of words w_i from w_1 to w_n, a list of predicate positions, and dependency parse tree information for the sentence. We treat role labeling and the sense identification as two separate tasks. For each predicate in a given sentence, the Role Subsystem outputs the list of predicted role tags for all words (SRL_i), and the Sense Subsystem outputs the sense tag of the predicate. The system is composed of five major components:

- Word Preprocessing and Word Derived Feature Convolution (Figure 2).
- Predicate Position Feature Convolution.

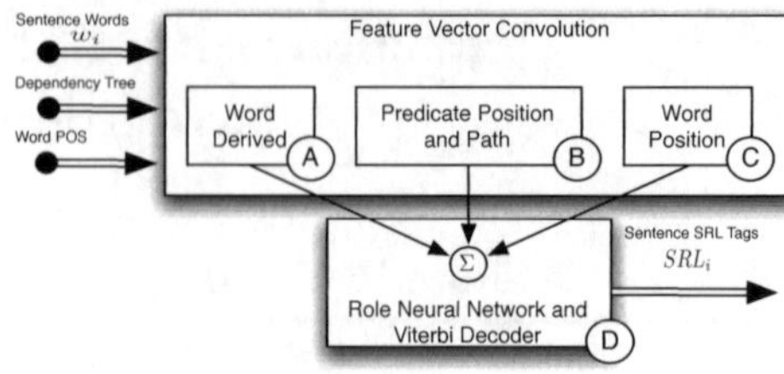

(a) Role Subsystem

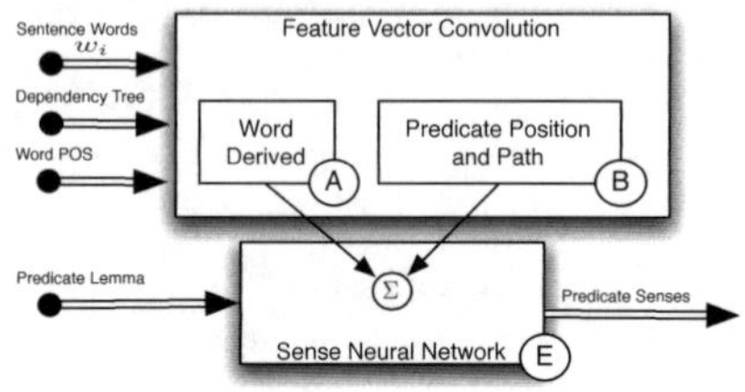

(b) Sense Subsystem

Figure 1: SRL Role and Sense Block Diagrams

- Word Position Feature Convolution.
- Neural Network and Viterbi (Figure 4).
- Predicate Sense Neural Network (Figure 5).

3.1 Word Derived Feature Convolution Section

The Word Derived Features and Convolution section, shown in Figure 2, is sourced by five features which are derived on a word by word basis.

The upper portion of Figure 2 depicts the process of looking up features from the words and parse tree information. The numeric information from the features for each word is concatenated together to form one long feature vector, shown in the diagram as a multi-shaded set of rectangles. Three words of feature information (the word and its two neighbors) from the Word Derived Feature Vector are multiplied by the the weights and bias of Θ_4 and stored in the Convolved Word Derived Feature Vector, for each word in the sentence. For the default convolution width of 300, this results in a long vector of $300 \cdot n$, where n is the number of words in the sentence.

Each feature lookup table contains an entry for *PADDING*. In order to allow the window to extend beyond boundaries of the sentence for early and late words the Feature Vector is padded with the *PADDING* value from each lookup table. If a fea-

ID	FORM	LEMMA	PLEMMA	POS	PPOS	FEAT	PFEAT	HEAD	PHEAD	DEPREL	PDEPREL	FILLPRED	PRED	A[announce]	A[close]
1	The	the	the	DT	DT	_	_	2	2	NMOD	NMOD	_	_	_	_
2	results	result	result	NNS	NNS	_	_	3	3	SBJ	SBJ	_	_	A1	_
3	were	be	be	VBD	VBD	_	_	0	0	ROOT	ROOT	_	_	_	_
4	announced	announce	announce	VBN	VBN	_	_	3	3	VC	VC	Y	announce.01	_	_
5	after	after	after	IN	IN	_	_	4	4	TMP	TMP	_	_	AM-TMP	_
6	the	the	the	DT	DT	_	_	8	8	NMOD	NMOD	_	_	_	_
7	stock	stock	stock	NN	NN	_	_	8	8	NMOD	NMOD	_	_	_	_
8	market	market	market	NN	NN	_	_	9	9	SBJ	SBJ	_	_	_	A1
9	closed	close	close	VBD	VBD	_	_	5	5	SUB	SUB	Y	close.02	_	_
10	.	.	.	.	.	_	_	3	3	P	P	_	_	_	_

Table 1: CoNLL format SRL Dependency Parse Input Test Sentence Example

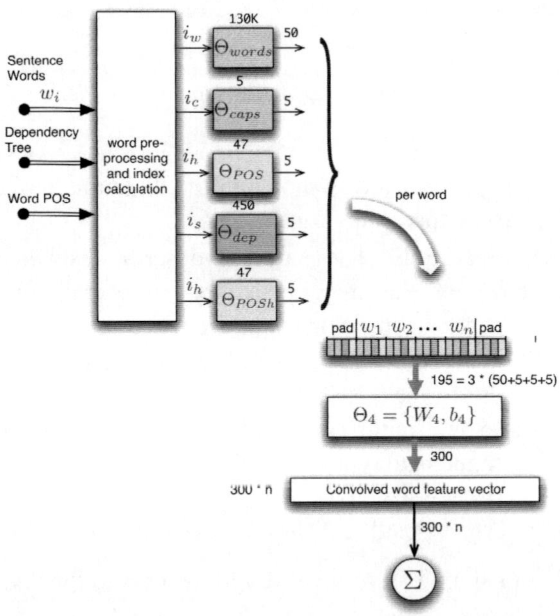

Figure 2: Word Preprocessing, Word Derived Features, and Word Derived Feature Convolution. (A) in figures 1(a) and 1(b).

ture is in the table, the associated vector is output, otherwise the vector corresponding to the special token *UNKNOWN* is output. The *PADDING* and *UNKNOWN* vectors are trained during supervised training.

To train the word representations from scratch, all except the 0.63% least common unique words from the training set are added to the lookup table. The remaining words are therefore trained as the UNKNOWN word, which can then be used to represent any word encountered outside the trained word list. For other features, the representation for the most probable token is used as the UNKNOWN representation.

The five types of word-derived features tested for the SRL Dependency Parse tagger are:

- Word Embeddings
- Capitalization
- POS tag of word
- Dependency Relation
- POS tag of head

3.1.1 Word Pre-processing

The input data provided for the CoNLL 2009 task has already gone through some initial tokenizing. This prevents tokenization differences of different systems from influencing the results, which are meant to allow comparison of the SRL tagging architecture itself. The Daisy pre-processor does not split hyphenated input words, so each input word will result in a single pre-processed word. Numeric values are collapsed to the single common *0* token, and words are lower-cased to create a word representation lookup word.

3.1.2 Word Embeddings

Words are transformed to numeric representations using a lookup table. Like all other feature lookup tables in the system, the word representation vectors can be initialized to small random values to start with, and then trained using the supervised training algorithm.

A method of training the word representations from untagged databases has been very successfully applied to create a starting set of vectors that can be used to initialize a network, which is then fine-tuned with supervised training to execute a specific task. By "pre-training" these word representations using large amounts of untagged text, very informative word relationships can be inexpensively extracted, and later used as the starting point for task specific application learning, see for example Hinton et al. [2006], Bengio et al. [2007] and Weston et al. [2012].

The word representations, or embeddings, used as input to the Daisy SRL System for the experiments described here were generated by Collobert et al. [2011] and were created using a pairwise ranking approach (Schapire and Singer [1998]).

3.1.3 Capitalization

Prior to lower casing, each word is checked for all capitals, initial capital, any capital, or no capitals, and this criteria is used to lookup a vector (default length 5) from the caps table.

3.1.4 Predicted Dependency Relation

The PDEPREL column from the training data, shown in table 1.

3.1.5 Predicted POS tag of word and of head

The Predicted Part-of-speech tag is provided in PPOS column of the training data. The head part of speech tag is found by following the PHEAD column and extracting the PPOS column. (see Table 1).

3.2 Predicate Position and Path Feature Convolution Section

Predicate Position and optional Path features are extracted on a per word basis and convolved, once per predicate (the outer loop of two).

3.2.1 Predicate Position Feature

The position of each word relative to the predicate being evaluated is represented by 25 vectors, based on distances of -12 to +12, and distances outside this range are saturated.

3.2.2 Dependency Path Feature

Information about the path from each word to a given predicate is maintained in a lookup table and is provided in the Predicate Position Convolution section as a per word feature.

Generic Path: The sequence of up and down transitions to traverse the tree from a word to a given predicate is referred to here as the *Generic Path*. The dependency parse trees for each of the two predicates from the example training sentence shown in Table 1 are diagrammed in Figure 3. The Generic

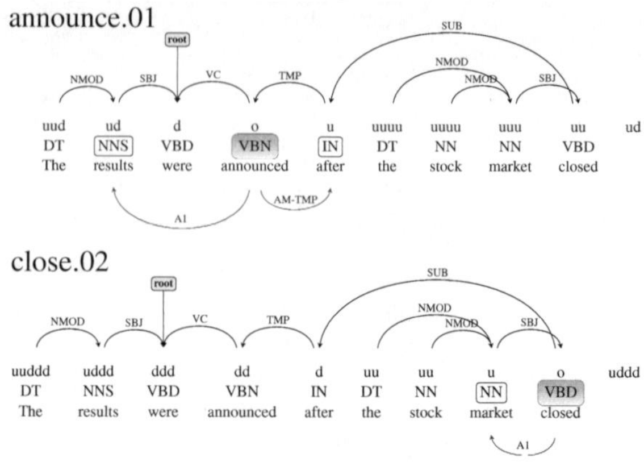

Figure 3: Dependency Parse and Generic Paths

Path for each word is shown in the diagram, above the part of speech tag for the word.

Labeled Path: These are path descriptions which include both the arc direction (Generic Path) and the dependency relation of the arc within the dependency tree. After several rounds of experimentation, we chose to include paths which occur at least five times in the training data, which resulted in about 77K unique path types.

3.3 Word Position Feature Convolution Section

The position of every word with respect to the specific word being evaluated is extracted once per word, per predicate (the inner loop of two). In a similar fashion to the predicate position feature, the position of each word relative to the word being evaluated is represented by 25 vectors, based on distances of -12 to +12, and distances outside this range are saturated.

3.4 Role Neural Network and Viterbi

Figure 4 shows the process of combining the Convolved Feature Vectors, processing with a neural network, and finding the most likely role sequence with a Viterbi detector. Both the Role and Sense neural networks are constructed with a single non-linear layer followed by an output layer. The parameters for each layer are referred to here as Θ, which includes a matrix of weights, W, and a vector of bias terms b. Each layer's output, prior to the activation function, can be calculated from the previous layer's activation output and parameters.

$$f_\Theta^l = W^{l-1} f_\Theta^{l-1} + b^{l-1} \quad (1)$$

The tanh function is used as the nonlinear activation function.

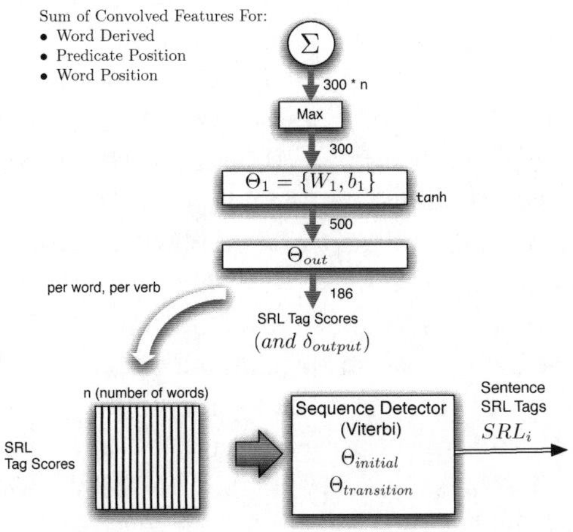

Figure 4: SRL Neural Network and Viterbi. (D) in figure 1(a).

The three Convolved Feature Vectors (diagrammed separately) are summed, then the maximum for each index within each group of 300 is determined. This results in a 300 element vector which will be the input to the Neural Network. A single layer neural network followed by a single output layer is used to create a "score" for each possible role "tag", for the word and predicate being analyzed. After running all words through the system for a single predicate, a matrix of SRL roles scores of size $tags \times words$ is created, which will be used as the input to the Viterbi sequence decoder.

3.5 Sequence Decoder (Viterbi)

The Viterbi decoding algorithm input is a matrix which consists of a vector of SRL role scores for each word. The algorithm is initialized with a learned set of weights per tag, and computes the log-likelihood of transitioning from each state to the next by applying a learned set of weights from the transition matrix.

3.6 Predicate Sense Neural Network

Figure 5 shows the process of combining the Convolved Feature Vectors, processing with a neural network, and finding the most likely sense for a given predicate. The neural network parameters for the sense subsystem are managed with a lookup table holding parameters for each lemma in the training set that is mapped to multiple senses.

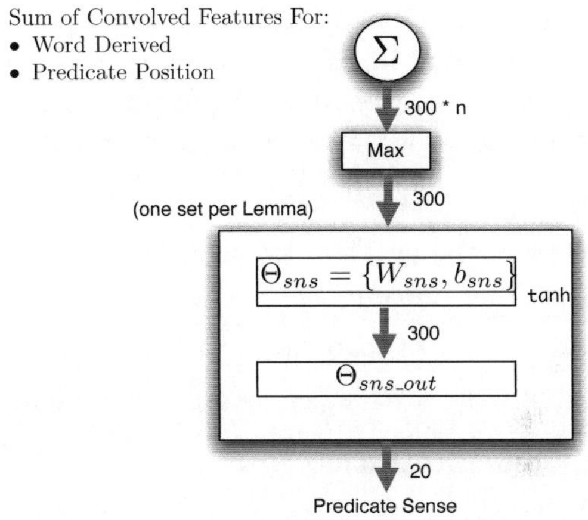

Figure 5: SRL Neural Network for Predicate Sense. (E) in figure1(b).

4 Sense Labeler Training and Forward Model Creation

Both the Role and Sense subsystems are trained using stochastic gradient descent. A forward pass is first run on the system, during which the indices of the maximum values of the sum of the convolutions layers (word-derived and predicate) are saved.

Back-propagation of the Sense Neural Network is based on minimizing a log-likelihood objective:

$$\log p(y|x,\Theta) = f[x,\Theta]_y - \log(\sum_j e^{(f[x,\Theta]_j)}) \quad (2)$$

The two Sense and Role subsystems have the same convolution structures (See figures 1(a) and 1(b)). Experiments run using a common structure for both tasks resulted in about 0.5% worse performance, so the the systems were kept independent.

A separate neural network was trained for each lemma found in the training data set, and the parameters for each network were stored in a lookup table. This results in very large memory requirements during training, especially since Adagrad (Duchi et al.

[2011] was used to decrease training time. To minimize memory requirements and training time, the sense for lemmas which always train to the same sense in the training data are stored in a dictionary. During forward processing, when a lemma is encountered that was not trained (and therefore is not in the parameter lookup table), the sense from the dictionary is output. If the lemma never occurred during training, it won't be in the dictionary, and the most commonly occurring sense of "01" is output by default.

5 Role Labeler Training and Forward Model Creation

During a forward pass, the activation layers and maxIndices are saved and reused during training.

5.1 Cost Calculation

The Viterbi parameters for initial score and transition probabilities are trained using the Sentence Level Log-Likelihood (SLL) cost function.

This cost function is based on Sentence Level Likelihood and is similar to equation 2, except the reference path score must be normalized by using the sum of the exponential of all path scores (the sum of unnormalized probabilities for *all* possible paths, instead of for all possible tags). A recursive method, developed in Rabiner [1989] and specified in Collobert et al. [2011], provides an important and efficient means of computing the sum of the exponential of all path scores. An intermediate vector, δ, is calculated, which will contain the unnormalized log probability that any path through the trellis will pass through a particular state k for the particular word t. The δ vectors have a dimension of N, the number of tags, and they are re-used for the gradient calculation during back-propagation.

5.2 Back-propagation

The recursion described in Collobert et al. [2011] is used to calculate Viterbi delta terms and gradients. The error is then back-propagated through the system in reverse, ending with the feature lookup tables. This is done for each word, for each predicate, requiring two nested loops for training a full sentence. The loop structure makes for long training times, roughly three days on a 2015 compute-optimized AWS core.

6 Results

6.1 Benchmark

The best ConLL 2009, English, SRL F1 score, is labeled Nugues, and the system is described in Björkelund et al. [2009]. To the best of our knowledge, the current state of the art for this dataset is represented by these results, and we therefore use them as a benchmark (See section 7). To generate these benchmark results, 20 features were used for argument identification, including the Dependency Relation Path, and Part of Speech of Dependency Relation Path. A reranker was then run on the output of multiple system outputs.

Table 2 compares the benchmark with a complete Daisy system using a labeled path, with a cutoff of 5, and two separate systems for sense and role labels. F1 scores are 0.41% higher for the WSJ Eval dataset, and 2.59% higher for the out of domain (OOD) Brown dataset.

System Description	WSJ F1	Brown F1
Benchmark (CoNLL2009)	85.63%	73.31%
Daisy	86.04%	75.90%

Table 2: SRL Dependency Parse Test F1

6.2 Metrics

In all experiments, we strictly followed the standard evaluation procedure of the CoNLL 2009 challenge. A simple validation procedure using the specified validation set was used to choose system hyper parameters, and the provided eval09.pl perl script was used to generate all system F1 scores. The system F1 score is the harmonic mean of precision and recall for both role and sense labels. Since we treated the predicate sense disambiguation and the predicate role assignment tasks as independent, it is interesting to view the performance of the two tasks separately. The predicate sense task requires a label for each given predicate, so a per predicate accuracy was calculated (SenseAcc). Similarly we generated a role label F1 score (RoleF1) that is independent of the sense labels. These subsystem performance metrics were also calculated on the CoNLL 2009 benchmark results for comparison.

6.3 Incremental Experiments and Results

Feature abbreviations used in the descriptions are shown in Table 3.

Abbrev.	Feature Description
W	words, initialized randomly prior to training
C	capitalization
P	Part of Speech
HP	Part of Speech of head word
DR	Dependency Relation
GP	Generic path
TW	words, initialized with pre-trained word embeddings prior to training
LP5	Labeled paths that occur at least five times in the training data.

Table 3: Feature Abbreviations

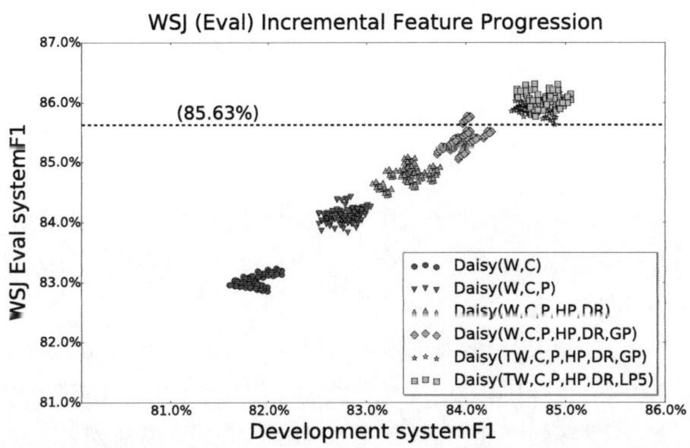

Figure 6: Scatter Plot of Dev F1 vs. Eval F1 for Various Feature Configurations (See also Table 4)

Incremental experiments were run to explore the benefits of adding increasingly more complex dependency-based features to the system.

We began with a basic configuration of only words (randomly initialized) and capitalization (W,C), Following this, a simple per-token part of speech was added (W,C,P). Information from the dependency parser is then added in two steps, first the head word part of speech and dependency relation (W,C,P,HP,DR), and next the generic path (W,C,P,HP,DR,GP). The word representations were then seeded with the pre-trained embeddings described in section 3.1.2 (TW,C,P,HP,DR,GP). Finally, the labeled path was used instead of the generic path, still seeding the words with pre-trained embeddings (TW,C,P,HP,DR,LP5).

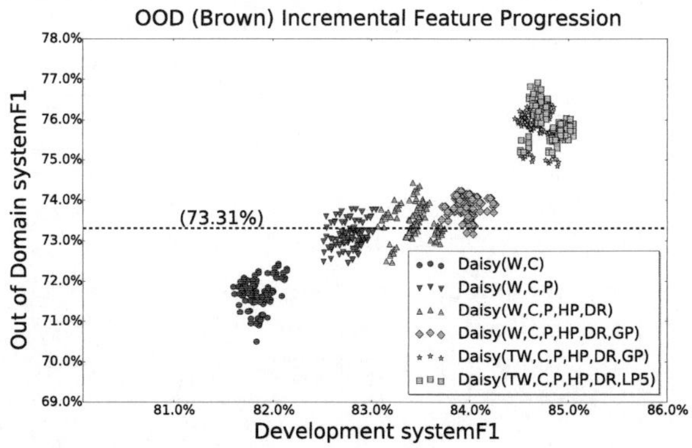

Figure 7: Dev F1 vs. Brown (OOD) F1 for Various Feature Configurations (See also Table 5)

For each system configuration, 12 role subsystems and 8 sense subsystems were trained and tested, using the WSJ development F1 score during training to determine the best model parameter state. After model generation, the WSJ development scores for different systems don't correlate well with the WSJ eval or Brown scores. For example, models with high development scores don't necessarily correspond to best scoring models for the WSJ or Brown data tests.

The CoNLL2009 results used as benchmarks were given as single data points so statistics are not available.

Figure 7 shows the relationship between the development and Evaluation F1 scores, as well as the general performance improvement as features were added.

Tables 4 and 5 show the statistical performance of the system with WSJ and Brown test data.

For the WSJ (evaluation) dataset, the role subsystem F1 improves much more dramatically than the sense subsystem as POS (+1.52%) and dependency parser information (+1.68%) is added. The mean System F1 score is -0.25% under the benchmark without the pre-trained word embeddings. Adding the embeddings boosts performance such that even the lowest scoring systems beat the benchmark, and the mean F1 score is about 0.41% higher.

System Description	SystemF1				RoleF1		SenseAcc	
	Min	Mean	(Δ)	Max	Mean	(Δ)	Mean	(Δ)
Daisy(W,C)	82.86	83.03		83.24	77.47		94.92	
Daisy(W,C,**P**)	83.83	84.12	(+1.09)	84.43	79.00	(+1.52)	95.15	(+0.23)
Daisy(W,C,P,**HP,DR**)	84.46	84.79	(+0.67)	85.10	79.92	(+0.92)	95.29	(+0.13)
Daisy(W,C,P,HP,DR,**GP**)	85.05	85.38	(+0.58)	85.78	80.69	(+0.76)	95.46	(+0.17)
Benchmark (CoNLL2009)		85.63	(+0.25)		81.00	(+0.31)	95.59	(+0.13)
Daisy(**TW**,C,P,HP,DR,GP)	85.64	85.92	(+0.29)	86.17	81.40	(+0.40)	95.66	(+0.07)
Daisy(TW,C,P,HP,DR,**LP5**)	85.77	86.04	(+0.13)	86.31	81.53	(+0.13)	95.77	(+0.11)

Table 4: Performance on WSJ Eval Dataset for Various System Configurations

System Description	SystemF1				RoleF1		SenseAcc	
	Min	Mean	(Δ)	Max	Mean	(Δ)	Mean	(Δ)
Daisy(W,C)	70.50	71.70		72.43	65.49		85.08	
Daisy(W,C,**P**)	72.45	73.13	(+1.43)	73.78	67.38	(+1.89)	85.66	(+0.59)
Benchmark (CoNLL2009)		73.31	(+0.18)		67.78	(+0.40)	85.23	(-0.43)
Daisy(W,C,P,**HP,DR**)	72.47	73.48	(+0.17)	74.43	67.87	(+0.09)	85.71	(+0.48)
Daisy(W,C,P,HP,DR,**GP**)	73.17	73.83	(+0.36)	74.23	68.21	(+0.34)	86.04	(+0.33)
Daisy(**TW**,C,P,HP,DR,GP)	74.85	75.80	(+1.97)	76.46	70.80	(+2.59)	86.72	(+0.68)
Daisy(TW,C,P,HP,DR,**LP5**)	75.19	75.90	(+0.09)	76.93	70.62	(-0.18)	87.40	(+0.69)

Table 5: Performance on Brown Dataset (OOD) for Various System Configurations

For the Brown (OOD) dataset, the role subsystem F1 improves significantly with POS and dependency parse information (+2.72%) while the sense subsystem benefits less (0.96%). The role subsystem dramatically improves when pre-trained words are added (2.59%), due in large part to a better ability to handle unseen words. The mean System F1 scores are higher than the benchmark as soon as dependency parser information is supplied, and the F1 is significantly better for the fully populated system (+2.59%).

7 Related Work

The same Semantic Role Labeling system used to generate the results used as our benchmark was later tested using improved dependency parsing in Björkelund et al. [2010]. Woodsend and Lapata [2014] explore text rewriting and compare results with the benchmark, which they accept as the current state-of-the-art.

Kanerva and Ginter [2014] use the CoNLL 2009 data as a benchmark for investigating the use of Finish and English word vector relationships, and the relationships of word vectors as they relate to semantic roles.

In Socher et al. [2013], the authors present a Recursive Neural Tensor Network (RNTN) which uses word vectors as a primary input and which is used to recursively generate a phrase tree structure for each sentence. The resulting structures are then further used to generate fine-grained sentiment analysis estimates.

Convolutional neural networks which include character level structures have been effectively used for sentiment analysis by dos Santos and Gatti [2014]. The characters are not pre-trained, and syntactic trees are not used as input to the network.

In Luong et al. [2013], words are broken down into morphemes as the input to a recursive neural network to capture morphological compositionality with the goal of improving the vector representations of scarce words.

The characteristics and semantic expressive power of various word embedding collections are investigated by Mikolov et al. [2013] and Chen et al. [2013].

8 Conclusion and Future Work

We have presented a dependency-based semantic role labeler using neural networks, inspired by Collobert et al. [2011] and others to reduce the use of hand-crafted features and make use of unsupervised techniques. Experimental evaluations show that our architecture improves the state of the art performance for this task significantly, for both in domain and out of domain test data. A key element of the system's performance is based on the use of features derived from syntactic dependency parses. The use of a dependency-based path feature, in particular, provides a significant boost in performance over simpler feature sets.

Promising future directions suggested by these results include whether proxies for the dependency-based features can be derived from a similar architecture without the direct need for a full dependency analysis, thus eliminating the pre-processing parser cost. Another future direction involves the predicate disambiguation system. Although this sense disambiguation task is part of the CoNLL 2009 SRL evaluation, it is more properly a word sense disambiguation problem. A more thorough investigation of sense disambiguation in the context of an SRL system is warranted.

References

Yoshua Bengio, Pascal Lamblin, Dan Popovici, and Hugo Larochelle. Greedy layer-wise training of deep networks. *Advances in neural information processing systems*, 19:153, 2007.

Anders Björkelund, Love Hafdell, and Pierre Nugues. Multilingual semantic role labeling. In *Proceedings of the Thirteenth Conference on Computational Natural Language Learning: Shared Task*, pages 43–48. Association for Computational Linguistics, 2009.

Anders Björkelund, Bernd Bohnet, Love Hafdell, and Pierre Nugues. A high-performance syntactic and semantic dependency parser. In *Proceedings of the 23rd International Conference on Computational Linguistics: Demonstrations*, pages 33–36. Association for Computational Linguistics, 2010.

Xavier Carreras and Lluís Màrquez. Introduction to the conll-2004 shared task: Semantic role labeling. In *Proceedings of the Eighth Conference on Computational Natural Language Learning, CoNLL 2004, Held in cooperation with HLT-NAACL 2004, Boston, Massachusetts, USA, May 6-7, 2004*, pages 89–97, 2004.

Xavier Carreras and Lluís Màrquez. Introduction to the conll-2005 shared task: Semantic role labeling. In *Proceedings of the Ninth Conference on Computational Natural Language Learning*, pages 152–164. Association for Computational Linguistics, 2005.

Yanqing Chen, Bryan Perozzi, Rami Al-Rfou, and Steven Skiena. The expressive power of word embeddings. *arXiv preprint arXiv:1301.3226*, 2013.

Ronan Collobert, Jason Weston, Léon Bottou, Michael Karlen, Koray Kavukcuoglu, and Pavel Kuksa. Natural language processing (almost) from scratch. *The Journal of Machine Learning Research*, 12:2493–2537, 2011.

Cıcero Nogueira dos Santos and Maıra Gatti. Deep convolutional neural networks for sentiment analysis of short texts. In *Proceedings of the 25th International Conference on Computational Linguistics (COLING), Dublin, Ireland*, 2014.

John Duchi, Elad Hazan, and Yoram Singer. Adaptive subgradient methods for online learning and stochastic optimization. *The Journal of Machine Learning Research*, 12:2121–2159, 2011.

Daniel Gildea and Daniel Jurafsky. Automatic labeling of semantic roles. *Computational Linguistics*, 28(3):245–288, 2002.

Jan Hajič, Massimiliano Ciaramita, Richard Johansson, Daisuke Kawahara, Maria Antònia Martí, Lluís Màrquez, Adam Meyers, Joakim Nivre, Sebastian Padó, Jan Štěpánek, et al. The conll-2009 shared task: Syntactic and semantic dependencies in multiple languages. In *Proceedings of the Thirteenth Conference on Computational Natural Language Learning: Shared Task*, pages 1–18. Association for Computational Linguistics, 2009.

Geoffrey Hinton, Simon Osindero, and Yee-Whye

Teh. A fast learning algorithm for deep belief nets. *Neural computation*, 18(7):1527–1554, 2006.

Jenna Kanerva and Filip Ginter. Post-hoc manipulations of vector space models with application to semantic role labeling. In *Proceedings of the 2nd Workshop on Continuous Vector Space Models and their Compositionality (CVSC)@ EACL*, pages 1–10, 2014.

Minh-Thang Luong, Richard Socher, and Christopher D Manning. Better word representations with recursive neural networks for morphology. *CoNLL-2013*, 104, 2013.

Tomas Mikolov, Wen-tau Yih, and Geoffrey Zweig. Linguistic regularities in continuous space word representations. In *Proceedings of NAACL-HLT*, pages 746–751, 2013.

Martha Palmer, Paul Kingsbury, and Daniel Gildea. The proposition bank: An annotated corpus of semantic roles. *Computational Linguistics*, 31(1): 71–106, 2005.

Lawrence Rabiner. A tutorial on hidden markov models and selected applications in speech recognition. *Proceedings of the IEEE*, 77(2):257–286, 1989.

William W Cohen Robert E Schapire and Yoram Singer. Learning to order things. In *Advances in Neural Information Processing Systems 10: Proceedings of the 1997 Conference*, volume 10, page 451. MIT Press, 1998.

Richard Socher, Alex Perelygin, Jean Y Wu, Jason Chuang, Christopher D Manning, Andrew Y Ng, and Christopher Potts. Recursive deep models for semantic compositionality over a sentiment treebank. In *Proceedings of the conference on empirical methods in natural language processing (EMNLP)*, volume 1631, page 1642. Citeseer, 2013.

Alex Waibel, Toshiyuki Hanazawa, Geoffrey Hinton, Kiyohiro Shikano, and Kevin J Lang. Phoneme recognition using time-delay neural networks. *Acoustics, Speech and Signal Processing, IEEE Transactions on*, 37(3):328–339, 1989.

Jason Weston, Frédéric Ratle, Hossein Mobahi, and Ronan Collobert. Deep learning via semi-supervised embedding. In *Neural Networks: Tricks of the Trade*, pages 639–655. Springer, 2012.

Kristian Woodsend and Mirella Lapata. Text rewriting improves semantic role labeling. *Journal of Artificial Intelligence Research*, pages 133–164, 2014.

A State-of-the-Art Mention-Pair Model for Coreference Resolution

Olga Uryupina[1] and **Alessandro Moschitti**[2,1]
[1]Department of Information Engineering and Computer Science, University of Trento,
[2]Qatar Computing Research Institute
uryupina@gmail.com, amoschitti@gmail.com

Abstract

Most recent studies on coreference resolution advocate accurate yet relatively complex models, relying on, for example, entity-mention or graph-based representations. As it has been convincingly demonstrated at the recent CoNLL 2012 shared task, such algorithms considerably outperform popular basic approaches, in particular mention-pair models. This study advocates a novel approach that keeps the simplicity of a mention-pair framework, while showing state-of-the-art results. Apart from being very efficient and straightforward to implement, our model facilitates experimental work on the pairwise classifier, in particular on feature engineering. The proposed model achieves the performance level of up to 61.82% (MELA F, v4 scorer) on the CoNLL test data, on par with complex state-of-the-art systems.

1 Introduction

The mention-pair model, as proposed by Soon et al. (2001) has been used for over a decade now. It combines a simple classifier trained to discriminate between coreferent and not-coreferent pairs of mentions ("links") with fast heuristic procedures for merging the classifier's decisions at the decoding stage. Several decoding heuristics have been advocated in the literature, the most commonly used ones including first-link (Soon et al., 2001) and best-link (Ng and Cardie, 2002).

Most state-of-the-art algorithms for coreference resolution, on the contrary, rely on complex modeling, ranging from entity-ranking to structural perceptron and other graph-based approaches (for an overview of state-of-the-art coreference resolvers, see (Ng, 2010; Pradhan et al., 2012)). Such algorithms show a clearly superior performance: thus, at the CoNLL-2012 shared task, the best-performing (Soon et al., 2001)-style system loses around 8% to the winning algorithm.

However, more traditional mention-pair approaches still have some important advantages. Thus, a mention-pair model is easy to implement and allows for fast prototyping. It relies on a simple binary classifier making it very fast to train compared to state-of-the-art models that are based on complex structural representations (Fernandes et al., 2012; Björkelund and Kuhn, 2014). This efficiency at the training step allows for straightforward automatic parameter optimization. Most importantly, mention-pair models can be useful for understanding low-level system behavior, and, in particular, for feature engineering. This can in turn help improve more complex models, since many of them rely on mention-pairs as their basic building blocks.

In this paper, we advocate a new easy-first mention-pair algorithm (EFMP): while it is based solely on pairs of mentions and does not attempt any global inference, it benefits from the decision propagation strategy to create a coreference partition. Augmented with the sieve-style prefiltering, the system achieves a performance level comparable to the state of the art.

The contribution of this paper is two-fold. First, we propose a novel decoding approach that combines predictions of the mention-pair classifier based on its confidence score, taking into account—in contrast to the previous studies, e.g. (Ng and Cardie, 2002; Stoyanov and Eisner, 2012; Björkelund and Kuhn, 2014)—both positive and negative links. We

*Proceedings of the Fourth Joint Conference on Lexical and Computational Semantics (*SEM 2015)*, pages 289–298,
Denver, Colorado, June 4–5, 2015.

thus propose a procedure for propagating positive and negative links to create the final coreference partition: we start from the most confident among all the classifier's decisions and iteratively construct coreference partitions by merging coreference chains (positive links) or blacklisting future merges (negative links). This decoding strategy is slower than the commonly used best-link model, but considerably faster than ILP-based decoding (Finkel and Manning, 2008; Denis and Baldridge, 2009).

Second, we show that our approach, being very fast and easy to implement, can be used for a variety of low-level experiments on coreference resolution, in particular, for studies on feature engineering or selection. Thus, we augment our system with two feature combination techniques, Jaccard Item Mining (Segond and Borgelt, 2011) and Entropy Guided Feature Inductions (Fernandes et al., 2012). While the latter has been used for coreference resolution before, Jaccard Item Mining (JIM), to our knowledge, has never been applied to any NLP task. The JIM algorithm has been developed within the data mining community and aims at finding combinations that tend to occur in a particular set of unlabeled transactions. In this paper, we introduce a post-filtering technique to re-score JIM output w.r.t. the class labels (±coreferent). We show empirically that JIM is more suitable for coreference: it provides smaller and more meaningful feature combinations leading to a better performance level.

The combination of our decoding approach with the JIM feature induction technique allows us to achieve a performance level of 61.82% on the CoNLL-2012 test data, just 1.5% percent below the (much more complex) winning system and above all the other submissions (cf. Table 4).

2 Related work

An improvement over the original mention-pair model (Soon et al., 2001) has been proposed by Ng and Cardie (2002). Their "best-link" algorithm picks the most confident antecedent for each anaphor. Unlike Ng and Cardie (2002), we do not process the input text from left to right incrementally, instead, we assess the confidence of all the proposed links at the same time ("easy-first") and keep track of negative assignments.

Our work has been motivated by more complex algorithms using the easy-first strategy, most importantly, by Stoyanov and Eisner (2012), Nicolae and Nicolae (2006) and Björkelund and Farkas (2012). There are two important differences between these studies and the Easy-First Mention-Pair model (EFMP): (i) EFMP does not evaluate links between entities or clusters, always operating on mention pairs instead; (ii) EFMP integrates both positive and negative assignments in its hierarchy of easy-to-hard decisions.

Being conceptually very simple, our algorithm allows for a straightforward integration of other techniques proposed in the literature, in particular, sieve-style prefiltering (Lee et al., 2011) and feature induction. Several recent studies have attempted exhaustive analysis of features and their impact on the overall performance (Recasens and Hovy, 2009; Uryupina, 2006; Bengtson and Roth, 2008; Durrett and Klein, 2013). We refer the reader to (Ng, 2010) for an overview of different features. Kobdani et al. (2010) create a framework that facilitates the engineering process for complex features. This approach, however, still relies on the human expertise for creating meaningful combinations. Versley et al. (2008) use kernel-based similarity as an implicit feature induction technique.

The only study we are aware of that investigates an explicit feature combination technique has been conducted by Fernandes et al. (2012). Their algorithm for Entropy-based feature induction (EFI), shows substantial improvement on the OntoNotes dataset. In the present work, we propose an alternative to EFI, based on the recent advances in Data Mining. We believe that Fernandes et al. (2012) have opened a very important research direction with their feature induction approach. We want therefore to evaluate EFI in a simpler and more straightforward mention-pair model—and compare it to our approach.

3 Easy-First Mention-Pair Model

In what follows, we describe our Easy-First Mention-Pair (EFMP) approach and then propose a solution for combining our model with manually engineered filters, inspired by Stanford "sieves" (Lee et al., 2011). EFMP is a decoding algorithm.

Algorithm 1 Easy-first decoding (EFMP)

```
Require: L = {< ana_l, ante_l, label_l, confidence_l >}: list
    of classified mention pairs
sort L according to confidence
for all l ∈ L do
    /* don't override prev. decisions */
    if chain(ana_l) == chain(ante_l) then
        continue
    if unlinked(chain(ana_l), chain(ante_l)) then
        continue
    /* update chains and unlink info */
    if label_l==not-coreferent then
        unlink(chain(ana_l), chain(ante_l))
    if label_l==coreferent then
        UpdateUnlinkInfo({chain(ana_l), chain(ante_l))
        MergeChains({chain(ana_l), chain(ante_l))
function UPDATEUNLINKINFO(chain_1, chain_2)
    for all c such as unlinked(c, chain_2) do
        unlink(c, chain_1)
function MERGECHAINS(chain_1, chain_2)
    for all m ∈ chain_2 do
        chain(m) = chain_1
```

At the encoding step, we generate mention-pairs in a straightforward exhaustive way: each candidate anaphor is paired with all the preceding candidate antecedents. Following the state of the art, we filter out mention pairs using the same sieve-style approach at both the encoding and the decoding steps (cf. Section 3.2 below).

3.1 Plain EFMP

Our EFMP approach addresses the clustering step of a coreference resolution process: as its input, it assumes a set of mention pairs for a given document, labeled as positive (two mentions corefer) or negative (two mentions do not corefer) by an external classifier. We also assume the classifier to output the confidence of its decisions.

The key idea behind EFMP is the processing of all the decisions, both positive and negative ones, in a specific order, according to the classifier's confidence. We start by sorting all the mention pairs by the confidence of the assigned label. We instantiate our clustering assigning each mention to its own cluster ("all singletons"), however, we do not prohibit potential links between any of them. Our EFMP module processes all the (sorted) mention pairs one-by-one, at each step performing one of the following operations, whenever possible:

- **link**: merge two clusters (includes propagating unlink information, cf. below)
- **unlink**: mark two given clusters to prohibit potential merge at any future step

These operations, however, are only performed if the system has no information about the possibility of (un)linking the two mentions at the given step.

Let us illustrate the approach with the following example:

(1) [Alice]$_1$ is showing [Zoe]$_2$ [her]$_3$ papers on coreference.

In this snippet, we collect three mentions ("Alice" (M_1), "Zoe" (M_2) and "her" (M_3)), forming three mention pairs.[1] A state-of-the-art pairwise coreference classifier would confidently label $< Alice, Zoe >$ as negative; and less confidently— $< Alice, her >$ and $< Zoe, her >$ as positive. The score for $< Alice, her >$ would be slightly higher: "Alice" is a subject and a first mention in the sentence. The EFMP module starts from three clusters: $C_1 = \{M_1\}$, $C_2 = \{M_2\}$, $C_3 = \{M_3\}$. At the first step, it registers the information, that C_1 and C_2 should never be merged ("unlink"). At the second step, it links M_1 and M_3, merging C_1 and C_3, thus producing a partition with two clusters: $C'_1 = \{M_1, M_3\}$, $C_2 = \{M_2\}$. It also propagates the previously collected unlinking information, registering the fact that C'_1 and C_2 should never be merged. At the next step, it tries to link M_2 and M_3. This, however, doesn't work, since the system has already collected some more reliable evidence that the corresponding clusters shouldn't be merged. As there are no more mention-pairs left, the system stops and outputs the last partition (C'_1, C_2).

3.2 EFMP with Sieves

The plain EFMP approach, as described above, assumes that all the mention pairs are labeled by the pairwise classifier. This has several potential issues. First, it requires sorting all the links: when mention-pairs are generated exhaustively, it amounts to the running time of $O(n^2 \log(n))$, where n is the total number of mentions. Second, the pairwise classifier has to be trained on a very biased dataset, containing

[1] We omit other mentions ("her papers" and "coreference") to simplify the presentation.

too many negative or irrelevant examples; this might decrease the performance and also requires substantial tuning of learning parameters.

To alleviate the problem, we pre-filter mention pairs aggressively, heuristically eliminating links that are either definitely positive (for example, pairs of same named entities), definitely negative (pairs with incompatible gender values) or "uninformative". The latter are pairs that we cannot realistically expect to be analyzed by our system, due to the limits of our feature representation. For example, a pair of two noun phrases sharing no common tokens and appearing far apart from each other might be either positive or negative, with the particular decision depending on a lot of factors, starting from the semantic compatibility of the two mentions ("car" and "relativity" can hardly be coreferent), but also including discourse-related factors and some suitably represented knowledge of other entities ("car" and "Ferrari" in different parts of a document talking about Formula 1 may refer to different entities). We believe that forcing our pairwise classifier to learn a labeling for such "uninformative" examples without providing adequate features might lead to inferior performance.

Our pre-filtering approach was inspired by the Stanford sieves algorithm (Lee et al., 2011), where several high-precision rules are applied in a specific order to filter out candidates. This approach has since then been used in several systems, most successfully by Fernandes et al. (2012) to filter out training data for coreference resolution classifiers. The idea of distinguishing between "informative" and "uninformative" instances has been implicitly adopted by many systems, restricting their search to a specific window. This approach is very common for pronominal anaphora, but it's also used by several general-purpose coreference resolvers (Fernandes et al., 2012; Stoyanov and Eisner, 2012).

All these rule-based decisions can be integrated into EFMP in a straightforward way. Thus, the uninformative pairs are simply excluded from the further processing. They do not produce training material and they are not processed by EFMP at the test time (consequently, mentions from such a pair may end up in the same cluster, as well as in two different ones, depending on other (un)links established by the system). This allows for a substantial reduction of the pairs to be processed at the decoding step (for example, in our setting described in Section 5.1 below, around 90% of all the pairs are eliminated as "uninformative"). The pairs, deemed positive or negative by the rule-based pre-filtering, do not contribute to the training data. At the test step, they are considered to be very confidently positive/negative instances, outscoring any test pairs, originating from the classifier output. Such pairs do not contribute to speeding up the EFMP part, however, they help improve the quality of our pairwise classifier, decreasing the bias towards negative instances in the data.

4 Techniques for generating feature combinations

Most state-of-the-art coreference resolution systems combine complex modeling with rich feature sets. While early data-driven approaches were essentially knowledge-poor (for example, the famous system of Soon et al. (2001) is based on 12 shallow features), modern algorithms rely on dozens of carefully engineered features, encoding various clues relevant for the task: from different measures of surface similarity, to morphological, syntactic, semantic and discourse properties, and world knowledge.

This study focuses on the automatic feature engineering task. We start from atomic features that are already encoded in a state-of-the-art toolkit (BART) and use a data mining technique, Jaccard item mining, to boost the system performance through automatic induction of complex features.

The features used by most coreference resolution systems are very heterogeneous. Some of them (for example, different measures of salience) encode insights from the linguistic theory, whereas others are purely data-driven (tokens). Some features are direct indicators for or against coreference (string matching vs. contra-indexing constraints), whereas others are supposed to provide more general information (individual properties of mentions). Some features are very frequent (mention types), whereas others are relatively rare (apposition). Finally, some features encode basic properties ("anaphor is a pronoun"), whereas others are combinations of such properties ("both anaphor and antecedent are pronouns and they have the same surface form"). Therefore, we specifically aim at designing an algorithm that is able to overcome these idiosyncrasies and provide meaningful combinations for such a heterogeneous set of atomic features.

4.1 Jaccard Item Mining

In this study, we adapt the Jaccard Item Mining (JIM) technique (Segond and Borgelt, 2011) to the coreference resolution task. Below we describe the JIM algorithm and our adjustment of JIM to the task of selecting meaningful features.

The Data Mining community has invested substantial efforts into Frequent Item Mining algorithms: techniques for finding frequent combinations of "items" in a "transaction database". We assume that a database is a set of item sets with some items often appearing together. Several approaches have been proposed to solve the task of enumerating all such frequently occurring combinations in a fast and efficient way, the most popular ones being Eclat and FP-growth. A typical application would be, for example, the task of finding similarities in shopping lists for different customers. We refer the reader to (Borgelt, 2012) for an overview of relevant approaches.

Frequent Item Mining algorithms output all the combinations with a frequency ("support") higher than a predefined threshold. If the original items are very heterogeneous, the output might get very noisy: for example, if there are some very frequent items, they will pollute most combinations and the interesting item sets will be difficult to find. To overcome this problem, Segond and Borgelt (2011) propose to use the Jaccard index as a measure of the item set quality. For a given set of items I, the Jaccard index $J_T(I)$ is defined as a ratio of the set's support over the number of transactions containing at least one item from the set:

$$J_T(I) = \frac{|\cap_{i \in I} K_T(\{i\})|}{|\cup_{i \in I} K_T(\{i\})|},$$

where $K_T(\{i\})$ is a set of transactions, containing the item i.

It is straightforward to see that $J_T(I)$ is an anti-monotone function. Therefore, standard frequent item mining algorithms can be easily adapted to cover the Jaccard index. In our experiments, we use a publicly available JIM implementation.[2]

[2]http://www.borgelt.net/jim.html

We recast the feature induction problem as a frequent item mining task. We start from atomic features (string, nominal and binary) and convert them into binary features that represent our items. Since our feature set is very heterogeneous, some items are very rare or, conversely, very frequent. We filter out all the items with the support below or above predefined thresholds. The frequent item mining approaches assume that all the transactions are equal. In our case, however, transactions correspond to training instances—and they come with the class labels. Since we are interested in the feature combinations that help distinguish between positive and negative examples, we perform two JIM runs, splitting the training data into the positive and negative parts. For each part, we induce all the combinations with the high Jaccard index ($J_T^+(I)$ and $J_T^-(I)$). After this step, we have two lists of items, each corresponding to feature combinations showing a good association strength for positive and negative examples respectively.

Both lists are then reranked, dividing the positive index over the negative one and vice versa:

$$score^+(I) = \frac{J_T^+(I)}{J_T^-(I)}, score^-(I) = \frac{J_T^-(I)}{J_T^+(I)}.$$

This reranking step helps us to filter out feature combinations that are either redundant or not indicative of coreference. For example, our atomic features already contain some combinations (e.g., `NEStringMatch` is a combination of `MentionType_Coarse` and `StringED`). Without the reranking step, we are getting numerous combinations reflecting peculiarities in the feature design. As the final JIM output, we take all the sets I with the scores exceeding some predefined thresholds ($score^+(I) > thr^+$ or $score^-(I) > thr^-$). Note that our $score$ measures are not monotone and cannot therefore be used in a fast Eclat-style algorithm (Borgelt, 2012) to directly provide $score$-optimal combinations.

To better align our approach with the Entropy Guided Feature Induction framework presented below, we convert our item sets back to the sets of atomic features, abstracting away from the particular values used for binarization.

The JIM-based feature induction algorithm relies on several parameters: the feature filtering thresholds (for removing too rare or too common features), the minimal Jaccard index for the JIM algorithm and the thresholds thr^+ and thr^- for selecting good item sets after the reranking step. We fit these parameters on the development set.

4.2 Entropy Guided Feature Induction

Fernandes et al. (2012) have proposed using Entropy Guided Feature Induction (EFI) for coreference resolution and have shown that it significantly improves the performance of their system. Below we provide a brief overview of the EFI approach, referring the reader to the original paper for further details.

The system works at two stages, using two different machine learning techniques. At the *first stage*, the EFI algorithm relies on a decision tree, generated from the training data, to obtain meaningful feature combinations. In particular, the algorithm extracts all the paths leading from the root of the induced tree to any node. Each node in a tree corresponds to a specific value assigned to some atomic feature and therefore each path corresponds to a conjunction of atomic features with assigned values. Fernandes et al. (2012) abstract over the values, thus, converting each path to a conjunction of atomic features. These conjunctions, or combinations, are then used to generate numerous binary features to be used by a linear classifier at the *second stage*.

Since the induced tree might get very large, the EFI algorithm might lead to conjunctions of too many atomic features, generating, in turn, too many binary features. To address the issue, Fernandes et al. (2012) prune their tree at the depth 5. In our implementation, we follow the algorithm of Fernandes et al. (2012) with no adjustments or alterations.

5 Experiments

Our first group of experiments assesses the quality of the baseline setting, with no feature combination techniques. We compare against the CoNLL submission of the BART group to make sure that our (Soon et al., 2001)-style mention-pair baseline shows an acceptable performance. We then evaluate the EFMP approach to confirm that it provides much higher performance figures and is on par with the state of the art. In our second experiment, we use EFMP to assess the impact of the feature combination techniques on the performance of a coreference resolution system.

5.1 Experimental Setup

We evaluate our approach on the English portion of the CoNLL-2012 dataset (Pradhan et al., 2012). To asses the system's performance, we use the official scorer, provided by the CoNLL organizers. However, the version used at the competition time (v4) was later found to contain errors and replaced with another implementation (v7). This procedure resulted in a performance drop for all the systems, but didn't affect their ranking. To facilitate comparison against previous and future studies, we report both v4 and v7 MELA scores. All the experiments are performed on automatically extracted mentions and use no gold information.

For our study, we use the publicly available BART toolkit (Uryupina et al., 2012). We have made several adjustments, starting from the configuration, suggested in the BART distribution for the OntoNotes/CoNLL data. Thus, we have modified the mention detection module, improving the treatment of coordinations and eliminating numeric named entities (PERCENT, MONEY etc). We have replaced the original `split` architecture with a single-classifier approach to be able to estimate the impact of our feature combination techniques in a more principled way. We have also replaced Decision Trees (Weka J48) with the LibLinear SVM package, to get a classifier outputting reliable confidence values, as needed by EFMP. We have considerably expanded the feature set, mainly reimplementing features from the winning system of CoNLL-2012 (Fernandes et al., 2012). Altogether, we have around 170 individual features (string, nominal or binary values), corresponding to around 20k features after the binarization step. The full list of our feature templates can be found at `http://bart-coref.eu/papers/sem15-suppl.pdf`.

Finally, we have augmented BART with a rule-based prefiltering module, motivated by Stanford Sieves (Lee et al., 2011), the winning approach of the CoNLL-2011 shared task. Our sieve-style prefiltering algorithm splits all the training instances into confidently positive, confidently negative, irrelevant and relevant. To implement the prefiltering

	development	test	
	v4	v4	v7
BART CoNLL-2012 submission			
	-	56.12	50.02
simplified reimplemented BART submission			
WEKA (j48)	56.02	55.84	49.83
SVM (Liblinear)	48.31	47.29	39.17
-*-, all features			
WEKA (j48)	56.53	55.98	49.84
SVM (Liblinear)	49.83	48.11	40.04
best-link, all features			
SVM (Liblinear)	59.71	59.03	55.21
EFMP, features from BART submission			
SVM (Liblinear)	57.40	56.16	50.65
EFMP, all features			
SVM (Liblinear)	60.02	59.12	55.38

Table 2: Baseline performance vs. plain EFMP: MELA score, different versions of the CoNLL scorer.

module, we have started with the original sieves and the version used by Fernandes et al. (2012). We have changed some sieves and introduced several additional filters (cf. Table 1).

5.2 Baselines vs. EFMP

Table 2 shows the performance levels for different baseline algorithms, learners and features on both CoNLL-2012 development and test sets. Note that the development set was used for parameter tuning and does not therefore provide an accurate estimation of the system's performance.

The results suggest that our simplified version of the BART CONLL-2012 system can be considered an adequate starting point: it only shows a very minor performance drop, compared to the original submission (we believe that this drop can be attributed to the simpler `no-split` architecture that we are adopting in this study). The (Soon et al., 2001)-style mention-pair model, however, suffers from several problems. First of all, its performance is simply not good enough: thus, the winners of the CoNLL-2012 shared task reported a v4 score of 63.37 on the test data. With a v4 score of 55.84, our system would have achieved the 12th place in the competition (out of 15+1). Second, this approach only works with the decision tree-based classifier: with SVMs, the performance gets much lower. We believe that this can be caused by several factors: (a) decision trees perform some sort of feature combinations, whereas Liblinear only relies on a sum of individual features for its classification and (b) the (Soon et al., 2001)-style model employs different sampling strategies for training and testing data (in fact, testing instance are sampled dynamically, based on the decisions made by the classifier so far), leading to a misfit between the two sets that is more problematic for Liblinear. Third, even with the decision trees, the system performance does not improve substantially when we add a lot of manually engineered high-quality features.

The EFMP model, on the contrary, shows promising performance figures. With an F-score of 59.12, the system would have achieved the 8th place in the CoNLL-2012 competition, within the cluster of very similarly performing systems on places 2–8(9). It must be stressed that EFMP is a very simple and fast algorithm, much less complex than any of the high-performing CoNLL systems.

We have also evaluated EFMP against a mention-pair model with the same sieve-style prefiltering and a best-link decoder (Table 2, row 6). As the results suggest, the best-link decoder shows a better performance level compared to (Soon et al., 2001), since it relies on the most confident positive links. The EFMP decoder, however, brings a further improvement, by incorporating and propagating information on confident negative links as well.

5.3 Feature combinations

In our second experiment, we investigate the applicability of JIM to coreference resolution, comparing it against EFI. The latter has been proven to yield a performance gain of up to 10%, leading to a system, significantly outperforming all the other competitors at the CoNLL-2012 shared task. While the impact of EFI on the system of Fernandes et al. (2012) cannot be underestimated, the following points need further clarifications: (a) the algorithm of Fernandes et al. (2012) shows only very moderate performance without EFI—it is not yet clear if EFI is equally beneficial for more competitive approaches; and (b) the system of Fernandes et al. (2012) relies on a relatively complex model—it is not clear how model-specific the benefits of EFI are.

Confidently negative	
Expletive	M_i or M_j is an expletive pronoun
Span	one mention spans over the other
Agreement	M_i and M_j disagree in number, gender or semantic class
Syntax	M_i and M_j violate contra indexing constraints (c-command etc)
SpeakerAliasProFalse	heuristics for 1/2 person pronouns, based on the `speaker` value
Pronouns	M_i is a pronoun, M_i and M_j disagree in person (respecting the `speaker`)
Confidently positive	
SpeakerAliasPro	heuristics for 1/2 person pronouns, based on the `speaker` value
SpeakerAliasNE	heuristics for 1 person pronouns (M_j) and NE (M_i), based on the `speaker`
SameNE	M_i and M_j are exactly matching NEs
Irrelevant	
ProNonpro	M_j is a pronoun, M_i is not a pronoun
DistantPro	M_j is a pronoun, M_i is more than thr_1 sentences away ($dist(M_j, M_i) > thr_1$)
DistantNP	M_j is a common NP, $dist(M_j, M_i) > thr_2$, head nouns of M_i and M_j differ
DistantNE	M_j is an NE, $dist(M_j, M_i) > thr_2$, M_i and M_j do not match

Table 1: Sieves for pre-filtering of mention pairs: each sieve is applied to a pair of mentions $\{M_i, M_j\}$, $i < j$, where M_i is a candidate antecedent and M_j is a candidate anaphor.

EFI and JIM use very different intuitions for combining atomic features. It is therefore not surprising, that the outputs of these two algorithms are different. Figure 1 summarizes the distribution of EFI vs. JIM-induced combinations of different lengths, normalized by the total number of combinations extracted by each method. EFI outputs around 20 times more sets than JIM (2k vs. 90). Most of them, however, are too long and do not provide good features. By definition, EFI cannot produce a lot of short combinations, since all the EFI paths must start from the root. JIM, on the contrary, tends to produce combinations of smaller lengths that are more likely to yield high-quality features.

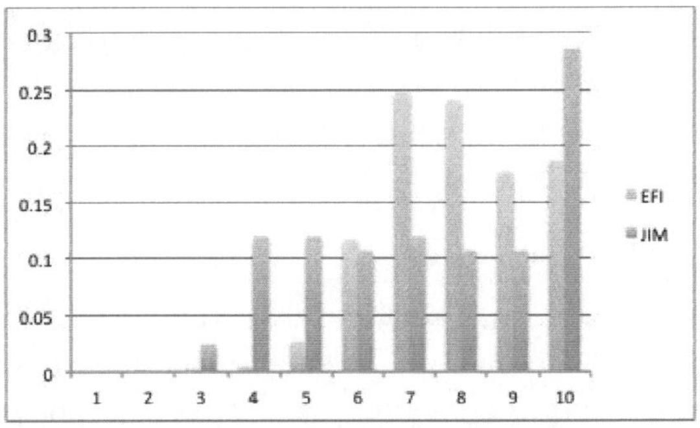

Figure 1: Normalized combination length for JIM and EFI: number of induced sets of size 1..9, 10+ divided by the total number of induced sets

Table 3 shows the performance of EFMP, augmented with EFI or JIM-induced features. We see that both techniques bring an improvement over the plain EFMP (significant, per-document t-test, $p < 0.05$). Even though JIM produces much fewer combinations, it still outperforms EFI ($p < 0.05$).

5.4 EFMP and State of the art

Table 4 compares the performance level of the EFMP approach, plain and enhanced with the JIM-based feature induction module, against the top 5 CoNLL-2012 systems on the CoNLL-2012 test set.

As the results show, the EFMP approach achieves results comparable to the state-of-the-art. At the same time, it's much faster than more complex approaches. The vast majority of high-performance coreference resolution systems (in particular, the CoNLL-2012 winning algorithm by Fernandes et al. (2012)) rely on complex structural representations and are therefore slow at the training stage. Our system only needs a simple binary mention-pair classifier that can be trained very efficiently. Some high-performance approaches rely on the same classifier, postponing a heavy global inference step to the decoding stage, for example, through Integer Linear Programming (Denis and Baldridge, 2009; Finkel

	development	test	
	v4	v4	v7
EFMP, all features, SVM			
none	60.02	59.12	55.38
EFI	61.66	60.75	57.56
JIM	62.53	61.82	59.14

Table 3: Feature combinations, JIM vs. EFI: MELA score, different versions of the CoNLL scorer.

	test	
	v4	v7
1 fernandes	63.37	60.65
EFMP+JIM	61.82	59.14
2 martschat	61.31	57.68
3 bjorkelund	61.24	57.42
EFMP	59.12	55.38
4 chang	60.18	56.10
5 chen	59.69	54.52

Table 4: EFMP and top-5 CoNLL-2012 systems: MELA score, systems ranked by the v7 score on the test set.

and Manning, 2008). While these systems have the same training requirements as EFMP, their decoding (ILP with binary variables) is known to be NP-complete. In practice, ILP-based approaches incorporating any forms of global modeling via transitivity constraints (Denis and Baldridge, 2009; Finkel and Manning, 2008) are known to be particularly slow. Our simple decoding algorithm runs in $O(p * log(p))$, where p is the total number of mention pairs: for the plain EFMP, $p = n * (n - 1)/2$, for the EFMP with sieves, $p = const * n$, where n is the number of mentions in the document.

6 Conclusion

In this study, we advocate an easy-first mention-pair model (EFMP). This approach combines the simplicity of mention-pair models with the high performance level of state-of-the-art systems. We believe that several research lines are open in the field of coreference resolution, ours being simple and allowing to focus more on low-level linguistic phenomena. Nevertheless, the approach shows a high performance level, despite the lack of any global inference (augmented with a feature induction module, our system would have achieved the second place at the CoNLL-2012 shared task, outperforming more complex algorithms). This suggests that there is still a lot of potential improvement that can be achieved within more complex frameworks, e.g., structural approaches that attempt at modeling links interdependence explicitly. One of our directions for future work involves comparing EFMP against other algorithms effectively combining positive and negative links, in particular, ILP-based approaches.

The proposed EFMP model allows for a straightforward investigation of possibilities for automatic feature induction. We have adapted the Jaccard Item Mining algorithm (JIM) to our task and compared its output against the Entropy-based Feature Induction (EFI) methodology proposed in the literature, showing that both techniques yield meaningful feature combinations and improve the system's performance. Yet, the JIM approach outputs smaller combinations, leading to a larger performance increase.

In our future work, we plan to focus further on the feature induction task, following several research directions. First, we want to apply automatic feature induction in a multilingual setting. Second, we plan to investigate other feature induction techniques: (i) comparing various similarity measures alternative to the Jaccard index in a JIM-style setting, (ii) trying to run EFI on different samples of the training set to obtain different decision trees and (iii) combining JIM and EFI-induced features. Finally, we want to verify our hypothesis that complex features represent meaningful linguistic combinations and as such can be used to enhance the performance level of more complex algorithms. This again would bridge the work on mention-pair and more advanced models.

Acknowledgments

This research is part of the Interactive sYstems for Answer Search (Iyas) project, conducted by the Arabic Language Technologies (ALT) group at the Qatar Computing Research Institute (QCRI) within the Qatar Foundation.

References

Eric Bengtson and Dan Roth. 2008. Understanding the value of features for coreference resolution. In *Proceedings of the Conference on Empirical Methods in Natural Language Processing*, EMNLP '08, pages 294–303, Stroudsburg, PA, USA. Association for Computational Linguistics.

Anders Björkelund and Richárd Farkas. 2012. Data-driven multilingual coreference resolution using resolver stacking. In *Joint Conference on EMNLP and CoNLL - Shared Task*, pages 49–55, Jeju Island, Korea, July. Association for Computational Linguistics.

Anders Björkelund and Jonas Kuhn. 2014. Learning structured perceptrons for coreference resolution with latent antecedents and non-local features. In *Proceedings of the 52nd Annual Meeting of the Association for Computational Linguistics (Volume 1: Long Papers)*, pages 47–57, Baltimore, Maryland, June. Association for Computational Linguistics.

Christian Borgelt. 2012. Frequent item set mining. *Wiley Interdisciplinary Reviews: Data Mining and Knowledge Discovery*, 2(6):437–456.

Pascal Denis and Jason Baldridge. 2009. Global joint models for coreference resolution and named entity classification. In *Procesamiento del Lenguaje Natural 42, Barcelona: SEPLN.*

Greg Durrett and Dan Klein. 2013. Easy victories and uphill battles in coreference resolution. In *Proceedings of the 2013 Conference on Empirical Methods in Natural Language Processing*, pages 1971–1982.

Eraldo Rezende Fernandes, Cícero Nogueira dos Santos, and Ruy Luiz Milidiú. 2012. Latent structure perceptron with feature induction for unrestricted coreference resolution. In *Joint Conference on EMNLP and CoNLL - Shared Task*, CoNLL '12, pages 41–48, Stroudsburg, PA, USA. Association for Computational Linguistics.

Jenny Rose Finkel and Christopher D. Manning. 2008. Enforcing transitivity in coreference resolution. In *Proceedings of the Annual Meeting of the Association for Computational Linguistics*, pages 45–48.

Hamidreza Kobdani, Hinrich Schütze, Andre Burkovski, Wiltrud Kessler, and Gunther Heidemann. 2010. Relational feature engineering of natural language processing. In *Proceedings of the 19th ACM Conference on Information and Knowledge Management (CIKM)*, pages 1705–1708.

Heeyoung Lee, Yves Peirsman, Angel Chang, Nathanael Chambers, Mihai Surdeanu, and Dan Jurafsky. 2011. Stanford's multi-pass sieve coreference resolution system at the CoNLL-2011 shared task. In *Proceedings of the Fifteenth Conference on Computational Natural Language Learning: Shared Task*, CONLL Shared Task '11, pages 28–34, Stroudsburg, PA, USA. Association for Computational Linguistics.

Vincent Ng and Claire Cardie. 2002. Improving machine learning approaches to coreference resolution. In *Proceedings of the 40th Annual Meeting of the Association for Computational Linguistics*, pages 104–111.

Vincent Ng. 2010. Supervised noun phrase coreference research: The first fifteen years. In *Proceedings of the 48th Annual Meeting of the Association for Computational Linguistics*, pages 1396–1411.

Cristina Nicolae and Gabriel Nicolae. 2006. Bestcut: A graph algorithm for coreference resolution. In *Proceedings of the 2006 Conference on Empirical Methods in Natural Language Processing*, EMNLP '06, pages 275–283, Stroudsburg, PA, USA. Association for Computational Linguistics.

Sameer Pradhan, Alessandro Moschitti, Nianwen Xue, Olga Uryupina, and Yuchen Zhang. 2012. CoNLL-2012 shared task: Modeling multilingual unrestricted coreference in OntoNotes. In *Proceedings of the Sixteenth Conference on Computational Natural Language Learning (CoNLL'12)*, Jeju, Korea.

Marta Recasens and Eduard Hovy. 2009. A deeper look into features for coreference resolution. In *Anaphora Processing and Applications (DAARC 2009)*.

Marc Segond and Christian Borgelt. 2011. Item set mining based on cover similarity. In *Proceedings of the 15th Pacific-Asia Conference on Knowledge Discovery and Data Mining (PAKDD 2011)*.

Wee Meng Soon, Hwee Tou Ng, and Daniel Chung Yong Lim. 2001. A machine learning approach to coreference resolution of noun phrases. *Computational Linguistic*, 27(4):521–544.

Veselin Stoyanov and Jason Eisner. 2012. Easy-first coreference resolution. In *Proceedings of the 24th International Conference on Computational Linguistics (COLING)*, pages 2519–2534.

Olga Uryupina, Alessandro Moschitti, and Massimo Poesio. 2012. BART goes multilingual: The UniTN / Essex submission to the CoNLL-2012 Shared Task. In *Proceedings of the Sixteenth Conference on Computational Natural Language Learning (CoNLL'12)*.

Olga Uryupina. 2006. Coreference resolution with and without linguistic knowledge. In *Proceedings of the Language Resources and Evaluation Conference (LREC'06)*.

Yannick Versley, Alessandro Moschitti, Massimo Poesio, and Xiaofeng Yang. 2008. Coreference systems based on kernels methods. In *Proceedings of the 22nd International Conference on Computational Linguistics (COLING)*, pages 961–968.

Resolving Discourse-Deictic Pronouns: A Two-Stage Approach to Do *It*

Sujay Kumar Jauhar
Carnegie Mellon University
Pittsburgh, PA 15213, USA
sjauhar@cs.cmu.edu

Raul D. Guerra
University of Maryland
College Park, MD 20742, USA
rguerra@cs.umd.edu

Edgar Gonzàlez
Google Research
Mountain View, CA 94043, USA
edgargip@google.com

Marta Recasens
Google Research
Mountain View, CA 94043, USA
recasens@google.com

Abstract

Discourse deixis is a linguistic phenomenon in which pronouns have verbal or clausal, rather than nominal, antecedents. Studies have estimated that between 5% and 10% of pronouns in non-conversational data are discourse deictic. However, current coreference resolution systems ignore this phenomenon. This paper presents an automatic system for the detection and resolution of discourse-deictic pronouns. We introduce a two-step approach that first recognizes instances of discourse-deictic pronouns, and then resolves them to their verbal antecedent. Both components rely on linguistically motivated features. We evaluate the components in isolation and in combination with two state-of-the-art coreference resolvers. Results show that our system outperforms several baselines, including the only comparable discourse deixis system, and leads to small but statistically significant improvements over the full coreference resolution systems. An error analysis lays bare the need for a less strict evaluation of this task.

1 Introduction

Coreference resolution is a central problem in Natural Language Processing with a broad range of applications such as summarization (Steinberger et al., 2007), textual entailment (Mirkin et al., 2010), information extraction (McCarthy and Lehnert, 1995), and dialogue systems (Strube and Müller, 2003). Traditionally, the resolution of noun phrases (NPs) has been the focus of coreference research (Ng, 2010). However, NPs are not the only participants in coreference, since verbal or clausal mentions can also take part in coreference relations. For example, consider:

(1) The United States says **it** may invite Israeli and Palestinian negotiators to Washington.

(2) Without planning **it** in advance, they chose to settle here.

In (1), the antecedent of the pronoun is an NP, while in (2) the antecedent[1] is a clause[2] (Webber, 1988). Current state-of-the-art coreference resolution systems (Lee et al., 2011; Fernandes et al., 2012; Durrett and Klein, 2014; Björkelund and Kuhn, 2014) focus on the former and ignore the latter cases.

Corpus studies across several languages (Eckert and Strube, 2000; Botley, 2006; Recasens, 2008) have estimated that between 5% and 10% of pronouns in non-conversational data, and up to 20% in conversational, have verbal antecedents. A coreference system that is able to handle discourse deixis will thus be more accurate, and benefit downstream applications.

In this paper we present an automatic system that processes discourse-deictic pronouns. We resolve the three pronouns *it*, *this* and *that*, which can appear in linguistic contexts that reflect the phenomenon illustrated in (2). Our system has a modular architecture consisting of two independent stages: classification and resolution. The first stage classifies a pronoun as discourse deictic (or not), and the second stage resolves discourse-deictic pronouns to verbal antecedents. Both stages use linguistically moti-

[1] Since the pronoun in (2) is cataphoric, it has a *postcedent* rather than an *antecedent*, but we use the two indistinctively.

[2] Following the OntoNotes convention, we represent clausal antecedents by their verbal head.

*Proceedings of the Fourth Joint Conference on Lexical and Computational Semantics (*SEM 2015)*, pages 299–308,
Denver, Colorado, June 4–5, 2015.

vated features.

We first evaluate our system by measuring the performance of the detection and resolution components in isolation. They outperform several baselines, including Müller's (2007) approach, which is the only other comparable discourse deixis system, to the best of our knowledge. We also measure the impact of our system on two state-of-the-art coreference resolution systems (Durrett and Klein, 2014; Björkelund and Kuhn, 2014). The results show the benefits of stacking a discourse deixis engine on top of NP coreference resolution.

Algorithm 1
Discourse deixis resolution of pronoun p

```
p_c(p) ← Θ_c(p)                          ▷ Classify
if p_c(p) > th_c then
    for v ← Candidates(p) do
        p_r(v, p) = Θ_r(v, p)            ▷ Resolve
    end for
    v_best ← arg max_v p_r(v, p)
    if p_r(v_best, p) > th_r then
        return v_best
    end if
end if
return ∅                    ▷ No verbal antecedent
```

2 Related Work

Coreference resolution systems mostly focus on NPs. Although some isolated efforts have been made to study discourse-deictic pronouns, they consist mostly of theoretical inquiries or corpus analyses. A few practical implementations have been proposed as well, but most rely on manual intervention or only apply to restricted domains.

Webber (1988) presents a seminal account of discourse-deictic pronouns. She catalogs how the usage of certain pronouns varies based on discourse context. She also provides an insight into the distinguishing characteristics of discourse deixis.

Several empirical studies have also been conducted to evaluate the prevalence of discourse deixis in corpora across languages. These have been applied to English for dialogues (Byron and Allen, 1998; Eckert and Strube, 2000) and news and literature (Botley, 2006), Danish and Italian (Navarretta and Olsen, 2008; Poesio and Artstein, 2008; Caselli and Prodanof, 2010), and Spanish (Recasens, 2008). These studies find that discourse deixis occurs in different languages, although prevalence depends on the domain in question. While discourse deixis can account for up to 20% of pronouns in dialogue and conversational text, a more general figure is between 5% to 10% for other genres.

In addition to a corpus analysis, Eckert and Strube (2000) provide a schema for performing discourse deixis resolution that they evaluate by measuring inter-annotator agreement on five dialogues from the Switchboard corpus. Byron (2002) presents an early attempt at a practical system that handles discourse deixis. However, it relies on sophisticated discourse and semantic features, thus only working with manual intervention in a limited domain.

The first fully automatic system to handle discourse-deictic pronouns was the one by Müller (2007). In contrast to our two-stage approach, it directly resolves pronouns to nominal or verbal antecedents. The author targets coreference resolution in dialogues, but includes several features that are equally applicable to text data—thus making a comparison to our system viable.

Chen et al. (2011) present another unified approach to dealing with entity and event coreference. Their system combines the predictions from seven distinct mention-pair resolvers, each of which focuses on a specific pair of mention types (NP, pronoun, verb). In particular, their verb-pronoun resolver falls within the scope of discourse deixis. Due to the tight coupling of multiple resolvers, a direct comparison with systems focusing on discourse deixis is hard. However, their features are among the ones considered in this work.

3 Our Approach

In this section we describe the architecture of our two-stage system, and then detail the features used in both stages.

3.1 System Architecture

We propose a two-stage approach for discourse deixis processing. Our system first classifies a potential pronoun as discourse deictic (or not), and then it optionally resolves discourse-deictic pronouns with their antecedent.

Feature	Description	Cla.	Res.	Mül.
Pronoun word	Word of p	•	-	
Demonstrative	p is *this* or *that*	•	-	•
Token position	Relative position of p in sentence	•		
Document position	Relative position of sentence containing p	-		
Verb presence	Sentences before p have verb	•		
Parent lemma	Lemma of parent of p if verb	•		
Parent & label	Lemma of parent and dependency label of p	•	•	
Tree depth	Depth of p in parse tree	-		
Pronoun path	Dependency label path of p to root	•	-	
⋆Negated parent	Parent of p is a negated verb	-		
⋆Parent transitivity	Transitivity of parent verb of p	•		
⋆Clause-governing parent	Probability of parent verb to govern a clause	•		
⋆Attribute lemma	Lemma of attribute of p	-		
⋆Attribute POS	POS of attribute of p	-		
Sentence distance	Number of sentences between v and p		•	•
Token distance	Log-distance between v and p in tokens		•	•
Verb distance	Number of verbs between v and p		-	
Relative position	v precedes p (anaphora/cataphora)		•	
Direct dominance	v is the immediate parent of p		•	
Dominance	v is an ancestor of p		•	•
Candidate path	Dependency label path of v to root		•	
⋆Negated candidate	v is negated		•	
⋆Candidate transitivity	Transitivity of v		•	•
⋆Clause-governing candidate	Probability of v to govern a clause		-	
⋆Right frontier	v is in the right frontier of p		•	•
⋆I-incompatibility	Attribute of p is a non-individual adjective		•	•
⋆Verb association strength	NPMI between v and parent verb of p		-	
⋆Selectional preference	Preference between v and parent verb of p		-	

Table 1: Features used for pronoun p and candidate v in the classification (Cla.) and resolution (Res.) stages. Features marked with • were selected, and those marked with - were discarded by feature selection. The last column (Mül.) contains the features used by Müller (2007). Features marked with $\star$ are described in Section 3.2.

More specifically, and as described in Algorithm 1, a classification model Θ_c is applied to each pronoun p to obtain its probability of being discourse deictic $p_c(p)$. If the probability is above a threshold th_c, the pronoun is considered for resolution. All verbs v in the current and n previous sentences[3] are considered as candidates. A resolution model Θ_r is applied to each candidate v to obtain its probability of being the antecedent of p, $p_r(v,p)$; if the candidate with the highest score v_{best} is above a threshold th_r, then it is returned as the antecedent. Otherwise, the pronoun remains unlinked.

Both components are implemented as maximum entropy classifiers. For simplicity, our approach is independent from the NP–NP coreference resolution component: competition between verbal and nominal antecedents is not considered.

3.2 Features

Table 1 gives an overview of the features that were used by the classification and resolution models. We consider all the features listed in the table, but some of them (marked with -) are pruned by feature selection (see Section 4.2). Real-valued features are

[3] A window of 3 sentences is used in our experiments.

quantized, and dependency label paths are considered up to length 2. Details for the more sophisticated features (marked with * in the table) follow.

Negated parent/candidate We consider a verb token to be *negated* if it has a child connected with a negation label.

Parent/candidate transitivity We consider a verb token to be *transitive* if it has a child with a direct object label.

Clause-governing parent/candidate This is the probability of the parent/candidate to have a clausal or verbal argument. Probabilities for every verbal lemma are estimated from the Google News corpus. We then use the logarithm of these probabilities as the feature values.

Attribute lemma/POS If the pronoun is the subject of a copular verb, we consider the lemma and POS of the attribute of this verb as features.

Right frontier Webber (1988) proposes the *right frontier* condition to restrict the set of candidates available as antecedents for discourse-deictic pronouns. We define this condition in terms of what Webber calls *discourse units*. These are minimal discourse segments, and a sequence of several units can also be nested and form a larger unit. She states that only units on the right frontier (i.e., not followed by another unit at the same nesting level) can be antecedents for such pronouns.

(3) [President Obama *arrived* in San Francisco on Sunday.] [[When he *held* a press conference,] he reported [he would meet with business leaders.]] [He thought **it** went well.]

In (3), where discourse units are marked by square brackets, the verbal heads of discourse segments that are on the right frontier are underlined, while the others are italicized to denote inaccessibility.

In our system, we approximate discourse units by sentences and clauses. The candidate antecedents are the respective verbal heads of these units. This feature triggers if the antecedent candidate occurs on the right frontier of the pronoun. Since we also consider cataphoric relations, we reverse the rule to check the left frontier for these cases.

I-incompatibility Eckert and Strube (2000) define an anaphor to be *I-incompatible* if it occurs in a context in which it "cannot refer to an individual object." Adjectives can be used as contextual cues for I-incompatible anaphors in copular constructions (4).

(4) **It** is true.

Similarly to Müller (2007), we define the *I-incompatibility score* of an adjective as its conditional probability of being the attribute of a non-nominal subject given that it occurs in a copular construction. This is estimated from the Google News corpus as the number of occurrences of the adjective in one of these patterns:

- `clausal subject + BE + ADJ` (*To read is healthy*)
- `IT + BE + ADJ + TO/THAT` (*It is healthy to read*)
- `nominalized`[4] `subject + BE + ADJ` (*The construction was suspended*)
- `-ing subject + BE + ADJ` (*Reading is healthy*)

divided by its number of occurrences in the pattern `BE + ADJ`. At classification time, if the pronoun is in a copular construction with an adjective attribute, the I-incompatibility score of the latter is used as feature.

Verb association strength To capture the strength of association between the candidate antecedent and the parent verb of the pronoun, we use the normalized pointwise mutual information of the two verbs co-occurring within a window of 3 sentences, estimated from counts in the Google News corpus.

Selectional preference We use selectional preference, as defined by Resnik (1997), to capture the degree to which the antecedent makes a reasonable substitute of the pronoun in the context of its parent verb. The selectional preference strength of verb ω is defined as $S_R(\omega) = KL(p(a|\omega) \parallel p(a))$, where KL denotes Kullback-Leibler divergence and a are all possible arguments of ω in the Google News corpus. Larger values of

[4]Nominalizations were identified using NOMLEX (Macleod et al., 1998).

Pronoun	Total	Discourse-Deictic
it	1310	75
that	400	120
this	365	57
Overall	2075	252

Table 2: Distribution of discourse-deictic pronouns in the test set of the CoNLL-2012 English corpus.

this quantity correspond to more selective predicates. Then, the selectional preference strength of a verb ω for a particular argument a is defined as $A_R(\omega, a) = p(a|\omega) \cdot \log(p(a|\omega)/p(a))/S_R(\omega)$. To account for nominalizations, verbs and nouns are stemmed following Porter (1980).

4 Evaluation

In this section we describe the setup for evaluating our system.

4.1 Dataset

We perform all our experiments on the English section of the CoNLL-2012 corpus (Pradhan et al., 2012), which is based on OntoNotes (Pradhan et al., 2007). It consists of 2384 documents (1.6M words) from a variety of domains: news, broadcast conversation, weblogs, etc. It is annotated with POS tags, syntax trees, word sense annotation, coreference relations, etc. The coreference layer includes verbal mentions.

Given these annotations, we consider a pronoun to be discourse deictic if the preceding mention in its coreference cluster is verbal, or if it is the first mention in the cluster and the next one is verbal. The distribution of potentially discourse-deictic pronouns (*it*, *this* and *that*) in the test set is summarized in Table 2.

For all our experiments we train, tune and test according to the CoNLL-2012 split of OntoNotes. The gold analyses provided for the shared task are used for training, and the system analyses for development and testing.

4.2 Experiments

We train the two components of our system separately. For each of them, a maximum entropy model is learned on the train partition. Feature selection and threshold tuning are performed by hill climbing on the development set. We use separate thresholds for *it*, *this*, and *that*, since their distributions in the corpus are quite different.

We perform two evaluations of our system: first classification and resolution are evaluated in isolation, and then both components are stacked on top of an NP coreference engine.

For classification, we measure system performance on standard precision (P), recall (R) and F1 of correctly predicting whether a pronoun is discourse deictic or not. For resolution, precision is computed as the fraction of predicted antecedents that are correct, and recall as the fraction of gold antecedents that are correctly predicted. To decouple the evaluation of both stages, we also include results with oracle classifications as input to the resolution stage.

Finally, we use the output of our system to extend the predictions of two state-of-the-art NP coreference systems:

- BERKELEY (Durrett and Klein, 2014), a joint model for coreference resolution, named entity recognition, and entity linking.
- HOTCOREF (Björkelund and Kuhn, 2014), a latent-antecedent model which exploits non-local features via beam search.

We only add our predictions for pronouns *it, this, that* that are output as singletons by the NP coreference system.

We report the standard coreference measures on the combined outputs using the updated CoNLL scorer v7 (Pradhan et al., 2014). Here, the systems are evaluated on all nominal, pronominal, and verbal mentions. The metrics include precision, recall and F1 for MUC, B^3 and $CEAF_e$, and the CoNLL metric, which is the arithmetic mean of the first three F1 scores.

4.3 Baselines

We compare our classification component against two baselines:

- ALL, which blindly classifies all mentions as discourse deictic.
- $NAIVE_c$, which classifies all *this* and *that* mentions as discourse deictic, and all *it* mentions as non-discourse-deictic. This is motivated by

	it			*that*			*this*			Overall		
	P	R	F1	P	R	F1	P	R	F1	P	R	F1
ALL	5.7	**100.0**	**10.8**	30.0	**100.0**	46.2	15.6	**100.0**	27.0	12.1	**100.0**	21.7
NAIVE$_c$	0.0	0.0	0.0	30.0	**100.0**	46.2	15.6	**100.0**	27.0	23.1	70.2	34.8
TWOSTAGE	**33.3**	4.0	7.1	**33.6**	77.5	**46.9**	**57.1**	21.1	**30.8**	**35.2**	42.9	**38.6**

Table 3: Classification evaluation (TWOSTAGE corresponds to our system).

	it			*that*			*this*			Overall		
	P	R	F1	P	R	F1	P	R	F1	P	R	F1
NAIVE$_r$	30.7	30.7	30.7	47.5	**47.5**	47.5	33.3	33.3	33.3	39.3	39.3	39.3
MÜLLER$_r$	30.7	30.7	30.7	47.8	45.0	46.4	43.9	43.9	43.9	41.6	40.5	41.0
TWOSTAGE	**46.3**	**33.3**	**38.8**	**59.6**	46.7	**52.3**	**59.1**	**45.6**	**51.5**	**55.7**	**42.5**	**48.2**

Table 4: Resolution evaluation with oracle classification (TWOSTAGE corresponds to our system).

	it			*that*			*this*			Overall		
	P	R	F1	P	R	F1	P	R	F1	P	R	F1
NAIVE$_r$	0.0	0.0	0.0	15.3	34.2	21.1	20.0	7.0	10.4	15.3	17.9	16.5
MÜLLER$_r$	0.0	0.0	0.0	16.7	36.7	22.9	20.0	7.0	10.4	16.5	19.0	17.7
TWOSTAGE	**14.3**	**1.3**	**2.4**	**21.5**	**40.0**	**28.0**	**46.2**	**10.5**	**17.1**	**22.6**	**21.8**	**22.2**

Table 5: Resolution evaluation with system classification (TWOSTAGE corresponds to our system).

the distribution of discourse deixis in the corpus (see Table 2).

For resolution, we use the baselines:

- NAIVE$_r$, which resolves a pronoun to the closest verb in the previous sentence. This is motivated by corpus analyses studying the position of discourse-deictic pronouns relative to their antecedents (Navarretta, 2011).
- MÜLLER$_r$, which is an equivalent maximum entropy model using the subset of our features also considered by Müller (2007). See column *Mül.* in Table 1.

Finally, when measuring the impact of our system on top of an NP coreference resolution engine, we consider the following baselines:

- NAIVE, which uses NAIVE$_c$ and NAIVE$_r$.
- MÜLLER, which does not include a classification stage, and uses MÜLLER$_r$ for resolution.
- ONESTAGE, which does not include a classification stage, and uses our complete feature set for resolution.[5]
- ORACLE, which outputs the gold annotations for discourse-deictic relations.

5 Results

The results for the classification stage are presented in Table 3, broken down by pronoun type. ALL performs the poorest overall, penalized by a precision just above 12%. Since in the case of *it* only 5.7% of the occurrences are discourse deictic, NAIVE$_c$ gets better results overall by always classifying *it* as non-deictic. Our TWOSTAGE system improves over NAIVE$_c$ by an additional 4% F1. However, the scores remain low—partly because of the difficulty of the problem (especially the class imbalance), and partly because despite using a rich set of features, most of them focus on local context and ignore cues at the discourse level. The classification of *it* is particularly difficult, reflecting the fact that the pronoun has a wide variety of usages in English.

[5]Feature selection and threshold tuning were done separately for this model. The exact subset of resolution features that were chosen is omitted for brevity.

The scores for resolution are shown in Tables 4 and 5. The former uses oracle classification whereas the latter uses the system output of our classifier.

With oracle classification, NAIVE$_r$ and MÜLLER$_r$ perform very similar, except for the case of *this*. Our TWOSTAGE resolver outperforms both of them for all pronouns and metrics, except for the recall of *that*. Overall, the difference in F1 is 9 points over NAIVE$_r$ and 7 points over MÜLLER$_r$. The evaluation actually penalizes recall for our system, since we do not take advantage of the fact that all considered pronouns are discourse deictic: we trust the threshold and do not force the assignment of an antecedent.

All the results are lower with system classification. Given that our classifier performs the best for *that*, the drop for this pronoun is not as high as for the other two. Again, *it* stands out as the hardest pronoun to resolve. Neither NAIVE$_r$ nor MÜLLER$_r$ recover any correct antecedent for *it*. TWOSTAGE obtains the highest scores across all pronouns and metrics.

Finally, Table 6 contains the coreference measures for end-to-end evaluation on top of the BERKELEY and HOTCOREF systems. The ORACLE row shows an upper bound of 2% in CoNLL score improvement. All three baselines—NAIVE, MÜLLER and ONESTAGE—actually cause a decrease of up to 0.9% CoNLL.

Our system TWOSTAGE achieves a small fraction of the headroom. The total number of discourse-deictic entities that it predicts on the test set is 248, of which 204 end up merged in the BERKELEY output, and 210 in HOTCOREF. This allows it to obtain the best B^3, $CEAF_e$ and CoNLL values, despite the fact that the low recall in the classification of discourse-deictic *it* reduces our margin for recall gains by one third. The drop in MUC highlights the difficulty of keeping the precision level, but our system is able to reach a better precision-recall balance than the other compared approaches.

We assess the statistical significance of the improvements of TWOSTAGE over BERKELEY and HOTCOREF using paired bootstrap resampling (Koehn, 2004) followed by two-tailed Wilcoxon signed-rank tests. All the differences are significant at the 1% level, except for the B^3 F1 differences.

Error type	**%**
System errors	
Classification	22.9
Resolution	20.0
Preprocessing	5.7
Annotation errors	
Missing	11.4
Multiple antecedents	20.0
System & Annotation errors	
Debatable	20.0
Overall	100.0

Table 7: Distribution of errors.

6 Error Analysis

In order to gain insight into the precision errors of our system, we manually analyzed 50 of its decisions on the CoNLL-2012 development set. Of these, 30% were correct, matching the gold annotation, as in (5).[6]

(5) Ah, we have *established* the year 2006 as Discover Hong Kong Year. Why is **that**?

The distribution of errors for the remaining cases is shown in Table 7. While half of the errors are due to actual errors in the model learned by our system—either in classification (6) or resolution (7)—or due to a pre-processing error, another third of them are not true errors but missing (8) or partial annotations (9)–(10) in the gold standard corpus.

(6) If pictures are taken without permission, **that** is to say, it will at all times be pursued by legal action, a big hassle.

(7) Do we even *know* if these two medications are going to be effective against a strain that hasn't even presented itself? Here's the important thing about **that**.

(8) You will be taken to stand before governors and kings. People will do **this** to you because you follow me.

[6]The pronoun to be resolved is in boldface, the antecedent annotated in the gold standard (if any) is in italics, and the antecedent predicted by our system is underlined.

		MUC			B^3			$CEAF_e$			CoNLL
		P	R	F1	P	R	F1	P	R	F1	F1
	Durrett and Klein (2014)	**72.61**	69.91	**71.23**	**61.18**	56.43	**58.71**	**56.16**	54.23	55.18	61.71
	+ NAIVE	70.10	**70.33**	70.21	58.64	**57.49**	58.06	52.02	**57.21**	54.50	60.92
	+ MÜLLER	71.57	70.18	70.86	60.15	57.02	58.54	54.55	55.86	55.20	61.53
BERKELEY	+ ONESTAGE	71.63	70.19	70.90	60.21	57.03	58.58	54.66	55.88	55.26	61.58
	+ TWOSTAGE	71.87	70.19	71.02	60.50	57.02	**58.71**	55.14	55.77	**55.45**	**61.73**
	+ ORACLE	*73.09*	*71.64*	*72.36*	*61.95*	*58.77*	*60.32*	*58.05*	*58.51*	*58.28*	*63.65*
	Björkelund and Kuhn (2014)	**74.30**	67.46	**70.72**	**62.71**	54.96	58.58	**59.40**	52.27	55.61	61.64
	+ NAIVE	71.38	**67.92**	69.61	59.72	**56.09**	57.85	54.14	**55.45**	54.79	60.75
	+ MÜLLER	73.11	67.74	70.32	61.51	55.58	58.39	57.32	54.00	55.61	61.44
HOTCOREF	+ ONESTAGE	73.15	67.79	70.37	61.54	55.61	58.43	57.35	54.02	55.64	61.48
	+ TWOSTAGE	73.49	67.77	70.51	61.94	55.58	**58.59**	58.14	53.93	**55.96**	**61.69**
	+ ORACLE	*74.79*	*69.20*	*71.88*	*63.59*	*57.33*	*60.30*	*61.33*	*56.87*	*59.02*	*63.73*

Table 6: End-to-end coreference resolution evaluation (TWOSTAGE corresponds to our system). All differences between the baseline system and TWOSTAGE are significant at the 1% level except for the B^3 F1 differences.

(9) At this point they've *wittled* it down to one aircraft and a missing crew of four individuals. So we've gone from several possible aircraft to one aircraft and from several missing airmen to four. So how much easier will **that** make it for you to unlock this case, do you think?

(10) What do you mean by *that*? Either she either passed out regurgitated. Something had happened. And on top of **that** now there's a statement...

The examples (8)–(10) show the difficulty of annotating discourse deixis relations under guidelines that require a unique verbal antecedent (Poesio and Artstein, 2008; Recasens, 2008). In our analysis we found several cases in which more than one antecedent is acceptable. This is usually the case when there is an elaboration (i.e., both the first clause and the follow-up clause restating or elaborating on the first one are acceptable antecedents, as in (9)) or a sequence of related and overlapping events. As pointed out by Poesio and Artstein (2008), "it is not completely clear the extent to which humans agree on the interpretation of such expressions," and the inconsistencies observed in the data are evidence of this.

Another class of hard cases are the discourse-deictic pronouns that are used for *packaging* a previous fragment or set of clauses (10). It is very hard to pick an antecedent for them, even deciding whether the antecedent is an NP or a clause (Francis, 1994).

Finally, in 20% of the cases the system and the annotation are in disagreement, but both decisions are debatable. In many of them, the system did not make any prediction, but the one in the gold annotation is incorrect. In (11), *act* is a more plausible antecedent for **that**.

(11) "Why didn't the Bank Board act sooner?" he *said*. "**That** is what Common Cause should ask be investigated."

As a result, even though our system obviously makes multiple mistakes in its decisions, we believe that the evaluation overpenalizes its performance due to the debatable and not always clear-cut annotations discussed above. Discourse deixis resolution is a hard problem in itself (the chances of selecting a wrong antecedent for a pronoun are many times greater than picking the right one), and this difficulty is accentuated by the problematic annotations in the training and test data.

Given the difficulty of identifying a single antecedent to discourse-deictic pronouns, as evidenced by the low inter-annotator agreement on this task, a more flexible evaluation measure for discourse deixis systems is needed.

7 Conclusion

We have presented an automatic system for discourse deixis resolution. The system works in two stages: first classifying pronouns as discourse deictic or not, and then assigning an antecedent.

Empirical evaluations show that our system outperforms naive baselines as well as the only existing comparable system. Additionally, when stacked on top of two different state-of-the-art NP coreference resolvers, our system yields improvements on the B^3, $CEAF_e$ and CoNLL measures. The results are still far from the upper bound achievable by an oracle. However, our research highlights the inconsistencies in the annotation of discourse deixis in existing resources, and thus the performance of our system is likely underestimated.

These inconsistencies call for future work to improve existing annotated corpora so that similar systems may be more fairly evaluated. Regarding our approach, a tighter integration between the NP and discourse deixis components could help them make more informed decisions. Other future research includes jointly learning the classification and resolution stages of our system, and exploring semi-supervised learning techniques to compensate for the paucity of annotated data. Finally, we would like to transfer our system to other languages.

Acknowledgments

This work was done when the first two authors were interns at Google. We would like to thank Greg Durrett and Anders Björkelund for kindly sharing the outputs of their systems. Thanks also go to Rajhans Samdani and the anonymous reviewers for their valuable comments and suggestions to improve the quality of the paper.

References

Anders Björkelund and Jonas Kuhn. 2014. Learning structured perceptrons for coreference resolution with latent antecedents and non-local features. In *Proceedings of ACL*, pages 47–57.

Simon Philip Botley. 2006. Indirect anaphora: Testing the limits of corpus-based linguistics. *International Journal of Corpus Linguistics*, 11(1):73–112.

Donna K Byron and James F Allen. 1998. Resolving demonstrative anaphora in the TRAINS93 corpus. In *Proceedings of the 2nd Colloquium on Discourse, Anaphora and Reference Resolution*.

Donna K Byron. 2002. Resolving pronominal reference to abstract entities. In *Proceedings of ACL*, pages 80–87.

Tommaso Caselli and Irina Prodanof. 2010. Annotating event anaphora: A case study. In *Proceedings of LREC*, pages 723–728.

Bin Chen, Jian Su, Sinno Jialin Pan, and Chew Lim Tan. 2011. A unified event coreference resolution by integrating multiple resolvers. In *Proceedings of IJCNLP*, pages 102–110.

Greg Durrett and Dan Klein. 2014. A joint model for entity analysis: Coreference, typing, and linking. *Transactions of the Association for Computational Linguistics*, 2:477–490.

Miriam Eckert and Michael Strube. 2000. Dialogue acts, synchronizing units, and anaphora resolution. *Journal of Semantics*, 17(1):51–89.

Eraldo Rezende Fernandes, Cícero Nogueira dos Santos, and Ruy Luiz Milidiú. 2012. Latent structure perceptron with feature induction for unrestricted coreference resolution. In *Proceedings of CoNLL: Shared Task*, pages 41–48.

Gill Francis. 1994. Labelling discourse: An aspect of nominal-group lexical cohesion. In M. Coulthard, editor, *Advances in Written Text Analysis*, pages 83–101. Routledge, London.

Philipp Koehn. 2004. Statistical significance tests for machine translation evaluation. In *Proceedings of EMNLP*, pages 388–395.

Heeyoung Lee, Yves Peirsman, Angel Chang, Nathanael Chambers, Mihai Surdeanu, and Dan Jurafsky. 2011. Stanford's multi-pass sieve coreference resolution system at the CoNLL-2011 Shared Task. In *Proceedings of CoNLL: Shared Task*, pages 28–34.

Catherine Macleod, Ralph Grishman, Adam Meyers, Leslie Barrett, and Ruth Reeves. 1998. NOMLEX: A lexicon of nominalizations. In *Proceedings of EURALEX*, pages 187–193.

Joseph F. McCarthy and Wendy G. Lehnert. 1995. Using decision trees for coreference resolution. In *Proceedings of IJCAI*, pages 1060–1065.

Shachar Mirkin, Jonathan Berant, Ido Dagan, and Eyal Shnarch. 2010. Recognising entailment within discourse. In *Proceedings of COLING*, pages 770–778.

Christoph Müller. 2007. Resolving *it*, *this*, and *that* in unrestricted multi-party dialog. In *Proceedings of ACL*, pages 816–823.

Costanza Navarretta and Sussi Olsen. 2008. Annotating abstract pronominal anaphora in the DAD project. In *Proceedings of LREC*, pages 2046–2052.

Costanza Navarretta. 2011. Antecedent and referent types of abstract pronominal anaphora. In *Proceedings of the Workshop Beyond Semantics: Corpus-based investigations of pragmatic and discourse phenomena*, pages 99–10.

Vincent Ng. 2010. Supervised noun phrase coreference research: The first fifteen years. In *Proceedings of ACL*, pages 1396–1411.

Massimo Poesio and Ron Artstein. 2008. Anaphoric annotation in the ARRAU corpus. In *Proceedings of LREC*, pages 1170–1174.

Martin F Porter. 1980. An algorithm for suffix stripping. *Program*, 14(3):130–137.

Sameer Pradhan, Lance Ramshaw, Ralph Weischedel, Jessica MacBride, and Linnea Micciulla. 2007. Unrestricted coreference: Identifying entities and events in OntoNotes. In *Proceedings of ICSC*, pages 446–453.

Sameer Pradhan, Alessandro Moschitti, Nianwen Xue, Olga Uryupina, and Yuchen Zhang. 2012. CoNLL-2012 Shared Task: Modeling multilingual unrestricted coreference in OntoNotes. In *Proceedings of CoNLL: Shared Task*, pages 1–40.

Sameer Pradhan, Xiaoqiang Luo, Marta Recasens, Eduard Hovy, Vincent Ng, and Michael Strube. 2014. Scoring coreference partitions of predicted mentions: A reference implementation. In *Proceedings of ACL*, pages 30–35.

Marta Recasens. 2008. Discourse deixis and coreference: Evidence from AnCora. In *Proceedings of the 2nd Workshop on Anaphora Resolution (WAR II)*, pages 73–82.

Philip Resnik. 1997. Selectional preference and sense disambiguation. In *Proceedings of the ACL SIGLEX Workshop on Tagging Text with Lexical Semantics: Why, What, and How*, pages 52–57.

Josef Steinberger, Massimo Poesio, Mijail A Kabadjov, and Karel Ježek. 2007. Two uses of anaphora resolution in summarization. *Information Processing & Management*, 43(6):1663–1680.

Michael Strube and Christoph Müller. 2003. A machine learning approach to pronoun resolution in spoken dialogue. In *Proceedings of ACL*, pages 168–175.

Bonnie L Webber. 1988. Discourse deixis: Reference to discourse segments. In *Proceedings of ACL*, pages 113–122.

Graph-based Coherence Modeling For Assessing Readability

Mohsen Mesgar and **Michael Strube**
Heidelberg Institute for Theoretical Studies gGmbH
Schloss-Wolfsbrunnenweg 35
69118 Heidelberg, Germany
(mohsen.mesgar|michael.strube)@h-its.org

Abstract

Readability depends on many factors ranging from shallow features like word length to semantic ones like coherence. We introduce novel graph-based coherence features based on frequent subgraphs and compare their ability to assess the readability of Wall Street Journal articles. In contrast to Pitler and Nenkova (2008) some of our graph-based features are significantly correlated with human judgments. We outperform Pitler and Nenkova (2008) in the readability ranking task by more than 5% accuracy thus establishing a new state-of-the-art on this dataset.

1 Introduction

Readability depends on many factors which enable readers to process a text. These factors can be used by readability assessment methods to quantify the difficulty of text understanding. Possible applications of readability assessment are automatic text summarization and simplification systems. Measuring readability can also be used in question answering and knowledge extraction systems to prune texts with low readability (Kate et al., 2010).

Many different text features have been used to assess readability. They include shallow features (Flesch, 1948; Kincaid et al., 1975), language modeling features (Si and Callan, 2001; Collins-Thompson and Callan, 2004), syntactic features (Schwarm and Ostendorf, 2005) and text flow or coherence (Barzilay and Lapata, 2008; Pitler and Nenkova, 2008). In a coherent text each sentence has some connections with other sentences. Although these local connections make the text more readable, the corresponding coherence features used in Pitler and Nenkova (2008) (Section 2) are not strongly correlated with human judgments.

The main goal of this paper is to introduce novel graph-based coherence features for assessing readability. To achieve this goal, we use the entity graph coherence model by Guinaudeau and Strube (2013) (Section 3.1.1) and follow two ideas. The first main idea is to use a graph representation of rhetorical relations between sentences of a text (Section 3.1.2) and to merge the entity graph and the rhetorical graph (Section 3.1.3). Hence we enrich the entity graph and consequently consider the distribution of two aspects of coherence (i.e. entities and discourse relations) simultaneously. The second main idea is to apply subgraph mining algorithms to find frequent subgraphs (i.e. patterns) in texts (Section 3.2). Subgraph mining has been successfully applied to other tasks, e.g. image processing (Nowozin et al., 2007) and language modeling (Biemann et al., 2012). We hypothesize that text coherence correlates with frequent subgraphs (vaguely reminding us of coherence patterns (Daneš, 1974)) and that the mined patterns are good predictors for readability ratings.

Our study is novel in introducing new and informative graph-based coherence features. We examine the predictive power of these feature in two experiments: first, readability rating prediction, and second, ranking texts according to the readability (Section 5).

*Proceedings of the Fourth Joint Conference on Lexical and Computational Semantics (*SEM 2015)*, pages 309–318,
Denver, Colorado, June 4–5, 2015.

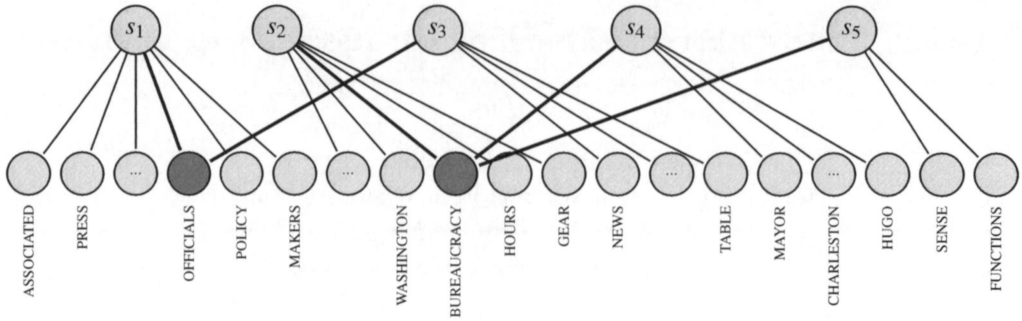

Figure 1: The entity graph representation of the text in Table 1. Dark entities are shared by the sentences.

2 Readability Assessment

The quality of a text depends on different factors which make the text easier to read. These factors range from shallow features like word length to semantic features like coherence. Readability assessment leads to two problems: distinguishing and recognizing readability levels of texts and predicting human readability ratings.

Pitler and Nenkova (2008) use all entity transitions of the entity grid model (Barzilay and Lapata, 2008) as coherence features. They compute the correlation between them and readability ratings and show that none of them is significantly correlated with human readability judgments. Indeed, none of these features on its own is a good predictor to measure coherence and to predict readability as well.

3 Method

We introduce the graph representation of a text and propose to use these graphs to model coherence.

3.1 Graphs

3.1.1 Entity Graph

Guinaudeau and Strube (2013) describe a graph-based version of the entity grid (Barzilay and Lapata, 2008) which models the interaction between entities and sentences as a bipartite graph. This graph contains two sets of nodes: sentences and entities. Sentence and entity nodes are connected if and only if the entity is mentioned in the sentence (Figure 1). Edges are weighted according to the grammatical role of the entity mentioned in the sentence.

Guinaudeau and Strube (2013) model entity transitions between sentences via a one-mode projection of the entity graph. The one-mode projection is a graph consisting of sentence nodes that are connected if and only if they have at least one entity in common in the entity graph. One-mode projections are directed as they follow the text order. Hence, backward edges never occur. Guinaudeau and Strube (2013) introduce three kinds of projections. The unweighted projection P_u^{ER} models the existence of the entity connections between sentences. The weighted projection P_w^{ER} uses the number of shared entities by sentences as a weight for the corresponding edge (Figure 2). P_{acc}^{ER} takes the grammatical function of entities in sentences into account as edge weights. Guinaudeau and Strube (2013) show that P_{acc}^{ER} does not perform well for readability assessment. It does not outperform P_w^{ER} in our

S1: The *[Associated] [Press]*'s *[earthquake] [coverage]* drew *[attention]* to a *[phenomenon]* that deserves some *[thought]* by public *[officials]* and other *[policy] [makers]*.

S2: Private *[relief] [agencies]*, such as the *[Salvation] [Army]* and *[Red] [Cross]*, mobilized almost instantly to help *[people]*, while the *[Washington] [bureaucracy]* "took *[hours]* getting into *[gear]*."

S3: One *[news]* show we saw *[yesterday]* even displayed 25 federal *[officials]* meeting around a *[table]*.

S4: We recall that the *[mayor]* of *[Charleston]* complained bitterly about the federal *[bureaucracy]*'s response to *[Hurricane Hugo]*.

S5: The *[sense]* grows that modern public *[bureaucracies]* simply don't perform their assigned *[functions]* well.

Table 1: A sample text from the Wall Street Journal dataset (Pitler and Nenkova, 2008).

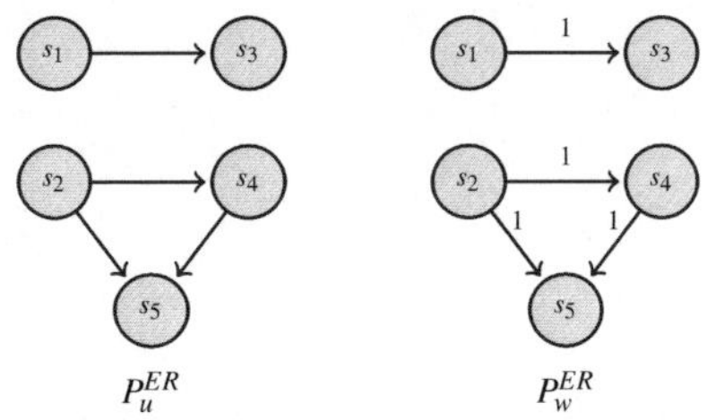

Figure 2: P_u^{ER}: unweighted, and P_w^{ER}: weighted projection graphs. In the weighted projection all edge weights are equal to one, because all sentences share one entity.

experiments as well. Thus, we do explain further details of P_w^{ER} here.

3.1.2 Discourse Relation Graph

Lin et al. (2011) and Lin (2011) use Rhetorical Structure Theory (RST) to describe and model coherence by considering the transitions between discourse relations. Inspired by the entity grid they expand the relation sequence into a two-dimensional matrix whose rows and columns are sentences and entities, respectively. The cell $\langle s_i, e_j \rangle$ corresponds to the set of discourse relations entity e_j is involved with in sentence s_i. These methods are based on entity transitions which, however, are intuitively implausible, because discourse relations connect sentences (or elementary discourse units).

Since discourse relations capture interactions between sentences (Table 2), we model these relations with a graph.

Relation	Arg1	Arg2
Implicit_Expansion	S1	S2
Explicit_Comparison	S2	S2
Implicit_Expansion	S2	S3
Implicit_Temporal	S3	S4
Implicit_Contingency	S4	S5

Table 2: PDTB-style discourse relations (Prasad et al., 2008) of the sample text in Table 1

A discourse relation graph is $P_u^{DR} = (V, R)$, where V is the set of sentence nodes and R is the edge set which represents all discourse relations in the text. Two sentence nodes are adjacent if and only if they are connected by at least one discourse relation. Intra-sentential discourse relations are represented as self-edges. We define P_w^{DR} as a weighted discourse relation graph whose edge weights are

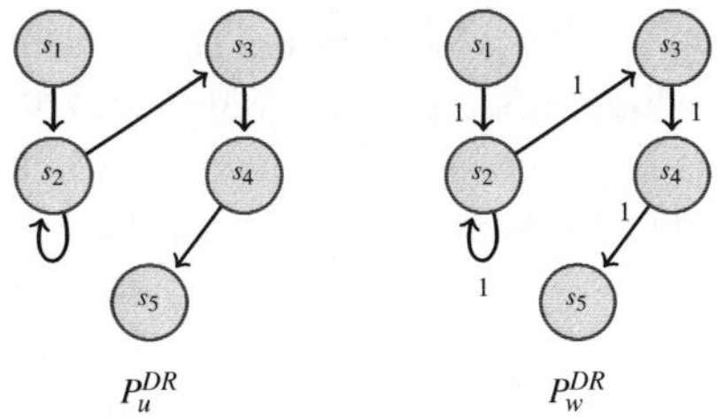

Figure 3: P_u^{DR}: unweighted, and P_w^{DR}: weighted discourse relation graphs.

the number of discourse relations between sentence nodes (Figure 3).

3.1.3 Combined Entity and Discourse Relation Graphs

Both projection and discourse relation graphs represent different types of connections. These graphs can be merged by employing basic operators.

We use the $\vee$ operator (logical OR) to combine the projection graph P_u^{ER} with the P_u^{DR} graph. The $\vee$ operator takes two sentence nodes and creates an edge between them if they are connected at least by one connection, whether entity transition (P_u^{ER}) or discourse relations (P_u^{DR}). The other basic logical operators (e.g. $\wedge$ or $\oplus$) lose connections. Hence we do not report on their performance. Inspired by linear regression models we combine the weighted graphs by adding ($+$) the edge weights in P_w^{ER} and P_w^{DR} (Figure 4).

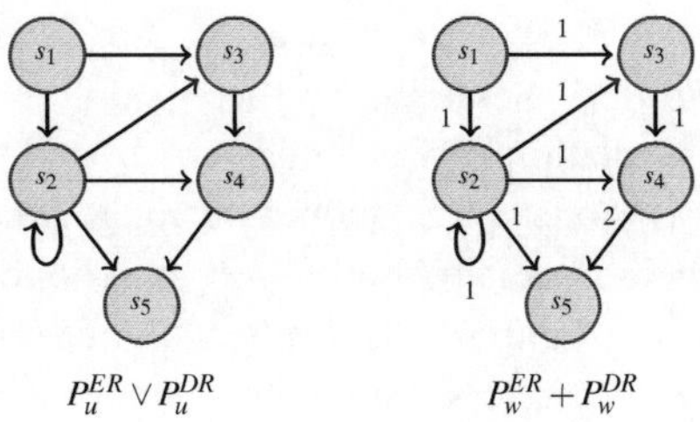

Figure 4: Combined entity and discourse relation graphs.

3.2 Coherence Features

We use the proposed graphs to introduce novel coherence features.

Average outdegree. Measures to which extent a sentence is connected with other sentences (Guinaudeau and Strube, 2013):

$$AvgOutDegree(P) = \frac{\sum_{s \in S} OutDegree(s)}{\|S\|}$$

where $OutDegree(s)$ is the sum of the weights associated with edges that leave node s and $\|S\|$ is the number of sentences in the text.

Number of components. The projection graph can be disconnected. A graph is *disconnected* if there are at least two nodes which are not reachable from each other (like s_1 and s_2 in Figure 2). A maximal non-empty connected subgraph in a graph is called *component*. Each projection graph in Figure 2 contains two components. Intuitively, projection graphs of a more coherent text should contain fewer number of components. The outdegree does not capture this type of connectivity. E.g., in Figure 5 the average outdegree of the two graphs is equal, while the left graph contains more components and should be less coherent.

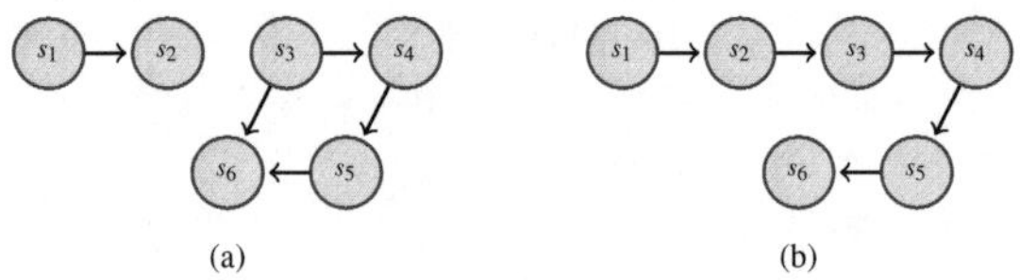

Figure 5: Two graphs with the same outdegree value. Graph (a) has two components. It is less coherent.

Frequent subgraphs. We hypothesize that particular coherence patterns show a correlation with readability. These patterns are encoded as subgraphs in graphs. An advantage is that coherence can be measured beyond simple sentence or node connectivity. We first define the graph concepts employed.

Isomorphic. Two graphs G and G' are *isomorphic*, if they fulfill two conditions: there should be a one-to-one association between nodes of G' and those of G, and two nodes of G' should be connected, if and only if their associated nodes in G are connected.

Subgraph. Graph G' is a *subgraph* of graph G, if G' is isomorphic to a graph whose nodes and edges are in G.

k-node subgraph. A subgraph with k nodes is called *k-node subgraph*.

Induced subgraph. The graph G' is an *induced subgraph* of graph G, if G' is a subgraph of G whose nodes are connected by all edges which connect the corresponding nodes in G (Figure 6). We always mean induced subgraphs when using the term subgraph.

Frequent subgraph & minimum support. Let $\zeta = \{G_1, G_2, \cdots, G_n\}$ be a database of n graphs. For

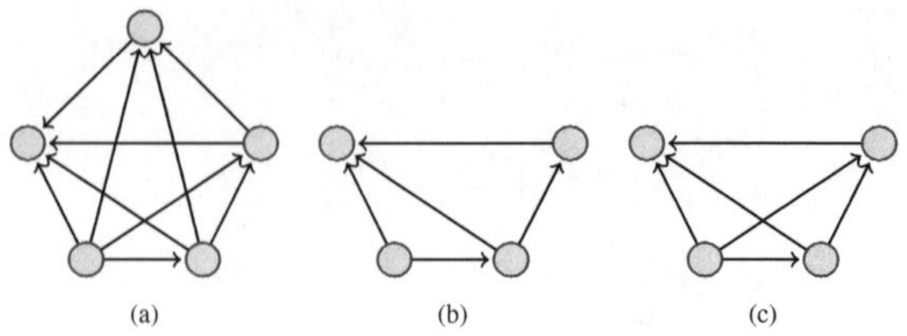

Figure 6: Both graphs (b) and (c) are subgraphs of (a). Only (c) is an induced subgraph of (a).

each subgraph sg, $support(sg)$ denotes the number of graphs (in ζ) which contain sg as a subgraph. A subgraph sg is a *frequent subgraph* if and only if $support(sg) > \lambda$, where λ is called *minimum support*.

Graph signature. Given a set of frequent subgraphs $\{sg_1, sg_2, ..., sg_m\}$, a graph signature for $G \in \zeta$ is the vector $\Phi(G) = (\varphi(sg_1, G), \varphi(sg_2, G), ..., \varphi(sg_m, G))$, where

$$\varphi(sg_i, G) = \frac{count(sg_i, G)}{\sum_{sg_j \in (sg_1, sg_2, ..., sg_m)} count(sg_j, G)}$$

Here $count(sg_i, G)$ is the number of occurrences of sg_i in graph G. We use the relative frequency $\varphi(sg_i, G)$ because it compares graphs with different numbers of nodes and different numbers of edges.

Subgraph features are divided into two categories: basic subgraphs and frequent large subgraphs.

Basic subgraphs. Instead of frequent subgraphs all possible 3-node subgraphs (Figure 7) are used as basic subgraphs because they are the smallest meaningful subgraphs that can model coherence patterns.

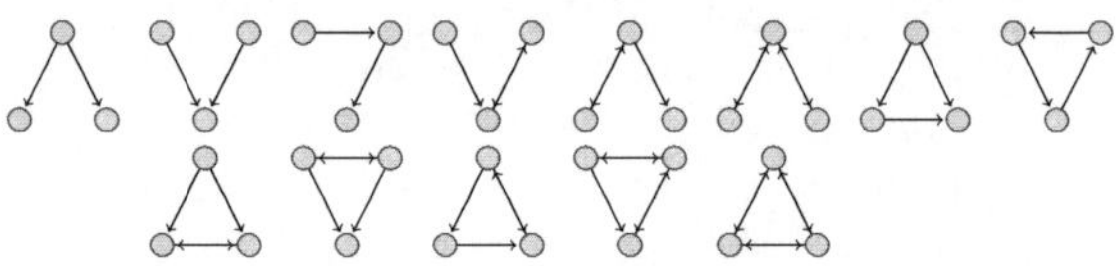

Figure 7: All possible directed 3-node subgraphs.

Because backward edges never occur in one-mode projections, only four subgraphs are feasible (Figure 8).

We interpret these subgraphs as follows:

- sg_1: The connection between a sentence and subsequent ones. In other words, at least two entities are mentioned in one sentence and the subsequent ones are about these entities.

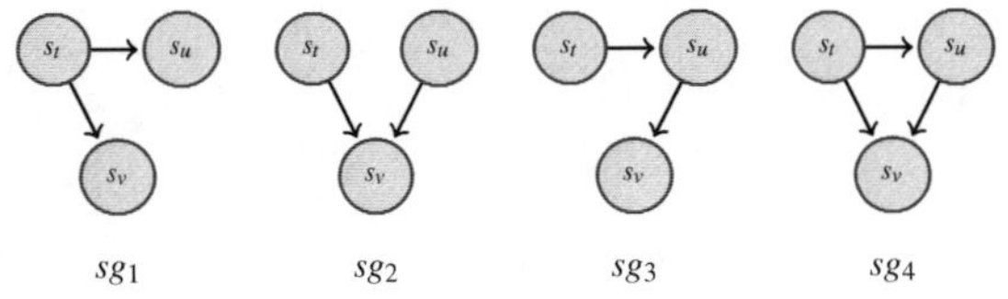

Figure 8: Feasible 3-node subgraph coherence features. Node labels illustrate the order of sentences. Sentence s_t occurs before sentence s_u, and sentence s_u occurs before sentence s_v (i.e. $t < u < v$).

- sg_2: Indicates that entities in s_t and s_u get connected to each other in s_v.
- sg_3: Each sentence tends to refer to the most prominent entity (focus of attention) in preceding sentences (Sidner, 1983; Grosz et al., 1995). The absence of a connection between s_t and s_v indicates that the entity connecting s_t and s_u is different from the entity connecting s_u and s_v. Therefore this subgraph approximately corresponds to the shift of the focus of attention.
- sg_4: Merges sg_1 and sg_3 and represents all connections of these two subgraphs.

We use these feasible 3-node subgraphs and compute the graph signature, Φ, of each $G \in \zeta$. We propose each $\varphi \in \Phi$ (i.e. relative frequency of each subgraph in G) as a connectivity feature of graph G to measure text coherence.

Frequent large subgraphs. Since we observe a strong correlation between basic subgraphs and human readability ratings (Table 4), we mine frequent large subgraphs of projection graphs. Our intuition is that larger subgraphs are more informative coherence patterns. Hence, we extend the coherence features from all feasible 3-node subgraphs to frequent k-node subgraphs. We first use an efficient subgraph mining algorithm to extract all subgraphs with size k and then compute the count of each subgraph as an induced subgraph in each graph $G \in \zeta$. We retain a subgraph sg, if it is frequent (i.e. $support(sg) > \lambda$). The result of these steps is a two-dimensional matrix whose rows represent graphs in ζ and columns represent frequent subgraphs with size k. The cell $\langle G_i, sg_j \rangle$ shows the count of sg_j in graph G_i. Given this matrix, we compute the graph signature of each $G \in \zeta$ and take each element of the graph signature as a coherence feature.

4 Experiments

4.1 Data

We use the dataset created by Pitler and Nenkova (2008) which consists of randomly selected articles from the Wall Street Journal corpus. The articles were rated by three humans on a scale from 1 to 5 for readability based on quality measures that are designed to estimate the coherence of articles. The final readability score of each article is the average of these three ratings.

We exclude three files from this dataset: `wsj--0382` does not exist in the Penn Treebank (Marcus et al., 1994)[1]. `wsj-2090` does not exist in the Penn Discource Treebank (Prasad et al., 2008). `wsj-1398` is a poem.

4.2 Settings

Entity graph. We use the gold parse trees in the Penn Treebank (Marcus et al., 1994) to extract all nouns in a document as mentions. We consider nouns with identical stem[2] as coreferent. We divide the edge weight between two sentence nodes s_i and s_j by their distance $j - i$ to decrease the importance of links that exist between non-adjacent sentences.

Discourse relation graph. We use gold PDTB-style discourse relations (Prasad et al., 2008). We filter out EntRel and NoRel relations.

Number of components. For counting the number of components in each projection graph, the Sage Math[3] package is used. This feature is computed on unweighted projections (i.e. P_u^{ER}).

Frequent subgraphs. Since subgraph mining is an NP-complete problem, different algorithms have been introduced to improve the performance of subgraph mining. We use the gSpan[4] algorithm (Yan and Han, 2002) to mine subgraphs of a graph database which contains P_u^{ER} projections. An advantage of using efficient subgraph mining algorithms is that we can exhaustively search very large subgraph spaces. A graph with $\|E\|$ edges, however, potentially has $\mathcal{O}(2^{\|E\|})$ subgraphs. Having sparse graphs

[1] Pitler and Nenkova (2008) also remove one file from their experiments. We assume that it is `wsj-0382`.

[2] We use Stanford CoreNLP (`http://nlp.stanford.edu/software/corenlp.shtml`)

[3] `http://sagemath.org/download-linux.html`

[4] We use the Java package: `http://www.cs.ucsb.edu/~xyan/software/gSpan.htm`

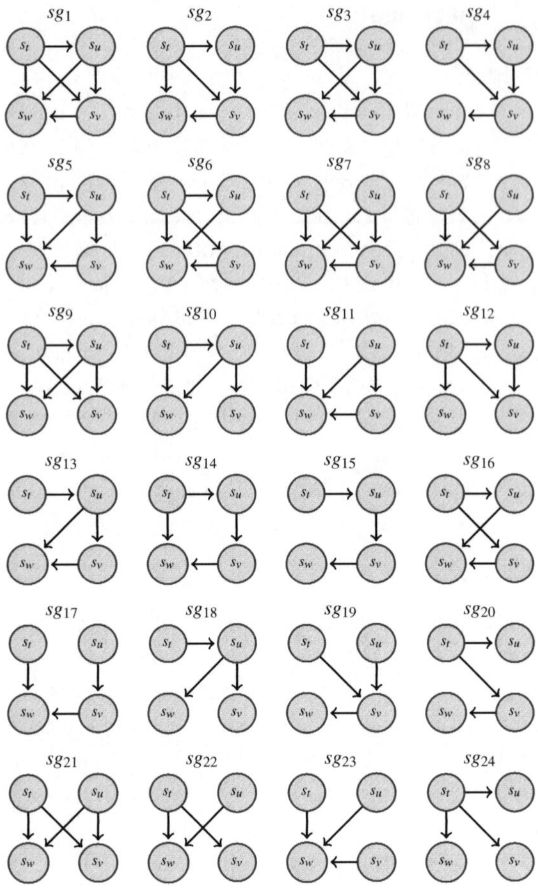

Figure 9: Frequent subgraphs with four nodes where $t < u < v < w$.

and using efficient subgraph mining algorithm lets us to search trough this space. We mine subgraphs with $k = 4$ and $\lambda = 0$ (Figure 9).

4.3 Evaluation

We evaluate on the following benchmark tasks.

Readability assessment. We use the Pearson correlation coefficient to find features correlated with readability scores. It takes feature values and readability scores of all articles and returns $-1 \leq \rho \leq +1$. A high value of $|\rho|$ shows a strong correlation. We report statistical significance on the 0.05-level[5].

Readability as ranking. We rank texts pairwise with respect to their readability. We define a classification problem with a set of text pairs and a label, which indicates whether the first text in a pair is more readable. We use every two texts whose human readability scores differ by at least 0.5. Each text is represented with its graph-based coherence features. We employ WEKA's linear support vector implementation (SMO) to classify the pairs. Performance is evaluated using 10-fold cross-validation.

[5]The results written in bold face (Section 5).

	ρ	p_value
Entity Graph		
P_u^{ER}	−0.013	0.949
P_w^{ER}	0.151	0.452
P_{acc}^{ER}	0.150	0.455
Discourse Relation Graph		
P_u^{DR}	0.150	0.455
P_w^{DR}	0.155	0.440
Combination of Entity and Discourse Relation		
$P_u^{ER} \vee P_u^{DR}$	0.083	0.681
$P_w^{ER} + P_u^{DR}$	0.185	0.356
$P_w^{ER} + P_w^{DR}$	0.187	0.350

Table 3: The correlation of the average outdegree of different graphs with human readability ratings.

5 Results

Readability assessment. We report the correlation of our coherence models encoded in graph features and compare them with Guinaudeau and Strube's (2013) entity graph as the state-of-the-art coherence model. Pitler and Nenkova (2008) show that the entity transition features extracted from the entity grid model (Barzilay and Lapata, 2008) on its own do not significantly predict human readability ratings. So we do not describe their results here.

The results for the outdegree feature is shown in Table 3. The average outdegree of P_w^{ER} is highly correlated with human readability ratings. This confirms the readability results of Guinaudeau and Strube (2013) on the Encyclopedia Britannica dataset. The outdegrees of discourse relation graphs are more strongly correlated with human readability ratings than the outdegree of the projections in the entity graph, suggesting that efficient graph-based encoding of discourse relations can measure readability well. The outdegree of the combined graph $P_w^{ER} + P_w^{DR}$ is highly correlated, showing that the interaction of entity connections and discourse relations is important for text coherence. However, none of the outdegree measures in this table are significantly correlated with human readability ratings, confirming the intuition that outdegree only measures node connectivity in graphs and it is not enough to measure readability.

	ρ	p_value
Number of Components	**−0.391**	**0.044**
Relative frequency of 3-node Subgraphs		
sg_1	0.310	0.116
sg_2	−0.325	0.098
$\mathbf{sg_3}$	**−0.384**	**0.048**
sg_4	0.108	0.592

Table 4: Number of components and subgraph sg_3 are significantly correlated to readability.

Table 4 shows the correlation of two features of projections[6]: The number of components has a strong and significant negative correlation with human readability ratings[7], suggesting that simple properties of graphs measure text coherence. The lower part of Table 4 shows the correlation of the relative frequency of 3-node subgraphs (see Figure 8). More readable articles have many sg_1 and few number of sg_2 patterns. Pattern sg_3 is significantly and negatively correlated with human readability judgments, confirming the intuition that many shifts in focus of attention make texts difficult to read.

Table 5 shows the correlation between the relative frequency of 4-node subgraphs and readability ratings. First, most subgraphs with less than four edges are negatively correlated with readability, except sg_{20} and sg_{24} which are weakly correlated with readability. Few connections between sentences make the text difficult to read.

Second, the highest positive and significant correlation of sg_{12} and the most negatively correlated subgraph sg_{11} show that different patterns of edges in subgraphs capture readability judgments. Stoddard (1991, p.29) explains this by the *ambiguity node* phenomenon: "[...] in some cases, there may be more than one logical, possible node for a given cohesive element in a text, in which case, a reader may see the resulting ambiguity but not be able to decide between the choices". E.g., in sg_{11} a reader may make a decision about the focus of attention in s_w, while in sg_{12} the focus of attention of s_w is the same as the focus of attention of s_t. This phenomenon can also be observed in all positively correlated subgraphs. If readers have to return to one point in the text, they prefer to return to a sentence which is the core of the preceding sentences. However, we should refrain of interpreting too much into these patterns.

[6]Although, the proposed features can be applied on all kind of presented graphs, we evaluate them (except outdegree) only on projections of the entity graph model. We leave the application to the other graph representations for future work.

[7]This supports Karamanis et al. (2009) who report that NOCB transitions in the centering model can be used for the sentence ordering task.

	number of edges	ρ	p_value
sg_1	6	0.103	0.609
sg_2	5	−0.212	0.288
sg_3	5	−0.176	0.380
sg_4	4	−0.257	0.196
sg_5	5	−0.140	0. 486
sg_6	5	0.200	0.317
$\mathbf{sg_7}$	**5**	**−0.402**	**0.038**
sg_8	4	−0.317	0.107
sg_9	5	0.153	0.446
sg_{10}	4	−0.238	0.232
$\mathbf{sg_{11}}$	**4**	**−0.509**	**0.007**
$\mathbf{sg_{12}}$	**4**	**0.449**	**0.019**
sg_{13}	4	−0.045	0.824
sg_{14}	4	−0.033	0.870
sg_{15}	3	−0.358	0.067
sg_{16}	4	−0.068	0.736
sg_{17}	3	−0.308	0.118
$\mathbf{sg_{18}}$	**3**	**−0.546**	**0.003**
$\mathbf{sg_{19}}$	**3**	**−0.601**	**0.001**
sg_{20}	3	0.094	0.641
sg_{21}	4	0.068	0.736
sg_{22}	3	−0.374	0.055
sg_{23}	3	−0.314	0.111
sg_{24}	3	0.100	0.620

Table 5: The correlation between the relative frequency of 4-node subgraphs and readability ratings.

Finally, we conclude that in all strongly negative correlated subgraphs, a subgraph suffers either from edge shortage or the *ambiguity node* phenomenon like sg_7.

Considering the correlation of 3-node subgraphs in Table 4 and 4-node subgraphs in Table 5, two results are noticeable. First, in large subgraphs there are more strongly correlated subgraphs than 3-node subgraphs, confirming our hypothesis that larger subgraphs convey coherence patterns with higher quality. Second, sg_{12} in 4-node subgraphs is more strongly and positively correlated than sg_4 in

3-node subgraphs, because sg_{12} captures more circumstances about s_t. The relative frequency of sg_{12} is more informative than sg_4's relative frequency.

Readability as ranking. Results of the readability ranking problem are shown in Table 6. Baseline features are entity transition features which are used as coherence features by Pitler and Nenkova (2008)[8].

Features	Accuracy
Baselines	
None (Majority class)	47.85%
Baseline features (Pitler and Nenkova, 2008)	83.25%
Graph-based Features	
Number of components	61.72%
Basic subgraphs (3-node)	79.43%
Frequent large subgraphs (4-node)	89.00%
Frequent basic + large subgraphs	88.52%
Baseline features + frequent large subgraphs	93.30%

Table 6: SVM prediction accuracy.

When classifying with graph signatures based on basic subgraphs, accuracy is lower than with the baseline coherence features. This is probably related to the entity grid features which represent grammatical role transitions of entities, while the basic subgraphs only models the occurrence of entities across sentences. Graph signatures based on large subgraphs improve the performance of basic subgraphs by around 10%. This high accuracy verifies that larger subgraphs capture coherence patterns with high quality. Combining basic (3-node) and large subgraphs (4-node) cannot improve the performance of the large subgraphs features. This probably is because basic subgraphs are implicitly included in larger subgraphs. The combination of coherence baseline features and frequent large subgraphs improves the accuracy.

6 Related Work

There is a research tradition developing metrics for readability and using these metrics to quantify how difficult it is to understand a document. Shallow features such as word, sentence and text length, which only capture superficial properties of a text, have been used traditionally (Flesch, 1948; Kincaid et al., 1975). De Clercq et al. (2014) use traditional shallow features and apply these to a new corpus annotated with two different methodologies. However, some studies indicate that shallow features do not precisely predict the readability of a text (Feng et al., 2009; Petersen and Ostendorf, 2009). Later studies introduce deeper (more semantic) features such as those obtained by language models (Si and Callan, 2001; Collins-Thompson and Callan, 2004) and syntactic features like the number of NPs in sentences or the height of the sentence's parse tree (Schwarm and Ostendorf, 2005; Heilman et al., 2007). Barzilay and Lapata (2008) propose an entity-based coherence model which operationalizes some of the intuitions behind the centering model (Grosz et al., 1995). Although this model works well on the sentence ordering and summary coherence rating tasks, it does not work well for readability assessment. Only when combining the entity grid with features taken from Schwarm and Ostendorf (2005) the entity grid performs competitively.

While most of these studies predict the readability level of documents, Pitler and Nenkova (2008) present a new readability dataset with *Wall Street Journal* articles, where each article is assigned human readability ratings. They analyze the correlation between different readability features and human readability scores. They show no correlation between entity-transition features and readability scores. In contrast to them we are able to report a statistically significant correlation between some entity-based features and human readability ratings.

7 Conclusions

We proposed graph-based coherence features based on the notion of frequent subgraphs. We analyzed these features on the dataset created by Pitler and Nenkova (2008) which associates human readability ratings with each document. We have shown that frequent subgraphs represent coherence patterns in a text. Larger subgraphs obtain a high and statistically significant correlation with human readability ratings.

Pitler and Nenkova (2008) did not achieve statistically significant (positive or negative) correlations between their features derived from the entity grid and human readability ratings. In contrast, some of

[8]The accuracy reported in their paper is 79.42%. Our reimplementation achieves higher accuracy, because our dataset has three articles less.

our automatically induced subgraphs have a strong statistically significant correlation. We also outperform Pitler and Nenkova (2008) in the readability ranking task by more than 5% accuracy thus establishing a new state-of-the-art on this dataset. We conclude that the graph-based representation (Guinaudeau and Strube, 2013) is a better and more informative starting point for assessing readability.

In future work, we plan to induce common subgraphs and apply our method to different datasets (e.g. the dataset created by De Clercq et al. (2014)) combined with other readability features (Schwarm and Ostendorf, 2005).

Acknowledgments

This work has been funded by the Klaus Tschira Foundation, Heidelberg, Germany. The first author has been supported by a HITS Ph.D. scholarship. We would like to thank our colleagues Benjamin Heinzerling, Yufang Hou, Sebastian Martschat, Nafise Moosavi, and Daraksha Parveen who commented on earlier drafts of this paper.

References

Regina Barzilay and Mirella Lapata. 2008. Modeling local coherence: An entity-based approach. *Computational Linguistics*, 34(1):1–34.

Chris Biemann, Stefanie Roos, and Karsten Weihe. 2012. Quantifying semantics using complex network analysis. In *Proceedings of the 24th International Conference on Computational Linguistics,* Mumbai, India, 8–15 December 2012, pages 263–278.

Kevyn Collins-Thompson and James P. Callan. 2004. A language modeling approach to predicting reading difficulty. In *Proceedings of the Human Language Technology Conference of the North American Chapter of the Association for Computational Linguistics,* Boston, Mass., 2–7 May 2004, pages 193–200.

František Daneš. 1974. Functional sentence perspective and the organization of the text. In F. Daneš, editor, *Papers on Functional Sentence Perspective*, pages 106–128. Prague: Academia.

Orphée De Clercq, Véronique Hoste, Bart Desmet, Philip Van Oosten, Martine De Cock, and Lieve Macken. 2014. Using the crowd for readability prediction. *Natural Language Engineering*, 20(3):293–325.

Lijun Feng, Noémie Elhadad, and Matt Huenerfauth. 2009. Cognitively motivated features for readability assessment. In *Proceedings of the 12th Conference of the European Chapter of the Association for Computational Linguistics,* Athens, Greece, 30 March – 3 April 2009, pages 229–237.

Rudolf Flesch. 1948. A new readability yardstick. *Journal of Applied Psychlogy*, 32:221–233.

Barbara J. Grosz, Aravind K. Joshi, and Scott Weinstein. 1995. Centering: A framework for modeling the local coherence of discourse. *Computational Linguistics*, 21(2):203–225.

Camille Guinaudeau and Michael Strube. 2013. Graph-based local coherence modeling. In *Proceedings of the 51st Annual Meeting of the Association for Computational Linguistics (Volume 1: Long Papers),* Sofia, Bulgaria, 4–9 August 2013, pages 93–103.

Michael J. Heilman, Kevyn Collins-Thompson, Jamie Callan, and Maxine Eskenazi. 2007. Combining lexical and grammatical features to improve readability measures for first and second language texts. In *Proceedings of Human Language Technologies 2007: The Conference of the North American Chapter of the Association for Computational Linguistics,* Rochester, N.Y., 22–27 April 2007, pages 460–467.

Nikiforos Karamanis, Chris Mellish, Massimo Poesio, and Jon Oberlander. 2009. Evaluating centering for information ordering using corpora. *Computational Linguistics*, 35(1):29–46.

Rohit Kate, Xiaoqiang Luo, Siddharth Patwardhan, Martin Franz, Radu Florian, Raymond Mooney, Salim Roukos, and Chris Welty. 2010. Learning to predict readability using diverse linguistic features. In *Proceedings of the 23rd International Conference on Computational Linguistics,* Beijing, China, 23–27 August 2010, pages 546–554.

J. Peter Kincaid, Robert P. Jr. Fishburne, Richard L. Rogers, and Brad S. Chisson. 1975. Derivation of new readability formulas (automated readability index, Fog count and Flesch reading ease formula) for navy enlisted personnel. Technical Report 8-75, Naval Technical Training Command, Naval Air Station Memphis-Millington, Tenn., February.

Ziheng Lin, Hwee Tou Ng, and Min-Yen Kan. 2011. Automatically evaluating text coherence using discourse relations. In *Proceedings of the 49th Annual Meeting of the Association for Computational Linguistics (Volume 1: Long Papers),* Portland, Oreg., 19–24 June 2011, pages 997–1006.

Ziheng Lin. 2011. *Discourse parsing: Inferring discourse structure, modeling coherence, and its applications*. Ph.D. thesis, Dept. of Computer Science, School of Computing, National University of Singapore.

Mitchell Marcus, Grace Kim, Mary Ann Marcinkiewicz, Robert MacIntyre, Ann Bies, Mark Ferguson, Karen

Katz, and Britta Schasberger. 1994. The Penn treebank: Annotating predicate argument structure. In *Proceedings of ARPA Speech and Natural Language Workshop*.

Sebastian Nowozin, Koji Tsuda, Takeaki Uno, Taku Kudo, and Gokhan BakIr. 2007. Weighted substructure mining for image analysis. In *Proceedings of the 2007 IEEE Computer Society Conference on Computer Vision and Pattern Recognition,* Minneapolis, Minn., 18-23 June 2007, pages 1–8.

Sarah E. Petersen and Mari Ostendorf. 2009. A machine learning approach to reading level assessment. *Computer Speech and Language*, 23(1):89–106.

Emily Pitler and Ani Nenkova. 2008. Revisiting readability: A unified framework for predicting text quality. In *Proceedings of the 2008 Conference on Empirical Methods in Natural Language Processing,* Waikiki, Honolulu, Hawaii, 25–27 October 2008, pages 186–195.

Rashmi Prasad, Nikhil Dinesh, Alan Lee, Eleni Miltsakaki, Livio Robaldo, Aravind Joshi, and Bonnie Webber. 2008. The Penn Discourse Treebank 2.0. In *Proceedings of the 6th International Conference on Language Resources and Evaluation,* Marrakech, Morocco, 26 May – 1 June 2008.

Sarah E. Schwarm and Mari Ostendorf. 2005. Reading level assessment using support vector machines and statistical language models. In *Proceedings of the 43rd Annual Meeting of the Association for Computational Linguistics,* Ann Arbor, Mich., 25–30 June 2005, pages 523–530.

Luo Si and Jamie Callan. 2001. A statistical model for scientific readability. In *Proceedings of the ACM 10th Conference on Information and Knowledge Management,* Atlanta, Georgia, 5–10 November 2001, pages 574–576.

Candace L. Sidner. 1983. Focusing in the comprehension of definite anaphora. In M. Brady and R.C. Berwick, editors, *Computational Models of Discourse*, pages 267–330. Cambridge, Mass.: MIT Press. Reprinted in: Grosz, Barbara J. et al. (Eds.) (1986). Readings in Natural Language Processing. Morgan Kaufman: Los Altos, Cal., pp.363-394.

Sally Stoddard. 1991. *Text and Texture: Patterns of Cohesion*. Ablex, Norwood, N.J.

Xifeng Yan and Jiawei Han. 2002. gSpan: Graph-based substructure pattern mining. In *Proceedings of the International Conference on Data Mining,* Maebashi City, Japan, 9–12 December 2002, pages 721–724.

Author Index

Ács, Judit, 165
Adler, Meni, 193
Aggarwal, Nitish, 92
Agirre, Eneko, 61, 101
Aletras, Nikolaos, 20
Alex, Adarsh, 228
Aluísio, Sandra, 216
Arrigo, Michael, 82
Asooja, Kartik, 92
Aussenac-Gilles, Nathalie, 30

Baldwin, Timothy, 106
Baroni, Marco, 199
Barrena, Ander, 101
Basu, Rupayan, 82
Bel, Núria, 182
Benamara, Farah, 147
Bird, Steven, 106
Boguraev, Branimir, 71
Bordea, Georgeta, 92
Botvinick, Matthew, 199
Buitelaar, Paul, 92
Burford, Clint, 106
By, Tomas, 82

Callison-Burch, Chris, 137
Carbonell, Jaime, 176
Clark, Micah, 82
Corman, Julien, 30

Dagan, Ido, 193
Dalton, Adam, 82
Danesh, Soheil, 117
Demberg, Vera, 205
Diab, Mona, 82, 137

Eger, Steffen, 127
Eichler, Kathrin, 193
Elfardy, Heba, 137

Exner, Peter, 239

Fauconnier, Jean-Philippe, 249
Feizabadi, Parvin Sadat, 40
Foland, William, 279

Gershman, Anatole, 176
Goldberg, Adele, 199
Gonzàlez Pellicer, Edgar, 299
Guerra, Raul, 299
Guo, Hongyu, 1
Gupta, Abhijeet, 153
Guthrie, Louise, 82

Heid, Christopher, 228
Hirschberg, Julia, 82
Hwang, Jena D., 51

Jauhar, Sujay Kumar, 299
Judea, Alex, 159
Jurgens, David, 182

Kamel, Mouna, 249
Kato, Yoshihide, 269
Klang, Marcus, 239
Kornai, Andras, 165
Kotlerman, Lili, 193

Le, Phong, 10
Long, Cotie, 199
Lopez de Lacalle, Oier, 61

Makrai, Márton, 165
Martin, James, 279
Martin, James H., 117
Martins de Matos, David, 176
Marujo, Luis, 176
Matsubara, Shigeki, 269
Mehler, Alexander, 127
Mendes, Pablo, 228

Mendes, Sara, 182
Mesgar, Mohsen, 309
Modi, Ashutosh, 205
Moschitti, Alessandro, 289
Mott, Greg, 228

Nastase, Vivi, 193
Navigli, Roberto, 182
Necsulescu, Silvia, 182
Nemeskey, Dávid Márk, 165
Neto, João, 176
Noh, Tae-Gil, 193
Nugues, Pierre, 239

Padó, Sebastian, 40, 153, 193
Pajkossy, Katalin, 165
Palmer, Martha, 51, 222
Paperno, Denis, 199
Perera, Sujan, 228
Pinkal, Manfred, 205
Poibeau, Thierry, 211
Prabhakaran, Vinodkumar, 71, 82
Prokofieva, Anna, 82

Rambow, Owen, 82
Recasens, Marta, 299
Recski, Gábor, 165
Ribeiro, Ricardo, 176
Ritter, Samuel, 199
Rudinger, Rachel, 205
Ruiz, Pablo, 211

Sanches Duran, Magali, 216
Schenk, Niko, 127
Schluter, Natalie, 259
Shaikh, Samira, 82
Sheth, Amit, 228
Shwartz, Vered, 193
Sobhani, Parinaz, 1
Soroa, Aitor, 101
Stevenson, Mark, 20
Strassel, Stephanie, 82
Strube, Michael, 159, 309
Strzalkowski, Tomek, 82
Sumner, Tamara, 117

Taboada, Maite, 147
Thirunarayan, Krishnaprasad, 228
Tracey, Jennifer, 82

Uryupina, Olga, 289
Utt, Jason, 153

Van Durme, Benjamin, 205
Vieu, Laure, 30

Werner, Gregory, 82
Wiebe, Janyce, 82
Wilks, Yorick, 82
Wu, Shumin, 222

Zhu, Xiaodan, 1
Zuidema, Willem, 10

Association for Computational Linguistics
209 N. Eighth Street
Stroudsburg, Pennsylvania 18360

CURRAN ASSOCIATES INC
proceedings.com